The Gorbachev Factor

The
Gorbachev
Factor

Archie Brown

Oxford University Press
1996

Oxford University Press, Walton Street, Oxford OX2 6DP
Oxford New York
Athens Auckland Bangkok Bombay
Calcutta Cape Town Dar es Salaam Delhi
Florence Hong Kong Istanbul Karachi
Kuala Lumpur Madras Madrid Melbourne
Mexico City Nairobi Paris Singapore
Taipei Tokyo Toronto
and associated companies in
Berlin Ibadan

Oxford is a trade mark of Oxford University Press

Published in the United States
by Oxford University Press Inc., New York

British Library Cataloguing in Publication Data
Data available

Library of Congress Cataloging in Publication Data
Brown, Archie, 1938–
The Gorbachev factor / Archie Brown.
Includes bibliographical references.
1. Soviet Union—Politics and government—1985–1991.
2. Gorbachev, Mikhail Sergeevich, 1931–   .   I. Title.
DK288.B76   1996   947.085'4'092—dc20   95–49061
ISBN 0–19–827344–4

1 3 5 7 9 10 8 6 4 2

Typeset by Hope Services (Abingdon) Ltd.
Printed in Great Britain
on acid-free paper by
Biddles Ltd.,
Guildford & King's Lynn

To my mother

Mary Yates Brown

and to the memory of my father

Alexander Douglas Brown

(1900–1979)

Contents

Preface   ix

List of Plates   xvii

Abbreviations   xviii

Note on Transliteration   xix

1 Introduction   1

2 The Making of a Reformist General Secretary   24

3 In the Portals of Power   53

4 The Power of Ideas and the Power of Appointment   89

5 Gorbachev and Economic Reform   130

6 Gorbachev and Political Transformation   155

7 Gorbachev and Foreign Policy   212

8 The National Question, the Coup, and the
   Collapse of the Soviet Union   252

9 Conclusions   306

Notes   319

Glossary   391

Index   393

Preface

THIS book is neither a history of the Gorbachev era nor a biography of Mikhail Gorbachev. It does, certainly, contain a good deal of information about Gorbachev's life and background, not all of it, I believe, familiar to the Western (or, for that matter, Russian) reader. It discusses, too, many of the major events of the final seven years of the Soviet system. But its main concern is to understand and interpret Gorbachev's contribution to the dramatic changes which took place in the Soviet Union and in that state's relations with the outside world in the second half of the 1980s and the beginning of the 1990s—a time in which East–West relations were transformed and Communist power came to an end in Eastern Europe. There is discussion, too, of Gorbachev's unavailing struggle to preserve any kind of a union in the former USSR in the face of growing nationalist assertiveness.

The most central task of this book, however, is to examine how important Gorbachev was as a mover or facilitator in the Soviet Union's transition from orthodox Communism to a different kind of political system. This involves discussing 'the Gorbachev factor' not only in terms of his contributions in different policy areas but in respect of his political power, outlook, and style. It entails considering the strength of the opposition to Gorbachev and the constraints upon his political actions at different times. It also necessitates making judgements about Gorbachev's mind-set and the development of his views over time.

Although these are not easy issues to settle, it is perhaps of at least some advantage that I have been paying attention to Gorbachev for a long time—well before it was common to do so in either the Soviet Union or the West. There were quizzical looks in my audience at Yale University when, in one of my Henry L. Stimson Lectures delivered there on 22 October 1980, I said: 'An event of extraordinary potential significance took place in Moscow yesterday—the promotion to full membership of the Politburo of Mikhail Sergeevich Gorbachev.' My reasons for saying this were twofold. The first was that I had come to the conclusion that any future General Secretary would, like his three predecessors, be drawn from the ranks of those I called 'senior secretaries', i.e. the small group of people who were both full members of the Politburo and Secretaries of the Central Committee. Gorbachev had just joined that category and he was by some twenty years the youngest member of the group.

Second, I was convinced that Gorbachev would be a serious reformer. It was a view I held long before it became fashionable and which I continued to hold after it had ceased to be fashionable, at any rate in Russia. My interest in

ix

Gorbachev stemmed from the time when he became a Secretary of the Central Committee of the Communist Party of the Soviet Union (CPSU) in 1978 at an unusually early age for anyone to join the party's top leadership during the Brezhnev years. It was enhanced by a long conversation I had in Oxford with Zdeněk Mlynář in June 1979. Mlynář (whom I first met in Prague in 1965) was a fellow student and close friend of Gorbachev in the Law Faculty of Moscow University from 1950 to 1955. Later he became one of the key Communist reformers during the 'Prague Spring' of 1968 and, later still, one of the initiators of Charter 77, the Czech opposition movement which helped to pave the way for the democratizing changes of 1989. He is the most reliable and perceptive source on Gorbachev's student years.

Discrimination and judgement are more than usually necessary in dealing with the available material on Gorbachev, some of which is of especially dubious validity. Misleading Soviet hagiography is less of a problem with Gorbachev than with any previous leader of the USSR. But a minority of Soviet emigrants who at one point or another in their career overlapped with Gorbachev—or who, in one case, graduated from Moscow University a few months before Gorbachev arrived—were unable to resist the temptation to write their 'inside' accounts at a time when the Western desire for knowledge of Gorbachev exceeded what they were equipped to supply. More generally, there is the comparatively new problem for a student of Soviet and Russian politics of the immense scope and great variety of source material emanating from the former Soviet Union itself. Taking account of the wealth of new sources of information on Gorbachev—of varying degrees of objectivity and subjectivity—now poses a major challenge.

In addition to the visits I paid to the Soviet Union over the last quarter-century of its existence (which became much more frequent during the Gorbachev era) as well as some half-dozen to Russia since the collapse of the USSR, I have tried, in common with other Western scholars, to keep up with the mass of new publications in the later Soviet and early post-Soviet periods. These are often frankly written and they embrace a very broad spectrum of opinion. Happily, they now include numerous political memoirs, in which a wide variety of views on Gorbachev are expressed. (Political autobiography was an extremely rare Sovietological resource in the past.) There was always a diversity of view in Moscow—not to speak of the rest of Russia or, more obviously, the other republics—but as recently as the first half of the 1980s one had to read between the lines of Soviet publications and supplement that reading with private conversations.

Other radically new sources in the last few years of the Soviet era included the results of competitive elections and the findings of public opinion surveys on politically sensitive issues—among them, information on the changing standing over time of Soviet politicians and institutions. Soviet and Russian survey data have to be used with great discrimination, for many newspaper opinion polls have been based on skewed samples. I have used data exclusively from the most professional of the institutions engaged in survey research, especially the All-Union Centre for the Study of Public Opinion (now the All-Russian Centre), founded in 1988 with Academician Tatyana Zaslavskaya as its first director, Boris Grushin as its deputy director, and Yury Levada (who succeeded Zaslavskaya as

Director in 1992) as one of its research leaders. The best survey data are a valuable corrective to the constructions of past consciousness made by Russians today on the basis of what they think now. They are also a necessary complement to the more impressionistic estimates of public opinion made by journalists who, nevertheless, in the perestroika period often threw light on the thinking of political activists and on that part of the intelligentsia with whom they came in contact. But both Western and Russian journalists frequently project backwards current attitudes without actually examining what people thought at the time. Thus, in recent years it has often been asserted that Gorbachev's popularity was a purely Western phenomenon and that he was deeply unpopular in Russia. Such an assertion is remote from the truth and does not, in fact, stand up to serious scrutiny. For the greater part of his time as Soviet leader, Gorbachev was the most popular politician in his country. Yet, a comment on Soviet public opinion by Oleg Gordievsky, the former KGB officer who became a British agent, is both representative of much recent writing and misleading: 'In the West [Gorbachev] became a hero, the first leader with the courage to pronounce that Communism was dead; but in the Soviet Union he was deeply unpopular and continued to be regarded as [a] typical provincial Party *apparatchik*, with a provincial brain and education . . .'.[1] Apart from the fact that a majority of Russians are not Muscovites and would not necessarily accept the superiority of metropolitan 'brains', the generalization about Gorbachev's domestic unpopularity is at odds with the evidence on public opinion in the Soviet Union, as should become clearer in the chapters that follow.

In Russia, as elsewhere, participants in the political process would often say on a non-attributable basis more than they would say on the record. It became, however, increasingly common in 1990–1 to find Soviet politicians—including those who were part of the executive—willing to speak on sensitive topics more openly, if anything, than their Western counterparts. This reflected, of course, not only the climate of greater frankness than hitherto but also the sharp political struggle which was going on. That struggle was not only between government and opposition, but also within the major institutions of the party-state, including, not least, the Communist Party itself. Following the collapse of the Soviet Union, there were even fewer constraints on the politicians of the perestroika era; the recollections of key participants in that political process, both published and oral, have become of enormous importance.

The sources over time came to embrace highly critical assessments of Gorbachev from conservative Communists and Russian nationalists, on the one hand, and from those who favoured speedier and more radical democratizing or marketizing change, on the other. The positive views of Gorbachev also come from people of very diverse political backgrounds. Thus, among reform-minded specialists in research institutes who worked for radical change from within the system, there was still up to and beyond the August 1991 coup a significant number of Gorbachev supporters. But there were positive evaluations, too, from among those who had had a much harder time in the past. The Russian Jewish writer Lev Razgon, who spent seventeen years in prison and labour camps, remarked at an informal meeting in Oxford in January 1990 that he said a prayer for Gorbachev every day. There is, however, no doubt that a sharp decline in

Gorbachev's popularity in the Soviet Union took place over a period of approximately two years before the abortive *putsch*.

While there are still some gaps in our knowledge of Gorbachev and of Gorbachev's Soviet Union, the main problem for the investigator who reads Russian is that of coping with the sheer volume of interesting and potentially relevant material available today rather than of deciphering the sub-text of the deliberately obscure or distorted communications which constituted the standard fare of Soviet citizens and students of the Soviet Union alike in the past. The materials now include the selective publication of documents from the archives of the perestroika era—from the Russian state authorities, on the one hand, and the Gorbachev Foundation, on the other.

So far as helpful conversations are concerned, I have already mentioned Zdeněk Mlynář, with whom I have had a number of interesting meetings at different points in his career. I have met Mikhail Gorbachev himself both in Moscow and in Oxford since he ceased to hold political office. I have also had numerous conversations with those who worked closely with Gorbachev, in which my focus was on his career up to the point at which he ceased to be President of a country—the Soviet Union—which itself then ceased to exist. I am not concerned in this book with Gorbachev's activities beyond that date— 25 December 1991—although I have made ample use of the significant new information on the Gorbachev era which has come to light over the subsequent three years and more.

In addition to the numerous talks I have had with those in Russia who had political and professional contact with Gorbachev, I have had discussions also with many Western politicians and senior diplomats who have dealt with him. On the Russian side, they have included four presidential aides—Anatoly Chernyaev, Georgy Shakhnazarov, Nikolay Petrakov, and Oleg Ozherelev. Chernyaev was a full-time aide to Gorbachev from 1986 to the end of his period as Soviet leader in 1991, Shakhnazarov from February 1988 until December 1991. Both men continue to work with Gorbachev—Chernyaev especially closely—at the Gorbachev Foundation. Petrakov was Gorbachev's aide on economic matters in 1990, but resigned at the end of that year. From soon after the August 1991 coup until the end of the Gorbachev (and Soviet) era in December of the same year he was back in Gorbachev's team as a member of the Political-Consultative Council of the President. Ozherelev was the economist who succeeded Petrakov as a presidential aide upon the latter's 1990 resignation. I have also had the benefit of speaking with Alexander Nikolaevich Yakovlev, a member of both the Central Committee Secretariat and the Politburo during the perestroika years and an influential ally of Gorbachev in the Soviet leadership at that time (later Vice-President of the Gorbachev Foundation and subsequently, until his resignation in March 1995, head of Ostankino television in Moscow); and Vadim Andreevich Medvedev, who, like Yakovlev, was a Politburo member and Secretary of the Central Committee, and whose co-operation with Gorbachev began several years before the latter became General Secretary. I have had a number of extremely helpful conversations with Andrey Grachev, who became a deputy head of the International Department of the Central Committee of the Soviet Communist Party in 1989 and, latterly, was Mikhail

Gorbachev's presidential press spokesman; since 1992 he has been attached to the Institute of World Economy and International Relations (IMEMO) and he is also a political commentator on *Moscow News* and on *New Times*. Also of value have been interviews with Pavel Palazhchenko, Gorbachev's interpreter at his summit meetings with American Presidents, and Alexander Likhotal, Gorbachev's adviser and press spokesman at the Gorbachev Foundation.

Other Soviet and Russian politicians and scholars with whom I have had especially numerous as well as particularly helpful discussions include, in alphabetical order, Yevgeny Ambartsumov, Fedor Burlatsky, Sergey Chugrov, German Diligensky, Leonid Gordon, Pavel Gratsiansky, Vladimir Guliev, Artemy Karapetyants, Grigory Karasin, Boris Kurashvili, Alexander Lebedev, Andrey Melville, Alexander Nikitin, Alexander Obolonsky, Mikhail Piskotin, Oleg Rumyantsev, Nikolay Shmelev, Nodari Simonia, Rair Simonyan, William Smirnov, Leonid Smirnyagin, and Ruben Yevstigneev. I have in addition had the benefit either of very useful interviews or of informal meetings with (among others) Anatoly Adamishin, Yury Afanasev, Abel Aganbegyan, Andrey Arsenev, Vadim Bakatin, the late Georgy Barabashev, Vladimir Baranovsky, Leonid Batkin, Yury Baturin, Nina Belyaeva, Nikolay Biryukov, Vladimir Bykov, Anatoly Danilitsky, Nikolay Deev, Vladimir Entin, Peter Ivantsov, General Oleg Kalugin, Karen Karagezyan, Yefim Khesin, Igor Klyamkin, Yelena Koronevskaya, Ivan Laptev, Otto Latsis, Yury Levada, Vladimir Lukin, Andranik Migranyan, Georgy Mirsky, the late Avgust Mishin, Vladik Nersesyants, Alexander Nikonov, Asan Nugmanov, Boris Pankin, Vladimir Pechatnov, Sergey Peregudov, Vladimir Popov, Vitaly Rassokhin, Lev Razgon, Anatoly Rybakov, Roald Sagdeev, the late Andrey Sakharov, Aleksey Shestopal, Yelena Shestopal, Lilia Shevtsova, Viktor Sheynis, Vyacheslav Shostakovsky, Alexander Shubin, Valery Slavinsky, Sergey Stankevich, Galina Starovoytova, the late Vladimir Tikhonov, Tatyana Tolstaya, Boris Topornin, Alexander Tsipko, Arkady Vaksberg, Vladimir Valkov, Alexander Veber, General Dmitry Volkogonov, Leonid Volkov, Alexander Maksimovich Yakovlev, Yegor Yakovlev, Tatyana Zaslavskaya, and Igor Zevelev.

It goes without saying that none of these scholars, writers, and politicians (several of whom come into more than one of those categories) can be held responsible for any of the conclusions I come to. They themselves differ very radically in their political views and in their attitudes to Gorbachev. In addition to the interviews I have conducted myself, I have made use of those of several of the best professional journalists in the field. In that connection, I should like to express my gratitude to Brian Lapping and Norma Percy, the makers of the excellent television documentary series *The Second Russian Revolution*, for the tapes of the interviews which they deposited in the St Antony's College Russian Centre Library and to them again and also to the British Library of Political and Economic Science for access to the transcripts of those interviews now held in the Special Collections at LSE. The extracts from the lengthy interviews used in the television programmes represented only a small part of this rich fund of material. (References to it are cited in the endnotes as *The Second Russian Revolution* transcripts.)

I have benefited, too, from many conversations with Western colleagues, especially at St Antony's College, Oxford, my academic home. Other Fellows in the Russian and East European Centre and graduate students alike have been a source of stimulus, as has—in a more general but very important way—the Warden of the College, Ralf Dahrendorf. For highly efficient help on a day-to-day basis I am enormously grateful to the Secretary and Librarian of the Russian Centre, Jackie Willcox. For drawing my attention to a number of important publications (particularly articles in Russian newspapers) which I might otherwise have missed I am indebted, first and foremost, to Martin Dewhirst (of Glasgow University) and also to Yitzhak Brudny (of Yale), to Riitta Heino and Alex Pravda in St Antony's, and to the excellent graduate students I have had the pleasure of supervising at Oxford. Among those in the latter category who have found material or checked references for me have been Warren Hatch, Raffaela Kluge, Neil Melvin, Martha Merritt, and Christian Schmidt. I owe a special debt to friends and professional colleagues who have taken the trouble to read particular chapters of this book and give me their comments. Andrey Grachev of IMEMO has read the whole book in draft, Artemy Karapetyants of Moscow University the first four chapters, Alexander Shubin of the Institute of General History (Moscow) Chapters 2 and 3, Robert E. Lane of Yale University Chapter 4, Włodzimierz Brus of Wolfson College, Oxford, Chapter 5, Alex Pravda of St Antony's Chapters 6 and 7, and another St Antony's colleague, Timothy Garton Ash, Chapter 7. These scholars are in no way responsible for any errors of judgement or of fact which may remain, but their generous advice has undoubtedly improved the text.

I have enjoyed the change of intellectual environment made possible by Visiting Professorships at Columbia University, New York (where, in the Fall semester of 1985 I had the opportunity to exchange views with a stimulating group of faculty and graduate students during Gorbachev's first year as Soviet leader), the University of Texas at Austin (in the 1990/1 academic year), and INSEAD, Fontainebleau (in the summer of 1991). All of these institutions provided conditions supportive of political research and a significant part of the work on the earlier chapters of this volume was done in Texas and France. I greatly appreciate, therefore, the initiatives of those who provided me with these highly congenial intellectual homes—Alfred C. Stepan, Robert Legvold, Marshall Shulman, and Seweryn Bialer at Columbia; James S. Fishkin, Robert D. King, and Michael Katz at the University of Texas; and Jonathan Story at INSEAD.

The work which follows draws on my research and reflection on 'the Gorbachev factor' over more than a decade, but in its book form it has its origins in an invitation I received from Alexander Dallin to give the second in an annual series of lectures established by the Center for Russian and East European Studies at Stanford University. I chose as the theme 'The Gorbachev Factor in Soviet Politics' and so what was, in effect, the first draft of a number of the chapters that follow was delivered at Stanford in a lecture series in April 1988. The warmth of the Californian climate was matched by the hospitality I received from Alex Dallin, Gail Lapidus, David Holloway, and others. I remain most grateful to them and sorry that I have kept them waiting so long for the book of the lectures. Given all that was subsequently to happen in the Soviet Union (culminating in the collapse of the union itself) and the truly extraordinary pace of change, it is obviously in many respects a quite different text from my original one.

Apologies for keeping them waiting are due even more to Oxford University Press, where I greatly appreciated Henry Hardy's enthusiasm for the project as well as his patience when the manuscript was much longer in coming than I predicted and he expected. I have enjoyed similar encouragement, support, and tolerance from his successor, Tim Barton. He has combined efficiency with friendly diplomacy and deserves credit (I hope) for finally extracting from me the manuscript I had been reluctant to draw a line under until I had taken full account of the never-ending flow of new information. In fact, more than enough is already known to make possible a quite detailed analysis and interpretation of the role played by Gorbachev in the history of the second half of the twentieth century.

I am glad to have this opportunity to thank the British Academy and their highly efficient and helpful staff (above all, Jane Lyddon) and the Economic and Social Research Council of the UK, who, between them, funded the majority of my study visits to the Soviet Union in the Gorbachev era. The British Academy, in particular, generously supported a series of visits to the Institute of State and Law of the Academy of Sciences in Moscow. Chapters 6 and 7 of this book, in particular, benefited also from an ESRC grant (R000231006) to several scholars, of whom I was one, for research on 'Soviet Economic Reform and its Relationship to Political Change'. In addition to the ESRC, the Hayter Fund of Oxford University and the Elliott Fund of the St Antony's College Russian Centre supported visits to the Institute of World Economy and International Relations in Moscow. The speed with which both the political climate and political institutions changed made relatively frequent first-hand contact especially valuable.

Finally, in any list of acknowledgements, I must mention the tolerance and suport of my family—even when Gorbachev has come between them and me—and thank, in particular, my wife, Pat, for compiling the index to this volume and our son, Douglas, for coming to the rescue on those occasions when my computer did something puzzling.

St Antony's College, Oxford ARCHIE BROWN

List of Plates

Gorbachev and Domestic Soviet Affairs

(between pp. 76 and 77)

1. An early picture of Raisa Titorenko and Mikhail Gorbachev
2. Mikhail Gorbachev and the Old Guard
3. Gorbachev meeting oil workers
4. Gorbachev at the Bolshevik Revolution anniversary parade
5. Alexander Yakovlev
6. Nikolay Ryzhkov
7. Yegor Ligachev
8. The opening of the Nineteenth Party Conference
9. Gorbachev voting at the first contested, union-wide elections in the Soviet Union
10. Gorbachev answering journalists' questions
11. Gorbachev signing the book of condolences for Andrey Sakharov
12. Rival chairmen Anatoly Lukyanov and Boris Yeltsin
13. The leaders of the coup against Gorbachev
14. Gorbachev's arrival in Moscow after the abortive coup attempt
15. Mikhail Gorbachev and Nursultan Nazarbaev, President of Kazakhstan
16, 17, 18   Different moods of Mikhail Gorbachev

Gorbachev in the International Arena

(between pp. 236 and 237)

19. Mikhail Gorbachev in Paris with President François Mitterrand
20. General Secretary Gorbachev and President Reagan signing the INF Treaty
21. Gorbachev being welcomed to Poland by General Wojciech Jaruzelski
22. Raisa and Mikhail Gorbachev with Margaret Thatcher at the Soviet Embassy, London
23. Mikhail Gorbachev and Felipe González, Prime Minister of Spain
24. Gorbachev with his aides Anatoly Chernyaev and Georgy Shakhnazarov
25. Gorbachev with President George Bush and American National Security Adviser Brent Scowcroft
26. Gorbachev and German Chancellor Helmut Kohl after signing a treaty of friendship and co-operation
27. Eduard Shevardnadze, Soviet Foreign Minister 1985–90.

Abbreviations

BBC SWB	British Broadcasting Corporation Summary of World Broadcasts
CPSU	Communist Party of the Soviet Union
FBIS	Foreign Broadcast Information Service (Washington)
Gosagroprom	Russian acronym for State Committee for the Agro-Industrial Complex (1985–9)
IMEMO	Russian acronym for Institute of World Economy and International Relations
INF	Intermediate-range Nuclear Forces
KGB	Russian initials for Committee of State Security (political police)
Komsomol	Russian acronym for Young Communist League
MGIMO	Moscow State Institute of International Relations
MVD	Ministry of Interior
NEP	New Economic Policy (introduced by Lenin in 1921)
NKVD	Russian acronym for People's Commissariat of Internal Affairs (a predecessor of the KGB)
OSCE	Organization for Security and Cooperation in Europe
Politburo	Political Bureau (of the Central Committee of the Communist Party), the highest policy-making body in the USSR for most of the Soviet era
RSFSR	Russian Socialist Federative Soviet Republic (what is now the Russian Federation)
SDI	Strategic Defence Initiative ('Star Wars')
TsEMI	Central Economic-Mathematical Institute
USSR	Union of Soviet Socialist Republics
VTsIOM	All-Russian (formerly All-Union) Centre for the Study of Public Opinion

Note on Transliteration

In transliteration from Russian there is usually a conflict between familiarity and consistency. In the Russian titles in the endnotes, I have adhered to the British Standard transliteration system (one which is used also by a number of major American publications). In the text of the book what readers will find is, for the most part, a modified version of that British Standard system, but which sometimes departs from it to accord with what is the most common English-language rendering of Russian names—thus, for example, Alexander, not Aleksandr, perestroika rather than perestroyka, and Volsky rather than Volskiy. The Russian soft sign has been omitted, rather than transliterated, except when it occurs in the titles of Russian articles or books in the endnotes and in the occasional Russian word in the text when that word has been italicized. An exception to the general rule of transliterating journal or book titles in full has been made for the monthly *Novy mir* which is more familiar in that form than as *Novyy mir*.

Chapter 1

Introduction

THE changes in what used to be the Soviet Union have been so great that it is easy to forget what the unreformed Soviet system was like and how modest were the expectations of significant innovation when Mikhail Gorbachev succeeded Konstantin Chernenko as top Soviet leader in March 1985. Neither Soviet citizens nor foreign observers imagined that the USSR was about to be transformed out of existence. While no one predicted, nor could they, all that was going to happen, those whose scepticism was greatest about the prospects for change were the first to be overtaken by events. Some, who in more recent years have castigated Gorbachev for his 'half-measures', have found it convenient to forget that the actual changes promoted or sanctioned by Gorbachev exceeded their wildest dreams, making a nonsense of predictions that he had neither the will nor the power to alter anything of consequence in the Soviet system.

When it became fashionable to react against the enthusiastic support for Gorbachev which was widespread in the late 1980s, the same observers who misread Gorbachev's intentions at the outset became the first to scorn an excessive concentration on the part played by Gorbachev while simultaneously, and with scant regard for logic, holding him personally responsible for all the major policy failures. And failures in the Gorbachev era there certainly were—especially of economic policy and in the relationships between the Soviet Union's constituent republics and the centre.

If the scale of the change in the Soviet Union during the Gorbachev years is considered with dispassion, what is most remarkable is the extent to which it occurred peacefully. Given the failure of all who had openly attacked the system from within the country to make any positive impact on policy outcomes prior to the late 1980s, it is doubtful if change of such magnitude could have taken place with so little violence—especially in Russia—in any way other than through the elevation of a serious reformer to the highest political office within the country. The prospect of a reformer becoming General Secretary—the very idea that such a thing was possible in principle—had been ruled out in advance by many Western observers and by such prominent exiles from the Soviet Union as the writers Alexander Solzhenitsyn and Alexander Zinoviev. Yet, it was the great power concentrated in the hands of the Communist Party leadership collectively and the General Secretary individually which made it critically important that someone of reformist disposition should attain the latter office. Without the promotion of a genuine reformer and highly skilled politician to the top Communist Party post in 1985, fundamental change in the Soviet Union would certainly have been delayed and could well have been bloodier as well as slower than the relatively speedy political evolution which occurred while Gorbachev was at the helm.

The General Secretaryship

The pre-reform Soviet system was one in which power flowed from the top down and in which the highest authority at each level was the party First Secretary. That was the case whether the unit of government was a union republic such as Lithuania or Georgia, a province of Russia such as the Sverdlovsk region or the Stavropol territory, a city, or a rural district. At the highest echelon of the system—the 'all-union' level—the most powerful person was, without doubt, the General Secretary of the Central Committee. The politician who attained that office was not only the acknowledged leader of the Communist Party but also in practice the chief executive within the country.

Only at the beginning of the Soviet epoch, and more ambiguously at the end of it, was the General Secretary not the most authoritative and powerful figure within the state as well as the Communist Party. In the earliest years of Soviet rule, Vladimir Lenin—who had led the Bolshevik faction of the revolutionary movement since 1903—was the acknowledged leader, even though his formal title was that of Chairman of the Council of People's Commissars (a body which in the post-Second World War period became the Council of Ministers). Although Joseph Stalin had become General Secretary of the Communist Party in 1922, it was only during periods of Lenin's physical incapacity and especially after Lenin's death in early 1924 that Stalin was able to use to the full the powers of the General Secretaryship. The right to appoint officials and the responsibility for execution of policy vested in the Secretariat of the Central Committee of the Communist Party were turned by Stalin into his personal prerogatives—powers concentrated in the office of the General Secretary, who stood at the top of the hierarchy of party secretaries spread across the country.

There were only six ruling General Secretaries in the entire seventy-four years of Soviet history. The power which Stalin acquired (and the way he used it) was of a different order from that of his successors. His willingness to employ ruthless terror against his potential rivals within the Communist Party as well as against enemies, real or imagined, in the broader society saw the Soviet Union move from an oligarchical rule in the 1920s—when Stalin was, however, already more than a first among equals—to a tyrannical personal dictatorship from the early 1930s until Stalin's death in March 1953. The Communist Party remained an important instrument of rule, but only as one among several such instruments, with the political police and the ministerial network playing no less crucial parts. Indeed, the statutes of the Communist Party—concerning, for example, how often Party Congresses or plenary sessions of the Central Committee should be held—were so blatantly disregarded by Stalin that immediately after his death it was not clear to all of his successors how potentially powerful the party organization still was and how control over it was the most important of all political resources in the Soviet system.[1]

Upon Stalin's death the Soviet Union reverted for a time to oligarchical rule, as a struggle for power took place among his successors. Latterly Stalin had been Chairman of the Council of Ministers as well as party leader and it was his successor in the former post, Georgy Malenkov, who seemed to the West to be Stalin's heir. But within two years Nikita Khrushchev, as First Secretary of the Central Committee (as the General Secretaryship was known between 1953 and 1966), had established his ascendancy. Although this was challenged in 1957 when some of the old guard—such as Malenkov, Vyacheslav Molotov, and Lazar Kaganovich—tried to overthrow him, Khrushchev was able to use his support in the ranks of the Central Committee to overcome what he called the 'so-called arithmetical majority' in the Politburo opposed to him. From that point on, but especially in the early 1960s, Khrushchev became a more domineering leader. Having added the post of Chairman of the Council of Ministers in 1958 to his party leadership, he proceeded to push through a number of policies which were not to the liking of most sectors of the political élite. Although Khrushchev did not instigate such radical changes to the Soviet system as Gorbachev was later to do, and though he himself accepted much more unquestioningly the fundamentals of that system, he was unpredictable and posed a threat to the security of tenure of party and state officials. This was in the end sufficient to bring together a coalition of high officials, including virtually the entire Politburo, to remove him from office in October 1964.[2]

Leonid Brezhnev, Khrushchev's successor, lasted eighteen years as Soviet leader by making sure that his style of leadership was as different as possible from Khrushchev's. Where Khrushchev was impetuous he was cautious; where Khrushchev did not hesitate to berate and demote party and state officials, or divide their powers and functions in half—as he did with all the regional party secretaries in 1962—Brezhnev was solicitous in his concern for the party apparatus; he made a boast and a virtue out of his policy of 'stability of cadres'. Whereas Khrushchev had not hesitated to take the lead on policy, Brezhnev was careful never to risk isolation on any issue and was a consensus-seeker within the Soviet top leadership. Yet, over time, Brezhnev was able to promote a greatly exaggerated account of his merits and achievements (to which public obeisance was paid, even if it never remotely reached the fervour or absurd extremes of the Stalin cult) and, having gradually succeeded in bringing into leadership positions more and more people personally indebted to him, he wielded greater power in the 1970s than he had possessed in the 1960s. At no time, however, did Brezhnev challenge the basic norms of the Soviet system; he was attentive to the particular interests of party officials, ministerial bureaucrats, the military, and the KGB, and shared their common interest in defending the system against any spontaneous political activity or independent political thought. While this approach was conducive to Brezhnev's political longevity, and by no means unattractive to the different branches of the Soviet establishment, it did nothing to tackle the underlying problems of the country; moreover, one person's 'stability of cadres' was another's promotion blockage. The 'era of stagnation' became, during the perestroika years, the most common way of referring to the Soviet Union under Brezhnev.[3]

When Yury Andropov succeeded Brezhnev, he was already 68 years of age and soon to be in failing health. More will be said about Andropov in the next two chapters, for he played an important part in advancing Gorbachev's career. He himself, however, was never likely to be an advocate of far-reaching political change of the kind which occurred in the Soviet Union in the second half of the 1980s. Fifteen years as head of the KGB had made Andropov suspicious of anything smacking of dissidence or political pluralism. He was, though, much less complacent than Brezhnev and prepared to contemplate reform within broader limits than those envisaged by his arch-conservative predecessor, albeit falling far short of what Gorbachev was prepared to implement. Andropov, in fact, altered the political agenda even within his short period of office by placing greater emphasis on discipline and on fighting corruption as well as by giving his blessing to some tentative moves in the direction of economic reform. There was also under Andropov a stepping-up of propaganda against alcoholism, although this was in practice contradicted and superseded by the introduction for the first time in years of a cheaper brand of vodka, which, as a sign of gratitude on the part of its consumers, became popularly known as 'Andropovka'. Although General Secretary only from Brezhnev's death in November 1982 until his own death in February 1984, Andropov did enough to demonstrate that the General Secretraryship was still the most important political office in the country, even if there were also quite clearly—in the post-Stalin era and following the forcible removal of Khrushchev—political limits on those powers.

The limits were more evident than the power during the thirteen-month incumbency of Andropov's successor, Konstantin Chernenko. As will be noted in greater detail in Chapter 3, Gorbachev was already at that time a possible alternative candidate to Chernenko and, indeed, Andropov's own choice for the succession. The caution of a majority in the Politburo who formed the main selectorate for the General Secretaryship, even though their choice had to be endorsed by the entire Central Committee, made them opt instead for the 72-year-old Chernenko, who clearly was not going to rock the boat to the extent that even Andropov had done (with his anti-corruption campaign and quite extensive personnel changes). A combination, however, of the failing health of Chernenko and the substantial foothold which Gorbachev already had in the Central Committee Secretariat meant that there was a stalemate in the leadership during the thirteen months between Chernenko's accession and his death in March 1985. Lip-service was paid to Chernenko as the supreme leader, but there was widespread awareness that this was no more than an interregnum and that if the real issues were to be tackled, it could only be when the physically declining Chernenko had departed from the scene.

Changing evaluations of Gorbachev

A remarkable amount has already been written about Mikhail Gorbachev and the fashionable view of him had already gone through three phases before his leadership and the Soviet Union itself came to an end. During the first two years or so—from 1985 until at least the end of 1986—the conventional wisdom in the West was that Gorbachev had introduced a change of style and that, in so far as he was a reformer, he was one of a technocratic type. No far-reaching changes in the Soviet political and economic system or in Soviet foreign policy could be expected.[4] That view was also quite widespread in Soviet liberal intellectual circles, although with the mass of the people Gorbachev's popularity was especially high during his first two years. (Indeed, contrary to what has been suggested both by many Western commentators and by Gorbachev's political enemies in Russia, Gorbachev was still the most popular and respected person in the Soviet Union five years after he had become General Secretary—a point which will be elaborated below.) His comparative youth and vigour made a striking contrast with the infirmity of his three predecessors and his televised meetings with ordinary citizens on the streets and in the countryside enhanced his popularity during the early stages of his General Secretaryship.

By 1987 most Western observers with reasonably open minds (although those with closed minds constituted an aggressively vocal minority[5]) could discern important developments taking place inside the leadership of the Soviet Communist Party. For some of them the turning-point was the January plenary session of the Central Committee which put political reform clearly on the agenda, for others it was the Central Committee meeting in June of the same year which endorsed the need for significant economic reform.[6] Within the Soviet Union itself, especially in intellectual circles, Gorbachev was from 1987 until early 1989 more widely than hitherto regarded as a great reformer. He was held in increasingly high esteem by Soviet democrats—who had previously been (and were subsequently to become again) very wary of him—and held in still higher regard by much of the outside world.

As one Eastern European country after another regained its autonomy and ended Communist rule, Gorbachev's popularity in the West actually grew throughout 1989. Acceptance of such a contraction of 'the Soviet bloc' was the most eloquent testimony to the seriousness of the 'New Thinking' on foreign policy which some Western sceptics had earlier dismissed as mere propaganda. The popularity of Gorbachev within the Soviet Union, however, reached its high point earlier with the advent of competitive elections to a new Soviet representative assembly and the convening of that body—the First Congress of People's Deputies—in the spring of 1989. Gorbachev's chairmanship of the sessions did not satisfy the conservative majority of the delegates, who were irritated by the fact that he gave the floor to representatives of the radical minority—and in particular Andrey Sakharov—more often than their numerical representation warranted. The liberals, for their part, did not like the extent to which Gorbachev dominated the proceedings, a domination which partly reflected the contradictory roles he was playing simultaneously—those of Communist Party leader, chief executive within the state, and, in effect, speaker of the fledgeling parliament.[7]

Moreover, concern about domestic economic and inter-ethnic problems, which were getting more rather than less severe, bulked larger in the minds of many Soviet citizens than the events in Eastern Europe. The latter had, however, two undesirable side-effects for Gorbachev. First, they greatly increased dissatisfaction with his policies in the army, not only on account of the loss—as some of his military critics saw it—of the fruits of victory in the Second World War but also because large numbers of officers and men had to return at short notice to woefully inadequate accommodation in the Soviet Union. Second, fired by the East European example, far more Soviet citizens than hitherto began to associate their misfortunes with the rule of the Communist Party. As leader of that party, Gorbachev could hardly escape some of the odium.

Thus, from the summer and autumn of 1989 in the Soviet Union and from early 1990 in the West the mood changed and a third stage of evaluation of Gorbachev was reached. Although Gorbachev's standing declined less in the West than in the Soviet Union, in the West, too, he was given reduced credit for managing a Soviet transition which had already gone further than anyone had envisaged in 1985. In the course of 1990 he was increasingly seen as part of the problem—an obstacle to the successful transformation of the Soviet system.[8] Yet, despite Gorbachev's greater popularity abroad than at home by the time he reached his last two years in office, and despite the growing opposition to him from both the radical democratic and the conservative Communist ends of the domestic political spectrum, in April 1990 he was still by a large margin the most respected political figure within the Soviet Union. It was not until May–June 1990 that Yeltsin's popularity moved ahead of Gorbachev's.[9] Over the previous year Gorbachev's support had declined, but not by so much within the country as a whole as in the groups with whom Western journalists most mingled. During the last two years and especially the last eighteen months in which Gorbachev held office, the drop in his popularity became steeper,[10] but most Western politicians—none of whom had turned their country upside down to the extent Gorbachev did—would have settled for being far more highly regarded than their nearest political rival five years after gaining office. One of the leading researchers (in post-Soviet Russia, the Director) of the most profes- sional of the public opinion research centres in the Soviet Union,[11] Yury Levada, noted in April 1990 that whereas 'a year ago' 55 per cent of the population had named Gorbachev as 'man of the year', in the spring of 1990 that had dropped to 46 per cent. Levada added, however, that, given the degree of exasperation and alienation in the society, that was a lot, 'the more so in that, so far as public opinion is concerned, he does not have any real rivals'. He noted, for instance, that only 16 per cent had named Boris Yeltsin—less than a third of those who had opted for Gorbachev.[12] By the summer of 1990 that had changed, but the change occurred much later in Gorbachev's leadership than is generally appreci- ated.[13] For much the greater part of his period of office as *de facto* chief executive, Gorbachev was the most highly esteemed politician in the Soviet Union.

The art of the impossible

It is as well, therefore, to bear in mind that *fashionable* opinion about Gorbachev—whether in Russia or in the West—has, for better or worse, not always been representative of Russian or Soviet society. While the fashionable opinions in each of the three phases of evaluation noted above were far from universal among those who offered public comment on the Soviet scene— whether in the West or the Soviet Union itself—at each stage of the Gorbachev era they were very widespread. Professional vantage-point, however, produced some variations. Thus, it was not accidental that Gorbachev's stock remained higher with Western politicians than with, in particular, the majority of economists specializing in Soviet affairs. No one, though, really needed to be an economist to see that the Soviet economy was going from bad to worse. The man and woman on the street anywhere between Minsk and Khabarovsk could have said the same. And since this was neither Stalin's nor Brezhnev's time but an era of Soviet history of unprecedented freedom, they frequently did.

Western politicians, however, did not base their judgements entirely on the state of the Soviet economy, but accorded a great deal of weight to changes in the language of politics, to new departures in Soviet foreign policy, and to political institutional change. With their understanding of politics as the art of the possible, they were constantly amazed to see Gorbachev pull off what seemed to them virtually *im*possible feats. In some ways they were more aware than many of the academic observers—and better aware, too, than a number of the new, radical, and (of necessity) relatively inexperienced politicians who emerged in the Soviet Union—of the framework of constraints within which Gorbachev was operating and of the balancing act which was at times demanded of him prior to the attempted coup.

Gorbachev behaved within the Soviet Union, as well as in his dealings with American and European leaders, more like a Western politician than any of his predecessors ever did. An appreciation of this, and a willingness to give Gorbachev a substantial share of the credit for the dramatic political changes, cut across party boundaries in the West. Such experienced politicians as François Mitterrand and Helmut Kohl, Ronald Reagan and George Bush, and Margaret Thatcher and Denis Healey sooner or later recognized that Gorbachev could transcend his political origins in the apparatus of the Soviet Communist Party. (Thatcher and Healey were among the first to see this and Kohl was a late but subsequently enthusiastic learner.[14])

The dissident movement and perestroika

The view that Gorbachev was capable of throwing off the shackles of Communist Party doctrine and organization had become more controversial by 1991. On the one hand, expectations had been raised by the ending of Communist rule in Eastern Europe in 1989–90 and, on the other hand, Gorbachev was judged more critically in the light of deepening Soviet economic, centre–periphery, and inter-ethnic problems. Some rewriting of Soviet history in the light of the latest perceptions got under way. Even before the failed coup, it was pointed out that many of the ideas being advanced in the Soviet Union were no different from those proclaimed by persecuted dissidents in the late 1960s and early 1970s. Indeed, both opponents and some of the more radical supporters of the reforms of the Gorbachev era drew attention, from their different standpoints, to the similarities. A Soviet journal of documents from the party archives actually printed in 1990 the text of a long letter previously known only in dissident literature—a plea for change written jointly by Andrey Sakharov, Valentin Turchin, and Roy Medvedev in 1970 and addressed to Brezhnev as party General Secretary, Aleksey Kosygin as Chairman of the Council of Ministers, and Nikolay Podgorny as Chairman of the Presidium of the Supreme

Soviet.[15] At the time there was a total lack of response on the part of the Soviet leadership to the demands of Sakharov, Turchin, and Medvedev, but in the period between 1985 and 1990 almost every issue raised by them so many years earlier was put on the political agenda and acted upon.

Much even of the political language of the 1970 document was to be echoed fifteen years later, whether the three authors' call for economic reform, democratization, and glasnost or their characterization of the period they were living through as one of 'stagnation' (*zastoy*). Even a number of the most specific suggestions were translated into political reality in the mid-1980s—for example, the call by Sakharov, Turchin, and Medvedev for the establishment of an institute for the study of public opinion.[16] Some of the proposals made were more modest than the actual political developments of the second half of the 1980s (by which time, of course, the agenda of Sakharov, in particular, had also become more radical). Thus, the twelfth of the fourteen points on which Sakharov, Turchin, and Medvedev called for action from the Soviet leadership in 1970 was for the '*gradual* introduction . . . of several candidates for each place in elections for party and soviet organs at all levels, including indirect elections' (emphasis added).[17] There is no suggestion that there should be more than one party in the political arena.

There is not the slightest doubt that many of the ideas which were openly discussed in the Soviet mass media in the second half of the 1980s, and in a number of cases translated into public policy, had first been aired in dissident circles. That, however, does not mean that this was a simple case of continuity, that the changes of the Gorbachev era were no more than a continuation of a process the dissidents had begun. It is not only that there was a total lack of positive response to the demands of Soviet dissidents between 1968 and 1985, but that the views of a good many reformers who had decided that discretion was the better part of valour, and who did not offer an open challenge to the authorities until such time as Gorbachev had made the Soviet Union safe for dissent, were little different from those of the dissidents. Such people were often referred to as 'within-system reformers', but since in the long run they were actually undermining the Soviet political and social order, the phenomenon they represented might equally or more appropriately—as Alexander Shtromas plausibly argued more than a decade ago—be called 'intrastructural dissent', as distinct from the 'extrastructural dissent' of the overt oppositionists.[18] So far as the latter were concerned, it is important to note that the dissident movement had been manifestly weakened by persecution over the decade and a half before Gorbachev became Soviet leader. The measures used against those who made their political dissent unambiguous and public ranged from compulsory exile to incarceration in labour camp or mental asylum. The *post hoc, ergo propter hoc* argument which sees the overt dissidents of the pre-Gorbachev era as the prime instigators of the changes of the second half of the 1980s ignores the fact that in the later Brezhnev years and under Andropov and Chernenko the Soviet dissident movement was at its lowest level of activity in two decades and had, to a large extent, been crushed.[19]

The leading Western specialist on Soviet dissidents, Peter Reddaway, writing in 1983 about the 'post-1979 purge of dissent', noted that 'the dissenting groups and movements . . . have made little or no headway among the mass of ordinary people in the Russian heartland'.[20] For that reason the Soviet leadership felt free to conduct 'the post-1979 purge of dissent' with the knowledge that it would 'not produce a large-scale internal backlash'.[21] 'Why', Reddaway asks, 'have ordinary Russian people been so inert?' He answers:

> First, the general demoralization and loss of autonomous values described so vividly by Andrey Amalrik and Alexander Zinoviev evidently still obtain.[22] Second, police controls remain overwhelmingly strong. And third, the regime's constant propaganda, relating all dissent to the malign influence of foreigners (or to mental illness), doubtless has a certain effect, if only over time.[23]

On the eve of perestroika, the leading dissidents were in prison and exile or, at best, under constant surveillance. None of their works could be published in the Soviet Union and by the first half of the 1980s the flow of protest letters and of *samizdat* (do-it-yourself) publications had been reduced to a trickle, as had emigration from the USSR. Alexander Solzhenitsyn had been sent into foreign exile as early as 1974 and Andrey Sakharov was banished to the city of Gorky (which has now been given back its old name of Nizhny Novgorod) in 1980. In the years immediately before Gorbachev became General Secretary even Roy Medvedev had KGB policemen sitting outside his apartment to prevent him meeting foreigners. That was notwithstanding the fact that, although he was a leading dissenter, his views represented a far less root-and-branch rejection of the Soviet system than did those of Solzhenitsyn and Sakharov (each from his very different perspective). By the autumn of 1991, the political turnaround had been such that Medvedev, who had been expelled from the Communist Party in 1969 and only readmitted to it in 1989, was protesting against the post-coup banning of the party by the Russian President (and former candidate member of the Politburo), Boris Yeltsin. In 1990 Medvedev had become a member of the CPSU Central Committee.

Solzhenitsyn—although he resisted calls for him to return to his homeland even after the failure of the August 1991 coup and the decision to quash the long-standing treason charge against him (and returned to Russia only in May 1994)—was able to publish in September 1990 in two mass-circulation Soviet newspapers his political programme, 'How to rebuild Russia'. His major books, including such a fundamental indictment of the Soviet system as *The Gulag Archipelago*, also appeared in Moscow editions while Gorbachev was still leader of the USSR.[24] Once a new openness and tolerance had begun to be practised, former dissidents played a significant part in carrying the process of change further. But that came after Gorbachev's breakthroughs of 1987 and 1988. The dissident movement retrospectively commanded much respect, but to see it as the prime agent of the changes in Russia and the Soviet Union as a whole which began in the mid-1980s is highly misleading and a product largely of wishful thinking.[25] (However, the fact that the dissidents were not decisive political actors at the time Gorbachev came to power does not mean that they were, in general, of no political consequence. They played a role in changing the political consciousness of a part of the intelligentsia.)

There was a tendency during the last two years of the Soviet Union's existence for citizens of the USSR to project backwards their criticism of Gorbachev as well as their support for more radically libertarian and democratic reformers—in particular, Sakharov. By the time of his death in December 1989, Sakharov was not only a prominent member of the Congress of People's Deputies but also the most respected upholder of democratic and liberal values in the country.[26] Yet less than a year before that a poll (in early 1989) of readers of *Literaturnaya gazeta*—a weekly newspaper read mainly by intellectuals—while it put Sakharov in second place as 'hero of the year' with 17 per cent support, placed him far behind Gorbachev, who was chosen by 68 per cent of respondents. When the same set of questions was put at that time in a national random sample (and thus, unlike the *Literaturnaya gazeta* survey, not biased towards the intelligentsia), only 1.5 per cent accorded heroic status to Sakharov.[27]

Popular reverence for Sakharov has become much greater after his death than it was in his lifetime,[28] although it was growing in the last year of his life. A large-scale public opinion survey conducted in December 1989, the month in which Sakharov died, asked Soviet respondents to name the man of the year.[29] (As distinct from the survey cited by Yury Levada—and noted above—this one invited answers not only about Soviet public figures, but about men from any country.) Some of the respondents were questioned shortly before Sakharov's death and others after it. Although foreign politicians figured in the list, pride of place was given to Russians. Sakharov was mentioned by 10.7 per cent of respondents and placed second only to Gorbachev (35.3 per cent) but ahead of Yeltsin—in third place at that time with 5.5 per cent. (A greater 'internationalism' was shown in answers to the question about the 'woman of the year', in which Margaret Thatcher, mentioned by almost 17 per cent of respondents, had a clear lead over her nearest rival.[30])

The impact made by Sakharov in the last year of his life, when he became for the first time a familiar figure for a mass Soviet public, does not mean that the earlier dissident movement had comparably influenced Soviet citizens. As late as March 1991 more than half of them were still either unfamiliar with the term 'dissident', or unable to say what the dissidents had struggled for. This is, of course, an indication of the relative efficiency of the KGB in the pre-perestroika years when they were successfully combating dissent. They had been able, to an extent, to seal off the mass of the people from the influence of dissenting views and to portray the dissidents as unpatriotic strangers within their own country. In the survey of March 1991, 71 per cent of citizens could not recall the name of a single dissident. (Among those who could, Sakharov and Solzhenitsyn were by far the best known.[31]) By the time that survey was conducted, Sakharov—fifteen months after his death—was placed above Gorbachev in respect of 'moral authority', as was now Boris Yeltsin. Asked to name people who 'in our time' have by their example and moral authority appreciably changed public opinion, Sakharov (named by 13 per cent) came in second place to Yeltsin (14 per cent), whereas Gorbachev came third (mentioned in this context by only 7 per cent of respondents).[32]

Yet, a mere fourteen months earlier—at a time when his popularity was already past its peak—Gorbachev was the only living person in the Soviet Union to be mentioned by a substantial number of Soviet citizens when they were asked (in a survey conducted by the same All-Union Centre for the Study of Public Opinion) to 'name the ten most outstanding people of all times and peoples'. Gorbachev was cited by 22.6 per cent of the population and occupied fourth place after Lenin (68 per cent), Marx (36.2 per cent), and Peter the Great (31.9 per cent).[33] To find Lenin and Marx enjoying the highest esteem of all would have been unthinkable in Poland, Hungary, or Czechoslovakia. It serves as a reminder of the important differences in political culture among the various Communist and post-Communist countries. In the Soviet context, however, it was also of interest that one-third of Soviet citizens did *not* in December 1989, when the survey was conducted, include Lenin in their list of the ten most outstanding people. Two or three years earlier support for Lenin would almost certainly have been still greater. Two or three years later, in contrast, Lenin's standing—while not as negligible as in the former Communist countries of Central Europe—had declined further.[34] An increasingly large number of Soviet citizens, in the wake of the August 1991 coup and its aftermath, had come to the conclusion that it was Lenin who must bear major responsibility for dispatching them on 'a road to nowhere' which they had traversed for over seventy years. But in the mid-1980s that was still the view of only a small minority of the population.

The social and political scene in Russia and most of the republics of the former Soviet Union changed with quite exceptional speed over the last six to seven years of existence of the Soviet state. There is ample evidence, too, of change in political attitudes and consciousness over the same period. It is important, therefore, to understand events in the early years of perestroika and Gorbachev's initiatives and political vocabulary at that time in their context, and not to view them exclusively through today's lenses. Much that was to become widely accepted in Russia and other successor states of the Soviet Union in the early 1990s was resisted in the mid-1980s—by public opinion as well as by the powerful bureaucratic institutions which were threatened by any move towards radical political and economic reform.

There were many stimuli to the changes which followed the succession of Gorbachev to the Soviet leadership in March 1985, including (some two or more years into perestroika) the moral and intellectual legacy of the dissidents of the 1960s and 1970s. But, as should emerge more fully in subsequent chapters, the choice of Gorbachev, rather than of any of the other people in the Communist Party leadership who could aspire to the party's (and at that time the country's) most powerful post, was of critical importance. Although this book does not concentrate exclusively on Gorbachev but attempts to put him in context, the main emphasis is, as the title indicates, on *the Gorbachev factor*. Such a focus is justified by the centrality of Gorbachev to the process of change.

A study in the politics of leadership cannot simultaneously be a study of everything else, although authors writing about Gorbachev tend to be accused (sometimes justly, sometimes not) of ignoring or playing down the importance of such major phenomena as the nationalities question or socio-economic developments. In focusing on Gorbachev's distinctive and fundamentally important contribution to political change in his country and in the wider world, I am far from unaware of this broader context. Indeed, writing some twenty years ago, I singled out as the 'major sources of tension and potential sources of tension . . . capable, in due course, of producing fundamental political change' in the Soviet Union, first, the nationalities problem (especially the growth of Russian nationalism and nationalism in the three Baltic states, Armenia, Georgia, and Western Ukraine); second, the potential threat of either workers or intelligentsia acquiring a stronger sense of group or class consciousness and acting as a social class 'in the sense of interacting politically and articulating collective demands'; and, third, demographic change whereby Russians stood to lose their overall majority within the Soviet Union and generational change which would bring into the party leadership people who had reached the age of political consciousness after the mass terror had ended and who might be 'more prepared to accept the risks entailed in political reform'.[35]

I am, accordingly, far from wishing to suggest that there are no other major themes to be explored or quite different books to be written about the demise of Communism in the Soviet Union in addition to work which examines the role of Mikhail Gorbachev. On the contrary, there is vastly more which needs to be elucidated about the social and political pre-conditions for the changes in the USSR and Russia after 1985.[36] The issue of the relations between the different nationalities within the Soviet Union, to which some attention is paid in later chapters of this book (especially Chapter 8), was such a prime factor in the breakdown of the classical Soviet system and the dissolution of the Soviet state that it will certainly attract further intensive work, in addition to the specialized recent studies which have already appeared.[37] The long-term decline in the rate of Soviet economic growth and the stagnation in the economy at the end of the 1970s and beginning of the 1980s is also a factor of prime importance in understanding the political change of the later 1980s, and it is one to which I return in Chapters 3 and 5. There is also, especially from 1987 onwards, a vital 'Yeltsin factor' in Soviet politics—quite apart from Yeltsin's overwhelming importance in early post-Soviet Russia. Although the Gorbachev–Yeltsin relationship is another recurring theme in the later chapters of this book (especially Chapters 6 and 8), Yeltsin's own role deserves study in greater depth and detail than is possible here.[38]

Learning, power, and pressure

There are numerous general accounts of the Gorbachev era[39] and several detailed political histories of the second half of the 1980s.[40] There are also some popular—although, for the most part, insubstantial—biographies of Gorbachev.[41] But there is still a paucity of political analyses which try to comprehend the evolution of Gorbachev's thinking and to identify and evaluate his personal contribution to change in Soviet political theory and political practice. Fathoming what Gorbachev thought when is a difficult part of the enterprise and one which cannot be determined simply by taking at face value all of his public statements at any given time.[42]

The proposals for political and economic change which Gorbachev endorsed between 1987 and 1991 (even before the coup and its aftermath) were so much more far-reaching and profound than those he put forward in his first two years as General Secretary as to call for explanation. Three major interpretations suggest themselves. They can be summarized as *learning, power,* and *pressure.* The first possible explanation is that Gorbachev *learned* with remarkable speed on the job and changed his entire outlook after becoming Soviet leader. A second explanation is that, as his *power* increased, so he was able to do more of the things he wanted to do but initially was constrained from doing. A third is that, unknowingly, he opened a Pandora's box out of which emerged pent-up grievances and new demands, under the *pressure* of which he had no choice but to buckle, going on to accommodate himself to change he was unable to resist.

None of these interpretations on its own provides an adequate explanation of the changing Soviet political agenda in the second half of the 1980s, although the first and third—or a combination of the two—have often been seen as sufficient by their proponents. Those explanations are especially favoured by Western students of the Soviet Union and political commentators who spent the first two years of Gorbachev's General Secretaryship assuring the world that the new leader would make only cosmetic or, at most, technocratic changes and would leave untouched the basics of the Soviet system. It was easier for them to claim that Gorbachev had changed utterly than to admit that they themselves had been utterly wrong. Alternatively—and this is one of the variants of the third interpretation—they could view Gorbachev as an orthodox Leninist, making what was only a tactical retreat, while remaining ready to restore familiar Communist norms when the time was ripe.[43]

At the outset of Gorbachev's General Secretaryship,[44] and, indeed, while Brezhnev was still alive,[45] I argued that Gorbachev would be a serious reformer, a view expressed at that time by only one other Western scholar, so far as I am aware.[46] Although it appeared to me that Gorbachev's impact on the Soviet system would be greater than that of any Soviet leader since Stalin, but of an altogether more enlightened nature, events were to move faster and more dramatically than I or anyone else predicted. They did not, however, do so in such a way as to make acceptable the first and third interpretations of the radicalization of the Soviet political agenda in the unqualified form in which they were stated above.

But while I argue in the next two chapters that Gorbachev's reformist disposition was not a new phenomenon—but one which pre-dated his General Secretaryship—I am far from wishing to deny that he underwent a profound *learning* process after becoming Soviet leader. His knowledge of the outside political world became far greater and his political ideas significantly altered during his years in office. That, too, will be one of the themes of the chapters which follow.[47] This links up with the stress which deserves to be placed on the importance of Gorbachev's increasing *power* between 1985 and 1989 for the radicalization of the Soviet reform agenda. A major reason why that enhanced power was significant was precisely because Gorbachev had a remarkably open mind for a politician who rose to the top through the ranks of the Soviet Communist Party bureaucracy. He was more willing to trust the evidence of his own eyes than the dogmas of traditional Marxism-Leninism. Accordingly, a number of policy positions and ideological tenets he had embraced by 1990—not to speak of his abandonment of the Communist Party in August 1991 following the failure of the attempted *putsch*—went well beyond what he could have envisaged himself accepting five years earlier.

The changing balance of power within the Soviet leadership and political system was crucially important, in the first instance, as an enabling factor. Between 1985 and 1989 Gorbachev was able to make these changes work to his advantage and to endorse publicly more radical propositions in 1989 than he dared espouse in 1985. From 1989 onwards, however, the changing power structure became a double-edged sword. Within the federal executive Gorbachev's powers increased, but the federal executive organs themselves were increasingly frustrated by new or newly emboldened institutional actors in other parts of the political system. The pluralization of Soviet politics had changed the rules of the game and provided new sources of *pressure* and influence upon Gorbachev. By 1990 they had changed to such an extent that the country's top leader could be openly attacked and defied; and, by 1991, in a number of areas of policy, major initiatives from the centre had to become a matter of prior negotiation with elected representatives of the republics. The turning-point was the introduction of contested elections in 1989 and their development into still freer elections the following year.[48] With that breakthrough, Soviet society—including political organizations and movements outside the Communist Party (and in some cases vehemently opposed to it)—acquired a hitherto unknown degree of autonomy. Among other things, that curtailed the power of the country's top leader in entirely new ways. Gorbachev had, to a remarkable extent, outwitted the traditional holders of institutional power who imposed constraints upon a Soviet leader's freedom of action, but he had also been responsible for the creation of new countervailing powers, more broadly based than any of the old ones and embodying many of the characteristics of political pluralism.

Even the increase of Gorbachev's power within the federal executive had its limits. It is true, as will be discussed in a later chapter, that with the creation of an executive presidency he reduced the direct power of the Politburo and the Central Committee of the Communist Party to conduct the affairs of state and their power to constrain the chief executive in his choice of policy options. Gorbachev had, however, only a small presidential apparatus and, so, for the implementation of policy he remained dependent both upon the entrenched government machine and, at lower levels, upon the party bureaucracy. As much of what he was trying to do was counter to the interests of those institutions, it is hardly surprising that there was a gap between the enunciation of policy and its execution. People who deemed it necessary to seize power from Gorbachev in August 1991, and who proved capable of putting him under house arrest as a prelude to establishing a new, highly authoritarian regime, were hardly likely to flinch from undermining his policies whenever opportunity arose at an earlier stage.

'Communism is unreformable'

One *non sequitur* in discussions of change in the Soviet Union should be disposed of at this early stage. That is the view that Gorbachev cannot be taken seriously as a reformer because there is no such thing as *reform communism*—'Communism is unreformable'. It does indeed make no sense to speak of *reform communism*. But that does not mean that a Communist system could not and did not become something different in kind—i.e. cease to be Communist in any meaningful sense of the term—while being led by a Communist reformer who became in due course a systemic transformer. Nor does it mean that reformers within a Communist system may not set in motion processes that lead to the replacement of that system by another. Evolutionary change is often in the long run more far-reaching in its effects than revolutionary upheaval, and the Gorbachev era was one of profound and—in a comparative context—surprisingly fast political evolution.

The Soviet Union, between the spring of 1989 and the summer of 1991, was in the throes of systemic transformation, and Gorbachev, as the leader of the country throughout a period of historic change, used a vocabulary which was a mixture of the old and the new. But in each year from 1985 to 1991 the proportion of new concepts to old in his political lexicon significantly increased. During that time he continued to refer to himself as a Communist (in public at least) and, with greater conviction, as a socialist. This was hardly surprising. An explicit renunciation of either identification would have had the probable effect of bringing forward the date of the coup. Indeed, until March 1990, when he became President, a coup in the 'constitutional' (or, more precisely, unconstitutional) sense would not even have been necessary. Gorbachev could have been removed—and surely would have been—at a moment's notice by the Central Committee of the Soviet Communist Party on the advice of the Politburo had he openly criticized either Communism or socialism, for his power until 1990 rested on the General Secretaryship of the Central Committee of the party. Following the introduction of competitive elections in 1989 and a new-style Supreme Soviet of which Gorbachev was Chairman, the process might not have been as straightforward as was the removal of Nikita Khrushchev in October 1964, but it would have been all too predictable an outcome if Gorbachev had attacked 'socialism' rather than redefining it.

In fact, the course he followed was a more subtle one than crude, counter-productive frontal attack. The views and policies he adopted moved further and further away from Communism in any meaningful sense of the term and—as is discussed in detail in later chapters—socialism was so redefined that it gradually came closer to social democracy of a West European variety than to Soviet-type socialism. Thus, the common criticism of Gorbachev that he refused to abandon an outmoded concept fails to pay due attention to the change in substance which lay behind some continuity of language and disregards the political context within which he was operating. A more telling criticism would be that, notwithstanding serious moves in the direction of political pluralism, the social democratic variant of socialism Gorbachev increasingly espoused remained in a number of respects at a conceptual rather than a practical level, for up to the coup the Soviet economy stayed highly centralized and overwhelmingly state-owned. It was also not unreasonable to criticize Gorbachev—even without the benefit of hindsight—for clinging too long to the Communist Party as an institution, although he had abandoned much of Communist ideology. The party, whose predominance had been taken for granted even by reformers until the late 1980s, had become increasingly discredited throughout the last two years of its existence prior to the coup. But Gorbachev's reasons for retaining the office of General Secretary for as long as he did (discussed in later chapters) had little or nothing to do with a continued attachment to a traditional Communist order which some of his critics imputed to him.

For both personal psychological and practical political reasons Gorbachev preferred to stretch the meaning of Communism to breaking-point and to engage in a gradual rethinking of what was meant by socialism. The process was, at any rate, gradual in the sense that there was no one moment at which he became a born-again democrat, but far from gradual if the extent of the change of doctrine between 1987 and 1991 is compared with the less profound doctrinal transformations (although changes there were) over the previous seventy years. By the time Gorbachev presented a new draft programme to the Central Committee of the Communist Party of the Soviet Union in the summer of 1991, his socialism had become fundamentally different from the body of doctrine he inherited in 1985.[49]

The chapters which follow constitute, then, both the study of a particular leader and, at a more general level, of leadership politics during a time of political transition. For the most part, comparisons between the attempt in the Soviet Union and attempts elsewhere to effect a transition to political democracy and a market economy are implicit rather than explicit, although I consider a number of the changes—and impediments to change—in relation to the body of knowledge and of generalizations to have emerged in the literature on transitions from authoritarian rule.

Obstacles to transformation: the inheritance

It is important to note—however briefly, at this stage of the argument—some of the enormous obstacles to the transformation of the Soviet system confronting any leader intent on changing it radically. Even many Soviet reformers who by the end of the 1980s were taking political pluralism for granted were extremely gloomy at the beginning of the Gorbachev era about the prospects of introducing it in the USSR. Centuries of authoritarian government in Russia—frequently autocratic and at other times oligarchic—had been followed by almost seventy years of Soviet rule. Although there were important differences between the totalitarian dictatorship of Stalin and the highly authoritarian but post-totalitarian Khrushchev and Brezhnev regimes which followed,[50] a great deal of conceptual stretching was involved in any attempt to attach the label 'pluralist' to the Soviet Union at any time earlier than the late 1980s.[51]

Political pluralism implies political organizations independent of the state (or, in the Soviet case, party-state), and to this Soviet leaders from Lenin to Chernenko were implacably opposed. Even a social pluralism encapsulated in the notion of 'civil society' can scarcely be said to have existed prior to the Gorbachev era. Civil society involves areas of autonomy for social groups and organizations, among the latter independent newspapers, publishing houses, universities, trade unions, and commercial enterprises.[52] It entails the right and possibility of proselytization for all kinds of associations, including churches and other voluntary bodies. In the Soviet Union, prior to the second half of the 1980s, the creation of any organization without the sanction and surveillance of the state was impermissible, even if that organization were not overtly political. The persecution of religion, and close monitoring of those churches which remained open, began with Lenin and was still continuing when Gorbachev became Soviet leader. Indeed, even Khrushchev, who as recently as the late 1980s was substantially rehabilitated, and accorded deserved respect in public as well as private for breaking the silence on the crimes of Stalin, was also a particularly ruthless closer of churches as he tried to make Soviet reality conform to his ideological predilections.[53]

Lacking experience not only of democracy in any meaningful sense of the term but also of political pluralism or even of civil society (except for the very limited pluralism and embryonic civil society emerging in the last decades before the 1917 Revolution),[54] Russia and the Soviet Union in 1985 did not appear to provide fruitful soil for the rapid growth of reform of a democratizing kind. If there was more to *The Russian Tradition* than the unremitting authoritarianism discussed in Tibor Szamuely's stimulating book of that title, that account of the historical relationship between state and society in Russia nevertheless contains a great deal of truth.[55] As Robert Conquest, in his summary of Szamuely's thesis, puts it:

> the circumstances of the past seven centuries in Russia had produced an order in which society as a whole had become totally dependent upon the state, and moved according to the subjective decisions taken by the state leadership. Moreover, the almost complete lack of any autonomous social and civic phenomena led to the absence of ideas of political adjustment and give-and-take among the State's opponents as well: so that there central peculiarities of Russian history produced the practice and principle of absolutism, of rule by decree, not only in the established order, but equally in the revolutionary tradition which opposed it.[56]

Similarly, seventy years of attempts to suppress the market and individual economic initiative—with the exception of the New Economic Policy (NEP) launched by Lenin in 1921 and ended by Stalin in 1928—left a society ill-equipped to adopt and accommodate itself to marketizing reforms. Apart from citizens of the three Baltic republics of Latvia, Lithuania, and Estonia—independent states between the wars—there was an almost total lack of first-hand experience in the Soviet Union of the workings of a market economy or even of independent peasant farming. Along with the institutional obstacles, discussed in a later chapter, that has been a formidable barrier to the successful implementation of economic reform and an important difference between, on the one hand, the Soviet Union (and its successor states) and, on the other, the Communist (now mainly post-Communist) regimes established in Eastern Europe and Asia after the Second World War.

Pre-conditions for democratization

In a number of respects, however, Soviet society was in 1985 at least better prepared for democratizing change than it had been a generation earlier, just after Stalin's death. In the intervening thirty years Soviet citizens had learned more about the outside world, partly through listening to foreign radio, partly through foreign travel—although trips abroad, especially to the West, were restricted to a small and privileged section of the population—and in part through their own censored mass media, which nevertheless conveyed more information about foreign countries than in Stalin's time.[57]

There had also been great social changes over the post-Stalin period. The process of urbanization continued and the Soviet Union moved from being a predominantly agricultural country to a predominantly industrial one. The industrial labour force consisted increasingly of second- and third-generation workers and not disorientated peasants forced into the towns. Educational levels rose and near-universal literacy was achieved. The number of Soviet citizens with higher education increased from 8.3 million in 1959 to 18.5 million in 1984.[58] In contrast with the communal radios and loudspeakers common in Stalin's time, by 1979 there were 544 radios per 1,000 people in the Soviet Union. Television, in the mean time, had become still more important. Whereas a mere 5 per cent of the population had access to television in 1960, by 1986 an estimated 93 per cent of households had television sets.[59] The total circulation of Soviet newspapers rose from 38.4 million in 1940 to 68.6 million in 1960 and then more than doubled within less than twenty years to 173 million in 1979.[60] While prior to the glasnost of the Gorbachev era the mass media were far less informative than they were subsequently to become, a significant minority of Soviet readers became adept at reading between the lines.

Alongside the 'pull' of a better-informed (albeit very inadequately informed) populace, there was also the 'push' of social deterioration in many spheres—appalling environmental pollution, increasing alcoholism and drunkenness, rising infant mortality rates, and lower life expectancy for adult males.[61] To these must be added the depressing indicator for Soviet leaders in the 1980s of a long-term decline in the rate of economic growth, a topic on which more will be said in Chapters 3 and 5.

Perhaps, however, the most important development of all in the years between 1953 and 1985 in preparing the way for what followed was the growth of privacy and the development of free discussion in small and informal groups. Over drinks and around kitchen tables the most diverse array of political views could be heard, ones which hardly anyone would have dared utter aloud in Stalin's time. The growth of freedom of expression in private circles preceded by two to three decades the achievement in the Gorbachev era of freedom of expression in public.[62] The Soviet literary scholar and dissident, the late Leonid Pinsky, in a conversation I had with him in Moscow in 1976, said that the most important social change in his view occurred when millions of people acquired the possibility 'to shut their own front door'. He was referring to the massive house-building programme of the Khrushchev years which enabled a large proportion of the urban population to move from communal apartments to single-family flats, acquiring at the same time the confidence to speak with a new freedom. T. H. Rigby, making a similar point about the conversations 'within trusted circles' which followed from this, is surely right when he observes: 'It was indeed a mighty leap from this private *glasnost'* to the public *glasnost'* of the late 1980s, but without the former as a jumping-off point that leap would have been out of the question.'[63]

Even under Stalin there were politically significant networks and relationships, not least of a 'patron–client' kind, and personal patronage continued in the post-Stalin period to modify the workings of the formal structures of the Soviet system.[64] But the Khrushchev and Brezhnev years saw the emergence also of 'opinion groupings' of like-minded people such as the anti-Stalinist readers of Alexander Tvardovsky's *Novy mir* in the 1960s and the very different collection of readers attracted by *Novy mir*'s rival periodical, *Oktyabr'*, the outlook of which at that time could reasonably be described as neo-Stalinist. The Khrushchev and Brezhnev eras saw, too, the coming together of informal groups or networks of people whose relations depended at least as much on broad similarity of political outlook as on personal friendship. Relationships of this kind existed within the heart of the Soviet establishment as well as in the broader society.

Important examples of such networks, with overlapping 'memberships', were the party intellectuals who worked as full-time consultants for Yury Andropov in the Socialist Countries Department of the Central Committee of the Communist Party in the 1960s, those who worked in Khrushchev's time with Politburo member Otto Kuusiinen on a revision of the 'bible' of Soviet doctrine, *The Fundamentals of Marxism-Leninism*, and those who spent some years in Prague working on the international Communist (but Soviet-dominated) journal, *World Marxist Review*.[65] Although the publications which emerged from these groups— not least *World Marxist Review*—were dreary and doctrinaire by any normal standard, the thoughts of some of the people in the groups developed well beyond what they were able to publish. Their ideas, which during the perestroika years became more radical, and their interactions were to attain a still greater importance in the second half of the 1980s, given Gorbachev's willingness to listen to their proposals.

Even within the party apparatus itself there was some diversity of view and there were reform-minded as well as conservative opinion groupings in Moscow which included members of the Central Committee apparatus. One surprising source of surreptitious fresh thinking was the International Department of the Central Committee, even though it remained headed until 1985 by Boris Ponomarev, an essentially conservative Communist who, nevertheless, tolerated different outlooks within his department. Almost by definition, this department contained people who knew Western languages and, in general, it had a higher proportion of well-educated and professionally competent specialists in its ranks than any other of the twenty or so departments of the Central Committee. It became a source of recruits to Gorbachev's team, at which point a number of people from the International Department were able to bring into the open views which had been able to reach the pre-Gorbachev leadership only in a watered-down version on documents bearing Ponomarev's signature. The most important example is Anatoly Chernyaev, who, despite the difference between his outlook and that of Ponomarev, was able to work alongside the latter as one of the deputy heads of the department during the second half of Ponomarev's long period in charge of it. (Ponomarev led the department from 1955 until he was removed by Gorbachev in 1985; Chernyaev was a deputy head of the department from 1970 until early 1986 when he became a full-time aide to Gorbachev.) If there was undoubtedly a tension within the department between, on the one hand, Communist ideologues and, on the other, enlightened officials of a pragmatic cast of mind, there were enough of the latter to make an impact upon the embryonic 'New Thinking'. One of the people who was close to Chernyaev, Andrey Grachev, is a case in point. In the perestroika era he was to be promoted to a deputy headship of the International Department and became, first, an informal Gorbachev adviser and later a formal one as presidential press secretary during Gorbachev's last months in office. Officials such as Chernyaev and Grachev had contacts with many of the heterodox thinkers within the research institutes which came under the jurisdiction of the International Department as well as with social democrats in Western Europe. The influences on *them* were of a diverse nature and did not exclude the indirect influence of the non-party, overt dissidents.[66] Reform-minded opinion groupings embraced both party intellectuals outside the apparatus and a minority of officials within it.

Although none of the informal groups of the Brezhnev years could take, other than covertly, the organizational steps which would have turned them into formal, campaigning ones, they—as well as the overt dissidents—helped to pave the way for the genuine and substantial element of political pluralism which had been attained in the Soviet Union by 1990–1. In Brezhnev's time the groups ranged from serious but frustrated reformers to backward-looking Russian nationalists. The former were located disproportionately in a number of research institutes, especially those concerned with international affairs. Many independent thinkers (as well as a proportion of time-servers) were to be found in three such institutes in particular—the Institute of Economics of the World Socialist System (renamed the Institute of International Economic and Political Studies in 1990), headed by Oleg Bogomolov from 1969 to the present day; the Institute of the United States and Canada, whose Director from its foundation in 1967 until 1995 was Georgy Arbatov; and the Institute of World Economy and International Relations (IMEMO), whose Director in the Brezhnev years was Nikolay Inozemtsev and whose successors have been Alexander Yakovlev, Yevgeny Primakov, and (since 1989) Vladen Martynov, two of whom—Yakovlev and Primakov—went on to play especially important leadership roles in Soviet and Russian politics. Within the Institute of Social Sciences, a body which came under the jurisdiction of the International Department and whose principal function was to train foreign Communists and students from Third World countries of 'socialist orientation', there was also a significant minority of scholars with ideas for political reform, among them Fedor Burlatsky and Alexander Galkin. Virtually every institute of the Academy of Sciences embraced people of different political views, and even one with a relatively conservative reputation, such as the Institute of State and Law in Moscow, could (and did) house a minority of scholars who favoured far-reaching political reform as well as many more who wished, in keeping with their profession as academic lawyers, to see greater respect for legal norms within the Soviet Union.

If Bogomolov's institute, in particular, and, to a lesser extent, IMEMO and the Institute of the United States and Canada were the major centres of reformist thought, the Russian nationalists also had their quasi-organizational bases. These included the editorial boards of the periodicals *Molodaya gvardiya* and *Nash sovremennik*—the leading organs of the Writers' Union of the Russian republic (RSFSR)—and the All-Russian Society for the Preservation of Historical and Cultural Monuments. Writers of Russian nationalist disposition actually had more success in the Brezhnev era than their liberal opponents in publishing works embracing values which were a far cry from Marxism-Leninism. Indeed, the authors of 'village prose' (*derevenshchiki*) formed the most important school of creative writing during the Brezhnev years.[67]

A division within the Russian intelligentsia between Westernizers and Russophiles (or Slavophiles, to use their older name), which had its origins in the nineteenth century, took on a renewed importance in the 1960s and 1970s.[68] It was to become a still more sharply divisive issue in the late 1980s, for by that time Gorbachev had made it clear that both his head and his heart were with the Westernizers, even if in his heart he had a place also for some of the Russophile writers of the 'rural prose' school. Gorbachev attempted to co-opt leading representatives from both of the warring camps and tried, with conspicuous lack of success, to make them more tolerant of one another.

Finally, it is important to underline a point which has already been made at least by implication—namely, that the Communist Party of the Soviet Union (CPSU) in the post-Stalin years was by no means the monolithically united body which its propagandists liked to pretend. (In an interesting convergence of images, the same view was diligently promoted by the cruder among anti-Communist propagandists abroad.[69]) Members of the party by the first half of the 1980s constituted a little over 6 per cent of the total Soviet population and about one in ten adults; citizens with a higher education were greatly over-represented within it. Membership of the CPSU did not carry the same social stigma as Communist Party membership frequently did in Eastern Europe. The Bolshevik Revolution of 1917, with all its disastrous consequences, was at least an indigenous revolution (or coup), whereas most of the countries of Eastern Europe were Communist only because such a regime had been imposed upon them by Soviet force of arms following the Second World War.[70]

People's reasons for joining the party were diverse, but the most common was that it was liable to further the individual's career. In some cases—such as employment in a responsible position in an institute concerned with international affairs—party membership virtually came with the job. To be told that a person belonged to the CPSU conveyed remarkably little about that individual's personal political beliefs. The Soviet Communist Party was nothing like a party in a competitive party system, but in reality a crucial part of the state structure. Indeed, both at the centre and in the republics and regions, the leading party organs were, in effect, also the highest instruments of state power. Until the

Gorbachev era a majority of Soviet constitutional lawyers argued that the party did not wield power as such but exercised only influence and persuasion. It was, however, clear to all serious students of the Soviet Union that, while influence and persuasion could also come into play, the party wielded not only power but power for which it could not be called to account. The Politburo was the highest policy-making body in the country and not merely the highest executive committee of the party, although its decision-making processes were shrouded in secrecy.

One Soviet academic lawyer who was to become at the end of the 1980s and beginning of the 1990s a prominent politician, Anatoly Sobchak—a radical deputy of the Supreme Soviet of the USSR who was elected Mayor of Leningrad (St Petersburg) in June 1991—belonged to the minority in his profession who viewed the Communist Party not as a normal political party but as a 'state structure'. He was, therefore, not alone in drawing the conclusion that it was possible to begin serious change in the Soviet Union only with reform of the Communist Party itself.[71] The position of the Communist Party in Soviet society was such that it was indeed very difficult for far-reaching reform to get under way anywhere else.

A revolution would have been another matter, but the party's controlling mechanisms in the unreformed Soviet system, including its penetration and subordination of the means of physical coercion—the military, the Committee of State Security (KGB), and the troops of the Ministry of Interior (MVD)—made a revolution a remote possibility. Since those who launched the attempted reform of the Soviet political and economic system in the mid-1980s were, overwhelmingly, members of the Communist Party, as were their most vehement opponents, an appreciation of the broad spectrum of views contained within that party is basic to an understanding of the Soviet political process in the first four years of the Gorbachev era.[72] Of course, once a substantial measure of political pluralism had been established, the containment of so many fundamentally different outlooks under the aegis of a single party became an anachronism, and by 1990—if not earlier—it was increasingly evident that within the ranks of the CPSU were not only different groups and factions but the seeds of a multi-party system, quite apart from the small parties formed in that same year by people who had never belonged to the Communist Party.

By 1991 many candidates backed by the Communist Party were unable to win crucial elections within Russia, not to speak of the Baltic or Caucasian republics. Yet the successful non-party candidates in the three most important Russian elections had all been members of the Communist Party until they resigned in 1990. Yeltsin, elected President of Russia, had been a party member since 1961 (and a party official from 1968 to 1987); Gavriil Popov, elected Mayor of Moscow, had joined the party in 1959; while only Sobchak was in a somewhat different category, having joined the CPSU as late as 1988 (following the Nineteenth Party Conference) in order to add his weight to the Gorbachev-led reformist tendency.[73]

A number of the themes introduced in this chapter will emerge again in the more detailed analysis of Gorbachev's leadership which follows. First of all, though, it is necessary over the next two chapters to examine the path Gorbachev took to the summit of power within the unreformed political system and to attempt to assess his ideas and intentions at the point at which he became the most powerful person within the Soviet party-state.

Chapter 2

The Making of a Reformist General Secretary

BEFORE Gorbachev could attempt to introduce fundamental change within the Soviet Union, he had to rise to the top within an essentially unreformed system. To many people, both in Russia and beyond, it seemed all too clear that no one of reformist disposition, or who was open to new ideas, could emerge from a background in the Communist Party apparatus with such an outlook or personality still intact. Such traits would either be knocked out of him on the way up or the person concerned would be eased out of the party apparatus before he had got very far. Yet, given the political resources that were concentrated in the hands of the Communist Party leadership and the political weakness of the overt dissidents, the best hope of changing the Soviet Union lay in a reformer climbing the greasy pole to the party leadership, however unlikely an occurrence this seemed during the years in which Leonid Brezhnev presided over a Communist oligarchy determined to nip in the bud even the slightest threat to the Soviet political status quo. Looking ahead at that time, more in hope than expectation, the leading Australian specialist on the Soviet Union, T. H. Rigby, observed:

> For the decisive steps to be taken which alone will make possible the shift from a mono-organisational system to one marked, in Leonard Schapiro's words, by 'the supremacy of law, civil liberties, the dignity of the individual and the liberty of the human spirit' . . . we must perhaps wait upon acts of outstanding intelligence, courage and imagination on the part of some future and, alas, difficult-to-discern Soviet leadership.[1]

The General Secretaryship, by the time Gorbachev attained that office, was (as noted in Chapter 1) no longer the all-powerful personal dictatorship that Stalin had made it, but its holder unquestionably possessed more power than any other individual within the Soviet Union. So far as the population as a whole, or even the millions of rank-and-file Communist Party members, were concerned, this was power without electoral or any other form of institutionalized political accountability. The General Secretary could not be forced to defend his actions or inaction against criticism within a parliament or even a representative party assembly. Single-candidate elections were the norm both inside the Communist Party and in the broader society. In other words, what happened in reality was that the incumbent officials of the ruling party *co-opted* newcomers to seats in soviets or party organs in what were 'elections' only in name. Moreover, even the slightest criticism of the General Secretary (and of the Communist Party as an institution) was taboo. The people the General Secretary had to concern himself with were the members of the Politburo (in effect, the ruling oligarchy) and the Central Committee (the broader party élite), as well as the most important other institutional interests—the military, the KGB, and the ministerial network.

Before Gorbachev reached this pinnacle of Soviet power, he had a long and, in his earliest years, difficult road to travel. It is with Gorbachev's formative experiences, his rise through the party ranks, the friendships and alliances he formed, and the evolution of his views before he became the sixth and last General Secretary of the Central Committee of the Communist Party of the Soviet Union that this chapter and the following one are concerned.

Every previous Soviet leader had been born before the 1917 revolution, and although three of them—Brezhnev (born in 1906), Andropov (born 1914), and Chernenko (born 1911)—were still children when it occurred, their generational experience was quite different from that of Gorbachev. In particular, his three predecessors had already embarked on serious political careers in Stalin's time and were marked for life by the fear they had known then and by culpability for the part they had played in imposing the Stalinist order. Brezhnev's predecessor, Khrushchev (born 1894), was much more heavily involved—and at a more senior level than any of them—in the repressions as First Secretary of the Moscow Communist Party organization in the 1930s (and again from 1949 until 1953), as First Secretary in the Ukraine in the 1940s, and as a Politburo member from 1939. Yet he it was who took the bold step in 1956 of exposing at least some of the crimes of Stalin at the Twentieth Congress of the Soviet Communist Party—an event which was to have a profound impact on party members of Gorbachev's generation.

Family background

Gorbachev, in contrast with all his predecessors as party leader, was a child of the Soviet system. He was born into a peasant family on 2 March 1931 in the Stavropol region of southern Russia in a small house on the edge of the village of Privolnoe.[2] Two of the misfortunes he suffered in childhood could easily have prevented his later advancement in the party hierarchy. The first was that he had lived in the family home of an 'enemy of the people'. The second problem—as potentially dangerous politically as it had been dangerous physically—was that the Stavropol territory was for a time occupied by the German army during the Second World War.

The first issue was sufficiently sensitive for a Soviet politician that it was not until November 1990 that Gorbachev revealed that not one but both of his grandfathers had been arrested on trumped-up political charges during Stalin's assault on the peasantry in the 1930s. His father's father, Andrey Gorbachev, was sent into exile to fell trees in the Irkutsk region of Siberia for failing to fulfil the plan for sowing in 1933 at a time when half of his family—three out of six children—'had died of starvation'.[3] His mother's father, Panteli Gopalko, was arrested in 1937 and imprisoned and interrogated for fourteen months, during which he confessed under extreme duress to things he had not done.[4] The

principal accusation against that grandfather—as dangerous as it was fanciful—
was that he had been active in the district centre of a Trotskyist organization.[5]
As a careful politician, Gorbachev disclosed different parts of his biography at
times of his own choosing to different audiences. Thus, in an interview for a
monthly journal carrying news of the current activities of the party Central
Committee as well as materials from the party archives, Gorbachev in May 1989
observed that both of his parents and also their parents on both sides were peasants and that his mother's father, Panteli Gopalko, was 'for many years chairman of a collective farm'.[6] The latter point indeed had been mentioned in
Gorbachev's official biography ever since he had become General Secretary of
the Communist Party. It was to an audience of intellectuals (writers, artists, and
film-makers) that Gorbachev first revealed in November 1990 that the same
grandfather had been among those caught up in the Stalin regime's state terror
against its own citizenry.[7] That second arrest within the family, followed as it
was by prison and torture rather than exile as in the case of his father's father,
appears to have been especially traumatic. Gorbachev was old enough to
remember that he had lived in the 'plague-stricken house' of an 'enemy of the
people' which no one—not even relatives and family friends—dared visit lest
the same fate befall them as had befallen his grandfather.[8] Writing in 1993,
Gorbachev recalled: 'every time that I filled out a document I had to write down
that my grandfather had been in jail. If I hadn't done so, I would have been
under suspicion.'[9]

The second hardship of Gorbachev's childhood which could have had an
adverse effect on his subsequent career, and would very probably have done so
in Stalin's time if his political career had already taken off by then, was the fact
that the Stavropol region was under German occupation from August 1942 until
January 1943.[10] For even longer it was close to one of the war fronts. During the
post-war Stalin years of spy-mania, it was a decided disadvantage to have lived
in an occupied area, even if—as in Gorbachev's case—the person concerned had
been a child at the time. It may be that Gorbachev's labour feats (described
below), along with those of his father and two other villagers in the later 1940s,
were part of a conscious effort to wipe the political slate clean, although they
doubtless stemmed also from real concern to make good the war losses and to
combat the extreme food shortages which had afflicted large parts of the Soviet
Union in the early post-war period. The war and the early post-war years were
ones of genuinely patriotic fervour in Russia.

Gorbachev's childhood coincided with the harshest years of Soviet history
and some of the most tragic times in the whole of Russian history. The forcible
collectivization of agriculture, followed by famine and the worst years of Stalin's
purges, took the lives of millions of peasants during the 1930s, including many
from the Stavropol region—among them (as already noted) members of
Gorbachev's own family. During the first two to three years of Gorbachev's life
as many as a third of the inhabitants of his native village of Privolnoe perished,
according to those who still live there today.[11] The Nazi invasion of the Soviet
Union in 1941 brought new horrors, although it also produced a patriotic spirit
of resistance which helped the society to recover, for a time at least, from the self-
inflicted wounds of the previous decade. Gorbachev's father, Sergey Andreevich,

served in the army, saw action on several fronts, and was twice wounded—on the second occasion in the battle for the town of Košice in Czechoslovakia—before being demobilized in 1946.[12]

Sergey Gorbachev died in 1976.[13] His widow—Gorbachev's mother—Maria Panteleevna died as recently as the spring of 1995. An Orthodox Christian who (unlike her husband) never had the opportunity to learn to read and write, she went along with the desire of Gorbachev's two grandmothers, both of whom were devoutly religious, to have her son secretly baptized. (The author of a book on Gorbachev's Stavropol years, who worked at various times under Gorbachev in the territorial party organization and as a journalist, cites Gorbachev as saying that the name 'Mikhail' was given to him by the priest; it was not the name his parents had intended to give him.[14]) On his mother's side, Gorbachev is of partly Ukrainian descent—as he chose to mention in an interview for Ukrainian television in December 1991 when he was trying desperately to keep Ukraine within a new and radically refashioned union which would replace the old Soviet Union.[15] His mother's own Russian speech was interspersed with many Ukrainian words.[16]

Gorbachev's wartime memories were of a time of great suffering for the civilian population—especially for those who lived close to the scene of battle.[17] He himself was aged 10 when the Soviet Union was invaded and 11 when the German army reached the Stavropol area. With almost all physically fit adult males called up for military service, the women and children left in the villages—including Gorbachev and his mother—were responsible for the harvest and were engaged in back-breaking toil from dawn until dusk.

In the first five post-war years, Gorbachev's schooling was combined with long summers of agricultural work, in which he came at the age of 15 an assistant at a machine-tractor station, working alongside his father.[18] The chances of a peasant boy from southern Russia entering Moscow University were quite slender, but a number of factors told in Gorbachev's favour. The most important single qualification was his award of the Order of Red Banner of Labour as an exemplary worker, especially when taken in conjunction with an excellent school record (both of which are discussed below). A necessary, although not sufficient, condition for the aspiring university student was a favourable report from his Komsomol (Young Communist League) branch, and this Gorbachev obtained.[19] Marginally helpful also was, perhaps, the fact that his father had joined the Communist Party during his army service in the Second World War,[20] but given that there were some six million party members in the Soviet Union at the beginning of the 1950s, it scarcely distinguished Gorbachev from his peers.

The post-war part of the Stalin era was not a time at which there was anything like as much affirmative action in favour of children from peasant and worker backgrounds, simply on the grounds of social class, as there had been at an earlier period of Stalin's rule.[21] This was, rather, the era of what Vera Dunham has called the 'Big Deal' between Stalin and a new Soviet 'middle class'—a social stratum that was 'totally stalinist, born out of Stalin's push for the industrialization, reeducation, and bureaucratization of the country, flesh of the flesh of Stalin's revolutions from above in the thirties, and ready to fill the vacuum created by Stalin's Great Purge and by the liquidation of the leninist generation of activists'.[22]

Gorbachev's parents were far removed socially and geographically from that new 'middle class', and their son's success in entering Moscow University was due very largely to his own abilities and efforts. Although even at this period of Soviet history there was an interest on the part of the authorities in having *some* students of peasant or worker origin, the chances of any particular boy or girl from those social groups reaching Moscow University were small. At school Gorbachev attained the top mark of five in all subjects except German, in which he got a four, and hence finished with a silver medal (in contrast to his future wife, who, coming from an equally unprivileged background, received top marks in all subjects and a gold medal).[23] If, however, class origins alone were of comparatively little advantage in the post-war Stalin years for gaining entry to the Soviet Union's most eminent educational institutions, to have earned an award for outstanding labour performance when still a teenager greatly strengthened Gorbachev's case for entry to Moscow University. It was especially his achievements as an exemplary worker, in combination with an excellent school record and Komsomol backing, which almost certainly played the decisive part in enabling him to enter Russia's oldest and most prestigious university and to move for the first time to the Soviet capital.[24]

It was in the summer of 1948 that Gorbachev established his credentials as an outstanding manual worker. Operating in a team of four comprising, besides himself, his village friend and contemporary, Alexander Yakovenko, and the fathers of the two boys, Sergey Gorbachev and Yakov Yakovenko, they produced a record harvest—five or six times the average—which resulted in each member of the brigade receiving a state award. For achieving the best result in the entire Stavropol territory, the two fathers were awarded the Order of Lenin and the sons, Mikhail and Alexander, the Order of the Red Banner of Labour.[25] According to Yakovenko, speaking in 1989, they worked 'twenty to twenty-two hours a day, only stopping when the dew set on the grass'.[26] (This included the time the two youths spent cleaning the combine harvesters at night.) Gorbachev's Order of the Red Banner of Labour was a very unusual honour for a teenager (he was 17 when he earned it), and of all his Soviet honours it was the one he most cherished.[27] When he wore it from time to time, it was one of his distinguishing marks as a student at Moscow University. (When at the end of the 1970s, before Gorbachev had become famous, I asked the Russian academic lawyer Pavel Gratsiansky, who had been a student in the Moscow University Law Faculty in the early 1950s, whether he remembered Gorbachev, he immediately replied 'Of course!' and mentioned the Order of the Red Banner as a major reason for recalling him. Other contemporaries have similar memories. Many of the older students, who had served in the war, had decorations, but such an order was most unusual for a student arriving in Moscow at the age of 19.[28]) Work on the land occupied the whole of Gorbachev's summers, but his schooling continued beyond the minimum leaving age. The village school at Privolnoe ended with the seventh grade and the nearest ten-year school was at Krasnogvardeysk (in those days called Molotovskoe). Gorbachev's parents arranged for him to live there in term-time, sharing a room with two other boys from the village. In that way Gorbachev was able to complete a ten-year schooling.[29]

Moscow University

Gorbachev's years in the Law Faculty of Moscow University from 1950 until 1955 were crucial ones for his intellectual development. Whatever the deficiencies of that faculty and the university in the last years of Stalin's life, they provided Gorbachev with a better education than was obtained by any of his colleagues in Brezhnev's Politburo, which he joined exactly thirty years after his university matriculation. Most Soviet leaders who served with Brezhnev had received only a narrowly vocational or party education and their paper qualifications were from provincial technical institutes and party schools or obtained by external study. Not one of Gorbachev's Politburo colleagues on the eve of Brezhnev's death a generation later had spent a full five years studying in a major Russian university. While this superior education gave Gorbachev certain advantages, it was also in some ways a handicap he had to overcome. The very fact that his scholastic experience was so markedly different from that of his colleagues in the years before he succeeded to the top leadership post indicates the general suspicion on the part of a majority of them of anyone who might turn out to be a closet intellectual or, at any rate, a person capable of engaging in independent political thought.

Gorbachev himself, when he arrived in Moscow with his provincial school education which had been interrupted by both the war and the post-war turmoil, was less well educated than many of his fellow students from professional families in Moscow, but within a year or two he had closed the gap.[30] The normal time taken by study for a first degree in the Soviet Union was five years and Gorbachev duly graduated—with distinction—in 1955. In between his arrival and departure far and away the most important event in his personal life was his meeting in 1951 with Raisa Maksimovna Titorenko and their marriage in 1953,[31] while much the most momentous occurrence in his political life, and in that of the entire country, was the death of Stalin on 5 March 1953.

Gorbachev, along with student friends, was among those for whom Stalin was still, above all, 'linked to victory in the war'. Much later he was to write: 'We could not know then the price that had been paid for that victory, nor what had taken place before it.'[32] Gorbachev was among the countless thousands who set off to see their lost leader lying in state: 'we joined the endless, slow-moving line of people and walked for a day and a night. It was morning when we reached the great hall where Stalin was laid out, and I saw him for the first time.'[33]

To be a Communist until March 1953 was to be a Stalinist. There were few exceptions. Gorbachev, in the last years of Stalin's life, was doubtless a long way away from making a connection between those stark injustices of which he was personally aware and the culpability of Stalin. (He was still further away from recognizing the fundamental flaws of the system as a whole and the responsibility for this of the person who more than any other had laid its foundations, Lenin.) As Alexander Yakovlev, an older man than Gorbachev and later one of the key reformers of the era of perestroika, put it: 'We all deeply believed in Stalin. We

deeply believed we were building a new society.'³⁴ Another future reformist colleague of Gorbachev, Eduard Shevardnadze, was typical of millions at that time
in knowing people who were being persecuted, believing them to be innocent,
but yet retaining faith in Stalin by persuading himself 'that Stalin did not know
about it'.³⁵ (Shevardnadze was much less typical, however, in marrying, while
Stalin was still alive, the daughter of an 'enemy of the people'—whose father had
been executed by firing squad in the 1930s—in spite of warnings that to do so
would ruin his career. Curiously, however, it was an aspect of Shevardnadze's
biography which he had in common with one of his later political critics, Yegor
Ligachev, who married in the early post-war years the daughter of a senior army
officer who had been arrested on false charges in 1936 and shot as an 'Anglo-
Japanese-German spy' in 1937.³⁶) Gorbachev himself, asked in 1992 when he
had begun to understand the real role played by the NKVD and its successor, the
KGB, replied that he had begun to feel it long ago—from the time his grandfather was under arrest for fourteen months, but that there was much that before
1956 remained obscure, adding that even his grandfather had said of his arrest:
'I am sure that Stalin does not know.'³⁷

The first half of Gorbachev's time at Moscow University coincided with
Stalin's 'anti-cosmopolitan' campaign. This, for Stalin and for many of his followers, was thinly disguised anti-Semitism. Gorbachev, who before Stalin's death
had become a Communist Party member (in 1952) and who was active in the
Komsomol of the Law Faculty and in his final year at the university a Komsomol
secretary,³⁸ did not, according to the most reliable accounts of his student life,
engage in witch-hunts, although he doubtless did not deviate from the 'general
line' of the party. Even his few critics from those years—whose acquaintanceship
with him was so distant as to make them unreliable sources—have not been able
to cite any convincing evidence of anti-Semitic actions or speeches by
Gorbachev.³⁹ Neither then nor subsequently has national chauvinism been a
character trait of Gorbachev. Indeed, one of his problems years later when he was
Soviet leader was that he underestimated the intensity of nationalist feelings and
assumed too readily that an extension of political and economic liberties within
the framework of a genuinely federal state would lead to a resolution of the
national question.

Among Gorbachev's closest friends in his Law Faculty class was the first for-
eigner he ever got to know, Zdeněk Mlynář.⁴⁰ Mlynář had arrived in Moscow as
a naïve, albeit highly intelligent, young Czech Communist. He was later to
become one of the most important of the 'Prague Spring' reformers (the principal author of the Action Programme of the Czechoslovak Communist Party published in April 1968) and later still one of the authors of 'Charter 77', which
became the basis of organized dissent in Czechoslovakia during the last twelve
years of the rule of Gustav Husák (who, with Moscow's blessing, had replaced
Alexander Dubček as leader of the Communist Party of Czechoslovakia in April
1969 and who in 1975 became President of Czechoslovakia).

In the same circle of close friends of Gorbachev was an older Jewish student
from an intelligentsia family, Vladimir Liberman, who had served in the war. In
more than one interview Liberman has pointed to the considerable risk
Gorbachev took in defending him when he was attacked at a party meeting in

early 1953 soon after Stalin had unveiled the 'doctors' plot'—an entirely fictitious plot by a group of 'murderer doctors' of Jewish origin who had set out to wreck the health of Soviet leaders.[41] The unveiling of this plot on 13 January 1953 looked very much like the first move in another massive purge—with Jews as the first victims. Liberman's Jewish origins appeared to be the sole motive for the attack on him by a fellow student and party member called Balasyan at a party meeting in the university. Gorbachev angrily came to Liberman's defence and called Balasyan 'a spineless animal', after which, said Liberman, 'all discussion about me ended'.[42] In that context it is worth citing Mlynář's comment in April 1985 that, as a student, Gorbachev had 'won an informal and spontaneous authority' and that he was 'not unaware of the fact', being conscious that he had got where he was 'thanks to his own powers and his own talent' and not to protection or social origin.[43]

Gorbachev's intellectual development at the university was promoted both by conversation with fellow students who had enjoyed a better school education and by at least a minority of the university teachers, especially some of those whose own higher education had occurred before the revolution. One of these was Serafim Vladimirovich Yuzhkov, whose historical lectures Gorbachev much enjoyed and who survived accusations of being a 'rootless cosmopolitan', only to die a natural death, albeit in the ominous year of 1952.[44] A favourite professor of both Gorbachev and Mlynář, and of many of the ablest students, was Stepan Fedorovich Kechekyan, who taught the history of political and legal thought.[45] Kechekyan was a scholar of genuine erudition and a man of gentle demeanour and kindly disposition—as I can personally testify.[46]

Mlynář, who got to know Gorbachev in his first year at Moscow University (and who sent him a picture postcard from Prague, which because of its foreign origins was delivered to Gorbachev as a 'suspicious object' by a policeman while he was working in the fields of his native village during the summer of 1951[47]), has noted that it was Gorbachev who, in their student years, opened his eyes to some of the discrepancies between Soviet propaganda and real life. When they studied the law relating to collective farms, Gorbachev told him how remote this was from what actually happened in the countryside and what role was played by 'common violence' in guaranteeing worker discipline on the farms.[48] When Mlynář saw the film *The Cossacks of Kuban* (the Kuban being an area of Russia embracing the Stavropol territory and neighbouring Krasnodar), which showed the tables of the peasantry bending under the weight of the abundance of food, it was again from Gorbachev that Mlynář learned what those tables were like in real life.[49] Mlynář has recalled, too, that a favourite expression of Gorbachev in his student years was one he had taken from Hegel, 'truth is always concrete', which he used not in any Hegelian, philosophical sense, but 'when a teacher or student talked hot air about general principles, conveniently forgetting how little they had in common with reality'.[50]

Yet, at the very outset of Gorbachev's General Secretaryship in 1985, Mlynář argued that Gorbachev was capable of thinking theoretically as well as of acting pragmatically. Moreover, unlike many Soviet students for whom Marxist theory had amounted to certain 'laws' which had to be learned parrot-fashion, Gorbachev had taken it seriously as a mode of analysis. He also caused some surprise as a party official in Stavropol by actually studying Lenin as distinct from having suitable quotations provided for him.[51] This interest in Marx and Lenin was still there when Gorbachev became General Secretary of the Communist Party a generation after he graduated from Moscow University. He thought of himself as a Marxist—and, indeed, as a Leninist—but his Marxism was flexible and undogmatic. When there was a conflict between theory and the evidence of his own eyes, he preferred to believe the latter. In an important speech three months before he became Soviet leader, Gorbachev criticized Soviet scholars who were not able 'to part company with obsolete conceptions and stereotypes', who tried to fit everything into 'preconceived schemes' and revolved 'in a circle of scholastic reasoning'.[52] He complained in general about attempts 'to squeeze new phenomena into a Procrustean bed of moribund conceptions'—which could have served as an epitaph for 99 per cent of the Soviet theoretical output that came under the rubric of Marxism-Leninism.[53] Writing less than a month after Gorbachev became Soviet leader, Mlynář observed: 'We are talking about a man who attributes more importance to his own experience, lived and felt, than to that which is decreed on paper.'[54]

No account of Gorbachev's politically significant encounters during his Moscow University years should omit mention of a student whom Gorbachev knew well at that time and who was to play an important part in political life once he had become General Secretary—Anatoly Lukyanov. Lukyanov was two years ahead of Gorbachev in the Law Faculty and graduated in 1953, but their paths frequently crossed, since he was for a time Gorbachev's superior in the university Komsomol. While Gorbachev's relations with Lukyanov were good, neither at university nor subsequently was he one of his close friends. Lukyanov's daughter has observed that the Gorbachev and Lukyanov families did not meet socially and that Gorbachev had never been in their home.[55] Nevertheless, their long-standing comradeship led Gorbachev to consider Lukyanov a political ally during his years as Soviet leader, as indeed he was for much of that period, although he had been an increasingly dubious one for one or two years before the coup. The fact that in August 1991 Lukyanov quite clearly failed to back Gorbachev and at that critical point was either an accessory to the *putsch* or a more active plotter was an especially severe blow for the Soviet President, given that, of all the people in senior positions in the political leadership during Gorbachev's years at the helm, Lukyanov was the one whom he had known longest and a person in whom he had placed great trust.

Gorbachev's most significant meeting of all during his years at Moscow University was with Raisa Maksimovna Titorenko, whom, as already noted, he first encountered in 1951. They met at a dance in a student club to which Gorbachev had been persuaded to come by his friends Vladimir Liberman and Yury Topilin.[56] The daughter of a Ukrainian father and Russian mother, Raisa Maksimovna was born in Rubtsovsk in the Altai region of southern Siberia in 1932, the eldest of three children.[57] The family, like Gorbachev's, suffered greatly during the 1930s. At a time when the more successful peasant farmers were treated as kulaks, Raisa Gorbachev's mother's family, which had not owned land of their own until after the revolution, were put into this category of 'rich peasants' and had their house and land confiscated. Later, her grandfather was accused of 'Trotskyism' and arrested. He simply 'disappeared without trace', and the family assumed he had died in a labour camp. Her grandmother, Raisa Gorbachev recalled in 1991, 'died of grief and hunger as the wife of an "enemy of the people" ' and her four children 'were left to the mercy of fate'.[58] It was as recently as early 1993 that Raisa and Mikhail Gorbachev learned the fate of her grandfather: 'He was shot dead—for no other reason than that he was a kulak.'[59]

Although a year younger than her future husband, Raisa Titorenko—as she was then—arrived at Moscow University a year earlier, aged 17, in 1949 and entered the Philosophical Faculty, from which she graduated in 1954. Her father had worked in railway construction and this meant that the family were constantly on the move during her childhood. Home was sometimes a carriage in a railway siding. When she completed her schooling, the family were living in Bashkiria. It was the second year in which gold medals had been awarded for top grades in all subjects and Raisa, in spite of her frequent changes of school, received one which gave her, in the words of the certificate, 'the right to enter institutes of higher education in the USSR without entry examination'.[60] She chose Moscow University and, like her future husband, saw the Soviet capital and the Kremlin for the first time when she arrived as an undergraduate.

When Raisa Gorbachev arrived in Britain on her first visit in December 1984, she surprised one of the officials meeting the Gorbachevs at the airport by saying how pleased she was to be in the land of Hobbes and Locke.[61] She has read widely and she prepared herself intellectually for each foreign visit. Valery Boldin, a Gorbachev aide who became in due course his presidential chief of staff and who betrayed him in August 1991, in an inaccurate book which attempts to portray every action of the Gorbachevs in the worst possible light, nevertheless notes that 'Raisa', when informed of the schedule of a foreign visit, 'would bury herself in books on the country in question. She would watch its movies, read its classics, study its culture and art, and learn about its museums and exhibitions.'[62]

Raisa Gorbachev also enjoyed teaching, which she did at the Stavropol Agricultural Institute in the 1960s and 1970s.[63] Her conversational style—in, for example, her tape-recorded volume of reminiscences and reflections—has echoes of the classroom and is often didactic. Her academic work had, however, an innovative character. At a time when sociology was barely recognized as a discipline in the Soviet Union, and most sociological studies took place under the rubric of philosophy, Raisa Gorbachev completed the Russian equivalent of a Ph.D. by undertaking an empirical sociological survey of the way of life of the Stavropol peasantry. She and her husband lived in Stavropol from 1955 until 1978 and it was in the 1960s that she conducted her research. It involved fieldwork in an unusually literal sense, since Raisa Gorbachev often had to make her way through the muddy expanses of Soviet farms to reach the doors of peasant homes in order to interview the occupants. Sometimes she went on foot and sometimes by motor-cycle.[64] Describing her work then as 'sociology with a human face' (the faces of the hundreds of people in the countryside whom she questioned on a wide variety of subjects), she 'came to understand many of our misfortunes and the questionable nature of many undisputed assertions and established concepts'.[65]

Her relationship with her husband, both intellectually and emotionally, has been an exceptionally close one, and her own professional work and increasing awareness of the gap between Marxist-Leninist theory and reality complemented his. At the time when Raisa Gorbachev was working on her dissertation, Gorbachev himself was rising through the party apparatus of the city of Stavropol. But in 1970 he became First Secretary of the party for the whole (mainly agricultural) region, at which point his wife's research on social conditions and public opinion in rural Stavropol became of direct relevance to him.[66]

Raisa Gorbachev turned her thesis into a book which was published under the title *The Way of Life of the Collective Farm Peasantry: A Sociological Study* in 1969.[67] This work was completed a year earlier than that, at a time when the Soviet leadership was engaged in a heresy-hunt as it reacted with extreme alarm to the 'Prague Spring'—not a propitious moment for objective social research. The manuscript was handed to the typesetter on 18 November 1968, some three months after Soviet troops invaded Czechoslovakia.[68] While there was little in it liable to have caused shock waves in Moscow, it was a work of solid empirical research and by no means mere apologetics. The usual contrast was made between pre-revolutionary illiteracy and the contemporary high literacy rates. Nevertheless, Raisa Gorbachev found—and duly recorded—an illiteracy level of 3.2 per cent of families in one of the villages she studied.[69] She had many critical remarks to make about the lack of basic amenities in rural localities and the continuing gap between town and countryside.[70] In keeping with the orthodoxy of the time, she stressed the importance of developing new Soviet traditions and customs, while noting that in fact there was a high degree of observance of religious holidays.[71] Some of the most striking passages in the book are devoted to gender inequality—a substantial section is entitled, 'On the Path to Sexual Equality'.[72] She takes issue with the well-known Soviet sociologist Boris Grushin (who, as noted in Chapter 1, today heads his own public opinion research centre in Moscow) and his junior colleague, Valentin Chikin (who twenty years later, as editor-in-chief of the newspaper, *Sovetskaya Rossiya*, was to become a severe critic of Gorbachev from a conservative Communist standpoint), for arguing in a book published in 1962 that the practice of giving dowries had become 'a rarity' in the Soviet Union. 'On the contrary!', writes Raisa Gorbachev, going on to state that in her sample of 289 young families, marriage dowries had been given in 206 cases. At the same time, she points out that the meaning and significance of the phenomenon had changed and that, in particular, it no longer played a role in the choice of partner.[73]

The break with Soviet tradition whereby Raisa Gorbachev in later years accompanied her husband on all his foreign travels, beginning with the 1984 visit to Britain (for which permission for her to come, too, had to be granted by the party General Secretary, Konstantin Chernenko), and most of his domestic trips, drew a good deal of criticism in Russia, but was welcomed abroad. For Gorbachev, it was a matter of letting 'everything happen naturally', although, as he put it some years later, to have in addition to perestroika the General Secretary being accompanied by his 'educated, energetic wife' was a 'second revolution', and he did not know which produced the sharper reaction.[74] On the one hand, this was another indication of the Gorbachevs' close relationship. On the other, it was an early manifestation of a strong Westernizing element in Gorbachev's political style. There was by Western standards nothing odd about leaders being accompanied by their spouses—only by Soviet ones.

In an interview with Soviet editors published in *Izvestiya* in September 1991, Gorbachev described his wife as someone who was capable of analysing the experiences she had lived through. He mentioned that, when several years earlier he had been asked a question about which issues he discussed with her and had replied 'all', that, apparently, had 'astounded many people'.[75] In fact, it so startled the Soviet establishment that when the interview Gorbachev had in mind— which he gave to Tom Brokaw of the American television company NBC in late 1987—was broadcast and published in *Pravda*, part of Brokaw's question and Gorbachev's answer was considered too sensitive to be transmitted by the Soviet mass media. Both Soviet television and the press did, it is worth noting, carry the essence of the point; that was already a sign of the changing times. Thus, when Brokaw commented on the fact that Raisa accompanied him everywhere and asked what issues of public life he discussed with her, Gorbachev's answer, 'We discuss *everything*', was broadcast both on Soviet television and radio and published in *Pravda*.[76] Brokaw, however, further inquired: 'Including Soviet affairs, at the highest level?', to which Gorbachev responded: 'I think I have answered your question in toto. We discuss everything.' That part of the interview was excluded from the Soviet domestic mass media, although broadcast by the Moscow World Service in English.[77]

Gorbachev's Moscow University years were important not only for the people he met, one of whom became his lifelong partner, and for the education he received, but because he was just a little more than half-way through his degree course when Stalin died. A somewhat greater political openness began to pervade student circles in the capital earlier than in most other parts of the Soviet Union. In a book published in 1980 (in which he did not mention Gorbachev),[78] Zdeněk Mlynář noted how the atmosphere altered in Moscow University between 1953 and 1955, after Stalin's death in March of the former year. He came to realize that even the Soviet citizens with whom he was personally well acquainted 'sensed and knew far more about the reality of Stalinist terror in their country than I had gathered from them while Stalin was still alive. In 1954 and 1955, such things were spoken of more and more openly.'[79] When Mlynář returned to Prague in 1955 he found that there was more fear there than there had been latterly in Moscow, where people were beginning to speak more freely among themselves and the political climate was changing 'under the influence of a slow but very real subliminal movement'.[80] The early post-Stalin years were also ones in which cultural life began to revive; a novel by Ilya Erenburg, *The Thaw*, published in 1954, gave its name to the era. Gorbachev was introduced to the cultural life of Moscow—theatre and poetry readings—above all by his wife, whose knowledge in that area exceeded his own (although as a schoolboy he had been an enthusiastic participant in amateur dramatics). It was during the Gorbachevs' university years that the then youthful poets Yevgeny Yevtushenko and Bella

Akhmadulina were first published to great acclaim, especially from young people.

As a student, Gorbachev took a dim view of the manners and political style of the typical Soviet bureaucrat. Throughout the university summer vacation of 1953 he worked in the office of a district procurator (prosecutor) in his home district of Krasnogvardeysk in the Stavropol region. In a letter to Raisa Titorenko, several months before their marriage, Gorbachev described his surroundings as 'disgusting', especially 'the manner of life of the local bosses'. He particularly disliked 'the acceptance of convention, subordination, with everything predetermined, the open impudence of officials and the arrogance'. He added: 'When you look at one of the local bosses you see nothing outstanding apart from his belly.'[81]

The Stavropol years

On graduation, Gorbachev returned to his native region and this time to the city of Stavropol, although in March 1955 he had been one of twelve law students selected to work in Moscow in the head office of the USSR Procuracy (an agency charged both with the prosecution of crime and with checking upon the legality of actions of public authorities). The function designated for these final-year students was that of supervising the KGB and other security organs. But in May of that year a government decree prohibited the use of young specialists in that branch of the state apparatus—according to Gorbachev, on the ostensible grounds that young people had been among the worst offenders in the 1930s in actually carrying out acts of repression.[82]

It was almost certainly fortunate for Gorbachev and for his subsequent intellectual and political development that this assignment to the headquarters of the Procuracy fell through. Since he had a law degree, and the practical vacation experience described above, his first job was, nevertheless, in the procuracy—in the Stavropol regional prosecutor's office. Gorbachev did not take long to make up his mind that he did not like it. He stayed for only ten days and wrote to his wife (who was still in Moscow and arrived in Stavropol a little later) that 'working in the prosecutor's office is not for me'.[83] He met some of the people he knew in the local Komsomol and, on the strength of his Komsomol experience at both school and university, was offered the job of deputy head of the department of propaganda and agitation in the regional Komsomol organization.[84] The transfer was not entirely straightforward. Before it was agreed, Gorbachev had 'a long and unpleasant conversation with the regional prosecutor', a man with whom he was later to have good relations.[85] Following further talks with the local procuracy, he informed his wife in a letter that, 'after berating me in every way, they have agreed to my leaving to join the regional Komsomol'.[86]

Thus began in 1955 Gorbachev's career as a full-time politician. In Khrushchev's time the Komsomol provided not only an introduction to bureaucratic politics but also, for an official involved in ideological and propaganda work as Gorbachev was, opportunities for public speaking and for learning the arts of persuasion. It was part of Gorbachev's apprenticeship as a politician who in later years was to impress Western publics rather more than their own politicians (with all the advantages of a lifetime of pluralist politics) were succeeding in doing. Since the Komsomol, even in the Khrushchev era, was a school of politics which produced also many a dull Soviet bureaucrat, the natural gifts—fortified and enhanced by his Moscow University years—which Gorbachev brought to his political career were, however, even more important than the nature of the work itself.

Many of the political skills and attributes necessary for a successful career in a comparatively free political system are dissimilar from those required for success in a highly authoritarian one. The degree of responsiveness to public opinion required in the one case is very different from the other. Skill in debate and public speaking ability more generally are clearly important in a democracy but counted for little in the unreformed Soviet political system. If they had, a Brezhnev or a Chernenko would never have made it to the top. Gorbachev, as he was later to show, possessed these talents in sufficient abundance to have brought him success in a pluralist political system if he had been born into one. They had for much of the time to lie fallow, emerging fully only in the second half of the 1980s. But some attributes are of value for politicians within authoritarian and pluralist regimes alike. These include intelligence, an ability to get along with people of different views and dispositions, and luck.

Andrey Sakharov, as one of the Soviet Union's greatest scientists as well as its most famous dissident, may be presumed to have been a fairly rigorous judge of the first of these attributes. Sakharov—who had been exiled to the city of Gorky in January 1980—was still there, and confined to hospital, when he watched one of Gorbachev's early television appearances in 1985. He told his room-mates: 'It looks as it our country's lucky. We've got an intelligent leader.'[87] When Sakharov first met Gorbachev in face-to-face discussion in 1988, he did not change that initial evaluation, assessing him then as 'intelligent, self-possessed and quick-witted in discussion'.[88] The Director of the Institute of the United States and Canada, Georgy Arbatov, who first encountered Gorbachev in the second half of the 1970s, found him to be 'bright and sensitive and in search of new ideas'.[89] Just one year before he became the highest-ranking Soviet diplomat to defect to the West, Arkady Shevchenko met Gorbachev, while holidaying at Kislovodsk, and, writing prior to Gorbachev's elevation to the General Secretaryship, described him as both 'intelligent' and 'open-minded'.[90] Similar observations were made by a great many of Gorbachev's interlocutors both before and after he became Soviet leader, although Western Sovietologists could be found who were ready to describe Gorbachev as 'merely an above-average product of the *nomenklatura* system'.[91]

The second attribute mentioned above—an ability to establish a personal rapport with different personality types and people of widely differing political views—was one which Gorbachev demonstrated in the international arena during his years in power when he established excellent personal relations not only with such prominent social democrats as Willy Brandt, François Mitterrand, and Felipe González but, quite strikingly, with the leading conservative politicians in the West—George Bush, Helmut Kohl, Margaret Thatcher, and even Ronald Reagan. It is hardly surprising, then, that in the years before 1985 Gorbachev was able to attract support and sympathy from politicians from different parts of the political spectrum within the Soviet Communist Party—from the conservative wing of the party in the shape of the highly influential Mikhail Suslov, from the more reform-minded Yury Andropov, and from such comparatively liberal party members as Eduard Shevardnadze and Alexander Yakovlev. More will be said later about Gorbachev's relations with all of them, especially the last two, who were to become key allies once Gorbachev become General Secretary.

Luck entered in mainly with Gorbachev's location. His native Stavropol—to which, according to his wife, he returned voluntarily from Moscow in 1955—is one of Russia's richer agricultural areas and it was easier for Gorbachev, as regional party First Secretary in the 1970s, to achieve good harvests there than it would have been in many another part of the country. Even more important, it contained a number of spas to which Politburo members from time to time descended and Gorbachev had both the duty (as local party chief) to meet these highly placed visitors and the opportunity to make a good impression. Stavropol also served Gorbachev better than Moscow during the greater part of the Brezhnev years inasmuch as it would have been more difficult for him to retain his independence of personality if he had gone through the rungs of the Komsomol and party bureaucracy in the Soviet capital. There the day-to-day pressures for conformity of thought as well as of public utterance would have been greater and he would have been more cut off from the real life of the country than he allowed himself to be in his native region.

Gorbachev's promotion within both Komsomol and Communist Party in the Stavropol territory was fast by the standards of the time. The Brezhnev era was one in which a great virtue was made out of 'stability of cadres'. If Brezhnev's consolidation of the status quo and postponement of all difficult decisions was undoubtedly bad for his country, it was splendidly attuned to the desires of its ageing bureaucracy. The security of tenure he gave to senior officials—after the life-threatening rule of Stalin and the job-threatening reorganizations of Khrushchev—made him the most congenial top leader the party and governmental apparatus ever had. The nostalgia of the old *apparatchiki* for the Brezhnev era became the greater with each successive year of perestroika.

While Gorbachev's promotion under Khrushchev and Brezhnev would not have been deemed especially fast in the 1930s, when there were many dead men's shoes to fill, it was, nevertheless, unusually quick for the years in which he in fact moved up through the hierarchy. A year after his initial appointment in the Komsomol apparatus, Gorbachev became in 1956 (at the age of 25) First Secretary of the Komsomol for the city of Stavropol, a post he held until 1958 when he became second secretary and, soon after, First Secretary of the regional Komsomol organization.[92] His career in the party apparatus began in 1962. As leader of the Komsomol for the entire Stavropol territory, his contacts with the Communist Party First Secretary for that region were close and frequent. The holder of this office was, quite fortunately for Gorbachev, an official still on his way up, Fedor Kulakov. He had been the regional party chief since 1960 and was to remain in that post until 1964 when, following Khrushchev's replacement by Brezhnev, he was promoted to be head of the Department of Agriculture of the Central Committee in Moscow. Later Kulakov became a Secretary of the Central Committee (1965) and a full member of the Politburo (1971), which meant, among other things, that Gorbachev had for the first time a friend in high places.

Kulakov's decision to bring Gorbachev into the party apparatus launched him on a career in that organization which formally ended only with his resignation from the General Secretaryship of the Soviet Communist Party in August 1991. His first post was as party regional organizer of the administration of collective and state farms, an office created by one of Khrushchev's reorganizations. From there he moved in 1963 to be head of the party organs department of the regional party committee, which meant that he was in charge of personnel policy and the selection of more junior party office-holders. Gorbachev's next promotion was in 1966 when, at the early age of 35, he became First Secretary of the Stavropol city party organization. In the meantime, just as it had been advantageous for Gorbachev that Kulakov had been a party official on the way up, it was also by this stage in his career convenient that Kulakov's replacement as party First Secretary for the Stavropol region was an official on the way down. Leonid Yefremov had been a candidate member of the Politburo in Khrushchev's time and for him to be sent from Moscow to Stavropol in 1964 was a clear indication that he was out of favour with the new Brezhnev leadership, although he appears to have been well respected in the Stavropol region.[93] When, in 1968, Gorbachev was moved from the leadership of the Stavropol city party to the second secretaryship of the party organization for the entire Stavropol region, it should have been clear that he was being groomed for the succession to Yefremov.[94] This promotion duly came in 1970 when Gorbachev was aged 39. Since important regional party first secretaryships carried with them a seat in the Central Committee, Gorbachev was elected to that body at the Twenty-Fourth Party Congress, held in 1971 just one month after his fortieth birthday.

The fifteen years between Gorbachev's return to Stavropol and his becoming the most powerful person in the region had been eventful ones in the wider world of Soviet politics. Crucially important was the de-Stalinization begun by Khrushchev. His 'secret speech' to the Twentieth Party Congress in early 1956—which was read aloud at Communist Party meetings at the time but not published in the Soviet Union (as distinct from the West, to which a copy quickly found its way) until Gorbachev himself was Soviet leader—had a profound effect on party members of Gorbachev's generation. Gorbachev, as a member of the Komsomol regional committee, had a better opportunity than the rank-and-file party member actually to read the Khrushchev speech. In his own words:

> The document containing Khrushchev's denunciations circulated briefly within the party, and then it was withdrawn. But I managed to get my hands on it. I was shocked, bewildered and lost. It wasn't an analysis, just facts, deadly facts. Many of us simply could not believe that such things could be true. For me it was easier. My family had itself been one of the victims of the repression of the 1930s.[95]

Khrushchev's criticism of Stalin was something which many older Communists found impossible to accept, but for the better-educated younger people—those between their late teens and early thirties in 1956—this was an important turning-point. The phrase 'children of the Twentieth Congress' was often used in later years in the Soviet Union to describe this political generation whose anti-Stalinist outlook took shape between 1956 and the early 1960s, for in 1961—at the Twenty-Second Party Congress—Khrushchev returned to the attack on Stalin and this time in open session. Another term used to describe the same group of people is *shestidesyatniki* ('people of the sixties').[96] Although the Twentieth Party Congress in 1956 was a starting-point for the rethinking of many of them, the 1960s was the decade in which they hoped for serious reform of the system; those hopes were, however, to be dashed. One can think of them as the *Novy mir* readers of the 1960s, for these were years in which that monthly journal stood alone for a more liberal and humanistic socialism at a time when conservative Communist and even neo-Stalinist views were gaining ground in other journals and in the mass media. Anti-Stalinism and a belief in the reformability of Communism were among the unifying values of the *shestidesyatniki*, although many of them had modified or abandoned entirely the second of those beliefs by the end of the 1980s. Numerous writers and readers of *Novy mir*, during that decade when it was under the inspired leadership of Alexander Tvardovsky, were greatly encouraged by the changes taking place in Czechoslovakia in 1968, and the Soviet military intervention in August of that year which put an end to the 'Prague Spring' was a severe blow to their aspirations. The decade ended dismally for the *shestidesyatniki* with the removal of Tvardovsky from the editorship of his journal and the breakup of the editorial board of *Novy mir*.

Although physically apart from the cultural excitements and struggles in Moscow and Leningrad during the 1960s, Mikhail and Raisa Gorbachev were not cut off intellectually. They read a great deal in Stavropol in the 1960s and 1970s, including Tvardovsky's *Novy mir*, the works of the *shestidesyatniki* generally, and the published writings of Alexander Solzhenitsyn.[97] When in late 1991 Gorbachev was asked whether he felt himself to be a man of the 'sixties generation' (a *shestidesyatnik*), he answered in one word: 'Yes'.[98]

The earliest Communist Party Congress Gorbachev attended as a delegate was the Twenty-Second, when Khrushchev enlarged upon the criticism of Stalin he had first voiced in 1956. At that Congress in 1961 Khrushchev introduced a new Party Programme which, to put it mildly, erred on the side of optimism. It envisaged the Soviet Union overtaking Western countries economically within a short period of years and stated that 'communism' (as distinct from 'socialism') would be built 'in the main' within the next two decades—i.e. by around 1980. At the time Gorbachev, on the eve of his thirtieth birthday, heard these pronouncements as a Congress delegate, he believed them. Later he characterized the programme as utopian. Speaking to Konstantin Chernenko's aide, Vadim Pechenev, in 1984, Gorbachev said: 'Now everything seems clear. With hindsight we are always impressive. . . . I myself, you know, voted for that Programme . . . and we believed in it then.'[99] The Party Congress of 1961 was not the first time Gorbachev had seen Khrushchev in action and had been impressed by him. He had heard him speak earlier when he attended the Thirteenth Congress of the Komsomol in Moscow in 1958. In a letter to his wife at that time, he said that he had found in that 1958 Congress 'vindication for all my worries, strivings and stress'.[100]

The impact of Khrushchev's exposure of some, at least, of the crimes of Stalin was greater among Moscow intellectuals than in the countryside. A colleague of Raisa Gorbachev's in the Philosophy Faculty of the Stavropol Agricultural Institute, who became friends with the Gorbachevs, observed: 'What brought us closer were the long discussions we had with Mikhail about Stalin. Even after the Twentieth Party Congress . . . comparatively few people in the provinces condemned Stalin. I was one, because I had seen the consequences of Stalin's politics at first hand. My mother was arrested in 1937.'[101]

Another feature of Gorbachev's Stavropol years which marked him off from most of his provincial contemporaries and which was to make an imprint on his political consciousness was his visits abroad. The least surprising of these were to other Communist countries, for it was customary for some regional party officials to be included in Soviet delegations. One such visit which may have involved Gorbachev in a measure of self-censorship of his views was a delegation to Prague in which he participated in late 1969.[102] It appears, however, that he accepted some of the distorted version of events presented in the Soviet mass media at that time. In an interview in December 1992 Gorbachev described his experience in 1969 as 'painful', adding: 'They doled us out very little information on what was going on.'[103] Later, he was to write that the delegation felt the resentment of the people of Czechoslovakia concerning the Soviet intervention in their affairs and that to say he felt 'uncomfortable' would be an understatement.[104] (Yegor Ligachev, at that time the First Secretary of the Tomsk regional committee of the Communist Party, was in the same delegation; this was the starting-point of the association between Gorbachev and Ligachev.[105]) Zdeněk Mlynář did not meet Gorbachev when his friend paid his first visit to Czechoslovakia, for by that time—in the aftermath of the Soviet invasion—he had been expelled from the Central Committee of the Czechoslovak Communist Party and had no access to a member of an official Soviet delegation. But on the eve of the Prague Spring Mlynář had paid a visit to Russia, during which he spent two days with the Gorbachevs at their home in Stavropol. At this 1967 meeting Mlynář discussed, among other things, the changes which the reformers within the Czechoslovak Communist Party hoped soon to introduce in their country. Gorbachev received these ideas sympathetically—Mlynář notes that they discussed them 'with mutual understanding'—for just as Gorbachev was 'in favour of a greater autonomy and responsibility for the republics and regions of the Soviet Union', so he was also supportive of 'the different countries having the possibility to proceed along their own specific roads of development'.[106] Gorbachev's suppression of any such heretical thoughts, together with an outward conformity with the anti-Prague Spring line of the Brezhnev leadership, would have become the more necessary to his survival in the party apparatus by the time he made his visit to Czechoslovakia in 1969, for in the meantime Mlynář's visit to Stavropol in 1967 had attracted the attention of the KGB; it had led in 1968 to a number of Gorbachev's and Mlynář's fellow students from the Moscow University Law Faculty in the 1950s being questioned by the security police about their relationship.[107]

The trips abroad were important not only for providing Gorbachev with the opportunity to see foreign countries, but for the possibilities they offered for 'networking'. Thus, for example, the Gorbachev–Ligachev relationship developed on friendly and co-operative lines for many years after their joint Prague experience. Given the fact that Gorbachev was the first of the two to rise high in the party hierarchy, the connection may have been more helpful to Ligachev than to Gorbachev, but there was a time (as will be noted in the next chapter) when there were definite advantages to Gorbachev in having the energetic Ligachev backing him for the party leadership. The way in which such contacts worked before Ligachev joined Gorbachev in the top leadership team during Andropov's General Secretaryship is usefully delineated by Ligachev:

> After that [their chance meeting on the delegation to Czechoslovakia], at the Central Committee plenums and at Party congresses when all the provincial Party secretaries gathered in Moscow, we would always have a friendly conversation, exchanging opinions on both particular and general matters. When Gorbachev became a secretary of the Central Committee, and then a member of the Politburo . . . I began to visit him frequently. Moreover, given the habits of the top political leadership under Brezhnev, Gorbachev in those years was the only member of the Politburo who could be found in his office until late at night.[108]

Meetings on delegations widened the range of contacts of ambitious party officials working far from Moscow, and Gorbachev himself was to call—once he had joined the top leadership team and, in particular, after he had become General Secretary of the Soviet Communist Party—on the services of those he had first met on foreign visits (or in the preparation for them). Apart from Ligachev (a mixed blessing), important cases in point are two men who were to become his aides in 1986 and 1988 respectively: Anatoly Chernyaev and Georgy Shakhnazarov. Chernyaev first met Gorbachev when they were on the same delegation to Belgium (and a shorter visit to Holland) in 1972.[109] At that time Chernyaev was a deputy head of the International Department of the party Central Committee, an office he held until 1986. Gorbachev was in the early years of his tenure as First Secretary of the Stavropol regional party committee and, according to Chernyaev, full of enthusiasm for improving the economy and social facilities of his native territory.[110] Indeed, Gorbachev was so busy expounding what needed to be done in Stavropol that, apparently, he scarcely noticed his surroundings on this, his first visit to the West.[111] Shakhnazarov, who was a deputy head of the Socialist Countries Department of the Central Committee between 1972 and 1986 (and First Deputy Head from 1986 to 1988), accompanied Gorbachev on visits to Eastern Europe, and took part in the briefings which preceded them, before as well as after Gorbachev became General Secretary.[112]

Especially important in terms of their impact on Gorbachev's political thinking were his visits to Western countries (with the perhaps surprising exception of the first). Untypically for a regional party secretary, he made two tourist trips to Western Europe in the 1970s in addition to visits as part of an official Soviet delegation. In her volume of reminiscences, Raisa Gorbachev speaks of going with her husband 'with a group of Soviet tourists' to Italy and France.[113] In an interview which the Gorbachevs later gave to *Paris Match*, they made it clear that the French trip in the summer of 1978 was one in which they were accompanied by only two other couples and that they travelled widely throughout France by car.[114] Gorbachev himself spoke about his Italian visit in the 1970s in an interview he gave in 1987.[115] He (and, from the evidence of her own reminiscences, his wife, too) was in a group of party workers who had been invited on holiday by the leadership of the Italian Communist Party. Their travels took them, among other places, to Sicily, Turin, and Florence.[116] It was during such trips, as Gorbachev was later to observe in conversation with his aides, that the discrepancy between Soviet propaganda concerning capitalist countries and the reality first came home to him.[117] In addition to his visits in the 1970s to Belgium, Holland, Italy, and France, Gorbachev travelled to West Germany for the first time in 1975 when he participated in the German Communist Party Congress in Stuttgart. He seems to have taken the opportunity to see some more of the country, for he was to refer on a number of subsequent occasions to a conversation he had during that visit with the owner of a petrol station near Frankfurt.[118]

Stavropol colleagues

In the 1960s Gorbachev—like his wife—studied for a second degree, but whereas she took a Ph.D. equivalent (candidate of sciences degree), his was a second first degree in a quite different subject from the Moscow one in law. With the aim of improving his specialist knowledge of agriculture, he took, by part-time study, a degree at the Stavropol Agricultural Institute, the institution in which his wife taught. It was taken in the Economics rather than Agronomy faculty of the institute and the thesis he wrote was on the economics of milk production.[119] The institute had a highly capable director between 1963 and 1978, whose ideas were unorthodox for that time. This was Alexander Nikonov, the son of a Russian father and a Latvian mother who grew up bilingual in Russian and Latvian in independent Latvia between the wars. Nikonov—who was the supervisor of Gorbachev's dissertation[120]—has affirmed that, unlike other party secretaries who frequently acquired academic qualifications by having theses written for them, Gorbachev did all his own work in the course of independent study for his second diploma.[121]

Although he was a Communist Minister of Agriculture in Latvia from 1951 until 1961, Nikonov was critical of Khrushchev's agricultural methods and fell foul also of the party First Secretary in Latvia, Arvid Pelshe, an old Bolshevik who had been a member of the Cheka (the ancestor of the KGB) in 1918 and who took over the Latvian party machine in 1959. In Nikonov's eyes, Pelshe was a 'Stalinist' who slavishly followed the Moscow party line. Nikonov has said that his opposition to excessively large collective farms led Pelshe to go so far as to accuse him of belonging to an 'anti-party group' and to threaten to bring him to trial.[122] Stavropol was for Nikonov an escape and a demotion, but also a more congenial political environment. He first encountered Gorbachev in 1963 and met him often thereafter.[123] Nikonov's practical and theoretical knowledge—especially of the work of some of the outstanding Soviet economists of the 1920s who had been purged in the 1930s—proved of value to Gorbachev, who frequently turned to him for advice during his time in the regional party apparatus in Stavropol.[124]

Later Nikonov wielded influence in Moscow during the years of Gorbachev's General Secretaryship and both then and earlier appears to have reinforced Gorbachev's view of the necessity to give the peasantry greater independence and control over the land they cultivated. Nikonov has recalled that Gorbachev, too, was opposed to Khrushchev's policy of combining small collective farms into larger units and the replacement of villages by agro-towns, which, as Gorbachev saw it, could only damage still further the self-confidence of the peasantry and their interest in their work.[125] With the support of Gorbachev, Nikonov in the mid-1980s, by which time he was President of the Lenin All-Union Academy of Agricultural Sciences in Moscow, played a crucial part in the rehabilitation of such talented Soviet economists of the 1920s as Alexander Chayanov and Nikolay Kondratev (known to Western economists as Kondratieff), both of whom were arrested in 1930 and died in prison camp in the late 1930s. Nikonov's first attempt in 1986 to have Chayanov rehabilitated met with a flat refusal from the Procurator-General. With the help of an academic lawyer, Nikonov went through the documents in the case of Chayanov and his colleagues and the ludicrous accusations against them, separating fact from fiction, and then approached Gorbachev. This was still a time when there was not even a pretence of separation of political and judicial powers and Gorbachev's word proved decisive. He immediately agreed that it was absurd that Chayanov and Kondratev had not been rehabilitated and issued an instruction that this process should be set in motion, and on 16 July 1987 the Military Collegium of the Supreme Court of the USSR formally pronounced them and others innocent of the charges against them and declared them to be fully rehabilitated.[126]

Another Gorbachev ally from his Stavropol years who was also to achieve prominence in Moscow once Gorbachev had become party leader was Vsevolod Murakhovsky, a Ukrainian who had served in the Soviet army between 1944 and 1950 and in a series of Komsomol and Communist Party posts in the Stavropol region from 1954 until 1985. Initially he was Gorbachev's superior in the Komsomol apparatus and then his subordinate within the party organization. When Gorbachev was elevated to a Secretaryship of the Central Committee in 1978, Murakhovsky succeeded him as party First Secretary for the Stavropol region. After Gorbachev had become General Secretary, Murakhovsky was appointed Chairman of a newly created State Committee for the Agro-Industrial Complex, which, however, failed to fulfil expectations.

Interesting evidence concerning Gorbachev's outlook at a time when he was still First Secretary of the Stavropol city (as distinct from the larger region) party organization has been provided by Mlynář, writing in 1985 about the two days he spent with the Gorbachevs in Stavropol in 1967, their first meeting since the fall of Khrushchev.[127] Apart from Gorbachev's sympathetic response to the plans of the reformists within the Czechoslovak Communist Party—noted above— Mlynář records that Gorbachev did not defend Khrushchev's record, objecting in particular to his administrative reorganizations of agricultural management and to the fact that—under the guise of decentralization—campaigns by, and arbitrary bureaucratic intervention from, the centre had still continued.[128] More than a quarter of a century later Gorbachev emphasized the other side of the Khrushchev coin, saying: 'I do not idealize Khrushchev but have a very high opinion of Nikita Sergeevich. To be the first to begin the assault on Stalinism, knowing who surrounds you—for that you need courage.'[129] At a conference devoted to an evaluation of Khrushchev on the centenary of his birth—held in the Gorbachev Foundation, chaired by Gorbachev, and attended by members of Khrushchev's family—Gorbachev said Khrushchev had to be understood in his 'given historical context'. He had taken 'the first steps towards improving the standard of living in the interests of ordinary people', and had 'begun the process of returning to the peasants their citizenship'. Above all, in 'an act of high civic courage', he had struck the first blow against Stalinism in his dramatic speech to the Twentieth Party Congress.[130]

During his years as party First Secretary for the Stavropol region between 1970 and 1978 Gorbachev was as pragmatic an innovator as the conservative temper of the times allowed. He supported what was called the 'link system' in agriculture, which involved giving a large measure of autonomy to a particular team or group of workers, including family groups, to farm a particular piece of land.[131] This was regarded with suspicion by some of those close to Brezhnev, being seen as a dilution of state or collectivized farms and a move in the direction of family farming, as in a sense it was. Indeed, it was comparatively rarely advocated in print in the 1970s until Gorbachev himself became Secretary responsible for agriculture within the Central Committee.[132] Gorbachev also gave support to innovative individuals in the Stavropol region, such as the entrepreneurial Viktor Postnikov (a native, like Gorbachev, of Privolnoe), for whom Gorbachev obtained permission to start a large-scale poultry farm with its own retail outlet in Stavropol. Postnikov got the idea in 1974 from the glossy American magazine *Amerika*, published for Soviet citizens and periodically on sale in the Soviet Union. There was a limit, however, to the amount of independence Gorbachev could accord to Postnikov's or any other enterprise in his capacity as regional party secretary. Postnikov has observed that he later frequently went to see Gorbachev when he was Central Committee Secretary with responsibility for agriculture and that it was especially from 1983, when Gorbachev's powers at the centre were extended under Andropov, that he was able to gain autonomy from the ministerial bureaucracy and feel he was 'master and owner' of the enterprise.[133] Gorbachev also fought the Ministry of Agriculture over the issue of fallow land. Against official insistence that every acre be farmed annually, he argued that productivity would be higher if part of the land of the Stavropol territory were to lie fallow each year.[134]

Gorbachev, however, paid due heed to signals from the Central Committee building in the capital. He engaged himself whole-heartedly in a more traditional harvesting campaign launched by Kulakov in Moscow. Kulakov chose his former party region of Stavropol and within it the Ipatovsky district, which also happened to be part of his Supreme Soviet constituency, for a widely publicized 'experiment'. His choice was also no doubt affected by his confidence in Gorbachev to organize the enterprise successfully and produce good results which would redound to Kulakov's favour (and also, incidentally, Gorbachev's). The idea was, as Zhores Medvedev relates in the best account of this episode, to reap the harvest far quicker than usual to avoid large losses of grain and to do this by sending in large mechanized units along with several party 'agitators'.[135]

This was a very different approach from the 'link' system Gorbachev had hitherto favoured and to which he was later to return, but it worked inasmuch as the harvest in the district was good in 1977 and a record-breaking one in 1978.[136] Like the majority of Soviet economic 'experiments' over the years, however, the Ipatovsky method did not produce results which could meaningfully be generalized, for so many specialist resources were poured into the effort that by definition a similar priority could not be given to all other agricultural areas. Many of them, moreover, had climatic conditions in which grain did not ripen simultaneously and where the Ipatovsky method would have been ineffective. But the Ipatovsky experiment achieved a narrower purpose. It brought awards to a number of agricultural workers and party officials in the Stavropol area, including the Order of the October Revolution for Gorbachev, and—in what was doubtless one of its primary aims—it yielded for Kulakov the still higher award of Hero of Socialist Labour.[137]

Gorbachev, however, was thinking more broadly about the problems of Soviet agriculture and the Soviet economy. In a lengthy memorandum which he sent to the Central Committee in May 1978, but which was published only in 1987, two years after Gorbachev had become General Secretary, he raised a number of fundamental issues.[138] This document (which occupies twenty-one pages of Gorbachev's collected writings and speeches) involved a risk on Gorbachev's part. It implicitly criticized the various ministries concerned with agriculture and it could easily be inferred from his criticisms that the party leadership as a whole had been remiss. Perhaps Gorbachev thought that two months after he had been awarded the Order of the October Revolution for his agricultural achievements was as good a moment as any to chance his arm. Some of his recommendations were of a detailed and technical nature, but in general they pointed to a deteriorating situation rather than one which was getting better all the time in accordance with the refrain of Brezhnevian propaganda. He complained about the slow growth of prices paid to the producer for agricultural products and of a declining rate of profit for collective and state farms, which meant that even in the Stavropol area they could no longer meet their economic needs from their own resources.[139]

Gorbachev stressed the need to raise agricultural productivity not by administrative methods but through a well-thought-out mechanism for material stimuli and material and technical provision.[140] He called for more local autonomy, and in a sentence which was very close in sentiments and terminology to a key passage in one of Andropov's agenda-setting speeches four and a half years later (soon after he had succeeded Brezhnev as Soviet leader), Gorbachev wrote: 'In our opinion it is necessary to give more independence to enterprises and associations in deciding various production and financial questions.'[141] He complained that in order to resolve small and perfectly clear issues it was necessary to possess 'gladiatorial capacities' to overcome the bureaucratic barriers. This had the further deleterious consequence that the central departments were so busy dealing with numerous trivial matters that they were not resolving questions of long-term significance.[142] Many of the ideas of perestroika, in its economic aspect, are, in fact, laid out in Gorbachev's 1978 memorandum, as the prominent reformist and sociologist Tatyana Zaslavskaya (who read the document for the first time only after its publication in 1987) remarked in an interview she gave in 1989.[143]

The price for plain speaking in one document had to be orthodoxy elsewhere. Thus, in the very same month, Gorbachev—along with party secretaries across the country—accorded lavish praise to the latest volume of Brezhnev's ghosted memoirs, *The Little Land*. In a speech to a Stavropol ideological conference in the same month—which, not surprisingly, Gorbachev did not include in his collected speeches published nine years later—he said that, 'in terms of the profundity of its ideological content, the breadth of its generalizations and the opinions expressed by the author, *The Little Land* has become a major event in public life'.[144] Other regional or republican party First Secretaries were more fulsome than Gorbachev about Brezhnev's achievements during the years in which attempts to project an image of Brezhnev as the embodiment of all political wisdom were being promoted from Moscow (even if these efforts were but a pale reflection of the personality cult of Stalin). Party First Secretaries from the southern union republics were especially lavish in their praise of Brezhnev, among them not only the old-style Communist Heydar Aliev in Azerbaijan but Gorbachev's near neighbour and friend, the reform-minded Eduard Shevardnadze in Georgia. It was a ritual in which all party secretaries had to indulge to a greater or lesser extent if they were to survive in the party apparatus, and both Gorbachev and Shevardnadze had hopes of promotion to the party leadership in Moscow which could only be achieved with Brezhnev's acquiescence, even if he were not to be the prime mover.

Gorbachev's backers

During Gorbachev's eight years (1970–8) as party chief of the Stavropol region, there were three senior figures in the Moscow leadership with especially close links to that area. One was, of course, Kulakov, who, as the Politburo member with particular responsibility for agriculture, continued to take a keen interest in the area in which he had served as First Secretary from 1960 until 1964 and who had the added advantage for Gorbachev of being on good terms with Brezhnev through his links with Brezhnev's most trusted subordinate, Konstantin Chernenko. Kulakov had worked alongside Chernenko in the Penza regional party committee between 1945 and 1947.[145] It can be taken for granted that Kulakov spoke well of Gorbachev within leadership circles during the 1970s, although he was not present to advocate his promotion when Gorbachev actually moved to Moscow, for the vacancy occurred as a result of Kulakov's death.

A second Gorbachev backer was Yury Andropov, Chairman of the KGB from 1967 until early 1982 and a full member of the Politburo from 1973. He had been born in the Stavropol region and frequently returned there. Andropov was a complex character who was a surprisingly popular Soviet leader at a man-on-the-street level during his fifteen months as General Secretary between November 1982 and his death in February 1984. Although he carried responsibility for the crushing of political dissent during the Brezhnev years, Andropov retained a desire for reform within certain limits and at the time of the succession to Brezhnev was the person in whom many people who subsequently became radical reformers in the Gorbachev era vested their hopes. Some of them had, in fact, worked closely with Andropov as his full-time consultants when he headed the Socialist Countries Department of the Central Committee from 1957 until 1967. That group of consultants has been described by Georgy Arbatov as 'one of the most outstanding "oases" of creative thought of that time (i.e. from the moment of its creation in 1961 until 1967 when Andropov transferred from the Central Committee to the KGB . . .)'.[146]

The best known among these consultants outside the Soviet Union over the past quarter of a century has probably been Arbatov himself, who became the first Director of the Institute of the United States and Canada in 1967[147] and who took a genuinely pro-*détente* line at home while defending orthodox Soviet positions abroad during the Brezhnev years. He retained his links with Andropov until the latter's death, although there was a rift between them for a time during Andropov's General Secretaryship.[148] Arbatov was a strong Gorbachev supporter during the earliest years of perestroika, but by 1990 had identified increasingly with the more overtly radical views of Boris Yeltsin.

Another of Andropov's former consultants in the Socialist Countries Department of the Central Committee who became an institute head was Oleg Bogomolov, who was appointed Director of the Institute of Economics of the World Socialist System in 1969. By 1990 it was evident that there was no longer such a thing as a world socialist system (if there ever had been) and the name was changed—as noted in Chapter 1—to the Institute of International Economic and Political Studies. Even under its old name, however, and even during Brezhnev's period of rule, the Bogomolov institute was a refuge for a number of independent thinkers who were to become very prominent proponents of transformative change in the Gorbachev era.[149]

The original head of Andropov's team of consultants in the Central Committee in 1961 was Fedor Burlatsky, a 'within-system' reformer who over many years tried to push wider the limits of the possible. Although Burlatsky's relations with Andropov virtually ceased when he left the Central Committee apparatus in 1965 (and moved to *Pravda*, from which he was dismissed in 1967), he welcomed Andropov's elevation to the party leadership in 1982 and his own influence became somewhat greater then than it had been in the later Brezhnev years. He played a still more prominent part in the Gorbachev era as a source of ideas for political institutional reform, as editor from March 1990 until August 1991 of the weekly newspaper *Literaturnaya gazeta*, and also as an active member of the Supreme Soviet of the USSR.[150]

The former consultant in the Socialist Countries Department of the Central Committee who was later to play the most influential role of them all during the years of Gorbachev's leadership was, however, Georgy Shakhnazarov. More will be said about Shakhnazarov later, for (as has already been noted in passing) he become in 1988 one of Gorbachev's full-time aides and even before that was an informal adviser. His opportunities to make an impact on Gorbachev's thinking were, accordingly, greater than those of any of the remaining participants in this network of anti-Stalinist Communists who had worked with Andropov a quarter of a century earlier.

Others from that group who achieved later prominence included Alexander

Bovin, for many years political commentator for the newspaper *Izvestiya*, and from late 1991 Soviet (and subsequently Russian) Ambassador to Israel after Israel's diplomatic relations with what was then still officially the USSR had been restored; Gennady Gerasimov, who achieved world-wide fame as Ministry of Foreign Affairs chief spokesman in the second half of the 1980s and as the Soviet official at summit meeting press conferences who, speaking in English, produced more quotable 'sound-bites' for the Western mass media than his American counterparts; Nikolay Shishlin, a shrewd political analyst who became one of the most liberal among senior figures in the Central Committee apparatus during the Gorbachev era; and the scholarly Lev Delyusin, for many years a China specialist in the Institute of Oriental Studies in Moscow.[151]

During the fifteen years in which Andropov headed the KGB he was evidently closer to people of a much less reformist disposition than his former party consultants, although the KGB, like other Soviet organizations, was not entirely homogeneous in its attitude to change within the Soviet system. Some of its well-travelled and well-educated members were better aware than most Soviet citizens of just how far behind the Western world Brezhnev's Soviet Union trailed. Moreover, when loyalties were later put to a stark test at the time of the August coup of 1991, a crucially important minority of KGB employees did not obey the orders of the *putschists*, who included their own chief, Vladimir Kryuchkov. It is worth adding that Kryuchkov himself had closer and longer-standing ties with Andropov than any of the party intellectuals discussed above. He served with him in the Soviet Embassy in Budapest in the mid-1950s—and was involved also, therefore, in the suppression of the Hungarian revolution of 1956—and subsequently in the Socialist Countries Department of the Central Committee, from whom he followed him to the KGB.

Andrey Sakharov, in the light of subsequent revelations, probably gave the KGB under Andropov more credit than it was due when, after castigating it for the persecution of dissidents during the 1970s and first half of the 1980s, he commented: 'On the other hand, precisely the KGB, thanks to its elite character, was almost the only force not affected by corruption and therefore opposed to the mafia. That duality was reflected in the personal fate and position of the leader of the KGB, Yu. V. Andropov.'[152] Andropov's life-style was, indeed, modest in comparison with others in the Brezhnev leadership team, and his anti-corruption sentiments, as Gorbachev has suggested, were probably genuine.[153] It is also the case that he launched an attack on corruption when he was politically strong enough to do so in 1982. But Andropov's particular selection of politicians with mafia connections was governed substantially by political expediency, and the KGB as a whole—according to Arkady Vaksberg, the author of *The Soviet Mafia*—was far from free of collusion with organized crime.[154]

Yet there was, as Sakharov suggested, a certain duality in Andropov's character. Although he proved himself capable of the ruthlessly efficient repression of organized dissent as KGB chief during the Brezhnev years, he remained less complacent about the regime's performance than did Brezhnev and his closest colleagues. Andropov's own brief period as party and national leader was to be one in which economic reform was tentatively placed on the political agenda for the first time since Aleksey Kosgyin had attempted the cautious introduction of some market criteria in 1965, a project which eventually floundered in 1968 when it suffered from guilt by association with the economic reforms of the Prague Spring being pursued by Ota Šik.

Andropov regularly took holidays and rest-cures at the spas and sanatoriums situated in the Stavropol territory. It was on one of these visits in April 1969 that Gorbachev was given the opportunity by Yefremov to meet him for the first time.[155] Once Gorbachev had become First Secretary of the region the following year, his meetings with Andropov became a regular feature of the latter's visits. While Soviet protocol demanded that the local party boss greet top leaders from Moscow, it is also clear that Andropov was attracted by Gorbachev's intelligence and personality. Arbatov recounts a conversation he had with Andropov in the spring of 1977 when the latter asked him whether he was familiar with the name 'Gorbachev'. Arbatov replied that he was not, and was told by Andropov that he was one of 'the completely new people with whom it is really possible to link our hopes for the future'.[156] Either in that same conversation with Arbatov or another one in the 1970s, Andropov described Gorbachev as a 'brilliant man working in Stavropol'.[157] Speaking in late 1991, Gorbachev said he did not wish to idealize Andropov 'and his ideological conceptions and participation in the struggle against dissidents—all that is clear', but he was a person of 'great intellect' with whom he (Gorbachev) had long-standing connections. 'I would not say', said Gorbachev, 'that we had a very close relationship, but I knew him well and we met regularly.'[158]

In addition to Kulakov and Andropov, those in high places in Moscow who thought well of Gorbachev during the 1970s included the powerful figure of Mikhail Suslov. Suslov was, in comparison with Andropov—not to speak of Gorbachev—an orthodox Communist of little imagination or intellectual curiosity. While addicted to power, he was less obsessed with its perquisites than Brezhnev and most members of the Brezhnev group. While generally supportive of Brezhnev, he stood somewhat apart from Brezhnev's circle of cronies and had an interest, as had Andropov, in checking the trend in the 1970s whereby the top leadership was gradually replenished with people who had close connections with Brezhnev personally. Suslov had been a Secretary of the Central Committee since 1949 and a full member of the Politburo from 1955. That combination of posts and his length of time at the top gave him great influence within the highest party echelons. Anatoly Chernyaev recalls how Suslov would pick up the telephone and say to the Soviet Minister of Foreign Affairs, 'Comrade Gromyko, prepare for such-and-such a date such-and-such materials' and put down the receiver without waiting for an answer.[159]

Suslov, like Andropov, had connections with Stavropol. He was one of Gorbachev's predecessors as First Secretary of the Stavropol regional party committee, a post he held from 1939 until 1944. He returned to Stavropol for holidays and Gorbachev himself has mentioned in the same breath Suslov and Andropov as senior party figures with whom he got acquainted in his years as party chief of the Stavropol region.[160] He appears to have met him for the first time when he went to Moscow in connection with his appointment as First Secretary of the Stavropol party organization in 1970.[161] For a Soviet politician who could establish good personal relations even with Western conservative politicians who had adopted positions as radically right wing as those of Ronald Reagan and Margaret Thatcher, there is no great mystery about his being able to be on good terms simultaneously with both Andropov and Suslov, whose relationship with each other was an uneasy one.[162] Gorbachev's interest both in learning from and in impressing Suslov and Andropov, and his attentiveness to such senior colleagues, were marks of a politician on the way up. On one occasion, in the summer of 1979, the Gorbachev family even accompanied the Suslov family on a trip together to a dacha which had once belonged to Stalin.[163] It is noteworthy that when Suslov died in January 1982 Gorbachev was the only Politburo member to stop and speak with each member of Suslov's family and that when Andropov was lying in state in February 1984 he was the only person in the top leadership to be shown on Soviet television sitting with Andropov's family.[164]

It was the relatively sudden death of Gorbachev's first important patron, Fedor Kulakov, that meant that a new Secretary of the Central Committee with responsibilities for agriculture needed to be chosen. Mikhail and Raisa Gorbachev celebrated the fortieth anniversary of the Kulakovs' wedding with them on 5 July, but on 17 July Kulakov died following a short illness and operation.[165] Kulakov, while already a full Politburo member as well as Secretary of the Central Committee, had continued to supervise agriculture, and there was a need for that particular gap to be filled. Gorbachev had probably vested some hopes in Kulakov himself becoming General Secretary, for given Brezhnev's declining health and the fact that at the age of 60 Kulakov was the youngest of the senior secretaries, he could well have been a candidate for the succession. At that time Andropov was still outside the party apparatus and it would not have been easy for him to move straight from the Chairmanship of the KGB to the General Secretaryship of the Central Committee of the party.

One of the first repercussions of Kulakov's death was that Gorbachev was granted the opportunity to address an assembly in Red Square for the first time; he delivered one of the orations at Kulakov's funeral there, the principal one being given by a senior member of the Politburo, Andrey Kirilenko.[166] It seems fairly clear that there was disagreement within the leadership about who should be the new Secretary responsible for agriculture and that Gorbachev was not Brezhnev's first choice. While the General Secretary had greater possibilities to promote his own nominees than had anyone else, and while he could, in effect, veto other people's suggestions, he was not able to place his preferred candidate in a leadership post on every occasion. In this instance disagreement is indicated by the length of time the position remained vacant; Kulakov died on 17 July 1978 and Gorbachev was still working in Stavropol in November. He was officially elected a Secretary of the Central Committee only on 27 November 1978, and, while the formal Central Committee decision sometimes disguised the fact that the person concerned had already taken up his new duties, that was not true in this case. Gorbachev's selection, with Suslov and Andropov as his principal supporters, may well have been part of a trade-off, for two of Brezhnev's closest colleagues, Konstantin Chernenko and Nikolay Tikhonov, were promoted at the same Central Committee plenum—Chernenko to full Politburo membership and Tikhonov to candidate membership.[167]

In the meantime, Gorbachev had been subjected to further close scrutiny by the most senior figures in the Soviet leadership. Zhores Medvedev has noted that Suslov, Andropov, and Kosygin all spent some time holidaying in Kislovodsk in the Stavropol region in August and September 1978;[168] on 17 September an especially intriguing meeting took place on the railway station of Mineralnye Vody, which was also within Gorbachev's domain. A special train carrying Brezhnev and Chernenko further south to Baku stopped there and they were met by Gorbachev, who was accompanied by Andropov. A two-hour discussion took place which was, in effect, a crucial job interview for Gorbachev. More remarkably, the participants in the discussion were the last four men to hold, in succession, the office of General Secretary of the Central Committee of the Soviet Communist Party.[16]

Chapter 3

In the Portals of Power

WHEN Gorbachev moved to Moscow as a Secretary of the Central Committee in November 1978, he became—at the age of 47—the youngest member of the predominantly elderly Soviet top leadership team. By virtue of his secretaryship, he was from now on entitled to attend meetings of the Politburo (though only full Politburo members could vote) in addition to meetings of the Secretariat. He also supervised the various ministries with responsibilities for agriculture as well as the Agricultural Department of the Central Committee.

He began to obtain much more information than he had before. It was at this time, Gorbachev has said, that he 'got access to closed materials and books by foreign authors which were available to high-up people who were on the right distribution list'. Although, however, his possibility of 'getting information was broader', it was 'still limited'.[1] The idea that he could have asked, for instance, to see the party archives on Czechoslovakia 1968 was absolutely 'out of the question'.[2] Equally, Gorbachev could not have cast doubt upon the main lines of any area of current policy without bringing his rise through the party hierarchy to an abrupt halt. Even in the realm for which he carried political responsibility—that of agriculture—he had to operate at the margins of policy so long as Brezhnev was alive. Under both Khrushchev and Brezhnev, agriculture had been an area in which the General Secretary himself took a special interest and over which he wielded authority. When Brezhnev was unable to exert himself independently, he had sufficient like-minded supporters in high places who were ready to invoke his name and office in defence of the status quo. Radical policy innovation was well-nigh impossible.

Brezhnev had been in deteriorating health for several years, but as his mental and physical decline proceeded, his sense of his own importance increased. The cardiologist to the Soviet political élite (and later Minister of Health), Yevgeny Chazov, has published a volume of memoirs in which he observes that Brezhnev's arteriosclerosis had destroyed his capacity for self-criticism.[3] There is not much evidence that critical self-appraisal had ever been one of Brezhnev's strong points, but by the end of the 1970s the awards with which he had himself festooned had reached new heights of absurdity. Already bedecked with medals, he needed little persuasion to accept the highest of all Soviet military awards, the Order of Victory, in 1978, or to receive in the same year the honour of being made a Hero of the Soviet Union for the third time. (He became a four-times 'Hero' in 1981.) According to Chazov, it was the

53

Minister of Defence, Dmitry Ustinov, who took the initiative in proposing the supreme military honour for the Soviet leader and the faithful Konstantin Chernenko who proposed the third gold star 'Hero' award.[4] The following year it was the turn of the Lenin Prize for Literature, the highest award for writers, to come Brezhnev's way; this was in honour of his slim volumes of ghosted memoirs. Brezhnev's supporters aimed to strengthen their own position by setting Brezhnev further apart from other colleagues in the party leadership. To some extent they succeeded. With the public at large, such awards did Brezhnev more harm than good (as Chazov recognizes), but for the Soviet establishment they were signs that Brezhnev's political, as distinct from physical, strength was not to be discounted.

A Brezhnev who was inactive for much of the time, but whose continuing presence was seen as a guarantee of stability, also suited admirably the most senior members of the Politburo, who had a good deal of *de facto* autonomy to run their own parts of the executive, provided they did not deviate from generally accepted Soviet norms. Suslov had been in the party leadership longer than Brezhnev and was the older of the two men, but in the second half of the 1970s he enjoyed better health than the party leader and was very content to continue wielding the powers of second secretary of the party. His post did not carry that title officially or in public, but it was, nevertheless, fully recognized within the Central Committee building and operated according to well-established convention.[5] Suslov, whose powers and length of time in the top party leadership were noted in the previous chapter, enjoyed substantial security of tenure. Although not a member of the 'Brezhnev group', but senior to all those who could be described as belonging to it, Suslov had been generally supportive of Brezhnev's brand of complacent, conservative Communism. So long as Brezhnev headed the party organization, Suslov could feel that both his own position and the system were secure.

Similarly, the three senior heads of state organizations who had entered the Politburo together in 1973—Yury Andropov, Andrey Gromyko, and Dmitry Ustinov—had no wish to rock the boat. Andropov did harbour ambitions to succeed Brezhnev, but while Suslov was in charge of the Secretariat he was unlikely to be wanted there,[6] and it would have been difficult for him to move straight from the Chairmanship of the KGB to the top party post. The irony of Andropov's stance was that he did not want Brezhnev's job to fall vacant until he himself could be the leading contender, but by the time this eventually happened in 1982 Andropov was on the verge of mortal illness which led to a more rapid deterioration of his health than had been the case with Brezhnev's. When informed in the mid-1970s of the gravity of the decline in Brezhnev's condition, Andropov's main concern was that this should not become an issue in the Politburo.[7] On the advice of Chazov, who argued that the condition of the General Secretary's health was so serious that the Politburo should know about it, Andropov had reluctantly discussed the issue with Suslov as early as 1975. He had been relieved when Suslov had agreed with him that it was important to preserve the political status quo in the country and that it would be harmful to widen the small circle of people who knew about Brezhnev's medical problems. Knowledge of the General Secretary's growing mental as well as physical incapacity might well, Andropov and Suslov feared, be put to political use by ambitious colleagues.[8]

Even more content with their present positions than Andropov, for they were older and had no aspirations to become party leader, were the Minister of Foreign Affairs, Gromyko, and the Minister of Defence, Ustinov. Enjoying good personal relations with Brezhnev and with each other, they had immense authority within their own ministries and in their interconnected areas of policy. Their actual power became still greater when Brezhnev himself could only spasmodically concentrate on foreign policy, defence, or any other area of political concern. Brezhnev's political power had increased from the time he came to office in 1964 until the mid-1970s, as he succeeded gradually in changing the composition of the party leadership to his liking and in removing his opponents. However, in his later years his day-to-day decision-making activity was negligible, although his formal authority had been advanced to the point where it was difficult for any initiative to be taken which had not received his personal endorsement. This was, indeed, a recipe for 'stagnation'—the term used after 1985 to describe the greater part of the Brezhnev era. The carefully promoted adulation of Brezhnev in the Soviet mass media—and the entire 'mini-cult' of his personality—was a device of his supporters, and of others who stood to gain from his continued presence, to counteract the evidence of his physical and intellectual frailty.

It was, however, deceptive inasmuch as the care devoted to keeping Brezhnev on a higher pinnacle of prestige than any of his Politburo colleagues did not correspond with the behind-the-scenes political reality of oligarchical rule. If the full and candidate members of the Politburo and Secretaries of the Central Committee—at any given time, some twenty-five people—constituted the top leadership team in the Soviet Union, the full Politburo members enjoyed higher standing and greater power than the others within that group. Although they constituted an oligarchy, there was a still narrower circle of 'inner oligarchs' in the Politburo which by no means embraced all of its members. Gorbachev has said: 'I only managed to insert my shoulder into that inner circle under Andropov.'[9] That was notwithstanding the fact that Gorbachev had become a full member of the Politburo, while retaining his Central Committee secretaryship, in November 1980—two years before Andropov became Soviet leader following the death of Brezhnev. The decision to send Soviet troops to fight in Afghanistan from December 1979, although formally endorsed by the Politburo, was taken, essentially, by Ustinov, Gromyko, and Andropov, in consultation with Brezhnev.[10] Boris Ponomarev, the head of the International Department of the Central Committee, was also consulted about the intervention and acquiesced. Anatoly Chernyaev, at that time a deputy head of the same department but of a different political disposition from Ponomarev, was informed by Georgy Kornienko, the First Deputy Minister of Foreign Affairs, that 'the initiator of intervention' was Gromyko who was enthusiastically supported by Ustinov'.[11] Shevardnadze has said that he and Gorbachev—who in 1979 were candidate members of the Politburo—first learned about the invasion from the mass media,[12] although that claim was called into question by the selective leaking of a 1979 Politburo document in late 1992.[13]

However that may be, it is clear that neither Gorbachev nor—still less—his like-minded colleague Shevardnadze could at the end of the 1970s exert decisive influence on major policy. A former aide to Konstantin Chernenko, Vadim Pechenev, has written that strategic decisions in the Soviet Union during Brezhnev's last years were taken by six senior members of the Politburo—Suslov, Ustinov, Gromyko, Andropov, Chernenko, and Brezhnev (with Brezhnev himself, for health reasons, playing the least active part of the six).[14] A witness hostile to Gorbachev (as, indeed, is Pechenev), Valery Legostaev, who was Ligachev's assistant, suggests that Gorbachev had insufficient experience to be qualified for the post of General Secretary in 1985. He observes: 'In 1979 he became a candidate member and then a member of the Politburo, but he did not enter its influential group.'[15] On many matters—among them the intervention in Afghanistan and foreign and defence issues more generally—even if the Politburo formally approved a policy, most of its members were not involved in the real decision-making process.[16] Politburo meetings in Brezhnev's later years had become extremely brief and formal and were not occasions for serious discussion, still less for questioning what had already been agreed within the inner circle. Gorbachev could either accept the decisions as *faits accomplis* and preserve the possibility of attaining the General Secretaryship—the post with the greatest potential power within the Soviet system—or challenge the judgements of the Politburo's inner circle and begin a descent from power which would have been strikingly faster than his rise through the party ranks.

By playing his part in maintaining collective solidarity on reprehensible decisions he was to reverse after he had become General Secretary—among them, the December 1979 intervention in Afghanistan and the exile to the city of Gorky of Andrey Sakharov in January 1980—Gorbachev occupied a position by no means so morally pure as that of the small band of Soviet dissidents who had courageously protested against oppressive actions such as these at the time they happened. There was, though, an important sense in which the activities of the within-system reformers and the overt dissidents were complementary, however much at odds they had earlier appeared to be. Indeed, the advance of the former within the highest party echelons after 1985 turned out to be a pre-condition for ending the marginality and persecution of the latter. Decisions such as the exile of Sakharov followed the logic of the Soviet system, and that system (as already noted briefly in Chapter 1) had proved remarkably impervious to assault from the small minority in Soviet society who, in the period between the mid-1960s and the mid-1980s, openly rejected it. In the short or medium term, the Soviet system could only be transformed, or subverted, from within that very system— by those working in the highest echelons of the Communist Party (in particular, the person at the apex of the party hierarchy) rather than in the broader society.

The same did not hold good for every Communist country; the strength of the social forces opposed to the system varied greatly from one to another. But the Soviet Union was not Poland, and prior to the late 1980s no organization remotely comparable to either the Catholic Church or Solidarity had succeeded in Russia in combining a mass base with genuine independence from the party-state. Although Gorbachev cast himself initially in the role of renewer and reformer of the Soviet system, before moving on to a realization that it required complete transformation, there was some point to the criticism of more traditional Soviet Communists that in reality he was undermining the foundations on which their power rested. The defenders of the old order were to realize this danger relatively early in the perestroika years—when Gorbachev seized the initiative and outmanœuvred them—and in the post-Soviet period the 'red-and-brown' alliance of unreconstructed Communists and Russian nationalists was to speak of bringing Gorbachev to trial for crimes against the motherland.[17] In contrast, the justification of the 'within-system reformers' in the Communist Party was that ultimately they found a standard-bearer who actually came to power and opened up hitherto unheard-of space for political innovation. Similarly, the justification, in the last resort, for Gorbachev's relative conformism in the Brezhnev years was that eventually he was able to become a transformative leader who changed the system fundamentally. Yet, the only way he could reach the apex of political power, and effect such change, was to play by the rules of the Soviet game (many of which were, in any event, second nature to him) until he got to the top.

Gorbachev's pre-1985 behaviour may be regarded as relatively conformist in comparison with, on the one hand, the activities of the overt dissidents and, on the other, the writings of the boldest of the within-system reformers (as a result of which even the latter could operate, at best, on the fringes of power). It also appears timid in comparison with his conduct once he had become General Secretary. The Gorbachev who was hailed for the boldness of his actions between 1987 and 1989 was, nevertheless, the same person who had displayed considerable caution before he attained the General Secretaryship.

Moreover, Gorbachev appears much less conformist if his behaviour is compared not with those who had little or no power to lose but with that of other members of the Soviet top leadership team in the years between 1978 and 1984. Not long after he arrived in Moscow, Gorbachev began to consult a wider range of experts than was customary within the Soviet leadership, including specialists outside the party apparatus. The range of these contacts was later to widen—especially from early 1982, by which time Gorbachev was himself a full member of the Politburo and Andropov had replaced Suslov, who had died in January of that year, in the Secretariat of the Central Committee. As a number of those who had contact with the leadership have testified, Gorbachev read more widely than his colleagues in the senior ranks of the party leadership. When Georgy Shakhnazarov first met Gorbachev, he was surprised to discover that the latter already knew him from his books, which, quite untypically for a Secretary of the Central Committee, Gorbachev had read.[18] Gorbachev also, along with his wife, took full advantage of the capital's cultural life; they were far more frequent attenders at the liveliest Moscow theatres (especially the Sovremennik, under the directorship of Oleg Yefremov, and the Taganka, under the direction until 1983 of Yury Lyubimov) than any others from within the top leadership circle.

Even while Brezhnev was still General Secretary, as he was for Gorbachev's first four years of work in the Central Committee apparatus, Gorbachev brought a different approach to the Secretariat and a zeal for change. Arkady Vaksberg, a legal specialist on the newspaper *Literaturnaya gazeta* and the author of *The Soviet*

Mafia, has recounted how an article he wrote soon after Gorbachev replaced Kulakov as the Secretary responsible for agriculture brought trouble on his head. He had written about the death of cattle on a large scale in the Vladimir region of Russia as the provincial officials and managers allowed the animals' feed to rot while they indulged themselves. Not only local party secretaries but the Central Committee Secretary with responsibilities for ideology, Mikhail Zimyanin, telephoned the newspaper to protest about Vaksberg's 'political error'. The editor-in-chief of *Literaturnaya gazeta*, the time-serving Alexander Chakovsky, insisted that Vaksberg publish a retraction that would contain 'a categorical dissociation from any of the general conclusions' he had reached. When he took a carefully worded draft text to Chakovsky the following morning, he found his editor in an excellent mood. He had just received a telephone call of congratulations from the recently appointed Central Committee Secretary, Mikhail Gorbachev, thanking the newspaper for 'its brave and hard-hitting piece', which, he said, would 'help him in the task of putting right the serious failings in the area for which he had been made responsible'.[19]

Gorbachev was, however, conscious of the limits within which he was working. He would encourage the publication of articles in newspapers which went further than the currently approved leadership line and beyond what he, as someone who was collectively bound by that line, could personally propose. Thus, Gorbachev wished to end the notoriously inefficient practices whereby, for example, tractor drivers on Soviet farms were paid on the basis of the number of hectares they ploughed. This gave them every incentive to plough quickly and shallowly and they had very little material interest in the final product of their labours.[20] As noted in Chapter 2, Gorbachev, in his Stavropol days, had supported both in print and in practice what was called the 'link' system, whereby a team of workers (which could be a family group) was given responsibility for farming a particular piece of land and for the entire crop-raising process from ploughing to reaping. Later Gorbachev was to develop this into the idea of the 'collective contract', whereby autonomous work teams and brigades were encouraged to make long-term contracts with their parent farms and were given operational independence to organize their own work and distribute the group's income among themselves; not least important, the income itself was to be based on production results (with a necessary minimum income guaranteed in years of bad weather). It was, however, not until several months after Andropov had succeeded Brezhnev as General Secretary that Gorbachev—in a speech at the city of Belgorod—could publicly advocate this as a policy which should be widely pursued.[21] On that occasion Gorbachev was addressing an important gathering of party officials from all of the republican and regional organizations, together with the republican ministers of agriculture and other senior officials with agricultural responsibilities. But he had already been preparing the way for this reform—which, because of the resistance of local officialdom, was never implemented on as wide a scale as he wished—much earlier than 1983. *Pravda*, whose commentary on agriculture Gorbachev was able to influence, began publishing in 1979 a series of articles calling attention to the loss of pride in work on the land of the Soviet peasantry and praising the 'link' system and the development of contractual relations between parent farms and teams of workers.[22]

One of the social scientists of an innovative turn of mind whom Gorbachev began to consult very early in his period as Secretary of the Central Committee with responsibility for agriculture was Vladimir Tikhonov. They met for the first time in 1978.[23] Tikhonov was an agricultural economist who was later to become one of the strongest advocates of independent co-operatives and of private enterprise. In due course he was chosen to head the movement of co-operators and entrepreneurs. What struck Tikhonov in 1978 was that, unusually for a Secretary of the Central Committee, Gorbachev read serious books, had a genuine interest in analysing the problems of agriculture, was ready to support the idea of independent enterprises within the agricultural sector, and, above all, was a good listener. Unlike other party functionaries, he did not interrupt a speaker just because he disagreed with what they were saying.[24]

The point about Gorbachev's ability to listen needs underlining, for some years later it was a common criticism of Gorbachev that he talked too much and did not listen sufficiently. It is true that, neither before he became General Secretary nor after, did Gorbachev break with the Soviet tradition that leaders' speeches should be (by Western standards) excessively long ones. It is also true that as the cross-pressures mounted on him in his last two years as Soviet leader he was a less patient listener than he had been earlier. That was especially so on public occasions which he felt a need to dominate and when he often talked more than he should have done. But it is a fundamental, albeit common, misunderstanding of Gorbachev as a politician to underestimate how much he learned precisely because he was prepared to listen to, and comprehend, a wide range of expert assessments and political views. The extent to which his views developed over time is evidence enough of his capacity for learning—and learning involved listening. In my own interviews with many specialists who were at different times consulted by Gorbachev, the vast majority commented on what, in the words of the Director of the Institute of State and Law in Moscow, was his 'extraordinary capacity for listening'.[25] The Mayor of St Petersburg, Anatoly Sobchak, who had already clashed with Gorbachev on several occasions by the time he published a volume of memoirs, nevertheless wrote there that 'Gorbachev is a person who knows how to listen. . . . His remarks draw you into conversation, you begin to forget about the time and how busy he is and, having fallen under his hypnotic charm, you start talking about things you did not intend to bring up.'[26]

Both before and after he became General Secretary it was Gorbachev's practice to summon groups of specialists for extended discussion sessions, during many of which Gorbachev—especially in the early days—would confine himself to asking questions in the course of meetings lasting several hours. While listening to many different views, Gorbachev was acutely sensitive to the limits of the politically possible at any given time. He also weighed the political strength as well as the cogency of argument of his interlocutors. It was possible for someone to leave Gorbachev believing that he or she had persuaded him intellectually, only to find that, in his public utterances on the topic, Gorbachev would say something different. That was not only because there could be a distinction under Soviet conditions between his political and his intellectual judgement but also because the views of any one specialist were highly unlikely to be the only ones he listened to. The range of evidence on the breadth and depth of his listening and political learning is by now quite formidable.[27]

Some of Gorbachev's contacts with social scientists who were critical of the status quo and who were subsequently to exercise greater influence in the perestroika years date from early 1982. It was then that he had a series of consultations with a number of scholars—sociologists as well as economists—with particular knowledge of agriculture in the run-up to a major policy pronouncement known as the 'Food Programme'. One of those specialists was Academician Tatyana Zaslavskaya, an economist-turned-sociologist from the Siberian branch of the Soviet Academy of Sciences; another was a more regular adviser, Alexander Nikonov, the former Director of the Stavropol Agricultural Institute, whose relations with Gorbachev were discussed in the previous chapter and who—with Gorbachev's encouragement—had moved to the Lenin All-Union Agricultural Academy in Moscow in 1978. Zaslavskaya, a bold reformer who received a party reprimand in Novosibirsk the following year, when a copy of a highly critical analysis of Soviet society which she presented in a seminar in Novosibirsk found its way into the Western press, assumed that Gorbachev had heard of her either from his wife—since Raisa Gorbachev's sociological research in the 1960s had been on rural society—or from Nikonov.[28] Although Zaslavskaya was not as close a Gorbachev adviser as has sometimes been suggested—in a book written in 1988 but published in 1990 she said that they had met 'five or six times' (subsequently, 'seven or eight times') and in small group, rather than one-to-one, discussions—there is no doubt that Gorbachev paid attention to her views and read her writings.[29] A major speech Gorbachev delivered in December 1984 (discussed later in this chapter) showed concrete evidence of Zaslavskaya's influence. It was also through Zaslavskaya that the economist Abel Aganbegyan, the Director of the Novosibirsk-based institute in which Zaslavskaya worked, was introduced to Gorbachev later in 1982.[30] Aganbegyan was subsequently to become a closer Gorbachev adviser—the most influential economist in the first stage of perestroika.

Gorbachev was explicit within these small group meetings about the limits to his freedom of action. When Zaslavskaya spoke her mind at the first meeting in a way that was 'not customary' at that time, and criticized the timidity of the draft agricultural programme, Gorbachev responded positively: 'In fact, he agreed with me and went on to say, "If only I could have written here everything I am thinking about".'[31] Zaslavskaya has described a three-hour meeting which she (a sociologist) and six economists had with Gorbachev in April 1982, in which they criticized the measures in the draft 'Food Programme' as piecemeal and half-hearted. But Gorbachev 'made it clear to us that he was not in a position at that time to pursue anything more radical'.[32] Zaslavskaya recalled Gorbachev saying that he would have been happy if even that draft programme were to be sent back from the ministries and the State Planning Committee looking still 'remotely similar to the original version', for he believed (rightly, as it turned out) that the programme was 'going to be emasculated even further'.[33] One of the issues being discussed was the setting-up of a State Committee for the Agro-Industrial Complex (Gosagroprom). Zaslavskaya expressed the view that this would be a worthwhile development if it replaced the existing ministries with responsibility for agriculture and did not simply become an umbrella organization which added an additional administrative layer to those already in existence. Gorbachev, indicating the political constraints within which he was operating, turned to an official from the Agricultural Department of the Central Committee who was accompanying him and asked: 'Do you think if I wrote that in the draft programme, I would still be sitting in this office?'[34]

Gorbachev's promotion between his arrival in Moscow in 1978 and his becoming General Secretary in 1985 was remarkably rapid for those years. The only other person who, between Brezhnev's accession to the General Secretaryship in 1964 and Gorbachev's succession to that office in 1985, moved in the space of two years from being an ordinary member of the Central Committee to full membership of the Politburo combined with a Secretaryship of the Central Committee was Konstantin Chernenko. Chernenko had become a Secretary of the Central Committee in 1976, a candidate member of the Politburo in 1977, and a full Politburo member in 1978. Gorbachev emulated this feat by becoming a Secretary of the Central Committee in 1978, a candidate member of the Politburo in 1979, and a full member in 1980. Full membership meant that he now, in principle, had a vote in Politburo meetings, but since in the last two years of Brezhnev's life these meetings had become shorter and more formal than ever—with votes scarcely ever taken—the enhancement of Gorbachev's status within the Central Committee apparatus was the most important aspect of the promotion.

If, in respect of the unusual three-stage promotion within successive years, Gorbachev's progress paralleled that of Chernenko, in one very important respect Gorbachev had far surpassed his predecessor. Chernenko was 64 before Brezhnev felt strong enough to promote to a Central Committee Secretaryship this loyal but colourless associate, with whom he had worked since their paths first crossed in Moldavia in the early 1950s. Gorbachev, in contrast, was 47 when he became a Secretary of the Central Committee and 49 when in October 1980 he became a senior secretary—that is to say, a secretary who was also a full member of the Politburo. The only other people in addition to Gorbachev and Chernenko (and, of course, the General Secretary Brezhnev) who held those joint ranks at that time were Mikhail Suslov and Andrey Kirilenko. Suslov, who was born in the Saratov region of Russia in 1902, was twenty-nine years older than Gorbachev. Kirilenko, a long-standing Brezhnev associate from the Ukraine, was twenty-five years Gorbachev's senior. Moreover, although this was not known outside narrow Kremlin circles at the time, he was fast losing his memory, failing to recall the names even of people very close to him and 'forgetting the most elementary things'.[35]

Given that Chernenko was the second youngest of the senior secretaries and that Gorbachev was a full twenty years his junior, it appeared that time was indeed on Gorbachev's side. In Soviet politics, however, there was many a slip 'twixt cup and lip, and the Brezhnev era provided quite a few examples of ambitious younger politicians being pushed aside to make way for an older man.[36] Gorbachev certainly could not take his progression to the top post for granted. All that the age disparity meant in the short run was that Gorbachev was the least influential of the senior secretaries. This began to change in a modest way from

January 1982 when Suslov died and his place was taken by Andropov (a switch which was formalized at a Central Committee plenum in April of that year) and, more strikingly, when Andropov succeeded Brezhnev as General Secretary after the death of the latter in November 1982.

Advancement under Andropov

Upon Andropov's accession to the top post, Chernenko took over the task of presiding at the weekly meetings of the Secretariat of the Central Committee. Andropov himself, as was normal with General Secretaries, chaired the Politburo—for as long as his health permitted. But even during Andropov's General Secretaryship (and regularly after Chernenko succeeded Andropov as party leader) Gorbachev 'sometimes led the sessions of the Secretariat'.[37] He began to make a strongly favourable impression on the more enlightened figures within the party apparatus, who fervently hoped that he would be Andropov's successor. Chernyaev was one such person. After taking part in a meeting in 1983 at which Gorbachev received the Iowa banker and farmer John Chrystal, Chernyaev reported to his superior, Ponomarev, that Gorbachev's performance had been 'brilliant, well-informed and extraordinary'. The 78-year-old head of the International Department (who had joined the Communist Party as long ago as 1919) rebuked Chernyaev for allowing himself to get carried away.[38] Chrystal, who met Gorbachev on a number of occasions, was, however, as impressed by him as Chernyaev had been.[39]

When Andropov succeeded Brezhnev as General Secretary, there was an immediate change of style and emphasis at the top of the Soviet political hierarchy. Gorbachev was soon to benefit from the changes. Andropov, as noted earlier, had placed high hopes in Gorbachev and had great respect for his ability. Gorbachev, in turn, had favoured Andropov as Brezhnev's successor. There is good reason to accept the view of the leading Kremlin doctor, Chazov, that there were, in effect, two opposed groups in the leadership from the time of Suslov's death in January 1980—one headed by Andropov and the other by Chernenko.[40] Gorbachev was clearly in the Andropov camp during that period. Chazov had also taken sides. He was careful to ensure that Andropov would be the first to learn of Brezhnev's death, believing it important for his succession prospects that he should immediately take charge when Brezhnev died. He assumed that the telephones of Brezhnev's dacha, where his death had occurred, might well be bugged and that if he had spoken openly by telephone about the death, either Vitaly Fedorchuk or Nikolay Shchelokov would have known within minutes. Fedorchuk, who had succeeded Andropov earlier in 1982 as head of the KGB, had not been Andropov's choice for the post. That became all the clearer when, in one of his first personnel changes after becoming General Secretary, Andropov replaced him with his own former subordinate at KGB headquarters, Viktor Chebrikov. Fedorchuk, a Ukrainian by nationality, had been in military intelligence—he was an officer in *Smersh* from 1943 until 1947—until 1970 when he became head of the Ukrainian KGB. His appointment as KGB chief for the entire Soviet Union was at the behest of Chernenko and Brezhnev. Shchelokov was the notoriously corrupt Minister of Interior who was very much part of the Brezhnev group and who had long-standing links to Chernenko, even though Chernenko did not share his life-style and 'contrived', in Ligachev's words, 'not to sully his reputation with corruption'.[41] To bypass these people and give Andropov a head-start in the succession race, Chazov got a message to Andropov that he should come at once to Brezhnev's dacha without telling him over the telephone that Brezhnev had died.[42]

As soon as he became General Secretary, Andropov put a new stress not only on discipline and fighting corruption but also on seeking ways to rejuvenate Soviet economic performance. Apart from a few selected areas to which the best human and material resources were directed—such as parts of the defence industry and the space programme—the Soviet economy had long compared unfavourably with its Western counterparts in terms of the *quality* of its output. From the beginning of the 1980s, however, it had become increasingly clear that even in *quantitative* terms the economy was now doing badly. Growth had virtually ceased from the end of the 1970s. Andropov was more prepared than Brezhnev had been to face up to this unpalatable fact. Although there remained important institutional and ideological obstacles to far-reaching economic reform, the change of leadership facilitated recognition of some of the serious deficiences of Soviet economic performance. That, in turn, created a climate of opinion within, at least, select party circles in which innovation could be contemplated.

While overt dissidents were given no respite during Andropov's General Secretaryship, a sharper distinction than had been common under Brezhnev was made between within-system criticism and overt dissent. For reform-minded specialists within the Communist Party there was a widening of the limits of the possible, even though there was the reverse of a let-up in the campaign to crush the already much-weakened dissident movement. Andropov had given some indication of this more nuanced approach to diversity of view within the Soviet system—while at the same time resisting anything resembling political pluralism as understood in the West—in the Lenin Anniversary Speech he delivered on 22 April 1982. On the one hand, he said that no society, whether capitalist or socialist, was without different points of view and different interests.[43] On the other hand, he went on to make the entirely orthodox point, in terms of traditional Soviet doctrine, that different interests under capitalism took the form of class antagonisms, whereas in socialist society there was neither private ownership of the means of production nor exploitative classes and, accordingly, the differences between different social groups did not become antagonistic ones.[44] The Soviet people, he said, would not agree to any opposition to the structure of their society and they were able to protect themselves from 'all kinds of renegades'.[45]

Although Andropov was more interested than either Khrushchev or Brezhnev had been in Marxist theory, he was still more concerned with getting the Soviet economy moving again. Among the earliest of important appointments made by him was that of Nikolay Ryzhkov, a man who had never worked in the party apparatus until he became a Secretary of the Central Committee in November 1982. His background was in engineering and his career had advanced steadily in Sverdlovsk from skilled worker to factory manager; latterly he headed the entire vast Uralmash complex of engineering plants. He had been summoned to Moscow in 1975 as First Deputy Minister of Heavy and Transport Machine-Building and at the time Andropov brought him into the party apparatus he was First Deputy Chairman of the State Planning Committee (Gosplan).

Andropov apparently believed that Gorbachev's political skills and knowledge of the party machine would be complemented by Ryzhkov's industrial experience and detailed understanding of the Soviet system of economic management. He held a joint meeting with Gorbachev and Ryzhkov in December 1982 at which he told Gorbachev that he was to extend his area of concern from agriculture to the economy as a whole and that he and Ryzhkov must work together.[46] Gorbachev had already shown a desire to broaden his interests to general economic issues but this, Ryzhkov notes in his memoirs, had been ill-received by the old guard in the Politburo.[47] Once the new General Secretary had charged Gorbachev with overseeing the entire economy, his colleagues had no option but to put up with it. The very fact that Andropov, rather than Chernenko, had succeeded Brezhnev meant that the Brezhnevite old guard was by this time on the defensive, although the rapid decline of Andropov's health during 1983 was to grant them a short additional lease of political life.

The collaboration between Gorbachev and Ryzhkov was initially, and indeed for several years, a happy one, notwithstanding the fact that by the end of the 1980s their views had moved further apart and their personal relations had become distant. Writing of the time when they worked together during Andropov's General Secretaryship, Ryzhkov says that they got along 'splendidly'. Their knowledge was indeed complementary, although he adds that Gorbachev did not like to admit that there was something he did not know or understand.[48] Ryzhkov was very conscious of Gorbachev's seniority to him at that time.[49] He had just become a Secretary of the Central Committee, whereas Gorbachev combined his secretaryship with full membership of the Politburo. Together, however, they examined proposals for change, some of which were solicited while others were sent on their authors' initiatives. They invited both scholars and factory managers to give their frank analyses of what needed to be done.[50] They studied 'about one hundred and ten memoranda' from institutes, ministries, and individuals, and among those whom they consulted in person were some of the people who were to emerge as key economic reformers once Gorbachev had become General Secretary. They included, Ryzhkov observes, such prominent figures as Aganbegyan, Arbatov, Bogomolov, Shatalin, Vladimir Tikhonov (not to be confused with the far more conservative Chairman of the Council of Ministers at that time, Nikolay Tikhonov), and Zaslavskaya—all of whom have been mentioned earlier in this book—as well as Leonid Abalkin, a serious economic reformer who was to become in 1986 the Director of the Institute of Economics of the Academy of Sciences, and Nikolay Petrakov, the Deputy Director of the Central Economic-Mathematical institute who had long been a proponent of marketizing reform.[51]

One thing Andropov, Gorbachev, and Ryzhkov could all agree on was the need, in some way, to decentralize the Soviet economy and give greater autonomy to factory managers and the heads of industrial associations. Thus, a number of 'experiments' were conducted whereby enterprises in selected industries were given expanded rights and were less subject to detailed tutelage from their ministerial overlords. While decentralization was desirable in itself, neither Gorbachev (at that time) nor Ryzhkov was sufficiently aware of the disruptive effects which could be produced by granting greater enterprise autonomy without changing the fundamentals of the economic system. These were later to become clearer when a more comprehensive measure designed to enhance the independence of factories and industrial associations, the Law on the State Enterprise (1987), was introduced by Gorbachev and Ryzhkov and had consequences far removed from those intended.

Economic 'experiments' in Soviet conditions were always somewhat artificial, for they involved not only special scrutiny on the part of the authorities but untypically favourable treatment for those enterprises which were part of the project. In August 1984, half a year after Andropov's death and Chernenko's succession, the Politburo passed judgement on the experiment which had been officially launched in July 1983 by Andropov, following preparatory work by Gorbachev and Ryzhkov.[52] Given that the new plan indicators and incentives came into operation only on 1 January 1984, that was an unrealistically short experimental time. The fact that it was then pronounced a 'qualified success' reflected Gorbachev's desire to move as quickly as possible to more wide-ranging reform. Looking back from his retirement on Andropov's 14 July 1983 decree widening the rights of industrial associations and enterprises and his 28 July decree on 'strengthening socialist work discipline', Ryzhkov goes so far as to view these decrees as the start of perestroika in its economic dimension.[53] Sensible measures, he adds, had, however, to be advocated in actual terms words 'dictated to us' (i.e. to Chernenko and Ryzhkov) 'by the all-powerful Ideology'. Why, he asks in retrospect, did discipline have to be 'without fail *socialist*'?[54]

Apart from bringing Ryzhkov into the Secretariat of the Central Committee in November 1982, Andropov made a number of other personnel changes, not all of which were necessarily to Gorbachev's advantage. Thus, Heydar Aliev, a career NKVD and KGB officer in his native Azerbaijan until he was appointed First Secretary of the Communist Party in Azerbaijan in 1969, was made a full member of the Politburo and brought to Moscow as First Deputy Chairman of the Council of Ministers at the same time as Ryzhkov was promoted. Aliev, although intelligent and adaptable (as he was to demonstrate by getting himself elected President in post-Soviet Azerbaijan), was no reformer and neither was Grigory Romanov, the First Secretary of the Leningrad party organization whom Andropov brought to Moscow as a Secretary of the Central Committee (he was already a Politburo member) in June 1983. There is ample evidence that Romanov was not well disposed towards Gorbachev, and the fact that this feeling was reciprocated was indicated by the speed with which Gorbachev removed him from the leadership once he had become General Secretary. These and other changes were made by Andropov in an effort to strengthen his own political position by bringing in people who were not Brezhnev protégés. The fact that he had spent fifteen years as head of the KGB, rather than in the Secretariat of the

Central Committee, meant that he lacked protégés in the party machine where he now needed them.

The only new appointment, however, that was to be of comparable importance in the future to that of Ryzhkov was the return to Moscow of Yegor Ligachev, the First Secretary of the Tomsk party organization. It was Gorbachev who was instrumental in bringing Ligachev in from the cold, as Ligachev himself acknowledged even after he had broken both politically and personally with Gorbachev. Ligachev had worked in the Central Committee apparatus in the early 1960s but since 1965 had been based far from Moscow in his native Siberia. His return took place in April 1983 and it was to a key position—the headship of the Department of Party Organizational Work. This was the department which supervised party officials up and down the country and, for anyone aspiring to the General Secretaryship, it was an exceptionally important office in which to have an ally. The ultimate decision at this stage was Andropov's, but Ligachev records his surprise that it was Gorbachev who first broached the subject with him and that he did this at a time when Chernenko, at that time number two to Andropov, was on holiday. The very same morning on which Ligachev saw Gorbachev he had a brief meeting with Andropov, who concluded his conversation with Ligachev by saying: 'Then we'll confirm you today at 11 o'clock at the Politburo.'[55] The decision had not in reality been taken quite so quickly. Two months earlier Gorbachev had been involved in a discussion about the position of head of the Party Organization department with Andropov and Gromyko (in the case of the latter, perhaps surprisingly, since he was Foreign Minister—but he was also a friend and ally of Andropov) and had said that they needed someone like Ligachev. Gromyko had readily agreed, but others may have taken more persuading. Gorbachev later told Ligachev of the delay, saying: 'Well, you know how it is; time was needed to clarify things, and so on. You know that Andropov studies the cadres thoroughly.'[56] Andropov doubtless studied the KGB as well as the party files on Ligachev. The fact that he was free of the taint of corruption was probably a telling point in his favour. Although some of Ligachev's political enemies in later years attempted to tar him with that brush, it was never very convincing and the more objective among Ligachev's opponents have rejected such accusations.

Ligachev was actually something of a puritan who wanted to reinvigorate the Soviet system, rather than reform it—still less change it fundamentally. Very early in the perestroika period, it became clear that he was a far more conservative Communist than Gorbachev. His immense energy and determination were, however, to be useful assets to Gorbachev over the two years following his return to the party headquarters in the spring of 1983. Gorbachev's confidence in him at that time was, none the less, much more crucial to the rise of Ligachev than was Ligachev's to the further elevation of Gorbachev. That was even more true in December 1983, when Ligachev was formally elected a Secretary of the Central Committee, than it had been in April. Some time before the December meeting of the Politburo which would consider the issue, Gorbachev had told Ligachev that he was 'adamant' that he be elected and that he was 'putting special effort into this question'.[57] Andropov was by then so ill that when Ligachev was summoned to his hospital bedside he scarcely recognized him. But the dying General

Secretary supported Ligachev for this promotion into the top leadership team not only because he approved of him personally but also because it would strengthen the position of Gorbachev.

Chernenko, who chaired the Politburo meeting which had to make the decision (after which 'election' by the Central Committee was a formality), referred to Andropov's view of Ligachev's suitability, but he himself—although second secretary—did not speak to Ligachev in the days leading up to the meeting and accepted his promotion without enthusiasm.[58] He could scarcely have been unaware that Andropov wished Gorbachev, not Chernenko, to succeed him, for it had already been clear to others that, before his health failed, Andropov was merely awaiting a suitable opportunity to remove Chernenko and replace him as 'second secretary' by Gorbachev.[59] Outwardly, according to Chazov, the relations between Andropov and Chernenko were 'almost friendly', but he observed that they both had to make a big effort 'in order to preserve the appearance of close, comradely relations'.[60] Chernenko had powerful allies in the old guard who were determined that he should not be removed to make way for Gorbachev as 'second secretary'. They had to treat Andropov's opinions with some respect, but any change in the balance of forces within the leadership beneficial to Gorbachev was unwelcome to them.

Many important decisions in Soviet politics at this time hung on the question of which senior person in the leadership would die first. This was a natural consequence of the entire top leadership team having been allowed to grow old together in Brezhnev's time. By the beginning of 1982, the year which saw the death of, first, Suslov and, later, Brezhnev, the average age of the Politburo had risen above 70. Andropov, a 'mere' 68 when he became Soviet leader, had begun to receive dialysis treatment for kidney deficiency as early as February 1983, four months after Brezhnev's death.[61] According to Ryzhkov, he was able to work properly for only eight months out of his fifteen as General Secretary; most of the remaining time he spent in hospital.[62] The accident of fate that saw Andropov's health go into steep decline just a little over a year before the same ill fortune caught up with Chernenko was decisive in ensuring that Gorbachev would not be Andropov's direct successor. Although Andropov made one last effort to make Gorbachev his heir apparent, his physical weakness by that time had undermined him politically. Only a few of the old guard suspected at this stage that Gorbachev might be a radical reformer. What they feared was that he would carry on where Andropov had left off in terms of fighting corruption and complacency and wield a new broom with such vigour that they would all be swept aside. Several of Andropov's most senior colleagues took it upon themselves, accordingly, to flout one of their dying leader's last wishes.

The Central Committee met in plenary session on 26–7 December 1983. It was at this session that a number of personnel changes, including Ligachev's election to a secretaryship of the Central Committee, were made.[63] Andropov was, of course, too ill to attend, but—with the help of his personal assistants—he had prepared a forceful speech which was distributed to those attending the session. However, as Angus Roxburgh notes in the best brief account of the episode, on 24 December Andropov had summoned his aide Arkady Volsky to his bedside and given him six additional paragraphs.[64] The last of these observed that he would not be able to chair meetings of the Politburo and the Secretariat in the near future and went on: 'I would therefore request members of the Central Committee to examine the question of entrusting the leadership of the Politburo and Secretariat to Mikhail Sergeyevich Gorbachev.'[65] This was a clear attempt to elevate Gorbachev above Chernenko and, in effect, to make plain that the younger man was Andropov's choice to succeed him.

Volsky, having consulted two other aides, who were as astonished as he was by the sensational addition to Andropov's speech, handed the original over to the head of the General Department of the Central Committee, Klavdy Bogolyubov (a more than averagely corrupt old Brezhnevite who enjoyed good relations with Chernenko),[66] having taken the precaution of making a photocopy first. When, however, he received the official text as a member of the Central Committee at the plenary session in the Kremlin two days later, he was shocked to discover that the last paragraph was missing. It had, Volsky added, been removed by the three people who, in his view, were running the country at that time, the second secretary, Chernenko; the Minister of Defence, Dmitry Ustinov; and the Chairman of the Council of Ministers, Nikolay Tikhonov. When Volsky approached them to ask what had happened to Andropov's last paragraph, he was told in no uncertain terms to mind his own business. He subsequently blamed himself, first, for not telephoning Andropov there and then to tell him what had occurred and, second, for telling Ryzhkov (who had heard rumours that something was amiss) that nothing had happened. He had, however, tried to reach Gorbachev to speak to him, but 'for the first time was not allowed' by the allies of the old guard 'to come up to him and talk to him'.[67] Volsky has given various accounts of his failure to get through either to Andropov or to Gorbachev by telephone. In one of the more colourful versions of the story, he told the American journalist David Remnick that he had said to Bogolyubov that he must telephone Andropov to tell him about the missing paragraph, to which Bogolyubov allegedly replied: 'Then that will be your last phone call.'[68]

By the time Volsky got back to his office, word had apparently reached Andropov of what had happened and he was incandescently angry. Volsky said: 'He cursed me very, very stridently' and said that 'I . . . and the other comrades should have stood up at the plenum . . . and said that he had written that last paragraph and then called him immediately.'[69] Years after this dramatic episode, Gorbachev acknowledged that he 'knew about the text', although Andropov had not discussed it with him in advance. At the same time, Gorbachev added, 'I did have a feeling of what his attitude towards me was like, he did devote attention to me. He gave me opportunities to display my initiatives and supported me . . .'.[70] But, commenting on the suppressed text in an interview conducted between the August coup and his resignation as Soviet President in December 1991, Gorbachev said: 'I never mentioned it to anyone.' He added: 'I know how things occurred in that old party. Frankly, that was no longer relevant . . . even though to be objective, one has to note that they did try to conceal this and they managed to hide it.'[71]

Gorbachev had not been personally involved in the attempt to push Chernenko aside and, in fact, did not yet feel entirely ready to become leader of his country. He told Vadim Medvedev (whose co-operation with Gorbachev had begun in 1980 when he was Rector of the party Academy of Social Sciences and who had been brought into the Central Committee by Andropov and Gorbachev as head of the Department of Science and Education in 1983) that he was 'not psychologically prepared for the role of first person' at the time when Chernenko was elected.[72] Accordingly, he reacted much more philosophically than Andropov to the action of his older colleagues, and it was he who went to the hospital to calm Andropov down.[73] Gorbachev was conscious also that he did not yet have a majority in the Politburo willing to support him.[74] Older members of the Politburo, as Medvedev observed, were much more concerned with their particular interests—personal, territorial, and departmental—than with the general good.[75] Thus, for example, the veteran Brezhnevite, Dinmukhamed Kunaev, who had been running Kazakhstan as his personal fiefdom since 1964, and the complacent and conservative Viktor Grishin, the First Secretary of the Moscow city party organization, could feel secure in their posts provided Chernenko was chosen as General Secretary. The Politburo members knew, when they elected Chernenko, that he had serious health problems, but, as the chief Kremlin doctor, Chazov, observed, expressing sentiments somewhat similar to Medvedev's, they were more concerned with their 'group and personal political interests' than with medical opinion.[76]

Gorbachev, in fact, made no bid for the leadership on Andropov's death and Chernenko was selected by the Politburo 'without any problem'.[77] Members of the Politburo were not unaware, however, that there was another *potential* candidate. The tough old Minister of Defence, Ustinov, was overheard (by Volsky) saying to the still older Nikolay Tikhonov that 'Kostya [Chernenko] will be more amenable than Misha [Gorbachev]'.[78] (Ustinov, who had been minister responsible for the armaments industry already in Stalin's time—and who had played a crucially important role during the Second World War—was, in the words of Vladimir Dolgikh,[79] 'permeated to the bone by the system'.[80] Tikhonov had been a friend of Brezhnev's since the 1930s, and Brezhnev had appointed him Chairman of the Council of Ministers in 1980 in succession to Aleksey Kosygin, even though by that time Tikhonov was 75.) Gorbachev, for his part, no doubt calculated that to stake all on a challenge to the older generation in the leadership at that moment would be a much riskier route to the General Secretaryship than biding his time. He could, after all, expect to become second secretary to Chernenko, provided he accepted the latter's accession to the General Secretaryship without demur.

Preparing for power

There was more opposition to Gorbachev becoming number two to Chernenko than perhaps he had bargained for. Politburo meetings were attended not only by members and candidate members of the Politburo but by the Secretaries of the Central Committee and by the aides to the senior figures within the Politburo. Among these witnesses of the first Politburo meeting to be chaired by the new General Secretary, a number have already recounted how there was an attempt to put a stop to the apparently inexorable rise of

Gorbachev. When it was proposed by Chernenko that Gorbachev should lead the Secretariat and that he should chair Politburo meetings when Chernenko was absent—which meant that he would be the *de facto* second secretary—Tikhonov led the opposition. Chernenko surprised a number of those present by the firmness of his support for Gorbachev. He may have been grateful for Gorbachev's acquiescence in his own elevation to the General Secretaryship. He may also have felt the need to have a much younger and more vigorous man in the position of second-in-command, especially in the light of his increasing frailty. The accounts of the meeting differ in respect of how many Politburo members supported Tikhonov (although several mention Grishin as being among them and others include Romanov as well), but they agree in affirming that no formal and final decision in favour of Gorbachev was taken. It was simply accepted that he would fulfil these functions for the time being and, as so often happened in Soviet politics, a temporary expedient became a longer-lasting arrangement. Gorbachev moved into Suslov's old room in the Central Committee building, which had been occupied, in turn, by Andropov and Chernenko when they had occupied the second secretary slot, and in the eyes of the party apparatus he had become the number two person in the Politburo, second only to the General Secretary.[81]

The top leadership at that time was unusual in that it contained only two senior secretaries apart from the General Secretary—that is to say, secretaries who were also full members of the Politburo. Under Andropov there had been three: Chernenko, Gorbachev, and Romanov; in the past there had sometimes been four or five. But Chernenko was not replaced, for it would have been impossible to reach agreement on who his replacement should be. Once Gorbachev had become second secretary, there was a political stalemate in the leadership. Gorbachev could carry with him the Secretariat—where Ligachev and Ryzhkov were especially important allies—but he was further away from having a majority in the Politburo.[82] Thus, neither the Gorbachev supporters nor those opposed to his advancement were strong enough to change the composition of the top leadership team. Since, as noted in Chapter 1, the supposed 'elections' by the Central Committee to positions in the Politburo and Secretariat were, in reality, *co-options* by the voting members of the Politburo, they depended upon a consensus within the Politburo *or* on a clearly dominant grouping which could impose its will *or* upon the presence of a particularly strong and determined General Secretary. Testimony that these conditions were absent during Chernenko's thirteen months as leader comes not only from some of the major political actors at that time but from the fact that throughout the period not a single person was promoted to full or candidate membership of the Politburo or to a secretaryship of the Central Committee, nor was anyone dismissed from the party's top leadership team. The number of voting members of the Politburo did decline by one in December 1984, but as a result of the death of Ustinov and not of any political decision. Ustinov's departure from the selectorate which would choose Chernenko's successor was, on balance, distinctly helpful to Gorbachev's chances, even though Romanov's authority *vis-à-vis* the military whom he supervised could be regarded as greater when there was no longer someone of Ustinov's prestige standing between him and them.[83]

Notwithstanding the reluctance of some of the senior members of the Politburo, upon the death of Andropov in February 1984, to see the powers of Gorbachev extended, he came to supervise a greater number of important areas of policy within the Secretariat than even Suslov had done, for in Suslov's time there had been more senior secretaries among whom functions had to be divided. Like Suslov before him, Gorbachev now became the senior secretary supervising the party organization and (for the first time) ideology and foreign policy, but he retained responsibility for the economy (which had never been part of Suslov's—or for that matter Chernenko's—domain). Romanov was primarily responsible for supervision of the military, the KGB, the Ministry of Interior, the Procuracy, and the Courts (as secretarial overlord of the Administrative Organs Department of the Central Committee), as well as of military industry. As such, he may have counted on the support of Ustinov, who carried great weight in Politburo deliberations. But since Romanov had been brought from Leningrad to Moscow by Andropov as recently as 1983, he had a lot of leeway to make up if he were ever to become a serious rival to Gorbachev, and Ustinov's death, while it may have left Romanov with more authority as military 'overlord', was to deprive him of a potential ally.

As it happened, the military played no independent role whatsoever when it came to the succession to Chernenko. Ustinov's voice had been an important one at the time of Brezhnev's and Andropov's deaths, but that owed more to his political seniority than to the military as an institutional interest, even though, as long as Ustinov was there, that interest was going to be strongly defended. It was an institution with which Gorbachev had no real links—a fact which did not help him in his relations with the military when, later as his country's leader, he pursued policies which caused the army concern. Gorbachev was too young to have served in the armed forces during the war and he did not do so thereafter; the time when he reached military age was one in which demobilization was taking precedence over recruitment. Romanov, who was eight years older than Gorbachev, had, in contrast, served in the Soviet army from 1941 until 1945.[84]

The stalemate during Chernenko's thirteen months as Soviet leader extended to policy as well as personnel. Ryzhkov has observed that right up to the time of Chernenko's death it was difficult for 'our team'—that is, the Gorbachev group— to get its way in the Politburo on any issue of principle.[85] When Gorbachev and his allies (especially Ryzhkov) were particularly anxious to get a decision adopted, they would not bring it forward as a resolution of the Secretariat (where, Politburo members knew, Gorbachev could command a majority) but would contrive to have it introduced as a proposal by Chernenko. Gorbachev and Ryzhkov were aware that, surprising though it may seem, Chernenko wished to acquire a reputation as an innovator. The best way in 1984 of getting something relatively new accepted was, accordingly, to persuade Chernenko that it was important that he, as party leader, should be seen as the initiator of that proposal. It could then be presented to the Politburo as Chernenko's idea.[86]

While Gorbachev did nothing to undermine Chernenko, there were several attempts to cut Gorbachev down to size and to prevent him from succeeding to the General Secretaryship. These did not take place at the time when Chernenko died—as has sometimes been suggested[87]—but earlier. The very first sign—of the traditional 'Kremlinological' kind—was the failure of *Pravda* and the other central newspapers to record that Gorbachev as well as Tikhonov had addressed the Central Committee plenum on 13 February 1984 which had elected Chernenko to the General Secretaryship. Tikhonov's speech proposing Chernenko was reported, but there was not so much as a mention of the fact that Gorbachev had spoken. It was only when the proceedings of the plenary session appeared in booklet form and in the pages of periodicals such as *Kommunist* and *Partiynaya zhizn'* some time later that the text of Gorbachev's address was published.[88]

Resistance to Gorbachev took other forms. It had been agreed in principle when Brezhnev was still alive that there should be a Central Committee plenary session (there were generally two or three such meetings each year) devoted to the issue of the scientific and technological revolution. Many books and articles were published in the Soviet Union on that subject even in the Brezhnev years, but few of them came close to stating the truth—that this 'revolution' was taking place elsewhere and that the Soviet Union was lagging far behind not only the developed world but also, and increasingly, the newly industrializing Asian countries. While a Central Committee plenum was hardly likely to solve the problem, in those days it was the main way in which a particular issue could be brought to the top of the political agenda. The idea was revived in the early summer of 1984 and it was agreed that such a plenum would be prepared and that Gorbachev would deliver the major report. Chernenko was just to say a few words at the beginning. A date was eventually fixed for the plenum on science and technology. It was to be held on 23 April 1985. A plenary session of the Central Committee was, indeed, held that day—the 'April plenum' which was the official launching-point of perestroika in the Gorbachev era—but by that time Chernenko, as Ryzhkov observes, had gone to join Stalin and Brezhnev in the Kremlin wall (their burial place).[89] Moreover, the plenum, when it finally took place, had to be of an even broader character than one devoted to science and technology.

Throughout the second half of 1984, however, Ryzhkov and Gorbachev worked intensively in preparation for the abortive science and technology plenary session of the Central Committee. In November of that year a working group chaired by Ryzhkov was set up to prepare for that projected plenum. A document was ready for presentation to the Politburo in January 1985, but by then Chernenko was too ill to preside and, says Ryzhkov, it would have been tactless to proceed without him.[90] Ligachev gives a more dramatic account of the same events, arguing that the Central Committee plenum was deliberately postponed by those who did not wish to see Gorbachev add to his prestige by presenting a major report and holding centre-stage. He quotes Gorbachev saying angrily to him in December 1984: 'Can you believe it? Trying to dump a subject so important for the country.'[91] According to the economist Abel Aganbegyan, who spent most of the summer of 1984 preparing an analysis for Gorbachev to use in his report to the science and technology plenum, it was at a Politburo meeting in January 1985 that the final decision was taken not to hold that plenary session until after a Party Congress had been convened.

It seems evident that the idea of such a plenum was not, in fact, ruled out until January, for Aganbegyan, whose home was then in Novosibirsk (where since 1967 he had been Director of the Institute of Economics and Organization of Industrial Production), recalled all too clearly that he had to miss seeing the New Year in with his family in Siberia because intensive work for the plenum which never took place was going on in Moscow even on 31 December 1984. It was in mid-January 1985 that Gorbachev told Aganbegyan and the group of specialists working on the report for the plenum that the Politburo had decided the meeting would not be held.[92] Instead, there was an attempt to bring forward the date of the next Party Congress from late February 1986 to the autumn of 1985. Chernenko's aide Pechenev and the editor of the journal *Kommunist*, Richard Kosolapov (described by Georgy Arbatov as a 'dogmatic (although also literate . . .) Stalinist' in whom Chernenko had unbounded faith, believing him to be an outstanding ideologist and theoretician[93]), had actively lobbied for this, for the composition of the Central Committee could be changed only at Party Congresses and they were afraid that Chernenko would not last out until 1986.[94] They were relying on him for their own promotion and to change the balance of forces at the top of the party against Gorbachev.

Aganbegyan concluded that Chernenko and the old guard, plus their hangers-on, were afraid of Gorbachev's growing prestige. Gorbachev's speech to a conference of ideological workers in December 1984 had made a big impression. As Aganbegyan put it: 'he made a very strong case—very strong by the standards of that time, and he came out as a new leader. Then came his triumphant visit to Britain, when he met Margaret Thatcher for the first time.'[95] These two events (both of which are discussed in greater detail below) created 'a certain impression on the older members of the Politburo' and they resolved to move Gorbachev 'aside a little bit'. If he were 'to become the hero of a new plenum which would have adopted important decisions, that, they were afraid, would reduce the prestige of Chernenko . . .'.[96] Since Chernenko's prestige was far from high to begin with, this might not have been too difficult. Perhaps more important is the fact that there were members of the Politburo, as well as those in Chernenko's entourage, who still hoped that Gorbachev's rise to the General Secretaryship might be slowed down or averted.

Ligachev argues that 'Andropov's protégés were in . . . an unstable position' during Chernenko's time as General Secretary and that in the early winter of 1984/5 'a chill of sorts between the general secretary and Gorbachev began to be felt quite keenly'.[97] It seems probable that those who were opposed to a Gorbachev succession were sowing seeds of doubt and discord in Chernenko's mind. Gorbachev was increasingly bypassed as Chernenko—or his aides—took matters straight to heads of department in the Central Committee. Although Gorbachev frequently had to chair the weekly Politburo meetings because Chernenko was not well enough to do so, this was conveyed to Gorbachev so short a time before the session as to deprive him of the opportunity of preparing for it: 'Suddenly, without notice, a half hour before the meeting, Gorbachev would be informed that the *gensek* was not coming and that he would have to chair the meeting.'[98] Later, in his speech to the Central Committee proposing Gorbachev as party leader, Gromyko was to say that Gorbachev had chaired the Politburo meetings 'brilliantly'.[99] But this was, in Ligachev's words, 'a very severe test for Gorbachev', especially 'if we take into account the fact that in the Politburo at the time there were people waiting for him to fail'.[100]

The chill emanating from the top became such that Ligachev took the initiative in telephoning Chernenko to tell him not to believe those who might be 'whispering all sorts of things against Gorbachev in his ear'.[101] Although Ligachev was later to regard Gorbachev as a traitor to the cause of Marxism-Leninism and the Communist Party, a view he had already formed by the time he published his memoirs, he succeeds in that book in recording objectively his feelings about Gorbachev at an earlier period. During the time of Chernenko's leadership he believed that 'only Gorbachev was worthy of occupying the highest post of general secretary of the Central Committee of the Communist Party'; accordingly, he deployed his considerable energy in gathering support for Gorbachev among the regional party secretaries who came under the jurisdiction of his Central Committee Department of Party Organizational Work.[102] Noting that, while Gorbachev was still prepared to wait for his time to come, he did not wait passively, Ryzhkov observes that the 'phenomenally active and tough' Ligachev was like 'a powerful tank' as he moved through the apparatus, replacing someone here and doing favours for someone else there, smoothing the path of Gorbachev's succession.[103] Ligachev, for his part, believed that his call to Chernenko helped to allay suspicion of Gorbachev, although the atmosphere at the time was such that he and Gorbachev did not speak aloud on some subjects—especially Chernenko's illness—in Gorbachev's office, 'but wrote to each other on scraps of paper'.[104] Even the second secretary of the Central Committee could not rule out the distinct possibility that his room was bugged. It was probably for the same reason that, on the eve of his actual election as General Secretary, Gorbachev and his wife discussed until four o'clock in the morning the topic of the succession not in their dacha but walking in the garden of the dacha, though late at night in the first half of March it is usually uncomfortably cold in the Moscow region.[105]

Although laden with responsibilities as Chernenko's health declined, and devoting a great deal of time to the problems of the Soviet economy in particular, Gorbachev began to take an increased interest in foreign affairs. While Andropov was still alive, in the summer of 1983, he had led a Soviet delegation to Canada. He had been impressed by what he saw—in particular the technological level of Canadian agriculture—but the most important outcome of the visit was that it resulted in the formation of a close political relationship between Gorbachev and Alexander Yakovlev. A former acting head of the Propaganda Department of the Central Committee, Yakovlev had fallen foul of the Brezhnevite old guard in the early 1970s and had incurred the wrath also of Russian nationalists with his vigorous opposition to their often chauvinistic views. In the light of this, he asked for an ambassadorial posting to an English-speaking country—a demotion in terms of the Soviet political system at that time. (As a very young man, Yakovlev had served in the Second World War as a company commander and had been invalided out, seriously wounded, in 1943, but later had the opportunity to learn English. He spent the greater part of 1959 as a mature student at Columbia University, New York.) He was sent to Canada in what was, in effect, a dignified exile as Soviet Ambassador. If he had been glad to leave Moscow in 1973, by 1983 he was anxious to get back, and he asked for Gorbachev's help in facilitating this. Gorbachev lost no time in responding to the request; shortly after Gorbachev's return to Moscow, Yakovlev was appointed to the influential post of Director of IMEMO, in which capacity he was to become one of the informal advisers of Gorbachev and a channel of ideas on both economic and foreign policy generated by the institute's researchers.[106] Yakovlev himself noted in an interview in 1990 that from the time of his return to Moscow from Canada his contacts with Gorbachev had been continuous.[107]

In the summer of 1984 Gorbachev led the Soviet delegation to the funeral of the Italian Communist Party leader, Enrico Berlinguer. Ever since the Soviet Union had used armed force to put an end to the 'Prague Spring', relations between the Italian party (PCI) and Moscow had ranged between cool and frigid. The PCI had been openly sympathetic to the reforms undertaken in Czechoslovakia in 1968 and had condemned the Soviet invasion. In the 1970s they were in the vanguard of what was called 'Eurocommunism', a brand of revisionist Communism which was anathema to the orthodox in Moscow on the grounds both of its suggestion that there could be more than one 'model' of socialism and its rejection of Soviet hegemony in the international Communist movement. By the 1980s, as the prominent American specialist on Italian politics, Joseph LaPalombara, has observed, the PCI had long abandoned both Leninism and revolutionary goals. Writing in 1987, he suggested that the Italian Communist Party had also 'largely buried Karl Marx, although in a relatively private and silent service to which the party militants were not invited'. It required, said LaPalombara apropos of the PCI, 'an act of will not to recognize that the only thing even mildly menacing about the Communist party today is its name'.[108] (Later the name was to go as well.) After his return from attending the funeral of the popular PCI leader in June 1984, Gorbachev was convinced of the need to establish normal relations with such a party. He had been impressed by the high level of support it enjoyed, as compared with Communist parties elsewhere in Western Europe, and rejected the view that slavish endorsement of whatever happened to be the current line of the Soviet Communist Party should be Moscow's criterion for judging the worth of a foreign Communist Party.[109] It was one of the major signs of changing times when, as foreign politicians gathered in Moscow for Chernenko's funeral in March 1985, Gorbachev, who had meetings with the major Western leaders, found time to meet only one European Communist leader—the Secretary-General of the Italian Communist Party, Alessandro Natta.[110] Ponomarev, the head of the International Department of the Central Committee and once a senior official in Stalin's Comintern, was perplexed by this. He asked a group of his colleagues in the International Department how it could be that, when tens of leaders of 'good' Communist parties had arrived in Moscow, Gorbachev received the leader only of the 'bad' Italians.[111]

If Gorbachev had been favourably impressed on his journeys to Canada and Italy, the most important of his visits prior to becoming General Secretary was still to come. That was the week he spent in Great Britain in December 1984. By that time he was universally recognized as a leading contender for the succession to the Soviet leadership, which, judging by what foreigners could see of

Chernenko, might not be so far off. The eyes of the world were thus on him as never before. The mass media of many Western countries followed him closely in Britain, while the British press, television, and radio gave the visit huge and highly positive coverage.[112] One novel feature was the presence of Raisa Gorbachev, whose attractive appearance and lively demeanour drew almost as much attention as her husband received—indeed, in the popular press, rather more. This attracted some adverse criticism in Moscow. As Mrs Gorbachev later wrote: 'When I returned home I heard people say: "Why did they sing your praises so highly over there? . . . What have you done to attract the West?" '[113] The Soviet mass media were more reticent than their Western counterparts in reporting the visit.[114] Nevertheless, Soviet television paid more attention to Gorbachev's activities in Britain than they usually devoted to a Soviet politician other than the General Secretary.

Gorbachev had prepared himself carefully to discuss foreign policy with the Prime Minister, Margaret Thatcher, and with British Members of Parliament, including the leaders of the Opposition parties. Inasmuch as any serious *faux pas* was going to be instantly relayed not only to the Western world but also to those who were waiting in Moscow and hoping that something would go wrong for him, Gorbachev—whose delegation included Alexander Yakovlev (at that time still Director of IMEMO and not yet a member of the Central Committee) and the nuclear physicist Yevgeny Velikhov—took a calculated risk in coming to a Western country at a time when he was heir apparent. He succeeded in conveying the impression to those British politicians and officials who met him that he was more flexible and open-minded than Soviet leaders with whom they had had dealings hitherto, while not actually departing from what was currently agreed policy in Moscow. It is probable that his performance impressed Gromyko, although Gromyko's subsequent support for Gorbachev almost certainly owed more to his desire to remain on the winning side in Soviet politics.[115] In the speech in which he was later to propose Gorbachev as General Secretary of the Central Committee of the Soviet Communist Party, Gromyko was untypically warm and enthusiastic. It was highly unusual for him to hold forth so animatedly in favour of anyone, not to speak of a relative newcomer in the party leadership who had been in Moscow for less than seven years. Gromyko, in contrast, had headed the Soviet delegation at the 1944 Dumbarton Oaks conference on the foundation of the United Nations, had dealt with every American President from Roosevelt to Reagan, and had been Soviet Minister of Foreign Affairs since 1957.

It is significant that in his speech of March 1985 Gromyko emphasized Gorbachev's flexibility, while indicating that this was, nevertheless, within approved limits; he could not imagine how far Gorbachev would before long push those limits. Gromyko remarked: 'You know, it often happens that problems—both internal and external—are very difficult to consider if you are guided by the law of "black and white". There may be intermediate colours, intermediate links, and intermediate decisions. And Mikhail Sergeevich [Gorbachev] is always able to come up with such decisions that correspond with the party line.'[116] Gromyko had, of course, equally little inkling of the extent to which Gorbachev was going to shake the Soviet military establishment when he added:

GORBACHEV AND DOMESTIC SOVIET AFFAIRS

1 *(right)* An early picture of Raisa Titorenko and Mikhail Gorbachev. They met as students at Moscow University in 1951 and were married in 1953.

2 *(below)* Mikhail Gorbachev and the aged leadership team he inherited, pictured in the Kremlin Palace of Congresses on 22 April 1985 at a meeting celebrating the 115th anniversary of the birth of Lenin. *Front row, left to right*: Ukranian party First Secretary Vladimir Shcherbitsky, Foreign Minister Andrey Gromyko, Gorbachev, and Moscow party First Secretary Viktor Grishin. Behind Gorbachev (*left*) is KGB Chairman Viktor Chebrikov, and (*right*) the long-serving head of the International Department of the Central Committee, Boris Ponomarev.

3 Gorbachev travelled widely around the Soviet Union during his first two years as leader. Here in 1985, he is meeting workers in the oil and gas industry in the Siberian region of Tyumen.

4 (*below*) A traditional Soviet scene. Gorbachev takes the salute for the first time at the anniversary of the Bolshevik Revolution on 7 November 1985.

5 Alexander Yakovlev, pictured here in early 1987, was given accelerated promotion by Gorbachev and became an especially influential reformer.

6 (*above*) Nikolay Ryzhkov, Chairman of the Council of Ministers and the most senior Soviet economic administrator, 1985-1990.

7 Yegor Ligachev, an energetic but conditional ally of Gorbachev in the earliest stages of his leadership, became an outspoken opponent of more radical reform. He is seen here addressing the Nineteenth Party Conference in 1988.

8 The opening of the Nineteenth Party Conference on 28 June 1988. *Front row, left to right*: Ligachev, Gorbachev and Gromyko. The conference was one of the most important events in Soviet history, and ended with Gorbachev pushing through far-reaching reform of the political system.

9 A smiling Gorbachev uses his vote in the first contested, union-wide elections to be held in the Soviet Union – on 26 March 1989 – for a new legislature, the Congress of People's Deputies of the USSR.

10 Unlike previous Soviet leaders, Gorbachev was accessible to journalists. Here he is answering correspondents' questions during a break in the proceedings of the Congress of People's Deputies of the USSR in November 1990.

11 (*below*) Gorbachev signs the book of condolences for Andrey Sakharov on 18 December 1989 at the Presidium of Academy of Sciences. In the last year of his life the distinguished Soviet physicist and leading dissident had become a prominent member of the Congress of People's Deputies, while remaining an ardent campaigner for human rights and for radical change in the Soviet system.

12 Rival chairmen. Anatoly Lukyanov (*left*), the Chairman of the Supreme Soviet of the USSR, and Boris Yeltsin, Chairman of the Supreme Soviet of the Russian Federation, were on less than friendly terms. They are pictured together here on 18 December 1990.

13 Unprepossessing putschists. The leaders of the coup against Gorbachev gave a press conference in Moscow on 19 August 1991. The five included in this photgraph are (*left to right*): Alexander Tizyakov, a prominent representative of military industry; Vasily Starodubtsev, a backward-looking spokesman for state and collective farms; Boris Pugo, the Minister of the Interior who committed suicide when the coup failed; Gennady Yanaev, Soviet Vice-President and a nervous acting president during the few days the coup lasted; and Oleg Baklanov, the head of the Soviet Union's military-industrial complex and one of the key figures in the plot to remove power from Gorbachev.

14 After being held under house arrest at Foros on the Crimean coast, President Gorbachev is pictured here arriving back in Moscow on the night of 21-22 August. On his left is Ivan Silaev, at that time Prime Minister of the Russian Federation, and behind (in striped shirt) Alexander Rutskoy, Vice-President of Russia.

15 As Gorbachev tried to prevent the breakup of the Soviet Union by negotiating a new voluntary union treaty with the leaders of the republics, an influential voice in favour of both preserving and renewing the union was that of Nursultan Nazarbaev, President (and for several years Communist Party First Secretary) of Kazakhstan. He is seen here with Gorbachev in the Kremlin in 1991.

Contrasting moods

16 (*right*) Gorbachev in confident
form, soon after being elected
President of the USSR.

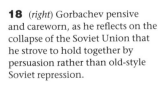

17 (*left*) Informal and relaxed, Gorbachev aboard the
Soviet presidential aircraft.

18 (*right*) Gorbachev pensive
and careworn, as he reflects on the
collapse of the Soviet Union that
he strove to hold together by
persuasion rather than old-style
Soviet repression.

'He always defends the point of view that the holy of holies for us all is to struggle for the cause of peace and to maintain our defence at the necessary level.'[117] Gromyko's support for Gorbachev was of undoubted value to him at the time of the succession, and the fact that he had been praised even by the 'iron lady'—as the Soviet press described Mrs Thatcher—probably counted for something with Gromyko (who a year earlier had been more than content to support Chernenko's elevation to the top post).[118]

Gorbachev, for his part, seems to have been impressed both by the level of attention he received in Britain—his meeting with the Prime Minister went on well beyond the time allotted for it in his programme—and by what he saw of the country and its political institutions. Several of those who worked closely with Gorbachev have said that he often thereafter referred to this visit as an eye-opening one for him.[119] He and Margaret Thatcher went on to establish what Gorbachev himself has called a 'good personal relationship', based on mutual respect, despite substantial divergences in their views.[120] The meeting was of significance not only for British–Soviet relations and for widening Gorbachev's political perspectives, but even for East–West relations more broadly. There had been no summit meeting between an American President and a Soviet General Secretary since 1979 and Ronald Reagan had shown little inclination to engage in dialogue with any leader of the 'evil empire'. He did, however, have an excellent political and personal relationship with Margaret Thatcher, and, when Gorbachev became General Secretary, she played an important part in persuading him that this was a Soviet leader of a different type from hitherto, one with whom it was possible to do business.[121] Indeed, the British Prime Minister did not wait for the heir apparent to come to power before making that point to Reagan. Within days of her meeting with Gorbachev in December 1984 she flew to the United States to convey her impressions directly to the American President.[122] The Secretary of State, George Shultz, later recalled: 'She was enthusiastic about Gorbachev, as had been clear from her public statements.' He noted, too: 'The president had immense confidence in her, and her views carried great weight.'[123]

Margaret Thatcher's celebrated remark—'I like Mr Gorbachev. We can do business together'[124]—was both calculated and genuine. It was calculated inasmuch as both the Prime Minister and the Foreign and Commonwealth Office *wanted* the visit to be seen as a success. They had reached the view already that it was desirable that Gorbachev, rather than an alternative candidate, should succeed Chernenko as Soviet leader.* The Prime Minister's remark was, however,

---

* I was, to a certain extent, involved in this process, having been invited to 10 Downing Street on 14 December 1984, the eve of Gorbachev's arrival in Britain, to speak specifically about Gorbachev to the Prime Minister and the Foreign Secretary, Sir Geoffrey Howe (the others invited were two economists, a foreign and defence policy specialist, and a businessman). That invitation had its origins much earlier—in a lengthy seminar at Chequers, held on 8 September 1983, for which a group of eight British academics prepared papers on the Soviet Union and Eastern Europe—which were read and annotated in advance by Mrs Thatcher—and were given the greater part of a day at the Prime Minister's country residence to put across their views to her. On the government side, other participants in the meeting included the Foreign Secretary (Howe), the Minister of Defence (Michael Heseltine), and the Minister of State at the Foreign and Commonwealth Office (Malcolm Rifkind). In my own paper on the Soviet political system and power structure I had identified Gorbachev not only as a likely future General Secretary but also as 'the best-educated member of the Politburo and probably the most open-minded' and 'the most hopeful choice from the point

not a matter of calculation alone; it reflected the fact that, for the first time, she had begun to establish a rapport with a Soviet politician and had taken to Gorbachev personally. Proof of this was that what she said in private corresponded with what she had announced in public.[125]

Gorbachev returned to Moscow a day earlier than planned. Having arrived in Britain on 15 December, he was due to fly home on the twenty-second. But Dmitry Ustinov died on 20 December and Gorbachev, evidently anxious to take part in the discussions concerning his successor, left the next day. He told his British governmental and parliamentary hosts that it was Ustinov's death that necessitated his premature return and, when asked by journalists why he was leaving early, it was he—rather than anyone in Moscow—who first gave the world the news that Ustinov had died. British politicians saw this as a sign of Gorbachev's self-confidence, as was the fact that he had a relaxed relationship with the other members of his group, 'who felt free to speak up, though there was no doubt who was in charge'.[126]

The day after Gorbachev's return to Moscow it was announced that the aged and relatively colourless Marshal Sergey Sokolov had been chosen as Minister of Defence. In so far as he had links with any of the leaders, they were with the senior secretary supervising the military, Grigory Romanov, for Sokolov had been commander of the Leningrad Military District in the 1960s at a time when Romanov was a Secretary (later First Secretary) of the Leningrad regional party organization. But Gorbachev probably felt he had little to fear from the 73-year-old Sokolov. Later, as General Secretary, he was to use the landing in May 1987 just off Red Square of a light plane, piloted by a young West German, Matthias Rust (whose unscheduled flight to within a stone's throw of the Kremlin amused rather than alarmed most Russians), as a convenient excuse for dismissing Sokolov as Minister of Defence, along with General Alexander Koldunov, the Chief of the Air Defence Forces.

If Gorbachev had taken a political risk in coming to a Western country and the accompanying glare of publicity at a time when it appeared that Chernenko might not have long to live, he had arguably taken an even greater chance less than a week before flying to London when he delivered a major speech to a conference on ideological work in Moscow. This speech of 10 December will be discussed further in the following chapter, for never before had Gorbachev introduced so many ideas which departed from the current orthodoxy and which were daring for the time. Indeed, the prospect of them being aired publicly was so alarming that 'literally on the eve of the conference Chernenko telephoned Gorbachev and proposed . . . cancelling it'. Vadim Medvedev, who first revealed this attempt to prevent the speech being delivered, notes that Gorbachev decisively rejected Chernenko's suggestion.[127] Among those who helped in the preparation of the lengthy address were Medvedev himself,

of view both of Soviet citizens and the outside world'. The importance of the 8 September 1983 seminar (which began at 9 o'clock in the morning and continued through a working lunch until 3.30 in the afternoon) is acknowledged by Margaret Thatcher in her memoirs, *The Downing Street Years* (HarperCollins, London, 1993), 450–3. I have touched on these 1983 and 1984 meetings at somewhat greater length than here in my review article, 'The Leader of the Prologue', *Times Literary Supplement*, 30 Aug. 1991, pp. 5–6 (repr. in Ferdinand Mount (ed.), *Communism* (Harvill, London, 1992), 293–300).

Alexander Yakovlev, and Nail Bikkenen (a theorist of Tatar nationality who in June 1987 was to become editor-in-chief of the journal *Kommunist*, turning it into still more the forum for debate which it had started to become a year earlier).[128] The speech caused something of a stir within the higher echelons of the Soviet Communist Party, although it was scarcely noticed in the West. Only half of it was published in *Pravda* and many of the most interesting and innovative passages were in the parts *Pravda*, with a circulation at that time of over ten million, missed out.[129] The text, however, was published promptly in booklet form in an edition of 100,000 copies.[130]

Most of the key concepts of the first few years of Gorbachev's General Secretaryship were well to the fore in this speech, which, though it was recognizably Marxist, embodied a critical Marxism which broke sharply with the apologetics of orthodox Soviet Marxism-Leninism. Not surprisingly, it was a mixture of the old and the new. The Communist Party as a whole still clung to the notion which had been accepted in Brezhnev's time that the Soviet Union had become a 'developed socialist society'. It was not until the Twenty-Seventh Party Congress in 1986, by which time he had been General Secretary for almost a year, that Gorbachev was able to say that the concept of 'developed socialism' had been a cloak for conservatism. The very title of the conference which Gorbachev addressed in December 1984 was 'The Perfecting of Developed Socialism and the Ideological Work of the Party in the Light of the Decisions of the June (1983) Plenum of the Central Committee of the CPSU'. Under that long-winded and far from promising rubric, Gorbachev had to put some of his radical proposals for change within the framework of attending to 'the problems of perfecting developed socialism'; that, he said, would be 'the basic criterion for evaluating the activity of social scientists'.[131] But what the 'perfecting of developed socialism' amounted to 'in the final analysis' was 'the widening of the possibilities for the development of the individual and the initiative of the Soviet person as master of his country, as worker and citizen'.[132] Konstantin Chernenko's aide at that time, Vadim Pechenev (who was removed by Gorbachev as soon as he became General Secretary), makes much in his memoirs of the fact that Gorbachev spoke of 'the perfecting of developed socialism'.[133] There was, however, nothing in the least surprising about that. Gorbachev, not yet being General Secretary, was in no position to revise the periodization of Soviet development which had become incorporated in party doctrine. (Later, as General Secretary, he was to alter that particular doctrinal tenet dramatically, arguing that the Soviet Union was at the stage of 'developing socialism', not that of 'developed socialism'.) It was, on the contrary, necessary for Gorbachev, at a time when Chernenko was still party leader, to use some of the current 'politically correct' phraseology when—and perhaps *especially* when—introducing new ideas into Soviet political discourse.

The speech of December 1984 in fact foreshadowed both political and economic reform. Gorbachev spoke at length about the need for democratization (what he meant by it will be taken up in the next chapter), glasnost, equality of all before the law, more self-government (*samoupravlenie*) at different levels of the Soviet political system, and the necessity for more space (*prostor*) to be opened up for the initiative of individual people and for 'healthy interests', work collectives, and local political organs.[134] The speech was the first to make extensive use of the term perestroika, and it introduced such favourite notions of the early Gorbachev era as *uskorenie* (acceleration) and 'the human factor'.[135]

Gorbachev referred in this speech to 'the slowdown of economic growth' at the end of the 1970s and the beginning of the 1980s and argued, in the terminology Marxists had used in analysis of the dynamics of development from one kind of socio-economic system to another, that this was a result of the lack of correspondence between production relations and the forces of production. The need for changes in production relations had not been spotted in good time and the unwarranted preservation of obsolete elements in these relations could 'bring about a deterioration of the economic and social situation'.[136] This critique was very much in line with, and fairly clearly influenced by, the writings of Zaslavskaya and other innovative Soviet social scientists.[137] In the same speech Gorbachev indicated the need to incorporate a substantial market element in the Soviet economy, although he used the term which was the nearest it was possible to get to market advocacy at that time, 'commodity-money relations'.[138] Vadim Medvedev, who participated in the writing of the speech, is just one of those who has confirmed that, by 'commodity-money relations', Gorbachev meant 'a socialist market' ('he could not use the term "market", but by commodity-money relations he meant the market').[139]

Not surprisingly, this speech caused a stir among party insiders. Pechenev has said that it 'was unambiguously perceived as a claim to political leadership' and that both Gorbachev's 'champions and his opponents understood it that way'. This followed from its breadth, the range of problems touched upon, and also from the confident manner of its presentation.[140] Mikhail Nenashev, chief editor of the newspaper *Sovetskaya Rossiya* (at that time one of the least hidebound newspapers, though after Nenashev's departure from the editorial chair in 1986 it was to become one of the most conservative), prepared an article, in the light of Gorbachev's speech, on the need for 'perestroika of ideological work'. Other newspapers, however, carried only dry reports, rather than commentary on the speech. Nenashev added: 'I was not very much surprised because I knew that many things said by Gorbachev were not supported by Chernenko and his associates.'[141] Vadim Medvedev described the speech of December 1984 as 'affirmation of Gorbachev's role as the Secretary responsible for ideology' and as having 'many fresh and undogmatic features', although couched within the old forms[142] (which included numerous citations of Lenin and one of Chernenko). The speech, said Medvedev, was 'regarded by quite a number of people as dangerous, as having gone too far'.[143]

Gorbachev took a calculated risk in making the speech, for the selectorate who would choose the next General Secretary—the voting members of the Politburo—were far from being a body of reformers. A majority were, on the contrary, hoping that things would go on pretty much as they had done. Gorbachev, however, was sincerely convinced of the need for change. He may well have felt, too, that, from his position of front runner, he could afford to give a lead; if his opponents tried to stop his progress, he would have a platform to take to the Central Committee as a whole. A number of members of the Central Committee—among them Boris Yeltsin[144] and Georgy

Arbatov[145]—have said that, on this occasion, if the Politburo had come up with any name other than that of Gorbachev when the succession finally occurred in March 1985, it would have been challenged by Central Committee members, themselves included, even though it was normal practice for the Central Committee to accept whatever the Politburo recommended. The mood in the country was also very much in favour of a break with the gerontocracy. As the person who had begun to push himself forward as a possible alternative to Gorbachev was the 70-year-old Moscow party First Secretary, Viktor Grishin, public opinion may even (untypically in the unreformed Soviet system) have counted for something in the minds of Soviet officials. In the view of Arbatov, if the Politburo had tried to foist another member of the old guard on the Central Committee, 'even some of the more conservative members . . . would have resisted it'. He added that it would have been quite another matter if they had known what kind of policies Gorbachev was going to pursue both domestically and internationally.[146]

Gorbachev, in the meantime—as his speech of December 1984 should have indicated to those who read it carefully—had decided that the Soviet system required serious political and economic reform. His views were to develop further after he became General Secretary—to the extent that he moved beyond reform of the system to the demolition of a number of its pillars—but the widespread contention that he was interested in nothing more in 1984–5 than acceleration of economic growth does not withstand serious scrutiny.[147] The political content of his December speech and other parts of the public record are examined more closely in the next chapter, but in private Gorbachev had already made his feelings clear. Alexander Yakovlev has recalled the long conversations he had with Gorbachev in Canada in the summer of 1983 when he was still Soviet Ambassador to Ottawa, saying 'we spoke very frankly about everything . . . the main point was that society had to change, that it had to be constructed on different principles'.[148] Adding that the ideas associated with perestroika did not arise simply spontaneously or by chance in March 1985, Yakovlev said that he knew they had been deeply maturing in Gorbachev for some time.[149]

Similarly, both Gorbachev and Shevardnadze have recalled a conversation in the Crimean resort of Pitsunda on an evening in December 1984 in which they had agreed that people in the Soviet Union could not go on living in the way they had. Gorbachev in 1990 quoted Shevardnadze with approval as having said then that 'everything had gone rotten'.[150] In his memoirs, published a year later, Shevardnadze wrote: ' "Everything's rotten. It has to be changed." I really did say that to Gorbachev on a winter evening in 1984 at Pitsunda, and I will not recant those words today.'[151] Gorbachev himself said to his wife on the eve of his succession to the General Secretaryship: 'We can't go on living in this way.'[152] Although within a few years of becoming General Secretary Gorbachev was to support policies he could not have envisaged himself advocating on the eve of his accession, his political agenda in late 1984 and early 1985—partly a hidden agenda, for he spoke more frankly to Shevardnadze at their annual winter holiday meetings than either man was in the habit of speaking in public[153]—was much more radical than the Soviet political establishment realized.[154]

What worried some of Gorbachev's opponents more than a reformism which many of them did not even comprehend was the likelihood of more rapid personnel change, involving demotion or loss of office for them, and the disciplinarian and anti-corruption parts of his platform. These themes had been much emphasized by Andropov during his short time as General Secretary, but had been pursued less seriously under Chernenko. In the last months, however, of Chernenko's life, when the weakness of his health meant that some of the reins of power fell into Gorbachev's hands, there was to be a sharp reminder of the disciplinarian element. The notoriously corrupt former Minister of Internal Affairs, Nikolay Shchelokov, had—despite his dismissal from office under Andropov— been enjoying a comfortable life under Chernenko (whom he had known for over thirty years). But in November 1984, in what was almost certainly intended as a prelude to bringing criminal charges against him, Shchelokov—who feared Gorbachev's coming to power and who had said of Gorbachev, 'That man must be destroyed'—was stripped of his military rank for bringing discredit to it and for abusing the ministerial office he had held.[155] The following month he committed suicide. The rumours in Moscow at the time that Shchelokov had taken his own life were confirmed in the memoirs of the Kremlin doctor, Chazov.[156] It seemed to Chazov that the suicide of such an old friend of the General Secretary as Shchelokov, following fast upon the death of Ustinov, made a deep impression on Chernenko.[157]

The succession

Traditional, non-competitive Soviet elections, oddly enough, were the scene of the last, ineffectual stand of the old guard opposed to Gorbachev. They also provided their own esoteric indications that Gorbachev was still in the strongest position to succeed Chernenko. The elections for the Supreme Soviet of the Russian republic were held in late February 1985. Viktor Grishin was pushing himself into the limelight as much as possible—in the view of Ligachev 'trying to instill the idea that he was the successor to the general secretary'[158] (no doubt with encouragement from Grigory Romanov, who could hope to replace Gorbachev as second secretary and heir apparent in a Grishin Politburo).[159] In particular, Grishin—taking advantage of his position as Moscow First Secretary—arranged for himself to be photographed beside a desperately ill Chernenko. The General Secretary had been removed from his sick-bed in order to go through the motions of voting and thus demonstrate to the world that the Soviet Union had a leader who was still alive—if only just. Grishin operated on the assumption that the person seen to be closest to the top leader would be perceived as the next most powerful. This ploy, however, backfired completely and made it still less likely that anyone other than Gorbachev would succeed Chernenko. Even many Soviet officials, not to mention the broader public, were strengthened in their view that there must be a generational change in the leadership if state funerals were not to become an annual ritual. It was all too obvious that Chernenko was going to die soon, and Grishin was only three years his junior. What Chazov has called 'the effort of Grishin to underline his closeness to Chernenko'[160] was, for Arbatov, 'just plain stupid',[161] for closeness to the ailing Chernenko had ceased to be an advantage.[162] (Ever since Chernenko had succeeded Andropov, the frailty of the aged Soviet leadership had become a subject of black humour in Moscow. One story told immediately after Andropov's funeral had Margaret Thatcher calling Ronald Reagan and saying: 'You should have come. They did it very well. I'm definitely coming back next year.' She did—for Chernenko's funeral—although Reagan again stayed away! Another story took the form of an announcement that at the most recent plenary session of the Central Committee a decision had been taken to elect Comrade X General Secretary and to bury him in the Kremlin wall.)

The elections, in fact, showed that Gorbachev was still in the leading position to succeed Chernenko. There were three different 'Kremlinological' indications of this, and these esoteric signs were not to be despised, for those who could read them obtained useful guidance at the time—and not only in retrospect—concerning the direction of the prevailing political winds. The first indicator came in January when *Pravda* published the numbers of constituencies which had nominated different leaders as well as a list showing which constituency nomination those leaders had accepted. So far as nominations were concerned, Chernenko received most, but in equal second place were Tikhonov and Gorbachev. The acceptance list placed Chernenko first, Tikhonov second, and Gorbachev third.[163] There was nothing spontaneous or accidental about this. Such placings were a reflection of a leader's position in the political hierarchy. As General Secretary, Chernenko had to have pride of place. Tikhonov owed his second place to his high state office as Chairman of the Council of Ministers. Since, however, he was aged 79 and, what is more, had never held party—as distinct from ministerial—office, he was in no sense a contender for the succession. Thus, among the small number of people who could even aspire to the General Secretaryship, Gorbachev led the field.

The second indicator was the order in which the election speeches were delivered. The addresses of Politburo members to selected prospective constituents were given on different days, with those at the top of the political hierarchy speaking closest to the election day. The last three speeches were by Gorbachev, Tikhonov, and Chernenko (whose speech had to be read for him, since he was too ill to appear in person).[164] The order of precedence was the same in late February as it had been in early January (in the list of nominations) and, indeed, as it had been in March 1984 when, shortly after Andropov's death, Politburo members had had to make their election speeches for the Supreme Soviet of the USSR.[165]

The third sign that Gorbachev was no ordinary member of the Politburo was that, contrary to past tradition, two Secretaries of the Central Committee, Ligachev and Ryzhkov—who were, of course, at that time his closest allies in the Secretariat—attended Gorbachev's election speech of February 1985. Since their presence did not, as one of the more experienced Secretaries, Dolgikh, noted, fit in with the 'totally sacred' traditional pattern which had evolved over time, 'people noticed that'.[166]

During January and February Chazov periodically telephoned Gorbachev to report on Chernenko's health. Being aware of Gorbachev's 'complicated relations with Chernenko', he was 'always surprised' by Gorbachev's informal requests to him to do everything in his power to save Chernenko and to preserve his health.[167] Chazov says that he did not, however, leave Gorbachev with any illusions, telling him that in the opinion of all the specialists Chernenko had 'only a few months, and perhaps less, to live'.[168] In fact Chernenko died, on 10 March, a Sunday evening, after having been in a coma for several days. It was Gorbachev who was the first to be told. Chazov called him at his dacha with the news.[169]

Although Gorbachev had been solicitous of Chernenko's health so long as he was alive, he and his ally, Ligachev, lost no time in setting in motion the wheels of the succession. As on previous occasions, this had to proceed in two stages. First, the Politburo had to decide whom they were going to recommend as General Secretary to the Central Committee, and then the Central Committee as a whole had to make the formal election. In principle, the possibility of opposition and divided votes in the Central Committee was not to be discounted (especially on this occasion if the Politburo had recommended someone other than Gorbachev), but in practice such elections had indeed been a formality. The real choice was made by the Politburo—or even by an inner circle within it who could then carry the Politburo as a whole with them—and the selection of Gorbachev was no exception. What was, however, without precedent was the speed and efficiency with which the operation was conducted. No General Secretary in Soviet history was chosen as quickly as was Gorbachev, although this merely made a likely outcome the more certain. Chernenko had died at 7.20 p.m. The head of the General Department of the Central Committee, Klavdy Bogolyubov—who had been exceptionally close to Chernenko and who, as we have already seen, was no friend of the Gorbachev camp[170]—had no choice but to respond to Gorbachev's instruction to call the Politburo members and Secretaries of the Central Committee to a meeting in the Kremlin that same evening.

Accounts by the participants in the Politburo meetings held that night and the following day differ somewhat in detail, but there are enough of them now for the essentials to be clear. The meeting on the Sunday evening did not formally constitute the Politburo's choice of General Secretary. It was convened, first, to hear a report from Chazov on the former leader's illness and death and, second, to discuss the composition of the funeral commission and, above all, who would head that commission. Ever since the death of Stalin the person who had been appointed to head the funeral commission of the previous General Secretary had become the party leader. Since this was the third death of a General Secretary within two and a half years, the precedents were fresh in the minds of the *cognoscenti* within the Soviet Union and of foreign observers. There was an important sense in which the choice of chairman of that commission was a pre-selection of the country's next leader.

There were good reasons from Gorbachev's point of view for holding the meeting at once. Three voting members of the Politburo had no chance of attending. The First Secretary of the party in Kazakhstan, Kunaev, could not possibly get from Alma-Ata to Moscow in time. There was still less chance of the Ukrainian party First Secretary, Vladimir Shcherbitsky, making it. He was in San Francisco, as head of a Soviet delegation visiting the United States, when the news came through.[171] The third person who could not attend was Vitaly Vorotnikov—the Chairman of the Council of Ministers of the Russian republic, who had been promoted to full membership of the Politburo under Andropov—who was snowbound in Yugoslavia. Of these three, none was close to Gorbachev, and two of them had been in the Brezhnev–Chernenko rather than Andropov–Gorbachev camp. Vorotnikov had taken it for granted that Gorbachev would be Chernenko's successor,[172] but the veteran Brezhnevites, Kunaev and Shcherbitsky, would have been happy to support an older, alternative candidate to Gorbachev, such as Grishin, if they had thought he had a serious chance of success. Even if they had been present, it is doubtful if they would have risked splitting the leadership, but their absence guaranteed that the succession was a very smooth one.

Most of the Politburo members and Secretaries of the Central Committee who were summoned to the Kremlin on that Sunday night were not told by telephone the reason for the urgency and they were too much part of the Soviet system to ask. It was not difficult, though, for them to guess that Chernenko had died. It was Gorbachev who gave that news to Grishin upon his arrival at the Kremlin, and he immediately, and artfully, took the opportunity to find out in advance of the formal meeting what Grishin's intentions were. Gorbachev did nothing so crude as to ask Grishin directly. Instead, he suggested to him that he, Grishin, organize the funeral commission.[173] Grishin expressed surprise, pointing out that it was traditional for the chairman of the funeral commission to be a Secretary of the Central Committee, rather than of a city committee, and that, in addition, it should be the person closest to the dead General Secretary. He concluded by saying to Gorbachev that 'you are that person'.[174] While the last point was true only in the sense that Gorbachev had been the second secretary, it was clear that Grishin had decided his own chances of success were so minimal that his best hope of survival in the top leadership team was to demonstrate support for Gorbachev.

How seriously Grishin's self-promotion should be taken is still unclear. Gorbachev himself, in spite of his asking Grishin if he wished to chair the funeral commission, has said that it never entered anyone's head that Grishin could be a candidate for the General Secretaryship.[175] That would appear to be not strictly accurate (although true at the time when the choice was actually made), inasmuch as Ligachev and Yeltsin, to name but two, seemed to have taken the idea seriously. Yeltsin, however, was at that time still a regional party secretary in Sverdlovsk and his account in his memoirs of the finding of a list compiled by Grishin of those who would support and oppose him in a bid for the General Secretaryship appears to be wholly fanciful.[176] Ligachev, although concerned about the extent to which Grishin was stepping up his activities in the winter of 1984/5 and 'beginning to claim almost openly a leading role in the Politburo',[177] was dismissive of Yeltsin's suggestion that such a list had been found. Saying that it sounded 'like a street rumour', he asked: 'Why make up a list when it's easy enough to memorize the names of a Politburo whose members can be counted on your fingertips?'[178]

Although Ligachev has also suggested that, even after the first meeting of the Politburo to choose a chairman of the funeral commission, the outcome was still uncertain, most other participants disagree. Gorbachev presided over the meeting from the outset and emerged as chairman of the funeral commission. The first person to mention his name—formally, at the Politburo meeting, as well as in the earlier informal encounter with Gorbachev—as the most appropriate person to chair the funeral commission was none other than Grishin, as Gorbachev himself later told his aide, Anatoly Chernyaev.[179] It was agreed that a Politburo meeting to select a new General Secretary would be held at 3 o'clock the following afternoon and that the Central Committee plenary session for the formal election would be at 5 p.m. In other words, a new leader was to be in place less than twenty-four hours after the death of the old one. Military planes were to bring members of the Central Committee from the far corners of the Soviet Union for the meeting[180]—just one more example of how the Communist Party called the tune and of the extent to which party and state were intertwined in the unreformed Soviet Union.

There is some disagreement even among those who were present at the Politburo meetings on the evening of 10 March and the afternoon of 11 March whether Gromyko had already made an important intervention in favour of Gorbachev at the earlier meeting to choose a chairman of the funeral commission, but there is no doubt that it was he who proposed Gorbachev at the Politburo meeting on 11 March (the day after Chernenko's death), held shortly before the Central Committee plenum at which Gromyko also made the main speech in favour of Gorbachev.[181] Ligachev, for example, regards the issue as still having been open until that Politburo meeting on 11 March—two hours before the Central Committee were due to convene—whereas Ryzhkov holds that everything was settled on the 10th.[182] In a formal sense—but perhaps only formally—Ligachev was correct, for the Politburo still had to vote specifically on the issue of the party leadership as had the Central Committee thereafter, and it was not yet public knowledge that Gorbachev had been selected to chair the funeral commission. It was only on the 11th that the outside world learned of Chernenko's death—and, then, later in the same day, that Gorbachev was his successor. Indeed, Dolgikh, who found himself sharing an elevator with Gorbachev on the way up to the Politburo meeting of 11 March, which was held in the Central Committee building on Staraya ploshchad (Old Square), jocularly asked him if he had prepared his speech from the throne yet. Gorbachev laughed and replied that he had assigned people to write a speech for whoever would be called upon to give it.[183]

Indeed, while one group of people close to Chernenko had sat up late at night writing Chernenko's obituary, another group had sat through the night preparing the acceptance speech to be delivered by the new General Secretary. The four authors of the speech 'to be delivered by whomever will be elected General Secretary' were Anatoly Lukyanov, at that time First Deputy Head of the General Department (and soon to head it, replacing Bogolyubov, when Gorbachev became General Secretary); Vadim Medvedev, the head of the Science and Education Department of the Central Committee; Vadim Zagladin, the First Deputy Head of the International Department; and Andrey Aleksandrov-Agentov, who had been foreign policy aide to three successive General Secretaries—Brezhnev, Andropov, and Chernenko—and who was to be kept on by Gorbachev until early 1986, when he replaced him by Anatoly Chernyaev.[184]

The first two were especially clearly identifiable as Gorbachev allies. The text of the speech suggests that they wrote it with Gorbachev very much in mind, although it was less bold and innovative than his more carefully thought-out and much longer speech to the ideology conference of December 1984. While the speech to the March Central Committee plenum had its full share of traditional elements, it did bring in two characteristic Gorbachevian themes, describing the development of democracy as one of the key tasks of intra-party policy and calling for the widening of glasnost in the work of party organizations, soviets, and state organizations.[185]

The fact that it was Gromyko who proposed Gorbachev for the General Secretaryship—and in the warmest possible terms—both at the Politburo meeting which preceded the Central Committee session and at the plenum made it that much harder for any doubters to speak up. Gorbachev already had the support of those who were hoping for both generational change and fresh ideas. Therefore, it was entirely to his advantage that the most senior representative of the older generation—the last survivor of the inner circle within Brezhnev's Politburo—should put his full weight behind him.[186] Among Gorbachev's qualities, singled out by Gromyko in his speech to the Central Committee, were his keen intelligence, analytical mind, broad erudition, political sensitivity (not seeing everything in 'black and white' terms), strong convictions, and directness, and an ability to establish a rapport, and a common language, with others. He also emphasized Gorbachev's experience of party work at various levels, his skill in chairmanship (of the Politburo and Secretariat), and, not least, his grasp of international issues.[187]

Neither at the Politburo meeting which preceded the plenary session of the Central Committee nor at the plenum was any voice raised against Gorbachev. He was unanimously elected by both bodies.[188] The process was little different from the successions to the General Secretaryship in 1982 and 1984, apart from the greater informality and liveliness of Gromyko's speeches in favour of Gorbachev and the sense of relief on the part of many in the Central Committee that the rule of sick old men was coming to an end (although a majority of them were to look back with nostalgia to the Brezhnev era before Gorbachev's time as General Secretary was over). The succession proceeded smoothly at the highest levels of the party hierarchy, not for lack of worries and doubts about Gorbachev on the part of roughly half the Politburo members, but because it was not their custom to come out in direct opposition against what was clearly the winning side. Accordingly, as Ryzhkov has emphasized, there was no battle for the leadership in March 1985 (although there had been many a skirmish behind the scenes over the previous two and a half years). The election of Gorbachev, as Ryzhkov aptly put it, was a revolutionary act, but revolutionary in essence, not in form: 'in form the election of the General Secretary was peaceful—and predetermined'.[189]

Thus, the Politburo and the Central Committee of the Soviet Communist Party had come to elect to the highest position within their ranks a man whom Ryzhkov, even after his estrangement from Gorbachev, described as 'an alien (*chuzhak*) in Brezhnev's Central Committee' and one who had not been corrupted by his years at the centre since 1978.[190] The system, as Ryzhkov observes, had 'created, nursed and formed' Gorbachev, and yet 'long ago Gorbachev had internally rebelled against the native System' (the capital letter is Ryzhkov's).[191] Gorbachev was, in the words of one of his later advisers, Andrey Grachev, 'a genetic error of the system'.[192]

Chapter 4

The Power of Ideas and
the Power of Appointment

THE years in which Gorbachev held the highest office within
the Soviet Union were a time not only of dramatic institutional and policy change but also of fundamentally changed thinking. The
Soviet regime had gone to much trouble and expense to keep threatening ideas
and information out of the country although technological advance was making
that increasingly difficult. The symbiotic relationship between Communist institutions and Leninist ideology had been crucial to the maintenance of the Soviet
system, and by embracing ideas that deviated from accepted orthodoxy
Gorbachev altered and undermined that system to an extent far greater than he
initially foresaw.

None of the ideas was, of course, *entirely* new. There were individuals and
small groups within the society who had for years held some of the views which
were promoted in the early stages of perestroika (although *their* beliefs, too, had
in almost every case changed by the end of the 1980s). But for ideas to become
politically effective within a closed and highly authoritarian political system
they needed bearers with some access to the seat of power or the means of communication. Within the centralized Soviet state, it was of decisive importance
that the new General Secretary was prepared to bring into positions of influence
and, in some cases, executive office people whose views diverged significantly
from the doctrinal certitudes which had held political and intellectual sway
under his predecessors. Thus, the potential power of ideas to transform the
Soviet system became a reality as a result of the General Secretary's power of
appointment. While this was not (as will be elaborated below) an unconstrained
power to appoint new people to positions of power and influence, the holder of
that office of General Secretary had, nevertheless, greater possibilities to do this
than anyone else. Although the promotion of new people did not automatically
mean the advancement of new ideas, it opened up that possibility in principle
and, in Gorbachev's case, in practice.

To appreciate the full extent of the ideational change between 1985 and 1991
it is necessary to be aware of the low starting-point. To the extent that one can
speak at all of public opinion in the Soviet Union in 1985—given the highly
restricted flow of information to the population and the equally rigorous curbs
on the public expression of independent ideas—it is clear that this was not yet a
country striving to cast off the mantle of Leninism and the rule of the
Communist Party. On the contrary, Lenin was still revered by the overwhelming
majority of the population[1]—especially in Russia—and the domination of the

Communist Party was taken for granted. Only a small minority of citizens had reached adulthood before the Bolshevik Revolution and could remember the embryonic political pluralism of the four Dumas which had functioned, successively, between 1906 and 1917. Among the older generation, moreover, many still compared their present improved conditions with the greater privations of earlier periods of *Soviet* history. They took pride also in the superpower status which the Soviet Union had acquired. Notwithstanding the fundamental flaws of the regime (which were readily apparent to Western eyes)—its lack of freedom, democracy, and accountability in the political domain and the irrationality and inefficiency of its economy—the population as a whole did not in 1985 reject the Soviet *system* (as distinct from grumbling in private about various aspects of its performance) any more than did their new leader, Mikhail Gorbachev. It would be fanciful in the extreme to see the changes which took place between 1985 and 1988 as a result of massive pressure from below.

Alexander Yakovlev, reflecting on the perestroika years in which he played an exceptionally important political role, concluded that Soviet society in 1985, although 'profoundly sick, did not wish to notice its illness' and outwardly appeared almost healthy.[2] One prominent outside observer of the Soviet scene, Seweryn Bialer, writing in the mid-1980s, observed that, in so far as the Soviet Union at that time faced a crisis, it was a 'crisis of effectiveness' rather than a 'systemic crisis' or a 'crisis of survival'.[3] In 1985 it was already clear to unbiased observers that the system was failing in crucially important ways, but it had, indeed, not yet reached crisis point—to continue with Yakovlev's medical analogy—whereby it was faced by imminent death or recovery. Gorbachev has himself given somewhat contradictory accounts of the condition of the Soviet system in 1985. Aware of the heavy price paid by the citizens of Russia and the other successor states for all the upheaval which occurred in the ten years that followed, he has often been anxious to suggest that there was no alternative to the path he took. On other occasions, he has noted that the system could have gone on in much the same way as before for a decade or longer during which he would have enjoyed the absolute authority as General Secretary which he voluntarily abandoned when he embraced transformative political change.

While Gorbachev was undoubtedly *right* to attempt to reform the system and to accept in due course that the task was not so much to secure its *recovery* or *renewal* as its *transformation*, this course of action was not forced upon him. The other members of the Politburo at the time of his election saw no need for far-reaching reform and, had any one of their number been elected General Secretary instead of Gorbachev, the Soviet Union would have postponed facing up to the fundamental problems of the system. The regime had, after all, been politically repressive and economically inefficient for the greater part of seven decades. Even though there were a number of signs of deterioration, there were also alternative ways of keeping the system going for some years. Unlike Gorbachev's reforms, they would not, however, have tackled the most fundamental problems or made the world a somewhat less dangerous place. As Shakhnazarov has observed, if we suppose that 'Grishin, Romanov or someone else from the "old guard" ' had been elected by the Politburo in March 1985, they might have gone so far as to attempt a 'Chinese variant' of combining economic reform with extreme authoritarianism. They would have preserved the Soviet Union, but among the high costs would have been the maintenance of tension within a bipolar international system and the continued risk of nuclear war.[4] There was, Shakhnazarov rightly insists, nothing inevitable about the Soviet Union embarking on a path of fundamental reform at the time it did, and there are serious problems with supposing that the coming to power of Gorbachev and the policies he pursued were economically determined.[5]

By 1990 the Soviet Union faced a crisis of survival. Whether the Soviet state was to be or not to be was indeed the question. That was not the issue when Gorbachev succeeded Chernenko as General Secretary five years earlier. It was, in fact, largely the unintended consequences of the most serious attempt in Soviet history to reform the system that turned dire problems into a real crisis of the system and one in which the survival of the Soviet state faced a test which it failed. Different groupings within Soviet society had different solutions to offer, and a great deal depended on which individuals and groups Gorbachev turned to for advice. If Bialer was right in suggesting that the Soviet Union did not yet in the mid-1980s face a 'crisis of survival', he was surprisingly wide of the mark when he wrote also in his book published in 1986: 'It is a tragedy of today's Russia that one cannot find evidence for the existence of any meaningful anti-Stalinist forces either in the establishment itself or in the various strata of Soviet society.'[6]

In fact, the main dividing line within the Soviet establishment at that time was between those who wished to undertake serious reform of the system and those who feared any attempt to do more than tinker with the status quo. Symbolically, this was often expressed in terms of 'Stalinism' and 'anti-Stalinism', not only to emphasize, as Khrushchev had done, the crimes of Stalin, but to go beyond the *ad hominem* simplicities of that speech and consider the defects of the system which had allowed Stalin and his cohorts to wreak such havoc. Behind the monolithic façade which the Soviet Communist Party presented to the outside world, there was a myriad of views, but the most basic divide was what Stephen Cohen, writing in 1985, called 'the confrontation between the forces of reformism and conservatism'.[7] While the latter did not actually want another Stalin, for that would have removed at a stroke the physical as well as the career security the Soviet conservatives had come to value, they were, nevertheless, opposed to any attempt to examine the murky past. Their resistance to reopening the issue of Stalin and Stalinism (not to speak of questioning Leninism, which was on virtually no one's agenda in 1985) was based partly on the assertion that Stalin's harsh measures had been appropriate in his time but also on the fear that the process of uncovering past misdeeds might get out of hand and undermine existing authority. In terms of bureaucratic politics, it would also mean (and within a very few years did mean) that the conservative Communists would be placed on the defensive, for the Stalin issue acquired a salience which made it one of the fundamental criteria for dividing reformers from those who did not wish to disturb the status quo.[8]

Very soon after the fall of Khrushchev it had become taboo to subject Stalin to the kind of criticism Khrushchev had made of him, and various mild euphemisms were employed to refer to the purges and mass terror. The term

'Stalinism' was outlawed and deemed to be an anti-Communist concoction. In private, however, there were many party intellectuals—including some in the apparatus of the Central Committee—who did use the term 'Stalinism' frequently and pejoratively. They might disagree among themselves on how far it was possible or even desirable to democratize the Soviet Union. But anti-Stalinism and a belief that the system was reformable were the threads which connected the reformers of the 1960s—the readers and many of the writers of Tvardovsky's *Novy mir*—with the reformers who were given their second chance after 1985.

In many instances they were the same people. A quite disproportionately important role in influencing the political agenda was played in the second half of the 1980s by party intellectuals in their late fifties and early sixties, people who had been aged around 40 at the time of the trial of the writers Andrey Sinyavsky and Yuly Daniel in early 1966—a major sign that cultural thaw was turning to freeze—and who had been in their twenties or early thirties in 1956 when Khrushchev had shattered the illusions of so many of them with his exposure of at least some of Stalin's criminal activities in his speech to the Twentieth Congress of the party.

While Gorbachev had long been known to his friends as an anti-Stalinist,[9] he could not unilaterally change the party line on Stalin. He was also aware how divisive was the issue of Soviet history, and it was no part of his early priorities to encourage debate on the Soviet past. When, however, in an interview he gave the French Communist newspaper *L'Humanité* on 4 February 1986, Gorbachev said—in reply to a question about Stalinism—that ' "Stalinism" is a concept thought up by enemies of Communism and widely used in order to slander the Soviet Union and socialism as a whole',[10] this was not a statement which should have been taken at face value. Many Western authors have assumed that Gorbachev meant exactly what he said in that interview and have, accordingly, postulated a still greater change in his views between 1986 and November 1987, when he was far more critical of Stalin (not to speak of 1989–91, by which time he had rejected virtually the entire Stalinist legacy along with most of Leninism), than actually occurred. Of course, Gorbachev's views did develop over time— even from 1986 to 1987. They had developed still further by the end of the decade, particularly in respect of his questioning of the fundamentals of Leninism, as distinct from its Stalinist excrescences. It is, however, a profound misunderstanding of Gorbachev's outlook in the mid-1980s to attach political significance to his remark to *L'Humanité*. Gorbachev was simply repeating what had been the standard line on Stalin adopted by the Communist Party leadership for more than twenty years (since shortly after the removal of Khrushchev) and which had not yet been changed. In his interview with the French newspaper, Gorbachev went on to say that the Twentieth Party Congress had thirty years earlier established its position on 'the cult of personality of Stalin', which had 'not been an easy decision for our party'.[11] Since the Twentieth Congress condemnation of Stalin had been played down throughout the Brezhnev era, this was in itself a minor break with convention. But the more essential point is that Gorbachev, even as General Secretary, had to prepare the ground for ideological change and could not unilaterally, on the eve of the party's Twenty-Seventh

Congress (which began later that month), change the line on Stalin and Stalinism. Reflecting in a broader context on his years as General Secretary, Gorbachev wrote in 1993: 'I came to understand the limitations on the freedom of action of a political leader—even if he is invested with the very widest authority.'[12]

There are two other general points which deserve emphasis here. The first is that, as the Estonian scholar Eero Loone has put it, in 'all studies of single ideology systems' one has 'to distinguish between sincere belief, the force of customary rhetoric and fundamental critique masquerading as a return to fundamentals'.[13] Until the system had been radically altered by the late 1980s, not only as a result of the development of freedom of expression but by the introduction of contested elections, most ideas for changing that system fundamentally had, indeed, to be presented as a return to Leninist first principles if they were to get off the ground in the real world of Soviet politics. Failure to appreciate that led a number of Western authors wildly astray in their analysis of Gorbachev's speeches and public statements.[14] The second point is that to look for complete consistency in Gorbachev's public political utterances—especially over time but even at particular, delicate moments of his leadership—is to apply an inappropriate criterion to the reformist leader of an authoritarian and ideologized state. Alexander Yakovlev, who was not only a Gorbachev ally but also a critic of Gorbachev's later tactical concessions to conservative Communist forces, nevertheless observed that in large part (although not in every aspect) 'the transformation was doomed to be inconsistent'. Speaking at the Vatican in January 1992, Yakovlev went on: 'A consistent radicalism in the first years of perestroika would have destroyed the very idea of comprehensive reform.'[15] The party and state machines, including the economic bureaucracy and (not least) the organs of repression, would have jointly mutinied and 'thrust the country back towards the worst times of Stalinism'.[16] It has often been remarked—and not without reason—that Gorbachev, as Soviet Communist Party chief and thus official guardian of Marxist-Leninist holy writ and as leader of a reform movement ready to question much of that doctrine, was in the uncomfortable position of being simultaneously both Pope and Luther. This was not, it may be added, a parallel which Yakovlev chose to draw in the Vatican.

Another aspect of the problem of assessing Gorbachev's public utterances, especially in his earliest years as Soviet leader, was that the Politburo he inherited from Chernenko—and to which he had to account for his actions—was about as far removed from notions of radical reformism as it was possible to be. Underpinning this highest executive committee of the Communist Party and of the country were the various 'apparats' of the Soviet system—vast bureaucratic structures with their own deeply ingrained norms, expectations, and patterns of behaviour. Even such a stern critic of Gorbachev as Boris Yeltsin noted:

> The chief problem of [Gorbachev's] launching of *perestroika* was that he was practically alone, surrounded by the authors and impressarios of Brezhnev's 'era of stagnation', who were determined to ensure the indestructibility of the old order of things. After a while, it became easier for him, and then he himself began to lag behind events. But at that all important initial moment of his

reforming initiative, he operated with amazing finesse. In no way did he frighten the old mafia of the Party *apparat*, which retained its power for a long time and which, if necessary, might have eaten any general secretary alive without so much as a hiccup.[17]

In so far as what occurred after March 1985 was a revolution—although that term is both ambiguous and somewhat misleading in the context of the time—it was a 'revolution from above' or a 'revolution from within'.[18] Gorbachev himself has described the process as 'revolutionary in its essence but evolutionary in its tempo'.[19] Justifying the description 'revolution from above', Gorbachev's aide Chernyaev points to the fact that it was the Communist Party which was to be the vanguard of Gorbachev's revolution, just as it had been the vanguard of Lenin's. Whether in the economy or cultural life, Gorbachev saw the party as leading the renovation of the Soviet state.[20] As compared with Lenin, however, Gorbachev had little option, since the Communist Party had long ceased to be a political party in the normal sense of the term and had become an integral, supreme power-wielding component of the state structure. Yakovlev has similarly argued that recognizing that this was a 'revolution from above' is crucial to an understanding of those years[21] (as, indeed, has Yeltsin).[22] Yakovlev draws attention to what he calls the 'simple truth' that the initiators of perestroika were 'a very narrow circle in the leadership of the party and state'.[23] The fact that it was a 'revolution from above' had, in his view, both advantages and pitfalls. On the one hand, it made possible the maintenance of political stability. On the other, it made impossible a root-and-branch critique of all that was wrong with the Soviet system.[24] Making a somewhat similar point, the British scholar John Gooding, employing his preferred terminology of 'revolution from within', has written: 'The very "withinness" of the revolution . . . vitiated its effectiveness, since it had to proceed under the auspices of that which it was in fact to undermine.'[25]

In some respects, the term 'revolution from above' is more misleading than 'revolution from within', for the highest party organs were never united in favour of radical change. Indeed, the Communist Party was deeply divided at every level, and different signals were being sent out from different parts of Gorbachev's Politburo—most obviously from Yegor Ligachev, on the one hand, and Alexander Yakovlev, on the other. What *is* clear, as Yakovlev suggests, is that it was Gorbachev and a small circle around him which launched the reform process that became known as perestroika. Making a different point against the use of the concept 'revolution from above', Gooding has aptly observed:

> revolutionaries-from-above from Peter [the Great] onward had modernized in defense of an existing political structure, imposing change upon a population which was treated as a passive object and never encouraged to see itself as a subject. Gorbachev's perestroika, by contrast, tried to activate the masses and to create a genuinely participatory society. The regeneration perestroika aimed at contained a distinct political component, and it was in fact as a *political* revolution that its major success was to be achieved.[26]

The term 'revolution' itself is ambiguous, for no matter how revolutionary was the essence of the changes in the Soviet Union in the second half of the

1980s, Gorbachev was a revolutionary neither by intent nor by temperament. He was, rather, a serious reformer—'a reformer by nature'[27]—who became in due course a systemic transformer. It was, however, as early as 1987 that Gorbachev had doubts about the capacity of the party to transform the country on the basis of the reformist principles he had espoused.[28] Yakovlev has said that it was in the same year that *he* realized the system was unreformable and had to be completely dismantled (although he did not put it in such stark terms at the time).[29] Expressing similar sentiments, Gorbachev has said: 'Just like reformers before me, I thought that we had a system that could be improved. Instead, I learned that we had a system that needed to be replaced.'[30]

If it was, in one sense, a weakness that Gorbachev, when he became General Secretary of the Soviet Communist Party, was ambivalent about the extent to which the system needed to be rebuilt on new foundations, it was an ambivalence which assisted the remarkably peaceful transition from an orthodox Communist regime to one of mixed government (a mixture of authoritarianism and democracy), of which the most important characteristic was political plu- ralism. It is truly remarkable that this occurred within the space of six years in a country well used to dictatorship and in which radical change had generally been accompanied by much bloodshed—far more than was spilt during Gorbachev's years in the Kremlin. As Gooding has remarked of Gorbachev: 'At once insider and outsider, apparatchik and revolutionary, true believer and icon- oclast, he would use his ambivalence as a vitally effective political weapon.'[31]

The seriousness of Gorbachev's desire to reform the Soviet system from the very outset of his General Secretaryship in 1985 was widely underestimated at the time. Even now it is a common misconception that Gorbachev was inter- ested *only* in faster economic growth and that he turned to significant reform, especially political reform, after the economic acceleration which he had sought failed to materialize. His contribution to the systemic transformation of the Soviet Union a few years later, while recognized by many at that time, has also been played down by power-holders in the post-Soviet successor states with an interest in the creation of a myth that accords them the central role in the process of democratizing a political system which in 1985 was (depending on how the terms are defined) at best highly authoritarian and at worst totali- tarian.

Gorbachev's specific role in economic reform, on the one hand, and political transformation, on the other, is the subject of the next two chapters, and the part he played in the fundamental revision and reorientation of Soviet foreign policy is the theme of Chapter 7. Our concern for the moment is with the linkages between personnel change and new ideas which made the subsequent changes in institutions and policy possible.

Although the Soviet system, for all its problems, was regarded both by the overwhelming majority of Soviet citizens and by most Western observers as sta- ble, it was at one and the same time in desperate need of fresh thinking and yet extremely vulnerable to new concepts. Its 'stability' rested in large part on the highly authoritarian character of the regime and on the relative passivity of a population with no experience of democratic alternatives, only of the still harsher totalitarian regime of Stalin. It is hardly surprising that the introduction of fresh ideas, free speech, freedom of assembly, and competitive elections into a multinational state with a vast accumulation of hitherto suppressed grievances turned a 'crisis of effectiveness'—or latent political crisis—into overt political crisis. What is more remarkable is that for five years, in spite of all the difficulties, Gorbachev largely succeeded in averting full-blown crises. These developed with a vengeance in 1990–1, although with a less bloody outcome than in former Yugoslavia.

A back-handed tribute to the power of ideas had been paid by the Soviet leadership prior to Gorbachev's coming to power in the lengths to which they went not only to promote official Marxism-Leninism—those parts of the writings of Marx and Lenin, together with suitable interpretative gloss, that fitted their political purposes—but also to keep out of circulation any heterodox political notions. Thus, there was strict censorship of the Soviet mass media, foreign radio was jammed, and each library of any consequence had its *spetskhran*, or special collection, which housed works which no ordinary reader was allowed to see, such as the analyses of Western specialists on the Soviet Union, the critiques of the Soviet system by Leon Trotsky, or literary works which called into question the fundamentals of that system, from George Orwell's *Animal Farm* and *Nineteen Eighty-Four* to Alexander Solzhenitsyn's *The Gulag Archipelago*. Foreigners were treated with suspicion and, particularly if they possessed knowledge of the Soviet Union, were subject to surveillance. Even when relaxation of such restrictions and pressures became official Soviet policy in the later 1980s, the KGB continued to be a 'state within a state' and that institution remained at best patchily responsive to the new guide-lines.[32]

Paradoxically, it was, in part, Gorbachev's misplaced confidence in the reformability of the Soviet system which enabled him to embrace new ideas far more boldly than any previous General Secretary and to struggle with conservative opponents of change within the Soviet establishment to have thinking which was radically new in the Soviet context accepted and acted upon. To some extent, these fresh ideas became a new orthodoxy, codified into a body of doctrine designated as 'New Thinking' or the 'New Political Thinking' (*Novoe politicheskoe myshlenie*). But the differences with the past, even in this respect, were far greater than the similarities. The new openness and open-mindedness were such that this was a fast-changing body of doctrine in which, for example, Gorbachev's 'socialist pluralism' quite soon became for radical commentators 'political pluralism', a concept accepted by Gorbachev himself some two and a half years after he had broken the taboo on regarding pluralism, however qualified, as anything other than a dangerous concoction of the Soviet Union's ideological enemies. In fact, it *was* a danger to the Soviet system as that system had operated since Lenin's time, and it was no part of Gorbachev's initial conception to introduce a fully-fledged political pluralism in which the Communist Party would become just one party competing with others for influence and power. Yet, having introduced the concept of pluralism in a qualified form, Gorbachev before long reached the view that the system had to be comprehensively transformed and that meant nothing less than its pluralization.

Like previous Soviet leaders, Gorbachev inherited a Politburo and Central Committee that could not instantly be changed and he had to carry his colleagues in these highest party organs with him. A Soviet leader in the post-Stalin period did not have the clear power of appointment to the Politburo possessed by an American President or British Prime Minister in relation to his or her Cabinet. Renewal of these highest party bodies depended, rather, on a process of collective co-option in which the voice of the General Secretary counted for much more than that of any other Politburo member but in which he had to carry with him a majority of that body's full members. (In addition to the full Politburo members, with voting rights, candidate members of the Politburo and those Secretaries of the Central Committee who were not also Politburo members attended its meetings and were entitled to speak but not to vote. Votes were actually rather uncommon; an attempt was made to achieve consensus. This was easier to attain under Brezhnev with his policy of minimal change and desire not to rock the boat than under Gorbachev when radical change was being placed on the political agenda and vested interests were threatened.)

A bold party leader could, nevertheless, within a few years change the composition of the top party organs. As General Secretary, his authority was greatest *vis-à-vis* the Secretariat of the Central Committee—the group of Secretaries who were responsible for the implementation of policy agreed in the Politburo and who had themselves great influence over appointments inside the party apparatus. Changes in the composition of the Politburo and Secretariat had to be formally approved at Central Committee plenary sessions which, for some years before Gorbachev became party leader, had normally been held only twice a year. Changes in the composition of this larger body, the Central Committee, could (with the exception of promotion of candidate members to full membership) be made only at Party Congresses, which the Rules of the Communist Party decreed must be held once every five years.

Gorbachev was, in some respects, fortunate that a Party Congress was due to be convened in early 1986, less than a year after he had assumed office. This provided an opportunity for introducing new blood. Since, however, he had elevated Yegor Ligachev to the position of *de facto* second secretary, in charge of the party organization, it was hardly surprising that even the new Central Committee formally 'elected' by the Twenty-Seventh Party Congress (held from 26 February to 6 March 1986) was far from being dominated by reformers, still less by radical reformers.

Changing the balance of influence

Gorbachev was, however, able to change the *balance of influence* within the leadership before he could change the *balance of power*. A General Secretary had a much freer hand in choosing his aides and advisers, both formal and informal, than he had in elevating an ally to the Politburo. Whereas the promotion of anyone to the Politburo or Secretariat of the Central Committee, or the appointment of a minister, needed the approval of the Politburo, the appointment of aides was entirely at the discretion of the General Secretary and required the sanction of no other body. This was still more evidently true of the General Secretary's consultations with informal, non-staff advisers. Every Soviet leader relied to some extent on outside specialists, but these experts were generally very conscious of what the leader wanted to hear. A three-stage filtering process meant that, in the first instance, only 'reliable' specialists whose views were unlikely to offer a significant challenge to the conventional wisdom of the party hierarchy were apt to be consulted; second, their recommendations were mediated by the permanent officials in the Central Committee department with responsibility for that particular area of policy; and, third, the specialists themselves engaged in self-censorship and—with rare exceptions—did not advocate radical change, since the most likely result of doing so would be to put an end to their privileged role.

In all three respects this consultative process changed under Gorbachev. He was prepared to listen to a broader range of specialists with fresh ideas, including some—such as Aganbegyan, Shatalin, and Zaslavskaya—who had received party reprimands in the past for excessive boldness. Especially in the earlier years of his leadership, Gorbachev was prepared to meet directly with specialists from academic institutes as well as from his own circle of full-time assistants, and he made it clear that he would actively welcome fresh ideas. Self-censorship drastically declined as it became evident that heterodox views expressed in official seminars or position papers would no longer blight a person's career but might even advance it. This change of atmosphere quickly made itself felt in the institutes of the Academy of Sciences, and specialists with ideas of their own who did not personally take part in seminars or discussions with Gorbachev were able to convey proposals to him either through his aides or through Alexander Yakovlev.

Gorbachev lost comparatively little time in replacing most of the aides he had inherited from his predecessors.[33] The long-standing foreign policy aide Andrey Alexandrov-Agentov, who had served Brezhnev, Andropov, and Chernenko in turn (and who was forced to make way for Chernyaev in early 1986), complained in his retirement that it was not possible to advise Gorbachev; he did not want to listen.[34] What this meant, however, was that Gorbachev was not particularly interested in the views of Alexandrov-Agentov. With his replacement, Chernyaev, it was an entirely different matter.

Andrey Grachev—himself a significant informal adviser of Gorbachev on foreign policy issues during the perestroika years, and a close and formal one in the last months of the Soviet Union when he was Gorbachev's presidential press spokesman—has described Chernyaev as 'the most faithful and reliable' of Gorbachev's assistants.[35] He recalls an occasion when Gorbachev went so far as to introduce Chernyaev to the Spanish Prime Minister, Felipe González, as his *alter ego*.[36] Ten years older than Gorbachev, Chernyaev had fought in the Second World War and taught in the History Faculty of Moscow University for a time before joining the party apparatus after Stalin's death. He belonged to the important group who had spent time in Prague—on the *World Marxist Review*—which had been an introduction to revisionist Communist and social democratic thought (notwithstanding, as noted in an earlier chapter, the relative orthodoxy of the journal they produced). Chernyaev, who had maintained links with people of critical views outside the party apparatus, worked exceptionally closely with Gorbachev from 1986 onwards. In the words of his former International Department colleague Grachev, he was 'a long-standing liberal political thinker who, in Gorbachev, finally acquired a person through whom he could try to realize many of the unsatisfied ambitions of his younger years'.[37] Chernyaev's outlook was known to Gorbachev before he appointed him. They had shared their critical views of the line taken by the International Department under Ponomarev and their approach to foreign policy was a common one.[38] With his experience of international affairs, Chernyaev was to become both an important vehicle of new ideas on foreign policy and an invaluable sounding-board for Gorbachev's opinions from the time of his appointment as principal foreign policy aide in February 1986. Chernyaev exemplifies the difference new appointments could make in terms of fresh ideas, dependent though that factor clearly is on *who* is appointed. He was one of the crucial contributors to the new thinking on foreign policy, although he himself, just before his appointment, was in no doubt about who would play the decisive role. In his diary for 18 January 1986, he wrote: 'And now we have got a rarity as leader: a clever person, educated, lively, honest, with ideas, with imagination. And brave.'[39]

Gorbachev appointed two aides in succession on ideological issues who, while by no means ready for fully-fledged democracy (as Gorbachev himself was not in 1985), were considerable improvements on those who had held that position on the General Secretary's staff in the past. The first was Georgy Lukich Smirnov, who had been a deputy head of the Propaganda Department of the Central Committee in the early 1970s when Alexander Yakovlev was First Deputy (prior to his ten years in Canada). It was probably on Yakovlev's recommendation that Gorbachev took Smirnov on, although Gorbachev, after he had become a Secretary of the Central Committee in 1978, had himself got to know Smirnov. Prior to that they had spoken only by telephone. Smirnov—who was in his early thirties at the time of Khrushchev's 'secret speech'—was one of those who felt himself to be a 'child of the Twentieth Party Congress'.[40] He retained an idealized view of Lenin—as did Gorbachev himself even after he had begun to undermine the foundations of Leninism. But there was no doubting the sincerity of Smirnov's anti-Stalinism. He ceased to be a Gorbachev aide in January 1987 when he was appointed Director of the Institute of Marxism-Leninism to restructure that 'citadel of dogmatism'.[41]

Smirnov was succeeded as Gorbachev's adviser on ideological issues by the intellectually more adventurous Ivan Frolov, whose career had hitherto been divided between scholarly and political work and who had acquired quite a good reputation as a philosopher of science. Twice a graduate of the 'Prague school of revisionism' (he served on the *World Marxist Review* from 1962 until 1965 and again in 1977–9), Frolov was very much a reformer from above, somewhat suspicious of the views of the mass of the people. As late as 1994 he was willing to go on record saying: 'I do not hide it: I am not a democrat . . . in principle I am on the side of a certain élitism and professionalism.'[42] Frolov was, however, both a contributor to fresh thinking while an aide to Gorbachev and at the same time a conduit for the ideas of others. Thus, for example, during this time Otto Latsis, an economic reformer of long standing, and his younger colleague on the party journal *Kommunist*, Yegor Gaydar (later Yeltsin's acting prime minister and advocate of the speediest possible transition to a market economy in post-Soviet Russia), presented Frolov with a large collection of papers on Russia's financial problems. Frolov was impressed by them and passed them on to Gorbachev: 'Mikhail Sergeevich also liked the articles, and they were sent on to the Politburo.'[43] There, however, they received an extremely cold reception. The attitude to scholarship in the Politburo, said Frolov, was hostile, and they were especially scornful of the social sciences. Notwithstanding Gorbachev's entirely sympathetic attitude to serious social analysis in general and to these documents in particular, the Politburo discussion ended with Gorbachev having to give way to the opposition—in the guise of a call for 'further reflection'—and the documents fell into limbo.[44]

Frolov, who had spent the year before joining Gorbachev's personal staff as editor of *Kommunist*, left to become editor-in-chief of *Pravda* in October 1989. Gorbachev had been wishing for some time to replace the relatively conservative Viktor Afanasev—who had edited *Pravda* since 1976 and whose lack of enthusiasm for political transformation was all too evident—with a nominee of his own.[45] In obtaining the Politburo's agreement to the appointment of Frolov, Gorbachev attempted to bolster the new editor's authority further by making him a Secretary of the Central Committee in December 1989 and a Politburo member in July 1990. This meant, at least, that Frolov—unlike his predecessor— did not have to take instructions from any Moscow or republican party secretary who cared to telephone.[46] Frolov remained *Pravda* editor until the August coup (although during the actual *putsch* he was in hospital in Germany), but the newspaper remained highly ambivalent about the kind of far-reaching reform Gorbachev was by then pressing, for its staff included many conservative Communists. It also no longer had pride of place among Russian newspapers, its loss of status mirroring that of the party.

The most important Gorbachev aide, apart from Chernyaev (whom he complemented, for they covered different territory), was, however, not Frolov, but Georgy Shakhnazarov, whose role will be a recurring theme in this book, for in terms of introduction of ideas for political reform he was more significant than Chernyaev and of almost comparable importance to Yakovlev. It was in early 1988 that Shakhnazarov was appointed a full-time Gorbachev aide, succeeding Viktor Sharapov, who became Ambassador to Bulgaria. Sharapov was a hold-over from Andropov's time as General Secretary. He had worked with Andropov over many years, first in the Socialist Countries Department of the Central Committee and later at the KGB. His functions as aide to the General Secretary— which Shakhnazarov inherited, but along with additional responsibilities—were to advise the party leader on developments in, and relations with, other Communist states. For many years a deputy head, and from 1986 to 1988 a First Deputy Head, of the Socialist Countries Department, Shakhnazarov had represented a more enlightened tendency within that department—as compared, for example, with his predecessor as First Deputy Head, Oleg Rakhmanin, who was strongly opposed even to the economic reforms undertaken in Hungary by János Kádár.[47]

Shakhnazarov's importance for Gorbachev was not only for his advice on East European affairs, but still more for his ideas on domestic political reform. Born into an Armenian family in Baku in 1924, Shakhnazarov is a man of many talents. After serving in the Soviet army during the Second World War, he studied law, in which he took a higher doctorate, and he became—along with Fedor Burlatsky—one of the two main advocates (from early in the Brezhnev era, but with little success then) of the institutionalization of a discipline of political science in the Soviet Union.[48] He, like Chernyaev and Frolov, worked for a time on the *World Marxist Review* in Prague, before returning to the Socialist Countries Department of the Central Committee (where, as noted in Chapter 2, he had earlier been a member of a team of consultants of the department head, Yury Andropov, before Andropov became KGB chief in 1967). Shakhnazarov is the author of poetry and of published works of science fiction (under the name Georgy Shakh) as well as of a wide range of political studies.

While a number of his pre-perestroika books contain far too much Leninist orthodoxy to satisfy many readers (including Shakhnazarov) today, his writings from those years often also include ideas which were then by no means common in official Soviet political literature. Thus, in a book published in 1972, Shakhnazarov advocated a much freer and fuller flow of information to Soviet citizens and, unusually for that time, wrote of the existence of different interests within Soviet society.[49] Shakhnazarov also anticipated some of the new thinking on foreign policy of the Gorbachev era. In May 1984 he published an important article in which humanistic considerations and universal values were given precedence over the 'class approach' traditionally sanctified by Marxism-Leninism. This was to become accepted doctrine under Gorbachev, but it was still a striking deviation from official orthodoxy at the time Shakhnazarov promulgated it. In the same article he formulated as a maxim for the nuclear era the proposition that 'political ends do not exist which would justify the use of means liable to lead to nuclear war'.[50]

Although it is not entirely easy to reconcile with some of his published works—which include, for example, criticism of the 'Prague Spring' with which in private he sympathized—Shakhnazarov was for long a closet social democrat within the Central Committee apparatus.[51] Crucially, this was a position that Gorbachev himself came round to in the course of his years in power. It was in December 1989 that Gorbachev first made explicit to Shakhnazarov his social democratic sympathies.[52] While Gorbachev still had to be rather more guarded in public, the previous month he had published in *Pravda* a significant article in which he stressed the diversity of manifestations of socialism and wrote explicitly and sympathetically about social democracy, from which 'we are striving to draw . . . whatever is appropriate for our society's conditions'.[53] Until Gorbachev became General Secretary Soviet leaders had held that, while there could be different *roads* to socialism, there was only *one socialism*—namely, that which existed in the Soviet Union and in the countries which had faithfully followed in its ideological footsteps.[54]

Shakhnazarov, writing in late 1991—after observing, correctly, that the Communist Party had not been an ordinary political party but 'in the fullest sense a state organization'—emphasized the enormous variety of tendencies to be found in that party ('from anarchist to monarchist').[55] One of the most numerically substantial of these tendencies was the social democratic, but only with Gorbachev's coming to power did it have the opportunity to make political headway. Dismissing the myth—increasingly disseminated both in Russia and abroad in 1991—that Gorbachev wished merely 'to perfect the system' while 'not touching its essence',[56] Shakhnazarov quoted verbatim from his December 1989 conversation with Gorbachev in which Gorbachev said:

> Don't think that something will stop me, that there is a threshold through which I shall not be able to pass. Everything that is needed for the very deepest transformation of the system I accept without embarrassment. I will go as far as it is necessary to go for that. And if we speak about the final goal, insofar as it is possible today to be definite, that is integration into the world community by peaceful means. By conviction I am close to social democracy.[57]

Given that Gorbachev was General Secretary of the Communist Party of the Soviet Union, which, historically, had seen social democrats as their most dangerous adversaries (Lenin—and not only Stalin—reserved his fiercest invective for those who were social democrats or 'democratic socialists' in the West European tradition), Gorbachev had already crossed a particularly difficult threshold. It was one, moreover, which it became increasingly plain to orthodox Communists that he had crossed. Many of them were later to feel both betrayed and outwitted. Three months after the collapse of the Soviet Union Ligachev complained: 'Gorbachev carried out a *putsch* against Marxism-Leninism and replaced it with social-democratism.'[58]

Shakhnazarov was granted the opportunity by Gorbachev to become one of the central figures in the elaboration of a fundamental reform of the Soviet political system in the spirit of social democracy. He played an important part in the preparation of the political reforms presented to the Nineteenth Party Conference in 1988 (discussed in Chapter 6). Moreover, along with Frolov, Shakhnazarov was one of the officials most responsible for work on a new Party Programme as well as for a declarative document, 'Towards a Humane, Democratic Socialism' which was adopted by the Twenty-Eighth Congress of the Communist Party in 1990. It was at this Congress that the decision was taken to produce a new official Programme to replace that adopted by the Twenty-Second Party Congress (1961) and in its revised version by the Twenty-Seventh Congress (1986). Much of the work on the 1986 document, which was not officially regarded as a new programme, but simply a revised version of the Party Programme produced in Khrushchev's time and adopted at the 1961 Party Congress, had been completed before Gorbachev became General Secretary. It certainly represented far less of a break with the past than the draft of an entirely new programme, on which, as Frolov has noted, work went on continuously between the end of 1990 and July 1991.[59] Even the latter, finally approved for publication by a Central Committee plenum, was, according to Frolov, 'very greatly deformed' as it passed through the hands of the Programme Commission.[60] By then the Communist Party was not only openly divided but engaged in bitter internal struggle and it was no longer determining the course of political developments in the country. Nevertheless, it is a historic fact that the draft programme—which was never endorsed, since the coup and the subsequent dissolution of the union-wide CPSU had occurred before an extraordinary Twenty-Ninth Congress of the party could be held in late 1991—had much more in common with West European social democracy than with traditional Soviet Marxism-Leninism.[61]

It would be wrong to end discussion of Gorbachev's choice of personal aides by conveying the impression that they were all wise ones. On the contrary, one of the worst of all Gorbachev's appointments (including even some of his later ones which are discussed in Chapter 8) turned out to be that of an aide. The appointment had already been made before he became General Secretary, and in the context of that time—1981—there was nothing surprising about it. The person concerned was Valery Boldin, who was then head of the agricultural section of *Pravda*. Since Gorbachev was still the Secretary of the Central Committee responsible for agriculture, this looked like a fairly routine choice, given the rules of the game of Soviet politics. Unfortunately, Boldin was a self-centred careerist whose every increase in power went to his head. Gorbachev's misplaced trust in him was such that, when he ceased to be his aide in 1987, he was moved to a position where he could do still more harm. Boldin became head of the General Department of the Central Committee, which controlled the flow of papers to the General Secretary. In 1990, once he had been elected President of the USSR by the Congress of People's Deputies, Gorbachev appointed Boldin as his chief of staff, so that once again he was acting as a gatekeeper with substantial control over which people and papers reached Gorbachev. Although Boldin played only a minor part in speech-writing, he was able to do much more damage by the bias he imparted to the information which reached Gorbachev. Through other aides and other sources, Gorbachev obtained a variety of views, but from Boldin it was the kind of misinformation which the KGB wished him to hear—dangerous concoctions about radical democrats planning marches to the Kremlin which would end with mass scaling of the Kremlin walls and about impending chaos in the Baltic states. Gorbachev trusted Boldin and accepted at face value some of the distorted evidence he presented to them. It was, therefore, a great shock to him, but not in retrospect to a number of his genuinely reformist allies, that Boldin joined Kryuchkov and the other *putschists* in August 1991.

Boldin not only did his utmost to skew the flow of information to Gorbachev in a conservative direction—especially dangerously on issues relating to the Baltic republics—but saw to it that a number of decisions of which he disapproved were not implemented. According to the Director of the Institute of General History of the Russian Academy of Sciences, Alexander Chubaryan, Boldin prevented the dispatch to the post-Communist Czech government of documents concerning Soviet–Czech relations in 1968 after Shevardnadze, Shakhnazarov, and (more remarkably) KGB Chairman Kryuchkov had signed a document authorizing their release.[62] As his self-importance increased, Boldin would, late in the Soviet period, see fit to deny access to Gorbachev even to the veteran agricultural specialist Alexander Nikonov, who protested in vain that he had known Gorbachev for more than twenty-five years.[63] Boldin's disloyalty to Gorbachev at the time of the August 1991 attempted coup, when he joined the conspirators, was compounded when he later published a mendacious book attacking the person who had promoted him so far above his deserts.[64]

Changing the balance of power

If official and unofficial advisers could be appointed by Gorbachev entirely at his own discretion, he had to use both his natural authority and the authority of the General Secretaryship—which raised a Soviet leader well above his Politburo colleagues—in order to alter to his advantage the composition of the highest Communist Party echelons. Changes in the headship of Central Committee departments, republican party First Secretaryships and, still more, secretaryships of the Central Committee and promotions to the Politburo altered the balance of power and not just that of influence. The distinction between power and influence is, of course, often a tenuous one, but real institutional power rested with, for example, the Secretary of the Central Committee responsible for party cadres and with any voting member of the Politburo—although the constant access to the General Secretary of a particularly trusted aide could make his influence worth more than the formal power of a less trusted member of the Politburo.

Of all those who began as informal advisers to Gorbachev and were then moved by him into positions of greater institutional power and authority, the most important was undoubtedly Alexander Yakovlev. Both before and after he had any formal position in the highest party organs, Yakovlev worked with Gorbachev on the formulation of policy and on his major speeches. In the period between 1985 and 1988 he was probably the most influential person in the Soviet Union, if Gorbachev is excluded on the grounds that *he* was the most important object of influence. Gorbachev listened to such a wide range of conflicting views and was so conscious of the need to avoid upsetting too drastically the delicate balance of forces within the Soviet establishment that there could be no question of his always accepting the advice of Yakovlev. The project of reforming the Soviet Union was Gorbachev's, and Yakovlev's participation in it owed everything to Gorbachev, however much he helped push forward the process. In the political context of the mid-1980s radical reform could not have been launched without constant pressure from—and not merely the acquiescence of—the General Secretary.

As the ultimate guardian of his own project of perestroika, Gorbachev felt justified in making concessions to conservative forces when this seemed necessary to keep the enterprise afloat. It was typical of his sleight of hand that he put the more conservative Yegor Ligachev in charge of the party organization, while not allowing him sole supervision of ideology. Normally the person who was recognized as 'second secretary' of the party (even though no post was formally designated as such) supervised both ideology and party cadres within the Secretariat. But after Yakovlev had joined the Politburo, he shared responsibility for ideology with Ligachev before both of them were superseded by Vadim Medvedev. Ligachev could think of himself as being the 'second secretary' since he chaired meetings of the Secretariat, but there was, to say the least, an ambiguity about his position. Having, however, satisfied Ligachev's desire for recognition, Gorbachev leant much more in Yakovlev's direction in terms of concrete policy and of the ideas to be found in his speeches.

It is worth noting, however, that while Gorbachev was closer to Yakovlev on, for example, issues of cultural policy, the role of the mass media, and the need for a radical revision of Soviet doctrine, he had genuine confidence, too, in Ligachev, seeing him initially not only as an energetic ally but also as someone committed to perestroika. As will be noted further on, the ambiguity of that term had great advantages for Gorbachev and for the reform process, but the fact that those who pledged loyalty to the idea often had vastly different notions of what it meant could also, in some instances, be a disadvantage. Thus, in late 1987 Gorbachev was still insisting that Ligachev was committed to perestroika, in spite (as Gorbachev accepted) of using unfortunate words and methods at times, whereas the most serious reformers in his entourage were in no doubt that the very essence of what Ligachev understood by perestroika was different from Gorbachev's and from *their* conception.[65] Later Boris Yeltsin, Alexander Yakovlev, and Eduard Shevardnadze were all to feel, at different times and in varying degrees, that their support of Gorbachev had not been sufficiently reciprocated, and Gorbachev is not beyond criticism on that score. But it was at least as much of an error to keep in his team for too long people with whom he had a good working relationship before he became General Secretary but who had become a political liability both in personal terms and by their retarding of the process of change. That applies, notably, to Ligachev and Ryzhkov as well as, still more, to Boldin.

In sharp contrast with Ligachev, whose contribution in the early stages of Gorbachev's General Secretaryship was ambiguous at best and who was soon to become a brake on transformative change, Yakovlev played an extraordinarily important part in helping Gorbachev to formulate his reformist project as well as in battling on its behalf in the corridors of power of the Central Committee. His ten years in Canada had broadened his vision, but it should not be forgotten that he had been a relatively senior official within the Central Committee apparatus before that lengthy diplomatic interlude in his career.[66] He knew who was who within the Central Committee apparatus (as did Chernyaev and Shakhnazarov) and, thanks partly to his time as Director of IMEMO, he had good contacts, too, with party intellectuals in the policy-oriented research institutes. Yakovlev became, accordingly, a conduit for the channelling of innovative ideas to Gorbachev, a function performed also by the most enlightened of his aides, especially—again—Chernyaev and Shakhnazarov.

Even in Gorbachev's first year as General Secretary there is some evidence that he was prepared to think the unthinkable, although not yet ready to do the unthinkable. At the end of 1985 Yakovlev wrote a memorandum to Gorbachev which proposed splitting the Communist Party in two in order to introduce competition into the political system.[67] This was an extraordinary idea in the context of the time, for the Communist Party had always punished with especial severity any 'splitters' within its ranks. It was, accordingly, an impractical suggestion less than nine months after the death of Chernenko. If Gorbachev had attempted to implement it, he would have been speedily removed from the General Secretaryship, and Yakovlev, instead of beginning his fast ascent to the Politburo, would have been banished from the ante-room of power. The very fact, however, that Gorbachev—having read and digested this memorandum and being already familiar with Yakovlev's general political outlook[68]—proceeded to accord Yakovlev accelerated promotion says much about his own openness to ideas for substantive political reform. The two parties about which Yakovlev was writing would have been an artificial creation at that time, although by 1990 (when Yakovlev also hesitated) the political context had changed dramatically. *Then* Gorbachev could and almost certainly should have taken the risk of splitting the party, whose deep ideological divisions had over the preceding few years come into the open, instead of papering over the cracks.

In his 1985 memorandum, Yakovlev suggested that one of the parties be called the Socialist Party and the other the People's Democratic Party, and that both should belong to a kind of popular front to be called the Union of Communists. This, perhaps, smacks not only of artificial social engineering from above but of a pseudo-multi-party system of the kind which existed in a number of the East European Communist states. But the proposal, however impractical, was intended to be a much more serious political reform than that.[69] Elections, which Yakovlev intended should be genuinely contested, were to be held every five years, and if the recommendation could have been implemented, a significant element of political pluralism would have been introduced into the political system at a time when that was still conspicuously lacking.

Gorbachev's response to Yakovlev's proposal is of some importance, for it gives the lie to the notion that he was then (and, according to careless observers, also later) still an unreconstructed Communist whose only concern was with improved economic efficiency. Writing in 1994, by which time the relations between Gorbachev and himself had become much more distant,[70] Yakovlev notes: 'The reaction of M. S. Gorbachev to this memorandum was calm and interested. But he considered the proposed measures to be premature.'[71] Speaking informally about this episode two years before he published in 1994 verbatim extracts from the memorandum, Yakovlev said that Gorbachev did not respond in writing to his document but did so orally. When asked what that response was, Yakovlev used just one word in Russian which requires two in English to capture its meaning, '*Rano*': 'Too soon!'[72] The fact that Gorbachev was completely unshocked by the proposal is significant in itself, for it would have been considered revisionist, or worse, by any of his predecessors. That he regarded it not as wrong, but as premature, is another indication that he had political as well as economic reform in view even in 1985.

If the part played by Yakovlev was extremely important for Gorbachev, Gorbachev's role was absolutely indispensable for Yakovlev. His career in the Communist Party hierarchy had come to an abrupt halt in the early 1970s; he was not in 1985 even a candidate member of the Central Committee. The Central Committee (elected by the Twenty-Sixth Party Congress in 1981) had 319 full members and 151 candidate members.[73] Thus, Yakovlev moved from being at the end of 1985 not within the top 470 party members in formal terms to being eighteen months later one of the top three in the party hierarchy. His promotion from non-membership of the Central Committee to full membership of the Politburo, together with a secretaryship of the Central Committee, was pushed through by Gorbachev at unprecedented speed. While by 1985—thanks also to Gorbachev—he was director of an important Moscow institute, Yakovlev held no position of political power. By June 1987 he was one of the four most powerful politicians in the country. After Gorbachev, Ligachev and Yakovlev were the leading people in the Communist Party, and the quartet was completed by Ryzhkov as Chairman of the Council of Ministers. In March 1986, at the same time as he became a member of the Central Committee, he was made a Secretary of that body, in January 1987 a candidate member of the Politburo, and in June a full member.

Only a determined General Secretary could elevate even the most trusted ally at such speed. It was the Soviet equivalent of being elected to the British House of Commons one year and becoming not only a Cabinet member but also the holder of one of the three major offices of state (after the prime ministership) the following year. Without such promotion Yakovlev's voice would still have been an enlightened one, but far less powerful. Thanks to Gorbachev, he was able to give direct support to the widening of the boundaries of the permissible in the mass media and cultural life, and to the new political thinking from his power base as a senior secretary. He also—in another link between the force of fresh thinking and the power of appointment—played a large part in replacing editors of newspapers and periodicals, generally by people far more reform-minded than their predecessors. Ligachev for one was extremely unhappy with the views subsequently expressed in a number of these publications and also complained 'around 1987' that 'Gorbachev was gradually being surrounded by people who were personally dependent on Yakovlev'.[74]

Gorbachev's use of his power of appointment, including the power he had devolved in that respect to Yakovlev, went hand in hand with the radicalization of the political agenda and the introduction of concepts previously taboo in Soviet political discourse. Not all of those promoted to high political office were, however, prepared for far-reaching change. Most, even of Central Committee members who had sincerely supported Gorbachev for the General Secretaryship, had done so partly to be on the winning side and partly in order to revitalize the old system. Thus, when Gorbachev promoted men in that category—such as the Chairman of the KGB, Viktor Chebrikov, who was advanced from candidate to full membership of the Politburo one month after Gorbachev became General Secretary, or two such crucial allies in 1984–5 as Ligachev, who became a senior secretary in April 1985, and Ryzhkov, who replaced Nikolay Tikhonov as Chairman of the Council of Ministers in September 1985—he found that, sooner or later, they refused to go along with the changes he was promoting or was prepared to endorse. They—and especially Ryzhkov—were prepared for reform within limits, but they stopped well short of the point at which such reform turned the system into something different in kind.

There was nothing, though, particularly inept about the promotion of Ligachev and Ryzhkov in the context of 1985. Gorbachev needed to remove the Brezhnevite old guard from the leadership, and the norms of the system were such that Politburo members had to be found from among people who already held a high party-state rank—a secretaryship of the Central Committee, candidate membership of the Politburo, or the headship of a particularly important Central Committee department, ministry, or state committee.

In so far as those were the rules of the game of Soviet politics, Gorbachev had to choose from a comparatively small pool of possible contenders for high office and one which contained scarcely any radical reformers. Quite apart from the norms of the system, Gorbachev needed, for his own purposes, people who knew where the levers of power were and how to use them. Thus, he had to find politicians with experience at high levels of the system who yet would be significantly different from those they replaced. That was a very difficult combination to achieve. One of the reasons why Yakovlev was so valuable for the new General Secretary was that he met both criteria admirably. With some such appointments Gorbachev succeeded, with others he failed. But he is more open to criticism for his 'cadres policy' after 1989 (discussed in Chapter 8), by which time he had a freer hand—as the society had become increasingly politicized and the boundaries of the political system broadened—than for his appointments between 1985 and 1988, several of which, by previous Soviet standards, were remarkably good, while others turned out to be little better than their predecessors.

At Secretariat and Politburo level the two outstandingly successful appointments from Gorbachev's standpoint as a reformer and as a new General Secretary needing to bolster his power base were those of Yakovlev and of Eduard Shevardnadze. Yakovlev's contribution has already been discussed, while Shevardnadze's much longer-standing friendship with Gorbachev has been touched upon in an earlier chapter. Shevardnadze's promotion to be Soviet Foreign Minister in the summer of 1985 deserves elaboration, however, for it was a master-stroke which took the Soviet establishment (not to mention Western diplomatic observers) by complete surprise. From his vantage-point at that time as a deputy head of the International Department of the Central Committee, Chernyaev wrote in his diary: 'Even for apparatchiks, close to the top, this was a bolt from the blue.'[75] Indeed, Shevardnadze has written that to say he himself was *surprised* to be informed of this impending move in a telephone call from Gorbachev in June 1985 would be a massive understatement.[76] As First Secretary of the Georgian party organization, he had made some visits abroad and had received foreign delegations in Tbilisi, but he was essentially without foreign policy experience. When he flew to Moscow the morning after the telephone call and in a meeting with Gorbachev produced many arguments against his being appointed Foreign Minister, not least his lack of experience, Gorbachev replied: 'No experience? Well, perhaps that's a good thing. Our foreign policy needs a fresh eye, courage, dynamism, innovative approaches. I have no doubt that my choice is right.'[77] Shevardnadze had, moreover, real political skills—not simply those of the Soviet bureaucrat, but flexibility and the capacity to establish a rapport with, and inspire trust in, his interlocutors (as even American Secretaries of State were to discover, to their surprise). He was also a politician of strikingly similar outlook to the new General Secretary. Shevardnadze has said that the main point underlying his acceptance of the Foreign Ministry was that he was Gorbachev's personal choice: 'I knew what he wanted, and knew that I wanted the same thing.'[78] Gorbachev correctly believed that Shevardnadze would be an able executant of an innovative foreign policy and his supporter on both domestic and international political issues within the Politburo, to which Shevardnadze was now promoted from candidate to full membership.

Gorbachev has often been accused of being indecisive—a charge not entirely without foundation (especially in economic policy, for reasons which are discussed in Chapters 5 and 8), but an over-simplification none the less. There was nothing indecisive about the way Gorbachev in his first few years in office removed from the Politburo and Secretariat of the Central Committee his opponents and brought in people on whom he thought he could rely. No General Secretary in Soviet history achieved such a substantial turnover of personnel in the highest party organs so early in his leadership. The very first Politburo member whose dismissal Gorbachev secured was Grigory Romanov, a senior secretary and a potential obstacle to far-reaching change who—at the time of his ousting in July 1985—was not the most obvious candidate for pensioning off in terms of age. Far from being of advanced years, he was in his early sixties and below the average age of the Politburo. Before the end of Gorbachev's first year two older Politburo members who were no friends of reform—Viktor Grishin and Nikolay Tikhonov—had joined Romanov in enforced retirement.[79] Gorbachev had to be sufficiently determined to convince the individual that he should offer his resignation or, alternatively, to persuade the Politburo as a whole that they should demand it.[80]

Many of Gorbachev's appointments were of people who, while somewhat more enlightened than their Politburo predecessors, were reluctant to embrace reform as radical as that which was acceptable to Yakovlev and Shevardnadze. They included men such as Lev Zaykov, a former Leningrad factory manager and party boss who (already a Central Committee member when Gorbachev became General Secretary) was speedily promoted to become by March 1986 both a Secretary of the Central Committee (overseeing the military and the armaments industry) and a full member of the Politburo; Georgy Razumovsky, a Gorbachev ally from Krasnodar who was brought into the Secretariat of the Central Committee in March 1986 (charged with overseeing party appointments at lower levels of the hierarchy) and into candidate membership of the Politburo in 1988; and Viktor Nikonov, a former agronomist and Minister of Agriculture in the Russian republic, who became the Secretary of the Central Committee with responsibility for agriculture in April 1985 and who from 1987 until 1989 held his secretaryship in conjunction with full membership of the Politburo.

Three more ambiguous appointments—with pluses and minuses from Gorbachev's point of view—were those of Vadim Medvedev, Boris Yeltsin, and Anatoly Dobrynin. Medvedev, who was extremely loyal to Gorbachev (and is still with him at the Gorbachev Foundation), was a serious economic reformer who, as noted earlier, was one of those who worked with him on his groundbreaking speech of December 1984. But on ideological and cultural issues, Medvedev was at times a liability for Gorbachev. Even on those matters a cautious reformer, rather than a reactionary, he failed to keep up with the rapidly changing public mood when he was the senior secretary responsible for ideology between 1988 and 1990.[81] The latter appointment was in many ways typical of the compromises in which Gorbachev engaged in order to prevent tensions between different wings of the Communist Party reaching extremes. Within the party bureaucracy the conservatives had a majority and they had not enjoyed the tug-of-war over ideology between Yakovlev and Ligachev between 1986 and 1988—all the less since, with Gorbachev leaning much more in Yakovlev's direction than Ligachev's, one supposed Marxist-Leninist verity after another had fallen by the wayside. As Medvedev's views fell between those of Yakovlev and Ligachev (although closer to the former than the latter), his appointment could be seen as a tactical master-stroke. Strategically, however, it was an error, for it came at a time when—as a result of decisions taken at the Nineteenth Party Conference (discussed in Chapter 6)—the rules of the game in Soviet politics were about to change and Yakovlev was better equipped than Medvedev to adapt to them.

The Yeltsin–Gorbachev relationship could be the subject of a monograph in itself, and can be discussed only briefly here (and at slightly greater length in Chapters 6 and 8). Yeltsin was very sensitive to status within the party hierarchy until shortly before his break with it. When he was offered the post of head of the Construction Department of the Central Committee in April 1985, his first thought was that the promotion was too modest. He headed the party organization in the heavily industrialized Sverdlovsk region, from where in the fairly recent past Andrey Kirilenko had become an influential Secretary of the Central Committee and Politburo member and from where Yakov Ryabov had been promoted straight from his Sverdlovsk First Secretaryship to a secretaryship of the Central Committee in 1976.[82] He was also very conscious of the fact that when Gorbachev had moved from his First Secretaryship of the Stavropol territorial party organization in 1978 and 'from a region, what's more, which in economic potential was considerably inferior to the Sverdlovsk region . . . *he* had been promoted to the rank of secretary of the central committee' (emphasis in original).[83] Yeltsin added: 'I think Gorbachev knew that this was on my mind, but neither of us gave any sign of it.'[84] Evidently Gorbachev was, indeed, aware of what Yeltsin was thinking, for in July 1985, just three months after his appointment as a department head, Yeltsin was promoted to a secretaryship of the Central Committee.

It is of some piquancy that Yeltsin was initially brought to Moscow at the bidding not so much of Gorbachev as of Ligachev, with whom Yeltsin was soon at loggerheads after he had become First Secretary of the Moscow Party organization later in the year. Gorbachev confirmed Ligachev's earlier assertion that this was so when, answering a question about Yeltsin in the summer of 1995, he said: 'I was, you know, very doubtful whether to take him or not.' But Ligachev, who had just returned from a visit to Sverdlovsk, had been most insistent that Yeltsin was just the person they needed.[85] Both Ligachev and Yeltsin were strong personalities, with a liking for getting their own way, and confrontation between them was not surprising. Perhaps both were bound to clash with Gorbachev also, sooner or later, although Chernyaev plausibly argued in a memorandum to Gorbachev that Ligachev had been the main culprit so far as the unhappy end of Yeltsin's Communist Party career was concerned.[86] After spending the second half of 1985 as a Secretary of the Central Committee, Yeltsin succeeded Grishin as First Secretary of the Moscow party organization in December of that year.[87] Yeltsin, in the first of his two volumes of reminiscences, assumes that Gorbachev was the prime mover in his appointment, but Vadim Medvedev is adamant that, just as it was Ligachev who played the major role in bringing Yeltsin from Sverdlovsk to Moscow, it was he who pushed for Yeltsin's appointment as Moscow First Secretary.[88] Although soon highly popular with Muscovites as a scourge of the local bureaucracy, Yeltsin made influential enemies among the bureaucrats whom he dismissed or who lived in fear of dismissal.

To his chagrin Yeltsin was not promoted from candidate to full membership of the Politburo, and Gorbachev had to listen to numerous complaints against him, not least from Ligachev, who at that time was the senior secretary supervising the party apparatus. Yeltsin between 1985 and 1987 saw himself as being in the advance guard of perestroika and by 1987 he felt he was entitled to more whole-hearted support from Gorbachev than he was given. This—as well as his open clashes with Ligachev and the party conservatives—was the background to his unscheduled speech at a Central Committee plenum in November 1987 which had been arranged to approve the draft of a speech Gorbachev would deliver at a solemn celebration of the Seventieth Anniversary of the Bolshevik Revolution.[89] By criticizing Ligachev openly, and Gorbachev by implication, on that occasion, Yeltsin began a process which led to the loss of his Moscow party post and candidate membership of the Politburo (although he remained a member of the Central Committee until his resignation from the Communist Party in 1990)—a train of events which in due course enhanced his national reputation and ended with his election to the presidency of Russia in June 1991.

The appointment of Dobrynin to a secretaryship of the Central Committee in March 1986 and to the headship of its International Department was not, in the longer run, as momentous an event as bringing Yeltsin to Moscow from the relative obscurity of Sverdlovsk turned out to be. But Dobrynin was a much better-known person than Yeltsin when he arrived in the Russian capital, for he had been a familiar figure on Soviet (as well as American) television news programmes as Ambassador of the USSR to Washington ever since 1962. (He had a baptism of fire in the United States, taking charge in Washington shortly before the Cuban missile crisis.) His whole career had been in the Ministry of Foreign Affairs and almost all of it concerned with America. Dobrynin had little interest in small countries and still less in small revolutionary movements in the Third World, which had been among the traditional concerns of the International Department. Although, for reasons which will be elaborated in Chapter 7, he never became the major player in Moscow politics which many Americans who had come to respect his professional competence in Washington expected, his appointment reflected Gorbachev's desire to give priority to improving state-to-state relations with Western countries and, in the first instance, with the United States. He also wished to see the International Department become a better source of alternative ideas on foreign policy than it had been under Ponomarev.

Sources of learning

As already noted, the International Department was not the homogeneous institution generally depicted in the specialist Western literature and it included highly capable individuals as well as its share of ideologues and of dead wood. It was a significant source of talent on which Gorbachev drew for his entourage and, almost by definition, it included people who knew something of the world outside the Soviet Union. Of those Gorbachev brought into his team, Chernyaev was the most important, although Grachev played an increasingly important role in the later stages of the Gorbachev era, and Vadim Zagladin, the First Deputy Head of the International Department of the Central Committee from 1975 until 1988 (and another alumnus of the *World Marxist Review* in Prague), became one of Gorbachev's advisers in 1988. Zagladin, however, had been too close to Brezhnev for too long to be entirely convincing as a new thinker, his intellectual agility notwithstanding.

The same could be said of Georgy Arbatov, the Director of the Institute of USA and Canada, although both he and his institute were able to put forward a wider range of policy proposals in the new atmosphere created by the succession of Gorbachev. The Russian Americanists both expanded the range of their vision and gained in influence during the first few years of Gorbachev's leadership.[90] Senior scholars at IMEMO had still easier access to Gorbachev and his circle, not least because Yakovlev had been its director from 1983 to 1985 and was succeeded by Yevgeny Primakov. The latter became an important Gorbachev adviser whose formal standing was enhanced by candidate membership of the Politburo in April 1989 and membership of Gorbachev's Presidential Council in March 1990. Primakov, almost alone among those who were close to Gorbachev, remained in a position of power in Yeltsin's team in the post-Soviet period (as head of Russia's Foreign Intelligence Service).

Of the three international institutes which (as already noted briefly in Chapter 1) offered influential advice both before the Gorbachev era and, with much greater frankness and efficacy, during it, the most radical was Oleg Bogomolov's Institute of Economics of the World Socialist System (from 1990 Institute of International Political and Economic Studies). Bogomolov himself, who had been rather less close to the pre-1985 leaderships than had the directors of IMEMO and the Institute of the USA and Canada, was also the boldest of the policy-oriented institute directors in those years—an early critic, for example, in a memorandum to the Brezhnev leadership of the Soviet military intervention in Afghanistan.[91] He was, furthermore, the most self-critical by 1990 for not doing more to oppose the system during the '18 years the party was headed by a dull-witted individual'.[92] This was despite the fact that his institute had been a haven for a higher proportion of capable and independent-minded social scientists than any other. That they were able to keep in touch with developments in the outside world (and especially Eastern Europe) through their professional work prepared them for their role as significant sources of new thinking during the Gorbachev years and as prominent political actors in the post-Soviet era.[93]

The Gorbachev era was the heyday of the *institutchiki*—the scholars who worked in policy-oriented research institutes.[94] A variety of institutes in addition to the three major Academy of Sciences ones with responsibility for international affairs played important advisory roles. They included the Institute of State and Law, the Central Economic-Mathematical Institute, the Institute of the International Workers' Movement, and the Institute of Social Sciences, which came under the jurisdiction of the International Department of the Central Committee.[95] Individual scholars in Soviet universities (especially the Law Faculties) and some institutes outside Moscow (most notably, the Institute of Economics of Industrial Production of the Siberian Academy of Sciences in Novosibirsk, from where the economist Abel Aganbegyan and the economic sociologist Tatyana Zaslavskaya were recruited, and the Sverdlovsk Juridical Institute[96]) also made significant contributions to the new political thinking, but the professionals in the Moscow institutes were in a privileged position.

From one point of view, their world was a small one. While some scholars from outside Moscow were part of reformist networks with good Moscow connections—Aganbegyan and Zaslavskaya are notable cases in point—most of the provincial social scientists and academic lawyers were at a big disadvantage in terms of access to the power-holders. The Muscovites, in contrast, knew each other and many of them had contacts with those in power, whether within the departments of the Central Committee or in Gorbachev's more immediate circle. From another point of view, they were part of a large world; the institutes were more numerous and employed far more people as researchers—divorced from teaching—than were to be found in any other capital city and far larger than could be supported by state funds in the post-Soviet era. If their size between 1985 and 1991 differentiated them from the post-Soviet scholarly world, their new-found freedom in those years distinguished them from their pre-1985 status. Until the Gorbachev era, the *institutchiki* had to engage in self-censorship and place limits on their criticisms and proposals for change if they were to survive. After 1985 they were able to cast off those shackles and were positively encouraged to produce innovative ideas. (Following the collapse of the Soviet Union in December 1991 the institutes found themselves, on the one hand, rather less consulted by the new Russian leadership than they had been by Gorbachev and his close colleagues and, on the other, losing many of their best, especially younger, scholars to the new commercial structures as inflation rose and salary differentials between the public and private sectors widened drastically.)

To recognize how important for Gorbachev and for policy innovation was the existence of many intelligent and relatively well-informed specialists in the research institutes should not, however, blind anyone to the crucial difference Gorbachev's coming to power made for *them*. Curiously, one author sees the Gorbachev accession and the activity of the international institutes (IMEMO, in particular) as *alternative* explanations of dramatic policy change in the second half of the 1980s rather than as *complementary* parts of a broader explanation which they clearly are.[97] To play down Gorbachev's importance in the 'foreign policy revolution' on the grounds that before late 1985 'there is no indication that he had developed a comprehensive conceptual or policy framework for foreign policy reform' is to miss several essential points.[98] In the Soviet political system it was inconceivable that an aspirant to the General Secretaryship could develop—in a process which would, after all, involve wide consultations—a comprehensive alternative foreign policy to that espoused by the existing General Secretary and the foreign policy establishment headed by Gromyko and Ponomarev. That, however, does not diminish the importance either of Gorbachev's mind-set or of his specific dissatisfaction with existing Soviet foreign policy, as compared with a Brezhnev, Andropov, Chernenko, Ustinov, Gromyko, Grishin, or Romanov. It was, moreover, not only Gorbachev's willingness to listen to specialist opinion from the institutes but also his appointments in the foreign policy realm which opened the way for the incorporation of new ideas in Soviet foreign policy and the elaboration within a very few years of a comprehensively different view of the Soviet Union's relations with the outside world than had prevailed hitherto.

In the sphere of external as well as internal policy, there was a clear linkage between Gorbachev's power of appointment and the power of fresh ideas with the latter, once the constraints on their expression were removed, demonstrating their capacity to overturn existing dogma and to alter political behaviour. Dismissals mattered no less than appointments, notably the removal of Gromyko (without, significantly, a word of public thanks—as Chernyaev noted—for his long service as Foreign Minister)[99] and Ponomarev, along with the aide to the General Secretary, Alexandrov-Agentov, and their replacement by Shevardnadze, Dobrynin, and Chernyaev. Gorbachev's promotion of Yakovlev was important for foreign policy as well as for domestic policy, for he was informally advising Gorbachev in both areas from the time of his return to Moscow from Ottawa in 1983 and, more formally, in external matters from 1988 when he became the Secretary of the Central Committee supervising international affairs.

Gorbachev undoubtedly learned much more than his predecessors from the specialists in the research institutes and it is worth asking why. There are, perhaps, four main reasons. In the first place, he was more conscious of the failures of Soviet society—not only in the economy, although that bulked large—and of Soviet foreign policy than any previous General Secretary (with the partial exception of Khrushchev), and perception of failure can be a very important stimulus to learning and fresh thought. Second, he had a more open mind than any of his predecessors as Soviet Communist Party leader and than all of the colleagues in the Politburo whom he inherited from Chernenko. Those scholars who took part in small-group meetings with him were well aware of this, although Gorbachev had to wait until he was in power before he could make what was, in effect, a plea for the opening-up of closed minds by promoting the need for 'new thinking'. Even so, there were many in the apparatus who reacted then in the same way as Boris Ponomarev, who declared that what was required was not 'new thinking' but 'correct thinking'—correct, that is to say, in traditional Marxist-Leninist terms.[100] But Gorbachev's new foreign policy appointments enhanced both the access to the leadership and the receptivity of those in charge of external policy to the ideas of the *institutchiki*.

A third reason (or complex of reasons) why Gorbachev learned more than his predecessors was that he had enormous energy, an insatiable appetite for work, and a great capacity for learning, which went together with an extremely retentive memory.[101] Even in his Stavropol days he liked working with scientists and scholars.[102] This continued to be the case when he arrived in Moscow and had a broader range of talents available to him. Already in Stavropol, too, local observers had seen plenty of evidence of the 'ebullient energy' which one of them, Boris Kuchmaev, suggests the future General Secretary inherited from his father.[103] This served him well during his years as Soviet leader, when the pressures were so diverse and intense that, in his own words, he 'lived through several lives'.[104] Drawing attention to Gorbachev's mental as well as physical energy, Alexander Yakovlev has described Gorbachev as a man 'whose imagination—in the good sense of the word, of course—is constantly working, constantly in action'.[105]

A fourth part of the explanation of Gorbachev's enhanced learning from the specialists he consulted was that, over and above the fact that they could speak to him more uninhibitedly than to his predecessors, their own views also developed during the second half of the 1980s. To some extent, it was a matter of being able to say in public (or to the leadership of the country) what they had previously felt secure in saying only to close friends, but there were few reform-minded party intellectuals whose ideas on what was either possible or desirable stood still during the Gorbachev era.[106] Their advocacy of ever-bolder and more far-reaching changes both in policy and of the system was useful for Gorbachev, given his own desire for change, but the evolution of their views also presented him with political problems. Thus, from 1990 many of them began to desert Gorbachev for the apparently more radically democratic camp of Yeltsin.

Learning from abroad

However important for Gorbachev were the ideas of party intellectuals from beyond the corridors of the Kremlin and the Central Committee, they were far from the only source of Gorbachev's political learning. The great significance of enlightened officials within the party apparatus has already been noted—for example, Chernyaev, Shakhnazarov, and, even more, Yakovlev (whom Gorbachev appointed head of the Propaganda Department of the Central Committee almost as soon as he became General Secretary). The influence of those officials both on Gorbachev and on party-state policy was more direct than that of the outside specialists. Yet there was another source of intellectual and political stimulus for Gorbachev, which was of comparable directness and at least as great importance. It is, furthermore, one which has received little attention in the Western specialist literature—namely, the contribution to the new political thinking made by Gorbachev's personal meetings with foreign leaders and by his visits abroad. These visits and meetings—beginning with Canada in 1983 and Britain in 1984, but which Gorbachev could conduct with a greater freedom from the time he became General Secretary in 1985—were on a different level from his earlier trips, when he had had no more than a tourist's eye view of the differences between Western Europe and the Soviet Union, important enough though that was for the development of his political consciousness. He told Shakhnazarov that it was his visits to Western Europe in the 1970s which had convinced him that the stories about capitalism having no future had nothing in common with reality.[107]

There was a clear discrepancy between the ideals of Communism in which Gorbachev had at one time genuinely believed[108] and the reality of the growing gap between Western Europe and the Soviet Union (to the disadvantage of the latter). There was likewise a tension between Gorbachev's desire to continue to think of himself as a Communist, or 'socialist' as that term had been understood in the Soviet Union, and his growing conviction of the necessity for greater political freedom and tolerance and of a substantial role for the market. The cognitive dissonance this produced led Gorbachev to seek to redefine socialism and to attempt to close the historic gap which had opened up between, on the one hand, Communists or Soviet-style socialists and, on the other, socialists who belonged to the very different social democratic tradition. For this reason two especially important foreign interlocutors for Gorbachev were Willy Brandt, the former German Chancellor and a Social Democrat, for whom Gorbachev (in common with many Russians) had the highest respect, and the Socialist (social democratic) Prime Minister of Spain, Felipe González—Gorbachev's favourite foreign leader among all the Prime Ministers or Presidents he met.[109]

Gorbachev, with his own intellectual journey in mind as much as Willy Brandt's, said of Brandt shortly after the latter's death: 'His principle was always to see the productive force of doubt. And doubt means a quest.'[110] Gorbachev has emphasized the extent to which he and Brandt saw eye to eye, and the transcript of one of their meetings bears witness to that.[111] Gorbachev explicitly states that Brandt's thought 'was one of the harbingers of the new thinking', and his great esteem for Brandt (whom he regarded as a personal friend) made it the easier for him to be influenced by his views.[112]

González, like Brandt, was living proof that outstanding politicians could make an enormous contribution to the consolidation of democracy in their country, following a period of authoritarian or (in the case of Hitler's Germany) totalitarian rule, that they could be totally committed to personal freedom and political tolerance, that they could preside over an essentially market economy and—still—consider themselves to be socialists. Andrey Grachev once asked Gorbachev which politician he felt closest to. His answer was unhesitating: González.[113] Gorbachev added that he also enjoyed friendly as well as professional relationships with George Bush, Helmut Kohl, Margaret Thatcher, and François Mitterrand, but González held first place in his affections.[114] Elaborating on Gorbachev's relationship with González, Grachev writes: 'He liked everything about the head of the Spanish government: his temperament, his openness, his youthfulness, his penchant for abstract, "philosophical" reflection. Above all, with his attachment to socialism González provided an "alibi" for the Gorbachevian "socialist choice".'[115] Gorbachev's discussions with González were always lengthy—some three to four hours—and included discourse on the nature of socialism.[116] In one such conversation—in Madrid in October of 1990—Gorbachev said that, if by socialism was meant a totalitarian regime in which people were no more than cogs in machines, then they were getting rid of such a socialism. But, he continued: 'For me socialism is a movement towards freedom, the development of democracy, the creation of conditions for a better life for the people, it is the raising of the human personality. In that sense I was and remain a socialist.'[117] In the course of that same conversation, González argued, among other things, that a market was the main instrument for achieving the socialist goals of better welfare, education, and pensions, although both he and Gorbachev agreed that there were areas of social life, including health care, which should not be subjected to the conditions of the market.[118]

Gorbachev saw González 'not only as an understanding partner but as an ideological ally' and he was, in the view of one who witnessed some of Gorbachev's conversations with González, very much influenced by him.[119] More recently Gorbachev has provided confirmation of that impact which had been discerned by a few of his closest advisers. He has said that González understood better than others what was happening in the Soviet Union and that as early as May 1986 the conversation they had in Moscow had a great influence on him. In their various meetings they had achieved a common understanding and good personal relations.[120] González is described by Gorbachev as 'an excellent man, blessed with many talents' and as 'a true democrat'.

Gorbachev's views developed also—although the influence was more indirect—in the course of discussions with Western leaders whose outlook was far removed from social democracy. This was true, for example, of his meetings with Margaret Thatcher, with whom he had vigorous arguments, although each respected the other.[121] The climate at their very first meeting in Britain in 1984, Gorbachev recalled in his memoirs, had been promising; they had cherished the contact and subsequently got along well, notwithstanding their sharp disagreements on many major issues. The Thatcher visit to the Soviet Union in late March and early April 1987 was particularly notable both for the length and the intensity of the discussions between the two leaders and for the further support which the British Prime Minister accorded Gorbachev personally. She spoke publicly in favour of perestroika while urging Gorbachev, both in private and public, to provide more evidence that the Soviet Union's foreign policy had changed. The accounts of the Thatcher–Gorbachev meetings given by Margaret Thatcher in *The Downing Street Years* and by Gorbachev's aide Anatoly Chernyaev in his diary-based memoirs tally remarkably well in respect both of the tone and the content of the exchanges.[122] One very important result of the meeting was that Gorbachev decided (and so informed a small group of his associates) that a much higher priority must be given to relations with Western Europe.[123]

Chernyaev observes that Gorbachev proceeded to put his own injunction into practice, the majority of his meetings with foreigners in 1987—a being with West European politicians. He adds: 'I think that [Gorbachev's] "personal" knowledge of Europe and understanding of its significance in the context of the policy of new thinking and his "bonding" in mutual trust with many influential European politicians made it easier for Gorbachev later to reach his historic decision—to agree to the unification of Germany.'[124] Gorbachev himself has written that he learned much from his participation in world politics, from co-operation 'with the greatest politicians of our times', and from personal contact with people who 'embodied the political and intellectual élite of the world'.[125] Chernyaev makes a similar point, writing that from the spring of 1986 Gorbachev had regular encounters with foreigners from a different 'intellectual tradition and political culture'. These meetings, he says, influenced the development of Gorbachev's 'new thinking'. He got to know another world and learned, in a favourite phrase of his, 'to reckon with reality'.[126]

Rethinking fundamentals

As head of the Soviet Communist Party Gorbachev got away with abandoning more central tenets of Leninist doctrine than would have seemed credible if anyone had suggested as much at the outset of his General Secretaryship. In some instances Gorbachev was the first person to break the taboo on using a concept which hitherto could be mentioned only pejoratively. In others he took up terms or ideas which had been brought into Soviet political discourse by the bolder specialists or political journalists. It is meaningless to compare the speed with which Gorbachev's views changed—and especially the timing of the public revelation of such changes—with that of any other actor on the Soviet political stage. He alone was General Secretary of the Soviet Communist Party and had he fallen from power at any time within the first four, and probably five, years of his leadership, it is virtually certain that the reform process, far from being speeded up, would have been put into sharp reverse. Party intellectuals, sitting in their studies, could become anti-Communists overnight—once, that is, Gorbachev had made the Soviet Union a freer and more tolerant place. So could the far from intellectual but undoubtedly courageous deposed party official Boris Yeltsin, whose removal from the leadership was a painful spur to agonizing reassessment of his beliefs and the start of a process which brought him into contact with former dissidents and other radicals. They helped to make his own critique of the Soviet system a more fundamental one (even though as President, in post-Soviet Russia, he was to surround himself with former Communists and to rely increasingly on people from the old party-state apparatus).

Gorbachev, in contrast with Yeltsin (before he assumed power) and with all others, had to combine his increasingly fundamental reappraisal of Soviet doctrine—including much that he himself had earlier taken for granted—with a political balancing act. He had to prevent those who were alarmed by the direction in which he was taking the country from regaining complete control of the levers of power which he had been gradually removing from their grasp. There were Soviet intellectuals who would sincerely, and even vehemently, have asserted before 1985 their commitment to the cause of socialism—although some had in mind a better or different 'socialism' from that which the Soviet Union had seen hitherto—who were, nevertheless, dismissive of Gorbachev by 1991 for clinging, as they saw it, to 'the socialist idea'. This was a failure to understand both the form and the substance of the change in Gorbachev's outlook which that term encapsulated. For Ligachev—from his relatively orthodox Communist position—it was a far cry from defining the Soviet Union as socialist and defending the *socialist system* to declaring allegiance to the much vaguer *socialist idea*.[127] Thus, the change of form was far from inconsequential, and the change of substance was even more significant.

A good many American commentators have joined with Gorbachev's Russian critics in happily writing him off as a conscious political transformer, or even as a serious innovator, because he did not renounce 'socialism' but, rather, professed allegiance to 'the socialist idea'. Such a strange misunderstanding of Gorbachev's political and intellectual journey has been much less in evidence in Britain, Germany, and Scandinavia, where social democracy has strong roots. In these countries there is a clearer understanding that 'socialism' has meant a great many different things in different places at different times as well as first-hand knowledge of the fact that the mainstream social democratic parties, far from representing a milder form of Bolshevism, embody a political outlook and practice totally at odds with it.[128] They are not, to borrow a felicitous phrase from the late Alec Nove—commenting, ironically, on Russian economists who had 'taken

to denouncing the West European welfare state in the crudest Chicago terms'—
'dangerous lefties who desire to travel the road to serfdom *slowly*'.[129]

Gorbachev did something more politically practicable than abandoning
'socialism' in a state in which the Communist Party held a monopoly of power—
and no less fundamental. He *redefined* it so radically that it became something
different in kind from Soviet-style socialism. In its later versions it could, perhaps, be criticized for being an excessively bland statement to which all reasonable people might subscribe, but that in itself distinguishes it sharply enough
from the Communist doctrine he inherited in 1985. Thus, for example,
Gorbachev said in 1992: 'I reached the conclusion that socialism is the quest for
social forms of life of humankind in which there would be present such important elements as individual freedom, private initiative and justice. Indeed, more
a code of morals.'[130] Meeting with writers and 'cultural workers' in the Kremlin
in November 1990, and speaking without a written text, Gorbachev told them
that he had just had 'a very long discussion' on the meaning of socialism with
Felipe González—'a convinced socialist who has . . . his own version, he has his
own thoughts'.[131] Gorbachev, for his part, said he continued to defend the idea
of socialism not just because he was General Secretary but because it meant
democracy and freedom.[132] Writing a year earlier (November 1989) in *Pravda*,
Gorbachev similarly declared: 'The idea of socialism, as we understand it today,
is above all the idea of freedom.'[133] This was about as far removed as it was possible to get from a description of what Soviet socialism had meant in practice and
equally distant, as a prescriptive emphasis, from what orthodox Soviet ideology
had chosen to stress. It is clear that Gorbachev could not have remained party
leader if he had renounced 'socialism'. It is equally clear that for psychological as
well as political reasons he had no wish to abandon the concept. What he
increasingly came to believe was that the West European 'democratic socialists'—and, for that matter, liberals—had done a far superior job of putting into
practice the ideals of socialism than had his Soviet predecessors.[134]

Gorbachev had taken Marx and Lenin seriously, not only at university (as
Mlynář has testified and as has been noted in Chapter 2) but also when a party
secretary in his native Stavropol region (as the Stavropol journalist Kuchmaev
has recorded).[135] More surprisingly, perhaps, he made time after he became
General Secretary to reread the later Lenin and the transcripts of the party congresses which took place while Lenin was still alive.[136] Gorbachev found inspiration in what he saw as Lenin's willingness to learn and develop and,
concretely, in his New Economic Policy launched in 1921.[137] He seemed
inclined to believe that Lenin had turned from being a revolutionary to a
reformer in his last years. Gorbachev had always had an idealized view of Lenin,
who in reality was scarcely less ruthless than Stalin, although—unlike Stalin—he
did not employ the weapon of terror against members of his own party. It was,
therefore, psychologically important for him—especially in the earliest years of
his General Secretaryship—to persuade himself that what he was doing was in
line with Lenin's thought before it had been distorted by Stalin. This was a
misperception, but it was one which was almost universally shared by Soviet
reformers (as distinct from such eminent dissidents as Andrey Sakharov and
Alexander Solzhenitsyn).

Gorbachev's former aide Georgy Smirnov (later Director of the Institute of Marxism-Leninism) coined the phrase, 'Not back to Lenin, but forward to Lenin'.[138] But illusions about Lenin went wider and deeper than that. Even Alexander Yakovlev said as late as 1989:[139]

> Perestroika requires a revival of genuine Leninism. Only now do we realize the full dimensions of Stalin's abandonment and distortion of Lenin's ideas, principles and practices. . . . Democracy, civil peace, and individual economic initiative were replaced by commands, repression, and bureaucracy. . . . And though Lenin did not live long enough to work out all the conceptions of socialism that we need, we are returning to his basic perceptions. In this sense, Lenin is a living adviser in our analysis of present-day problems.[140]

What this statement of allegiance to Lenin indicates is that the differences in the development of the political perceptions of Yakovlev and Gorbachev are by no means as clear-cut as has sometimes been suggested. Perhaps by this time Yakovlev was saying in public (even though the interview was for publication in a *Western* book) something he no longer believed in private (as happened on occasion with Gorbachev). But his words surely serve also as an illustration of the fact that it was difficult for any senior party reformer—and, much more so, the party leader—to accept that Lenin's project had been a gigantic mistake from the outset.[141]

In Gorbachev's case there was a real tension between his growing attraction to social democracy of the West European kind and the lip-service he still paid to Lenin. The way Gorbachev resolved this was to read into Lenin what he wanted to find and to project some of his own developing ideas on to him. That was not entirely a new phenomenon in the Soviet Union. There was a sense in which different people created their own 'Lenin', as could be seen in even some of the highly esoteric debates which took place before 1985.[142] Different versions of Leninist orthodoxy were promoted by different specialists and the divergences became much more overt and dramatic after 1985. Projecting on to Lenin what he wanted to be in Lenin's mind not only served a stress-reducing psychological function for Gorbachev but also, until 1989, an important political one. He had to be able to defend himself against his most dangerous enemies, who in those years were still conservative Communists with reason to suspect that Gorbachev had embarked on a non-Leninist course. Even with the population as a whole, reference to Lenin did a reformer no harm during the first four years of perestroika, for—as already noted—Lenin was still regarded by a majority of Russians in 1989 as the greatest person who had ever lived.

Gorbachev had ceased to be a Leninist without consciously rejecting Lenin. His growing acceptance of the kind of political beliefs held by a Brandt or González was quite incompatible with Leninism. West European 'democratic socialism' of the social democratic variety cannot meaningfully be placed in the same conceptual category either as Leninism or as the particular development of that doctrine which became known in the Soviet Union as Marxism-Leninism. In view of the historic rift between Communism and West European social democracy, that was already clear enough, but it has become still more obvious in the light of the evolution of the social democratic parties since the Second

World War which has reduced their distinctiveness as compared with other mainstream West European political parties and has brought about 'a progressive ideological assimilation between social democracy and liberalism'.[143]

Just as Molière's *bourgeois gentilhomme* was speaking prose without knowing it, so Gorbachev had begun to use the language of social democracy before he fully realized he was doing so. When he did recognize (in the course of 1988–9) that he felt closer to a social democratic variant of socialism than to Bolshevism,[144] no great point of substance was involved in the misplaced esteem he retained for Lenin personally.[145] Admittedly, that was to become more damaging to him in 1990–1, as the strength of radical democrats grew and Lenin— formerly a symbolic figure whom all could agree to admire—increasingly became a symbol of what divided the old and the new currents in Soviet society. For the General Secretary of the Central Committee of the Communist Party it was, of course, politically as well as psychologically more difficult to discard the Founding Father than it was for virtually anyone else.

Yet Gorbachev parted company with Leninism if not with his image of Lenin. It was not simply that he had developed an especial affinity with Western politicians whose similarity of outlook with the founder of the Soviet state could be conjured up only by the most fevered imagination. At least as important, he had consciously rejected from the earliest days of his leadership the *psychology* of Bolshevism—hostility to all compromise and coalition-building except as a temporary expedient; the view that the end justifies the means; and the attitude to political opponents of *kto kogo* (which may be freely translated as 'who will crush whom'). Indeed, both for Gorbachev and for the advisers closest to him 'neo-Bolshevism' became a term of abuse. It was applied not only to their hardline Communist enemies but to some of their opponents in the ranks of the radical democrats whose attitude to all who disagreed with them appeared to have something in common with Bolshevik psychology, however far removed were their policy goals from those of the Bolsheviks. Asked to define 'neo-Bolshevism', Gorbachev responded that it meant 'to act unconstitutionally, using violence, in the face of the law and democratic procedures'.[146] He also criticized the original Bolsheviks for not trying to 'unite the whole spectrum of democratic forces' after the February 1917 revolution: 'Instead, they moved towards a split, particularly with the left social-revolutionaries. They should have worked with them and the Mensheviks.'[147]

A conceptual revolution

Beginning with the aspiration to reform—rather than dismantle—the Soviet system, Gorbachev believed that getting rid of outworn dogma was a necessary part of the reformist and cleansing project. That was a central theme of his speech to the ideology conference in December 1984 which has already been touched upon in the previous chapter.[148] Many of the doctrinal changes he was to elaborate in the course of his first two years as General Secretary were given their first serious airing on that occasion. Indeed, some of them found more radical expression then than in his 1985 speeches after he had become General Secretary. It is probable that, with Chernenko ill and Gorbachev occupying the number two place in the party, he felt less inhibited in giving vent to his own opinions than in the earliest months of his General Secretaryship when every statement would be taken to represent the views of the leadership as a whole. Later, of course, Gorbachev's views were to move beyond the stage in his intellectual journey he had reached on the eve of attaining the top party post, and his removal of the old guard from the Politburo freed him from some of the political constraints upon expressing them. Nevertheless, the extent to which Gorbachev broke new ideological ground in December 1984 demonstrated considerable boldness, given that he was providing ammunition for his more conservative enemies.[149] Three concepts in particular, which came to have a special place in Soviet political discourse of the Gorbachev era, were emphasized in that speech several months before Gorbachev succeeded Chernenko. These were: perestroika, acceleration (*uskorenie*), and glasnost.

Two of the three were to remain points of reference over the next six years, although their meanings were broadened and radicalized during that time. The exception was *uskorenie*, which, excessively employed in the first two to three years after Gorbachev became General Secretary, fell into disuse. The notion of economic acceleration (which according to Nikolay Ryzhkov had its origins in a commission chaired by his predecessor, Tikhonov, during Chernenko's General Secretaryship)[150] had virtually disappeared by the time of the Nineteenth Party Conference in the summer of 1988. Ryzhkov was, and remained, an advocate of socio-economic 'acceleration', but he argues that *uskorenie* (not simply the term but any possibility of translating it into practice) was killed off by the 'senseless political acceleration' which came to assume a higher priority for Gorbachev.[151]

Certainly the term was dropped by Gorbachev in 1988, the very point at which he began to move well beyond any kind of political reform which had been seen in the Soviet Union hitherto and set in motion more basic changes which were to alter the character of the political system fundamentally. At the outset of the Gorbachev era *uskorenie* had connotations of 'getting the country moving again', following the now openly admitted 'stagnation' of the later Brezhnev era. But three years on it was becoming politically counter-productive not only because there was little sign of economic acceleration taking place but also because it was becoming clearer that such acceleration was, in principle, incompatible with the transition from a 'command economy' to one in which the market had a large role to play. Economic indicators were likely to get worse before they got better in such a period of dislocation. (Gorbachev, it should be said, during the years he spoke of 'acceleration', usually went out of his way to emphasize that this meant qualitative change—for example, increased labour productivity rather than simply raising output by meeting overall quantitative targets in the old Soviet way. Indeed, when a conference was held on 11 June 1985 at which many of the materials prepared for the aborted Central Committee plenum—the politics of which were discussed in Chapter 3—were finally presented, its stated theme was 'problems of acceleration of scientific-technological progress'.[152]) It would appear that the last time Gorbachev used the word 'acceleration' in one of his speeches was in April 1988.[153]

Of the three key terms in Gorbachev's speech of December 1984 the one which was to serve as an overall conceptual umbrella for the reform process launched the following year was perestroika—best translated as reconstruction or restructuring but about to enter many languages other than Russian as an untranslated neologism. This was a word for which Gorbachev had long had a liking and which he made use of well before his collaboration with Alexander Yakovlev began. It had cropped up in his speeches and writings of the 1970s and early 1980s, often in the context of the need for 'psychological restructuring' on the part of those engaged in economic activity at all levels.[154] By the time of his December 1984 speech, however, the meaning had shifted. 'Today,' Gorbachev declared then, 'one of the important issues on the agenda is a perestroika of the forms and methods of running the economy.'[155] Gorbachev was no longer talking only about psychological adjustment, but about structural change, albeit still in the context of the economic system. By the time of his June 1985 speech to the conference on science and technology, the scope of perestroika has become more far-reaching: 'An acceleration of scientific and technological progress insistently demands a profound perestroika of the system of planning and administration, of the entire economic mechanism. Without all of that, what we are talking about today may remain only pious wishes.'[156]

In a speech to an audience of workers in the Russian industrial city of Togliatti on 8 April 1986 Gorbachev greatly broadened the meaning of perestroika.[157] Indeed, Vadim Medvedev has observed that this was the first use of perestroika 'in the all-embracing sense' which was to become familiar both in the Soviet Union and the outside world.[158] In this speech, Gorbachev said that perestroika had to occur everywhere 'in each work collective, in management, in party and state organs, including the Politburo and the government'.[159] By the January plenary session of the Central Committee in 1987—which launched serious *political* reform—perestroika had still more clearly become a concept connoting significant reform of the entire Soviet system. Indicating that many more changes were in store, Gorbachev said that perestroika was only just beginning and linked its further progress with that of democratization, both the 'further democratization of Soviet society' and greater intra-party democracy. Significantly, he said that the electoral system could not remain untouched by perestroika.[160] Speaking one month after that plenum, Gorbachev adverted to the important question 'troubling us all'—how to make perestroika irreversible. The answer was to extend it to all spheres—economic, social, political, administrative, and spiritual, and to engage the whole people in that task. There was only one path to take to achieve this, that of a 'broad democratization of Soviet society'.[161]

The term perestroika was later to be dismissed as absurd by some Western writers who welcomed the collapse of the Soviet system they had never expected to live to see and by many within the post-Soviet Russian leadership who wished to distinguish their own reforms from Gorbachev's.[162] But such wisdom of hindsight merely obscures a failure, whether involuntary or wilful, to understand the political context of 1985 and to appreciate the advantages of a concept which, amazingly aptly, served the cause of changing the Soviet system during the first three to four years after Gorbachev became General Secretary. At the time Gorbachev became leader even the word 'reform' was taboo. Ever since Kosygin's

economic reform of 1965 had been buried in the wake of the more radical political and economic reforms in Czechoslovakia in 1968, Soviet economic reformers had to use such euphemisms as 'the perfecting of the economic mechanism'
if they wished to give voice to any mildly reformist thoughts in the mass media.
It was Gorbachev himself who broke this taboo in his speech to the Twenty-
Seventh Party Congress in February 1986. Speaking of the economy, he not only
used the word 'reform', but said that 'a radical reform is necessary'.[163]

Precisely because it did not carry ideological baggage—not even a direct association with the 'reformism' against which the Communist revolutionary tradition had defined itself—perestroika was an inspired choice of term with which
to begin the reform of the Soviet system. Its ambiguity and vagueness (while they
could at times pose problems for Gorbachev as well as for his conservative opponents) initially smoothed the path of reform, for any attempt to change radically
the political and economic system was bound to impinge upon the interests of
powerful institutions and individuals. Perestroika, however, could be readily
accepted even by those whose interests it was subsequently to undermine, for it
was open to interpretation as a mild tinkering with the 'superstructure' (in
Marxist terms) of the Soviet state. At the other extreme, it could be viewed as a
reconstruction of the system from the foundations up—*constructing anew* the
political and economic system. For Gorbachev himself perestroika at the outset
meant more than the first of these connotations but much less than the second.
By 1987, accepting that 'perestroika is a word with many meanings', he wrote
that 'the one which expresses its essence most accurately . . . is revolution', since
the 'qualitatively new' and radical changes which the Soviet Union required constituted 'a revolutionary task'.[164] These words, written for Gorbachev's book
Perestroika in the summer of 1987, retain their ambiguity, and that work was very
far from being Gorbachev's last word on the kind of changes which were
required in his country. By the following year he was talking with his closest
allies about something still closer to a fundamental reconstruction of the system,
although sometimes his words in public (especially during his ill-fated tactical
retreat in the winter of 1990–1) belied this. Moreover, the change of goals and of
meaning was veiled by linguistic continuity: the Soviet Union was still pursuing
'perestroika'.

The ambiguity of the term meant that in the earliest years of Gorbachev's
leadership everyone could be for perestroika—from the editor of *Pravda*, Viktor
Afanasev, and the even more conservative editor of *Sovetskaya Rossiya*, Valentin
Chikin (nominated for that post by Alexander Yakovlev, as he later ruefully
admitted),[165] to the former dissident and purest of liberals, Andrey Sakharov. By
the time the majority of officials within the party and government bureaucracy
and the greater part of the army and KGB officer corps realized that perestroika
was deeply damaging to their institutional interests, it was almost too late.
Gorbachev could still have been overthrown, but the costs were growing higher
in each of the first four years of his General Secretaryship. These were years, as
noted in Chapter 1, when Gorbachev was the most popular politician in the
country, and by 1989 many of the old guard had been removed from positions
of power, while popular participation in politics had been qualitatively
enhanced with the introduction of contested elections.

The third key concept introduced by Gorbachev in December 1984 was glasnost. While best translated as openness, or transparency, the term lends itself to more than one interpretation. It could, as Alec Nove for one pointed out, 'mean that party and government should act more openly, explain and publish more' without of itself implying that 'unofficial voices will be heard'.[166] Alternatively, it could be interpreted to mean something close to freedom of information and freedom of speech. Dissidents, including the most famous of them—Sakharov and Solzhenitsyn—had in the past called for glasnost, even though a much earlier dissident, the nineteenth-century radical Nikolay Chernyshevsky, writing during the reign of Alexander II, said: '*Glasnost* is a bureaucratic expression, a substitute for freedom of speech.'[167]

In the more restrictive sense—and without any serious intention of translating the notion into practice—glasnost was advocated even by Leonid Brezhnev as long ago as 1974. In an 'election' speech that summer, Brezhnev said that 'the raising of the political culture of the workers and the widening of glasnost in the work of party, soviet, and economic organs' had become especially topical.[168] Gorbachev is also on record as having spoken of the need for glasnost as early as 1974.[169] At that time his formulation was only a small improvement on Brezhnev's. The term even appeared in Article 9 of the 1977 Soviet Constitution, attracting little attention abroad and having no practical effect at home.[170] When in December 1984 Gorbachev took up the notion of glasnost more seriously and turned it into a broader conception, he did so in the context of emphasizing also the need for 'unity of word and deed'. While his 1984 formulation was still some way short of freedom of speech, it was an advance on what had been heard before from Soviet leaders, reflecting the development of Gorbachev's views over the previous decade which had included his first important visits to the West and also the simple fact that as number two to the dying Chernenko he was less constrained than he had been earlier. On 10 December he said: 'An inalienable component of socialist democracy is glasnost. Broad, timely, and frank information is testimony of faith in people, of respect for their minds and feelings and for their capacity to work things out themselves in one situation or another.'[171]

The most important point about according glasnost a central place in the fresh thinking Gorbachev was already beginning to espouse publicly in 1984, and which developed apace from 1986, was that this was a facilitating concept. It was one which, given the necessary level of sincerity of the section of the party leadership advocating it, enabled writers and journalists to push its limits ever wider. (At the highest levels, the real supporters were only—but crucially—Gorbachev, Yakovlev, and Shevardnadze, and even they initially saw glasnost more as a gift from above than as a right which could be asserted from below.) What the concept came to connote changed in the course of the Gorbachev era, so that—following the first session of the Congress of People's Deputies in the spring of 1989, when all manner of previously forbidden views were aired on live television—glasnost had evolved in meaning to such an extent that it came to be either synonymous with or (better) superseded by freedom of speech and publication.[172] But even from 1987 a 'glasnost from below' had begun to develop in which, increasingly, what was published in the press or monthly journals was not necessarily what the party leadership wanted to hear.

Gorbachev even introduced the term 'democratization' in December 1984, arguing the need to give a 'new impulse to the democratization of our social and economic life'.[173] This was, however, not yet the kind of democratization of the political system he was to begin to advocate in 1987–8; the emphasis was, rather, on a greater 'democracy' at the work-place, extending the rights of work collectives, and on enhancing the role and significance of such 'social organizations' as the Komsomol and trade unions.[174] In an earlier section of the same speech, Gorbachev called for a 'widening and deepening of socialist democracy'.[175] But 'socialist democracy' was a traditional Soviet term which distinguished *their* kind of democracy from *bourgeois* democracy. Gorbachev's formulation was not, of course, a complacent one. What he had in mind then was a need to reactivate the soviets and to regenerate party committees and primary organizations, so that the full-time party *apparatchiki* did not continue to usurp most serious decision-making. But this was limited reform within the boundaries of the old system.[176]

To argue that the Soviet Union was in need of further 'democratization' was more novel, but it was not until the January plenary session of the Central Committee in 1987 that 'the further democratization of Soviet society' was presented as the most urgent task facing the Communist Party. The concrete political reforms, and Gorbachev's struggle to achieve them, is one of the themes of Chapter 6, but in the present context what is important is that, following his passing reference to 'democratization' in 1984, his extension of the scope and significance of that concept within two years of becoming General Secretary offered enormous opportunities to radical reformers. Under the rubric of 'democratization'—which now had the imprimatur of the General Secretary—many hitherto scarcely imaginable proposals for political change could be contemplated.

Conceptual change is an important species of political innovation in any society and immeasurably more important in a system, such as the Soviet one, in which all political actions were required to adhere to an officially sanctified ideology than in a liberal democracy. There could be esoteric argument within the Soviet ideology and different leaders would emphasize different parts of Marxism-Leninism at different times, putting it on occasion in the service of pragmatism. Even if, however, Soviet leaders had traditionally manipulated the ideology while expressing undying fealty to it, Marxism-Leninism also placed limits on their freedom of action and, still more, upon the categories in which they thought. Leninism could be selectively codified as Marxism-Leninism by its ideological guardians under the watchful eye of the party leadership. It could be bent in this direction or that, but there were certain concepts which were incompatible with it—and which before Gorbachev became General Secretary were almost literally unthinkable within the ruling circles. In Communist states, and especially one such as the Soviet Union where there were many true believers, it was even more blatantly true than in Western systems that the beliefs and actions of political actors are 'partly constituted by their concepts' and language is for them 'an arena of political action'.[177]

With this in mind, it is difficult to overestimate the importance of the fact that Gorbachev introduced into Soviet political discourse concepts which undermined both the traditional ideological and institutional pillars of the system and which were, indeed, much more revolutionary in the Soviet context than 'perestroika'. Of these concepts the most crucial is *pluralism*, for it was to the extent that the Soviet political system became pluralist that it had become different in kind from what it had been for seventy years, notwithstanding the many other changes which took place during that time.

So many Soviet theoreticians—with the party leaders joining in from time to time—had anathematized the concept of pluralism that a politician as interested in ideas as Gorbachev could not but have been aware that he was opening up an entirely new range of possibilities when he broke the taboo on using the term (other than as one of abuse). So long as 'pluralism' was automatically rejected as an alien and hostile concept in the Soviet Union, Gorbachev's reforms—including, not least, glasnost—were especially vulnerable to attack. Becoming the first Soviet person to use the term pluralism, other than pejoratively—in remarks intended for, and duly reported by, the mass media—Gorbachev spoke in July 1987 of the need for a 'socialist pluralism [*plyuralizm sotsialisticheskiy*], so to speak' within Soviet newspapers, so that they would not be dominated by narrow cliques but would be open to broader representation.[178] Even the General Secretary had to smuggle 'pluralism' into a speech to representatives of the mass media, writers, and artists almost surreptitiously, and he was well aware that it would be seized upon and developed by many of those present. Gorbachev continued to use the term, but until February 1990 he qualified it as 'socialist pluralism' or a 'pluralism of opinion',[179] Logically, his first public acceptance of *political pluralism*—which implies the freedom to organize both interest groups and political parties—came in the speech he delivered to the Central Committee of the Communist Party in February 1990 advocating the removal of the article of the Soviet Constitution which accorded that party the leading role in the political system.[180]

Once Gorbachev had either introduced new concepts or voiced his approval for them, they increasingly took on a life of their own, for Gorbachev's institutional changes as well as his ideological innovation had deprived the Soviet authorities of the means of maintaining their former control over what could be publicly said or published. This greatly irked even Gorbachev at times and, when he was under especially intense pressure from the conservative forces still deeply embedded in the Soviet establishment, he could castigate radical democrats or nationalists in terms which contradicted the new concepts whose entry into political discourse and the political struggle he had made possible. Not all of Gorbachev's zig-zags, whether in political appointments or in political language, were efficacious, but given the intense cross-pressures to which he was subjected, they were not entirely avoidable.

As the occupant of the highest office within the system and as the system's most powerful critic, as Pope and Luther, Gorbachev sometimes genuinely sought centre ground when under attack from opposite directions (especially in the winter of 1990–1) and at other times merely purported to be a centrist while moving a radically reformist agenda forward. Gorbachev's public political language—and, to a significant but decreasing extent, his thinking—was a mixture of the old and the new, but since his predecessors' thinking consisted of the old and the old, it was the novel ideas which must be accorded weight. That is especially so since words once uttered (even if, on occasion, contradicted) could not be withdrawn, and in the first few years of his leadership, when the system remained such that a General Secretary's words counted for more than anyone else's, Gorbachev was to demonstrate anew the power of ideas.[181]

Speaking about change in the Soviet Union, Gorbachev more than once emphasized the need for a process which 'was revolutionary in its essence but evolutionary in its tempo'.[182] In this sense, what happened in the realm of ideas between 1985 and 1991 was, indeed, both evolutionary and revolutionary. Concepts which were bold in the Soviet context of 1986 or 1987, albeit hardly revolutionary in conception, had by 1990–1 turned standard Soviet doctrine on its head. Thus, support for a 'socialist rule-of-law state' became advocacy simply of a state based upon the rule of law. Support for a 'socialist market' gradually became advocacy of a 'market economy' and in the case already highlighted—in some ways the most dramatic break with Marxism-Leninism of all—promotion of the idea of 'socialist pluralism' or a 'pluralism of opinion' became acceptance of 'political pluralism'.[183]

What generally happened was that Gorbachev would introduce or endorse a concept which had previously been banished from Soviet political discourse, but within his first few years as General Secretary he would attach the adjective 'socialist' to it. Reform-minded intellectuals would seize on the concepts and elaborate them; by 1988 the more radical among them were dropping the 'socialist' qualifier. Such instances illustrate a more general point made by the historian Keith Michael Baker: 'language can say more than any individual actor intends; meanings can be appropriated and extended by others in unanticipated ways'.[184] That statement itself has to be qualified in the Soviet context. Until the Gorbachev era, control 'from above' over the language of politics, while not absolute, was sufficient to impose strict limits on the ways in which ideas, within an ideocratic state, could be interpreted. It may be that 'meanings (and those who depend upon them) are always implicitly at risk',[185] but within unreformed Communist systems the leaderships succeeded in minimizing those risks. It was the relative and growing political tolerance within the Soviet Union after 1985 which compressed the normal historical period in which concepts change their meaning radically.

Even in his choice of terms, however, Gorbachev was trying to avoid the constraints upon thought as well as on speech involved in sticking to the traditional Soviet vocabulary. It is especially noteworthy that the new key concepts introduced by Gorbachev or those close to him did not, in fact, come from the Marxist-Leninist lexicon. That is clearly true, for example, of perestroika, glasnost, democratization, pluralism, a rule-of-law state, checks and balances, the non-pejorative use of market, even acceleration. Indeed, many of them had been regarded by Leninists as specifically bourgeois notions. What was striking about Gorbachev was not only that, having launched many ideas alien to Marxism-Leninism, but with a 'socialist' or other qualification, he would take them up two years later in their revised form with all reservations removed. It was also that, even when he used the adjective 'socialist', this was nothing like as restrictive as it would have been in the past, for—as we have seen—Gorbachev's adoption of the rather vague term 'the socialist idea' represented at the same time a move away from attachment to 'the socialist system' as a specific economic and political order developed over seven decades in the Soviet Union. Indeed, by 1988 at the latest (for he was already beginning to have such heretical thoughts in 1987) he had reached the conclusion—which he regarded as in no way incompatible with adherence to 'the socialist idea'—that it was necessary to *change the system*.[186]

Chapter 5

Gorbachev and Economic Reform

GORBACHEV's two major failures were in economic reform and in resolution of the 'national question' in the Soviet Union. Yet this statement has to be qualified by the observation that the problems involved were so intractable that any idea that a new leader could have come along and 'solved' them would be the height of naïvety. In so far as Gorbachev had choices as well as severe constraints upon his freedom of action in these areas, they were extraordinarily hard choices (however simple they may have appeared to some of his armchair critics). Both economic reform, on the one hand, and union-republican and nationality relations, on the other, were spheres in which Gorbachev was subject to sharply conflicting pressures. The contradictory demands came from powerful institutional interests and social forces which had the capacity, advertently or inadvertently, to bring the entire process of reform to an end well before the abortive coup of August 1991.

Thus, although Gorbachev made significant mistakes in both of these areas, there were more serious errors he avoided that could have led to an earlier show-down and the likelihood of a return to Soviet Communism of a traditional and thoroughly oppressive type. Too seldom, Andrey Grachev remarks, is the question posed: how many possible *coups d'état* did Gorbachev manage to avoid in the years before the unsuccessful August 1991 *putsch*?[1] For the greater part of Gorbachev's time as Soviet leader, there would have been no need for any tanks—'a secret vote at the highest echelon of the party leadership would have sufficed'.[2] Of these two areas of understandable failure, it is to the vicissitudes of economic reform that I now turn, for the nationalities issue is discussed in later chapters (especially Chapter 8).

The tension between two contradictory aims—improving the system and constructing the system on different principles—was especially acute in the economic sphere. Whereas, with institutional change in its political dimension it was possible to move from reformist to transformative change almost imperceptibly—and to do so, moreover, during Gorbachev's first five years, with strong popular support—the economic system went from bad to worse under the weight of this contradiction. The resultant shortages and frustrations contributed substantially to Gorbachev's rapidly declining support during the greater part of his last two years as Soviet leader.

A command economy and a market economy operate on fundamentally different principles. All attempts to find a half-way house between an administered economy with its central plans and a market economy governed by the law of supply and demand have proved fruitless. That is not, of course, to say that there are (or should be) 'perfect market economies' any more than the Soviet Union had a 'perfect command economy'. Market economies in Western countries are regulated and market principles are not generally extended to all spheres of social life. Equally, not all economic activity in the Soviet Union depended on political decisions or on central planning. There were areas, ranging from private tuition in teachers' own homes to the sale of agricultural produce from peasants' private plots, where market forces rather than planners' preferences were the determinants of economic transactions. Yet, experience thus far suggests that an economic system must be *predominantly* one thing or the other—either essentially a command economy or essentially a market economy, with the latter having proved to be the more efficient.

While the command economy never worked well, it did, however, work after a fashion so long as the Soviet regime was either totalitarian or highly authoritarian. When there was fear of repression and the Communist Party and ministries had real power and authority, there was sufficient responsiveness to instructions from above for goods to be produced and exchanged and economic growth to occur. But once the fear of repression was removed and the institutional supports of the command economy were undermined, production fell, hoarding increased, and shortages grew.[3] Gorbachev's dilemma was the greater inasmuch as, once he realized that he had to move to a system in which the market was the main regulator of economic life, he needed to deny the Communist Party its economic functions and controls. Yet he still needed the Communist Party as the instrument of implementation of policy in the absence of any executive organs other than the economic ministries.

There are two further general points worth stressing at the outset, although their validity will only become clearer in the course of this chapter and the next. The first is that, since Gorbachev was not a dictator and as his reforms and innovations were resisted every inch of the way, what is sometimes identified as 'Gorbachev's policy'—in particular, 'Gorbachev's economic policy'—may be a misnomer, since neither the policy settled upon at any given time nor (still less) its outcome was necessarily what Gorbachev wished to see. There were areas where he lost a number of battles or in which seeming victory at what appeared to be the point of authoritative decision (whether within the Politburo or in the Central Committee) was turned into defeat through his lack of control over the execution of policy.

Second, and more specifically, these points are linked to the complexity of the institutional networks and the strength of the bureaucratic agencies whose support was necessary for the implementation of policy in particular spheres. It is no accident that it was Soviet *foreign* policy which Gorbachev was able to transform most comprehensively, for here (and the point is elaborated in Chapter 7) he was himself able to be a key executant of policy in numerous meetings with his chief-executive counterparts in other countries (including nine summit meetings with Presidents of the United States). But more important, there was only one major Soviet agency for the execution of foreign policy, the Ministry of Foreign Affairs,[4] and that Gorbachev was able to turn into a relatively pliable instrument of his policy preferences by the appointment of Eduard

Shevardnadze, a like-minded ally, as Minister. The other area in which Gorbachev had great success, notwithstanding fierce resistance (as Chapters 6, 8, and 9 make clear), was in political reform, leading on to transformative change of the political system. Here the institutional obstacles to fundamental innovation were far greater than in foreign policy-making, but the introduction of glasnost and its development into freedom of speech, followed by the crucial decision in 1988—duly implemented in 1989—to introduce contested elections, were in themselves decisive breakthroughs which also altered the balance of forces in favour of more far-reaching change.

It was in the attempted radical reconstruction of the economic system that Gorbachev encountered the most effective resistance on the part of agencies whose co-operation was necessary both for the everyday running of the economy and for the implementation of reform. This came both from the ministerial network and from the Communist Party *apparat*. Stephen Whitefield, the author of the major book on the Soviet Union's industrial ministries (indeed, the *only* one to analyse at length their place in the structure of power), points to the unavailing attempts of successive political leaders to make these ministries as subordinate to the top party leadership in practice as they were in theory.[5] Writing about the pre-Gorbachev era, Alexander Yakovlev put the same point succinctly: 'The party apparatus and the apparatus of coercion retained levers sufficient to curb any particular economic official but not the economic apparatus as a whole.'[6] For Whitefield 'the ability of the ministries to control the reform process, even when directed by energetic and serious reformers like Gorbachev and his entourage rather than the compromised and weak politicians of the Brezhnev era is final proof of their centrality within the old system . . .'.[7] The industrial power they commanded 'severely constrained the politicians, and radical anti-ministerialism was both difficult and dangerous' for all who embarked on it.[8] Through their continued ability to control the implementation stage of the policy process, the ministries were able, Whitefield argues, to defeat Gorbachev's attempted economic reform, as they had defeated previous, less comprehensive reformers before him.[9]

The Communist Party *apparat* was scarcely more responsive to the demands for economic reform than the ministries. Ligachev made no secret of his hostility to the market and his opposition—as the person in charge of the party organization and of ideology (along with Yakovlev, although as a Politburo member earlier than Yakovlev, Ligachev was initially the senior ideological partner)— counted for a great deal. It fully matched the views and interests of a majority of party officials at lower levels where party officials played, among other parts, the role of fixers and economic brokers.[10] It was entirely typical that, among the earliest contacts—co-operative and friendly at that time—in the 1970s of Yeltsin and Gorbachev as First Secretaries respectively of the industrial Sverdlovsk region and the agricultural Stavropol territory should be telephone conversations whereby, in the absence of a market, they had to attempt to compensate for the shortcomings of the Soviet economic system. 'Quite often', Yeltsin noted, 'we needed to extend each other a helping hand: metal and timber from the Urals, food products from Stavropol.'[11] Regional party leaders were reluctant to give up these functions—which, given the starting-point of an irrational economic system—were among the more useful jobs they did and which, if performed successfully, could enhance their local prestige. Moreover, their unwillingness to abandon intervention in economic decision-making was the less surprising, since even in the perestroika era they 'continued to be held responsible by higher organs for the economic performance of their region'[12] as well as being blamed for shortages by their local populations, who felt increasingly able to voice their grievances.

Acceptance of the power of these entrenched interests may raise the objection that in the economic sphere, as in the Soviet system generally, reform was not what was needed; what was required was the replacement of one system by another. Whatever the merits of such a proposition in principle, it was irrelevant to the real world of Soviet politics. In the first place, Gorbachev—and, for that matter, even the most enlightened of his advisers—initially *believed* the system was reformable and one of his first acts as leader was to put economic reform on the political agenda; that is part of the reality that cannot be wished away, even with the benefit of hindsight. Second, there was *no other way* than through reform of the existing system that its transformation could *begin*. Not only the industrial ministries but (more immediately threatening for a General Secretary) the Communist Party leadership and the party apparatus, the military, and the KGB were committed to the command economy and powerfully opposed to anything smacking of capitalism. No Soviet leader—even if one were to make the highly implausible assumption that his aim from the outset was to build capitalism—could begin other than with a piecemeal attack on the power of existing economic institutions and by attempting to change attitudes to the market. Third, reform is not a single and for-all action but a *process*[13] and, among other things, a learning process, in which there is both collective and individual learning, with different lessons being drawn by different political actors.[14] It was entirely possible, in principle, that *reform* of the economy could have led to the *replacement* of the Soviet economic system by a different and market-oriented system, as half-measures failed to work and the system began to combine some of the disadvantages—rather than the advantages—of both the command economy and the market economy. Indeed, in terms of the evolution of ideas, such learning occurred, although translating the ideas into practice proved much more difficult. In the last two to three years of the Soviet era there was also some spontaneous adaptation by many existing party-state institutions as they began to hedge their bets on the future of the system and to protect their privileges and resources. Thus, as controls from above loosened, state bureaucrats began to create new and, with some distortions, market-oriented structures—in particular a multiplicity of banks which became instruments of the defence and, indeed, the enhancement of their economic interests.[15] Thus, even in the relatively unsuccessful sphere of economic reform, the extent of change in the Soviet Union by 1990–1 was far greater than had been predicted at the beginning of perestroika.

Most Western observers had very modest expectations in 1985–6 and did not expect Gorbachev to venture much beyond technocratic reform while continuing to reject market-oriented change.[16] The precedents, it was repeatedly pointed out, were not propitious. The history of economic reform in the Soviet Union was one of shattered dreams and of hopes which were all too soon to be deceived.

R
Conclusion

(Indeed, some might wish to extend that generalization not just to economic reform but to reform more broadly and to the whole of Russian—not just Soviet—history.) But the Soviet record in economic reform was plain for all to read. From the New Economic Policy of the 1920s, when Lenin made substantial concessions to the market, to Khrushchev's attempts to remove the bureaucratic dead-weight of the ministries from the Soviet economic system once and for all, to the 'Kosygin reform' of 1965, which made modest concessions to market ideas by making respectable, for example, the concept of profit, the result was the same. The policies were abandoned or reversed and a centralized Soviet economy continued its attempt to defy the law of supply and demand.

New stimuli to reform

It was the Kosygin reform and the Soviet experience of the later 1960s which was most frequently invoked as a reason why economic policy under Gorbachev was unlikely to produce anything more than minor change in the economic mechanism. But in many respects the Kosygin–Gorbachev analogy was a flawed one. There were at least four major differences between the second half of the 1960s and the second half of the 1980s which improved the chances of far-reaching economic reform being undertaken in the Gorbachev era.

First, the objective economic trends were much worse by the 1980s than they were in 1965. Gorbachev himself indicated quite early on in his General Secretaryship the stimulus this had provided to reform. In his book *Perestroika*, published in 1987, he wrote: 'In the last fifteen years the national income growth rates had declined by more than a half and by the beginning of the eighties had fallen to a level close to economic stagnation.'[17] Even the official Soviet statistics showed an annual growth rate which was declining significantly from one decade to the next between the 1950s and the first half of the 1980s, with an average rate of growth of net material product of 3.5 per cent between 1981 and 1985 as compared with 6.6 per cent for 1961–5. The CIA estimates suggested a steeper decline—from 5.1 per cent average growth of gross national product in 1961–5 to 1.9 per cent in 1981–5.[18] However, the official Soviet (and even CIA) figures disguised the depth of the problem. Abel Aganbegyan, Gorbachev's most influential economic adviser in the earliest years of perestroika, after noting how Soviet statistics took insufficient account of hidden price increases through changes in the range of products (which became dearer but without a corresponding improvement in quality), observed that there was, in effect, 'a zero growth rate' between 1981 and 1985.[19]

The impressive work of the Latvian-born economist Girsh Khanin, whose fundamental challenge to official Soviet statistics had kept him on the fringes of the Soviet economics profession until the Gorbachev era, suggests that there was already *negative* growth in Brezhnev's last years, 1979–82.[20] (This , however, was not the stimulus to Andropov's minor and Gorbachev's major reform efforts, for the leadership themselves were unaware of the depth of the problem and relied on official statistics, which, in any event, showed a sufficiently discouraging trend from their point of view.) It was a literary journal—*Novy mir*—rather than an economic one which published the first comprehensive challenge to official

Soviet statistics. The joint authors were Khanin and a prominent economic journalist, Vasily Selyunin. Their article, entitled 'Cunning Figures', contended that, whereas the authorized figures showed almost a ninety-fold increase in Soviet national income from 1928 to 1986, in reality the increase was between six and seven times—surely, Alec Nove observed, 'the largest downward amendment in growth rates known to recorded history'.[21] While Soviet growth statistics were, and remain, a subject of debate unlikely ever to be completely resolved (partly because of false reporting at different levels of the system and probably to a varying extent over time), increasingly Khanin's figures were accepted as being a far closer reflection of reality than those produced by the State Committee on Statistics.[22]

A second difference between the 1960s and the 1980s which had nothing to do with Gorbachev—like the objective decline in Soviet economic performance (no matter which set of statistics one chose to believe)—concerned what had been happening in the meantime in other Communist countries. Kosygin had no alternative experience and models to draw upon when he was trying to reform the command economy. By 1965 no significant economic reform had been introduced in any Communist country, although serious discussion of reform had already taken place in Poland, Czechoslovakia, and Hungary. Indeed, in so far as any other Communist state was making the running between 1965 and 1968, it was Czechoslovakia, and when the Czech plans for economic reform were accompanied by more far-reaching political change than the Soviet Politburo was prepared to tolerate, that turned out to be the final nail in the coffin of Kosygin's reform. The 'Prague Spring' and its crushing by Soviet military intervention in August 1968 strengthened the hand of Soviet domestic opponents of change and put reformers very much on the defensive as conservative Communists set about tarring them with the brush of 'revisionism' and 'opportunism'.

By 1985 the international Communist context was quite different from what it had been in the late 1960s. At that earlier time China was another negative factor from the standpoint of Soviet reformers and, indeed, of the Soviet leadership as a whole. The Chinese were in the throes of their 'Cultural Revolution' and were condemning even the most half-hearted innovation in the Soviet Union as 'revisionist'. By the mid-1980s, in contrast, China had embarked on an economic reform substantially more radical and consistent than anything seen up to that point in Russia.[23] This, and especially the impressive speed at which China had raised its agricultural production, attracted a lot of interest in Moscow. In addition to China, the Soviet Union by the second half of the 1980s could draw on the diverse experiences of economic reform in Eastern Europe, especially in Hungary, where a reform—launched in 1968—had gone through several stages and, for all its serious limitations, had produced striking improvements in agriculture in particular (as a result of a mixture of semi-private and public enterprise and of concessions to the market).[24]

Thus, the political context for reform was very different in the mid-1980s from the mid-1960s, and to the objective difference of a more clearly declining Soviet growth rate must be added the subjective difference in perceptions of the Soviet leadership. Gorbachev was frequently to speak of the 'pre-crisis situation' which had prevailed in the Soviet Union in the early 1980s, and he and others in the leadership had taken note of the very real crisis for a ruling Communist Party which had occurred in Poland in 1980–1 when massive protest from below, and the formation of an independent trade union-cum-political movement, Solidarity, had for a time called into question the continued existence of the Communist regime. The case of Poland, as a warning example, cropped up quite frequently in the conversations and, to a lesser extent, the writings of Soviet party intellectuals from the early to mid-1980s.[25] This, too, constituted a major perceptual difference between the time when Kosygin was attempting to introduce limited economic reform and the Gorbachev era.

The third major difference between the 1960s and the 1980s related directly to the Gorbachev factor and is suggested by the very fact that the economic reform launched in 1965 was known as the 'Kosygin reform'. It was, indeed, the Chairman of the Council of Ministers of the USSR, Kosygin, and not the General Secretary[26] of the Central Committee of the Communist Party, Brezhnev, who was pushing for economic reform in the mid-1960s. However powerful the Soviet ministerial network may have been *collectively*, the Chairman of the Council of Ministers was less powerful *individually* than the party General Secretary. The fact that Brezhnev was responsive to those party and state bureaucrats who were apprehensive about economic reform and that he failed, to put it at its lowest, to give his backing to Kosygin's mildly reformist efforts was enough to ensure that eventually they came to nothing.[27] It was thus important that twenty years later it was the General Secretary, Gorbachev, who was committed to economic reform and the Chairman of the Council of Ministers, Tikhonov, who was extremely reluctant to depart from well-worn paths.[28] It was, accordingly, not at all surprising that Gorbachev took the initiative in replacing Tikhonov by Ryzhkov in September 1985. As Chairman, Ryzhkov, it is true, was able to exercise great power in the economic field over the next five (and especially next four) years. That was partly because he was in day-to-day charge of the vast economic apparatus, but it was also in no small measure because Gorbachev until 1989 had confidence in him.[29]

Fourth, Gorbachev's perestroika, even in 1985–6—and, much more obviously, by 1987–8—was a far more comprehensive notion of reform than that envisaged by Kosygin. The obstacles to a serious marketizing economic reform were enormous. The ministries, in their opposition to such reform, could count on the support of a majority of regional party secretaries as well as on the military and the managers of the defence industry.[30] Even as late as 1990, by which time the economic reform agenda had been radicalized along with the opinions of a substantial section of the public, Gorbachev was faced by an informal alliance of all the institutional interests which had done relatively well out of the command economy.[31] An awakened public opinion in which people began to assert their rights both as citizens and as consumers was a direct threat to these interests. Glasnost and democratization, while regarded as desirable political goals in themselves by Gorbachev (whose understanding, as noted in the previous chapter, of what was meant by those notions broadened over time), were seen by him also as a necessary means of putting pressure on the institutions opposed to essential economic change.

Confidence in the unreformed economic system was severely undermined by the swingeing attacks made on it by such reformist economists as Nikolay Shmelev, Gavriil Popov, and Vasily Selyunin.[32] A minority of independent-minded academic lawyers also made notable contributions to the critique of the existing system and produced proposals for far-reaching reform.[33] The preparation of public opinion for radical economic reform was the more important inasmuch as on its own this was (in the short term, at least) a threat to 'rights' to which Soviet workers had become accustomed. These included the expectation of job security (which for some years had meant not only a guarantee of employment in general but, broadly speaking, the possibility of continuing to work where one had always worked) and the practice of charging low and subsidized prices for basic foodstuffs and services, including rents, heating, and lighting. Political reform, in contrast, whether in the realm of glasnost or that of extension of the electoral principle (including the introduction of shop-floor elections whereby in many factories workers were given the opportunity to elect their foremen and, in some instances, even the factory managers)[34] offered workers, in common with other citizens, an extension of their rights. One lesson which Gorbachev, as well as his supporters, appeared to have learned from the failure of Kosygin's attempted innovations was that it was no longer enough to attempt to introduce economic reform in isolation from the rest of political and social life if the forces of economic conservatism were to be defeated.

The movement from glasnost to freedom of speech and the broadening of the meaning of 'democratization' were also, however, double-edged swords so far as Gorbachev was concerned, for they led to a polarization of Soviet politics which in some ways made economic reform more difficult. The change of political climate provided opportunities not only for those who came to espouse 'shock therapy' transition to a market economy to propose more drastic remedies than Gorbachev could easily accept but also for those who were fundamentally opposed to marketization to campaign for retention of the traditional Soviet economic model. Gorbachev's dilemma was expressed wryly by David Dyker in his book on the economic dimension of perestroika when he wrote: 'It is hard to dispute Gorbachev's conclusion that economic reform would not be possible without political reform. What is less clear is whether economic reform is possible *with* political reform.'[35]

On markets and mixed economies

In fact, though the economic *performance* which resulted was dismally disappointing, and far removed from what Gorbachev had hoped for, the economic *reform* was radicalized during his years in office in several basic dimensions. These included economic aspects of the conceptual revolution (already discussed, but mainly with reference to political concepts, in the previous chapter), abolition of the institutions of the Communist Party responsible for supervising economic activity, concrete changes in property relations, and concessions to the market. So far as concepts were concerned, Gorbachev himself moved from the euphemism for a market of 'commodity-money relations'[36] to speaking of a 'socialist market'; he then began to talk increasingly about the need for a 'regulated market economy' and, often latterly, simply a 'market economy'. Until at least 1987, however, he was thinking in terms of market elements playing a subordinate role in an essentially planned economy.[37] It was only after the June 1987 plenary session of the Central Committee devoted to economic reform that Gorbachev began openly to advocate a market, at that time still a 'socialist market'. He did, however, insinuate the word 'market' into his major speech to the June plenum in a passage which combined obeisance to 'strengthening socialism in reality' with recommendation of the use of a variety of market instruments.[38]

By November 1988 Gorbachev was complaining that vulgarized views of the socialist state had led to an undervaluing of the role of the market under socialism.[39] Addressing the First Congress of People's Deputies on 30 May 1989, Gorbachev went further and said that no better or more democratic alternative had been found to the market and that the socialist economy could not manage without it.[40] In his concluding words to the same Congress on 9 June he emphasized that he was a strong supporter of the market, but that he could never agree with those who held that the market could regulate everything. Not even in capitalist countries did the view prevail that the market could automatically solve all problems.[41] By 1989, and subsequently, Gorbachev accepted a predominantly market economy which would, however, be regulated in the West European manner and would be a 'mixed economy' in terms of ownership. This was in keeping with the development of his views in the direction of social democracy which has already been noted in the previous chapter. After ceasing to be General Secretary of the Soviet Communist Party, Gorbachev was naturally in a position to be much more open about this. Asked in an interview in early 1993 if he was still a Communist, Gorbachev replied: 'If you look at my pronouncements, then it will become clear that my political sympathies belong to social democracy and the idea of a welfare state of the kind to be found in the Federal Republic of Germany.'[42]

Gorbachev's acceptance, as General Secretary, of the notion (as well as the developing reality) of a 'mixed economy' was another highly significant conceptual break with the past, for it meant embracing co-operative and even private, as well as state, ownership and abandoning insistence that all ownership be 'socialist'.[43] A number of Russian intellectuals—including some who but a few years earlier were still 'builders of communism'—were airily dismissive of Gorbachev's support for a *regulated* market economy, although a year after Gorbachev's departure from political office Yegor Gaydar, who, as he remarked, could 'scarcely be suspected by anyone of conservatism and of disliking the market', was to observe that 'throughout the world the market is regulated'.[44] Gorbachev's acceptance of a 'mixed economy' and of a 'regulated market economy' brought him far closer to an acquiescence with Western practice and with an important strand in Western thinking than his critics acknowledged.

Although the term 'mixed economy' more usually refers to a mixed ownership system—that is, both private and public (or state) enterprise[45]—it can also be employed, as it is in an important article by Robert A. Dahl, to denote a significant measure of state intervention in the economy.[46] Dahl argues not only that a socialist command economy is incompatible with democracy but that a strictly free market is also incompatible with democratic political rule. So far as the historical evidence is concerned, just as no country with a socialist command economy has ever been democratic, so, Dahl contends, no democracy has ever had a market economy whose workings were not altered in certain respects by state intervention.[47] Since one way or another 'the victims of free markets are likely to influence the government . . . to adopt interventionist policies intended to mitigate the harm' done to them, a strictly free market could only be created or maintained by resort to 'guardianship or elite rule, or to put it more bluntly, by an authoritarian dictatorship'.[48] In remarks fully consonant with those of America's leading democratic theorist, Gorbachev told the Socialist International congress (the annual gathering of West European-style social democratic parties) in Berlin in September 1992: 'the market economy should not be perceived as an end in itself, but rather as a means of achieving certain goals. And the market is not identical with democracy, or liberty with the market economy.'[49]

When Gorbachev succeeded Chernenko, the issue of curbing the excesses of the market economy was far from his mind. What he was seeking was a very partial marketization of the Soviet economy, and the main emphasis was on *uskorenie*, acceleration, meaning a qualitative improvement in economic growth. By late 1989, however, when he invited the well-known 'marketeer' Nikolay Petrakov to become his aide and economic adviser, Gorbachev's views had evolved to the point of acceptance that the market should be the major (but not sole) economic regulator. From the outset of his General Secretaryship there is no doubt that he was the member of the Politburo most committed to far-reaching economic reform. His allies at that time, Ryzhkov and especially Ligachev, had more limited aims in view, and every other member of the Politburo—until the elevation of Shevardnadze in the summer of 1985—was an opponent of even the most limited marketizing reform. (Ligachev staked out his position clearly. As early as the summer of 1986 he dismissed the idea of movement towards the market on the grounds that a 'market economy' always and everywhere led to 'injustice and inequality'.[50]) Even such a harsh Western critic of the later Gorbachev as Anders Åslund quite aptly entitled his careful study of the first three and a half years of perestroika *Gorbachev's Struggle for Economic Reform*.[51] The title is a useful reminder that the push for economic reform came from Gorbachev himself and that it was always an uphill struggle against sceptical or more conservative colleagues and against deeply entrenched vested interests. As Gorbachev put it in a 1993 interview: 'The party bureaucracy, the ministries and all the feudal lords were resisting. Even the industrial bosses and the managers were afraid of losing their power.'[52]

Gorbachev from the earliest days of his General Secretaryship was interested in moving in the direction of 'market socialism'. The idea of combining plan and market, dear to the heart of many (subsequently disillusioned) East European reformers, has never worked satisfactorily in practice, and before the end of his time in office Gorbachev, too, had lost faith in the state planning component, although he did not go so far as some of his former Communist Party comrades who exchanged the ideological certitudes of Marx and Lenin for those of Hayek and Friedman. Even in the earlier part of his General Secretaryship Gorbachev was, however, acutely conscious that the Soviet economy was over-centralized, that more decision-making must be devolved to the work-place, that the country was technologically backward (except in a few privileged areas such as space and military research), and that an agricultural reform in which the peasantry would gain control of the land they farmed and be freed from the petty tutelage of local party secretaries was essential.

Economic policy-making

The concrete policies which emerged to put those principles into practice were, however, inadequate. It is sometimes argued that this was because there was not an overall strategy for economic reform with a carefully worked-out conception of its stages. That is a misleading over-simplification in two respects. On the one hand, the divisions within the leadership were such—with Gorbachev even by 1986 still in a minority in the Politburo in favouring a measure of marketization—that there was no possibility of genuine agreement on strategy and, accordingly, all talk of 'sequencing' was the stuff of Western academic seminars rather than of Kremlin politics. There was a great deal of trial and error (with error bulking much larger here than in foreign policy, political reform, or cultural policy) as well as inconsistency which reflected fundamental disagreements within the Soviet leadership and the ascendancy of particular viewpoints at different times.

On the other hand, notwithstanding those difficulties, a set of guide-lines for the future was adopted by the party leadership in June 1987. Called the *Basic Positions* (*Osnovnye polozheniya*), it was seen as quite radical at that time, even though it was doomed to be overtaken by events. It was welcomed by the late Ed Hewett (who was to become the chief specialist adviser on Soviet affairs in the Bush administration) for stating its principles 'with a clarity that can be attained only in the early stages of a reform' before (Hewett added realistically) 'the actual legislation that makes up the reform is crafted, with all the inevitable compromises, and before the implementation of the reform forces even more, possibly fatal, compromises'.[53] The *Basic Positions* retained central planning but attempted to remove micro-economic management from the hands of the planners. While Hewett was concerned that its radicalism might be compromised in political practice, in fact it was to become clearer to Gorbachev (if not Ryzhkov) over the next two years that the *Basic Positions* were not radical enough. This was particularly true of the price reform, since it was impossible to judge the efficiency of any industrial enterprise so long as highly artificial prices provided no possibility of assessing whether the factory was making a profit or a loss in real terms. The compromise position adopted by the *Basic Positions* was that prices would be decided by negotiation and contract between enterprises and that the State Committee on Prices would henceforth simply determine and enforce the rules governing this process.[54] It was always likely, however, that the State Committee on Prices would not be content with the role of umpire and that the rules themselves would be bent by large and powerful enterprises—often monopolistic suppliers—to force up prices and stoke inflation.[55]

Policy innovation: alcohol and agriculture

A number of policy changes had already been adopted on a piecemeal basis before the promulgation of the *Basic Positions*. The first concrete economic measure was introduced as early as May 1985 and, curiously enough, neither Gorbachev nor Ryzhkov were the prime movers, although Gorbachev's name was strongly associated with it and he has continued to defend the principle, as distinct from the implementation, of the policy.[56] This was the launching of the anti-alcohol struggle, which involved not only a campaign and exhortation against alcohol abuse (as had occurred often enough in the Soviet past) but also concrete measures to limit the production, sale, and distribution of alcohol. Thus, many shops were no longer allowed to sell alcohol, numerous vodka distilleries were closed, and even many vineyards were destroyed (in, for example, Georgia, although drunkenness had been less of a problem there than in the spirit-drinking Slavic parts of the Soviet Union). The new rules forbade the serving of alcohol in restaurants before 2 o'clock in the afternoon, and even official Soviet receptions—from those graced by the party leadership to those held in Soviet embassies abroad—became alcohol-free (or, in the first stage of relaxation of the stipulations, at least vodka-free). The setting of such an example was a break with the past, although one which was not appreciated by all of the hosts, not to speak of their guests.

Among Gorbachev's Politburo colleagues and close associates, there was a clear perception that the principal protagonists of the anti-alcohol measures were Yegor Ligachev and the Chairman of the Committee of Party Control and Politburo member, Mikhail Solomentsev.[57] Ryzhkov notes that the form the campaign took was determined by Ligachev and Solomentsev, but that Gorbachev strongly supported it, for he was concerned to improve the moral atmosphere.[58] The Slavic parts of the Soviet Union had among the highest rates of alcohol consumption in the world and the situation had got worse during the Brezhnev years. Indeed, notwithstanding periodic propaganda efforts to warn of the dangers of excessive drinking, it would scarcely be going too far to say that for Brezhnev alcohol was a convenient pain-killer for the ills of Soviet society, a substitute for reform, and a vital contributor to the Soviet exchequer. Since the state had a monopoly over the manufacture of alcoholic drinks and could fix a price which included, in effect, a very large element of taxation, it made an enormous contribution to the Soviet budget. In fact, the revenue from this source was greater than the total the Soviet state received in income tax.[59]

Gorbachev recognized the problem of alcoholism and drunkenness to be a major one, and as an extremely moderate drinker himself (at receptions and dinners even before and after the clampdown on alcohol consumption he would take a maximum of two glasses of wine) he could not be accused of hypocrisy. His inclination to do battle with alcohol may also have been reinforced by his wife. Raisa Gorbachev's passionate opposition to excessive drinking arose from distress over the chronic alcoholism of her brother, to whom in childhood she had been particularly close.[60] With Gorbachev's endorsement of the anti-alcohol policy, even Shevardnadze, from wine-drinking Georgia (and attending the crucial Politburo meeting at that time still as a candidate member), did not, against his better judgement, speak up against the measures.[61] Gorbachev put his full weight behind the policy in public, in speeches and meetings that were more widely publicized than those of any of his Politburo colleagues, and accordingly the General Secretary became firmly associated in the public mind with the excesses of the anti-drinking measures. He was jocularly referred to as the *mineral'nyy sekretar'* (mineral-water-drinking secretary) rather than *general'nyy sekretar'* (General Secretary). Initially approved of in principle by a majority of Russians, especially by women, the anti-alcohol struggle was to become increasingly unpopular.

It can be argued, and has been, that the policy was not a total failure.[62] In spite of the huge increase in illicit distilling, there is some reason to believe that this did not wholly fill the gap left by the drastic cut-back in state production and that consequently total alcohol consumption was reduced.[63] It is even suggested that the long decline in Soviet male life expectancy (which many analysts had associated with increasingly heavy drinking) was temporarily reversed between 1985 and 1988. Certainly the official figures indicate this to have been the case and they show also a reduction in the number of new in-patients suffering from severe alcoholism as well as substantial reductions in the rates of accidents at work and of death on the roads.[64] While it would be unwise to place total faith in the Soviet statistics even of the perestroika era, it is likely that some improvement in these respects did occur, if only because it had become so much more difficult and inconvenient for the average person to purchase alcohol. Some of the hardest drinkers, however, turned to substances more dangerous than vodka and that was not the only unintended consequence of the policy. The Soviet economic reformer Nikolay Shmelev argued that 'our semi-prohibition will have the same effects as American prohibition', by which he meant both the large-scale production of *samogon* (moonshine) and the stimulus to organized crime.[65]

The greatest set-back for Gorbachev, however, was the enormous hole in the Soviet state budget left by this loss of revenue, since no tax was paid on the home-made brews to which so many drinkers turned. It was not only Russian alcoholics but the Ministry of Finance which faced a liquidity crisis. As Shmelev observed in early 1988: 'By giving away its revenue to the bootlegger, the government in the last two years has sharply increased its budgetary imbalance and incurred a deficit which is today being covered in a most dangerous and unhealthy way, by the printing press.'[66] The rigours of the anti-alcohol policy were gradually pared away from 1988 onwards, mainly as a result of the damage done to the state budget but in part also because the central authorities no longer had the same power to dictate to a revitalized society and to determine policy for the entire Soviet Union as was still possible in 1985.[67]

An area in which Gorbachev, not surprisingly, was the initiator of early policy innovation was agriculture. Although still by no means entirely a free agent, he was less constrained than hitherto. Gorbachev was an admirer of the Hungarian agricultural reform, which combined some of the advantages of large-scale agricultural production with the granting of a great deal of autonomy to co-operatives to buy equipment and sell their produce relatively freely, while granting individual members of the co-operative the possibility to diversify into other production in seasons when they had time on their hands. The overall result had been a substantial improvement in living standards in the countryside and a far better supply of foodstuffs to the towns than in the Soviet Union or in pre-reform Hungary. Some time before he became General Secretary, Gorbachev had—in the course of an extended visit to Hungary in his capacity as Secretary of the Central Committee supervising agriculture—expressed considerable enthusiasm for what he saw on Hungarian farms. At the end of his visit, his Hungarian counterpart plucked up the courage to ask him why, if he liked the Hungarian reform so much, a similar policy was not being pursued in the Soviet Union. Gorbachev answered: 'Unfortunately, in the course of the last fifty years the Russian peasant has had all the independence knocked out of him.'[68] What Gorbachev had in mind was that, in the wake of forcible collectivization, a demoralized, and increasingly ageing, rural work-force had taken the place of an independent peasantry. This, however, was only one of the problems for Gorbachev when he was still only a Central Committee Secretary. As already noted in Chapter 3, he put the other constraint upon him quite graphically when, in response to Tatyana Zaslavskaya's suggestion made in 1982 that the setting-up of a State Committee for the Agro-Industrial Complex (Gosagroprom) would be worth while only if it took the place of, and was not an addition to, the existing ministries with agricultural responsibilities, he asked rhetorically whether, if he wrote that into the draft 'Food Programme', he would 'still be sitting in this office'.[69]

As General Secretary Gorbachev did what he had felt unable even to recommend three years earlier. In November 1985 he secured the abolition of five ministries and one state committee and set up in their place a State Committee for the Agro-Industrial Complex. Moreover, as its chairman he appointed his former Stavropol colleague Vsevolod Murakhovsky. Unfortunately, in spite of Murakhovsky's best intentions, Gosagroprom both at the centre and in the regions did develop into yet another large bureaucracy and achieved virtually none of the results Gorbachev and his advisers had hoped for. This may have been partly because, in Moscow's corridors of power, the new Secretary of the Central Committee with responsibility for agriculture, Viktor Nikonov (who had been Minister of Agriculture for the Russian republic from 1983 to 1985), counted for more than the Ukrainian Murakhovsky, freshly arrived from Stavropol and whose first post in Moscow this was. Nikonov, though, was one of Gorbachev's least inspired appointments. His speeches indicated that he was less well disposed to radical agricultural reform than either Gorbachev or Murakhovsky.[70] It becomes a puzzle why Gorbachev should have appointed *that* Nikonov to such a key position. Gorbachev's agricultural mentor, Alexander Nikonov, would have been another matter, but—apart from age considerations—he was ruled out because, as a minimum, he would have had to be a member of the Central Committee before it would have been possible to contemplate elevating him to a secretaryship of that body.[71] The rules and conventions of Soviet politics thus still greatly restricted Gorbachev's choice of personnel for senior party posts, the more so since they all required collective Politburo approval and were not in his individual gift. Even so, the appointment of Viktor Nikonov was a mistake and Murakhovsky was also a relative failure. Gosagroprom was abolished in early 1989 and many of its functions were transferred from all-union to republican jurisdiction.

Gorbachev's other attempt to tackle the problem of under-productivity in Soviet agriculture was to return to the idea of contract leasing between groups of farmers (including family groups) and their parent state farm (*sovkhoz*) or collective farm (*kolkhoz*). He had first (as already noted in Chapter 3) won the support of Andropov to air this idea in March 1983, but now he was in a position to take it up when far more levers of power were at his disposal and to insert it into as authoritative a document (in the conditions then prevailing) as the Central Committee's political report to the Twenty-Seventh Congress of the CPSU, which Gorbachev delivered on 25 February 1986. In that major speech he expressed approval for the wide diffusion of the 'contract and accord system at the level of the brigade, link, and family' and said that those involved should be provided for the contracted period with the means of production, including land.[72] In practice, this approach continued to be frustrated by the unwillingness of district party secretaries and collective and state farm chairmen to allow the best land to be farmed free from their interference by independent groups of agricultural workers; by some apathy on the part of the peasantry themselves; and by the reliance of even those workers who did want to take advantage of the new opportunities on the dubious goodwill of the farm bosses for the supply of equipment. Thus, the policy of 'contracting-out' of the collective and state farm system was subject to severe limitations.

It is often argued that Gorbachev should have begun with greater agricultural change as the Chinese and Hungarians did when they started their economic reform. The desirability of a radical reform of Soviet agriculture was not in doubt, but the comparison with China and Hungary begs many questions. Among the substantial differences between them and the Soviet Union, the most basic was that the latter had been a Communist country for an entire generation longer. In China and Hungary there were people in the countryside who still remembered what it was like to farm independently. That was not the case in the Soviet Union. In addition, in Russia there had been a flight from the land of many of the youngest and ablest potential workers and Soviet farming was accordingly much more heavily dependent on capital equipment than was China, where a labour-intensive agriculture could rapidly produce results once the shackles were removed from the peasantry. And, as compared with Hungary, Russia—not to speak of the Soviet Union as a whole—was a vast country where the transport and marketing of agricultural produce was an altogether more formidable task. In fact, Gorbachev *did* begin with an administrative reform of agriculture, but nothing as radical as the Hungarian reform which might usefully have been introduced in some parts of the Soviet Union, such as the Baltic states or Georgia. But neither the organizational change embodied in Agroprom nor the encouragement of contractual leasing came close to fulfilling his expectations.

One of those who thought Gorbachev should have devoted more time to agriculture and pushed through a radical reform at an early stage was Alexander Nikonov.[73] He accepted that this would still have been extremely difficult because of the vested interests involved and on account of Ryzhkov's approach, which was 'that of a technocrat who saw everything through the prism of a factory manager'.[74] However, in Nikonov's view, because Gorbachev's top priorities were to begin political reform, to weaken his conservative enemies, and 'to end the Cold War', he did not or could not devote enough time to agriculture when he still had the power to bring changes about.[75]

By the later 1980s there was a growing demand from the most radical reformers for fully-fledged private farming and the sale of land, although other reformers resisted this on the grounds that the only people who would be able to afford to buy land would be 'the mafia', corrupt officials, and foreigners. Even late in the Gorbachev era only a minority of the population as a whole (21 per cent) favoured the private buying and selling of agricultural land.[76] Gorbachev on this question was with the majority rather than the radical minority. As late as November 1990 he spoke against the private ownership of the land, although leasing of land even for a hundred years he was happy to accept; at the same time he proposed that each Soviet republic should take its own decision, preferably by referendum, on whether or not the people wished to return to private land ownership.[77] Most Russians made, and have continued to make, a distinction between large-scale and small-scale private ownership of land. By 1991 over 80 per cent of the population were ready to accept private ownership of small plots of land, but less than 40 per cent supported private ownership of large plots. That, moreover, was a higher percentage than in any previous year of the Gorbachev era and higher also than in the post-Soviet period. Support for private ownership of large tracts of land declined from 1991 to 1992 and by 1993 it was down further (only 24 per cent of the population approving).[78]

Economic legislation

Private economic activity, whether by individuals or under the guise of co-operatives, was, however, supported by Gorbachev. In 1986 a struggle was going on between those who wished to stigmatize all forms of private economic activity as 'speculation' (as, judging from his speeches, Ligachev did) and those who wished to legalize it. An early interim measure was the Law on Individual Labour Activity of November 1986, which legalized both family-based and individual enterprise of the kind which was already being undertaken on the black or grey market. It included such activities as car and television repairs, private tuition, and taxi services. This was still, however, a very limited measure; those engaged in it were supposed to do it only part-time and, although that stipulation soon fell by the wayside, by 1989 the people involved still numbered just 300,000.[79] A much more far-reaching, marketizing piece of legislation was the Law on Co-operatives adopted in May 1988.[80] A co-operative could henceforth be set up entirely independently. It required a minimum of three members but there was no maximum. Although hired labour was not allowed, this was merely a formal concession to traditional ideology, for the co-operatives (which were soon to become indistinguishable from private companies) 'could employ an unlimited number of non-members on a contract basis'.[81] Non-state economic activity and leaseholds were given a further boost by the Law on Leaseholds of 1989 and the Law on Land passed in 1990. But in some ways the most important new idea in the Soviet context had been expressed by the then Director of the Institute of State and Law in Moscow, Vladimir Kudryavtsev, as early as December 1986. After referring to the need for further development of traders' and consumers' co-operatives and for a general law on 'the unifying principles of socialist management', he added: 'Of the two possible principles, "You may do only what is permitted" and "You may do everything that is not forbidden", priority should be given to the latter inasmuch as it unleashes the initiative and activism of people.'[82] Kudryavtsev had frequent contact with Gorbachev, who was entirely at one with him on this issue. Before long Gorbachev was to give public voice to this principle—a sharp break with Soviet tradition which also turned out to be in tune with the developing reality of everyday life.[83] The maxim that everything was permitted that the law did not specifically forbid was explicitly written into three major pieces of economic legislation—the Law on Individual Labour Activity (1986), the Law on the State Enterprise (1987), and the Law on Co-operatives (1988).[84]

Gorbachev consulted widely with economists (as well as with other social scientists and with academic lawyers) in the period between his elevation to the leadership in March 1985 and the June plenum of the Central Committee in 1987 in which he called for a radicalization of economic reform. Although he did not—prior to Petrakov's appointment almost five years after he became General Secretary—have a full-time aide with specialist knowledge of economics, the economic adviser he consulted most frequently during the period preceding the June 1987 plenum was Aganbegyan. Within the administration, he worked particularly closely with Ryzhkov, who in the earliest months of the Gorbachev era was the Secretary of the Central Committee with special responsibility for the economy and, from September 1985, Chairman of the Council of Ministers. Given that Gorbachev had to concern himself with every aspect of politics (with foreign policy bulking increasingly large), it was Ryzhkov, rather than Gorbachev, who was in day-to-day charge of the management of the Soviet economy, although Gorbachev never stood as aloof from economic decision-making as Yeltsin was to do as President of post-Soviet Russia.

One of the first of the problems to be addressed by the new leadership was that of technological lag. Ryzhkov has related how, in the run-up to the June 1985 conference on science and technology, he and Gorbachev went back to the proposals from many different quarters they had studied when they were preparing for the abortive Central Committee plenum on science and technology in Chernenko's time (the politics of which were discussed in Chapter 3). They would, said Ryzhkov, argue about which examples and arguments should be used and which should not. They were considering so many different memoranda and papers that they would not fit even on the substantial desk in Gorbachev's office. Therefore, they spread them out on the floor and examined them, jackets off, in what Ryzhkov calls 'a rather creative atmosphere', on their knees![85]

In his speech of June 1985, Gorbachev (as noted in Chapter 4) called for a perestroika of the entire economic mechanism.[86] He also attacked various ministries and state committees, including Gosplan and the Ministry of Finance, for interfering even in the 'economic experiments' whereby certain enterprises had been accorded greater independence.[87] (Aganbegyan, who had taken part in the preparation of major speeches to be delivered by previous party leaders—from Brezhnev to Chernenko—has commented on how differently Gorbachev worked. Whereas none of his predecessors put in an appearance with the academic specialists who were doing the detailed work, Gorbachev met with them 'quite frequently' and 'took part in the preparation of these materials'.[88]) The speech of June 1985 did not, however, raise overtly anything as radical as even a partial marketization of the economy and later it was to be criticized for its technocratic limitations. Five years on Bogomolov was to argue that the entire thrust of the June report and meeting (which had almost the status of a Central Committee plenum) was wrong 'because it was purely technocratic'. This was linked by Bogomolov to Gorbachev's excessive reliance on Ryzhkov at that time so far as economic issues were concerned.[89]

The illusion that decentralization of decision-making to the industrial enterprise could produce better results without being accompanied by a much more substantial marketization—including, in particular, demonopolization and price liberalization—was carried forward into one of the legislative centre-pieces of early economic reform: the Law on the State Enterprise (Association) adopted by the Supreme Soviet less than a week after the June 1987 Central Committee plenum.[90] In principle, this law gave much more autonomy to the managers of factories and of industrial associations, and to some extent it did so in reality. They were able to have greater control over their own wages bill while continuing to be subject only to the 'soft budget constraints' which the leading Hungarian economist János Kornai was the first to identify as one of the most central problems of socialist economic systems. Moreover, 'state orders' (which kept the factory order-books full) took the place of the former ministerial directives. The most important deficiency of all, perhaps, was that, in the absence of a general price liberalization and competition, the enterprises were freer than hitherto to charge higher prices for production of no higher quality than in the past. In general, the Enterprise Law fuelled inflation, promoted inter-enterprise debt and failure to pay taxes to the central budget, and did much more harm than good.

The radicalization of reform

Soviet economic policy in the first few years of Gorbachev's leadership, while moving cautiously towards a greater acceptance of the market and non-state forms of ownership, reflected the fundamental disagreements within the leadership, in which Gorbachev's own views did not necessarily prevail. When a new Five-Year-Plan (to commence in 1986) was being considered in the Politburo, a first version was rejected and a revised plan prepared. But most of the work on both versions had been done under the aegis of the Chairman of the Council of Ministers, Nikolay Tikhonov, and the Chairman of Gosplan, Nikolay Baybakov, both of whom had only recently—in the autumn of 1985—been removed from office on Gorbachev's initiative. Gorbachev sought the opinion of Aganbegyan on the revised document and Aganbegyan told him that the figures were too conservative and did not reflect the social strategy which had been enunciated at the April 1985 Central Committee plenum and the June conference on science and technology. Later Aganbegyan was told by some of those who had attended the Politburo meeting in November 1985 which considered the revised plan that Gorbachev had spoken up for the ideas that he and other like-minded people had prepared for him, but the Politburo decided to accept the revised document as the basis of the plan in spite of these objections. Aganbegyan took the first opportunity that arose to ask Gorbachev why this had happened, to which Gorbachev gave the revealing reply: 'What could I do, they had me surrounded.'[91]

Between the June plenum of 1987 and the summer of 1989 Gorbachev was less involved in economic policy-making than he had been before and than he was to be again from the middle of 1989 and especially in 1990.[92] Aganbegyan saw much less of him[93] during those two years and had ceased to be Gorbachev's first-choice economic adviser by the time Gorbachev decided to make more time for economic issues. In the interim foreign policy and the radicalization of political reform had been Gorbachev's major preoccupations. Although his energy and capacity for work were such that he could never leave economic matters entirely to Ryzhkov, Gorbachev was restrained not only by the other demands on his time and by his confidence in Ryzhkov but also by his growing acceptance of the idea that the Communist Party should cease to interfere in the actual running of the economy. His most striking initiative demonstrating his seriousness about curtailing the party's economic role was the abolition in September 1988 (along the lines of a memorandum dated 24 August which Gorbachev sent to the Politburo) of the departments of the Central Committee which supervised the economic ministries and the different sectors of the economy.[94] This was in the context of an overall reduction of the number of Central Committee departments from twenty to nine and a diminution of the powers of the party secretariat which will be discussed further in the next chapter. The problem with this was that, even if it removed one layer of high-level bureaucracy, it left the ministries more unchecked than ever and made Gorbachev more dependent on the reforming zeal, or lack of it, of the Chairman of the Council of Ministers. Gorbachev may have been counting on the new legislature, which the Nineteenth Party Conference had recently agreed should be elected the following spring, to act as a fresh and more effective check on ministerial power.

It was during 1988 that Leonid Abalkin supplanted Aganbegyan as the most influential economist in the country. Abalkin, though not a radical, had a reputation as a serious reformer. Director of the Institute of Economics of the Academy of Sciences since 1986, he was also president of the Soviet Chess Federation. At the Nineteenth Party Conference he had irritated Gorbachev by claiming in a critical speech that perestroika had not achieved much thus far and that no economic breakthrough had taken place.[95] Ryzhkov, in contrast, liked Abalkin's speech and in the interval afterwards—at a time when Abalkin was standing alone and feeling cold-shouldered even by people who knew him—greeted him warmly.[96] He subsequently involved him more closely in government discussions and in July 1989 a State Commission on Economic Reform was set up and Abalkin was invited by Ryzhkov to chair it. He met with Ryzhkov on successive days (but not with Gorbachev) and agreed to take the job on, provided he could retain (without salary) his Directorship of the Institute of Economics. To this Ryzhkov readily consented, adding that it would even be useful for his new work. Ryzhkov underlined the seriousness of the assignment by giving Abalkin at the same time the rank of deputy prime minister.[97]

Abalkin and Ryzhkov continued to enjoy harmonious relations, but the former's new position in the government distanced him from the radical economic reformers outside, the more so since it appeared to them that Abalkin had been co-opted by the government and was increasingly a spokesman for the cautious policy they associated with Ryzhkov. It was in late 1989 that Gorbachev became convinced that more radical measures were required than Ryzhkov was ready to countenance and that his confidence in the Chairman of the Council of Ministers began to diminish.[98] In December 1989 he spoke with Nikolay Petrakov and, after telling him that he had a great need for someone who was familiar with marketization issues, invited him to become his aide and adviser on these matters. Petrakov asked Gorbachev if he was familiar with his beliefs and got the reply: 'Of course.'[99]

Petrakov, who was then in his early fifties, was one of the most senior and respected 'marketeers' among professional Russian economists. Although Deputy Director of the Central Economic-Mathematical Institute (TsEMI), he had had numerous brushes with the authorities in the past. In 1971 he had been accused of 'standing on bourgeois positions' because of his advocacy of marketization and his support for the Czech economic reforms associated with the name of Ota Šik. In the aftermath of the 'Prague Spring' Petrakov belonged to a group of scholars who had become deeply suspect in the eyes of the Soviet establishment. For some years his articles were either refused publication, strictly censored, or appeared only because he used Aesopian language.[100] Since Gorbachev had come to power, Petrakov—in common with millions of other Soviet citizens—had been free as never before to express his heterodox views. He had taken part in several discussion meetings with Gorbachev, the first of them in Chernenko's time, and Gorbachev was very well aware of his commitment to the market. Petrakov, in turn, had been greatly impressed by Gorbachev's ability to grasp the issues.[101] There was no doubt in Petrakov's mind that Gorbachev himself was committed to transition to the market and that his choice of him as his first-ever economic aide (as distinct from *ad hoc* adviser, which had been the position of Aganbegyan and others) was ample confirmation of his resolve.[102] 'The very fact that he offered me the job', said Petrakov, 'demonstrates that Gorbachev had realised the need to go over to the market economy, because everyone knows me as an economist who believes in the market . . . I never made a secret of it and of course he was aware of that . . . He understood that there is no alternative to the market economy . . . the big question is how to go over to the market.'[103]

Ryzhkov, in spite of a professed commitment to a market economy in the long term, was in everyday practice a more effective opponent of radical economic reform than the more conservative Ligachev because, unlike Ligachev, he headed the apparatus responsible for its implementation. Petrakov recounted a conversation he had with Ryzhkov after he became Gorbachev's aide in which he told him that there was no need for a State Committee on Prices and that it should be abolished. Ryzhkov replied: 'You're right, but in a few years time.' Petrakov responded: 'Nikolay Ivanovich, you talk about the market as we used to talk about communism—it's always sometime later!'[104] Gorbachev, in contrast, in selecting Petrakov as his economic aide, had, in the latter's view, 'chosen the course of moving towards the market economy in a very short period'.[105]

During 1990 Gorbachev had innumerable discussions with Petrakov, and his knowledge of economic issues increased substantially. Although his actual experience of a market economy was limited to brief visits abroad, economists who worked especially closely with him—above all, Petrakov—do not subscribe to the simplistic view to be found in some Western circles that it was Gorbachev's lack of grasp of economics which was the cause of the Soviet Union's economic problems.[106] Gorbachev was always in the position of having to weigh what might be economically desirable against what was politically feasible.[107] As Vadim Bakatin—one of the ablest politicians to work with Gorbachev, for a time an exceptionally liberal Minister of Interior, and, after the failed August coup of 1991, the person who was charged with cutting the KGB down to size—put it, speaking about the perestroika project as a whole: 'We did not have a well thought out plan. Nor could we ever have one. Sometimes these were half-measures. Sometimes concessions had to be made to one set of forces or another. Gorbachev could never ignore the real existence of certain forces in society.'[108] Even so, Gorbachev took great risks at times, not least over the '500 Days Programme' (discussed later in this chapter and in Chapter 8).

The Soviet Union's deteriorating economic plight by 1990 owed much to the fact that, without the fear and coercion the old order had instilled (which under Brezhnev were already in decline and which virtually disappeared under Gorbachev), the traditional instruments of economic power were working worse than ever; the system was somehow in limbo—neither a functioning command economy nor yet a market economy. Concrete economic outcomes were the result of the struggle for power and resources among the major economic interests, and the entire battleground was supervised by a ministerial system with no interest in facilitating a move to a market economy and by a Chairman of the Council of Ministers in principle committed to such a transition but who wished to take his time about getting there. By 1990 the party and governmental apparatus were in widespread covert—and often open—revolt against Gorbachev. As Petrakov observed, it was highly unusual that in a year of a good harvest, as there had been in 1990, there should have been a bread shortage. This he attributed to lack of co-operation by the government and local officials, with the local *party* officials in particular having not the slightest desire to help Gorbachev.[109]

The '500 Days Programme': advance and retreat

The most dramatic episode in the history of attempted economic reform of the Gorbachev era occurred in the late summer and early autumn of 1990. Since this involved, first, an apparent total break with the existing system on Gorbachev's part and, then, a temporary accommodation with its most powerful institutional interests, it is a crucial period in the *politics* of transition—one which in the end damaged Gorbachev greatly—and as such is dealt with also in later chapters. In May 1990 Boris Yeltsin had been elected Chairman of the Supreme Soviet of the Russian republic, and the struggle between Russian institutions and the central (all-union) authorities was beginning to add a wholly new dimension to the centre–republican discord which had hitherto been confined mainly to the Baltic and Caucasian republics. The all-union legislature had instructed the government to prepare a new version of their economic programme by September and the Russian legislature had called for a programme of economic reform specifically for Russia—also by September. The young economist Grigory Yavlinsky, who had been given primary responsibility for the elaboration of the Russian programme, reached the conclusion that it did not make sense to do so in isolation from the rest of the union because of the closeness of inter-republican ties. He spoke with Petrakov and they agreed that it would be absurd to have different programmes for transition to a market economy for the Soviet Union as a whole, for Russia, for Ukraine, and for each of the other republics.[110]

Petrakov invited Yavlinsky to prepare a paper which he would show to Gorbachev, who became 'very excited' when he read it and asked to see Yavlinsky immediately.[111] Gorbachev was attracted not only by the idea of a single and radical programme for transition to a market economy but by the fact that a representative of the 'Russian' team had recognized the need for co-operation with the all-union authorities. He saw an opportunity for a renewal of co-operative relations with Yeltsin (who in May 1990 had overtaken Gorbachev as the most popular politician in the country)[112] and for putting together a coalition strong enough to win the battle for marketization. Gorbachev telephoned Yeltsin to urge him to make the team of radical economists a joint (Soviet Union–Russian Republic) one, and, after taking several hours to think about it, Yeltsin signed the document setting up the group which Yavlinsky brought to him.[113] Getting the additional signature of the Chairman of the Council of Ministers of the Russian republic, Ivan Silaev, was then a formality. The most difficult task for Gorbachev was to get the signature of *his* Chairman of the Council of Ministers, Ryzhkov, who was being asked to approve the setting-up of a rival team to the government one led by Abalkin. Ryzhkov had no desire to be presented with a programme more radical than his own and no faith in the prospects for harmony between Yeltsin (whom he had known since they had both worked in Sverdlovsk and from whom he had become increasingly alienated) and Gorbachev. Ryzhkov has explained that he signed most reluctantly and mainly because he was persuaded by his deputies that he would be blamed as the one person preventing an accord between the leader of the entire country and the leader of its largest republic if he did not.[114]

The working team became known as the Shatalin–Yavlinsky group (or sometimes the 'Shatalin group' after the more senior of the two economists). Everyone on it was a convinced marketeer, although half the nominees came from Gorbachev and half from Yeltsin. From the Gorbachev side the most formidable figures were Petrakov and Shatalin; Yeltsin's nominees included Yegor Gaydar and Boris Fedorov (later to become important politicians in the post-Soviet Russian government) as well as Yavlinsky. But because these were essentially like-minded radicals, they did not divide along Gorbachev–Yeltsin lines. Whereas Yeltsin adopted a hands-off approach, Gorbachev took an intense interest in the work of the team as it proceeded in a dacha near Moscow throughout August.

Several times a day, although on holiday, he would telephone both Petrakov and Shatalin to ask detailed questions about how things were going.[115]

After intense work the group produced what became unofficially known as the '500 Days Programme' (originally, before Yavlinsky joined forces with Petrakov, it was to have been 400 days) and which had the official title 'Transition to the Market: Conception and Programme'.[116] This main report was a 238-page document which did not once mention 'socialism' and made no concessions to traditional Soviet ideology. It incorporated the ideas of large-scale privatization, a great devolution of power to the republics, and the speedy construction of market institutions. An accompanying volume contained draft legislation for the legal acts which the authors believed would be necessary during the transition period. Gorbachev initially approved the documents both privately and publicly, and in the course of long discussion made some amendments of his own to them.[117] They spelled the end of state socialism and were utterly inconsistent with the idea that Gorbachev was still a Communist in any meaningful sense of the term, even though he was still General Secretary of the Communist Party of the Soviet Union! In fact, one of the more striking features of this episode is that he had entirely bypassed the party. The joint Union–Russian team had been set up without as much as a glance in the direction of the Politburo. In March 1990 Gorbachev had become President of the Soviet Union and he was making the most of that presidential power. The political backlash, together with second thoughts on Gorbachev's part, was still to come—and is one of the themes of Chapter 8. What is important in the present context is that Gorbachev accepted these radical marketizing and privatizing proposals in principle, even thought he later feared that they devolved so much power to the republics that they might hasten the dissolution of the union. That was an argument which was pressed on him very strongly, by Abalkin and Ryzhkov, among many others.[118] It is probable, although by no means certain, that the opposite was the case; they represented one of the last chances of holding a union together, whether as a loose federation or as a confederation.

The significance of the documents was as much political as economic. While one of the distinguishing marks of the '500 Days Programme' was that it had a precise timetable which other programmatic documents had lacked, the target dates were almost certainly unrealistic. Part of the argument for adhering—in the face of immense difficulties and attacks—to the Shatalin–Yavlinsky programme was that this might maintain the momentum for political and economic transformation and sustain a coalition of radically reformist forces.[119] Abalkin was among the most scathing of those who pointed to the over-optimism of the *Transition to the Market* team, saying that, if they really could bring the country out of deep economic crisis in five hundred days, he would raise a monument to them and regularly lay flowers at it.[120]

Under intense political pressure, which at the very least must have been an additional stimulus to the second thoughts which he has said that he began to have independently,[121] Gorbachev looked for a way of retaining the essence of the Shatalin–Yavlinsky programme while making some concessions to his critics. Ryzhkov had threatened to resign and to take the whole government with him. The military and the KGB—a cut in whose budgets was explicitly recommended in the 500-days document—were equally adamant that the programme was unacceptable, and the party apparatus at both the central and the local level was opposed to it. Gorbachev turned once again to Aganbegyan and asked him to draft a compromise programme which incorporated something of the Ryzhkov government view while retaining the essence of Shatalin's. This went through more than one variant and was approved by the Supreme Soviet of the USSR in October. Although Aganbegyan had succeeded in maintaining the pro-Shatalin bias of what was now known as the 'President's programme'—while removing the firm deadlines, restoring some of the revenue-gathering powers that had been removed from the union authorities, and incorporating some figures from Ryzhkov's programme—the compromise was unsatisfactory. The backtracking offended Yeltsin (some of whose close subordinates were, in any event, unhappy about his renewed alliance with Gorbachev), and Shatalin and the entire team expressed their dissatisfaction.[122]

As more concessions were made to conservative forces in the winter of 1990–1, Petrakov resigned in late December as Gorbachev's economic aide and was replaced by the less radical Oleg Ozherelev. Gorbachev finally, but in the opinion of Petrakov and others belatedly, decided to replace Ryzhkov; as he was on the point of doing so Ryzhkov suffered a serious but non-fatal heart attack, which, however, made his departure the more certain. As his successor (with the new title of Prime Minister), Gorbachev, after widespread consultations, chose the Minister of Finance, Valentin Pavlov.[123] Far from being an improvement on Ryzhkov, however, Pavlov turned out to be a disastrous appointment.

During 1991 Gorbachev attempted to keep in play several economic options, while his major concentration was on the political task of securing a new Union Treaty as a basis for holding the Soviet state together. He was guilty both of some indecision and of attempting to conduct three different, and conflicting, strategies simultaneously. First, he gave ostensible support to the policy of his Prime Minister, Pavlov, although by February 1991 he had realized that his appointment had been an error.[124] Second, he gave his blessing to a trip to the United States made by Grigory Yavlinsky, who—as one of the main authors of the '500 Days Programme'—was pursuing a quite different policy and was seeking to win the financial and political support of the United States administration for a rapid transition to the market in the Soviet Union.[125] In a third different approach, Gorbachev was conducting discussions with leaders of the other republics (and in particular Yeltsin and Nazarbaev) about radical changes in the Soviet government which would include the removal of Pavlov and his replacement as Prime Minister by, preferably, Nazarbaev.[126]

Between the appointment of Pavlov at the beginning of the year and the August coup of 1991 Soviet economic policy was poised uneasily between Gorbachev's desire to move more quickly to a market economy and to secure Western aid to ease the process and the reluctance of the Soviet government to give up any more of its levers of power. The growing strength of Yeltsin and of the institutions of the Russian presidency and legislature tied Gorbachev's hands further. When he came to London for a G7 summit in June 1991, the lack of coherence of the policies he presented—seeking non-existent middle ground between Yavlinsky's proposals which had received an encouraging response in the United States and the policies of Pavlov's government—was duly noted by his Western interlocutors, who showered Gorbachev with kind words but did not translate them into concrete economic assistance. Entirely understandable though that was, given that the Pavlov government was still in office, it weakened Gorbachev's authority further and strengthened the resolve of those from both sides of the political divide—but especially the hardliners—who wished to remove him.

Chapter 6

Gorbachev and Political Transformation

A CENTRAL thesis of this book has been that from the outset of his General Secretaryship Gorbachev was seriously interested in political change as well as economic reform,[1] but that in the course of the struggle to introduce it, he came to realize that reform was not enough and that the political system had to be comprehensively transformed. Reform within the limits of the Communist system was, it became increasingly clear, an unstable stopping-point.[2] It provoked so much resistance that a reformist leader was always likely to be faced, as Gorbachev was, with a choice between abandoning the attempt or accepting that the initial reforms could only be a stepping-stone on the way to something more fundamental. The *most* Gorbachev could envisage even up to 1987[3] was movement towards a socialist market economy and political reform up to the limits of the 'Prague Spring', although Czechoslovakia 1968 was not at that time a conscious reference point for Gorbachev.[4] However, the independent adoption of such views by the General Secretary of the Soviet Communist Party was already a large step forward and a highly significant deviation from previous Soviet theory and practice.

What is meant here by the Czech analogy is that the Communist Party would allow more debate within its own ranks and in the broader society and a fuller flow of information, together with a certain amount of interest group activity, but would ultimately retain institutional control over the levers of power. Although Gorbachev used the term *demokratizatsiya* (democratization), even in his major speech of December 1984, at that time it did not have the same denotation as it had for him by the late 1980s. In the earliest years of his General Secretaryship it signified a desire to breathe new life into existing institutions and to remove the formalism of intra-party life and in the activity of soviets. It meant that professional party or state functionaries should no longer be able simply to usurp the rights of discussion and deliberation which nominally belonged to party committees and soviets at the various levels of the party-state hierarchy.[5]

Although Gorbachev called this 'democratization', in reality what he was working for at that time was a *liberalization*.[6] It was a stage of redefining and extending rights which already existed on paper, whether in the Soviet Constitution of 1977 or in the *Rules of the Communist Party of the Soviet Union*, but which had been ignored in practice.[7] The elections that took place in the Soviet Union as a whole in 1989 and in the union republics in 1990 and 1991 went beyond liberalization and were a crucial part of the breakthrough to *democratization*. These elections—in the great majority of constituencies even in 1989—were multi-candidate, genuinely contested, and by secret ballot, and were preceded by vigorous debate. So far as Russia is concerned, they attracted far higher public interest and voter participation than any elections held in the post-Soviet period.

The very fact that Gorbachev stressed the need for *demokratizatsiya* was a stimulus to the democratization process, for those who wished to move in that direction could quote the General Secretary in support, although the system was such that initiatives from the top were still the main motor of change in the first four years of perestroika. What Gorbachev meant by *democratization* changed over time and by 1988–9 signified movement towards pluralist democracy—even before that was stated in so many words. Since Gorbachev sometimes took one step back for tactical reasons before moving two steps forward—and occasionally even two steps back, most notoriously and ill-advisedly in the winter of 1990–1—it is easy to find quotations from quite late in his General Secretaryship which supposedly demonstrate that his thinking had not changed significantly from his earlier years in office. Outside observers have to be as sensitive as Gorbachev's colleagues were to the fact that some speeches reflected his aspirations and developing political views more than others.

Of course, a speech in which obeisance was paid to traditional Communist Party norms—followed by no change of behaviour to the patterns of the past—could only very temporarily appease party conservatives, while lip-service from time to time to the concepts of an earlier era, such as 'democratic centralism', diminished his authority in the eyes of radical democrats. Yet there was no point at which it would have been safe for Gorbachev, even after he had become intellectually convinced that political systems of a West European type had major advantages over Communist systems, to take a resolute and entirely consistent line in favour of pluralist democracy. (That is not to say, however, that he should have refused to take the risk—although risk it would have been—of breaking openly with the hardliners and splitting the Communist Party at the Twenty-Eighth Party Congress in 1990, especially since, with the benefit of hindsight, it is all the clearer that seeking a temporary accommodation with the forces of conservatism in the autumn of that year did not work.)

While deploring Gorbachev's zig-zags and political manœuvring, some of his conservative Communist opponents understood what Gorbachev was doing better than did his critics in the ranks of the radical democrats (most of whom were neither particularly radical nor noticeably democratic until Gorbachev had taken the danger out of public criticism). Thus, Ligachev observes in his memoirs:

> I remember a wonderful speech Gorbachev gave in Kiev about the Party, one that could have become the foundation for the energetic Party activity to renew itself and cleanse its ranks. The general secretary, however, never again mentioned this speech: he spoke, signed off, and forgot. When I reminded him of his Kiev speech and of the fact that its theses should be implemented, Gorbachev changed the subject. There were many such occasions. I got the feeling that this was not inadvertent but rather an element of political

tactics—to voice some thesis to placate various social strata and political tendencies, but to carry on a different line in deeds.[8]

In comparison with all the transitions to political pluralism and greater or lesser degrees of democracy which have taken place in the world over the past two decades or more, the Soviet Union represented a quite exceptionally daunting challenge. Even the overt dissidents between the mid-1960s and mid-1980s had, on the whole, advocated liberalization rather than democratization. Their aims were generally rather modest by the standard of the later 1980s—such as, for example, the demand that the political authorities obey their own Soviet laws and constitution. Moreover, as has been noted in an earlier chapter, the dissidents had been all but eliminated as a movement (as distinct from small and isolated groups) by the time Gorbachev came to power and did not represent a threat to the power of the party-state, although they acted as the conscience of the morally reflective part of the population. All those tempted publicly to oppose specific major policies, not to speak of attempting to transform the fundamentals of the system from below, had been left in no doubt that persecution would follow. Even in the post-Stalin period a number of such people (incomparably fewer, of course, than in Stalin's time) died in Soviet labour camps. Only the most famous avoided prison, but even they did not succeed in breaking down the walls of the system. Solzhenitsyn, who came closest with his powerful writings (some of which were officially published from the early to the mid-1960s and thereafter only in *samizdat* and *tamizdat*), was deported from Russia in February 1974 and did not return until May 1994. Sakharov was exiled from Moscow to the city of Gorky (which was closed to foreigners, thus preventing his direct communication with foreign journalists) from 1980 until 1986.

Need for fourfold transformation

The problem for any Russian reformer was that the Soviet Union required a *fourfold transformation*. And no other country in the world which has embarked on the course of transition to democracy has had such a complicated, quadruple task. Gorbachev did not initially, it should be emphasized, have such a fundamental transformation in view. While in due course he came to admire the Spanish transition to democracy, that was not his reference point when he was elected General Secretary. His reformist project changed gradually and not all of the elements to be discussed were part of it from the outset. He was, however, aware from the beginning of his leadership of the need for significant—albeit, initially, not system-transforming—change in three of the four areas outlined below. The apparent exception was the third, where, in company not only with the rest of the party leadership but also with most Russian reformers in the mid-1980s, he seemed insufficiently aware of the potentially explosive strength of national sentiment and of the need to develop special institutional arrangements if all or most of the Soviet Union were to be held together on the basis of consent rather than coercion. As Gorbachev's project evolved and became qualitatively different from what he had had in mind in March 1985, he was faced by the virtually insuperable task of undertaking four more or less simultaneous transformations. The dilemma was the greater inasmuch as any three of these basic changes were likely to be undermined by the absence of a fourth, yet, as each was implemented, its side-effects produced complications in the other spheres.

The *first* transformation in terms of importance, and the one to which Gorbachev at least as early as the beginning of 1987 gave priority, was that of the political system. This element did not so fundamentally distinguish the Soviet Union from what was required of authoritarian regimes of 'the right'. They, too, required basic change in their political systems, but generally *only* that, for market institutions were already in place. However, even if the term 'totalitarian' as a description of the Soviet Union is reserved for the atomized society and mas- [1] sive repressions of Stalin's time, there was a difference between the 'post-totalitarian authoritarianism' of a *Communist* state and an authoritarian regime in which the party and political police had never permeated so thoroughly all walks of life.[9] Yet if the political system were to be transformed into one of pluralist democracy, this would involve competitive elections, freedom of group organization, the establishment of representative assemblies in which critical voices could be heard, subordination of the most powerful institutions to a rule of law, and real diversity in the mass media, prerequisites so radical that they were not seen as realistic goals by even the boldest reformers in the Soviet Union of 1985.

The *second* necessary transformation involved the need to move from a command economy with virtually 100 per cent state ownership of the means of production to a market economy with a substantial private sector. This element alone did not distinguish the Soviet Union fundamentally from other Communist systems in process of transition, although some—as noted in the previous chapter—had already gone further in modifying the command economy than had the Soviet state by the time Gorbachev came to power. The need for marketization *did*, however, distinguish the USSR from all of the states, whether in southern Europe or Latin America, which had made more or less successful transitions from authoritarianism to democracy by the mid-1980s.

It was, though, the combination of the first two requirements with the necessity of a *third* transformation—and its linkage with a fourth—which distinguished the Soviet transition from every other. This was the need to transform inter-ethnic and centre–periphery relations in a country with well over one hundred different ethnic groups, living for the most part in their historic homelands (although some of them had been exiled far from there by Stalin). Specifically, the political system could not be successfully democratized without some resolution of the 'national question', since throughout the Soviet period, as well as in Imperial Russia, the political aspirations of the more self-conscious nations within Soviet, and earlier imperial, borders had been rigorously suppressed. Alternatives had to be found to a repressive unitary state which purported to be a federation but did not in reality come anywhere near meeting the requirements of federalism. The two main alternatives in principle, no matter how difficult they were to attain in practice, were either a genuinely federal union or a looser confederation.[10]

But there was a *fourth* transformation required which, in some respects, was essential if the other three were to work but which, like each of the others, was also capable of complicating the transition. That was the need to transform Soviet foreign policy. It is well known that there were, in effect, two Soviet economies: one—privileged and pampered and in a number of areas up to world standards—devoted to military production and defence-related industry; and the other—starved of capital, new technology, and esteem—constituting the civilian industrial sector and supposedly providing for the needs of the ill-served Soviet consumer. For domestic transformation to be carried through there had to be the kind of change in international relations which would facilitate a reordering of Soviet economic priorities at home. The problem for Soviet leaders was that to tamper with the rationale for their huge military expenditure was to put at risk the only basis they had found thus far for ensuring that the Western world treated them with a grudging respect. It was clear to many foreign and Soviet observers that the USSR's superpower status depended (apart from the size and natural resources of the country) entirely upon its military strength—certainly not on the efficiency of the Soviet economy or the attractiveness to foreigners of the Communist political model (apart from some Third World revolutionaries who saw in Leninism a way of seizing and holding on to power). Paul Kennedy put the Soviet quandary well in *The Rise and Fall of the Great Powers* when he wrote: 'Without its massive military power, it counts for little in the world; *with* its massive military power, it makes others feel insecure and hurts its own economic prospects. It is a grim dilemma.'[11]

Writing early in the Gorbachev era, even the perceptive Kennedy did not expect that any Soviet leader would attempt to change the ideological base of the economic system or offer a fundamental challenge to the privileged position of the Soviet military and defence industry. Kennedy held that 'it is highly unlikely that even an energetic regime in Moscow would either abandon "scientific socialism" in order to boost the economy or drastically cut the burdens of defense expenditures and thereby affect the military core of the Soviet state'.[12] But Gorbachev's innovatory zeal was soon to outpace Western expectations. If the domestic political and economic transition to anything approximating democracy and a market economy were ever to take place, it required an end to the hostility that had characterized East–West relations and a massive reduction in the share of the budget taken by the defence sector. In his determination to tackle the problem of the militarization of the Soviet economy, 'Gorbachev', Chernyaev has argued, 'was moved not only by moral and humanitarian convictions; he had decided that social and economic reform would not be possible unless the role of the military-industrial complex was radically reduced'.[13] Shakhnazarov makes the interconnected point the other way round: 'it was impossible without political reform to get rid of the enormous burden of militarism.'[14] This was one major reason why political reform became a priority for Gorbachev. To bring the military budget under control was essential if marketizing reform and democratization were to begin to be bolstered by signs of an improving standard of living for the Soviet citizen. That material improvement was, to say the least, inadequately realized, even though it became, if anything, the more desirable once Gorbachev's political reforms had actually been introduced and people acquired a new political currency in the form of votes in elections whose results (unlike those in the unreformed Soviet system) were not predetermined. It was also important—certainly for Gorbachev himself and the radically reformist minority within the Soviet leadership—that the Soviet Union be integrated as a partner into both the international community and the international economy as a way of reducing the likelihood of a return to the unreconstructed Communist past with its combination of political oligarchy and economic autarky.

Since the first of these components has been discussed in the previous chapter and foreign policy is the subject of the next, the remainder of this chapter is concerned mainly with the domestic political system and the extent to which the prerequisites for a pluralization and democratization of the polity were met. The closely related nationalities question, while touched upon here, is treated at greater length in Chapter 8. However, one illustration of just how interlinked *all four* elements of a comprehensive transformation of the Soviet system were in reality was the change in foreign policy which led to acceptance of the independence of the East European states and fundamental changes in *their* political and economic systems and relations with the West and the Soviet Union. This had an immediate effect in the Soviet Union itself, not only in strengthening the conservative backlash against Gorbachev's policies but in raising further the expectations of those nations most bent on achieving sovereign statehood. Thus, in the Baltic states a widespread reaction was that what had been possible for Poland, Hungary, and (the then) Czechoslovakia should apply no less to Estonia, Latvia, and Lithuania. Even if the Soviet Union had been a more nationally homogeneous society, the problems of democratizing it after such a long period of totalitarian and authoritarian rule would have been immense, but they were enormously complicated by the aspirations of a number of the nations within the Soviet multinational state to break away entirely from the USSR. The tensions this provoked both at the centre and in particular republics left the reformers within the leadership—and Gorbachev, in particular—attempting to cope with the most contradictory and intense cross-pressures.

The stages of political transformation

Although I am more concerned in this chapter with offering an interpretation of political change, and Gorbachev's specific role in it, than with providing a detailed chronological account of the changes,[15] some key stages in the evolution of reform into transformative change must be highlighted. It is possible to divide the Gorbachev era into six different phases. The first three, which occupied the greater part of Gorbachev's time as Soviet leader, are covered in this chapter. They embrace the period in which the pluralization of the system took place, along with a substantial degree of democratization, so that by the end of the third phase the political order Gorbachev inherited in 1985 had been transformed. Discussion of the remaining three phases is to be found in Chapter 8 which, in addition to an analysis of the complex national question, is concerned with the political backlash against the earlier changes, the events leading up to the attempted coup, and the aftermath of that failed *putsch*. The six more or less distinct phases are: *first*, that of preparing the ground for reform (1985–6); *second*, radical political reform (1987–8); *third*, transformation at home and abroad (from early 1989 to the autumn of 1990); *fourth*, Gorbachev's 'turn to the right' (in the winter of 1990–1); *fifth*, the Novo-Ogarevo process (the attempt to achieve voluntary agreement on a new union treaty, April–August 1991); and *sixth*, from coup to collapse (the disintegration of the union, August–December 1991).

This is, of course, a retrospective view. Initially Gorbachev, while indeed preparing the ground for reform (by dint, for example, of several key appointments), was not seeking the kind of transformation of the system which he was later to embrace—still less the disintegration of the union which occurred. Gorbachev's own understanding of his project changed over time, as his early liberalization and the first steps of democratization stimulated a radicalization not only of his own ideas but of those around him. At the same time the process brought into being new social forces which were able to influence the country's political agenda, so that if it was still in 1988 largely set on the basis of internal struggle within the Communist Party, this was ceasing to be true by 1989 and was clearly not the case by 1990.[16] While the process called for constant adaptation on Gorbachev's part, it was more than unthinking improvisation. In due course, Gorbachev was to reject the essential features of Communism and to embrace social democracy. So long as he held office as General Secretary of the Soviet Communist Party (a necessity, in Gorbachev's view, if control of the party apparatus was to be kept out of the hands of those who would use it to turn back the political clock), he could not say so publicly. But both intellectually—as he made clear not only in private but also in his public adoption of concepts at odds with Marxism-Leninism[17]—and in political practice Gorbachev abandoned *Communism* (as distinct from the Communist Party, which, during the second half of his period in office, he hoped to turn into a democratic socialist party).

Preparing the ground

The first phase, that of *clearing the ground for reform*, occupied the whole of 1985–6. While Gorbachev began with an attempt to reinvigorate the Soviet economy—as something on which all members of the leadership team he inherited could agree—by 1986 he was moving towards giving priority to political over economic reform, not only because he believed that the former was a precondition of the latter but also because he thought liberalization and a broadening of the scope of political activity of existing partially moribund organizations, such as soviets and party committees (as distinct from the professional *apparat* which had usurped many of their powers), were desirable aims in themselves.

As I have attempted to show already in Chapter 4, personnel change and policy innovation went hand in hand, the former being a necessary, albeit not sufficient, condition for the latter. Just one year after Gorbachev became General Secretary—that is to say, immediately following the Twenty-Seventh Party Congress held in late February and early March 1986—there were twelve new faces out of twenty-seven in the Soviet top leadership team (full and candidate members of the Politburo and Secretaries of the Central Committee). For the first time in a quarter of a century it included a woman, Aleksandra Biryukova.[18] Within the larger party élite—that is, the members of the Central Committee— 44 per cent of those elected in 1986 were new as compared with approximately

28 per cent of newcomers in Brezhnev's last Central Committee chosen at the Twenty-Sixth Congress in 1981.[19] Of course, in his promotions policy Gorbachev (in so far as he had the most powerful voice in elevations to the Politburo and Secretariat)[20] was selecting from a pool of talent not of his own choosing, since the norms of the Soviet system were such that no one could mount several rungs of the ladder in one leap. It is hardly surprising, therefore, that new faces did not automatically translate into fresh ideas, the generation of which remained the concern only of the radical minority within the leadership. That minority included, of course, Gorbachev himself, even though he had also to play the role of even-handed arbiter in Politburo disputes.

Nevertheless, some of the essential groundwork for reform was, indeed, laid by Gorbachev in 1985–6 by virtue of his appointments policy. At the level of the Politburo and Secretariat, in addition to the co-option of a number of con-ditional allies, the two key promotions were those of Yakovlev and Shevardnadze, who were both whole-hearted Gorbachev supporters and ready for reform every bit as radical as Gorbachev was prepared to endorse. Yeltsin's appointment as Moscow First Secretary in December 1985 and entry into the ranks of the candidate members of the Politburo two months later was more ambiguous, not then such an obvious strengthening of the radical reformist tendency as it might have seemed five years on. In fighting corruption in Moscow, dismissing many local officials, allowing traders selling fruit and veg-etables to set up booths on the streets of the city, and attacking excesses of party privilege, he had dealt some hefty blows to the Moscow establishment, and gained popularity with Muscovites in the process, but he still took the basic institutional framework for granted. It was Gorbachev who was to do far more to change *the system*.

While a supporter at that time of Gorbachev, Yeltsin was still in an early stage of his political evolution. He did not have anything like as far-reaching a con-ception of reform as had Yakovlev, in particular, and Shevardnadze. Moreover, he was a less important Gorbachev ally in the Politburo, for he was exceptionally silent in the meetings of that body.[21] This may have had something to do with the fact that Yeltsin remained a candidate member of the Politburo even as late as 1987 and that he resented not being accorded voting membership,[22] but there is ample evidence that he had less to say than other party officials of the same rank and made no contribution to the elaboration of the new thinking on domestic or foreign policy.[23]

Apart from the appointments Gorbachev made to the top leadership team and, no less important, his success in dismissing such obstacles to change as Grishin, Romanov, and Tikhonov (as noted in Chapter 4), there were important developments in the mass media and cultural life. While Gorbachev envisaged glasnost initially in terms of increasing and diversifying the flow of information to the public—rather than as anything resembling complete freedom of speech and publication—and, as such, desirable in itself, he saw it also as an *instrument* in his struggle against conservative forces within the party-state bureaucracy. Instrumentally, it was a way of establishing contact with the society and of win-ning their support in his battle with the party conservatives. Later the concept acquired a broader meaning for Gorbachev, as for many others within the society, and he recognized it as one of the particularly valuable ends of the process he had begun and not merely a means.

In a paradoxical way, the disastrous accident at the Chernobyl nuclear power station in April 1986 was a stimulus to the further development of glasnost. The paradox lay in the fact that the initial Soviet reaction was a complete negation of glasnost and an apparent return to the bad old ways. The leadership itself did not at first realize how serious the catastrophe had been,[24] for both at the plant level and at the level of the regional political authorities there was an attempt to play down the scale of the disaster. Gorbachev, complaining about the sketchiness of the information the leadership received, has said that, if they acted too late, it was due to ignorance rather than irresponsibility.[25] It would also, however, appear that, when they did begin to learn more, they were concerned, as Alexander Yakovlev has observed, to avoid mass panic.[26] Authorities in Western countries, too, have tended to belittle the extent of nuclear disasters, but with a relatively free mass media they have become increasingly unsuccessful in doing so.[27]

Nevertheless, the fact that news of Chernobyl came first from the West rather than from within the Soviet Union made talk of glasnost ring hollow. What turned out to be the world's worst nuclear accident to date occurred on 26 April and it was not until the evening of 28 April that it was publicly acknowledged by Moscow in a minimally informative announcement on Soviet television. It was later still (30 April) before the Moscow newspapers acknowledged in two official sentences that an accident at Chernobyl had occurred.[28] Before long the Soviet press—or, to be precise, a significant segment of it—was to become less supine. The bolder Soviet journalists and scholars drew lessons from the catalogue of irresponsibility the Chernobyl disaster embodied, beginning with the careless work at the nuclear power station itself, moving on to the failure to provide adequate and timely information about the nature and scale of the disaster, and linking the need for genuine glasnost with that for greater public accountability.[29] Questioned about Chernobyl in late 1991, Gorbachev observed that 'this event shook us immensely' and agreed that 'it was in fact a turning point' in terms of the development of greater openness.[30]

The summer of 1986 certainly saw the beginnings of a significantly fuller flow of information and argument. In this first phase of perestroika there remained, however, a strong element of guided glasnost, as a number of changes of editors of periodicals were made at the behest of the Propaganda Department of the Central Committee, headed by Alexander Yakovlev. The most important cases in point were the nomination of Vitaly Korotich as editor of *Ogonek* and of Yegor Yakovlev to the editorship of *Moscow News*, following which these two weeklies altered their character radically and became for several years the most critical of the unreformed Soviet system and of conservatism within the Communist Party. Also of consequence was the replacement in the same year of Richard Kosolapov, the orthodox Marxist-Leninist editor of *Kommunist*, by the more enlightened Ivan Frolov, who later (as noted in a previous chapter) was to become an aide to Gorbachev and then editor of *Pravda*. In the first issue of *Kommunist* under Frolov's editorship, there appeared an official Central Committee criticism of the journal's performance hitherto, and in his second issue, as if to draw attention to the change of course, articles by such serious reformers as Tatyana Zaslavskaya and Otto Latsis were published.[31]

Among other important changes in 1986 were the editorships of two of the most important of the 'thick journals', *Novy mir* (to which the liberal Russian nationalist and campaigning environmentalist Sergey Zalygin was appointed) and *Znamya*, whose editor from the October 1986 issue was the liberal Georgy Baklanov.[32] (No less important in the latter case was the appointment as Baklanov's deputy of Vladimir Lakshin, a justly respected *shestidesyatnik* ('man of the sixties') who had been a deputy of Tvardovsky on *Novy mir* between 1962 and 1970 when that journal alone had found the collective courage to criticize some aspects of the status quo and, more particularly, the Stalinist past.) These prestigious literary monthlies regularly carried one or two long articles on current affairs, and over the next few years many of them broke completely new ground. Alongside these articles, in the greater part of each issue devoted to creative literature the most politically sensitive forbidden works—from Orwell (none of whose works had previously been published in the Soviet Union) to Solzhenitsyn (only a small part of whose writings had hitherto appeared in Soviet editions)—were introduced to Russian readers.

There was encouragement of change also in the cultural unions, where a movement from below had the tacit support both of Alexander Yakovlev (whose power increased from March 1986 when he became a Secretary of the Central Committee) and of the new head of the Culture Department, Yury Voronov, who had been appointed to that post by Gorbachev after having fallen into disfavour for a time in the Brezhnev years.[33] An important breakthrough occurred in May 1986 when major changes took place at the Congress of the Cinema Workers' Union, with Elem Klimov, a director whose own films had suffered severely from censorship and delayed distribution, becoming First Secretary. According to Klimov, Gorbachev sat through half a day of the Congress and Alexander Yakovlev attended the entire proceedings.[34] The presence of these leaders was a clear indication of political and moral support from the reformist wing of the party leadership for the proponents of change in the film industry. By the time the Writers' Union held their Congress in June 1986 the conservative forces had organized their defences better and the change at the top was less radical. Nevertheless, the time-serving Georgy Markov lost his position as First Secretary to Vladimir Karpov, who was no radical but had a stronger claim to integrity.[35] Later in 1986 liberal elements within the theatrical world followed the earlier example of the film-makers and asserted their cultural freedom and organizational autonomy. An entirely new Russian Theatre Workers' Union was formed on the initiative of the prominent actor Mikhail Ulyanov, the theatre director Oleg Yefremov, and the playwright Mikhail Shatrov, in an act of rebellion against the conservative All-Russian Theatre Society. Ulyanov, who was to be a forceful voice on the side of freedom of speech and democratization later in the perestroika period, became the first head of the new union.

An important signal both to the Soviet intelligentsia and to the outside world that a new attitude was beginning to be adopted to freedom of conscience and dissident political activity was the decision in December 1986 to release from exile Andrey Sakharov. Gorbachev had 'long ago', according to Chernyaev, felt uncomfortable about Sakharov's banishment from Moscow,[36] and with the help of Alexander Yakovlev he set about preparing opinion in the Politburo for putting an end to this arbitrary decision of the Brezhnev leadership in 1980. Nikolay Shishlin and Andrey Grachev, both at that time working in the International Information Department of the Central Committee, were entrusted by Yakovlev with the task of producing arguments which would persuade the Politburo to put an end to Sakharov's exile.[37] Gorbachev could not afford to upset the more conservative members of the Politburo too much at a time when he was attempting to get their agreement for a report he wished to present to the forthcoming (January 1987) Central Committee plenum which would radicalize the political reform agenda, and so the ground for the Sakharov decision had to be prepared carefully.[38]

Gorbachev and Yakovlev were, says Grachev, aware that neither the democratization of the country nor normal relations with the outside world would be possible so long as Sakharov remained in exile.[39] But 'the delicateness also of the problem was indicated by Yakovlev's conspiratorial tone as he formulated the task for us'.[40] Among other things, Shishlin and Grachev had to make sure the KGB did not know what was afoot, and thus they could not go to the KGB's archives to obtain Sakharov's political writings published in the West, since it would have been extremely unwise 'to prick up the ears of [KGB Chairman] Chebrikov in whose hands the fate of the exile continued to lie'.[41] Given the norms of the Soviet system and the body which had to be persuaded, Yakovlev's emissaries had to demonstrate not that Sakharov's exile was either immoral or illegal—for that would have cut no ice in the Politburo—but that it was 'inexpedient' for the Soviet state. Thus, the authors of the memorandum emphasized the political and moral damage which their country suffered from Sakharov's continuing exile, and, having laid hands on enough of his works (one or them Grachev had in his own apartment, having bought it abroad), they proceeded by selective quotation to show that there was a great deal in common between Sakharov's ideas and arguments and the Soviet 'New Political Thinking'.[42]

By 1 December 1986, when Gorbachev raised the matter at the Politburo, he had got the agreement in principle of the ruling group to put an end to the banishment of Sakharov.[43] On 16 December Gorbachev telephoned Sakharov (a telephone having been specially installed in the latter's Gorky apartment so that he could receive the call) and informed him that—along with his wife, Yelena Bonner, who had been as active as Sakharov in the dissident movement—he was free to return to Moscow and to 'go back to your patriotic work'.[44] By 'patriotic work' Gorbachev no doubt had in mind Sakharov's great distinction as a physicist and the prestige of Soviet science, but Sakharov spent even more time in the years that were left to him on his more *strictly* patriotic work—since as a scientist he was part of an international body of scholars—of attempting to bring Soviet observance of human rights up to acceptable standards of decency.

Gorbachev must have realized that Sakharov would continue to speak out on these issues, for, having thanked the Soviet leader for ending his exile, Sakharov immediately raised the issue of the dissident Anatoly Marchenko, who had died in prison earlier that month. He also spoke about the other prisoners of conscience concerning whom he had written to Gorbachev in a letter of 23 October

1986 in which he had also complained about his illegal exile and had asked to be allowed to return to Moscow.[45] From Gorbachev's answers to Sakharov in the course of the telephone call it was clear that he had read that letter, and it is probable that this provided the final stimulus to him to act to put an end to Sakharov's isolation. On the same day as his brief conversation with Sakharov (which was ended by the latter, not by the General Secretary)[46] Gorbachev held a meeting of heads of Central Committee departments and reported to them that he had called Sakharov and had invited him to return to Moscow. Chernyaev, who was there, noted that a majority of the senior party officials present greeted this news with a 'sarcastic smirk'.[47]

Radical political reform

The second phase was one of *radical political reform*. It began with the January plenum of the Central Committee in 1987 and continued throughout 1988. During the latter year an event of quite exceptional importance—the Nineteenth Conference of the Communist Party—greatly radicalized the political agenda and prepared the way for the more far-reaching changes of the following two years. It was in the course of the preparatory work for this gathering that Gorbachev, in consultation with his inner circle of advisers, took the firm decision to move towards contested elections and the creation of a new legislature to replace the existing, purely decorative Supreme Soviet, decisions which were then given the authoritative imprimatur of the conference, thanks largely to its skilful political management by Gorbachev.

Of great consequence as the first major step towards democratization was, however, the January 1987 plenum of the Central Committee. Its controversial character within the leadership was indicated by the fact that this plenary session was postponed three times before the January date was finally agreed.[48] Gorbachev's speech to the plenum was much more radical than his report to the Twenty-Seventh Party Congress just under a year earlier and it was the most significant address by a Soviet leader since Khrushchev's speeches denouncing Stalin delivered to the Twentieth Congress in 1956 and to the Twenty-Second Congress in 1961. Gorbachev produced his most far-reaching critique so far of Soviet theory and practice. Political thinking, he observed, had remained largely fixed 'at the level of the 1930s–1940s' when 'vigorous debates and creative ideas disappeared . . . while authoritarian evaluations and opinions became unquestionable truths'.[49] He emphasized more than ever the need for democratization, using language that (in conventional Soviet terms) was highly revisionist. After saying that the society and system were only at the initial stage of perestroika, he declared: 'Perestroika itself is possible only through democracy and due to democracy. It is only in this way that it is possible to give scope to socialism's most powerful creative force—free labour and free thought in a free country.'[50] Gorbachev proposed, furthermore, concrete measures of political reform. These were to include the introduction of more than one candidate for party secretaryships at all levels from the district up to the union republic in elections that would be conducted by secret ballot in party committees.

He also announced that it was 'the Politburo's opinion' that there should be, in addition, 'further democratization' of 'the formation of the central leading bodies of the party', and this, said Gorbachev, was 'wholly logical'.[51] The greater vagueness of the proposal concerning the election of the highest party organs was understandable. If the Central Committee, left to its own devices, elected the Politburo—rather than endorsing Politburo recommendations on its own composition, in which the voice of the General Secretary had traditionally been by far the most influential—Gorbachev would have been handing to more conservative forces additional powers at the very time he was trying to weaken their position. His ideal was to get an overwhelmingly reformist Central Committee elected before seriously entrusting them with the choice of members of the Politburo and Secretariat which they already enjoyed in theory. A premature 'democratization' of the Central Committee would have slowed or prevented the broader democratization of the political system. It was only through making use of the traditional authority vested in the office of the General Secretary and the real powers of the General Secretaryship that Gorbachev was able during his first four years in office (and especially his third and fourth years) to push through changes which were against the interests of the party apparatus, notwithstanding the fact that party officials constituted the overwhelming majority of members of the Central Committee.

Dissatisfied as he was with the results of the Twenty-Seventh Party Congress, Gorbachev persuaded his Politburo colleagues that there should be a special all-union party conference held in the summer of 1988, and he announced this decision to the January 1987 Central Committee plenum. The purpose of the conference, he told them, would be to monitor the course of economic reform and 'to discuss matters of further democratizing the life of the party and society as a whole'.[52] Gorbachev was thus already in early 1987 beginning to think about the need for liberalizing or democratizing measures that would go beyond simply greater intra-party democracy, although he was also conscious of the necessity for further change within the party itself. To help that process along, he hoped to be able to alter the make-up of the Central Committee at the following year's conference. Another Party Congress (officially held at five-year intervals) could not be convened so soon after the last one, and all-union party conferences were second only to congresses in the hierarchy of party authority. The last one had been held as long ago as 1941, but in the earlier Soviet period they had been more frequent and had sometimes made changes to the composition of the Central Committee.

In the remainder of 1987, following the January plenary session of the Central Committee, the most important domestic political events were the June 1987 plenum (discussed in Chapter 5), which radicalized economic reform but in a manner which produced unintended and harmful consequences, and the run-up to the seventieth anniversary of the Bolshevik revolution, which in October–November 1987 saw both a re-evaluation of seven decades of Soviet history and the first overt criticism of the party leadership by Boris Yeltsin. That latter event not only exacerbated the already bad relations between Yeltsin and Ligachev but made certain Yeltsin's removal from his Moscow party post and candidate membership of the Politburo. It was also the beginning of a breach between Yeltsin and Gorbachev which developed into the rivalry that was to play an increasingly important part in the fate of the Soviet Union. From this point on, neither man was at his most rational when contemplating the other, and while—in the face of the conservative backlash against Gorbachev's reforms—a political alliance between them would subsequently have made sense, it was something which they were able to sustain only for a matter of months in two separate periods of co-operation in the late summer of 1990 and the spring and early summer of 1991.

Gorbachev spent much time and effort on the report he was to present on the seventieth anniversary of the Bolshevik revolution, but in its final form it needed the approval, first, of the Politburo and then (much more formally) of the Central Committee before it could be delivered on what was to be a celebratory occasion in November 1987. The Politburo discussed Gorbachev's draft on several occasions and made a number of 'corrections' to it.[53] While speaking in private with Chernyaev, Gorbachev whole-heartedly condemned Stalin (as 'not simply 1937' but 'an entire system' which still had to be overcome), but in the Politburo he accepted a watering-down of the criticism of the past and especially of Stalinism in response to criticism from Ligachev, Gromyko, Solomentsev, and Vorotnikov.[54] The Politburo still included a substantial group who were highly defensive about the Soviet past, as they were to demonstrate again during the 'Nina Andreeva affair' (discussed below) less than half a year later. Gromyko, already quite a senior official in Stalin's time, was a prime case in point, as was Ligachev, who as early as the summer of 1986 had expressed disquiet about what he saw as an excessively disrespectful attitude to Soviet achievements even of the Stalin years.[55] Gorbachev's speech—delivered in the Kremlin Palace of Congresses to a joint celebratory meeting of the Central Committee of the CPSU and the Supreme Soviets of the USSR and of the Russian republic—was entitled 'October and Perestroika: the Revolution Continues'.[56] In the circumstances it was something of a compromise which did not entirely satisfy either those who wanted a sharp break with the past or, still less, those who wished to continue to think well of Stalin. Gorbachev concluded his speech with ringing words which read ironically in the light of the further departures from Communist orthodoxy which he was soon to make: 'We are on our way to a new world—the world of communism. From that path we shall never digress!'[57]

This finale brought Gorbachev 'stormy and prolonged applause', the stock-in-trade reaction to speeches by previous General Secretaries but a response which was soon to become a thing of the past for Gorbachev when he addressed party audiences. Earlier in his speech, Gorbachev had succeeded in breaking some new ground. He took the first steps towards rehabilitating both Nikolay Bukharin (the old Bolshevik[58] whom Lenin had described as 'the favourite of the whole party' and who was executed at Stalin's behest in 1938 following one of the most notorious of the show trials)[59] and Nikita Khrushchev, and declared that Stalin's guilt in relation to the massive repressions and illegality was 'immense and unpardonable' and should serve as a lesson 'for all generations'.[60] Importantly, he observed that the rehabilitation of Stalin's victims had virtually ceased in the mid-1960s and he announced the setting-up of a new commission (to be headed, although that was not mentioned in Gorbachev's speech, by Alexander Yakovlev) to examine the still unresolved cases of victims of repression.[61]

The break with Yeltsin This Gorbachev speech of 2 November was almost overshadowed by the Central Committee plenary session that preceded it, when he presented—on 21 October—his draft to the Central Committee. The Central Committee members duly approved that version, which had already been sanctioned by the Politburo, and the meeting—which had been convened for the sole purpose of ratifying this important party document—was about to disperse when Yeltsin indicated that he wished to speak. Ligachev, who was chairing the proceedings, tried to prevent him from taking the floor, but Gorbachev—without knowing what was to come—intervened on Yeltsin's behalf.[62]

Yeltsin's entirely unscheduled speech (already touched upon briefly in Chapter 4) turned out to be the beginning of the end of his career in the Communist Party—a process which by 1989, when the first contested elections at the national level were held in the Soviet Union, worked to his advantage, but which in the short term played into the hands of his conservative enemies. Yeltsin broke with the form which Central Committee meetings had hitherto taken, even though the substance of his criticisms was mild by his own later standards and by the standards of speeches by Gorbachev's conservative critics in the Central Committee some three years later. Yeltsin, however, complained about the lack of implementation of decisions taken in the first two years of perestroika, of the lack of support he received from the Central Committee Secretariat (and opposition from Ligachev, in particular, which indeed amounted to 'bullying' in the disinterested view of a reformist Central Committee official close to Gorbachev, rather than to Yeltsin[63]), and about what he regarded as a growth in the glorification of the General Secretary on the part of a number of full members of the Politburo.[64]

A whole series of speakers took the floor to criticize him, beginning with Ligachev, who mentioned (as he was to do again the following year—this time in public—at the Nineteenth Party Conference) that he was one of those who had proposed bringing Yeltsin from Sverdlovsk to a more senior post in Moscow.[65] A regional party secretary from Ukraine, Fedor Morgun, said that, if Ligachev was guilty of anything, it was precisely that.[66] The critics included the leading reformers Yakovlev and Shevardnadze, as well as Gorbachev himself, who spoke last. Yakovlev, in an interview some three years later, said: 'I was not convinced that Yeltsin had adopted a democratic position at that time. I was under the impression that his position was conservative. History will decide whether I was right or wrong.'[67] One of those who was most severe on Yeltsin was the Chairman of the Council of Ministers, Ryzhkov, who—as he pointed out—had known Yeltsin for a long time, since they had both been public figures in the same city of Sverdlovsk.[68] Ryzhkov accused Yeltsin of 'political nihilism', of getting carried away by the fact that he was being cited on foreign radio, of wanting to distance himself from the political leadership, and of having developed inordinate personal ambitions.[69]

To the extent that the last point was true—years later Yeltsin was to say that 'perhaps being first was always part of my nature'[70]—it was far from obvious at the time that Yeltsin had chosen the way in which he was most likely to further those ambitions. Indeed, even the following year he was to make an appeal for 'political rehabilitation', asking the Nineteenth Party Conference to rehabilitate

rehabilitate

him 'in the eyes of Communists' and 'in the spirit of perestroika'.[71] This had the appearance, since he remained, after all, a member of the Central Committee (albeit an outsider within that body), of a plea for promotion to the Politburo.[72] As late as 1988, in other words, it appeared to Yeltsin, as well as to his critics, that a serious political career could not be made outside the higher echelons of the Communist Party. At the October 1987 plenum Gorbachev had given Yeltsin the opportunity to reply to his numerous critics before summing up himself. Yeltsin said that he had 'no doubts about the strategic and political line of the party', but he returned to several of his specific criticisms, including that of glorification of the General Secretary. This, he said, was a criticism not of the Politburo as a whole but of 'two or three comrades', even though he believed they were speaking 'from the heart'.[73]

In his reply Gorbachev revealed that Yeltsin had written to him while he was on holiday in the south, threatening to resign and requesting a meeting with him. In a telephone conversation Gorbachev had urged Yeltsin to continue to work as normal until after the November anniversary celebrations of the seventieth anniversary of the Bolshevik Revolution and, he said, they had agreed that they would meet after that. Yeltsin had warned Gorbachev that, if he did not agree to meet him, he would take the issue to the Central Committee, but so far as Gorbachev was concerned they had decided to hold their discussion the following month. Gorbachev said that he had not, accordingly, expected Yeltsin to choose this inappropriate occasion on which to speak, showing thereby a lack of respect for him and for their agreement.[74] Anatoly Chernyaev records in his memoirs that he was with Gorbachev in the Crimea when Yeltsin's letter arrived and that he was present in Gorbachev's room when the subsequent telephone conversation took place; he reports Gorbachev saying to him that Yeltsin had agreed 'not to fret' between then and the public holiday.[75] Yeltsin several years later, in conversation with Alexander Yakovlev, denied having made any such agreement with Gorbachev.[76] It seems likely either that Yeltsin's memory was at fault or that Gorbachev and Yeltsin had ended their telephone conversation with a different understanding of what had been agreed even at the time. The latter explanation is offered by another Politburo member, Vadim Medvedev, who says that the words used by Gorbachev about his proposed meeting with Yeltsin were '*posle prazdnika*', or 'after the celebration (public holiday)', which Yeltsin had interpreted in his own way to mean 7 October, which was then the Day of the Constitution (celebrating the Stalin Constitution of 1936), although, Medvedev adds, no one else saw that date in such a celebratory light.[77]

If this was a misunderstanding, it would appear to be a momentous one, but Yeltsin had been particularly riled by the treatment he had received from Ligachev—who was always more assertive when in charge of the party organization while Gorbachev was on holiday—and it could only have been a matter of time before his patience snapped. The origins of the October episode, according to Alexander Yakovlev, lay in Ligachev's persistent attempts to gain control over the Moscow party organization which Yeltsin headed and in a particularly severe clash in the Politburo in August when Ligachev was presiding over it in Gorbachev's absence.[78] Vadim Medvedev believes that the problem went much deeper than that. Confirming Ligachev's statement on more than one occasion that it was he who was the prime mover in bringing Yeltsin from Sverdlovsk to the Central Committee, Medvedev suggests that Ligachev had reckoned that Yeltsin would be 'his man' in Moscow, whereas in fact Yeltsin resented (as he made clear in his memoirs) being initially only a department head of the Central Committee and later, as Moscow First Secretary, being expected by Ligachev to subordinate himself to him as well as to Gorbachev.[79] The problem was, Medvedev suggests with good reason, that in temperament and personality Ligachev and Yeltsin were very similar to one another.[80] They were categorical in their judgements, authoritarian in their methods of leadership, and rigid in their practical actions.[81]

Gorbachev, whose relations with Yeltsin had, in Medvedev's view, been reserved from the outset—'since there was too great a difference in their style of work and behaviour'—was particularly irritated by one passage in Yeltsin's October speech in which the Moscow Party First Secretary had said that the people had gained nothing over the past two years. That, Gorbachev retorted, was an irresponsible statement. An 'entirely new atmosphere in the party and in the country' had been created and they were coming out of a long period of stagnation. How was it that a candidate member of the Politburo had failed to notice that?[82]

It was not at the time the custom to publish verbatim accounts of the proceedings of Central Committee plenary sessions, and it was a year and a half later that the full stenographic report of the October 1987 plenum appeared in a party journal. In the meantime, and especially in the weeks immediately after the October plenum, rumours of what Yeltsin had said abounded. Most of them were false and exaggerated the scale of his criticisms, but they were damaging for Gorbachev. In retrospect, he must have regretted failing to find time to meet with Yeltsin ahead of the plenum or, failing that, to publish promptly the transcript of the proceedings.[83] Earlier at that same plenum, Gorbachev, after covering the main points to be included in his speech commemorating the seventieth anniversary of the Bolshevik Revolution, had strongly attacked conservative forces within the party who were paying lip-service to perestroika but actually obstructing change. As Angus Roxburgh has observed, there could hardly have been 'a clearer statement of Gorbachev's radicalism, yet within the hour he was forced to become a centrist'.[84] In the short run, Yeltsin's unexpected intervention strengthened the conservative forces in the party. Whereas immediately prior to Yeltsin's speech Gorbachev had attacked *only* the conservatives, he and his leading ally in the fight for domestic political reform, Yakovlev, were now placed on the defensive. In Roxburgh's words, 'Yeltsin had handed the right a victory by forcing Gorbachev to take up a more centrist position, at least publicly.'[85]

A week after Gorbachev delivered the anniversary speech on 2 November, Yeltsin became ill and was taken to hospital. Yet two days later Gorbachev insisted that he attend a meeting of the Moscow city party committee. Although Ligachev led the pack of Yeltsin's accusers at that meeting—which ended with Yeltsin being removed from the office of First Secretary of the Moscow party organization—the fact that Yeltsin was forced to attend against the advice of his doctors (and under sedation) was one of the least creditable episodes of Gorbachev's career. The denunciations of Yeltsin by local party officials whom he had dismissed or offended were fiercer than the criticism he had faced at the Central Committee and were all too reminiscent of former Soviet times.[86] Gorbachev had the grace to look embarrassed, as well he might, by the ferocity of the verbal attacks on Yeltsin as the party apparatus took its revenge and it was he who took Yeltsin by the arm and helped him out of the hall after Ligachev and all Yeltsin's other accusers had left in triumph.[87]

The Nina Andreeva affair Yeltsin was replaced as Moscow Party First Secretary by Lev Zaykov, a former First Secretary of the Leningrad regional party organization who had made his earlier career in military industry. His appointment, in keeping with the general aftermath of Yeltsin's *démarche*, had bolstered the position of the more conservative forces within the leadership.[88] Just, however, as Yeltsin had acted rashly (to his own short-term detriment), so Ligachev and his allies were to overreach themselves less than six months later. The episode became known as the 'Nina Andreeva affair' and Gorbachev made shrewd and determined use of it in order not only to recapture the ground he had lost with Yeltsin's resignation but also to put the party conservatives on the defensive once again.

A long letter from a hitherto-unknown lecturer at a Leningrad chemical institute, Nina Andreeva, appeared in the newspaper *Sovetskaya Rossiya* on 13 March 1988. From a neo-Stalinist standpoint, she criticized the growing tendency to fill in the 'blank spots' in Soviet history with what to the detached observer were objective facts but which she interpreted as denigration of a mainly heroic Soviet past. She attacked Westernizing liberals in Soviet society and, by implication, also blamed Jews for most of Russia's troubles. Of the several people of Jewish origin mentioned in her article, the only one to escape criticism was Karl Marx.[89] In essence, the letter—which had been professionally rewritten as an article by a *Sovetskaya Rossiya* journalist in consultation with officials in the Central Committee apparatus—was an attack on the main thrust of Gorbachev's reforms and a plea to turn the clock back to the political practices and ideological beliefs characteristic of the unreformed Soviet system. Its importance lay in the fact that it was immediately interpreted, both by those who welcomed it and those whom it shocked, as a much more authoritative document than its apparent authorship by an obscure Leningrad teacher would suggest. (When the letter was first discussed among Politburo members, Vadim Medvedev and Lev Zaykov—both from Leningrad—were asked who Nina Andreeva was, and they had to confess they did not have the faintest idea, thus fuelling the unwarranted suspicion that the name was a pseudonym.[90])

Russian intellectuals suspected that the letter had support within the leadership, and in that they were right. Many of them also believed that it reflected a significant shift in the balance of forces within the highest echelons of the party. That judgement was, to say the least, premature. The Andreeva letter was not a reflection of a change at the top but an intended stimulus to such a shift. Those who sponsored it were attempting to put a stop to the kind of perestroika which embodied radical reform and called the Soviet past into question, and the fruit of their and Andreeva's labours was, accordingly, characterized by Gorbachev and Yakovlev as an 'anti-perestroika manifesto'.

The date of its publication had been chosen carefully by officials within the Central Committee apparatus, who had conspired with Valentin Chikin, the editor of *Sovetskaya Rossiya*, to supervise the rewriting of the letter and ensure that it would have maximum impact. It appeared on a Sunday and the day before Gorbachev left for a visit to Yugoslavia and Yakovlev for Mongolia. Ligachev was, accordingly, in sole charge of the party apparatus and of ideological concerns. Although he was later to deny that he had anything to do with the Andreeva letter until after it had appeared, the weight of evidence suggests that he was involved both before and after. What is, at any rate, beyond doubt is that he was quick to praise it, describing it as 'a benchmark for what we need in our ideology today' and urging journalists 'to seek inspiration in the article'.[91] Presiding over a meeting within the Central Committee on the Monday, the first working day after its appearance, Ligachev described the article as a fine example of party journalism and urged its republication in local newspapers.[92] It was not only many local newspapers which were, indeed, quick to republish, but the East German party newspaper *Neues Deutschland* which did so, evidently heartened by this reiteration of old dogmas and warnings against new departures from them. The very fact that the article was not rebutted in the Soviet Union during the days which followed—as a result of the absence of Gorbachev and Yakovlev from Moscow at the crucial time—strengthened the gloomy view of reformist intellectuals that there had been a change of party line and that the 'Moscow Spring' was ending.[93]

Very few of those who were to proclaim themselves to be democrats and to castigate Gorbachev for his 'half-measures' two years later put their heads above the parapet over the three weeks following the publication of the Andreeva letter.[94] Old habits of prudence rapidly reasserted themselves in the face of an apparent signal of change in the balance of forces at the top of the party hierarchy and of a return to a time when dissenting intellectuals would no longer be treated with tolerance.[95] One of the small minority of bodies to protest was the Film-Makers' Union, following the initiative of the playwright Alexander Gelman.[96] Gorbachev realized that a gauntlet had been thrown down which he would have to pick up when he discovered that a substantial number of Politburo members thoroughly approved of the article.[97]

Having returned to Moscow on 18 March, Gorbachev first discussed the Andreeva letter with a majority of Politburo members during the interval of the Congress of Collective Farm Workers being held in the Kremlin and which was addressed by him on 23 March.[98] It became immediately clear that the publication was very much in tune with the thoughts of an alarmingly large number of his colleagues, among them Vorotnikov, Ligachev, Gromyko, Solomentsev, and Nikonov.[99] Gorbachev took the issue to a formal meeting of the Politburo on 24 March and discussion of the *Sovetskaya Rossiya* publication continued over two days.[100] At the Politburo meeting the KGB Chairman, Chebrikov, who complained about the scheming 'of our ideological adversary', was essentially on Andreeva's side,[101] while Lukyanov added his voice to those of her supporters—an especially unwelcome surprise for Gorbachev.[102] (This should have been a warning to him not to place much faith in Lukyanov, in spite of the fact that they had known each other for so long, but it was one which he did not heed.

All of the other Politburo members who supported the Andreeva letter were removed from positions of power before 1991, but Lukyanov was there right up to the August coup, during which he betrayed Gorbachev. Latterly, it should be added, he had his own power base as Chairman of the Supreme Soviet of the USSR.) In March–April 1988, the time of the Nina Andreeva affair, the traditional authority of the General Secretaryship was still an important factor in Soviet politics, and, taken in conjunction with Gorbachev's personal high standing then, enabled him to overcome numerically strong opposition within the Communist Party's highest policy-making body. Politburo members hesitated to continue to defy the party leader on something on which he clearly felt strongly.

Gorbachev insisted upon every Politburo member stating his position on the article. Yakovlev (in a detailed, twenty-minute-long rebuttal of the *Sovetskaya Rossiya* publication), Ryzhkov (who resented Ligachev's interference from the party secretariat in the affairs of the Council of Ministers), Shevardnadze ('vividly and, as always, emotionally', according to Vadim Medvedev[103]), and Medvedev attacked the article especially vehemently, and Gorbachev was able to put its supporters, including Ligachev, on the defensive.[104] Gorbachev and Yakovlev were already in agreement that the Andreeva letter required a formal reply, and the Politburo duly assented to the publication of an authoritative, unsigned response to be printed in *Pravda*.[105] Without mentioning Andreeva by name—as recognition that the article had been much more than the expression of an individual's political opinions—the *Pravda* article rebutted the *Sovetskaya Rossiya* 'letter' point by point. Drafted mainly by Yakovlev, but with the participation of Gorbachev, it appeared on 5 April, following which the radical wing of the intelligentsia found its voice once again. The Andreeva affair was an important example of the extent to which commitment to radical political change, including continuing support for glasnost, still depended—three years after his coming to power—on Gorbachev and how little reliance could be placed at this time on democratic pressure from below to combat attempts by party conservatives to launch a counter-reformation.[106]

Throughout the Politburo meeting Gorbachev stressed that his concern was not with the individual views of Nina Andreeva but with the way her views had been promoted as an example which others should follow. Alluding to the support that the Andreeva letter had received from within the Central Committee apparatus and its Secretariat, Gorbachev said that this had taught him a lesson that he had not been sufficiently close to those bodies. He had, he said, never attended a meeting of the Secretariat since becoming General Secretary, although Brezhnev occasionally had done so.[107] (In Brezhnev's time the weekly meetings of the Secretariat of the Central Committee were normally chaired by Suslov, and during the first three years of the Gorbachev era it was Ligachev who presided over them.) Gorbachev had always carefully examined the agenda of Secretariat meetings and discussed issues of principle arising in them, but evidently that was not enough. Therefore, he said, he had not adequately fulfilled all of his responsibilities as General Secretary and had to engage in self-criticism.[108] This exercise in apparent humility was, however, another way of saying that the Secretariat had been allowed too loose a rein. Their very next meeting was chaired by Gorbachev.[109] More dramatic changes were to follow.

Within a very few months the Central Committee party apparatus was drastically cut in size and the Secretariat ceased to meet as a body.

The Nineteenth Party Conference An immediate result of the Andreeva affair was that, while Ligachev remained in charge of the party organization and was still jointly, along with Yakovlev, in charge of ideology, he lost his share in the supervision of the press to Yakovlev, who now had primary responsibility within the Central Committee Secretariat for the mass media.[110] Many writers and journalists, ashamed of their timidity during the period when it had looked as if a price might have to be paid for the publication of critical views, took full advantage of this change to push wider the boundaries of glasnost in the run-up to the Party Conference which was held from 28 June until 1 July 1988. In the meantime, foreign policy successes (discussed in the next chapter) had further enhanced Gorbachev's popularity. The Geneva accords on the ending of the Soviet intervention in Afghanistan had been signed on 14 April and the phased withdrawal of Soviet troops had begun in May; at the end of that month the extent to which East–West relations had changed dramatically for the better was emphasized when Ronald Reagan arrived in Moscow for a fourth summit meeting with Gorbachev.

In the early months of 1988 Gorbachev's political language manifested old as well as new thinking. (This remained true to some extent even after the Nineteenth Party Conference, but by then the new had a greater predominance over the old.) In a speech Gorbachev made to a Central Committee plenum in February 1988, every third phrase, as Shakhnazarov puts it in his volume of political reflections and memoirs, could have been used by those who argued that Gorbachev wished to do no more than to ' "touch up" socialism', but he qualified such statements with remarks which had not been heard 'from a high party tribune in the course of many decades'.[111] Thus, for example, Gorbachev spoke of the 'guiding and leading role of the party' as an 'indispensable condition of the functioning and development of socialist society', but he went on to say that the party must use that leading role in order to effect 'deep transformations' and 'employing only democratic methods of work'. Similarly, while still describing Marxism-Leninism as 'the scientific base of the party's approach to an understanding of social development and the practice of Communist construction', Gorbachev also said: 'there cannot and must not be any limitation on scientific enquiry. Questions of theory cannot and must not be decided by any kind of decrees. The free competition of intellects is essential.'[112]

The preparation of documents to be presented to the Nineteenth Party Conference provided a major opportunity for such serious argument and for the radicalization of political reform. Indeed, the resolutions passed and decisions taken by the conference at Gorbachev's instigation set the Soviet Union on a course of transition from reformist to transformative change of the political system. It was, moreover, during intense discussions with his reformist allies in the months preceding the conference that Gorbachev's own position was further radicalized. While not only Gorbachev's thinking but that of even the most radical of his advisers still contained some traditional elements, more concepts taken from Western democratic thought and practice entered Soviet political discourse. Alexander Yakovlev and Georgy Shakhnazarov were especially influential in elaborating proposals for reform of the political system, and others who played an important part in the discussions and preparation of documents before and during the conference included Vadim Medvedev, Anatoly Lukyanov, Ivan Frolov, Anatoly Chernyaev, and the editor of *Kommunist*, Nail Bikkenen.[113]

The strong nostalgia for the past of leading party figures, demonstrated by their sympathy with the sentiments expressed in the Andreeva letter, had also played a part in sharpening Gorbachev's radically reformist position. Between 11 and 18 April 1988, as part of the preparation for the Nineteenth Party Conference and also to underline the necessity of combating the support which had been manifested in party circles for the Andreeva viewpoint, Gorbachev held a series of three meetings with regional party first secretaries (some 150 key officials, with approximately fifty attending each meeting).[114] He drew attention to the significance of moving to a state based upon the rule of law, pointing out that this meant that every person and all institutions must be subordinate to the law, including the Politburo.[115] The influence of democratic practice in non-Communist countries and of his conversations with Western politicians was apparent when Gorbachev told his audience of party officials in one of these off-the-record talks that 'the whole world criticizes us for the fact that the party rules the country regardless of the law' and because only a part of the society (meaning Communist Party members) had a share in real power.[116] According to Chernyaev, as early as these April meetings Gorbachev introduced the idea which became policy at the Nineteenth Party Conference that party secretaries at all levels of the hierarchy should also chair the corresponding local soviet, *but* if they failed to be elected to the soviet they would have to resign their party post as well.[117] In this way, the non-party majority of the population were to be given, in effect, a veto on the holders of party posts (as well as on membership of the local councils and higher legislative bodies), one which would have been anomalous in a competitive party system but was a step forward in a one-party state.

Before the Nineteenth Party Conference began, 'theses' to be presented to it in the name of the Central Committee were published.[118] Although they represented a further modest step in the radicalization of reform, they did not include the most dramatic changes which were to be announced by Gorbachev himself at the actual conference. Most of the detailed preliminary work on the draft theses had been done by Gorbachev's aides Georgy Shakhnazarov and Ivan Frolov, working in the Novo-Ogarevo dacha outside Moscow and keeping in close touch with the General Secretary.[119] A Politburo meeting on 19 May broadly approved their work, although there were some specific objections. Thus, for example, Ligachev said that to the 'all-human interests' noted in the document it was necessary to add 'class interests'.[120] (The final version of the theses would appear to have eliminated that entire sentence. The document did not mention class interests or values, but did—in the context of international relations—refer to 'the primacy of law and common human morality'.[121]) Perhaps the most serious set-back was that several Politburo members spoke out 'against the co-option of new members of the Central Committee' and Gorbachev did not insist on having his way.[122] In Shakhnazarov's view, this 'later played a fateful role, hampering reform of the party'.[123]

Against that, it must be said that subsequent changes in the composition of the Central Committee and the Politburo at the Twenty-Eighth Party Congress in 1990 still did not give Gorbachev a majority of genuine supporters within either of those bodies. His own views had moved increasingly in a social democratic direction, while a majority in the party apparatus were primarily concerned about the loss of power the drastic reforms already entailed for them. They complained about the way Gorbachev had pushed change through without taking account of their views, holding that this amounted to a lack of democracy in the party. As has been noted above, however, if the party apparatus had been able to exercise 'democratic control' over Gorbachev, it would have been in defence of their vested interests and in direct conflict with the democratization of the society.[124]

If Gorbachev *had* insisted on replenishment of the Central Committee at the Nineteenth Conference, that would have helped him only if the new members had come from the radical minority among the conference delegates and it is highly unlikely that he could have staved off a showdown at some stage or other between the forces favouring fundamental change and those whose nostalgia for the status quo ante was growing stronger by the day. Gorbachev would also, if the changes were to have done him any good, have had to supervise the choice of new members himself, taking advice from such allies as Yakovlev, Shakhnazarov, and Chernyaev. This would have brought forward the date of the open break with Ligachev (which would have been welcomed by Yakovlev and like-minded colleagues who found Gorbachev's patience with Ligachev both irritating and anomalous), for he still supervised the party organization and would have bitterly resented being bypassed on a key issue of 'cadres policy'. But in 1988, to a much greater extent than in 1990, the traditional authority granted to a General Secretary still worked in Gorbachev's favour, and in Shakhnazarov's view the Nineteenth Party Conference represented a 'unique chance' to renew the party leadership, for Gorbachev retained sufficient influence to have been able to persuade the party conference to vote for the names he proposed.[125]

The conference itself widened the boundaries of debate in Soviet politics. Politburo members—among them Gromyko, Solomentsev, and Ligachev—were criticized by name in speeches which were reported at length on television. Yeltsin, in his speech, brought his dispute with Ligachev into the open, and Ligachev responded with a vigorous onslaught on Yeltsin.[126] Gorbachev was not yet criticized directly, but several speakers (above all, the conservative writer Yury Bondarev) were highly critical of him implicitly. The Nineteenth Party Conference, however, and the months which followed it—prior to the convening of the First Congress of People's Deputies the following May—can be regarded as the high point of Gorbachev's power within the system. He dominated the conference to a greater extent than he had the Party Congress of 1986, frequently contributing to the discussion and often engaging in a dialogue with particular speakers to hammer home points he wished to emphasize.[127] The fact that Gorbachev was able to wield so much power between the summer of 1988 and spring of 1989 (as compared with 1985–6, when he had to proceed more cautiously) supports the generalization that the power of Soviet General Secretaries increased over time—not from one incumbent to the next (for Stalin wielded a power, including that of life or death of his 'colleagues', that was incomparably greater than any of his successors) but within each incumbency.[128] This was, not least, because it took a General Secretary a number of years (but fewer than usual in Gorbachev's case) to remove foot-dragging colleagues whom he had inherited and to use his *de facto* power of appointment to bring in more of his own supporters.[129]

It can, of course, be readily observed that by 1990–1 Gorbachev was far less in control than he had been two years earlier, and that fewer levers of power by that time were concentrated in the office of General Secretary. That, however—as I argue below—was a direct result of far-reaching changes pushed through by Gorbachev himself, as a consequence of which the Soviet system had become different in kind. Generalizations about the polity based on its operating rules as a closed system of co-option and appointment from above did not, and could not, apply to a system in which contested elections, combined with freedom of expression, had radically changed the rules of the political game. Once a broader Soviet public had been given the opportunity for the first time to become genuine participants in the political process and republican political leaders had been put in place by their own electorates rather than by the General Secretary and the Politburo, it followed that the all-union party leader was operating in a transformed system in which some of the most crucial of his former prerogatives no longer fell within his jurisdiction.

Later, as President of the USSR, Gorbachev was frequently accused of trying to concentrate too much power in his hands. He could legitimately respond (and frequently did) that if he had been interested in nothing but power he had absolutely no need to change the unreformed Soviet system, for it endowed the General Secretary with powers beyond the dreams of most national leaders. Even that view should be qualified, however, with the addendum that the General Secretary enjoyed such enormous power and authority so long as he did not challenge the fundamentals of the system. Given the extent to which Gorbachev had done so by the end of the Nineteenth Party Conference, it is a tribute to his political skills that he remained as strong as he then was. As the projected reforms of 1988 were actually introduced, Gorbachev found himself under attack not only from radical democrats who had, for the first time, been given a public platform and legitimated political voice, but from within the General Secretary's traditional power base of the party apparatus.

The Nineteenth Party Conference passed a series of resolutions, each of which had been discussed in conference commissions presided over by senior members of the Politburo. The most path-breaking resolutions emerged from the commission chaired by Gorbachev, in keeping with the logic of party power whereby the political weight of the General Secretary had to be brought to bear if anything radically new was to be accepted. The two resolutions Gorbachev specifically sponsored and introduced were on the 'deepening of perestroika' (which embraced not only economic reform but foreign policy) and on 'the democratization of Soviet society and reform of the political system'. The other resolutions passed were on the 'struggle against bureaucratism' (the product of a commission chaired by Ligachev), on relations between the nationalities (chaired by Ryzhkov), on glasnost (chaired by Yakovlev), and on legal reform, the commission on which was presided over by the unlikely figure of Gromyko, who was still (although not for much longer) Chairman of the Presidium of the Supreme Soviet.[130] Taken together, the resolutions embraced many of the ideas for far-reaching reform which had been aired over the previous months (but not hitherto adopted as policy) and introduced several more which went far beyond what had previously been heard from an authoritative Soviet forum.

By the time the next Party Congress (in principle a still more authoritative assembly than an all-union party conference) met in 1990, what was decided was no longer of such consequence for Soviet citizens or of comparable interest to the outside observer, for the Communist Party no longer held a monopoly of power in the society. In mid-1988, however, what happened in the highest party forum was of enormous significance for the country as a whole and, as it turned out, for the outside world. The Communist Party leadership still set the political agenda, deciding which ideas that had been floated in the mass media or that had emerged among groups of specialists in particular 'policy networks' would be taken up and become authoritative public policy.[131] But within that leadership Gorbachev and a group of like-minded associates (whose influence depended entirely on their access to, and the political sympathy of, the General Secretary) were far more important as political innovators than the rest of the top echelon of the party put together.

Thus, a member of Gorbachev's personal staff, Shakhnazarov, who had been appointed specifically to advise him on reform of the political system, exercised more influence than a majority of his nominal political seniors who were full members of the Politburo. It should not, however, be forgotten that the latter still had the collective power to oust the General Secretary from office (together, needless to say, with his advisers) had they worked in consort and had they not been humoured and cajoled by Gorbachev into becoming part of a coalition for far-reaching change in which few of them wholly believed. As the record of the Politburo meeting in which the Nina Andreeva letter was discussed showed, Gorbachev would make the most of his authority as General Secretary while engaging also in genuine persuasion to achieve what would then bear a resemblance to consensus among Politburo members, even if some of them were by the end of a long discussion merely suppressing their doubts.[132]

Contested elections and the democratization process The most decisive break with the past was the decision to introduce contested elections for a new legislature which would replace the existing Supreme Soviet, a body which met infrequently and rubber-stamped legislation at the behest of the executive. The resolution 'On democratization of Soviet society and reform of the political system' called, *inter alia*, for the ensuring of 'unrestricted nomination of candidates, broad and free discussion of them, the inclusion on the ballot papers of a larger number of candidates than seats and strict observance of the democratic procedures of elections'.[133] The elections were to be for a new 'outer' legislative body, the Congress of People's Deputies of the USSR, which would, in turn, elect a smaller 'inner' body, a bicameral Supreme Soviet, which would be the standing legislature (meeting for some eight months of the year, in contrast with the old, unreformed Supreme Soviet, which was in session for fewer than eight days each year). The Congress of People's Deputies was to include members chosen directly by political and social organizations—including the Communist Party, the Komsomol, and trade unions—as well as those to be elected from national and territorial constituencies. Since one of the other points emphasized in the resolution was the necessity of forming a 'socialist state based upon the rule of law' (*sotsialisticheskoe pravovoe gosudarstvo*),[134] the decisions of the party conference did not, logically enough, have legal force until appropriate laws had been passed by the legislature. As this was still the unreformed Supreme Soviet, it was not, however, difficult to get the desired response from that body. In December a number of constitutional amendments were passed and the proportion of deputies to be elected from territorial constituencies was fixed at two-thirds, with one-third to be chosen by public organizations.[135] Of the 2,250 deputies, 750 were to be elected from different parts of the country on the basis of equal numbers of electors per constituency, and hence of population density, and 750 from the national-territorial formations—from union republics down to the so-called 'autonomous regions'—which meant that on that particular slate the small Estonian republic returned as many deputies as the enormous Russian one. The most controversial group of deputies to be included in the new law were the 750 to be selected by public organizations, among which the Communist Party was allocated 100 seats. Nevertheless, the inclusion of the Academy of Sciences and various cultural organizations (for example, the writers', theatre workers', and film-makers' unions) among the bodies entitled to select deputies helped to provide the new legislature with some of its most distinguished and non-conformist members.[136]

The actual working of this new legislature is discussed briefly in the next section—which deals with the stage at which change moved beyond conceptual innovation to institutional transformation—but the nature of the 'historic compromise' it represented is worth considering in the broader context of transitions from authoritarianism to democracy. Even at the time, and to a greater extent in retrospective assessments in post-Soviet Russia, the reservation of seats for deputies selected by 'public organizations' and the indirect nature of the election of the Supreme Soviet (by the Congress of People's Deputies) attracted criticism. By 1990, moreover, Gorbachev himself was in no doubt that there should be direct elections for the Supreme Soviet *in future* and that there should be no seats reserved for the Communist Party or any other organization.[137] The decisions taken at the party conference in the summer of 1988 and the new electoral law in December of that year established, in other words, what could only be transitional electoral procedures and a transitional legislature. The advantage, however, of the forms they took in the concrete conditions of the Soviet Union little more than three years after Gorbachev came to power deserves emphasis. It was almost as if the proponents of radical change had drawn their own conclusions, in certain important respects, from the maxims to be found in the general literature on transitions from authoritarianism to democracy. That is not, it goes without saying, to suggest that Gorbachev was guided by the writings of students of comparative politics rather than by his own individual political judgement and instinct. The point is rather that Western and Russian commentators should have been more sensitive than many of them appear to have been to the framework of political constraints within which Gorbachev was operating. On the whole, the criticisms came later; the decisions of the Nineteenth Party Conference caused surprise rather than disappointment at the time. When the decision to have contested elections for a new legislature was first announced, observers were divided between those who saw this as a remarkably radical change and those who did not believe that the Soviet leadership could be serious about actually subjecting party officials to the risk of electoral defeat. Yet what is crucial is that Gorbachev had succeeded in combining genuine institutional breakthrough with enough reassurance for vested interests within the Soviet élite to enable him to get these far-reaching changes accepted and implemented.

It is difficult to see why anyone should have expected Russia to move from extreme authoritarianism and pseudo-elections to fully-fledged democracy and totally free elections in one fell swoop.[138] The criticism in Russia a few years later that the 1989 elections fell short of that ideal came mainly from intellectuals who had transferred their allegiance from Gorbachev to Yeltsin. It must be linked either to very short memories on their part or a lack of understanding of the political context within which Gorbachev was operating in 1988, the very year in which most of Gorbachev's critics had been silenced by a single article in the newspaper *Sovetskaya Rossiya*,[139] and only found their voices once again after Gorbachev had made it clear that this was no change of official line and that he really had made the Soviet Union safe for dissent.

The introduction of elections which, in the main, were genuinely contested was the decisive turning point in terms of the transformation of the Soviet system, undermining such pillars of the Communist system as 'democratic centralism' and the *nomenklatura* system of party appointments, and introducing substantial elements of pluralism and democracy into what had hitherto been an overwhelmingly authoritarian regime. While great differences exist between the Soviet transition and the transitions from authoritarianism in southern Europe and Latin America (some of which were pointed out earlier in this chapter), there are also certain common features. The division often observed in the literature on transitions between 'hardliners' and 'softliners' within the old élite, with the real pressure for change coming from the society, was of only very limited relevance to the Soviet Union during Gorbachev's first three years. Gorbachev and his closest associates within the Communist Party leadership were not 'softliners' responding to pressures from below but the *prime movers* introducing change from above. Nevertheless, nothing was more obvious than the fact that the Soviet élite was deeply divided and that only a minority within the Politburo and the Central Committee and its departments, not to speak of the KGB and the army, were in favour of change as far-reaching as Gorbachev was prepared to countenance.[140] With each radicalizing step of perestroika the divisions came ever more clearly into the open. Reflecting on transitions from right-wing authoritarian regimes, Guillermo O'Donnell and Philippe C. Schmitter have observed: 'Once liberalization has been chosen—for whatever reason and under whatever degree of control by incumbents—one factor emerges which hangs like a sword of Damocles over the possible outcome. This is the fear of a coup that would not only cut short the transition but impose a regression to an even more restrictive and repressive mode of governance.'[141]

Such a coup was, after all, attempted in the Soviet Union in August 1991, and the only way in which its leaders could have maintained control for a period of years, as distinct from the few days they actually lasted as a self-appointed ruling committee, would have been to impose a regime harsher than Brezhnev's, for in the years between 1988 and 1991 many Soviet citizens had lost the habits of obedience and conformity. Moreover, Gorbachev even earlier had been very conscious of the possibility of a 'coup', although one of a different kind from that which eventually occurred. What he could not afford to forget was the fate of Khrushchev in October 1964, which had demonstrated that there were definite limits in the post-Stalin era even to a General Secretary's power. The removal of Khrushchev had not, strictly speaking, been a coup at all, but rather an example of the Communist Party élite (the inner élite of the Politburo and the outer élite of the Central Committee) exercising not only their *de facto* power but also the right which the Party Rules gave them to depose one General Secretary and to choose another.[142]

Democratization is not the same as democracy; it is a process leading to democracy. In Britain, the classical case of gradual democratization, this process took roughly a century from the First Reform Act of 1832 to the Representation of the People Act of 1928, which gave women the vote at the same age as men.[143] (Female enfranchisement occurred in 1918, but with a voting age of 30 for women, whereas for men it was 21.) Democratization 'on the installment plan' is, O'Donnell and Schmitter observe, one way of 'tranquilizing the hard-liners' in transitions from authoritarian rule,[144] but instalments at such long intervals as in Britain were an increasingly unrealistic option for the Soviet Union once liberalization had raised expectations and especially after Communist regimes in the 'fraternal countries' of Eastern Europe had been more unambiguously cast aside from 1989. In the last two decades of the twentieth century it is fair to say that 'liberalization mentally evokes democratization, and democratization is signaled by elections'.[145] Moreover, 'liberalization without democratization only raises expectations and rekindles impatience'.[146]

While stimulating popular expectations with his introduction of contested elections, Gorbachev had at the same time to provide reassurances for the old élite, including 'tranquillizers' for the hardliners. Every step he took was under the watchful eye of the party high command, whom he had to cajole or persuade, and not alienate, unless and until he could establish an alternative power base. When Gorbachev became President of the USSR in March 1990, on a vote of the Congress of People's Deputies of the USSR, he greatly reduced, but without entirely eliminating, his dependence on the Communist Party for his continuation in office. Thereafter, he more frequently bypassed the highest party institutions and less often went out of his way to persuade them of the rightness of the decisions he had taken or wished to take since power had passed from party to state institutions in a number of important respects. But before the new institutions were created, and in the absence of anything more than the most embryonic and fragile civil society, Gorbachev in 1988 had to make movement towards competitive elections appear less than a major threat to the party élite even as he took the step which, more than any other, was to undermine their power.

Accordingly, at the local level, the idea of genuine elections for soviets was combined with the proposal that the local party First Secretary would normally preside over the soviet, although (as noted earlier) that meant that if he failed to be elected to the soviet, he would be liable to lose his party office as well. At the time of the Nineteenth Party Conference Shakhnazarov was among those who objected to the idea that the regional, city, or district party secretary should be expected to be chairman of the soviets to be elected at each of those levels. Gorbachev's response was to say that the situation would turn out in exactly the way Shakhnazarov wanted—that is to say, in the rejection of many party secretaries by the electorate—but 'if we want to get these decisions adopted this is the approach we have to take'.[147] Otherwise there would be strong objections from those who were to be removed from power. Gorbachev believed that 'progressive-minded and forward-looking people . . . would be elected anyway' and that, while they would survive under the new system, many conservative Communists among the party officials would not.[148] So far as the all-union legislature was concerned, the reserving of 100 seats for important party members meant that the great majority of members of the Politburo and Secretariat of the Central Committee would be among those who could rely on a safe passage into the Congress of People's Deputies. (It was, however, an act of excessive caution that the Central Committee selectorate was presented with only one hundred candidates for one hundred places, even if under the electoral system adopted two more candidates than places would have meant the loss of Ligachev and Yakovlev, who attracted the largest number of negative votes, although each had a substantial body of support in the party and, on those grounds, a good claim to a seat in the legislature.[149])

Furthermore, with the 2,250 deputies in the Congress acting as an electoral college to choose the Supreme Soviet, the higher party echelons could feel confident that this method of indirect election would keep inconvenient radicals out of the smaller and permanently functioning part of the legislature, even if a number were elected to the Congress of People's Deputies. Whatever the defects of these arrangements as compared with elections and parliaments in thriving democracies, they did combine some reassurance to vested interests within the old élite with a genuine measure of democratization inasmuch as for the first time the public as a whole were to be given a right to veto the candidate approved by the Communist Party authorities and in many cases to elect a deputy to whom the party apparatus was opposed. Moreover, these elections were to a legislature which was being granted real powers, not to a cipher such as the unreformed Supreme Soviet.[150]

It was one thing for the Nineteenth Party Conference to approve in principle the idea of having elections with more than one candidate for a new legislature as well as a radical reduction in the size of the Central Committee apparatus and another for these decisions to be put into practice. According to Ivan Laptev (in an interview in 1990 shortly before he moved from being editor-in-chief of *Izvestiya* to becoming Chairman of one of the chambers of the Supreme Soviet), party officials had 'felt fine' about the resolutions they had passed because they had thought 'the tasks are so enormous that it will take us ten years to tackle them'.[151] Thus, they imagined that they would be safe in their posts for another decade or so. But at the end of his closing speech to the conference Gorbachev pulled a piece of paper from his jacket pocket in which he proposed one more resolution which, says Laptev, 'was a surprise for everyone'.[152] It said that the amendments to the Constitution, needed to put the political changes into effect, should be made at the next session of the Supreme Soviet, that the new legislature should be functioning by April 1989, and that the reductions in the size of the party apparatus should take place before the end of 1988.[153] Gorbachev, having presented this stark resolution (which he admitted had been 'formulated quickly'),[154] said: 'I think it is simply vitally necessary to adopt the resolution. Is that right, comrades?' His audience agreed, whereupon he put the issue to the vote.[155] With cunning timing, Gorbachev had bounced the delegates into voting unanimously for momentous political change after all debate had appeared to be over and they were about to stand to sing the 'Internationale'.[156] Some of those who had raised their hands to vote for the beginning of the end of the party's monopoly of power were within minutes viewing what they had done with foreboding. Gorbachev was aware that a decision of fundamental importance had been taken,[157] but so—when it was too late to fight it—were many of the delegates. Laptev recalled that as he left the conference he heard 'major party workers', especially from the regions, saying: 'what have we done?'[158]

 Central Committee reorganization Gorbachev lost no time in putting into effect the radical restructuring of the Central Committee apparatus and cutting the size of the paid party apparatus at all levels of the hierarchy, starting with the Central Committee. In a memorandum to the Politburo of 24 August 1988,[159] Gorbachev recommended the abolition of the branch economic departments of the Central Committee (such as, for example, the Department for Heavy Industry and Energy), each of which had acted as overseer of the work of several ministries. The reorganization took place in October 1988 with the number of Central Committee Departments being cut from twenty to nine.[160] Apart from a new Socio-Economic Department the only other department now concerned with economic matters was the Agricultural Department. Gorbachev was motivated not only by a general desire to cut the size of the party apparatus but to hand over much of the task of maintaining political control over the ministries to the new legislature whose creation had been agreed by the Nineteenth Party Conference. The relationship between the ministries and their corresponding Central Committee department had, for the most part, been a cosy one and the extent to which the former could be said to be controlled by the latter was very limited.[161]

The new legislature was, in fact, to be a more challenging critic of the economic ministries than the party apparatus had been. Furthermore, by seeking a new basis of political authority in the Soviet Union through an elected legislature Gorbachev was to make it 'no longer possible for the industrial apparatus to utilize the camouflage of party power as a means of resisting reform'.[162] The abolition of most of the economic departments of the Central Committee and their counterparts at lower levels of the party apparatus was also intended, in keeping with the principles of the economic reform, to prevent the party from duplicating the work of state institutions and to allow the economy to become more self-regulating. If the former of those aims was largely realized, the latter was not, for the ministries and their industrial components proved remarkably adept at maintaining their power and privileges while making the necessary concessions to new stimuli and demands.[163]

Another significant aspect of the reorganization of the Central Committee apparatus was the abolition of the Department for Relations with Communist and Workers' Parties of Socialist Countries (normally known simply as the Socialist Countries Department) and its incorporation as a section within the International Department. This was part of the growing tendency to treat other Communist states as sovereign entities rather than as parts of a Soviet empire requiring strict political controls and separate administrative arrangements from other foreign countries. Valentin Falin succeeded Anatoly Dobrynin as head of the reorganized and enlarged International Department.[164]

Perhaps the most momentous of the party reforms introduced in the autumn of 1988, so far as domestic Soviet politics were concerned, was the downgrading of the Secretariat of the Central Committee and its replacement by six new Central Committee commissions. In principle, and to some extent in practice, these commissions gave party members outside the apparatus greater opportunities to influence policy, but since the party's authority within the society was before long to come into question, it is hardly surprising that their power never equalled that of the old Secretariat. Given Gorbachev's serious interest in creating a law-governed state, it is probable that their powers were never intended (unlike those of the Secretariat) to rival those of official state institutions. Ligachev, who deplored the changes, later wrote: 'The cleverness, whether intended or not, lay in the fact that no one made any mention of eliminating Secretariat meetings or seemed to be attacking them. The commissions were established, and the Secretariat's meetings simply ended of their own accord. The Party was deprived of an operating staff for its leaders.'[165] The Secretariat, which had traditionally met weekly, usually under the chairmanship of the *de facto* second secretary of the party, had been responsible both for supervising the work of the Central Committee apparatus and for ensuring the implementation of party policy in the country. For the next year and more, as Ligachev indicated, it virtually ceased to meet as a body and its functions passed to the Central Committee commissions.

The chairman of each commission became, in a sense, the overlord of that area of policy within the Central Committee apparatus, although how much this meant in practice varied from one policy area to another. One of the most interesting appointments was that of Vadim Medvedev as chairman of the commission on ideology, since previously Ligachev and Yakovlev had shared responsibility for this sphere. The 'dual curatorship of the ideological sphere of Ligachev and Yakovlev', observed Medvedev, had failed to work not only because of their conflicting positions but also on account of their personal characteristics, including their pride and an unwillingness to compromise.[166] They were now both replaced by a reformer more cautious than Yakovlev but substantially more willing to contemplate far-reaching change than was

Ligachev. The time was, however, past when even a coherent ideological line from the party leadership could 'work'; a significant sector of society had found its voice and was unwilling to respond automatically to guide-lines from above. The tension which had existed between Yakovlev and Ligachev, while disturbing from the point of view of the party bureaucracy, may even have served a useful purpose in the pluralization of the Soviet system. The very fact that the Politburo and Secretariat of the Central Committee were speaking with discordant voices provided the mass media with choices to which they responded in a variety of ways. In the conditions of a one-party state this was greatly to be preferred to an agreed line coming down from on high.

Yakovlev, in a significant move (which he himself welcomed),[167] became chairman of the commission on international affairs (and, thus, the party over-seer—after Gorbachev—of foreign policy) and Ligachev was side-tracked into heading the agricultural commission. A Gorbachev ally, although not a particularly effective one, Razumovsky, who had already been supervising party appointments, now chaired the commission on party construction and cadres policy and Slyunkov, who was somewhat more of a reformer than Ryzhkov, became chairman of the commission on social and economic policy. In the worst appointment, Chebrikov, who had been removed from the chairmanship of the KGB in the guise of being promoted to a secretaryship of the Central Committee, became chairman of the legal commission. While Chebrikov's KGB background made him manifestly unfit to supervise any transition to a law-governed state, his appointment may be seen as part of a two-stage process of putting him out of political harm's way. Exactly one year later—in September 1989—he was dropped from the Politburo, Secretariat, and his headship of the legal commission.[168]

Transformation at home and abroad

The third phase, *transformation at home and abroad,* began in early 1989 with the campaign for the first-ever contested union-wide elections since the creation of the USSR and included the election itself in March and the huge impact made by the body it elected, especially at its initial session. This political phase saw also the boost to political pluralism given both by subsequent sessions of the Congress and the new-style Supreme Soviet and the elections for republican legislatures in 1990. It embraced, too, the collapse of Communism in Eastern Europe and that, in turn, had a profound influence on public opinion within the Soviet Union. This remarkable period, decisive for the pluralization of Soviet politics, came to an end in October–November 1990 when Gorbachev made what became known as his 'turn to the right'.*

---

* The terms 'right' and 'left' have been largely avoided throughout this book mainly because of their imprecision. But the use of 'right' and 'left' in public political discourse during the last years of the Soviet Union was one interesting example of the language of Soviet dissidents becoming dominant within the mainstream of Soviet politics. For the dissidents, those who challenged the status quo were the 'left', or progressives, and those who defended it were the 'right', or conservatives, while those who wished to go back to a still harsher Soviet regime were the 'extreme right', neo-Stalinists or reactionaries. Western conservatives of a neo-liberal tendency found it hard to come to terms with a political language whereby admirers of the economic policies of Margaret Thatcher were described as being on the 'left' of the political spectrum and hardline Communists were called

Having failed in his initial aim of using the Nineteenth Party Conference to change the composition of the Central Committee, Gorbachev was faced by the problem that an increasing number of the members of that body which retained the power—if it could be collectively mobilized—to remove him from office had lost the positions that brought about their membership in the first place. This ageing group of 'dead souls' was, therefore, a likely repository of disgruntlement and a potential source of support for a rival to Gorbachev, should any attempt be made to remove him from the General Secretaryship. Stalin's solution to the presence of potential enemies on the Central Committee had been to have them arrested and shot; Khrushchev replaced them at Party Congresses; Gorbachev became the first Soviet leader to *persuade* large numbers of Central Committee members to *retire* in between Congresses. At the Central Committee plenum held on 25 April 1989 a request signed by seventy-four full members of the Central Committee and twenty-four candidate members that they be freed from their duties as Central Committee members was duly granted by the plenum.[169] Among those to take the last step in their departure from the political scene in this manner were Andrey Gromyko, Vladimir Dolgikh, Nikolay Tikhonov, Boris Ponomarev, and the conservative ideologist Petr Fedoseev, who, as Vice-President of the Academy of Sciences, had helped to keep the social sciences in an especially sorry state prior to Gorbachev's coming to power.[170] At the same plenum twenty-four candidate members of the Central Committee—including the scientist Yevgeny Velikhov and the head of the International Department, Valentin Falin—were promoted to full membership.

That important plenary session of the Central Committee was convened in between the first contested all-union elections in the Soviet Union and the first convocation of the body they elected, the Congress of People's Deputies of the USSR, which was held from 25 May until 9 June. The run-up to the election on 26 March was a time of more overt political struggle than had occurred even in 1988 as radical candidates tried to secure enough support to get their names on the ballot paper and conservative party officials resisted them. In some cases reformers were able to secure sponsorship by one or another public organization when they had failed to be adopted as a candidate for a territorial constituency. Moscow was a scene of particular political struggle, with Boris Yeltsin fighting for a city-wide seat against a candidate who was clearly favoured by the party

---

'conservatives'. A common response was to blame Western observers for this distortion of political language. They, however, were merely trying to avoid the still greater confusion that would have arisen if, when commenting on statements by their Russian interlocutors, they had turned on their heads the meanings of the terms the latter used. Many unreconstructed Marxist-Leninists in the Soviet Union also took umbrage at being labelled conservatives, but the very partially reconstructed Yegor Ligachev made a virtue out of necessity in words which offer some solace to Western conservatives: 'The notion of a gradual mastery of innovation associated with so-called conservative thinking is, in fact, society's defense reaction against political extremism. People throughout the world understand this, and it is one reason why conservative parties are so popular in developed bourgeois countries' (Ligachev, *Inside Gorbachev's Kremlin*, 124). Ligachev goes on to make clear that, from his point of view, it was in 1989 that 'political extremism' became increasingly dominant in the Soviet Union. The fact that it was necessary to write above of 'Western conservatives of a *neo-liberal* tendency' indicates the ambiguity of the notion of conservatism in the West as well, not least in Britain and the United States over the last two decades. An important strand within conservative thinking, indeed, rejects the idea that the economic liberalism of nineteenth-century Manchester or late twentieth-century Chicago should properly be called 'conservative'.

apparatus, Yevgeny Brakov, the manager of the large Zil car-manufacturing plant. With Communist Party officialdom doing all in their power to help Brakov and discredit Yeltsin, the result suggested that their efforts had been counter-productive. Yeltsin was elected, having received almost 90 per cent of the vote from the 83.5 per cent of Muscovites who came to the polls.[171]

The 1989 Election and the First Congress In the literature comparing transitions from authoritarian rule the concept of the *founding election* occupies a prominent place.[172] The term is generally reserved for the first *multi-party election*. Of the three sets of contested elections in Russia in 1989, 1990, and 1991, none, however, fulfilled that criterion. (Even in 1989 and, still more, in 1990 Popular Front candidates were particularly successful in a minority of non-Russian republics—notably the Baltic states—and the loose umbrella organization 'Democratic Russia' helped to get Boris Yeltsin elected to the Russian presidency in 1991. These were not, however, multi-party elections.) The first multi-party elections in Russia (and then in what was no more than a 'quasi-multi-party system'[173]) came two years after the end of the Soviet Union—in December 1993. They were characterized by apathy and low turn-out as well as by the success of nationalists and Communists.[174]

There was no comparison between the mass enthusiasm which greeted the 1989 all-union election and the disillusionment of late 1993. This suggests that the term *founding election* is a concept of doubtful value in the Soviet and Russian context. If it is to be used at all, it may most meaningfully be applied to the *first-ever contested all-union elections* of March 1989.[175] While the 1990 election in Russia was, in some respects, more democratic, it was also—so far as the Russian republic was concerned (although in this respect Russia was the exception rather than the rule among the Soviet republics)—for a two-tier legislature, in which a Congress of People's Deputies of the Russian republic elected the Russian Supreme Soviet. No seats were reserved for institutional interests (the 'public organizations') by 1990, which, from the standpoint of democracy, could be regarded as a step forward, although it was from that third of the deputies in the all-union Congress that in 1989 some of the most outstanding public figures (especially from the intelligentsia) found their way into the legislature. Indeed, there were undoubtedly more people of genuine distinction elected to the Congress of People's Deputies of the USSR than to its Russian equivalent a year later.[176] Both in 1989 and 1990 the great majority of deputies were members of the Communist Party, but that was, of course, no indication that they were like-minded people. At the very first Congress of People's Deputies of the USSR in 1989 groups of very different political orientation—including the radical Inter-Regional Group of Deputies, whose leading figures included Sakharov, Yeltsin, and the historian Yury Afanasev—had been formed and members of the Communist Party were numerically dominant in all of them. If any further proof were needed that the monolithic unity of the Communist Party was a myth (at least at the ideational level, for until 1988–9 a unity of action had generally been maintained), these new and overt cleavages showed with a fresh clarity how unfounded was the notion of the party as a body of people of similar political outlook.[177]

The turn-out of voters was significantly higher in 1989 than in 1990—89.8 per cent in the Soviet Union as a whole and 87 per cent in Russia as compared with 77 per cent in the election to the Congress of People's Deputies of the Russian republic in 1990[178]—and that was not only because in rural areas party officials were more able to exercise their traditional authority in the former year than the latter. Participation rates dropped in both Moscow and Leningrad (in the case of the former from 83.5 per cent to 70 per cent). This suggested a growth of disillusionment with politics—even though political life had become pluralist and partly democratized—which was subsequently to accelerate in the first half of the 1990s. It also indicates that the high point of election fever came, not altogether surprisingly, in 1989, when elections involving genuine competition possessed the attraction of extreme novelty, representing a radical break with past Soviet practice.

While some of the organizations accorded the right to make elections to the Congress of People's Deputies of the USSR did so with a minimum of argument among their members, others became forums for intense debate in the new and highly politicized atmosphere. The Central Committee of the Communist Party—in a plenary session to which Gorbachev invited also non-members of the Central Committee—was, as already noted, presented with just 100 names to vote on for the 100 seats it had been allocated as an organization in the legislature. This was clearly much more an act of reassurance for the old élite than a manifestation of the new democracy. But even in this case, in a break with tradition, the number of votes of the Central Committee members for these named candidates was published. Each had to secure more than 50 per cent support to go forward. All the candidates were elected, more than half of them unanimously. The less controversial a public figure the person had been, the more likely that candidate was to attract no negative votes. But twelve negative votes were cast against Gorbachev (the announcement of which was another step in the secularization of Soviet politics) and fifty-nine against Alexander Yakovlev, but it was Ligachev who attracted the highest number of votes against him by his Central Committee colleagues: seventy-eight. This provided Yeltsin with one of his favourite lines: what would have happened if the party had nominated not one hundred, but one hundred and one candidates for the hundred seats available to it?[179]

Among the most vigorously contested political battles within an institution accorded the right to elect deputies to the legislature was that involving the Academy of Sciences. Although Andrey Sakharov had been nominated by some sixty scientific institutes, the Presidium of the Academy did not include his name on a list of twenty-three candidates for twenty places which it sent to its electorate of scientists and scholars. In response the Academy voters struck out fifteen of the names presented to them, giving the required 50 per cent support to only eight of the candidates. These results necessitated a second round of voting and this time the list included the names of some of the Soviet Union's most prominent reformers. Among those to be elected from it were Sakharov; the head of Soviet space research Roald Sagdeev; and the radical economic reformer and writer Nikolay Shmelev, who topped the poll.[180] Virtually everyone elected on the Academy list was now close to the liberal or radically reformist end of the political spectrum.

In the territorial constituencies, the electoral process varied widely from one part of the country to another. The Communist Party apparatus was much more successful in Soviet Central Asia than in the major European cities in getting its favoured candidates elected. In the latter cases the efforts of party officials to support a particular candidate frequently rebounded against them. Alongside Yeltsin's victory in Moscow, the most spectacular failure of the apparatus was in Leningrad, where the First Secretary of the regional party organization and candidate member of the Politburo, Yury Solovev, was defeated. In the major cities of Moscow, Leningrad, and Kiev an anti-apparatus vote was clearly discernible. At the same Central Committee meeting on 25 April at which, as noted above, a substantial number of its older members resigned, the anger of a party bureaucracy beginning to see itself as an endangered species came out strongly.

Many regional party secretaries blamed economic shortages, the central party leadership, lack of party unity, and the press for the set-backs they had suffered. One reactionary regional secretary and former Central Committee department head, Alexander Melnikov, was particularly vociferous in his complaints about how ordinary people had been led astray by 'a massive onslaught from the mass media'.[181] The defeated Leningrad party chief, Solovev, noted that 'not one of the six leaders of the party and soviet in Leningrad and its region assembled the necessary number of votes'.[182] This, he observed, was not unique to Leningrad, and the only pattern he detected in such votes against the local establishments was that they had been cast 'in major industrial, scientific, and cultural centres'.[183] That scarcely augured well for the future of the Communist Party, even if the party leadership could still count upon a large majority within the new legislature in most votes. Gorbachev continued to argue in public in favour of the Communist Party retaining its 'leading role', but in his closing speech to the First Congress of People's Deputies on 9 June he observed that, if it was going to be a vanguard party, then it must 'reconstruct itself faster than society'.[184]

The results of the 1989 union-wide elections were welcomed by Gorbachev. Even the defeat of Communist Party officials was seen by him both as justification and as concrete evidence of the success of his electoral reform.[185] Yet, while contested elections were especially dangerous for party bureaucrats opposed to change, they were a double-edged sword also for Gorbachev. On the one hand, the breakthrough in Soviet politics whereby it became clear that it was possible to triumph *against* the wishes of the party apparatus added democratic substance to perestroika and enhanced Gorbachev's credibility as a serious reformer at home and abroad. On the other, from this time onwards Gorbachev's power could never be the same again. That was not only because there was now a legislature much less compliant than its predecessor, but also because the party structure was the only machinery Gorbachev possessed for implementing policy. Its undermining in contested elections was, thus, at one level a triumph for Gorbachev and, at another, the beginning of the diminution of his own power.

If the elections that brought the deputies to the Palace of Congresses in Moscow were a crucial step in the process of democratization, the First Congress itself broke new frontiers in public freedom of speech. What made the breaking of one taboo after another of major political consequence—as party leaders, the KGB, nationalities policy, and the behaviour of the Soviet military, among other formerly forbidden targets, were trenchantly criticized—was that the entire proceedings were broadcast live on television and radio. The decision to do this was Gorbachev's and it was comparable in importance only to his informing the 87.6 per cent of deputies who were Communist Party members on the eve of the First Congress that they would not be expected to speak or vote according to a party line, but were free to express their own views. The speeches were heard by an estimated audience of between ninety and one hundred million people.[186]

The tone of the Congress of People's Deputies was set on the first day, shortly after Gorbachev was proposed as Chairman of the Supreme Soviet. One of the very first speakers to be called to the rostrum by Gorbachev was Sakharov, who protested against the fact that only the General Secretary was being nominated for that position and argued that there should be a competitive election. Sakharov said that he did 'not see anyone else who could lead our country', but added that his support for Gorbachev was 'of a conditional nature'.[187] Though many conservative as well as liberal voices were heard at the Congress of People's Deputies, the radicals from Moscow and the Baltic republics were given a greater share of speaking time than their minority representation within the total body of deputies strictly warranted. This was partly a tribute to their determination and articulateness, but it could not have happened without Gorbachev's guidance and support from the chair and his uphill struggle to create a spirit of tolerance in an assembly whose atmosphere was often highly charged.[188]

In the event, a challenge was mounted to Gorbachev for the new position of Chairman of the Supreme Soviet (the Speakership of that body) by a self-proposed engineer-designer from the Leningrad region, Alexander Obolensky. A non-party member (who later, with the formation of new political parties, joined the Social Democrats), Obolensky attacked the privileges attached to the *nomenklatura* which, he said, gave them an interest in the maintenance of the existing system and also provided a convenient lever for maintaining control over them. Obolensky, who, like Sakharov, was concerned to establish a precedent of competition for all high political offices, was able to make his case at length, but, in a vote as to whether his name should appear on the ballot, a majority of deputies—1,415—voted against, although a significant minority—689 (there were 33 abstentions)—voted in favour. In the secret ballot which followed, simply for or against the one nominee, Gorbachev was supported by 95.6 per cent of those who voted, with 87 votes cast against him.[189]

One of the most important, and controversial, parts of the work of the First Congress of People's Deputies was the election of the Supreme Soviet—the smaller and more permanently functioning part of the legislature. A radical deputy, Yury Afanasev (who had been elected in a highly competitive election to represent a district in the Moscow region), made a combative speech in which he said that the deputies had chosen an inner body that was no better than the Supreme Soviet of Stalin's and Brezhnev's time. That was a considerable exaggeration. Many of the republics and regions put forward only as many candidates as would fill the number of seats to which they were entitled in the Soviet of the Union and the Soviet of Nationalities, and so the conservative majority in the Congress of People's Deputies had no choice but to endorse them. This ensured that a significant minority of outspoken critics—from, for example, Estonia,

Latvia, Lithuania, Georgia, and Armenia—made their way into the Supreme Soviet. The principal cause of the dissatisfaction of Afanasev and of other radicals was the fate of the Moscow slate of candidates. Endorsing the principle of competitive elections, the Moscow group of deputies put up fifty-five candidates for its allotted twenty-nine places in the Soviet of the Union and twelve candidates for its eleven seats in the Soviet of Nationalities. This gave the regional party secretaries and their like-minded colleagues, who formed a majority in the Congress, an opportunity to take their revenge on the most outspoken Moscow intellectuals and to cross out the names, for example, of Gavriil Popov, Tatyana Zaslavskaya, and an articulate newcomer (unknown to a broader Russian public until he was elected to the Congress), Sergey Stankevich. Even so, the former dissident Roy Medvedev and the serious proponent of reformist ideas Fedor Burlatsky were among the twenty-nine from Moscow who made their way into the Soviet of the Union.

By far the greatest cause of outrage was the fact that Boris Yeltsin finished twelfth in the election for the Soviet of Nationalities and so became the *only* Moscow nominee for that body to fail to be elected, in spite of his having been supported in the elections to the Congress of People's Deputies by the overwhelming majority of Muscovites. Notwithstanding the breach in his relations with Yeltsin, Gorbachev was aware that this was a politically damaging outcome which seriously threatened the legitimacy of the new legislature. When one of the deputies who had been elected from the Russian slate, the Siberian lawyer Aleksey Kazannik, resigned to make way for Yeltsin, Gorbachev seized upon that unexpected initiative with relief and lost little time in guiding the Congress to accede to the replacement of Kazannik by Yeltsin.[190]

In spite of the problems the First Congress of People's Deputies posed for Gorbachev, he was, according to his aide Shakhnazarov, very satisfied with it, believing that 'the new system he had built . . . had begun working'.[191] At the time Gorbachev remarked: 'At long last we now have a normal political structure, a normal political environment, where people can argue and they do not use knives against each other, they continue to co-operate.'[192] Whereas in the past a Soviet leader would have made sure that critical voices were speedily suppressed, Gorbachev was ready to argue with those with whom he disagreed. In Shakhnazarov's words: 'It was a real political struggle, a struggle waged in words, a conflict of ideas, that is what made that situation fundamentally new.'[193] For Gorbachev, Shakhnazarov adds, the achievement of this was 'a moment of political triumph'.[194]

Anatoly Lukyanov, whose relationship with Gorbachev went back (as noted in Chapter 2) to the Moscow University Law Faculty in the early 1950s, was elected First Deputy Chairman of the Supreme Soviet. During the last months of the existence of the unreformed Supreme Soviet (from September 1988 until May 1989), he had been First Deputy to Gorbachev when the latter was Chairman of the old Presidium of the Supreme Soviet. As time went by, Gorbachev increasingly delegated the Chairmanship of the sessions of the new Supreme Soviet and even those of the less frequently convened Congresses of People's Deputies to Lukyanov, for the burden of being head of state, chief executive of the country, General Secretary of the ruling party, commander-in-chief of the armed forces (an office which went along with the General Secretaryship until March 1990, after which it was held by Gorbachev in his capacity as president), *and*, in effect, Speaker of the legislature was an intolerable one.

Challenging party power Only Gorbachev in the early stages of activity of the Congress of People's Deputies and the new Supreme Soviet had, however, sufficient authority to chair the sessions and ensure that all the major (and sharply conflicting) points of view were given a hearing. This was, in many respects, however, a thankless task and contributed to a decline in Gorbachev's popularity which began in 1989 and accelerated in 1990. The special authority attached to the top leader in the Soviet Union—who was both head of state and chief executive—may have been dented for a portion of the tens of millions of television viewers who saw him attacked by hitherto unknown deputies while Gorbachev responded mildly and generally with reasoned argument. This was hardly in keeping with the traditional Russian view of a strong leader (although, to an outside observer, it was none the worse for that).[195] More certainly, Gorbachev—as a participant in the debates as well as umpire—could not avoid offending a part of the deputies in almost every session he chaired. The conservative majority among them objected to Gorbachev allowing Sakharov and other radicals so many opportunities to speak, given their relatively small numbers in the Congress of People's Deputies, while the radicals felt that Gorbachev too often brushed aside their concerns. This was notably the case when Gorbachev rebuffed Sakharov shortly before the latter's death in December 1989 when Sakharov tried to present him with a petition calling for the scrapping of Article 6 of the Soviet Constitution, which enshrined the 'leading and guiding role' of the Communist Party within the political system.

Gorbachev's irritation was enhanced by the fact that he fully accepted that the leading role of the party had to be removed from the Constitution, but he wanted to do this at a time of his own choosing when executive power could be transferred from the Communist Party to elected state executive organs.[196] In effect, party power in 1990 was being transferred to the soviets, which at the all-union level were able to become something closer to a parliament than the Soviet Union had ever seen, but could not simultaneously perform the functions of an executive. Given, however, that the amendment or abolition of Article 6 had been made a test of commitment to democratization by the radical deputies in the Soviet legislature, Gorbachev allowed their pressure to determine the timing of the change.[197]

While Gorbachev's awareness that the party's monopoly of power had to be removed in due course preceded by some time Sakharov's raising of the issue in the Congress of People's Deputies, the very fact that the Communist Party *still* *played* a leading role within the political system meant that he could not accede to a demand made from the floor of the legislature, and supported by only a minority of deputies, before he had persuaded the party Central Committee that the Communists' special position within the Constitution and the society should no longer be guaranteed. Gorbachev eventually did get the agreement of the Central Committee to make that change in February 1990 and the following month the section of Article 6 which set the Communist Party above all other potential parties or groups was duly repealed by the Congress of People's Deputies.

In private Gorbachev had realized at least since 1988 that Article 6 in its old form would have to go, but he had envisaged its removal as but a component part of the adoption of a completely new constitution. As noted in an earlier chapter, he had not even rejected in principle but held to be 'premature' Alexander Yakovlev's proposal, made as long ago as 1985, to divide the Communist Party in two. More recently, Gorbachev has said that, in principle, the decision to give up the Communist Party's monopoly of power was taken at the time of the Nineteenth Party Conference (in the summer of 1988), but that it was necessary to prepare the transfer of power and that timing was crucial.[198]

That this was not just a later rationalization of failure to take action to curb the party's 'leading role' is borne out by participants in the preparations for the Nineteenth Party Conference. Anatoly Chernyaev and Ivan Laptev, both of whom were among them, were in no doubt that by 1988 Gorbachev had accepted, as part of the logic of the changes he was introducing, that Article 6 would eventually have to be removed. According to Chernyaev, from the time of that conference Gorbachev recognized that there must be a multi-party system as well as free elections, although he could not yet speak about the former publicly: 'he wanted to choose the right time.'[199] Speaking in similar terms about Gorbachev's awareness of the need to remove Article 6, Laptev has observed that as a 'very shrewd politician he knew that we should not put it forward before the time was ripe'.[200] The problem was, however, that when the time was as yet scarcely ripe for the Communist Party establishment—in early 1990—it was already overripe for a society which had seen Communist Parties removed not only from their constitutionally decreed 'leading role' but from actual power in Eastern Europe in the course of 1989.

The crucial linkage between transformation within the Soviet Union and in Eastern Europe was that, on the one hand, the change in Soviet foreign policy was a *sine qua non* of the non-violent removal, Romania apart, of Communist regimes in the Warsaw Pact countries, while, on the other, the sight on Soviet television screens of Communist regimes being overthrown in Eastern Europe made the connection for many Russians between their own misfortunes and Communist rule. The Balts did not need any lessons in anti-Communism, but they took encouragement from the fact that Soviet troops did not intervene to prevent one East European country after another from regaining its independence. This strengthened their belief that independence for Lithuania, Latvia, and Estonia were becoming increasingly realistic possibilities and hence the willingness of a substantial proportion of their populations to struggle to achieve that goal.

The amendment of Article 6 in March 1990 was part of a more general process by which Gorbachev was transferring the basis of authority within the country from the party to the state—and doing so by evolutionary means. In the unreformed Soviet political system there was a *de facto* fusion of party and state, inasmuch as the Politburo was in reality the highest body of state power, whatever the Soviet Constitution said. (The Council of Ministers and its Presidium had a great deal of authority so far as economic decision-making was concerned, but foreign policy, for instance, was discussed there extremely rarely and on those occasions purely as a formality.[201]) With the creation of the Congress of People's Deputies as an important part of a developing political pluralism, the Communist Party's position became more anomalous and ambiguous.

The process of gradual transfer of power from party to state was taken a significant step further when Gorbachev became President of the Soviet Union in March 1990. That post, which is discussed below, took precedence over the party General Secretaryship, although the distinction was somewhat blurred by the fact that Gorbachev continued to hold the party leadership along with his new presidential office. The new legislature elected in 1989 was itself, however, a far more serious political institution than its Soviet predecessors, one which top party and state officials could no longer take entirely for granted. The Chairman of the Council of Ministers and leading Politburo member, Nikolay Ryzhkov, was soon to discover this when nine of his nominations in June 1989 for ministerial office were rejected by the newly established committees and commissions of the Congress of People's Deputies and the Supreme Soviet.[202] Indeed, so much had things changed that Ryzhkov, in his memoirs, takes satisfaction from the fact that *only* nine (or 13 per cent) out of his sixty-nine nominations of heads of ministries or state committees were 'killed off' by the legislature.[203] In comparison with confirmatory processes in Western parliaments, the new Soviet legislature had, in fact, demonstrated remarkable muscle, and Ryzhkov, however reluctantly, accepted their right to exercise these powers and came up with new names. Another aspect of the move from party to state rule was that, as Ryzhkov emphasizes, he was now in charge of 'an *independent* government', one which he was to continue to head for the next year and a half (emphasis in original).[204] The abolition by Gorbachev in the previous autumn of most of the Central Committee departments which had overseen the work of economic ministries, together with the new accountability of the Council of Ministers to an elected legislature, meant not only that the government would be subjected to more open criticism than hitherto but also that the lines of responsibility were clearer than they had been in previous Soviet times.

For Gorbachev the party General Secretaryship had been a crucial source of power, enabling him to drive through reform during the first four years of perestroika. However, the dilemma posed by his relationship with a party apparatus which had accepted radical reform with great reluctance, and was showing increasing determination to prevent that from turning into system-transformation, became increasingly acute in 1990. As the Communist Party became subject to more and more criticism, Gorbachev's popular standing suffered because he remained at the head of that party. A number of his aides and well-wishers of seriously reformist disposition[205] advised Gorbachev to split the General Secretaryship from the presidency. This he was unwilling to do, partly because he saw the party still as his power base but, even more, because of his concern with what could be made of it in the hands of someone else. He believed that if he ceded the General Secretaryship it could be used as a countervailing force against him, against the presidency as an institution, and against the process of political transformation. Gorbachev, in conversation with Shakhnazarov in April 1990, recognized that his *authority* would be greater if he occupied only the

presidency and gave up the General Secretaryship. But he feared the consequences both for his *power* and for the process of change if he were no longer
party leader. He argued that to do other than hold on to both offices at that time
might produce 'dual power and, still worse, bloodshed'.²⁰⁶ A month later
Gorbachev told Chernyaev that '70 per cent of the apparatus of the Central
Committee and of the Central Committee itself are against me and hate me' and
in early July 1990 he expressed himself to that same aide even more colourfully,
saying: 'You mustn't let go of the reins of a mangy, mad dog'! If he were to do
that, Gorbachev continued, the entire party machine would be turned against
him.²⁰⁷

Gorbachev was certain that if he were to relinquish the General Secretaryship
his successor in that post would be no reformer and that, whereas he himself
could neutralize the party machine by remaining as party leader, it could be a
more formidable reactionary force if the levers of power were controlled by a successor of quite different political disposition. For him to give up the General
Secretaryship, Gorbachev told a Czech journalist in the summer of 1990, 'would
play into the hands of those who want to liquidate perestroika'.²⁰⁸ Or, as he put
it more than a year after losing office (in an article entitled 'I Do not Know Happy
Reformers'): 'I tried to do everything so that the CPSU did not fall into the hands
of destructive forces.'²⁰⁹ He was well aware, he added, that by retaining the
General Secretaryship he was attracting fire on himself.

The Soviet Communist Party had greater reserves of power to draw on than
the Communist parties of Eastern Europe and, in comparison with them, even a
low-level form of legitimacy based on the fact that the overwhelming majority
of Soviet citizens had known no other system and the fact that the Bolshevik
seizure of power in 1917 had been an indigenous revolution rather than the foreign imposition which Communist rule was throughout most of Eastern Europe.
(The East European leaders, indeed, remained highly dependent on the Soviet
party and its leadership to sustain them in power by force of arms if necessary.)
Gorbachev had reason not to be rushed into giving up his position at the head
of the party. At the Third Congress of People's Deputies, held in March 1990,
which removed the Communist Party's leading role within the political system
from Article 6 of the Constitution and created the new office of President, a
majority of deputies voted in favour of an amendment to the Constitution stating that 'the person elected to the post of President of the USSR must not hold
any other political or state posts'. There were 1,303 votes in favour of the amendment and only 607 against. However, the result fell short of the 1,497 votes
needed to effect a constitutional change.²¹⁰ What is significant in the present
context is that the majority of those who voted to separate the General
Secretaryship from the presidency were conservative Communists who clearly
believed that this would work to their advantage. It was an alliance between
them and the radical democrats which produced a result that came close to set-
tling the issue for Gorbachev in the way he feared.

What is remarkable in the case of the Soviet transition from highly authoritarian rule by a Communist oligarchy is that the decisive moves towards liberalization and the first important steps in the democratization process were made
by Gorbachev *before* there were broadly based social pressures for such change.

Provided he had *not* attempted a serious liberalization or democratization of the Soviet system, he could have strengthened his position within the party-state structures using the traditional prerogatives of the General Secretary, removing opponents or insufficiently enthusiastic supporters one by one. The idea that Gorbachev embarked on liberalization in order to strengthen his power as such makes little sense, although to the extent that he was serious about democratization he did need to move his power base from the party apparatus to new state institutions.[211] Indeed, in his early years as General Secretary (not least in 1987) Gorbachev was engaged in a process of educating and provoking a still largely inert society to press from below for change. The new institutional arrangements which the party leadership approved in principle between May and December 1988 were, however, to be the last such major decisions to be taken in the Soviet period in the absence of serious popular demands.

The election campaign for the Congress of People's Deputies and the broadcasting of the argumentative First Congress went a long way towards politicizing Soviet citizens and radicalizing a significant part of the population. With every taboo on freedom of speech having been broken by the radical minority among the new deputies, the broader public also lost any remaining inhibitions about voicing their complaints. Apart from the strongly held grievances of particular national groups (discussed in Chapter 8), it was the gap between expectations of economic improvement and the continuing shortages in an economy poised uneasily between plan and market which provoked the greatest discontent. Even some of the economic developments which, in a longer-term perspective, could be regarded as positive, such as the legalization of co-operatives, had rapidly ceased to be popular as the number of co-operatives grew. In most cases these were private trading or service concerns which found it convenient to fly under the co-operative flag at a time when only the smallest-scale private enterprise was legal. Rightly or wrongly, many citizens believed that the co-operatives added to the shortages and introduced a new element of exploitation by buying up scarce products at subsidized prices in the state shops and selling them at inflated prices.

Prior to the liberalization of prices by Yegor Gaydar immediately after the collapse of the Soviet Union, shortages were a more serious manifestation of the failures of the economy than rapidly rising prices, although prices were also going up, albeit on a modest scale as compared with post-Soviet Russia. The final straw for coal-miners at a pit in Western Siberia on 10 July 1989 was to come off a shift and discover there was no soap.[212] Their strike marked the beginning of a series of miners' strikes which were to embrace other mines in the Siberian Kuzbass, Vorkuta in the north, and the Donbass in Ukraine. The miners demanded improved living and working conditions, better supplies, greater control over their work-place, and curbs on the co-operative movement.

The strikes presented a serious political challenge to Ryzhkov's government and to Gorbachev as well as to the new Supreme Soviet. The government's response was largely conciliatory, and most of the immediate demands of the miners were met in principle, although by no means all of the promises extracted in negotiations were kept. (Five years later, well into the post-Soviet era, miners' working conditions remained appalling.) While 'most strikes under perestroika remained overwhelmingly non-political', it was a significant social development when miners formed their own autonomous organizations to press their claims and to defend their collective interests.[213] Such actions reflected not only their sense of outrage but the loss of fear which was one of the most important developments of the Gorbachev era. Shakhnazarov (whose career in the Central Committee apparatus began in Khrushchev's time and continued under Brezhnev) went so far as to observe: it 'never even occurred' to Gorbachev to use force against striking miners, whereas 'Brezhnev and Khrushchev wouldn't have hesitated for a single minute'.[214] It was, moreover, of considerable political consequence that the Supreme Soviet on 9 October 1989 recognized the right to strike, for this was a break with the traditional Soviet sophistry that no such right was necessary or possible because workers in a workers' state could not go on strike against themselves.

From party to state power As dissatisfaction grew within the society and the new toleration of criticism and dissent led to the political articulation of discontent, Gorbachev and those of his advisers most committed to far-reaching change became conscious of the need to move further in transferring power from the party to the state. This had already been done, to a considerable extent, at the legislative level, but not in terms of executive power. As Chairman of the Supreme Soviet, Gorbachev occupied a hybrid position. He was *de facto* chief executive by virtue of being General Secretary of the ruling party, but at the same time chairing the legislature and not infrequently responding to its criticisms of decisions of the party hierarchy. The way out was seen in the creation of an executive presidency, introducing into Russian political discourse even the term *Prezident*. The Russian *Predsedatel'* had a very similar meaning, but that was Gorbachev's title as Chairman, or President, of the Supreme Soviet, and a new name was sought to convey the extent of the institutional innovation.

What was more difficult was to decide on the form which the presidency and related presidential institutions would take. The two main models which were discussed within Gorbachev's circle of advisers and among the closest of his Politburo colleagues were the system adopted by the Fifth French Republic and that of the United States of America. Gorbachev initially favoured the American model, partly, he argued, because the government needed the authority of the President at its head if it was to be able to implement difficult decisions and also because the United States had a federal system, as had, or aspired to have, the Soviet Union. (By 1990 substantial power had been devolved to or had been simply asserted by the republics.) Among those who offered advice, Georgy Shakhnazarov favoured the French model, while a majority of his colleagues favoured an American-style presidency.[215] The advantage of the French system, in Shakhnazarov's view, was that having a government headed by a premier rather than by the President would free Gorbachev from being swamped by detail and having to make far too many decisions. The American system whereby the President was *de facto* head of government as well as head of state was, Shakhnazarov argued, more suitable for a country enjoying the political and economic stability of the United States than for one in flux, and facing acute economic problems and challenges to its statehood, as was the Soviet Union. The form chosen was a hybrid, somewhat closer to the French than to the American model, inasmuch as there was to be a Prime Minister and, under him, a Council (later Cabinet) of Ministers.[216] Yet the Congress of People's Deputies and Supreme Soviet continued in principle to wield power which overlapped with that of the presidency and there was no constitutional court to adjudicate on the demarcation of powers. (The nearest thing to it, and itself a significant concession to the need for checks and balances within the political system, was the setting up of a Committee for Supervision of the USSR Constitution, chaired by a legal theorist, Sergey Alekseev, for many years the prominent head of a group of academic lawyers at the Sverdlovsk Juridical Institute.) The outcome was, on the whole, unsatisfactory, inasmuch as Gorbachev as President continued to be held responsible for all policy decisions, whether he had been involved in them or not, although many deputies took seriously also the need to hold the government accountable to parliament.

The idea of a presidency had been discussed between Gorbachev and his aides already in 1988 during the preparations for the Nineteenth Party Conference, but at that time Gorbachev had preferred the idea of the Congress of People's Deputies and combining the Chairmanship of that body with the General Secretaryship, the former post being seen by him then as an *alternative* to a presidency. In this, he was influenced by Lukyanov, who had romantic illusions about the early Soviet period, and part of the appeal of these institutions for Gorbachev in 1988 (as distinct from 1990) was precisely that the new political structures were *not* a copy of Western institutions.[217] He was also against the creation of a presidency then because he feared it might be said that he had begun the whole process of perestroika simply in order to become the Soviet Union's first President.[218]

At that time Yakovlev and Shakhnazarov had been among the strongest advocates of moving to a presidential system, while Lukyanov had favoured a 'republic of soviets', and Boldin, later Gorbachev's chief of staff as President and at that time head of the General Department of the Central Committee, had 'as always, preserved a mysterious vagueness'.[219] It became increasingly clear to Gorbachev and his allies that the transfer of power from party to state which had taken place at legislative level needed to be matched by a similar transfer of executive power. Moreover, Gorbachev's power had to be strengthened *vis-à-vis* both the Communist Party and the Congress of People's Deputies. In keeping with the general willingness to seek specialist advice, characteristic of policy-making during the Gorbachev era, the Institute of State and Law of the Academy of Sciences and the Presidium of the Supreme Soviet were charged with undertaking a joint project to compare the French and American presidential systems.[220]

Until he assumed the presidency of the USSR, Gorbachev remained vulnerable to replacement as General Secretary of the Central Committee of the Soviet Communist Party, the undiluted source of his power[221] prior to his becoming Chairman of the Supreme Soviet of the USSR at the First Congress of People's Deputies in 1989, although that post scarcely provided him with enough political armour to rebuff a determined Politburo and Central Committee intent on removing him from office. Once Gorbachev became President in March 1990, he convened Politburo meetings far less frequently than before (once a month instead of almost every week), although meetings of the Secretariat then became more frequent. Following the reorganization of the party apparatus in the autumn of 1988 there had been, as Ligachev complained, a period of about a year in which the Secretariat did not meet once.[222] Thereafter, sessions were convened sporadically by Vadim Medvedev, who, as the senior secretary in charge of ideology, was now the unofficial number two in the party. *Weekly* meetings of the Secretariat—which at one time had been the norm—were resumed only after the Twenty-Eighth Party Congress in the summer of 1990. They were then chaired by Vladimir Ivashko, who (with Gorbachev's backing) had been elected at the Congress as deputy General Secretary of the party, convincingly defeating Ligachev, who had stood against him. The aim was to have an official who would remove some of the organizational burden from Gorbachev without being a threat or a rival to him. (Ivashko, a Ukrainian, had succeeded Shcherbitsky as First Secretary of the Communist Party of Ukraine in December 1989.) The resumption of the activity of the Secretariat owed something, no doubt, to a growing realization that the Communist Party as an institution was in crisis; to an increasing paralysis of the party apparatus;[223] to the fact that Ligachev was no longer entitled even to attend, still less to lead, the sessions (he ceased to be a member of the Central Committee in 1990); and to Gorbachev's above-noted increasing unwillingness to convene Politburo meetings, which left a gap in collective deliberation at the top of the party hierarchy that the Secretariat attempted to fill.

While the decisions of the Nineteenth Party Conference in 1988 had marked the beginning of the end of the Communist Party's monopoly of power—a process which reached its logical political conclusion with the removal of the party's leading role from Article 6 of the Soviet Constitution in March 1990—there had, paradoxically, been a revitalization of intra-party life during the first five years of perestroika. This continued even as the party bureaucracy came to believe, with good reason, that its hold on power was under severe threat. Whereas in the Brezhnev years and during the short Andropov and Chernenko General Secretaryships, typically there were only two (and sometimes three) Central Committee plenums a year, under Gorbachev the number increased sharply. They were occasions for Gorbachev to radicalize the political agenda, but latterly—with the party no longer in control of that agenda—they were also forums at which he was subjected to severe criticism by alarmed and often angry Central Committee members. Whereas in 1985 there were four (one of them occasioned by the death of Chernenko), in 1986 two, and in 1987 three plenary sessions of the Central Committee,[224] that number increased as the issues dividing party members became still sharper. In 1988 there were five, in 1989 eight, and in 1990 five plenums.[225] During the period of less than eight months that the Communist Party of the Soviet Union survived in 1991 there were three plenary sessions of the Central Committee—in January, April, and July.[226]

Even though 1988 saw the decisions taken which would lead to the demise of the unaccountable hegemony of the Communist Party, the Politburo—still more than the Central Committee—was a much livelier political institution under Gorbachev than it had ever been previously. It was only seriously downgraded from the time Gorbachev became President of the USSR in March 1990 when two new state institutions, the Presidential Council and the Federation Council (seen at the time as functional substitutes for the Politburo), were created. It is noteworthy that during the first five years of his leadership Gorbachev kept in the Politburo people of strong personalities and of very different views. This was partly, no doubt, because he felt constrained to do so, but, still more, because he chose to have a broad representation of opinion and counted on his skills of persuasion to carry both wings of the party with him in the process of fundamental, yet evolutionary, change. Alexander Yakovlev, Eduard Shevardnadze, Yegor Ligachev, and Nikolay Ryzhkov—to name but the most prominent—were people with minds of their own and strong enough personalities to take a firm stand on many issues.

Yakovlev pointed to both the positive and negative aspects of this when he wrote: 'Under Gorbachev there was a sufficiently democratic atmosphere in the Politburo. That helped, but in a certain sense also "hindered" reforms, making them half-hearted, insufficiently precise, and delayed.'[227] The criticism is understandable, especially from the standpoint of the most radical of Gorbachev's Politburo appointees, for the process of consensus-seeking within a Politburo which contained relatively conservative Communists as well as committed reformers was bound to dilute or delay many measures. Listening to, and to some extent taking account of, the various points of view was also, however, a necessary part of building a coalition for change, and without that coalition-building the turning-points of the Nineteenth Party Conference in 1988 and the union-wide contested elections of 1989 would not have been reached. The more serious problem was that from early 1990 (or even from 1989) Gorbachev needed to build a *different* and broader coalition, one which drew in the new political forces whose emergence in Soviet society his reforms had made possible. Building bridges to them would have given greater dynamism to the process of transformation than attempting to retain the confidence—a forlorn hope, given all that had gone before—of the highest party and state functionaries.

The fact that Gorbachev *wanted* to bring together people from different parts of the political spectrum was underlined when he drew upon a wider range of opinion than existed in the Politburo with his—this time unfettered—appointments to the Presidential Council, even though (as noted below) its composition was far from optimal. But until March 1990—that is to say, for the first five years of Gorbachev's leadership—the Politburo remained the highest collective policy-making body in the country. It met 187 times in the period between the Twenty-Seventh Party Congress in February–March 1986 and the Twenty-Eighth Party Congress in June 1990 as compared with 238 times in the longer period between the Twenty-Sixth and Twenty-Seventh Congresses (1981–6).[228] But a slight reduction in the number of sessions is not the main point; the distinction is in the nature of the meetings. For years before Gorbachev came to power, it had been not unusual for Politburo meetings to be over in an hour, and at times half an hour, as the members rubber-stamped decisions taken by an inner group of members (as noted in Chapter 3) or in the Central Committee apparatus. In contrast, Politburo meetings, in which real issues were argued over, not infrequently lasted 10–12 hours in the Gorbachev era—and two days (as noted earlier) in the case of the Nina Andreeva letter.[229]

Both before and after Gorbachev became President, however, he had a 'kitchen cabinet' or narrow group of trusted colleagues on which he particularly relied. This should not be confused with an 'inner cabinet' of the Politburo, for it was broader in composition than the Politburo and was a sounding-board rather than a decision-making body. It met informally, often late in the evening, and included aides (although not all of them) as well as Politburo members (a still smaller proportion of that body). Its most regular members were Alexander Yakovlev and Vadim Medvedev from the Politburo, Anatoly Chernyaev, Georgy Shakhnazarov, and (for a time) Ivan Frolov from his aides, Valery Boldin (who was successively a Gorbachev aide, head of the General Department of the Central Committee, chief of staff to the President, and his betrayer when he joined the *putschists* in August 1991), and Yevgeny Primakov (Yakovlev's successor as Director of IMEMO, Chairman of the Soviet of the Union in 1989–90, and a candidate member of the Politburo during that same period, and in post-Soviet Russia Yeltsin's chief of the Foreign Intelligence Service). This core group had its limitations, especially in the shape of Boldin, as well as considerable merits. But when taken as a whole, it was clearly of a more radically reformist disposition than either the Politburo or the legislature elected in 1989 (although the latter included a minority of deputies more radical than anyone in Gorbachev's 'narrow circle').[230]

As a leader, Gorbachev liked to listen to a range of ideas and in his early years as General Secretary these would frequently (as noted in earlier chapters) include the views of social scientists from research institutes. Those meetings became less frequent as ever-more-pressing problems crowded on to the political agenda, although in 1990 Gorbachev renewed his interest in hearing the ideas of academic economists. The most prominent cases in point were Nikolay Petrakov, who was Gorbachev's aide during those twelve months, and Stanislav Shatalin, who was his choice to head the team of economists he set up jointly with Yeltsin (the outcome of which is discussed, in its different aspects, in both Chapters 5 and 8). Gorbachev would also from time to time convene more formal meetings with representatives of the intelligentsia, in which a sometimes excessively long introductory preamble by Gorbachev would be followed by comments and questions from his audience.

Electing a president   Gorbachev's election as President divided both the intelligentsia and the more democratic members of the Congress of People's Deputies. While a majority of the latter appeared to favour the presidency as an institution, some argued that it should only be introduced once a multi-party system was in place. Others stressed that there should be competition for the post and preferably in an election by the whole people. If Gorbachev had made surprisingly few major political errors during his first five years as General Secretary—the time when he could have been replaced at a moment's notice by the party high command and had therefore to consider the limits of their tolerance as well as the desirability of radical change—it can fairly be argued that in 1990 he made up for this with miscalculations on several fundamental issues. His greatest mistake was the tactical alliance he formed with conservative elements within the party-state leadership in the winter of 1990–1 (discussed in Chapter 8, as is the nationalities question, on which, despite almost insuperable difficulties, Gorbachev can also be faulted).

Even before that, however, when Gorbachev was faced with three important choices, he selected the more cautious option when the bolder might have further enhanced the process of democratic institution-building as well as his own chances of remaining a key political actor. That is not for a moment to suggest that the choices were straightforward ones. Nor is it to deny that if he had gone for the bolder variant in any or all of these cases, he would have been taking a serious risk. Picking the more daring option could have led to his removal from office all the sooner or even to an earlier, and more dangerous, attempted *putsch*. Yet at the time the bolder alternatives seemed to some (although far from all) of Gorbachev's more radical advisers the better way forward and, in retrospect, still more attractive, since it had become clear in the meantime that his caution in 1990 produced consequences very different from those he intended. A major reason for Gorbachev's greater caution in 1990 than in 1988, when he had acted boldly, was that in the earlier year the intelligentsia, and all the forces favouring reform, were still solidly behind him, whereas by 1990 they were rapidly deserting his camp for that of Yeltsin. With enemies on the 'left' as well as the 'right', Gorbachev began to steer a more centrist course.

The first of these difficult choices resulted in Gorbachev's opting for election as President by the Congress of People's Deputies rather than by the whole people. One reason for going for the quick installation of presidential power was a widespread realization that, with the Baltic states intent on breaking away from the Soviet Union and economic difficulties worsening, the Soviet Union was reaching the point of crisis. There was, so it was plausibly argued, no time to be lost in forming an executive authority superior to the increasingly discredited Communist Party whose apparatus (apart from an enlightened minority within it) was desperate to claw back the power that was slipping from its grasp. The second reason for allowing election by the deputies rather than the entire citizenry, albeit one which Gorbachev did not wish to admit even to himself though it was surely present at some level in his mind, was that by this time his popularity was in decline and Yeltsin's on the rise; accordingly, the possibility of Gorbachev actually losing such an election could by no means be ruled out. Against that second argument it is worth reiterating that it was not until May 1990 that, according to the most reliable survey research, Yeltsin actually moved ahead of Gorbachev in popular standing.[231] Moreover, the General Secretary would probably have enjoyed a surge of support if he had taken the risk of being the first leader in Russian history to give the people the opportunity freely and democratically to remove him from power. If he *had* lost, his reputation as the greatest democratizer of Russia would even have been strengthened. Moreover, if Yeltsin had thereafter abided by the rules of the democratic game (admittedly, an uncertain conjecture in the light of his later behaviour), it is possible that Gorbachev's defeat would have been a short-term one. Yeltsin, as *Soviet* President, would have been faced by the intractable problems with which Gorbachev continued to wrestle for another year and a half. Having taken this further step in the democratization of the highly authoritarian political system he inherited, Gorbachev's chances of returning to office would thereby have been stronger than they subsequently were after his forced resignation in December 1991.

If, on the contrary (as seems more likely than not), Gorbachev had *won* the support of the people as a whole in an election in the spring of 1990, he would have been in a stronger political position than he was after being elected by the legislature (with less than overwhelming support).[232] It is also the case that Gorbachev would have been even freer of control by the Politburo and Central Committee of the Communist Party than he subsequently became if he had been elected by the people as a whole—one reason why (a minority of radical reformists apart) the higher echelons of the party did everything they could to discourage Gorbachev from holding a general election. But Gorbachev's allies were also, on the whole, in favour of his speedy election by the Congress of People's Deputies—'more for pragmatic than for principled motives', as Vadim Medvedev puts it, since their belief was that this would produce the speediest strengthening of his executive power. Medvedev was among those who, in retrospect (and with all the wisdom of hindsight), recognized that this had been a mistake.[233] A decision in principle was taken that in future all presidential elections should be by universal suffrage, but arguments concerning the acute and urgent nature of the problems facing the country prevailed as reasons why the election of the first President should be hurried through. Ironically, whereas many of the most radical elements in the democratic opposition in Russia favoured popular elections for the presidency, radical democrats in some other Communist countries in transition—most notably, Hungary—opposed the direct election of the President by the people as a whole. They did so partly on the basis that this would produce an excessively strong presidency *vis-à-vis* parliament and, still more, because a radical 'Communist' reformer, rather than an overtly non-Communist politician, would be likely to win such an election.[234]

In Russia, too, there were important voices even among deputies committed to the development of political pluralism favouring, for different reasons, the election of Gorbachev as President by the Congress of People's Deputies. That was not, however, in keeping with the general view of the Inter-Regional Group of Deputies, a grouping of some of the major democratic forces within the Soviet legislature (although a majority of their members, including Yeltsin, were still members of the Communist Party in March 1990). This body was, on the whole, in favour of direct popular election of the Soviet President. Among the important dissentient voices from within their ranks were those of the Leningrad academic lawyer (later Mayor of St Petersburg) Anatoly Sobchak; the economist, Nikolay Shmelev; the future leader of Russia's Democratic Party, Nikolay Travkin; the prominent physicist, Academician Vitaly Goldansky; and one of the most respected authorities on Russian literature and culture, Academician Dmitry Likhachev.

Likhachev—President since 1987 of the Cultural Foundation, one of the social organizations entitled to elect deputies—was perhaps the most influential of all those who intervened on the side of electing Gorbachev to the presidency without delay. Old enough to remember the two Russian revolutions of 1917, Likhachev compared Russia's current situation to February of that year and warned of the danger of civil war if Gorbachev were not elected President.

Moreover while Likhachev had never been a party member (and had, moreover, been imprisoned in the late 1920s for his participation in a student discussion group), he insisted on the importance of Gorbachev holding the party leadership jointly with the presidency to avoid a dangerous division within the executive power. Sobchak would have preferred to grant Gorbachev presidential powers as a temporary measure without actually giving him the title of President until a new Constitution had been adopted on the grounds that this would have been an incentive to him to speed up the work of the Constitutional Commission, of which Sobchak was a member. Since there was, however, little support for that idea, Sobchak argued instead for Gorbachev's speedy election by the Congress in order to overcome the 'undoubted paralysis of state executive power'.[235] In the end Gorbachev was elected President unopposed, but by only 59 per cent of the deputies and with a margin of only 206 more votes than he needed.[236] Talk of civil war, however sincere in Likhachev's case, was an exaggeration, but it reflected the lack of confidence on a part of the democratic forces in their ability to withstand the backlash from the party-state apparatus unless they bolstered Gorbachev's state powers and thus in some measure reduced his dependence on the fragile support of the Central Committee.

Gorbachev himself, according to both his critic on many issues, Sobchak, and his ally, Shakhnazarov, made no attempts behind the scenes to win votes either by conducting negotiations with different groups or by offering deals.[237] He was, as Sobchak later revealed, ill at the time of his election as President, but as a matter both of pride and of political prudence, he concealed the illness from almost all rather than seek specialist help. In Sobchak's view, the Kremlin doctors would have wanted to put Gorbachev (who normally enjoyed robust health) in hospital, so he consulted not them, but only the medically qualified deputies.[238] Among the various arguments adduced against Gorbachev's elevation to the new executive presidency, the one which most irked him was the accusation that he was attempting to accumulate dictatorial powers in his hands. Half an hour after he had been sworn in as the first (and, as it turned out, last) Soviet President on 15 March 1990, Gorbachev reflected on this in a conversation with his wife, Raisa, and his aides, Chernyaev, Shakhnazarov, and Frolov. He had, he said, undermined the truly dictatorial powers he had inherited as leader of the Communist Party and subjected them to parliamentary control, and 'yet even now . . . some stupid people believe that I need the presidency so that I can order people around'. Gorbachev continued: 'If that was what I wanted I would just have remained general secretary and could have ordered people around for another ten or fifteen years!'[239] Sobchak fully endorsed that view in his memoirs, observing: 'for a dictator it is not necessary to undertake deep transformations in society and not necessary to awaken society from its Communist lethargy. Dictators, arriving in power, do not begin with democratic reforms and with attempts to place legal limits on their own absolute authority.'[240]

The failure to split the party Understandable though Gorbachev's decision was to take the speedier route to presidential power, especially as he was coming under increasing attack from within the Communist Party, it was, on balance, a mistake not to take the risk of calling for a union-wide election. The second equally difficult decision where Gorbachev in 1990 probably made the wrong choice was in his preference for postponing or avoiding a formal split within the Communist Party and trying instead to win the party over to acceptance of an increasingly social democratic programme. Although the party embraced a still greater variety of political outlooks, its two major components were by 1989–90 a social democratic tendency and the traditionalist Communist. The main concern of those who adhered to the latter was to defend the power structure which had served its *nomenklatura* beneficiaries so well. It was not so much commitment to a more undiluted socialism, except inasmuch as they defined socialism in terms of the power structure that had existed before Gorbachev began his reforms. As Alexander Yakovlev, from an immediate post-coup perspective in August 1991, put it ironically, with reference to the party and state officials who had taken part in the abortive *putsch*, 'I am against, say, the socialist choice, against, say, Marxism, but I believe in it more than they, those who defend it.'[241]

As noted above, a majority of these more orthodox Communists attempted to separate the General Secretaryship from the presidency at the Third Congress of People's Deputies in March 1990, believing that this would strengthen them and weaken Gorbachev. Thus, there is a case for saying that by clinging to the party leadership, Gorbachev (as he himself believed at the time) was safeguarding the transformative process, even as he paid a price for this in terms of his own popularity. His opponents were also, however, ambivalent as to whether they would fare better without him, for on more than one occasion, when under severe attack at Central Committee plenums, Gorbachev threatened to resign, and each time his enemies lacked the determination and self-confidence to take him at his word. It is probable that the optimal moment for Gorbachev to have forced a split in the Communist Party would have been at the Twenty-Eighth Party Congress in July 1990. He made a speech which encapsulated the transformation of the political system which was taking place and which was anathema to much of his audience. He was given a frosty reception for statements such as 'A civil society of free people is replacing the Stalinist model of socialism' and 'The political system is being radically transformed, genuine democracy is being established, with free elections, a multi-party system and human rights, real people's power is being reborn'.[242]

At a meeting in between sessions with a large group of city and district party secretaries Gorbachev was furiously attacked and when he asked them what was intended to be a rhetorical question, 'What are you saying, then? Is our entire course wrong?', they replied 'Yes! Yes! Yes!'[243] Gorbachev came close at this time to making the break with those in the Communist Party who were fundamentally opposed to political transformation, authorizing Shakhnazarov to begin discussions with leading liberals, including some who had (along with Yeltsin) just left the Communist Party, with a view to forming a new coalition with them.[244] But having persuaded the Congress to vote for policies with which a majority of the delegates were clearly out of sympathy, Gorbachev understandably believed that he was winning the party over to acceptance of his increasingly social democratic position. The victory, however, was a hollow one. In the short term, Gorbachev created an informal 'centre-left coalition', inasmuch as he bypassed the party organization when, along with Yeltsin, he set up the Shatalin–Yavlinsky group to produce their plan for a swift transition to a market economy. But when the backlash to the '500 Days Programme' became intense, he retreated and before long was sucked into forming a 'centre-right coalition'. Thereby, without doing enough to satisfy the conservatives, he found himself making dangerous concessions to the dominant views within the party-state apparatus as the '500 Days Programme' presented them with a new focal point for their backlash. The time had passed when it was politically wise to paper over the deep cracks within the Communist Party. If Gorbachev had precipitated a split at the Twenty-Eighth Congress, he would, of course, have been taking a risk, for traditionally the Soviet Communist Party did not forgive splitters. The struggle for power between the old guard and the new would still have been intense. But he could have emerged as the leader of a democratic socialist party which had rid itself of all the most backward-looking elements in the CPSU. Whether a majority of party members would have followed Gorbachev is far from certain, but he could have counted on having a party of several million people behind him—quite possibly a majority of rank-and-file members, although only a minority of the full-time party functionaries. Splitting the Communist Party would at one and the same time have given a great impetus to the development of a competitive party system and a new lease of life to Gorbachev's own flagging domestic political standing.

Coalition-building and the new institutions The third decision even before the 1990–1 winter of discontent (but in important respects a prelude to it), in which Gorbachev eschewed the bolder option was his retreat, following initial approval, from the '500 Days Programme'. The problems with that programme and the pressures for backing away from whole-hearted endorsement of it are discussed elsewhere in this book, and Gorbachev's decision is again understandable. Even if, however, as noted in Chapter 5, the programme would have had to be amended in practice, since it was undoubtedly over-optimistic, it would probably have been better for Gorbachev to leave that to 'life itself' (to use a phrase to which Gorbachev, like Khrushchev before him, was partial) rather than for him personally to sound the retreat in a compromise which failed to resolve either the economic or political impasse. Apart from his own genuine second thoughts about the viability and desirability of the '500 Days Programme', Gorbachev was subjected to the most intense pressures (see Chapters 5 and 8) from the party-state machine not to go along with it.

Gorbachev, however, was constantly forced to fight on two or more fronts. He could never satisfy the demands of the most radical critics on the liberal or democratic 'left', who were free to ignore, in a way Gorbachev was not, the formidable institutional obstacles to peaceful revolutionary, as distinct from speedy evolutionary, change. Accordingly, he did not feel he could allow the conservative majority within the party apparatus to consolidate themselves organizationally in ways beyond his control. As Gorbachev, for these reasons, refused to give up the General Secretaryship of the Central Committee of the CPSU, pressure increased for the creation of a separate party organization for the Russian republic. Sensing that this could become a second centre within the party and one which would be a counterweight against his leadership of the union-wide Communist Party, Gorbachev tried to hold that process back. It was not easy to do so, for the RSFSR was the only Soviet republic which did not have a party organization of its own. This had hardly appeared to matter in pre-perestroika days, when party officials in Russia felt their interests were fully taken care of by the all-union leadership, but a combination of their dissatisfaction with Gorbachev and the growing independence of the Communist Parties in other republics made the demand for a Russian Communist Party unstoppable.

Already in 1989 the pressure for such a party organization was growing and Gorbachev succeeded in pre-empting it for a time by creating instead a Russian Bureau of the Central Committee of the CPSU with none other than himself at its head.[245] By April 1990, however, the Leningrad party organization held a conference with a view to establishing a Russian party, and Gorbachev, realizing that this was a battle he could not win, ceased opposing their aim in the hope of retaining some leverage over them. A conference of Russian Communists in Moscow in June established a Russian Communist Party (soon renaming the conference the First Congress of the RCP) and elected the conservative Ivan Polozkov as their First Secretary.[246] Russian reformers within the Communist Party, who wanted to have nothing to do with this new party organization which purported to speak in their name, had already formed their own 'Democratic Platform' within the all-union party and in the same month as the First Congress of the RCP they held the Second All-Union Conference of the 'Democratic Platform in the CPSU'.[247] The monolithic unity of the Communist Party, which had long been a myth in the realm of ideas, was now just as clearly a thing of the past at the organizational level.

Alongside his effort to avoid isolation from either wing of the Communist Party while moving the process of political transformation forward, Gorbachev attempted to put to use in the process of coalition-building the new state institutions which had been created at the same time as the executive presidency. He included within the Presidential Council, which was in essence an advisory body to the President, a mixture of people and executive functions as well as those who held no political office whatsoever. Thus, they included from the legislature Anatoly Lukyanov, who, having been First Deputy Chairman of the Supreme Soviet when Gorbachev was Chairman, succeeded to the Chairmanship when he became President of the USSR, thus relieving Gorbachev of the burden of chairing the parliament, while considerably increasing his own influence over the passage of legislation; and Yevgeny Primakov, the Chairman of the Soviet of the Union, who was also a member of Gorbachev's informal circle of advisers. From the ministerial network were included Ryzhkov, as Chairman of the Council of Ministers, together with the Minister of Foreign Affairs, Shevardnadze; the able and liberal Minister of the Interior, Bakatin; the Minister of Defence, Yazov; the KGB chief, Kryuchkov; and the Chairman of the State Planning Commission, Maslyukov. From the party apparatus (although not ex officio but rather as people in whom Gorbachev reposed trust) came Alexander Yakovlev, a senior Secretary of the Central Committee (he was later joined by Vadim Medvedev), and Valery Boldin, who at the time of his appointment was about to move from heading the Central Committee's General Department to becoming chief of staff to the President.

Other appointments included two contrasting pairs. From the literary intelligentsia, Gorbachev plucked not only the Russian writer of nationalist orientation (and religious believer) Valentin Rasputin, but also the Kirghiz novelist and internationalist Chingiz Aitmatov, who had made full use of poetic licence in a speech to the First Congress of People's Deputies in 1989 when he named, among other countries, Norway, Spain, Canada—and even Switzerland—as fine examples of socialism.[248] He had justified this unorthodox approach by saying: 'The social protection and level of welfare of those societies are something we can only dream about. This is real and, if you like, worker trade-union socialism, although these countries do not call themselves socialist, but are none the worse for that.'[249] A similar contrast lay in the choice of the market-oriented economist Stanislav Shatalin, by this time a publicly proclaimed social democrat, alongside a spokesman for workers suspicious of the consequences of marketizing the economy, Veniamin Yarin. Gorbachev evidently believed that, if he could carry this disparate body of people with him, he would be able to unite sufficiently broad sections of the population behind far-reaching changes.[250]

Unfortunately, however, the mix did not work. Even when Gorbachev could persuade or charm individual members of the Presidential Council, the body as a whole had no collective power. When they agreed on the desirability of a course of action, they had no supporting structures capable of carrying the policy into effect.[251] The other body which was created at this time—also as an advisory institution attached to the presidency—was the Federation Council. It consisted of the Presidents or Chairmen of the Supreme Soviets of the union republics; later (as will be seen in Chapter 8), it increased in importance and outlived the Presidential Council. Whereas Gorbachev personally decided upon the composition of the Presidential Council (although the Chairman of the Council of Ministers was a member ex officio), the composition of the Federation Council was determined from below—by the fifteen union republics. The apparent loser in this process was the Communist Party, for the Politburo had been collectively co-opted by the existing party leadership, even if the General Secretary's voice counted for much more than anyone else's. Now, the party high command had no say in the make-up of either of the two bodies which together, on the face of it, were supplanting the Politburo.

The gainer, however, was not Gorbachev. With almost all of the economic departments of the Central Committee having been abolished in 1988 and the Politburo now downgraded as well, the ministries—although subject to criticism both from the legislature and the mass media—actually increased their power within the executive.[252] It had become more important than ever for Gorbachev to have a government that was responsive to him as well as to the rapidly changing society. Even if there were to be both a President and Prime Minister, as in Fifth Republic France, the best way for Gorbachev to have kept pace with the new public mood and at the same time increase his control over policy outcomes would have been to install a Prime Minister and government committed to the transformation process. The creation of the presidency was, indeed, the optimal time to form a coalition government, one which would have brought into positions of executive power such newly prominent politicians as Sobchak and perhaps, in key economic posts, Petrakov and Shatalin. Ideally, since the policy (as distinct from personal) differences between them were not great at this time, Gorbachev would have co-opted Yeltsin, although whether Yeltsin would have been willing in March 1990 to accept even one of the most important portfolios in a union-wide government must remain doubtful. As early as the summer of 1989, before either a presidency or a vice-presidency had actually been created, Shakhnazarov suggested to Gorbachev that it was, perhaps, an opportune time to satisfy Yeltsin's ambition and make him Vice-President. Gorbachev replied that Yeltsin would not be prepared to play that role, adding that Shakhnazarov did not know Yeltsin: 'He has inordinate pride. He needs full power and for the sake of that he is ready for anything.'[253] By the time of the creation of the presidency and the Presidential Council in 1990 it was, at any rate, high time to bring into leading positions several *popular* politicians,[254] for this was a period in between Communist orthodoxy and post-Soviet disillusionment when there still *were* popular politicians in Russia.

The Presidential Council might more usefully have been formed as a Presidential Cabinet of the most senior ministers (on the lines of the distinction between Cabinet and government as a whole in Britain). For although Gorbachev was now more independent of the party apparatus, he was actually in a weaker position when it came to the implementation of policy than he had been in the days when the Politburo was the functional equivalent of the British Cabinet and when there were officials at all levels sufficiently imbued with party discipline to implement decisions passed down the hierarchy. The alternative to such a Cabinet would have been to build up a substantial executive office of the presidency, drawing upon the American example. Even such an apparatus, however, would have had to rely on the ministries and local councils—to the extent that the power-broking role of the Communist Party in the localities was being phased out—unless an entire parallel, vertical chain of command were to have been created. What Gorbachev did not fully realize was that, as he removed the executive power which the Communist Party had exercised *de facto*, he was becoming more, rather than less, dependent upon the ministerial network. It was of exceptional importance, accordingly, to make wide-ranging changes at the top of the ministerial hierarchy and to integrate its leading figures in the Presidential Council or Cabinet without diluting what could then be a serious executive institution with free-floating intellectuals who were not in a position to give orders to anyone.

It was not, of course, easy—to put it mildly—to create entirely new political institutions while coping with conflicting pressures from all sides. Boldin, who (on Gorbachev's insistence) had a seat on the Presidential Council, had also—as presidential chief of staff—responsibility for organizing the support staff of the President. This duty he discharged in the interests of his own power aggrandizement, his main concern being to ensure that all documents passed through his hands, giving him the ability to decide which information—sometimes so one-sided or misleading as to amount to misinformation—found its way to Gorbachev. Thanks to Shakhnazarov, Chernyaev, and Petrakov, whose titles changed from aides to the General Secretary to aides to the President and whose access to the holder of those two offices remained frequent, Gorbachev was not entirely dependent on Boldin.[255] But there is no doubt that Boldin's activity as gatekeeper made its own contribution to unfortunate decisions and, still more, to non-decisions.

The shortcomings of the new institutions attached to the presidency did not constitute the only problems posed for Gorbachev's actual political control. As the political system had become increasingly pluralist, Gorbachev could only very partially set the political agenda. He was frequently responding both to the initiatives of others and to unexpected crises. While he was gradually dismantling the power of the Communist Party, a new phenomenon of oppositional demonstrations on the streets of Moscow, directed partly against Gorbachev himself (the first one on a substantial scale occurring on 25 February 1990), made him less willing to escape entirely from the party's embrace, since it appeared that he was being spurned by the radical democrats.[256] As opposition grew, there was a tension between, on the one hand, Gorbachev the party boss and product of the party machine and, on the other, Gorbachev the well-read and well-informed new thinker.[257] It was the extent to which, however, taking his period in power as a whole, Gorbachev rose above his background in the party apparatus which made him the transformational leader he was.[258] For all the mistakes which Gorbachev understandably made in the course of entering uncharted political territory, he had, nevertheless, played a decisive role in moving the system from party to state rule and from monism to pluralism. His consensus-seeking political style, and skill at forestalling premature revolt by those whose institutional interests he was undermining, could at times (not least in 1990) be a serious drawback. Yet, for the greater part of his leadership, it was an indispensable condition of the Soviet Union's remarkably peaceful political transformation.

Chapter 7

Gorbachev and Foreign Policy

TWO views were aired quite prominently in the West when Gorbachev became General Secretary of the Soviet Communist Party. One was that, given the seriousness of Soviet domestic problems, he would concentrate all his energies on the home front and pursue a low-key foreign policy marked by continuity with the past. The other view was that in the face of severe internal difficulties the Soviet Union would pursue a more vigorously adventurous, and even expansionist, policy abroad. These forecasts were, of course, contradictory. All that they had in common was that they both turned out to be wrong.

Gorbachev, in fact, saw more clearly than any of his predecessors the links between domestic and foreign policy. Thus, although he had never in party forums hitherto challenged the conventional Soviet attitude to political opposition and dissent (had he done so he would not have become General Secretary), he was psychologically ready to change this policy. He appreciated that as long as the Soviet Union persecuted dissidents—the most striking example (discussed in the previous chapter) being Andrey Sakharov's internal exile—Soviet relations with Western democracies would still be tense and based on mistrust. Gorbachev was equally well aware that, while the Soviet Union devoted a quite disproportionate part of its national income to the army, military industry, and the security forces, this would mean not only a continuation of international tension but also the frustration of domestic reform.[1] On the one hand, it distorted the Soviet economy and left civilian industry as a poor relation to the defence sector, while the gap between the Soviet Union and the West in terms of technological innovation widened in the West's favour. On the other, it meant that the military-industrial complex carried too much weight within the society and polity.[2] Thus, the issue of reducing international tension was closely bound up with that of regeneration of the domestic economy and changing the balance of influence within the political system.

The key appointments

The link between the new political actors and new thinking—the power of appointment and the power of ideas—which has been discussed in Chapter 4 was nowhere more clearly to be seen than in foreign policy. Gorbachev was able to have a decisive impact on the development of ideas on the Soviet Union's relationship with the outside world and on the actual conduct of Soviet foreign policy by virtue of some half-dozen key appointments. These were the elevation of Eduard Shevardnadze to the post of Foreign Minister, in succession to Andrey Gromyko, in the summer of 1985;[3] the replacement of Boris Ponomarev as head of the International Department by Anatoly Dobrynin in 1986; the promotion of Alexander Yakovlev to Politburo and Secretariat membership (with oversight of international affairs from the autumn of 1988, although even before that he participated in foreign policy discussions as well as domestic policy-making); the replacement of Konstantin Rusakov by Vadim Medvedev as head of the Socialist Countries Department of the Central Committee in 1986, together with the promotion of Georgy Shakhnazarov to be First Deputy Head of that department; and the appointment of Anatoly Chernyaev as Gorbachev's foreign policy aide in 1986, with Shakhnazarov joining him as a Gorbachev aide two years later.

From this group Shevardnadze and Yakovlev were especially important, and Chernyaev's role (in spite of his less elevated political standing) was next in significance, given his personal closeness to Gorbachev and his experience of international affairs. Shakhnazarov, although an adviser also on Eastern Europe, was—as noted in Chapters 4 and 6—even more important for his work on domestic political reform once he joined Gorbachev's personal staff. The same is, to a lesser extent, true of Vadim Medvedev. Although he was in charge of the Socialist Countries Department of the Central Committee from early 1986 until the autumn of 1988 (when he became the Secretary of the Central Committee overseeing ideology), he was also part of Gorbachev's inner circle on domestic issues, including—as already seen in Chapter 6—the group which worked on the documents presented to the crucially important Nineteenth Party Conference. However, these six people were, in varying degrees, vital players in Gorbachev's foreign policy team, and, working through them, Gorbachev could implement the policies he wished in a way which was not possible in many key areas of domestic politics—in economic policy, in particular.[4]

As has already been noted in Chapter 5, any attempted radical transformation of the Soviet economic system was bound to run into a myriad of obstacles in the shape of the Chairman of the Council of Ministers, the large number of ministries with their vested interests, the party secretariats at all levels of the administrative hierarchy with a strong stake in the status quo, and the industrial managers, many of whom were dominant figures in Soviet-style 'company towns'. Even if an enlightened policy could reach the stage of being enacted (in itself no easy matter), there were endless opportunities to water it down or distort it during the implementation stage of the policy process. In contrast, the one agency responsible for the actual conduct of foreign policy—at least so far as East–West relations were concerned (for the Socialist Countries Department was also involved in state-to-state relations, given the inextricable links between party and state, with other Communist countries)—was the Ministry of Foreign Affairs.

The role of the International Department of the Central Committee in this area is sometimes overstated. Chernyaev, who spent sixteen years as deputy head of that department (1970–86), has emphasized that his department 'knew everything', for it had full access to 'closed information' (including reports from the

KGB and military spies), but it 'was not in charge of foreign policy'.[5] That was the responsibility of Gromyko, not Ponomarev.[6] Against that, it is important to note that the International Department played a greater role in relations with the Third World than with developed Western countries and this was the one area in which it got more or less directly involved in state-to-state relations. Its main concern, however, was to maintain ties with political movements and parties in the outside world. Vadim Medvedev has written that, prior to the appointment of Dobrynin to head it in early 1986, 'the International Department had been occupied almost exclusively with parties and movements', but Gorbachev decided 'to reorientate the department to general problems of international politics'.[7] This, though, was something for which the International Department was 'absolutely unprepared', and so in the elaboration and, still more, the implementation of foreign policy, the Ministry of Foreign Affairs continued to hold sway.[8]

The main way in which the International Department had played a role in East–West relations, apart from the contact with non-ruling parties, had been through the participation of its head and deputy heads in speech-writing for the General Secretary, especially in the Brezhnev era. Yet, from the time Gromyko became a full member of the Politburo in 1973, the political weight of the Ministry of Foreign Affairs increased and Gromyko then not only outranked Ponomarev in formal party terms but counted for more informally with Brezhnev, Andropov, and Chernenko in turn and had greater influence in the formulation of foreign policy as well as its execution.[9]

Thus, the replacement of Gromyko by Shevardnadze as Foreign Minister was more crucial than the replacement of Ponomarev by Dobrynin as head of the International Department, but the latter appointment was also not without significance. Dobrynin held the post from early 1986 until late 1988, when he was retired (and became a Gorbachev adviser) to make way for Valentin Falin, a German specialist who had previously served both in the Ministry of Foreign Affairs and the Central Committee and who had been a successful Soviet Ambassador to the Federal Republic of Germany from 1971 to 1978. Falin (unlike Dobrynin in 1986) did not receive promotion to a secretaryship of the Central Committee. This meant that from the autumn of 1988 there was a certain downgrading of the International Department which coincided with the abolition of almost all of the Central Committee departments overseeing economic ministries. Even before that, however, Dobrynin had not been a dominant figure in foreign policy-making. His main importance lay in the fact that he was not Ponomarev and that he was much more of a pragmatist than an ideologue.

The fact, then, that it was through the Ministry of Foreign Affairs that East–West relations were conducted made it easier for Gorbachev to become the decisive figure in Soviet foreign policy-making as compared with his difficulties in the face of the institutional complexity of economic policy. Although—in addition to the International Department and the Socialist Countries Department of the Central Committee—the Ministry of Defence and the KGB not only had views on foreign policy issues but could also, on occasion, pursue policies which undermined the credibility of Gorbachev and the Minister of Foreign Affairs, the latter ministry was the main institution over which the

General Secretary needed to exert control if he were to play a decisive part in this policy area. In the early years of Gromyko's tenure as Foreign Minister, Khrushchev was very much the dominant figure in the determination of Soviet policy, even though some of his foreign initiatives played their part in his subsequent undoing in 1964.[10] By 1973, in contrast, when Gromyko became a member of the Politburo, he already had sixteen years of experience as Foreign Minister behind him, and so it is hardly surprising that he became an increasingly formidable figure within his own domain. It was thus crucially important that Gorbachev made it one of his earliest priorities to remove Gromyko from the field in which by 1985 he had worked for almost half a century.[11] The appointment of Shevardnadze not only gave Gorbachev a like-minded ally who could be relied upon to co-operate with him closely but one who, until he had mastered an exceptionally complex brief, had less foreign policy experience than Gorbachev himself.

There was, however, another factor which was very important for Gorbachev. He was 'categorically opposed to the appointment of a diplomat; he wanted a politician'.[12] The distinction between a politician and an official (civil servant) was not a particularly easy one to make in Soviet conditions, but someone who had been the party first secretary of one of the less conformist Soviet republics (Shevardnadze's native Georgia), and who—like Gorbachev himself—had a natural aptitude for politics, was going to be a different kind of Foreign Minister not only from Shevardnadze's predecessor, Gromyko, but from his successor, the relatively liberal but excessively cautious Alexander Bessmertnykh. Bessmertnykh, a stop-gap appointment when Shevardnadze unexpectedly resigned his post in December 1990, had been a career diplomat whose main speciality, like that of Dobrynin, was the United States. When his greatest test came with the August coup of 1991, discretion for Bessmertnykh (in the form of a diplomatic illness) turned out to be the better part of valour, even though he was not in sympathy with the *putschists*. This brought to an end his short-lived political career.[13]

In choosing Shevardnadze, then, Gorbachev had in mind a number of criteria and the appointment was more than simply the promotion of a friend and supporter. He wanted a politician both because that person could instantly be promoted to full membership of the Politburo (which besides providing Gorbachev with a valuable ally would add to his weight as minister) and because he would have the necessary feel for politics and the responsiveness of a politician in his dealings with Western leaders and foreign ministers. The result was exactly what Gorbachev had hoped for. Sir Geoffrey Howe (then British Foreign Secretary) remarked that when he was talking with Shevardnadze he felt he was talking to a fellow politician, not a bureaucrat.[14] Gorbachev's close aide Chernyaev—while rightly dismissive of any suggestion that Gorbachev was pursuing Shevardnadze's foreign policy, rather than the other way round—has acknowledged that Shevardnadze personally 'made a huge contribution to the realization of the policy'.[15] Chernyaev's view of Shevardnadze was of someone who was both intelligent and sincere and 'with a completely different style from the "Gromykoesque" cadres'.[16]

The other reason for Gorbachev's dominance in foreign policy—apart from the role of the Ministry of Foreign Affairs and its responsiveness to Gorbachev's views once Shevardnadze was installed at its head—was that the acceleration in the speed of international diplomacy (from faster air travel to special telecommunications with other world leaders) had for some time been enhancing the role of chief executives in the conduct of foreign policy at the expense of their foreign ministers. The decrepitude of Brezhnev from the late 1970s and of his successors, Andropov and Chernenko, had somewhat obscured that general trend, but, with a fit Soviet leader installed in the Kremlin, it became clear that highest-level talks with the USSR meant talks with Gorbachev and he was soon in great demand from would-be foreign interlocutors. Indeed, given the popularity in the outside world which Gorbachev attained early in his General Secretaryship, Western political leaders were not averse to attempting to boost their own flagging popularity with a Gorbachev visit to their country or a trip to Moscow for a photo-opportunity, as well as discussions, in the Kremlin. As a result both of the demands upon his time and of his own interests and volition, Gorbachev was exceptionally active in foreign policy—not only in its elaboration behind the scenes but also in its conduct (in his meetings with presidents and prime ministers)—even as compared with Khrushchev or with Brezhnev when the latter was still in full possession of his faculties.

Thus, for example, Gorbachev did not allow a single year of his General Secretaryship to go by without holding summit talks with the American President; there were nine such meetings, five with Ronald Reagan and four with George Bush, in the period of less than seven years during which Gorbachev was Soviet leader.[17] The last US–Soviet summit meeting before Gorbachev became General Secretary had been between Brezhnev and Carter at Vienna in 1979, and—as compared with Gorbachev's three meetings with US Presidents on American soil—the *only* previous summits for which a Soviet General Secretary travelled to the United States had been Khrushchev's meeting with Eisenhower in 1959 and Brezhnev's with Nixon in 1973. In addition to his discussions with American presidents, Gorbachev had a very full programme of meetings with European and Asian leaders, the latter including—unusually in the context of recently preceding Soviet history—the Chinese and Japanese. Gorbachev re-established civil relations with the Chinese leadership, although they were alarmed by the processes of liberalization and democratization in the Soviet Union and their consequences, as they saw it, of the fall of Communism in Eastern Europe. With the Japanese Gorbachev was prepared for compromise on the issue of the Kurile islands—which the Japanese insistently made a stumbling-block to improved relations with the Soviet Union—but by the time he visited Tokyo in 1991 he was politically too weak (with Russia asserting its rights against the Union) to bargain.[18] While, in general, Soviet–Asian relations under Gorbachev did not produce much that was dramatically new, one novel element was the establishment not only of diplomatic relations but also of increasingly significant economic relations with South Korea.[19]

Given the extraordinary foreign policy activism of the Soviet Union under Gorbachev, his new Foreign Minister, too, had a demanding and important role to play, one which Shevardnadze performed with skill and integrity, in the process winning the respect and even affection of his foreign counterparts.[20] Shevardnadze's relative openness and frankness made a startling contrast with

Gromyko's political style. Gromyko—who inherited the sobriquet 'Mr *Nyet*', first applied to Stalin's Foreign Minister, Vyacheslav Molotov[21]—played his cards so close to his chest that he once paused carefully before answering a Western diplomat who asked him if he had had a good breakfast with a noncommittal 'Perhaps'.[22]

Western leaders, foreign ministers, and senior officials responded with diverse and mixed emotions to the new style of Soviet foreign policy, for the change of manner was immediate, whereas changes of substance were not so instantaneous. While, in general, they welcomed dealing with Soviet counterparts with whom they could have real conversations not overladen with dogma, they realized that they could no longer rely on the ineptitude of Soviet propaganda to give them a walk-over victory in any battle for public opinion. By early 1986 the American Secretary of State, George Shultz, had reached several important conclusions—that 'the Soviets were managing their foreign policy in an entirely new way', that Gorbachev had 'great capability and agility and toughness', that he had proved to be 'a skillful and adroit tactician in the politics of the Politburo' who 'had quickly put his own people in key spots', and that Gorbachev (*pace* Soviet experts in the US government who 'were forever counselling President Reagan that the Soviets had an inferiority complex') did '*not* have an inferiority complex'.[23] In the United States, still more than Western Europe, there was, however, disagreement as to whether this new kind of Soviet leader was to be welcomed or regarded as highly dangerous.[24]

Apart from a strong top foreign policy team, the new and self-confident Soviet leader had another advantage in international affairs that was not available to anything like the same extent in domestic—especially (again) economic—policy. This was the fact that the Soviet Union was well supplied with high-quality specialists on international relations and foreign countries, both within government and in the various policy-oriented institutes already discussed in earlier chapters.[25] First and foremost, however, these specialists were to be found in the Ministry of Foreign Affairs itself, where there was no shortage of relatively enlightened and capable people who had not had the opportunity to exercise their talents or political judgement to the full under Gromyko. Part of the change in Soviet foreign policy, and its successful implementation, was due to the advancement in the careers of some of these officials—for example, the promotion to the rank of deputy foreign minister of both Anatoly Adamishin and Vladimir Petrovsky in 1986.[26] (The personal style of Gorbachev and Shevardnadze—so different from that of their predecessors—was, of course, even more important in signalling to foreign governments the early change that had taken place in the tone of Soviet foreign policy.) Rising educational levels in the Soviet Union in the post-Stalin era were clearly reflected in the staffs of the Ministry of Foreign Affairs and the Central Committee's International Department, many of the officials being graduates of élite educational institutions—especially MGIMO (the Moscow State Institute of International Relations), which was a source of recruitment also for the KGB. In many respects, the Soviet diplomatic establishment by the mid-1980s was as professionally competent as its Western counterparts, although, of course, it included old thinkers as well as new thinkers and, until the Gorbachev era, even the latter often found themselves defending the indefensible.

The International Department, while perceived by some Soviet diplomats as harbouring a larger share of conservative Communists than Gromyko's ministry, was also not lacking in able and highly-qualified personnel.[27] A majority of the younger members of that supposed citadel of Communist orthodoxy were able to effect a smooth transfer in post-Soviet Russia to the staff of the present-day Russian Ministry of Foreign Affairs.[28] It is of significance also that during the perestroika period Gorbachev drew a number of his aides and advisers from the ranks of the International Department. In addition to Chernyaev—the most influential of them—and Grachev, they included the long-serving First Deputy Head of the International Department, Vadim Zagladin, who moved from that post in 1988 to become a Gorbachev adviser. (Like Chernyaev, he is still working with Gorbachev—in his Foundation.) Although Zagladin's successful career under Brezhnev made him seem increasingly like a time-server, he had been a genuine enthusiast for change in Khrushchev's time and it is possible that he recaptured some of that zeal under Gorbachev.[29]

It is noteworthy that, though Gorbachev drew extensively for advice upon specialists in the academic institutes concerned with international affairs, he preferred to draw for his staff appointments upon officials in the party apparatus. At least in the early part of Gorbachev's leadership, the norms of the system were still sufficiently strongly entrenched to make it difficult for him to do anything other than that; at a later stage, especially when he became President of the USSR in 1990, Gorbachev had a freer hand in appointments. His invitation (discussed in Chapter 5) in late 1989 to the academic economist Nikolay Petrakov to become his aide on economic policy was one of the relatively rare examples of his recruiting a full-time staff member outside the ranks of officialdom.[30] While his domestic policy might have benefited from a greater boldness in that respect, little harm was done to his foreign policy by reliance on insiders for the filling of staff positions. He was, in fact, able to construct an efficient and open-minded foreign policy team, all of whom (including, not least, Shevardnadze and Yakovlev) had extensive experience as party officials. They themselves, however (Yakovlev, in particular), as well as Gorbachev, made use of experts from the research institutes to a greater extent than ever before when considering policy options.

Thus, for example, in his role as Gorbachev's principal foreign policy aide, Chernyaev—on the eve of Gorbachev's announcement of his support for the policy of the United States following the Iraqi invasion of Kuwait in 1990—called together several academic specialists on international issues and, although opinion among them was divided, summed up in favour of those who advocated a strong line, including the possible use of force as a last resort, against Saddam Hussein.[31] This was at a time when the Middle Eastern specialists in the Ministry of Foreign Affairs were still opposed to a policy which they believed would undermine the relationships they had built up over many years with radical regimes in the region. Shevardnadze was also prepared to overrule those officials and was supportive of the American position. Indeed, he was more unambiguously willing to countenance the use of force than was Gorbachev.[32] The Soviet leader acceded to the request of Yevgeny Primakov (former Director of the Institute of Oriental Studies of the Soviet Academy of Sciences and subsequently Yakovlev's successor as Director of IMEMO) to use his powers of persuasion and his Middle Eastern contacts to convince Saddam of the necessity of withdrawing his troops from Kuwait and thus avoid the onslaught which awaited them. The intervention of Primakov—at that time a member of Gorbachev's Presidential Council and later head of Yeltsin's Foreign Intelligence Service—irritated Shevardnadze, but turned out to be of no avail.[33] Gorbachev, having taken a firm line against *Soviet* military intervention in other countries during his time as leader, had a clear preference for a political solution to this and other crises, the more especially as it occurred in late 1990, when he was already under strong pressure from conservative forces (including the military) in the Soviet Union. The general support of Gorbachev and Shevardnadze for the American position *vis-à-vis* Iraq, nevertheless, held fast, although it added to the growing resentment in Russian nationalist and orthodox Communist circles towards both of them.[34]

One of Gorbachev's ideas concerning the making of foreign policy was that the International Department should become much more of a think-tank for the Soviet leadership than it had been hitherto. This would involve it in paying less attention to revolutionary movements in the Third World and engaging more proactively in fresh thinking on central issues for the Soviet leadership, including that of East–West relations. He wanted the department's relationship to the Ministry of Foreign Affairs to be complementary rather than competing, but, nevertheless, for it to offer alternative ideas.[35] His desire both to shift the focus further in the direction of East–West relations and to maintain harmony with the Foreign Ministry was reflected in the choice of Dobrynin as head of the International Department (with the rank of Secretary of the Central Committee) and of Georgy Kornienko—who, like Dobrynin, had spent his entire career in the diplomatic service (from 1977 to 1986 as First Deputy Minister of Foreign Affairs)—to be First Deputy Head of the International Department. Kornienko, however, as his later statements were to illustrate, was rather more at home with the half-truths and deceptions of the Gromyko era than with the Gorbachevian new thinking.[36] Dobrynin had the reputation of being a relatively liberal and highly capable diplomat; the good relations he had established with his near-neighbour Yakovlev during the latter's ten years as Soviet Ambassador to Canada may also—given Gorbachev's willingness to listen to Yakovlev's advice—have played a part in his being brought into a senior position in the Central Committee apparatus. According to Chernyaev, 'Gorbachev chose Dobrynin not only because he did not like Ponomarev—and didn't like his views and Comintern attitudes and wanted to establish equality of rights in the international Communist movement—but because he wanted an experienced diplomat who would turn the International Department into an organization which would deal with foreign policy generally.'[37]

The Dobrynin appointment, while it had the desired effect of downgrading interest in revolutionary movements, did not, in other respects, live up to Gorbachev's expectations (or to those of his Washington admirers, who had over his many years as Soviet Ambassador acquired a high regard for his diplomatic finesse). Dobrynin had been so long in the United States that he knew the

Washington corridors of power better than those of Moscow. His lack of connections within the Central Committee apparatus meant that he never carried as much weight there as his formal rank would, on the face of it, have suggested. He was also primarily not an ideas man but a skilful executant of policy. He remained, moreover, fascinated with the United States, and while he now had, in principle, responsibility within the Communist Party for the whole world—including Europe, to which Gorbachev wished to devote increasing attention—Dobrynin liked nothing better than meeting visiting American delegations.[38] He 'was much more familiar with the reality of the United States than with the reality of his own country',[39] and, although the International Department's responsibilities included an attempt to build relations with West European social democrats[40] as well as Communist Parties and Third World revolutionary movements, these remained something of a mystery to Dobrynin, since they were all political forces which were absent from American political life.[41]

It was not only, however, the appointment of Dobrynin which prevented the International Department from becoming an important independent source of information and ideas to the Ministry of Foreign Affairs. This, Chernyaev points out, might have occurred if Gromyko had still been Foreign Minister. But once Gorbachev had appointed Shevardnadze, the International Department was doomed to play a subordinate role, given Shevardnadze's long-standing friendship with Gorbachev and the congruity of their ideas and general outlook.[42] Dobrynin was 'very loyal and good-natured' and his relationship with Shevardnadze and the Ministry of Foreign Affairs was co-operative.[43] The atmosphere changed when Falin became head of the International Department in 1988. He tried to make it the kind of department, offering alternative proposals, which Gorbachev had originally envisaged. But 'Shevardnadze simply ignored Falin' and from the very outset their relations were bad.[44] There was, in fact, strong resentment on Falin's part that on many important issues the Department was bypassed by the Soviet leader and his Foreign Minister. That apart, the essence of Falin's (and Kornienko's) general critique of the foreign policy of Gorbachev and of its conduct both by Gorbachev and by Shevardnadze was that—in their attachment to universal values and all-human interests—they neglected to defend with sufficient vigour *Soviet* 'national interests' and did not bargain nearly hard enough, whether over a united Germany or on arms control.[45]

New thinking

The salience of new ideas in Soviet politics during the Gorbachev era has already been emphasized in Chapter 4, but with particular reference to new ideas about the political system. Yet the new thinking on foreign policy was certainly no less important and was quick to produce results. With Gorbachev in charge and a new foreign policy team in place, the leadership both generated and encouraged innovative ideas. It was also responsive to fresh thinking emanating from within the Foreign Ministry and Central Committee apparatus and from the broader community of *mezhdunarodniki* (specialists on international relations and foreign countries). The rethinking was fundamental and provided a conceptual framework for changed Soviet political behaviour.

While Gorbachev's major speech to the Twenty-Seventh Party Congress in early 1986 did not yet set out an internally coherent new foreign policy, it nevertheless contained some significantly new elements, including a reference to the war in Afghanistan as a 'bleeding wound' which was his first public hint that he was determined to put an end to that Soviet military intervention. He emphasized that so far as relations with the United States were concerned, the only security worthy of the name was mutual security, while at the same time stressing that 'reasonable sufficiency' (rather than matching the potential adversary in all particulars) should henceforth be the criterion for judging Soviet military expenditure.[46] (That doctrine was resented by many in the military at the time and later violently attacked by the more conservative among them. According to General Albert Makashov, the most serious blow against the armed forces of the Soviet Union was delivered by none other than their commander-in-chief, Gorbachev. As the 'initiator of the doctrine of "reasonable sufficiency", he, in essence, began the planned reduction of the military potential of the country, and later even its destruction'.[47]) Gorbachev also provided an early indication of the more multipolar Soviet foreign policy he intended to follow, observing that 'one must not in world politics restrict oneself to relations with just one country alone, even if it is a very important one'. To do so, '*as experience shows*, only encourages the arrogance of strength' (emphasis added).[48] This was not only a criticism of the United States but an indirect criticism of Gromyko's foreign policy, as was Gorbachev's remark that 'continuity in foreign policy has nothing in common with the simple repetition of what has gone before, especially in the approach to *problems that have accumulated*' (emphasis added).[49]

The most important element in Soviet new thinking on foreign policy was a humanistic universalism. A relatively early expression of this was Gorbachev's speech to an international group of dignitaries assembled in Moscow in February 1987 for a forum called 'For a Nuclear-Free World, for the Survival of Mankind',[50] and it was authoritatively elaborated at the Nineteenth Party Conference in the summer of 1988[51] and in Gorbachev's speech to the United Nations in December of that year.[52] This was quite at odds with the old Soviet pseudo-internationalism whereby lip-service to a 'class approach' to international relations and references to 'proletarian internationalism' and 'socialist internationalism' were coded language for putting the interests of the Soviet Union first and above all other concerns. These euphemisms were manifestations of an ideologized perception of national interest in which there was virtually no conflict between Marxism-Leninism and the interests of the Soviet Union as a great power. That was not surprising, since the Soviet Communist Party leadership were, collectively, the chief interpreters of Marxist-Leninist ideology with responsibility both to guard and to 'creatively develop' it. Soviet institutions and Soviet doctrine had become so intermixed that Marxism-Leninism provided the ideological cement which held the power structure together while the Communist Party provided structural supports for the ideology.

The concept of a 'class approach' had, needless to say, nothing in common with listening to the demands of actual workers, which, on the face of it, it might appear to imply. As recently as 1980–1, the Soviet leadership had demonstrated this once again with their nervous and hostile reaction to the rise of Solidarity in

Poland, a movement supported at that time by the great majority of Polish manual workers.[53] However spurious the notions of a 'class approach' and 'proletarian internationalism' had been, the reality behind the rhetoric was a view of the
world as divided into two permanently hostile camps, one which saw East–West
relations in terms of *kto kogo* or as a zero-sum-game.[54] As Robert Legvold has put
it, what Gorbachev had done was to 'set aside the holiest of Soviet foreign policy concepts, the notion that the most elemental dynamic of international politics resides in the tension between two historic social orders—socialism and
capitalism'.[55]

The idea of the inevitability of war between these two different systems had
already been abandoned in Khrushchev's time and since then the notion of
'peaceful coexistence' had been advanced. But the promulgation of that idea had
almost invariably been accompanied—especially in documents for domestic
Soviet consumption—by the admonition that this meant a heightening rather
than a slackening of the class struggle. (What it also acknowledged was the necessity of avoiding actual war with NATO countries, as distinct from ideological struggle.) As early as 1985, when the new edition of the Communist Party Programme
was being prepared for adoption at the Twenty-Seventh Party Congress in early
1986, a conscious decision was taken by Gorbachev to abandon the definition of
peaceful coexistence between states with different social systems as a 'specific form
of class struggle'.[56] Gorbachev's emphasis on interdependence, universal values,
and 'all-human' interests was quite different from that old formulation and genuinely new so far as the top leadership was concerned.[57]

Precisely because the subordination of class interests and values to universal
ones was so much at odds with classical Marxism-Leninism, Gorbachev was at
pains to claim that Lenin had made a similar assessment (however uncharacter-
istic of Lenin's thought this may have been). In a meeting with writers in
October 1986 Gorbachev spoke about how Lenin had expressed an 'idea of colossal depth' concerning 'the priority of the interests of social development, of all-
human values, over the interests of one or another class'.[58] But the passage from
Lenin on which Gorbachev—and, following him, a number of Soviet commentators—drew was not, as Stephen Shenfield has pointed out, postulating conflict
between 'working-class' and 'general social' interests and did not even include
the words 'all-human values'.[59] Even at this early stage of the new leadership,
Shenfield could appositely observe that 'Gorbachev's "new thinking" has
enabled moral absolutism to establish a precarious foothold in the fortress of official ideology'.[60] Elaborating on the theme of universal interests and values in his
book *Perestroika*, published in 1987, Gorbachev spoke about reading Lenin 'in a
new way' and drawing inspiration from him and his ability 'to get at the root of
things'. Stretching this point still further he went on:

> Being the leader of the party of the proletariat, and theoretically and politi-
> cally substantiating the latter's revolutionary tasks, Lenin could see further,
> he could go beyond their class-imposed limits. More than once he spoke
> about the priority of interests common to all humanity over class interests. It
> is only now that we have come to comprehend the entire depth and signifi-
> cance of these ideas.[61]

While, as I have suggested in an earlier chapter, Gorbachev retained an idealized view of Lenin while departing more and more from the essentials of Leninism, the passage just quoted is an example of the *instrumental* use of Lenin which was common to Soviet politicians until, at least, the last year or two before the collapse of the USSR. Lenin had to be pressed into service to legitimize whatever doctrinal pronouncement or major action they wished to undertake in foreign or domestic policy. When making foreign policy pronouncements which had ideological implications, Gorbachev was conscious of addressing two very different audiences—on the one side, a domestic one in which the main threat (during his first five years in office, at least) came from conservative Communist forces who viewed with alarm his abandonment of Marxist-Leninist orthodoxy and his undermining of the pillars of the Communist system and, on the other side, a foreign audience which was likely to be unimpressed by references to Lenin and was more interested in the depth and extent of the change in Soviet doctrine and what bearing this would have on Soviet behaviour.

The notion of universal values and interests, and their special salience in the nuclear age, had probably not first entered Gorbachev's consciousness as a result of rereading Lenin (even though he *did*, when already General Secretary, reread a number of Lenin's publications of the NEP period). These ideas had been formulated earlier by Soviet intellectuals—notably by Andrey Sakharov but also (and of more direct influence on Gorbachev and his closest colleagues) by people on the liberal wing of the party intelligentsia, including Fedor Burlatsky and Georgy Shakhnazarov.[62] But it was only with Gorbachev's acceptance of them that they became authoritative (albeit, in terms of traditional Marxism-Leninism, highly revisionist) doctrine.[63] For many Soviet officials, especially in the military establishment, it was hard to come to terms with Gorbachev's abandonment of past Soviet certitudes. Even General Dmitriy Volkogonov, later a close ally of Boris Yeltsin and the author of a highly critical biography of Lenin, wrote a letter to Gorbachev in 1987 'protesting sharply against the pacifism in the conception of the new thinking'.[64] (In his two-volume biography of Lenin published in 1994, Volkogonov complains—on the basis of selective evidence and ignoring the main thrust of Gorbachev's thought—that Gorbachev continued to adhere to Leninism, but, as his earlier attribution to Gorbachev of quasi-pacifist views should have made clear, Gorbachev's mode of thinking was very different from Lenin's, even though he continued to hold Lenin in misplaced esteem.[65])

In many cases, the contributors to new thinking on foreign policy were also those with innovative ideas on domestic reform. The acceptance of the possibility of establishing interdependent and even harmonious relations between 'capitalist' and 'socialist' systems went along, naturally enough, with a redefinition of those terms. Both 'socialism' and 'capitalism' were concepts which had been employed to describe a wide variety of political and economic realities, including 'socialist' and 'capitalist' *dictatorships*, but in their social democratic and liberal democratic variants the dividing line between 'democratic socialism' and 'democratic capitalism' became quite a fine one. Gorbachev, with his new emphasis on global concerns and universal values, was, in effect, abandoning the idea of a final victory of Communism and legitimizing both a political and economic diversity and an international co-operation which transcended ideological divisions. He was, in a sense, embracing the idea of *convergence of social systems* which had been prematurely, and mainly erroneously, discerned by a number of Western commentators in the Brezhnev era and roundly denounced—also for the wrong reasons—by Soviet ideologists. What is more, this convergence in the Gorbachev era became increasingly a political reality, but not in the way which had been envisaged in convergence theory, with its assumption of movement from both directions towards a median position between archetypal capitalist and Communist systems. The movement, on the contrary, came almost entirely from the Soviet side, with Western liberal and democratic norms being gradually accepted as superior to traditional Soviet ones. Indeed, as T. H. Rigby has noted, the words 'normal' and 'civilised' began to be 'applied to practices and conditions *not* found in the USSR, and most tellingly in the phrase "in the civilised countries" '.[66]

Gorbachev himself made much use of the terms 'civilization' and 'civilized'—for example, in a major article he published in *Pravda* in November 1989 he used the word 'civilization' or a derivative of it on ten separate occasions.[67] Emphasizing that the Soviet Union was part of human civilization, with a responsibility for conserving it, he went on to say that they had in the past underestimated the importance of much that had been developed by humankind over the centuries. He continued: 'Such achievements of civilization include not only simple norms of morality and justice, but also principles of formal law, that is, the equality of all before the law, individual rights and freedoms, and the principles of commodity production and equivalent exchange based on the operation of the law of value.'[68] (Here we have references both to the rule of law and to the market as part of 'civilization', the former advocated unambiguously and the latter in a more convoluted form.) Unlike some Soviet writers and social scientists—who were by this time abandoning the concept of socialism—Gorbachev linked the development of socialism with the progress of civilization,[69] arguing: 'Democracy and freedom—these are the great values of human civilization which we inherit and are filling with socialist content.'[70] He recognized, however, that 'in terms of general civilization we were left in a past technological epoch in a number of important spheres', while 'the countries of the West were making the transition to another—the era of high technology, of fundamentally new relationships between science and production, of new forms of social provision for people and even of their way of life'.[71]

Alongside a fresh evaluation of the achievements of Western countries and of world civilization as a whole went a new attitude to individual countries' right to choose their own form of government, an aspect of the new thinking on foreign policy which was clearly of special importance for international relations. Most foreign observers, nevertheless, found it hard to believe that this indicated any willingness on the Soviet Union's part to slacken its control over the countries of Eastern Europe, still less to allow a genuine freedom of choice to the Warsaw Pact states. Yet it was immediately after speaking about 'world socialism' (and its current difficulties) and about how relations between the Soviet Union and the 'socialist commonwealth' were beginning to be freed from 'the stratification of the past' that Gorbachev went on, in his major speech to the Nineteenth Party Conference in June 1988, to say: 'A key place in the new thinking is occupied by the concept of freedom of choice. We are convinced of the universality of that principle for international relations when the main and general world problem has become the very survival of civilization.'[72]

In his speech to the United Nations in December of the same year Gorbachev returned to the theme of freedom of choice and in New York his words attracted still more attention than had similar ones in Moscow. He said:

> For us the necessity of the principle of freedom of choice is clear. Denying that right of peoples, no matter what the pretext for doing so, no matter what words are used to conceal it, means infringing even that unstable balance that it has been possible to achieve. Freedom of choice is a universal principle and there should be no exceptions.[73]

It is hardly surprising that these words of Gorbachev's were accepted as an invitation to seek a genuine independence by the peoples of East-Central Europe. The one thing which had kept the populations quiescent—for most of the time— was the apparently certain knowledge that an attempt to change the fundamentals of the system would lead both to Soviet military intervention and the imposition of a still more oppressive regime than that which had existed before. This, at any rate, appeared to be the lesson of the crushing of the 'Prague Spring', even though the Czech reforms had constituted a process of peaceful change initiated from within the Communist Party. (The Hungarian Revolution of 1956, in contrast, led within a few years to an amelioration of the system against which Hungarians had rebelled, but the cost in lost lives as a result of the bloody suppression of the revolution—and the severity of the crackdown during the remaining years of the 1950s—was sufficiently high to deter any further major attempt to assert a greater independence until the Czechs attempted to do things differently twelve years later.) While Gorbachev's words in 1988 had unintended consequences—at that time he still hoped to see reformist Communists with a similar outlook to his own come out on top in Eastern Europe—he had not in that year lost control, but was, on the contrary, making things happen.[74] His decisions in 1988, in both domestic and foreign policy, were of decisive importance and a crucial stimulus to further change, whereas a year or two later he was increasingly responding to events. His words at the Nineteenth Party Conference and in his UN speech quoted above were so different from any previous statement by a Soviet leader and so apparently unambiguous that a sufficiently large number of East Europeans began to contemplate putting matters to the test to see whether Gorbachev's actions—or, more precisely, non-actions—would match his pronouncements.

The new behaviour and its stimuli

Before we turn to consider briefly the changes brought about by Soviet new thinking on foreign policy, a prior question is: what produced the changed Soviet thinking and behaviour in the first place? In earlier chapters we have seen how Gorbachev's thinking (and that of some of his principal advisers) concerning the outside world had altered as a result of their foreign travels, especially in

Western Europe, and of their meetings with foreign politicians, again especially Europeans. The enhanced knowledge of the West gained by Soviet officials and by academics in the policy-oriented institutes by the time Gorbachev came to power has also been noted, and this, too, had its impact on Gorbachev, Yakovlev, and Shevardnadze, given their openness to fresh ideas and willingness to listen to experts from outside as well as within the ministerial and Central Committee apparatus. Attention has already been paid to the reassessment by Gorbachev and his closest colleagues of past Soviet failures and of the extent to which the Soviet Union was lagging economically, technologically, and in terms of the everyday life-style of its citizens as compared with the West (and, so far as technology was concerned, even with the newly industrialized countries of Asia). Such evaluations of the seriousness of the Soviet Union's domestic problems led to an emphasis on the need for radical domestic change, which in Gorbachev's view necessitated a very different international climate from that in which he came to power.

Yet there is an alternative explanation of all that was new in Soviet thinking and behaviour which is accepted unquestioningly by many American politicians and commentators, by a smaller proportion of their West European counterparts, and even by some Russians. That is the view that the change in the Soviet Union was induced by the intensification of the arms race inaugurated by Ronald Reagan after he entered the White House in 1980 and, in particular, by his Strategic Defence Initiative (SDI or, in popular parlance, 'Star Wars') announced in 1983. For Gorbachev the possibility of the arms race entering a still more highly automated, dangerous, and expensive stage *was* a further argument for the kind of policy innovation which would break the deadlock and end the vicious spiral. The Soviet leadership as a whole did not believe that the United States would succeed in fulfilling Reagan's dream of creating a foolproof defensive shield which would prevent all nuclear missiles from reaching their intended targets, but some of them were extremely concerned that the technological spin-offs from the research and development being undertaken would be sufficient to put the Soviet Union at a military disadvantage. The head of Soviet space research, Roald Sagdeev, an outstanding physicist who was a representative of the scientific community rather than the military-industrial complex but whose work brought him into constant contact with the latter, was one of those who argued that SDI would not work and that it would be a colossal waste of money for the Soviet Union to attempt to emulate Reagan's venture. He took the view that the 'Americans oversold SDI' and the 'Russians overbought it' in the sense of exaggerating the threat it imposed. When he heard a leading official in the Soviet space industry telling Gorbachev that 'we are losing time while doing nothing to build our own counterpart to the American SDI program', Sagdeev says he 'almost died from suppressing my laughter'.[75] (Sagdeev has, since 1990, lived in the United States. He moved from the Soviet Union, as he put it, as part *not* of 'the brain drain' but of 'the heart drain'; he had married Susan Eisenhower, the granddaughter of the American President who, in his valedictory speech, put into circulation the concept of the 'military-industrial complex'. For Sagdeev that complex was even more of a reality in the Soviet Union than in the United States.[76])

While Gorbachev was far from alone in the Soviet leadership in being alarmed by the policies of the Reagan administration, he was the only person in the Politburo (until he himself became General Secretary and was able several months later to promote Shevardnadze to full membership) to draw the conclusion that Soviet as well as American policy had to change. Other Russian leaders had reacted to increased American military spending in traditional ways and the fact that Gorbachev came to power when he did was totally unconnected with the policies of the Reagan administration in general and SDI in particular. For Gorbachev the likely spin-offs from SDI and the additional burdens this would impose on the Soviet economy did indeed represent additional reasons for seeking not only arms control agreements but also a dramatic improvement in the climate of Soviet–American relations. The Gorbachev factor was, however, much more decisive here than the Reagan factor. Reagan's policies had done nothing to change Soviet policy for the better during his first term of office. Had not the health of two successive General Secretaries—both of them chosen during Reagan's first term—deteriorated rapidly, leading to their deaths, Gorbachev would not have come to power at all while Reagan was still in the White House.

Indeed, far from making the Soviet leadership more conciliatory and on the look-out for a dovish General Secretary, the immediate effect of Reagan's speech in March 1983 proposing 'an all-out, Manhattan Project-like campaign to develop comprehensive, space-based anti-ballistic-missile' defences for the United States[77] was a heightening of international tension. Some senior Soviet officials began to believe that the West might be preparing for a pre-emptive strike on the Soviet Union. This suspicion was, paradoxically, strengthened when a Soviet plane shot down the Korean civilian airliner KAL 007 on 1 September 1983 after it had blundered into Soviet air-space. Not only at the time, but several years later, the Soviet military believed that the plane was engaged in military reconnaissance.[78] The British Prime Minister and Foreign Secretary were informed by their source in the KGB, Oleg Gordievsky, that what Geoffrey Howe described in his memoirs as 'simplistic overreaction' in the United States 'came near to convincing Moscow, Andropov included, that the whole incident had somehow been contrived, as a cunning trap, by the CIA'.[79] The author of a careful study of the causes and consequences of the KAL 007 crisis, Alexander Dallin, observes that it heightened mutual Soviet–American suspicion and that 'the outrage, both genuine and sham' that the two sides directed at each other 'served to place them even further apart'.[80]

Howe notes that a few weeks later Gordievsky informed British intelligence that there were Soviet fears that a NATO exercise due to take place from 2 to 11 November, which was to simulate a crisis leading to nuclear conflict, could be preparation for 'a real-life nuclear strike'.[81] As a result of Gordievsky's warnings, NATO changed some aspects of the exercise 'so as to leave the Soviets in no doubt that it was only an exercise', while 'Gordievsky's own reports to his nominal masters reinforced the message, and the crisis passed'.[82] This account is confirmed in Gordievsky's own memoirs.[83] The dangerous level of Moscow nervousness—which raised, in principle, the possibility of a pre-emptive Soviet strike—was conveyed by the British Prime Minister and Foreign Secretary to their American counterparts and to other leaders.[84] In early 1984, however, the atmosphere remained tense, and in January Vladimir Kryuchkov, at that time in charge of foreign intelligence in the KGB (later its Chairman, 1988–91), told a KGB conference in Moscow that the White House was engaged 'in the psychological preparation of the population for nuclear war'.[85] As a leading Washington analyst of Soviet and American security policy observed, it was assumed during the first term of the Reagan administration that 'war could only come about through some Soviet action that the United States failed to deter . . . the possibility of inadvertent war was discounted. Confrontational policies and high tension were seen as enhancing deterrence, and not as making war more likely.'[86] Little serious attention was devoted to the way in which American policy might be *perceived* in Moscow and to the possibility of inadvertent world war.[87]

The high-risk policies being pursued by the Reagan administration were, indeed, more damaging to the Soviet than to the American economy, given both US technological superiority and the fact that the effort to maintain military parity demanded a substantially higher proportion of Soviet than of American national income. Nevertheless, from the standpoint of the Moscow leadership, the economic danger (in so far as they appreciated it) seemed to be some time in the future, whereas the military and political threat appeared immediate. For Gromyko and Ustinov Washington's policies served as an excuse to continue an intransigent policy and to build up the Soviet military machine. Gorbachev, alone in the Politburo, drew different conclusions from the others, but he did not reveal them to his Politburo colleagues, still less to a broader public, until after he had become General Secretary. Even then, Gorbachev—as a former senior International Department official has observed—'needed courage to reverse the dominant mood in the top political echelon of the Soviet leadership'.[88]

Neither Reagan's policies nor the increased tension—contrary, as already noted, to some Western mythology—played a part in bringing Gorbachev to power. The first vacancy to occur in the General Secretaryship after the launching of SDI came with the death of Andropov in February 1984. He was succeeded not by Gorbachev but by Chernenko, who was chosen by the old guard precisely because he represented continuity with the past—especially the Brezhnevite past—and he was particularly warmly supported by Gromyko and the hardline Minister of Defence, Ustinov. Both of these political veterans, whose careers as important officials stretched back to Stalin's time, knew that they could continue to run Soviet foreign and defence policy along traditional lines as long as Chernenko was there.

It was the accident of fate which saw the collapse of Chernenko's health, and his death a mere thirteen months after coming to office, which brought Gorbachev to power in March 1985. It is not certain that he would have succeeded Chernenko even then but for another important death within the aged Soviet oligarchy—that of Ustinov in December 1984. Certainly if Ustinov and Gromyko had imagined for a moment that Gorbachev would change Soviet military and foreign policy to anything like the extent he did, they would have employed their considerable political weight to stop his rise to power before he reached the point of becoming the obvious heir apparent to Chernenko. At the time when Gorbachev became Soviet leader, Ustinov's successor as Minister of

Defence, Marshal Sokolov, was not even a candidate member of the Politburo, because there had been no Central Committee meeting in the interval since Ustinov's death at which he could have been accorded such a position.

When Gorbachev *was* chosen to succeed Chernenko, this was, then, not because the Soviet party-state élite were responding to Reagan's foreign and defence policy. In the first place, Gorbachev and his supporters (as has been described in Chapter 3) seized the initiative and had Gorbachev chosen as Chairman of Chernenko's funeral commission (and putative successor) before all members of the Politburo had a chance to reach Moscow and participate in the deliberations. Second, Gorbachev had given no hint to any members of the top leadership team either at the time of his election or earlier that he would deviate from the existing Soviet military policy of matching the United States whatever the cost and risks involved.[89] With an eye, no doubt, to the votes he would need at some future date from that selectorate (at a time when Ustinov was still alive), he spoke in the Politburo in favour of the Soviet Union needing to take an 'offensive position' in the propaganda war which followed the shooting-down of the South Korean passenger airliner in the late summer of 1983.[90] Gorbachev was to speak also, in his Politburo acceptance remarks of 11 March 1985, following the decision to recommend him to the Central Com-mittee as next General Secretary, of raising 'the economic *and military might* of the motherland' (emphasis added).[91]

Third, inasmuch as Politburo members had a choice and in so far as Central Committee opinion had been canvassed, Gorbachev was selected as a modernizer who would give dynamism to Soviet policy, not radically transform it. His own intentions, as has been argued in earlier chapters, were reformist rather than transformative at the outset, and he played down even the reformism at the Politburo meeting which chose him to succeed Chernenko. In a passage which reads oddly in the light of the radical changes Gorbachev was soon to embrace, he said: 'We do not need to change policy. It is a true, correct, fully Leninist policy. We need to raise the tempo, move forward, expose shortcomings and overcome them, to see clearly our radiant future.'[92] Even the most conservative Communist in the Politburo could have found nothing remotely worrying, or smacking of a change of course, in such cosily reassuring rhetoric. (Gorbachev was a complex politician operating in a complicated political environment, and these emollient words were less indicative of his thinking at the time than the far more critical and wide-ranging analysis of the level of Soviet economic and social development he had made in his major speech—discussed in earlier chapters—of December 1984 to a conference on ideology in Moscow.) Fourth, while Gorbachev's diplomatic success in Britain in December 1984, just after the Moscow conference, somewhat strengthened his qualifications for the General Secretaryship, foreign and defence policy were not at issue in the election.[93] The traditional concerns about place and patronage—who would be the gainers and who the losers in the domestic Soviet political struggle—were very much to the fore, and this time they were accompanied by a sense that the rule of old men (and the ritual of annual funerals of the top leader) could not continue if the Soviet Union was to avoid becoming a laughing-stock and also by an awareness on the part of at least a section of the leadership that the slowdown in Soviet economic growth was assuming the dimensions of a major problem.

It was the good fortune of President Reagan and of the West generally that Gorbachev came to power in 1985,[94] but there is not a shred of evidence that would justify seeing it as a consequence of Reagan's policy during his first administration.[95] Gorbachev was, after all, the fourth Soviet General Secretary (albeit the only fully fit one) to coincide with Reagan's period in office, but the first to interpret the intensification of the arms race not as a reason for the Soviet Union to step up its military efforts but as an additional reason for seeking a new basis for trust in East–West relations. Thus, while there is something in the argument, provided it is not overstated, that saw the American willingness to outspend the Soviet Union in the search for new weapons systems as *one* of the stimuli to *Gorbachev's* policy innovations,[96] there is no reason to suppose that Andropov or Chernenko would have acted in the same way had they lived longer or that any politically conceivable alternative candidate for the General Secretaryship in the mid-1980s would have acted as Gorbachev did. It was Gorbachev's different outlook and his encouragement of fresh thinking that produced the innovative Soviet foreign policy. That is especially true of Gorbachev's first four years in power—before the pressure of events in Eastern Europe constrained his choices and presented him with stark alternatives, to which, however (and crucially), he responded with behaviour consistent with the precepts of the new thinking.

Soviet-American relations

While, ultimately, it was developments in Europe—and especially Gorbachev's acceptance both of the independence which East European states asserted in 1989–90 and of the reunification of Germany—which ended the Cold War, the breakthrough to new levels of trust and co-operation with the West had already been made by 1988. During the first phase of Gorbachev's leadership the Soviet Union was more preoccupied with the relationship with the United States than with that with Western Europe and Gorbachev had much more expertise at his disposal on the former than on the latter. Improvement in the Soviet–US relationship, indeed, moved faster than that with most of the countries of Western Europe.[97] This was particularly true of relations with the United States while Ronald Reagan was still in the White House. Among the varied advice offered to Gorbachev in the earliest days of his General Secretaryship was the suggestion that he could afford to sit out the remainder of the Reagan presidency and not concern himself unduly about what was seen in Moscow as Reagan's obduracy.[98] But Gorbachev rejected this line, taking the view that it was especially important to establish a rapport with the conservative Reagan if real change was to be achieved. His briefings on the American political scene had enabled him to realize the advantages of winning the trust of a conservative Republican administration. Later he could imagine the kind of outrage which would have greeted any Democratic president who established as cordial relations with a General Secretary of the Soviet Communist Party as, first, Ronald Reagan and, subsequently, George Bush did. (Following his summit meeting with Gorbachev in Moscow in the summer of 1988, Reagan sent a note in which he wrote 'To Mikhail from Ron', and Gorbachev responded in similarly familiar terms.[99])

Gorbachev and Reagan had, moreover, one controversial viewpoint in common—a desire to achieve the total elimination of nuclear weapons. Within their respective administrations there were many who regarded this goal as unrealistic, even utopian, and among some of Reagan's European allies—most notably, Margaret Thatcher in Britain and François Mitterrand in France—the idea was regarded with horror. That aspect of SDI—Reagan's belief that it could lead to the abolition of nuclear weapons—was especially strenuously resisted by Mrs Thatcher, who took the view that it was impossible to disinvent nuclear weapons and emphasized Soviet superiority in conventional forces and chemical weapons. She was also, of course, especially unwilling, as were the French, to see the end of a small and exclusive 'nuclear club', of which Britain and France were members and which appeared to elevate them above other middle-ranking world powers.[100] Gorbachev's nuclear worries had been greatly heightened by the Chernobyl catastrophe in 1986. George Shultz later noted Gorbachev's 'seemingly genuine horror' concerning 'the devastation that would occur if nuclear power plants became targets in a conventional war much less a full nuclear exchange'. Shultz, in a memorandum to President Reagan, observed how 'deeply affected' Gorbachev had been by Chernobyl and remarked on the fact that it had 'left a strong anti-nuclear streak in Gorbachev's thinking'.[101] Chernobyl did make a very real impact on Gorbachev, but he had also decided early on to link it to the still greater danger of nuclear war. He did so publicly on numerous occasions. Moreover, in a speech to the staff of the Ministry of Foreign Affairs a month after the Chernobyl accident which—apart from some excerpts which appeared in the Ministry's specialist journal more than a year later—remained unpublished until 1993, Gorbachev spoke about Chernobyl as a tragedy but also as an opportunity to mobilize anti-militarist opinion, adding: 'if the peaceful atom is attended by such risk, what does that say about the nuclear weapon!'[102]

After the Geneva summit of November 1985, in which Gorbachev and Reagan got on well in personal terms, but achieved little more than that, came the far more dramatic Reykjavik meeting of October 1986. The idea of holding a summit devoted primarily to disarmament measures and to convene it either in London or Reykjavik was Gorbachev's and was first voiced by him to Chernyaev on his summer vacation in the Crimea in 1986.[103] (Gorbachev worked almost as much during his vacations as when in Moscow, but took the opportunity to read, reflect, and think ahead in a way which was scarcely possible when he was shuttling between the Kremlin and the Central Committee building, given the number of people anxious to see him and the vast quantity of documents which crossed the desks of his two offices.) Shevardnadze was also on holiday at the time, but elsewhere, and so Gorbachev went ahead on his own, though informing the First Deputy Foreign Minister, Anatoly Kovalev, who was in charge of the ministry during Shevardnadze's absence.[104]

One of Gorbachev's most skilful political moves in building a coalition for change in foreign and defence policy had been to give a prominent role in the policy process and in the detailed conduct of negotiations to Marshal Sergey Akhromeev, the respected Chief of the General Staff.[105] Later Gorbachev was to lose the support of a large part of the military and, indeed, of Akhromeev himself, but in the earlier stages of his leadership his co-option of Akhromeev, who enjoyed high esteem in the armed forces and possessed the kind of expertise on military issues which Gorbachev needed, stood him in good stead. The draft document which the Soviet side took to Reykjavik was initially prepared by Akhromeev, along with Yuly Vorontsov (like Kovalev, a First Deputy Foreign Minister) and Georgy Kornienko, recently moved from the Foreign Ministry to the First Deputy Headship of the International Department of the Central Committee (who, as noted above, was later to become disenchanted with Gorbachev's concessionary foreign policy), and presented to the Politburo by Dobrynin.[106]

In the actual negotiations between the Soviet and American working parties at Reykjavik, which went on through the night and narrowed down the range of disagreements to be discussed in the sessions involving Gorbachev and Reagan, Akhromeev was the most authoritative figure on the Soviet side. At a dinner with George Shultz in 1987, Akhromeev told the American Secretary of State that, alongside his part in the defence of Leningrad during the Second World War, the proudest days of his life had been those spent working with Gorbachev.[107] By the following year, however, Akhromeev was alarmed by the size of the unilateral cuts in Soviet conventional forces which Gorbachev was prepared to make and he resigned as Chief of the General Staff as Gorbachev made them public in his United Nations speech of December 1988. (Shevardnadze found Akhromeev a difficult colleague, saying that 'he was the one who made [arms control] so difficult',[108] but Gorbachev had to involve the military in the decision-making process. Any military representative would have been bound to take a sceptical, if not hostile, view of the scale of the cuts Gorbachev and Shevardnadze were contemplating; and for as long as Gorbachev was able to keep Akhromeev aboard and associated with his arms control policies, he had some protection from his military critics. Moreover, Akhromeev—in contrast with a substantial part of the military-industrial complex—was an influential proponent of the view of leading scientists such as Sagdeev that the Soviet Union had no need to pursue its own SDI programme, and that any such effort would be a colossal waste of money.[109]) Even after his resignation as Chief of Staff, Akhromeev continued to serve as an adviser to Gorbachev, although by 1990–1 he was concerned still more by the prospect of the breakup of the USSR. His growing conviction that everything he had fought for from the Second World War onwards was being destroyed led him to support the August coup of 1991 and to commit suicide when it failed.

The Reykjavik summit came close to concluding an agreement on the elimination of wide ranges of weapons. Gorbachev had a far surer grasp of the technicalities than had Reagan, for whom, however, at the end his pet project of SDI—which several years later was abandoned by the United States—was the one thing which stood between the leaders and an accord. That agreement would, however, have been so far-reaching and so sudden that it would have had a very hostile reception at governmental level from a number of America's European allies (although it would almost certainly have won more support than criticism from their electorates). At one point in the negotiations Reagan offered to eliminate not just ballistic missiles but all nuclear weapons, a proposal to which Gorbachev readily assented.[110] The Soviet leader, however, made every element in the package which had been agreed conditional upon a strict interpretation of the Anti-Ballistic Missile Treaty of 1972, insisting that work on SDI be confined to the laboratory.[111] This Reagan refused to do, and the summit ended—unlike any of the others between Gorbachev and an American President—with both leaders having difficulty in concealing their anger.[112]

Gorbachev, nevertheless, went straight to a press conference at which even experienced journalists looked shaken by the apparent total failure of a super-power summit meeting, in the course of which expectations of a great break-through had been raised. He gave a virtuoso performance and, instead of telling the world's mass media that 'one can't deal with that U.S. administration', which was what Shevardnadze had expected him to say,[113] he described the Soviet posi-tion and American responses in detail and managed to find much that was pos-itive. He told Shevardnadze that it was only when he saw how worried-looking were the faces in front of him that he decided that he must 'be constructive'.[114] It was a good example of Gorbachev's responsiveness to the mood of a meeting and of his feel for politics. He had also succeeded in getting in first with the Soviet side of the story. What is more, most of the Reykjavik proposals—which moved far beyond the arms control agreements of the Brezhnev era—were to be agreed upon over the next few years.

A more surprising result was that Reykjavik did not sour the Reagan–Gorbachev relationship. Indeed, Gorbachev trusted Reagan more from that time onwards, and the way he spoke about him in private to close colleagues was much more respectful after Reykjavik than before.[115] Chernyaev cites an instance not long before the Reykjavik summit in which a prominent Western politician, in a meeting with Gorbachev, described Reagan as 'a fool and a clown', to which Gorbachev responded that it was a pity that such a person should be at the head of a superpower.[116] After Reykjavik, Chernyaev never heard Gorbachev even in private express or agree with such sentiments con-cerning Reagan.[117] Reagan's attitude to Gorbachev, notwithstanding his tempo-rary anger over Gorbachev making SDI a sticking-point at Reykjavik, also became increasingly positive. After his presidency was over, he said: 'Looking back now, it's clear that there was a chemistry between Gorbachev and me that produced something very close to a friendship. He was a tough, hard bargainer. He was a Russian patriot who loved his country. We could—and did—debate from oppo-site sides of the ideological spectrum. But there was a chemistry that kept our conversations on a man-to-man basis, without hate or hostility. I liked Gorbachev even though he was a dedicated Communist and I was a confirmed capitalist.'[118] (Reagan goes on, with a mixture of truth and exaggeration, to depict Gorbachev as 'different from the Communists who had preceded him to the top of the Kremlin hierarchy' because he was 'the first not to push Soviet expansionism, the first to agree to destroy nuclear weapons, the first to suggest a free market and to support open elections and freedom of expression',[119] with-out seeing any contradiction between that description and depicting Gorbachev as 'a dedicated Communist'.)

An important contributory factor to the improvement in Soviet–US relations was Gorbachev's determination to end Soviet military involvement in Afghanistan. The Soviet intervention in December 1979 had added to the already worsening relations between the two superpowers at that time. Since this had involved moving beyond what had been recognized as the Soviet sphere of influence since the end of the Second World War—and interpreted by Stalin to mean total Soviet control—it attracted more concern and condemnation in Washington than had the crushing of the 'Prague Spring' in 1968.[120] When Georgy Arbatov, the Director of the Institute of the USA and Canada, told Gorbachev—in the course of a meeting soon after his election as General Secretary in March 1985 (and before the April plenum which marked the official beginning of perestroika)—that the Soviet Union should put an end to its military involvement in Afghanistan, Gorbachev replied that he was already thinking about that.[121]

For Gorbachev the real question when he became General Secretary was not whether to end Soviet military involvement in Afghanistan but how. As early as 17 October 1985 Gorbachev put to the Politburo the proposal that Soviet troops should get out and received approval in principle for this.[122] Chernyaev, in his memoirs, expresses regret that Gorbachev did not make the decision public at the time, but it is clear that he wished to obtain something from the United States in return for a Soviet withdrawal—in particular, a cessation of the US supply of weapons to the anti-government forces in Afghanistan. In July 1986 the Soviet Union announced the pull-out of 8,000 troops and from the beginning of 1987 publicly encouraged a process of reconciliation between the warring parties in Afghanistan. In April 1987 Gorbachev told George Shultz that the Soviet Union wanted to leave Afghanistan 'but the United States kept putting "sticks in the spokes" '.[123] In July of the same year Gorbachev announced in the course of an interview with an Indonesian newspaper that 'in principle, Soviet troop withdrawal from Afghanistan has been decided upon'.[124] The Soviet military were reluctant to leave Afghanistan in a manner which looked like a defeat, and there remained a gap between the decision in principle and actual Soviet behaviour on the ground. Indeed, during 1985 and 1986 Soviet military activities in Afghanistan intensified. But as Gorbachev's position within the leadership became stronger throughout 1987, with Yakovlev a full member of the Politburo as well as a Secretary of the Central Committee from June of that year, he was unwilling to brook further delay.

Yakovlev has confirmed that right from the start of his leadership Gorbachev's 'view was that a peaceful withdrawal should be effected'. Those who were reluctant to accept this did not oppose him on principle but found a multitude of practical reasons for slowing down the process. In the Politburo commission on Afghanistan, of which Yakovlev was a member and which met 'every week or ten days', Akhromeev and Varennikov from the military and Chebrikov and Kryuchkov from the KGB would put forward 'seemingly objective and reasonable arguments'.[125] But 'when you put them all together, day after day . . . it became apparent that they were deliberately holding things up, spinning things out in order to put off the moment when it would be possible to say: That is it, we are getting out.'[126] In contrast with Yakovlev, Kornienko (who was a member of the same Politburo commission) argues that Shevardnadze shared with Kryuchkov a desire to safeguard the position of the head of the Afghan government, Mohammad Najibullah, whereas he and Akhromeev were prepared to see a more broadly based coalition which might well exclude Najibullah. According to Kornienko, Shevardnadze was guilty of foot-dragging on the withdrawal from Afghanistan, and Chernyaev also notes Shevardnadze siding with the Minister of Defence, Yazov, and the Chairman of the KGB, Kryuchkov, in offering continued support to Najibullah, although Shevardnadze's Western interlocutors gained no such impression.[127] What is not really in doubt is the decisive role of Gorbachev in ending the Soviet military intervention in Afghanistan. Asked who had the final say, Yakovlev replied: 'Mikhail Sergeyevich [Gorbachev]—of course he had the final say. Enough hesitation, he said, the troops must be withdrawn—that's all there is to it. They must be withdrawn.'[128]

Shevardnadze drew George Shultz aside before going into a larger meeting in Washington on 16 September 1987 to tell him: 'We will leave Afghanistan.'[129] Shevardnadze asked for American help to attempt to ensure that there would be 'a neutral, nonaligned Afghanistan' and not 'a reactionary fundamentalist Islamic regime', but made it clear that a firm decision had, in any event, been taken. As Shultz put it in his memoirs: 'Gorbachev and Shevardnadze had both said publicly on earlier occasions that the Soviets would withdraw from Afghanistan, but we saw no evidence on the ground to lend credence to their statements. This private assurance was different. I had enough confidence by this time in my relationship with Shevardnadze that I knew he would not deliberately mislead me.'[130] The following April in Geneva agreements were signed involving Afghanistan and Pakistan as well as the Soviet Union and the United States on the total withdrawal of Soviet troops and on a pledge of mutual restraint in the supply of arms to the combatants. The Soviet forces began to leave Afghanistan in substantial numbers the following month and the withdrawal was completed by the set date of 15 February 1989.

The firm decision which Shevardnadze had conveyed to Shultz in September 1987 smoothed the way for the remaining two major summit meetings Gorbachev held with Reagan—in Washington in December 1987 and Moscow at the end of May 1988. (They also had a fifth meeting on 7 December 1988, the day before Gorbachev made his major speech to the United Nations quoted earlier in this chapter.) In his desire to remove medium-range nuclear missiles from Europe, Gorbachev made a major concession to the policy of the Reagan administration by removing the linkage between this issue and SDI. There were three main reasons for this. First, it was clear to Gorbachev that there was a limit to the progress he could make with Reagan on arms control so long as he made SDI a sticking-point. Second, he had been exposed to the arguments of Sagdeev and other scientific specialists that the Soviet side had been making more of a fuss about SDI than it deserved. Third, he may well have felt that, given a sufficient improvement in relations between the Soviet Union and the United States, domestic opinion in the USA would be unwilling to sustain the rising costs of SDI. This change of tack made possible the successful negotiation of the INF Treaty, signed at the Washington summit in December 1987, which eliminated intermediate as well as shorter-range missiles from Europe.

The value of summit meetings was twofold. On the one hand, they provided the possibility for the top leaders to take the measure of each other and, as happened in the case of Gorbachev and two successive American Presidents, to establish a personal rapport. On the other hand—and at least as important—they provided deadlines by which progress should be made (by the foreign ministers and other officials in a series of advance meetings), whether on arms control measures or on moving closer to a common position on areas of conflict. An initial summit could be justified simply in terms of meeting the first of these requirements, but thereafter summit meetings were liable to be judged as failures if they did not produce concrete results. An exception was Reykjavik, in that it was seen as a failed summit at the time, but later regarded as more of a breakthrough than a breakdown since it showed that accord between the United States and the Soviet Union on measures of disarmament could go far beyond the limited horizons of arms control negotiators in Geneva, Vienna, or elsewhere.[131] The American Secretary of State, George Shultz, was later to describe Reykjavik as 'the most remarkable superpower meeting ever held'[132] and his Soviet counterpart, Eduard Shevardnadze, was to write of the 'enormous significance' of the Reykjavik meeting, which had 'exerted a strong influence on our perceptions of . . . what was possible in Soviet–American relations and in world politics'.[133]

The Washington summit in December 1987 achieved a goal which had been set out by Ronald Reagan in 1981 and regarded then as unrealistic both in Western Europe and in the Soviet Union—the elimination of an entire category of nuclear weapons, the removal of the Soviet SS-20s as well as the Western cruise and Pershing missiles which were subsequently deployed in response to them. In this, as other instances, the cuts were asymmetrical, involving the destruction of approximately four times as many warheads on the Soviet as on the American side, since the Soviet Union had deployed more in the first place.[134] Although this was, understandably, interpreted by Reagan as a vindication of the position he had taken six years earlier, he was to discover that, like Gorbachev, he had opponents 'on the right', albeit far less of a serious threat than Gorbachev's enemies. For many of these critics the whole point of Reagan's zero option was that it would never be taken up; no Soviet leader would ever dare admit that it had been a mistake to install the Soviet SS-20s in the first place, thus justifying the installation and retention of American medium-range missiles in Western Europe. While Gorbachev was making the bigger concessions in an agreement which was in the interest of both sides, Reagan and—still more—his Secretary of State, George Shultz, were criticized by Senators Robert Dole, Dan Quayle, and (it goes without saying) Jesse Helms, among others, for agreeing to the INF Treaty. The Chairman of a right-wing pressure group, the Conservative Caucus, published an article in the *New York Times* in which he ridiculed the idea that Gorbachev was 'a new kind of Soviet leader' who 'no longer seeks world conquests' and described the summit meetings and arms control agreements as 'treasonous'.[135]

The dramatic change for the better which took place in the Soviet Union, Eastern Europe, and in East–West relations began with Gorbachev, but it depended on his finding Western partners who were not so ideologically blinkered that they failed to see the changes taking place in Soviet policy or so boneheaded that they would not take 'yes' for an answer. In contrast to his right-wing critics, Reagan had been, as Shultz put it, 'willing to recognize an opportunity for a good deal and a changed situation when he saw one', while Gorbachev had been 'perceptive enough' to recognize the problems and 'bold enough to be deci-

GORBACHEV IN THE INTERNATIONAL ARENA

19 Gorbachev's first visit to a Western country as General Secretary of the Soviet Communist Party was to France. He is pictured here in Paris with French President François Mitterand.

20 (*below*) General Secretary Gorbachev and President Reagan signing the INF Treaty on the elimination of medium- and short-range missiles in Washington on 8 December 1987.

21 Gorbachev being welcomed to Warsaw on 28 June 1986 by the Polish leader – and head of the Polish United Workers' Party – General Wojciech Jaruzelski. Whereas Gorbachev's relations with a number of East European Communist leaders were uneasy, his relationship with Jaruzelski was based on mutual respect.

22 (*below*) One of the less predictable international friendships was that between Mikhail Gorbachev and Margaret Thatcher. But having established a rapport at their first meeting in December 1984, they continued to enjoy good relations, notwithstanding some sharp differences over policy. This picture of Raisa Gorbachev, the British Prime Minister and the Soviet leader (with interpreters behind them) was taken in the London Embassy of the USSR during the Gorbachevs' two-day visit to Britain in April 1989.

23 Of all the foreign leaders with whom he came in contact, Gorbachev was especially close to the Spanish Prime Minister Filipe González (*left*), their conversations playing an important part in the evolution of Gorbachev's views towards a more social-democratic conception of socialism.

24 (*above*) Gorbachev with the two most politically substantial and influential of his aides – on the right Anatoly Chernyaev, his principal aide on foreign policy and a former deputy head of the International Department of the Central Committee and, centre, Georgy Shakhnazarov, an important adviser on reform of the political system and, as a former deputy head of the Socialist Countries Department of the Central Committee, on Eastern Europe.

25 (*left*) Gorbachev in relaxed mood with President George Bush and (far right) American National Security Advisor Brent Scowcroft. Pavel Palazhchenko, to the left of Gorbachev, is interpreting.

26 The good personal and political relations established, after a shaky start, between Mikhail Gorbachev and German Chancellor Helmut Kohl played a significant part in smoothing the way for the peaceful unification of Germany. In this picture Gorbachev and Kohl are seen exchanging pens after signing a treaty of friendship and co-operaton between their countries in November 1990.

27 Eduard Shevardnadze, a Gorbachev ally and his surprise choice as Soviet Foreign Minister in 1985, quickly won both international and domestic popularity. Later he came under severe pressure from Soviet hard-liners and he resigned his post, warning of the danger of a coming dictatorship, in a dramatic speech to the Congress of People's Deputies on 20 December 1990.

sive in dealing with the critical foreign policy issues we faced'.[136] The conservative American opponents of the foreign policy of Shultz and Reagan—and of the arch-enemy, Gorbachev—would later have the gall to claim some credit for winning the Cold War. It is, however, clear that, if Reagan and Shultz had been unwise enough to listen to them, the opportunity to change the character of East–West relations presented by Gorbachev's leadership would have been missed.

The events of the next few years in Eastern Europe and the Soviet Union were to make the dire warnings of America's conservative ideologues at the time of the Washington summit even more absurd in retrospect than they appeared at the time. With one exception, rationality was on the side of the Soviet and American negotiators. The exception was the White House's insistence that the INF Treaty agreement must be signed at 1.45 p.m. on 8 December 1987, the first day of the summit meeting. Why the signing had to take place at precisely that time was as much of a mystery to Shultz and his team as to his Soviet counterparts who, nevertheless, went along with the proposal. It later turned out this had been the decision of Nancy Reagan, relying on the recommendations of her Californian astrologer.[137]

Among the issues which Gorbachev—in sharp contrast with his predecessors—addressed in the course of his meetings with Reagan and Shultz and subsequently with Bush and Baker were the Soviet superiority in conventional forces and the need for asymmetrical cuts not only in nuclear missiles but in troop levels as well, the need to eliminate chemical weapons, acceptance of strict verification procedures in arms control (including rigorous on-site inspection), and the legitimacy of the topic of human rights in international diplomacy. By accepting—as did Shevardnadze in his meetings with Shultz—that the human rights issues had a regular place on the agenda (in contrast with the previous defensive Soviet insistence, which implicitly conceded the vulnerability of their position, that they were entirely the 'internal affair' of the Soviet Union), Gorbachev not only took the opportunity to attack aspects of the American record at home and abroad but also, and more importantly, brought into harmony his domestic and foreign policy objectives. Liberalization and a greater tolerance—more specifically, movement towards a state based upon the rule of law and the attainment of religious freedom and freedom to travel abroad and of emigration—were assisted at home by the need of Gorbachev and Shevardnadze to be able to defend the Soviet human rights record in their meetings with foreign interlocutors, European as well as American.

The other respect in which foreign policy came to the aid of Gorbachev domestically was that reducing international tension and the danger of war was enormously popular in Russia and throughout the Soviet Union. This threat had always seemed more tangible to Soviet than to American citizens, given that many of the most horrendous battles of the Second World War had been fought on Soviet territory. Moreover, years of warnings by Soviet propagandists of the imperialist threat had derived a new salience from the 'Second Cold War', as the period from the last years of the 1970s until the coming to power of Gorbachev came to be called.[138] Alongside an often cynical official lip-service to peace— which the party-state machine, in general, and the KGB, in particular, attempted to manipulate for their own ends—existed a real yearning for a more assured peace on the part of the great majority of Russians. Thus, Reagan's visit to Moscow in the summer of 1988 symbolized for Soviet citizens the qualitative change for the better which had taken place in East–West relations.

Gorbachev's foreign policy contributed substantially to his popularity in the Soviet Union, as well as abroad, during the first four to five years of his leadership. It was only from 1989 that serious survey research on the comparative standing of Soviet politicians, including Gorbachev, was undertaken by the most professional of Soviet public opinion polling organizations—the All-Union (now All-Russian) Centre for the Study of Public Opinion. As late as December of that year 81 per cent of citizens in Russia fully or partly approved of the activity of Gorbachev, with the comparable figure for the Soviet Union as a whole being 84 per cent.[139] And, as noted in Chapter 1, when Russians were asked to choose—in an open-ended survey, conducted in the same month—'the person of the year', Gorbachev received more than three times as much support as his nearest rival, Andrey Sakharov.[140] While it is virtually certain that Gorbachev's standing was as high, or higher, in 1988 (the precipitous drop in his domestic popularity, as noted in an earlier chapter, took place during his last two years in office) as in 1989, no comparably reliable survey data for that year are available. The impression he made on American public opinion can, however, be documented over a longer time period. Harris polls showed that in mid-1986 51 per cent of American respondents had 'a favourable impression' of Gorbachev, that this favourable rating had risen to 72 per cent on the eve of Reagan's visit to Moscow in May 1988 and to 83 per cent after it.[141] The impact of Gorbachev's domestic and foreign policy changes on American public opinion was reflected in the fact that, whereas at the beginning of the 1980s an overwhelming majority of Americans were in favour of 'getting tougher' with the Soviet Union, by late 1987 this had changed to a similar majority saying that the United States should 'try harder to reduce tensions' with the rival superpower.[142]

By 1990 Soviet citizens had already come to take it for granted that there would be no nuclear war, and domestic problems took increasing precedence over the international situation. The award to Gorbachev in October 1990 of the Nobel Peace Prize, although certainly deserved, was by that time of little or no benefit to him at home. This, as has already been indicated, was in sharp contrast to 1988 when Gorbachev's domestic standing was still being enhanced by the fact that he had brought the Soviet Union's sworn enemy, Ronald Reagan, to Moscow in peace and friendship. Asked by a reporter inside the Kremlin grounds whether he still believed that the Soviet Union was an 'evil empire' (the term he had used in 1983), the American President replied: 'No, I was talking about another time, another era.'[143] The Moscow summit was not especially notable for its substance but strong on both visual and verbal symbolism. The world's cameras were on Gorbachev and Reagan as they walked together on Red Square and on Reagan, standing in front of a bust of Lenin, as he addressed a large audience of students at Moscow University. The American President told them not only that it was time that the Berlin Wall was removed but also that they were 'living in one of the most exciting, hopeful times in Soviet history'.[144]

Partly, no doubt, because they were more vulnerable than Reagan had been to attacks from the conservative Republican ultras, but also because they (understandably) wished to conduct a policy review, George Bush and his Secretary of State, James Baker, began by displaying suspicion of the warm relations their predecessors had established with Gorbachev and Shevardnadze.[145] As Shultz observed in his memoirs: 'George Bush and Jim Baker seemed concerned and wary that Ronald Reagan and I had become too impressed with Soviet personalities—Gorbachev, Shevardnadze—too ready to believe that genuine change was occurring in the Soviet Union. . . . I was apprehensive that the "new team" did not understand or accept that the cold war was over.'[146] There was indeed a lull in US–Soviet relations in the early months of 1989 which greatly concerned Gorbachev, who had to be reassured by his West European partners—most notably, Margaret Thatcher and Helmut Kohl—that this would only be temporary, and that before long Bush would be at least as forthcoming as Reagan had been.[147] In the face of the available evidence, Bush's caution was excessive, and, as Michael Beschloss and Strobe Talbott have observed, 'when he belatedly began to engage with Gorbachev that May [1989], he appeared to be doing so under pressure from public opinion, Congress, and his NATO allies'.[148]

Eventually, Gorbachev's relations with Bush and Shevardnadze's with Baker were to be no less friendly than those with Reagan and Shultz.[149] Indeed, Gorbachev's discussions with Bush had more substance than his conversations with Reagan, given that Bush came much closer to matching Gorbachev's grasp of the issues—and far surpassed it on the detailed workings of market economics. Baker and Shevardnadze were the first to meet and to establish warm relations. By September 1989 the American Secretary of State had become highly impressed by Shevardnadze's willingness to be influenced by a strong argument and to defend that position subsequently in Moscow as well as by his candour about Soviet mistakes and problems.[150] It was, though, not until the first Gorbachev–Bush summit—held off the coast of Malta at the beginning of December 1989—that relations of trust were established between the Soviet and American chief executives. The collapse of the Berlin Wall the previous month and the Soviet acceptance of this had strengthened Gorbachev's standing in the West, but it did nothing to help him at home. On the contrary, Gorbachev's position was now weaker in important respects than it had been during the Reagan years. He was already being criticized in the Soviet Union both by hardliners and by more overtly radical reformers (although not yet as severely attacked as he was to be the following winter); the economy—now obeying the rules neither of plan nor market—was in worse shape than when he had become General Secretary; there had been inter-ethnic violence in the Caucasus and Central Asia, as well as large-scale miners' strikes in Russia and Ukraine; and Communist regimes—as well as the Berlin Wall—had begun to crumble in East-Central Europe.

Although Gorbachev was left with a weak hand to play in any negotiations, he played it with panache. He was helped by Bush's desire not to undermine Gorbachev's domestic position in any way—his stated intention 'not to dance on the [Berlin] wall'.[151] Bush had been convinced in the course of the preceding months—as the Soviet leadership made clear that it would not intervene militarily to put a stop to regime change in Eastern Europe—that the new thinking was being matched by a completely new pattern of behaviour. The so-called 'Brezhnev doctrine'—the Soviet rationalization, following their military intervention to put an end to the 'Prague Spring', that the Soviet Union and other Warsaw Pact states had a right and duty to intervene to 'defend socialism' in any part of the 'socialist commonwealth' where the Communist system was threatened—had been totally rejected. It had been replaced, as the Soviet Foreign Ministry spokesman, Gennady Gerasimov, quipped, by the 'Sinatra doctrine'—letting the East Europeans do it *their* way.[152] By the end of the Malta summit, during which turbulent weather and waves had kept President Bush marooned on his ship for half a day, Gerasimov (who, although speaking in English rather than his native Russian, almost invariably came up with a more quotable phrase than his American counterpart, Marlin Fitzwater) was able to announce: 'We buried the Cold War at the bottom of the Mediterranean Sea.'[153]

Malta, as the first summit meeting between Gorbachev and Bush (although they had met earlier when Bush was Vice-President and President-elect), resulted in a stronger personal relationship between them. Gorbachev was impressed by the knowledge both Bush and (still more) Baker displayed of the Soviet Union's economic problems and by the fact that they appeared to have made their choice to support perestroika and its principal author.[154] In public the new accord was symbolized by the fact that for the first time a Soviet leader and an American President gave a joint press conference.[155] Bush (who 'was affected more than most world leaders by personal relations') found that, for his part, 'he actually liked and . . . could do business with the Soviet leader'.[156]

This rapport, and Bush's sympathy for Gorbachev's increasingly difficult domestic predicament, resulted in some concessions being made from the American as well as the Soviet side when the two presidents (Gorbachev having become Soviet President in March 1990) met next in Washington and Camp David at the end of May and beginning of June 1990. The further collapse of Communist regimes in Eastern Europe and especially Germany's movement towards reunification had added to the discontent in the Soviet military, the KGB, and the party apparatus, already caused by the growing political pluralism which threatened them at home. Yet Gorbachev was continuing to lose ground among his former democratically inclined supporters as well. The election of Yeltsin as Chairman of the Supreme Soviet of the Russian republic on the eve of his departure for Canada and the United States had done nothing to improve his mood.

Germany (discussed in the next section) bulked large in the Washington summit talks, and this was an issue—especially the prospect of a united Germany in NATO, which was what the United States was seeking—that was acutely sensitive for Gorbachev in terms of his domestic political battles. With an eye on his declining support at home, he was also extremely anxious to have the Soviet Union granted Most Favoured Nation status in its trading relations with the United States. Bush, with *his* domestic critics in mind, initially rejected the idea of offering MFN standing until the Soviet Union had passed an emigration law and had lifted the economic blockade which had been imposed on Lithuania after it had declared its sovereignty. Both Shevardnadze, in his talks with Baker, and Gorbachev, in his negotiations with Bush, far from disguising their weakening position, made it count in their favour. The American President and Secretary of State much preferred dealing with them not only to any hardline Soviet alternative leaders but also to the relatively unknown quantity represented by Yeltsin, who was not yet, in any case, as authoritative a figure as he was to become a year later after he had been elected President of Russia by the people as a whole. Thus, Bush gave way on the issue of Most Favoured Nation status but told Gorbachev that he wished to link it in his public statement both to ending the Lithuanian blockade and the enactment of the emigration law. Gorbachev protested that this would weaken his position at home and Bush again relented, mentioning only one of the issues in his public statement and in a sufficiently tactful way as to minimize the damage to Gorbachev.[157] The summit saw also the signing of agreements on chemical weapons and nuclear testing as well as a compromise statement on the strategic arms treaty which had not yet been concluded.[158]

By the time Bush came to Moscow just over a year later—at the end of July 1991—Yeltsin had been elected Russian President and Gorbachev's position was in danger (with the coup less than a month away, in greater danger than he knew). Nevertheless, Bush's substantive discussions were with Gorbachev, not with the Russian President. Agreement on strategic arms had been reached by Soviet and American negotiators at Geneva, and Gorbachev and Bush were able to sign at last the START treaty. Yeltsin tried to command as much of Bush's attention as possible and succeeded thereby in annoying not only Gorbachev, which was predictable, but also Bush, who complained he had been 'ambushed'.[159]

The Bush administration was both then and later criticized by important opinion groupings within the United States—not only on the extreme right—for focusing for too long on Gorbachev and the Soviet Union rather than on Yeltsin and the new Russian authorities. But, contrary to the suggestion of the critics that some unspecified opportunities were lost thereby, nothing was lost and a great deal was gained. Enormous damage would have been done to East–West relations—and particularly the US–Russian relationship—in the post-Soviet era if the United States could have been shown to have been an active participant in the breakup of the Soviet Union. Whereas some of the USSR's successor states—most notably, Estonia, Latvia, and Lithuania and, to a lesser extent, Ukraine—could take pride in their newly independent status, for Russia 'independence' was a much more ambiguous outcome of the political struggle. To the extent that Russia dominated the Union, the breakup of the USSR represented for Russians a loss of territory, statehood, and superpower status.

Given that Russian nationalists were in any event to blame the West in general and the United States in particular (together, of course, with Gorbachev and Yeltsin) for the destruction of the Soviet Union, it was highly prudent of the Bush administration to give them few substantive grounds for doing so. That became the more significant a matter within a very few years, by which time a majority of Russian citizens were very openly regretting the disappearance of the Soviet Union and taking no pride in their 'independence' within reduced and porous borders.[160] The only point, in fact, at which the American President could reasonably be accused of giving a push to the fissiparous process was when, several days before the referendum on Ukrainian independence held on 1 December 1991, he let it be known that, following a 'yes' vote, the United States would recognize Ukrainian independence 'expeditiously' without waiting for any reaction from Moscow.[161] Bush was by this time responding increasingly to the domestic critics who blamed him for not having done enough to encourage the various independence movements and at the same time overcompensating for a speech he had made in Kiev just after the Moscow summit in the summer of 1991 when he had gone out of his way to laud Gorbachev's achievements to a sceptical Ukrainian audience and had infuriated some of them by adding: 'Freedom is not the same as independence. Americans will not support those who seek independence in order to replace a far-off tyranny with a local despotism. They will not aid those who promote a suicidal nationalism based on ethnic hatred.'[162]

Gorbachev and Europe

While there is no doubting the importance of the Soviet–American relationship, especially in the realm of arms control, the most profound changes of the Gorbachev era took place within Europe and in the Soviet Union's relations with European countries, both West and East. The radical improvement came, in the first instance, with the countries of Western Europe and was consolidated by the Kremlin's changing attitude to Eastern Europe. The new levels of trust established between Gorbachev and his West European counterparts made it easier for him to accept the unambiguous rejection of Communism (which in a much more incremental—and of necessity, given his position at the head of the Soviet Communist Party, inconsistent—way he was rejecting himself) in the Warsaw Pact countries and the breakup both of that military alliance and of its economic counterpart, Comecon. Equally, the fact that Soviet troops stayed in their barracks as the East Europeans changed their regimes was the final proof even for the doubters in Western Europe (of whom by this time there were comparatively few, except in France) of the genuineness of the Gorbachevian new thinking, marked as it now was by renunciation of the use of force to maintain Soviet hegemony in a part of the world where it had held sway ever since the end of the Second World War.

In a confidential speech to the staff of the Ministry of Foreign Affairs on 23 May 1986,[163] Gorbachev criticized the inertia of thinking which had characterized past Soviet policy towards Europe and said that the Soviet Union must not see Europe 'through the prism of its relations with the United States of America'.[164] More generally, he argued that it was 'inexcusable to think that the partner [in negotiations] is more stupid than we are' and it was necessary to get away from the 'senseless obduracy' which had led to Soviet representatives being named 'Mr *Nyet*'.[165] Gorbachev gave a significant place in this speech to the need to change relations with the countries of Eastern Europe, arguing that these must be based on respect for 'their experience and merits' and involve less smugness on the Soviet side: 'It is impermissible to think that we can teach everyone. No one gave us that right.'[166]

The good personal relations Gorbachev established with, for example, Felipe

González, Margaret Thatcher, François Mitterrand, and (after an awkward start) Helmut Kohl have been discussed in an earlier chapter. The Gorbachev–Kohl dialogues constituted the most important relationship of the later Gorbachev era, and their developing friendship played a significant part in the peaceful reunification of Germany. Gorbachev's most important European interlocutor of his earlier years in power, so far as East–West relations were concerned, was, however, Margaret Thatcher. While, as noted in a previous chapter, Gorbachev's conversations with Felipe González were more influential in terms of the development of his own thinking—in a social democratic direction—Margaret Thatcher was able to become a more important partner of the Soviet Union, on the one side, and the United States, on the other, than any British Prime Minister since Churchill. This was the single most important and constructive achievement of her prime ministership. It is ironical that such notable predecessors as Harold Macmillan, the author of *The Middle Way*, and the middle-of-the-road Harold Wilson, both of whom aspired to play the role of honest broker between the superpowers, made only modest headway in that regard in the case of Macmillan[167] and much less in Wilson's,[168] whereas the more right-wing Margaret Thatcher did have an impact both on Gorbachev's thinking and on Ronald Reagan's view of Gorbachev and the seriousness of his reformist intentions.[169] Her plain speaking with Gorbachev gave him a sharper perception of how past Soviet policy looked from Western Europe, and her personal support for Gorbachev in public and private in the West was especially important *vis-à-vis* the Reagan administration in the earliest period of Gorbachev's leadership, given her impeccably anti-Soviet credentials and Reagan's regard for her judgement.[170] Gorbachev, both at the time and in retrospect, placed special value on Thatcher's public support for the changes in Soviet domestic and foreign policy he had brought about, observing that, her militant anti-Communism and commitment to ideological struggle on behalf of the West notwithstanding, she had 'honestly tried to help us by mobilizing the West's help for perestroika'.[171] As was noted in Chapter 4, he resolved after her 1987 visit to Moscow to devote still more attention than hitherto to Western Europe.[172]

Two days after the departure of the British Prime Minister from Moscow in the spring of 1987, Gorbachev spoke to a small group of his aides and associates about Europe. According to Anatoly Chernyaev, Gorbachev's 'powerful turn towards Western Europe' was an 'important consequence' of his conversations with Thatcher.[173] Describing Western Europe as 'our basic partner', Gorbachev said: 'Perhaps I am wrong, but it seems to me that we study Europe badly and we know it badly.'[174] In the course of these remarks Gorbachev proposed establishing a centre for research on Europe. (The following year a new Institute of Europe was indeed established in Moscow, although—perhaps by way of demonstrating Gorbachev's point that there were fewer high-quality specialists on Europe than on the United States—it was a Deputy Director of Arbatov's Institute of the USA and Canada, Vitaly Zhurkin, who became the first Director of the Institute of Europe. Zhurkin was, however, an appropriate enough choice in that he was at least a serious contributor to the new thinking on foreign policy.) Not a single question could be decided without the involvement of Europe, said Gorbachev, and there were great possibilities for step-by-step improvements in Soviet–West

European relations. Indeed, 'without such a partner as Western Europe, we will not turn [the Soviet Union] around'.[175] Gorbachev's actions on Europe matched his words. The majority of his meetings in 1987–8 were with West European politicians.[176]

So far as Western Europe was concerned, the unification of Germany—which, although an *indirect* rather than intentional result of Gorbachev's changed foreign policy, could not have come about when it did without his ultimate acquiescence—was the most important consequence of the Soviet new thinking and new behaviour. Chronologically—and in terms of political logic also (since it was the most sensitive European issue of all for the Soviet leadership)—this came after the breakthrough to independence had been made by most of the countries of Eastern Europe. But although the speed with which it then happened took almost everyone by surprise, including the Soviet leader, Gorbachev had played his part in stimulating hopes of reunification not only with his 'freedom to choose' speeches of 1988 but on two occasions in 1987.

In a meeting with the West German President, Richard von Weizsacker, in July 1987, Gorbachev became the first Soviet leader since the war to indicate that the division of Germany might be anything other than permanent. When von Weizsacker raised—'almost just for the record', as he later told Timothy Garton Ash—the issue of German unity, Gorbachev replied that 'history would decide what would happen in a hundred years'.[177] In his book *Perestroika*, published later in 1987, Gorbachev seemed far from wishing to hasten the process of German unification. Discussing the two German states, he said 'one should proceed from existing realities and not engage in incendiary speculations'. Nevertheless, he repeated virtually verbatim what he had said to von Weizsacker: 'Both [German states] have drawn lessons from history, and each of them can contribute to the affairs of Europe and the world. And what there will be in a hundred years is for history to decide.'[178]

The very fact that Gorbachev had shifted the Soviet position away from rigid adherence to the notion of two permanently divided German states was significant, and in spite of his placing a hypothetical German reunification in the distant future, his statements of 1987 may constitute some evidence at least to bolster the controversial assertion of Chernyaev (who had been a participant in many private conversations on foreign policy with Gorbachev) that Gorbachev's words to von Weizsacker represented a 'signal' that 'was accepted'. Chernyaev continues: 'Knowing him [Gorbachev], I can affirm that inwardly he was already then, and some time earlier even, convinced that without a resolution of the German question and without a restoration of historically conditioned normal relations between the two great nations of Europe no healthy international situation would result.'[179] It is easy, of course, unconsciously to project backwards views one has come to accept only later, and by no means always simple even for the individual in question to recall when he or she reached a particular intellectual position. For what it is worth, however, Alexander Yakovlev—in a remark fully consonant with Chernyaev's—said in early 1992 that Gorbachev had already accepted from the very outset of his General Secretaryship in 1985 that Germany would become reunited.[180] In so far as this was the case, it seems likely, though, that Gorbachev envisaged Germany being reunited only after the division in Europe as a whole had been ended.[181]

The Chernyaev–Yakovlev view is rejected by Vyacheslav Dashichev, one of the innovative policy-oriented academics in Bogomolov's institute in Moscow, who wrote a memorandum as early as 1987 in which he argued that 'the continued existence of two German states was very negative for the Soviet Union' and that the time had come 'to consider and discuss the option of reunification'.[182] This received short shrift from the International Department both then and subsequently. So far as Gorbachev's position is concerned, Dashichev's view is somewhat contradictory. On the one hand, he observes that in 1988–9, 'despite the attempts by Falin, Ligachev[183] and others to hinder them, Shevardnadze and Gorbachev were gradually succeeding in forging a realistic foreign policy, free of the dogmas and burdens of the Stalinist era', while, on the other hand, arguing (following a reference to Ligachev and Falin) that 'Gorbachev, too, remained mired in traditional stereotypes of foreign policy thinking on the German question'.[184] This interpretation is strenuously rejected by Chernyaev, writing in the same volume as Dashichev. After noting how Soviet–German relations lagged behind the improved relationship between the Soviet Union and other West European countries in the period between 1986 and 1988, Chernyaev observes that this was due to Gorbachev's wish to teach Kohl and the Germans a lesson after the German Chancellor had made his ill-advised comparison between Gorbachev and Goebbels as propagandists— which Gorbachev, hardly surprisingly, regarded as insulting—in 1986.[185] Thus, it was not until October 1988 that Kohl was able to visit Moscow. The discussions he held there turned out to be a good example of Gorbachev's unwillingness to bear lasting grudges (with the perhaps understandable exception of his relations with Boris Yeltsin), especially when *amour propre* could get in the way of serious policy. To the surprise of Chernyaev, the October 1988 talks between Gorbachev and Kohl 'produced a mutual trust, which quickly developed into a genuine friendship' as well as demonstrating Gorbachev's 'courage in making the break with Marxism-Leninism in favour of pragmatism and common-sense'.[186]

There is no doubt that the speed of German reunification—far faster than Gorbachev (or for that matter Margaret Thatcher or François Mitterrand) wished—was forced by events in Central Europe when regime transformation in Hungary and Poland, and the opening of the Hungarian border which allowed East Germans to travel westwards, was followed by the opening of the Berlin Wall in November 1989. Even Dashichev, with his somewhat critical view of Gorbachev, accepts that it was Gorbachev who took the crucial step when he told Helmut Kohl in February 1990 that it was up to the Germans to determine in what kind of state they would live and the speed at which it would be attained. He notes, too, that Gorbachev and Shevardnadze had to keep an eye over their shoulders at 'the political and military *nomenklatura*' who were making intimidatory noises about sell-outs to an alleged enemy.[187] Within the International Department of the Central Committee, as well as in military circles, there was a strong feeling that Gorbachev and Shevardnadze had not been sufficiently 'professional' and that a harder bargain could have been struck with the Germans in return for such a prize as reunification, one which a few years earlier had seemed but a distant dream.[188] In a longer historical perspective, however, Gorbachev is likely to be given credit not only for keeping Soviet troops in their barracks and not obstructing the process of speedy reunification once it had begun but also for not driving a bargain so hard that it would have added a final sad chapter to the history of Russian–German relations in the twentieth century. Instead, he extracted the Soviet Union from an alarmingly difficult situation which was changing so fast on the ground that a divided Germany could have been maintained only by the convincing threat of Soviet military action. To eschew such an option and make a virtue out of necessity—given Gorbachev's firm intention to use only peaceful means—may be stigmatized as no more than the diplomacy of decline. Yet it was no mean achievement. With the partial exception of the British, no *West* European imperial power in the post-Second World War period accepted the end of empire with as much political aplomb or as little bloodshed as was involved in Gorbachev's diplomacy. Indeed, so far as the 'outer empire' was concerned, only in Romania was blood spilled, and that by Romanians.[189] In the particular case of Germany, Gorbachev's conduct of relations left behind a fund of German goodwill both for him and for Russia.[190]

While the United States played a significant role in the negotiations—in particular, by standing strongly behind Kohl in insisting that a united Germany should be in NATO, a particularly difficult pill for the Soviet leadership to swallow—the most crucial negotiations took place between Gorbachev and Kohl.[191] In summit talks with President Bush at the end of May 1990, Gorbachev had conceded (to the visible consternation of Falin, who was present) that it 'should be up to the Germans' to 'choose their alliances' after reunification.[192] Gorbachev subsequently, however, qualified that concession. Looking for a face-saving formula, he told the Supreme Soviet in Moscow on 12 June that a united Germany in NATO would be acceptable if the military forces in East Germany retained 'associate membership' of the Warsaw Pact during a transition period.[193] Gorbachev had virtually conceded the point that 'freedom to choose' meant that a united Germany could elect to be in NATO in talks he had with Kohl in February 1990,[194] but movement in that direction came under fierce criticism not only from within the Soviet foreign policy and military establishment but also from inside the Community Party apparatus. Thus, Ligachev, in a speech to the March 1990 plenum of the Central Committee, complained vigorously that, while 'the socialist commonwealth' was falling apart, the NATO bloc was being strengthened. Returning to his well-rehearsed disagreement with the new thinking on foreign policy, he added that if a united Germany joined NATO it would not be possible 'after that to affirm that international relations in our time do not have a class character'.[195] Domestic opposition notwithstanding, the principle of a united Germany, free to belong to NATO, became definitive—and public— Soviet policy following Kohl's visit to the Soviet Union in mid-July 1990, during which Gorbachev and the German Chancellor held fruitful and remarkably friendly talks both in Moscow and in Gorbachev's native Stavropol territory.[196]

This was not quite the end of the bargaining. Possibly, as Garton Ash has suggested, stung by criticism from Falin and others that true professionals would have struck a harder bargain, 'Gorbachev haggled hard on the telephone with Kohl in early September, securing a round DM 12 billion plus a further DM 3 billion credit, to cover the costs of the Soviet troops in the . . . territory of the former GDR and their relocation to the Soviet Union'.[197] In what Hannes Adomeit, with studied understatement, has called 'two of the most expensive telephone conversations in recent Russian–German history' on 7 and 10 September, Kohl and Gorbachev had settled on a figure substantially higher than the Germans had earlier in the year expected to pay, although significantly lower than the bill presented (as a negotiating ploy) by the Soviet ambassador to Bonn, Vladislav Terekhov, on 5 September.[198] Kohl saw financial help to, and economic co-operation with, the Soviet Union as an integral part of the comprehensive package he had agreed with Gorbachev, and he was to demonstrate both his gratitude and good faith by being the 'most outspoken proponent of G-7 assistance for Soviet economic reform' in 1991 and by ensuring that Germany remained the most economically supportive partner of Russia in the post-Soviet period.[199]

Eastern Europe

So far as the ending of Soviet limitations on the sovereignty of the states of Eastern Europe as a whole is concerned, the Gorbachev factor was decisive. Many books and articles have been and are being written on the collapse of Communism in the former Soviet bloc and on the variations from one country to another in the way in which Communist regimes finally fell as well as on the post-Communist transitions to greater or lesser degrees of democracy.[200] These transformations of political and economic systems offer scope for interesting comparisons. But there is no need to search far to find the main stimuli to change. These were the relative failure of the regimes both in economic terms and in terms of political socialization of the population into acceptance of Communist values.[201] Western Europe presented far more attractive and successful economic and political models than anything on offer from the Soviet Union. It is true that the perception of West European success was stronger in the 1970s and 1980s than it had been in the late 1940s or 1950s, but what had changed most dramatically by the late 1980s was the Soviet political system and Soviet foreign policy priorities. The essential point is that the Communist regimes of Eastern Europe existed because the Soviet Union had put them in place—by force of arms or threat of force—and had been ready to intervene to sustain them in power. The sudden collapse of the systems, accordingly, requires no elaborate explanation, although the internal situation varied greatly from one to another in ways which are beyond the scope of this book. The stimulus of radical reform in the Soviet Union, the new Moscow doctrine of 'freedom to choose', and, *above all*, the growing (and accurate) perception that the Soviet Union would no longer intervene to uphold Communist Party rule were the main factors explaining the *timing* of the overthrow of Communist systems throughout East and Central Europe in 1989 and 1990.

With the partial exceptions of Hungary and Poland—which in several important respects deviated significantly from Soviet-type Communism even before Gorbachev came to power—the transformation of Eastern Europe at the end of the 1980s was, then, a fairly direct consequence of the transformation of Soviet policy. I recall former active participants in the Czechoslovak reform movement of the 1960s telling me in Prague in the mid-1970s that 'nothing will change here until things change in the Soviet Union'. Fatalistic this may have been, but it was also an essentially accurate prediction. Without Gorbachev the present Prime Minister of the Czech Republic, Václav Klaus, would still, in all probability, be a fairly obscure economist working for the Academy of Sciences in Communist Czechoslovakia.[202] It is one thing to recognize that the Communist systems of the Soviet Union itself and of Eastern Europe lacked long-term viability; it is another to imagine that, had Gorbachev not come to power in 1985, 'then some other Soviet reformer would have in all probability emerged as the leader in the mid-1980s'.[203] The correlation of forces within the leadership of the Soviet Communist Party at the time Gorbachev became General Secretary (discussed in earlier chapters) suggests that the contrary is true.

Even for Gorbachev the process of adaptation to the idea that the East European states could be entirely independent of the Soviet Union was a gradual one. He may, as Chernyaev has noted, have been critical of the petty tutelage which the Soviet Union attempted to maintain both over the international Communist movement as a whole and over the parties in power in Eastern Europe.[204] But his initial preference was for like-minded leaders of Communist Parties to come to power in Eastern Europe—certainly not for the overthrow of Communist regimes and advent of new governments which would be understandably anxious (in the light of the post-war history of their countries) to break rather than reform their relations with the Soviet Union. Indeed, in his earliest years as Soviet leader, Gorbachev on occasion criticized East European Communist leaders for adopting policies which were, apparently, more of a threat to the ultimate control of the Communist Party than those he was prepared to endorse in the Soviet Union at that stage. Thus, Todor Zhivkov, the Bulgarian party leader—who, along with the Communist leadership in Czechoslovakia, fell into the category of those who expressed 'hypocritical approval' of the Soviet perestroika[205]—found himself mildly chastised by Gorbachev at a meeting in the Kremlin on 16 October 1987 for having endorsed a policy whereby, in theory at least, the Communist Party of Bulgaria would no longer be 'the principal subject of power' and for supporting a division of powers, as distinct from differentiation of functions, between party and state.[206] Gorbachev also warned Zhivkov—no doubt on the basis of information either from the KGB or the Socialist Countries Department of the Central Committee—that around him there were people of a 'pro-Western orientation'.[207] A few years later Gorbachev's own conservative domestic critics were accusing him not simply of having a 'pro-Western orientation' but of betraying Soviet interests to the West.[208] Gorbachev, nevertheless, played many different roles in the conduct of foreign policy, and the sentiments he expressed in private meetings with East European leaders in his capacity as the number one party leader in Communist Europe changed only gradually. In this area, as in others, 1988 (and particularly the Nineteenth Party Conference) was a turning-point.

Yet Gorbachev had strong political reasons for wishing to see the post-1988 political evolution of Eastern Europe lead to a new type of genuinely co-operative relationship with the Soviet Union rather than the total break which could only be interpreted by his enemies as 'the loss' of Eastern Europe. As noted in the previous chapter, Brezhnev did not in 1968 believe that he could survive as Soviet General Secretary if the 'Prague Spring' were not stopped in its tracks,[209] and yet that was as nothing compared with the changes of 1989. Whatever the long-term importance of the developments in Czechoslovakia in 1968, they consisted of radical reform in *one* Warsaw Pact country in which the Communist Party still retained a 'leading role' (albeit redefined) and which was not even proposing to leave the Warsaw Pact. It is hardly surprising, therefore, that Gorbachev had to be concerned about his political survival if *every* Eastern European country asserted its independence and non-Communist and anti-Soviet governments came to power. This accounts for the fact that, while Gorbachev, on the one hand, asserted 'freedom to choose', he attempted, on the other, to manage the process of change and looked for Eastern European leaders who would have the capacity to preside over evolutionary, rather than revolutionary, change. Partly for that reason he valued Poland's General Wojciech Jaruzelski more than most of the East European party chiefs.[210] He had earlier admired Kádár at a time when he was leading the most reformist ruling party in the bloc, but his support for him weakened as it became clear that Kádár could not keep pace with the demands for more far-reaching liberalization in Hungary which led to his replacement by Károly Grósz in May 1988.[211] Gorbachev, however, paid too much attention to a leader's standing within the ruling élite of his country and too little attention at this stage to the relations between regime and society.[212]

Gorbachev had no time for Ceauşescu and was exasperated by Honecker, but in the earliest stage of his leadership—in May 1985—the new General Secretary, speaking in private with Honecker, actually voiced traditional Soviet sentiments which he would soon publicly disown when he said: 'There is only one model, Marxist-Leninist socialism.'[213] Having accepted that, ultimately the other ruling parties had to make their own decisions without Soviet interference, Gorbachev was, nevertheless, irritated by Honecker's growing disapproval of the Soviet reforms, which became more ill-disguised the further they proceeded. Gorbachev did not overtly attack Honecker, but indirectly made clear his view that he was lagging behind the tide of history when he made his well-known remark at the celebrations of the fortieth anniversary of the foundation of the GDR that 'life punishes those who come late'.[214] Gorbachev himself did not realize then how close to its end was the Communist regime in Eastern Germany, he was still looking forward to its liberalization.[215]

The key to change in Eastern Europe was Gorbachev's decision in principle to abandon Soviet foreign military interventions and his refusal to contemplate resort to them, even when the Soviet Union was faced with an utterly changed relationship with the area it had controlled since the end of the Second World War. The fact that the East European leaders should no longer imagine that the Soviet Union would send tanks to their rescue if they failed to establish a *modus vivendi* with their own populations was conveyed to some of them as early as their very first meetings with Gorbachev in 1985.[216] The information that there would be no future resort to the use of Soviet force of arms in Eastern Europe was conveyed more formally to the leaders of the Comecon countries when they met in Moscow in November 1986.[217] This was not, of course, news that the East European Communist leaders were in any hurry to share with their own peoples.

It was precisely the perception that behind them stood the might of the Soviet army which kept them in power. Once it was realized—as it was by 1989—that even those Soviet soldiers stationed in East-Central Europe (who were especially numerous in East Germany) would have orders to remain in their barracks rather than suppress popular demonstrations calling for an end to the Communist regimes, everything else followed. Once again Gorbachev had turned Leninism—with its view that the (Communist) end justified the means (however violent)—on its head. Now, the means not only justified the ends,[218] but determined them. By 'rejecting coercive intervention', Gorbachev 'broke with the traditional view of Eastern Europe as a region to be held at any cost', and it was 'Gorbachev's policy revolution that opened up the road of peaceful transition from imposed communism to independence and political choice'.[219]

Although Gorbachev and the Soviet leadership had to respond piecemeal to change which in 1989–90 undoubtedly went further and faster than they had bargained for, both the new thinking and the new relationships which had been established over the preceding four years worked together to ensure that wisdom would prevail. The anti-militarist element in the new thinking, together with acceptance of the right of sovereign states to choose their own form of government, prevailed mainly because they were values which Gorbachev had come to hold and take seriously. Moreover, at any time after his United Nations speech of December 1988 a Soviet military intervention in Eastern Europe would have involved such a discrepancy between word and deed as to destroy the credibility that Gorbachev had built up in the outside world. When it came to the point of decision, the military option was not, in fact, even considered, so far had the thinking of the top leadership moved on from the 'Brezhnev doctrine'. That this should have been so owed much also to the relations of trust which Gorbachev had established with Western European and American leaders. The 'enemy image' had disappeared not only from Soviet propaganda but from the minds of Gorbachev and the small group of politicians who exercised decisive influence over the new foreign policy. And just as there were intimate links between domestic reform and external policy, so there was a complementarity between policy towards the two halves of Europe.

A Germany which had in 1989 given Gorbachev a hero's welcome, and one led by Helmut Kohl, seemed more like a friend than a threat. Thus, its *de facto* incorporation of the former GDR in the act of unification was no longer unthinkable. The abandonment not only of Soviet control but of Soviet guidance of the rest of Eastern Europe represented, of course, a giant failure of Soviet policy over more than forty years. It was not, however, a failure on the part of Gorbachev, although interpreted as such by his conservative domestic enemies. The 'loss' of Eastern Europe was foreordained by the manner in which it had been acquired and governed. But who actually lost? Vadim Medvedev has pointed out that the West gained because it was no longer faced by a hostile Warsaw Pact in Eastern Europe, the countries of Eastern Europe gained because they were now independent, and, he argues, Russia also gained because it was saved from massive military expenditure and was no longer responsible, and held accountable, for everything which happened in Eastern Europe.[220] And were there losers? Yes, Medvedev replies, the losers were those forces with an interest in confrontation—ideological, political, and military—and who wished to preserve authoritarian regimes.[221] There were enough of such losers to make it a remarkable political achievement that Gorbachev survived as Soviet leader for two years after most of East-Central Europe had rejected the Soviet link. Still more of an achievement was the change he had introduced in the fundamentals of Soviet foreign policy which had made possible the transformation of the East European political landscape. Most important of all was his refusal to attempt to stem the democratic tide which flowed from Berlin to Prague even when it threatened to overwhelm him.

Chapter 8

The National Question, the Coup, and the Collapse of the Soviet Union

I HAVE suggested already (in Chapter 6) that if the Communist system was to be dismantled in the Soviet Union and replaced by a relatively democratic polity and some kind of market economy, this required a fourfold transformation. Three of these transformations—that of the economic system (where only limited progress was made under Gorbachev), the political system, and foreign policy (in both of which fundamental changes took place)—have been discussed in Chapters 5, 6, and 7. The fourth element in the transition, the need to transform national and centre–periphery relations in the Soviet Union, has been touched upon at various points throughout the book, and in this chapter becomes a major focus of attention.

In several respects the nationalities issue was the most intractable problem of all. There are powerful reasons for supposing that it almost guaranteed that what would *not* emerge from perestroika was a democratic and intact Soviet state, such was the legacy of historic grievances of the various nationalities. Indeed, Robert Conquest has written that to anyone 'with even a moderate knowledge of Soviet nationality problems' it had long been evident that 'a "democratic Soviet Union" would be a contradiction in terms'.[1] Although it was no part of Gorbachev's intention to stimulate the breakup of the Soviet Union and since he was, nevertheless, to become serious about its democratization, it is hardly surprising, then, that he failed to reconcile these two goals, not to mention harmonizing them with the other key elements involved in the transformation of the Soviet system. For those to whom the preservation of Soviet statehood (or the maintenance of the approximate boundaries of the old Russian empire) took precedence over all other values, it followed that Gorbachev should never have embarked on perestroika—or, at least, the serious democratizing element within it which got under way from 1988. There were many who held to that standpoint in the last years of the Soviet Union and who hold that position in Russia today. It is more surprising to encounter in the West the view that Gorbachev's 'decision to introduce some form of democracy to the USSR proved disastrous', since it led to the collapse of the union and, 'whatever its failings, the USSR's survival did ensure that interethnic and intercommunal violence was limited to the odd street brawl or sublimated into political or sporting rivalries'.[2]

Yet if that judgement is highly questionable, it is at least different from the more common over-simplification that there were straightforward answers to the national question and that nothing but Gorbachev's myopia prevented him from seeing them. Certainly, Gorbachev made mistakes in this area, but his

actions must be seen in a political context in which he was fiercely criticized—
and, in effect, twice overthrown (in August and December 1991)—by two opposing groups espousing mutually exclusive views. One group insisted that he
defend the union against the seepage of political power and authority from the
centre to the republics and the other demanded self-rule or total independence
from the union.

A common misconception was that the nationality problem could be overcome, and imperial rule replaced by democratic government, through recognition of the absolute right of self-determination of nations.[3] The argument was
flawed in three fundamental respects. First, it generally ignored the fact that
many national territories within the *Russian* republic were no less part of the
Russian *empire* than the fourteen non-Russian union republics. Indeed, several of
the latter had a longer and more harmonious association with Russia than the
former and had not been subject to such recent imperial conquest.[4] Second, and
following on from that, the absolute right of self-determination based on nationhood raised the possibility of almost infinite regress. Not only the Soviet Union,
but Russia itself, was home to more than one hundred different nationalities,
and within every territory named after a particular nationality—which might
assert a right to independent statehood—there were ethnic minorities who
could, in principle, make their own claims to sovereignty.[5] So intermixed were
the nationalities in almost every administrative–territorial unit bearing the name
of one particular nation that self-determination based on nationhood could easily become (and already, to some degree, has become—in the former USSR as well
as in former Yugoslavia) a recipe for a series of civil wars. Third, there was no necessary congruence between the achievement of 'national self-determination' and
democratic and accountable government. Political leaders in Soviet Central Asia,
who had professed loyalty to Marxism-Leninism over many years and had only
reluctantly gone along with Gorbachev's reforms, generally imposed more
authoritarian regimes in the early post-Soviet years than in the period 1989–91,
once they were released from the constraints imposed by reformist and (latterly)
partially democratic Soviet authorities in Moscow. They may by then have felt a
greater need to crush all opposition as well as having a freer hand to do so with
impunity. They had shown no enthusiasm for independent statehood—until in
1991 it was thrust upon them—for fear that their record as Communist place-
men would make it impossible to preserve their positions in successor states
which would be professedly Islamic.[6]

None of this suggests *either* that the answer to the 'nationality problem' was
to preserve the union at all costs *or* that it necessitated welcoming every assertion of national independence to the point that the fifteen union republics (and
Soviet successor states) would themselves disintegrate, leading to the creation of
tens or even scores of purportedly independent countries. The art of politics lay
in maintaining levels of integration and co-operation as high as could be made
compatible with the consent of the governed and in reaching agreement on the
optimal locus of decision-making for particular areas of policy. This required a
willingness to argue and negotiate rather than resort to brute force. Gorbachev
for his part attempted to argue, cajole, and, finally, to negotiate, and though
he did not go far enough for some of the republics most committed to outright

independence, he went too far for representatives of powerful institutional interests who were determined, whatever the cost in terms of coercion and lost lives,
to maintain the integrity of the Soviet state, thus provoking the coup against
him in August 1991. Ironically, it was Boris Yeltsin—seen during the last years of
the USSR as the champion of oppressed nationalities (as to some extent in
1990–1 he was)—rather than Mikhail Gorbachev who resorted to force on a bar-
baric scale, reminiscent of a more distant Soviet and Russian past, when he lost
patience in late 1994 with the *de facto* independence which the rulers of
Chechnya had asserted throughout the post-Soviet period and authorized the
shelling and bombing of the civilian population, who died in their thousands,
and left the Chechen capital of Grozny looking like Stalingrad after the German
bombardment in the Second World War.[7]

State boundaries and democratic transitions

Yet before further attention is devoted to the acuteness and specificities of
the Soviet nationality problem, there is a more general consideration which has
escaped the attention of most of Gorbachev's critics, although it is widely
accepted among perceptive students of transitions to democracy. This is that an
authoritarian state or empire in which there is no agreement on the part of the
overwhelming majority of citizens on the boundaries of their state or political
entity is, at best, enormously handicapped and, at worst, doomed to failure in an
attempted transition to democracy. Dunkwart Rustow developed the argument
a quarter of a century ago when (not long after the crushing of the Prague Spring)
the democratization of Communist systems was not his main reference point. He
maintained that what he called 'national unity' is the 'single background condition' for transition to democracy. Making it plain that this does not necessitate
agreement on political goals, he goes on:

> It simply means that the vast majority of citizens in a democracy-to-be must
> have no doubt or mental reservations as to which political community they
> belong to. This excludes situations of latent secession, as in the late Habsburg
> and Ottoman Empires or in many African states today, and, conversely, situ-
> ations of serious aspirations for merger as in many Arab states. Democracy is
> a system of rule by temporary majorities. In order that rulers and policies may
> freely change, the boundaries must endure, the composition of the citizenry
> be continuous.[8]

While a consolidated democracy can live with some uncertainty regarding the
future boundaries of the state—as the examples in recent times of, for example, Britain,[9] Belgium, and Canada demonstrate—such uncertainty can be fatal
for a nascent democratic movement and dangerous even for an unconsolidated
democracy. In the case of Spain, where the boundaries of the state were challenged by the Basque nationalist movement and accompanied by terrorism in
the early (and, indeed, more recent) years of the Spanish democracy,[10] what
was probably decisive in enabling democratic rule to become consolidated was
the responsible behaviour of serious politicians. No national political party
used the increase in violence to deny the legitimacy of the democratic regime

or to claim that the problem could be handled better by a return to authoritarianism.[11]

Part of the general difficulty is that, as Dahl and Tufte put it, 'democratic goals conflict, and no single unit or kind of unit can best serve these goals'.[12] Moreover, no matter how skilfully constructed the political units of a democratic polity might be, they 'will never perfectly correspond to the interests of every citizen'.[13] Democratic theory assumes a political process taking place within a given political entity. It still has relatively little to say on how the units themselves should be determined.[14] The problem is not that reasoned judgements about which alternative units are better than others cannot be made, but that 'they are very likely to be inconclusive and highly disputable'.[15] Boundaries can go a long way towards determining substantive political outcomes, yet in even the most democratic states these boundaries were normally established in the first instance by far from democratic means.[16] In the words of the late Sir Ivor Jennings: 'the people cannot decide until somebody decides who are the people.'[17] Yet the fact 'that democratic methods cannot be brought to bear on the determination of political boundaries, even though this is usually an important political decision . . . has the effect of rendering controversies over boundaries among the most intractable and bitter types of political conflict'.[18]

The national question in Soviet context

To 'resolve' the nationalities question and the boundaries of the polity in the specific context of the Soviet Union was an extraordinarily difficult task, rendered more complicated by the fact that the attempt had to be made concurrently with the processes of democratization, marketization, and, not least, the transformation of foreign policy. That last change in Soviet policy brought about a demonstration effect from Eastern Europe for nations within the Soviet Union aspiring to independent statehood, making them increasingly reluctant to accept the more gradualist approach to possible secession which Gorbachev urged upon them. At the same time the sweeping-aside of Communist regimes in the former Warsaw Pact countries, as the latter attained full political independence, transmitted danger signals to the party-state authorities in Moscow and those in the republics who depended upon Moscow's hegemony.

Arguing in 1990 for recognition that the Soviet state needed to be turned 'into a genuinely voluntary confederation or commonwealth',[19] Zbigniew Brzezinski observed: 'The stark reality is that the Soviet Union can either remain a Great Russian empire or move toward a multinational democracy. But it cannot do both.'[20] While that statement was clearly true, it did not follow that an arrangement as loose as a confederation was the choice of a majority of the population—even of a majority within most of the Soviet republics. Nor was it necessarily the case that the disintegration which occurred was more in the interests of a majority of Soviet citizens than the preservation of some kind of union. To be compatible with democracy and the consent of the governed, it would, though, have had to be both a *smaller* and a *different* kind of union from that which had existed hitherto.

What was, however, beyond question was the reality of crucial disharmony on the issue of statehood. The Soviet Union spectacularly illustrated Rustow's generalization about the problem of lack of agreement on the part of substantial minorities[21] concerning the legitimacy of the state borders and Dahl's related point on the impossibility of determining boundaries of the polity which would be in the best interests of everybody.[22] The disagreement was convincingly demonstrated when, at Gorbachev's instigation, a referendum was held in March 1991 on the question, 'Do you believe it essential to preserve the USSR as a renewed federation of equal sovereign republics in which the rights and freedoms of a person of any nationality will be fully guaranteed?', and six out of the fifteen republics refused to conduct it. These were Estonia, Latvia, Lithuania, Armenia, Georgia, and Moldova. Nevertheless, answers in the affirmative did not fall below 70 per cent in any of the nine republics in which the question was put (even in Ukraine) and the overall proportion of the population answering 'yes' was 76.4 per cent.[23] Moreover, 80 per cent of the total adult population of the Soviet Union (over 148.5 million people) took part in the referendum.[24] Independent statehood, combined with confederation, was not the choice of a majority of Soviet citizens—even a majority in most of the non-Russian republics—as late as March 1991.

Thus, Gorbachev's efforts to maintain a union on the basis of a transformed federation were not necessarily misplaced. The actions of particular politicians—including, not least, the *putschists* of August 1991 and the three leaders of Russia, Ukraine, and Belorussia (Yeltsin, Kravchuk, and Shushkevich) who met in December of the same year unilaterally to pronounce the death of the union—played an enormous part, in conjunction with the bitter legacy of the Soviet past, to doom those efforts to failure. It is also arguable that Gorbachev was too late in undertaking the quest for a new union treaty which would put membership of a genuinely federal (or, in some instances, consociational or quasi-confederal) state on the foundation of a freshly negotiated agreement. His other mistake—although more understandable in political context than in the abstract—was not to treat Estonia, Latvia, and Lithuania as special cases, at least not until too late in the day.[25] The West, for its part, had never recognized the forcible incorporation of these Baltic states into the Soviet Union in 1940 and there was no likelihood that they could be kept within the USSR on a voluntary basis.

It is virtually certain, accordingly, that the *entire* Soviet Union could not have been held together, in the course of liberalization followed by democratization, even had the leadership in general and Gorbachev in particular been better prepared for the development of separatist sentiments than they were. What is also, however, beyond doubt is that whereas political reconstruction and economic reform were placed on the political agenda from above—by Gorbachev and his allies—the national question forced its way on to that agenda from below. Gorbachev was not unaware that this was a very sensitive issue in the Soviet Union. A great many different nationalities lived in his native Stavropol territory and tensions among them surfaced from time to time. Yet, in common with his closest associates, he did not realize—at the time when he embarked on reform of the system—that nationalism would place fundamental strains both on the union and on the democratization process. Even Shevardnadze, who, both as a Georgian himself and as the former First Secretary of the Georgian party organization was conscious of the strong sense of national identity of Georgians as well as that of the ethnic minorities within Georgia, has said that in 1985 he 'believed that the nationalities issue . . . had been resolved'. From the outset, said Shevardnadze, Gorbachev and his closest associates had far-reaching ideas for change, but they 'never expected an upsurge of emotional and ethnic factors'.[26]

In so far as Gorbachev recognized that there was a serious nationalities issue—and by 1988 he was in no doubt about it—his answer to the problem was twofold. First, that national chauvinism must be combated and that a genuine internationalism must prevail, so that people of different nationalities could feel comfortable in any part of the Soviet Union. Second, he argued that the Soviet Union had hitherto been a unitary state which merely purported to be a federation and that they must move from pseudo-federation to genuine federalism. Later—from April 1991—he showed still greater flexibility in being prepared to contemplate an asymmetrical relationship between the republics and the federal authorities, whereby some of the component parts of the Soviet Union (which was itself to be renamed) would have the rights accruing to a unit of a federation and others would have something closer to a confederal relationship with Moscow.[27]

The Soviet Union in the post-Stalin era had been held together by a combination of concessions to national consciousness and readiness on the part of the KGB, fully backed by the party leadership, to suppress with severity any expression of political nationalism. Union republics had a number of rights in the post-Stalin period—many of them formal, but not all of them meaningless—including their own party organizations (led by a First Secretary who, almost always after the death of Stalin, was a member of the titular nationality of the republic), their own ministries (with, of course, only limited powers), Supreme Soviet, and Academy of Sciences, and some protection for their national languages. These benefits accrued, first and foremost, to the republican political élites. But the promotion of education, including a substantial higher education sector, helped to create native intelligentsias where they had scarcely existed before 1917, while industrialization turned peasants into factory workers and urbanized them, strengthening thereby the representation of the titular nationality of the republic in major towns. As Ronald Suny has put it: 'Between center and periphery, power relations were always unequal and limiting, but in the 74 years of Soviet power, the subject nationalities gained their own subsidized intelligentsias, institutionalized in republican universities and academies of sciences, as well as a new demographic presence in their own capital cities.'[28]

Moreover, the very fact that the administrative–territorial division of the Soviet Union was constructed on the basis of national homelands, whether that of the fifteen union republics or of the so-called autonomous republics and autonomous regions within these republics (especially the huge Russian republic), provided structural supports for national consciousness—in some cases, notably in Central Asia, helping to develop a sense of nationhood where little had existed prior to the Bolshevik Revolution. The fact that some concessions were made to national consciousness (as distinct from national independence) in the pre-Gorbachev era had played a part in making public manifestations of nationalist discontent relatively rare occurrences. But still more important in preventing mass protests had been the overt or latent threat of repression by the party-state authorities. Both Gorbachev and his supporters in the all-union leadership underestimated the role that coercion had played in keeping the nationalities issue under control. There were parts of the Soviet Union—not least the Baltic states and western Ukraine—where the apparent quiescence of the majority of inhabitants owed much to a realistic assessment of what was politically feasible prior to the Gorbachev era and to the sure knowledge that the pursuit of separatism would lead to imprisonment or worse. Once expectations had been aroused as a result, at home, of glasnost and political reform, and, abroad, of a gradual abandonment of Soviet hegemony over the countries of Eastern Europe, revised assessments could be made within Soviet republics of the possible costs and benefits of supporting national independence.

Some of the most positive elements in Gorbachev's reform programme had, accordingly, the paradoxical effect of bringing national tensions to the surface of political life and, in that sense, exacerbating the national problem. Liberalization made people less afraid of retribution when they spoke out on the injustices suffered by their nation in the past, glasnost in the mass media brought to light and spread knowledge of past persecutions of entire nations within the Soviet Union (or of their foremost representatives among politicians and the intelligentsia), while democratization provided hitherto unimaginable opportunities actually to vote for those who espoused the national cause.

Because the Soviet Union collapsed relatively suddenly in 1991, many authors have, however, contended that there never was a 'Soviet' identity as distinct from the specific national ones of Russians, Ukrainians, Armenians, and others. This is almost certainly wrong. The serious survey research that might have helped to resolve the argument only became possible in the last years of the Soviet Union, and so some conjecture is involved in discussion of earlier periods.[29] In general, though, it is not only possible but commonplace for individuals to have *several* foci of identification (including a feeling of belonging to both smaller and larger territorial units), whether Wales and Britain, California and the United States, or Armenia and the USSR. The opinions of citizens of the Soviet Union in late 1991 cannot simply be projected backwards to bolster the assumption that a sense of Soviet identity never existed. It would be foolish, on the one hand, to imagine that 'the Soviet people' made up the happy family of nations portrayed in Soviet propaganda and, on the other, to deny the role of coercion in bringing into being and maintaining the USSR. Yet, for most of those who lived in the Soviet Union, a subjective acceptance of Soviet identity went alongside a sense of specific national consciousness (whether Russian, Ukrainian, Georgian, or other) and accompanied the objective reality of their living in the Soviet state. Although any rejection of that identity provoked (until the Gorbachev era) severe sanctions, the fact that in the course of seventy years the overwhelming majority of the population had not lived anywhere other than the USSR meant that the Soviet identification was taken for granted. It depended as much on habit and the absence of realistic alternatives as on coercion. There were, of course, substantial differences from one nationality to another, and certainly there is no reason to suppose that most Estonians, Latvians, or Lithuanians ever willingly accepted being Soviet citizens.

For Russians it was an especially straightforward matter to identify with the Soviet Union. It covered more or less the same territory as the Russian empire which preceded it. And in the Soviet Union, albeit to a lesser extent than in Imperial Russia, Russians held a preponderance of top positions.[30] But the identification went much wider than that. Shakhnazarov—a Russified Armenian born in the Azeri capital of Baku who, as a soldier during the Second World War, took part in the liberation of parts of Ukraine, Belorussia, and Lithuania from German occupation—has observed that he and his comrades-in-arms had no sense that these places (any less than Baku or Moscow, where Shakhnazarov had spent most of his life) were anything other than part of their 'homeland'.[31] What was true of a majority of Soviet citizens in wartime also appears to be valid for much of the post-war period, when people of different nationalities continued to take great pride in that victory, after immense suffering, over the Nazi invaders, as well as in the rebuilding of their country, in winning the race to put the first person in space,[32] in the achievements of Soviet sportsmen and women (in which the particular nationality of an Olympic gold medallist was not the most salient consideration), and, indeed, in their post-Stalin superpower status and military might (until the negative side of that last achievement was revealed during the Gorbachev era).

Pride in Soviet exploits, and acceptance of a Soviet as well as a specific national identity, was bolstered also by ignorance—varying over time and from one part of the USSR to another—about the outside world. It became clearer than ever before to the Soviet population in the Gorbachev era just how far behind the West the USSR remained both in terms of standard of living and of personal liberty. The attitude to the union, however, depended significantly on the reference group of particular Soviet nationalities. The Baltic peoples were a special case of disaffection with the Soviet state not only (albeit crucially) because they had the experience of independent statehood between the two world wars and had been forcibly incorporated in the Soviet Union in 1940 but also because they compared their conditions with those of the neighbouring Scandinavian countries. The Soviet Union could not but come out badly in a comparison with the style of life (including far superior *public* services) and political freedom enjoyed by the smaller democracies of northern Europe. The Soviet Central Asian republics, in contrast, for all their legitimate grievances, had little reason to envy their immediate Asian neighbours, whether in Afghanistan or China. (In the case of the latter, it might be argued that this ceased to be the case very late in the Soviet era, but such an argument involves turning a blind eye to dictatorship and ignoring the Tiananmen Square massacre of 1989.)

The greater knowledge of Soviet failures which became widespread during the Gorbachev era, combined with a debunking of Marxism-Leninism, produced something of an ideological vacuum which nationalism was the most obvious candidate to fill. Nationalist sentiment was also promoted and manipulated by ambitious politicians, including Communists who had been anything but reformers (the first post-Communist President of Ukraine, Leonid Kravchuk, being a prime example) but who sought a new basis of legitimation which would enable them to continue in power. '*Nomenklatura* nationalism' made instrumental use of national feelings in order to bolster the position of local political élites who had become more afraid of their own peoples than of Moscow.

National conflicts and political cross-pressures

The last three phases into which the Gorbachev era can be divided (the first three were discussed in Chapter 6 and brought the story up to the end of the summer of 1990) will be considered below and the national question figures prominently in all of them. Before examining, however, the last fifteen months of the Soviet Union's existence, it is necessary to look briefly at the development of national conflicts, especially those involving a greater or lesser degree of violence, in the period up to what has become known as Gorbachev's 'turn to the right' in the autumn of 1990. Gorbachev is frequently blamed for the use of force by the army or Ministry of Interior troops, although he scarcely had any direct responsibility for the bloodshed. There is scope for argument about the degree of his *indirect* responsibility for the violence of the reprisals against Azeris in Baku in January 1990 following a pogrom of Armenians and for the deaths in Vilnius a year later when Soviet troops took over the television centre, and these issues will be discussed below.[33] One group of critics, however, holds him personally responsible for killings in Baku, Tbilisi, Vilnius, and Riga, while the other group blames him for a quasi-pacifist reluctance to use legitimate force in order to maintain the integrity of the state over which he presided. As is not uncommon in discussions of Gorbachev, the criticisms are as irreconcilable as they are simplistic and ill-informed.

Warning-signals from Alma-Ata

The first serious conflict with nationalist overtones during the Gorbachev era occurred in the Kazakh capital of Alma-Ata (now Almaty) in December 1986. Gorbachev had secured the removal from the first secretaryship of Kazakhstan of one of Brezhnev's closest cronies in the Politburo, Dinmukhamed Kunaev, and presented it to the Politburo not as a dismissal, but as a case of Kunaev (who was 73) wanting to retire.[34] Untypically, however, Kunaev's replacement was not a Kazakh but a Russian, Gennady Kolbin. He had been second secretary of the Georgian party organization from 1975 to 1983, a time when Eduard Shevardnadze was First Secretary. Kolbin had enjoyed excellent relations with Shevardnadze, from whom, he said, he had 'learned a lot'.[35] The Soviet Foreign Minister's approval of Kolbin, in turn, was important, given Shevardnadze's closeness to Gorbachev. Kolbin's years in Georgia also meant that he was a Russian with experience of 'nationality questions', although even in Kazakhstan, a republic where there were almost as many Russians as members of the titular nationality, that hardly compensated for the new republican First Secretary's lack of knowledge of the Kazakh language.

Nor did it prevent his appointment being greeted with riots in Alma-Ata, in which many people were injured and some killed, both demonstrators and police. Accounts differ as to the number of deaths, but a commission of investigation in Kazakhstan reported in 1990 that the demonstration had been peaceful initially and excessive force had been used to put it down.[36] According to Kolbin, Gorbachev strove to prevent that from happening. He telephoned the newly appointed First Secretary several times during the demonstration and insisted that no force should be used against the demonstrators.[37] Kolbin has said that Gorbachev criticized him 'in no uncertain terms' even 'for using water-cannons'; any use of force, he told him, must be precluded. This somewhat rose-tinted version cannot, however, be taken entirely at face value, for Gorbachev himself has said that in Alma-Ata in 1986 he 'acted, in general, according to the old rules' and that 'at the dawn of perestroika we were still far from being what we became'.[38] Kolbin survived this inauspicious start and later succeeded in improving his relations with the local population. He was not moved from Alma-Ata to Moscow until the summer of 1989, although Gorbachev recognized that his appointment to the Kazakhstan party leadership had been a big mistake.[39]

While the selection of a non-Kazakh made it possible to mobilize crowds of protesters, the demonstrations also owed much to the anxiety among those who had been part of a large and corrupt network within Kunaev's clan that the privileges and profitable relationships they had enjoyed were about to end. The protests were provoked, indirectly, by Kunaev himself. The Kazakhs were not agreed on a successor to Kunaev and it was the retiring First Secretary who specifically recommended Gorbachev to choose a non-Kazakh.[40] Kunaev was especially insistent that Nursultan Nazarbaev, who at that time was Chairman of the Council of Ministers in Kazakhstan and who eventually succeeded Kolbin in June 1989, should not become the new First Secretary and did everything in his power to persuade the Moscow leadership that Nazarbaev's rise should be stopped.[41] Later Nazarbaev was to become an important political actor at the all-union level as well as a dominant figure in his native Kazakhstan and a politician for whom Gorbachev had a lot of respect. But in 1986 Kunaev not only succeeded in postponing Nazarbaev's succession, but also did nothing to calm the subsequent protests against the selection of a non-Kazakh.[42] The Soviet leadership did not, however, learn as much as they might from this manifestation of hurt national pride. Gorbachev has noted that, in the aftermath of the Alma-Ata riots, the Politburo—when it met on 25 December—did nothing to explore the real reasons for these events, but was concerned, as in the past, with countering the danger of a 'spontaneously erupting nationalism'.[43]

Gorbachev's desire to depart from the traditionally harsh Soviet ways of dealing even with peaceful protests was more successfully in evidence the following summer when Moscow itself saw its first nationality-based demonstration of the perestroika era. In support of their long-standing demand that they be allowed to return to the Crimea, from which they had been expelled at the end of the Second World War, Crimean Tatars demonstrated in Red Square in July 1987. The Soviet police acted with unprecedented restraint, although *The Times* correspondent in Moscow observed: 'Comments heard on Red Square yesterday suggest there would have been a popular mandate for the police to have broken up the demonstration with whatever force they considered necessary.'[44] A nine-person commission chaired by Gromyko (at that time Chairman of the Presidium of the Supreme Soviet and the longest-serving member of the Politburo) was set up to investigate the Tatars' complaints. Its results were unsatisfactory so far as the main demand of the Tatars was concerned, although more support for the Tatar language and culture in the Central Asian republics to which they had been exiled was promised and a very gradual return of Tatars to the Crimea continued to take place.[45] While Gromyko, on the whole, lived up to his reputation as 'Mr Nyet', the Soviet leadership took into account opposition within the Crimea to a return of the Tatars *en masse*. There were worries, too, that 'acceding to these ultimate Tatar demands would produce undesirable effects in other ethnically contested areas' as well as causing problems with people who had made their homes in those parts of the Crimea where the Tatars had formerly lived.[46]

Nagorno-Karabakh and the Armenian–Azeri dispute

If the Tatar issue raised problems between different Soviet republics and was not one for which there was a simple solution available to Moscow, that applied all the more strongly to the conflict over Nagorno-Karabakh between Armenians and Azeris. The fact that the predominantly Armenian enclave of Nagorno-Karabakh within Azerbaijan came under the jurisdiction of the Azeri authorities in Baku had long been a sore point for Armenians, and it was not just in the Gorbachev era that Armenian outrage was expressed. As was noted by Arkady Volsky—who was to become in 1988 Moscow's envoy to Nagorno-Karabakh—it was an issue which had long been smouldering and 'once every ten to twelve years it erupted'. The difference from the Gorbachev era was that in the past the authorities made 'short work . . . of restoring order'.[47] Some people would be arrested, others expelled from the party, and 'a lot of sweet sugary talk about the great friendship of the peoples' would continue, although 'it was all false'.[48] But while the sources of tension long preceded perestroika, there is no doubt that by 1988 the new political atmosphere in the Soviet Union and the liberalization which occurred under Gorbachev emboldened Armenians to make a determined attempt to right what they regarded as a historic wrong.

The Armenians in Nagorno-Karabakh had good cause for their discontent. The region was economically impoverished and exploited by the authorities in Baku, while Armenian culture was suppressed. Despite its closeness to the border with Armenia, the people of Nagorno-Karabakh could not receive television broadcasts from Yerevan and the teaching of Armenian history was suppressed in the schools. The land itself, however, was the subject of conflicting claims by Azeris and Armenians, each side utterly convinced that historically it belonged to them. It was, and is, a dispute comparable to that between Israelis and Palestinians in terms of each side's passionate belief that history and morality are on their side and, thus, no easier to resolve.[49] A deep religious divide added emotive force to the claims of the parties, Armenians being among the earliest peoples to embrace Christianity while the Azeris are predominantly Shiite Muslims.

It was in February 1988 that Nagorno-Karabakh became a major issue in Soviet politics and Azeri–Armenian tensions reached boiling point. First, the regional soviet of Nagorno-Karabakh requested that the territory, 80 per cent of whose inhabitants were Armenian, be transferred to the jurisdiction of the Armenian republic. Huge demonstrations were held in the Armenian capital of Yerevan in support of this demand, and tensions rose between Azeris and the substantial Armenian minority in other parts of Azerbaijan, escalating into inter-ethnic violence. In the industrial city of Sumgait, near Baku, at least thirty-two people were killed, twenty-six of them Armenians, while many more Armenians were injured or had their homes wrecked or looted.[50] This led to Armenian attacks on Azeris in Nagorno-Karabakh and in Armenia itself, and to migrations, based on fear, of both Armenians and Azeris. The presence of a substantial number of Azeri refugees in Baku fuelled nationalist passions there.[51]

As relations between Azeris and Armenians deteriorated, the Soviet Politburo decided, at Gorbachev's suggestion, to send Ligachev to Baku to meet the Central Committee of the Communist Party of Azerbaijan and Yakovlev to Yerevan to address the Armenian Central Committee. The basic position taken (subsequently partly contradicted by the Law on Secession adopted in April 1990)[52] was that there should be no redrawing of national and territorial borders, since, in Ligachev's words, 'to violate that principle would open up a path for a multitude of bloody conflicts',[53] but that a political solution should be found by responding to any other legitimate grievances of particular national groups, provided that they did not thereby promote national exclusiveness.[54] Gorbachev's instinctive inclination towards consensus-building in the Politburo led him to support the idea of Yakovlev being accompanied to Yerevan by the more conservative Dolgikh, while Ligachev was partnered in Baku by the more reform-minded Razumovsky. The results were not exactly what Gorbachev desired. Ligachev, with his emphasis on the inviolability of existing territorial boundaries—notwithstanding his remarks on the need to pay attention to 'the lawful demands of all national and ethnic groups in the population'[55]—was perceived in Azerbaijan as coming down essentially on the Azeri side of the argument. Yakovlev, stressing in his speech in Yerevan the dangers to perestroika of conservatism but omitting to reiterate the Politburo's line on the danger of changing national territorial borders, was believed in Armenia to be more sympathetic to their national cause.

Persuasion and diplomacy having failed to resolve the dispute, Gorbachev resorted to direct rule by Moscow over Nagorno-Karabakh. Although this could be only a temporary expedient, it was one which produced more favourable conditions for the inhabitants of the enclave than they had endured earlier. Arkady Volsky, the former aide to Andropov and Chernenko, whose background was in industrial administration and who headed the department of the Central Committee responsible for the machine-building industry from 1985 until 1988, first visited Nagorno-Karabakh in that capacity in March 1988, since the plants located there had stopped working.[56] It came as a great surprise to him, however, when Gorbachev invited him for a talk and told him that his help was needed in Nagorno-Karabakh. He spent almost a year and a half there from July 1988 until November of the following year, and in 1989 was head of a Committee of Special Administration which implemented Moscow's direct rule of the territory. Among the improvements he brought about, with the approval of the all-union authorities, were the acquisition of Armenian textbooks, the provision of access to Armenian television, the teaching of Armenian history in the schools, and the opening of a theatre which produced plays in the Armenian language. At the end of November 1989 the special committee ruling Nagorno-Karabakh was dissolved by Moscow and the administration of the territory became once again the responsibility of Azerbaijan.[57]

None of this, however, ended the tensions elsewhere in Azerbaijan or in Armenia. The Azeris believed that Gorbachev was favouring the Armenians, and the Armenians, who had initially been supportive of Gorbachev, came to believe that he was pro-Azeri. Even-handedness, combined with some exasperation and occasional tactlessness in his dealings with the protagonists, led to Gorbachev being blamed by both sides. His main concern, however, was with the preservation of elementary order and the prevention of bloodshed—an almost impossible task once the first wave of killings had taken place and passions had been aroused, but one which could not have been met simply by coming down unambiguously on the side of one nation rather than the other. When several Russian generals from the Ministry of Interior were taken hostage by Azeri militants who were ready to kill them unless five arrested Azeris were released in exchange, Volsky was given conflicting advice from different parts of the leadership in Moscow: 'Take them by storm. Or negotiate.'[58] Gorbachev was firmly on the side (which prevailed) of avoiding bloodshed—telling Volsky: 'hold on, try to prevent bloodshed, please try'—even though, as Volsky later put it, 'for a great power . . . it's a loss of face to exchange generals for hooligans'.[59]

One of the worst atrocities—a pogrom of Armenians in Baku in January 1990 which caused at least sixty deaths—led several days later to a disproportionate response which was also too late to save the Armenians. It was directed at the supporters of the Popular Front in Azerbaijan, who were held, on the one hand, to be morally responsible for the deaths of the Armenians and, on the other, to be a threat to the integrity of the Soviet state. There is, however, no reason to believe that those killed by the reckless actions of Soviet troops in Baku were personally guilty of the massacre some days earlier of the Armenians. The official death-count following this retaliatory measure was eighty-three, but Azeri nationalists claimed that several hundred people had been killed.[60] The need to take firm action against the Popular Front in Azerbaijan was urged upon Gorbachev by Yevgeny Primakov, who had arrived in the capital of Azerbaijan on 14 January, the day after the pogrom of the Armenians, but the indiscriminate nature of the onslaught which followed was the responsibility of the Soviet senior officers on the spot.[61] Gorbachev, nevertheless, while deploring such extensive loss of life, continued to defend the accompanying declaration of a state of emergency in Baku, with its concomitant introduction of troops, and claimed that, but for action to stop the atrocities, the number of victims would have been still higher.[62] There are circumstances, he declared in January 1995, when 'it is necessary to bring in troops'.[63] Because these harsh measures were regarded even by liberal intellectuals in Russia as a response to the persecution of the Armenians, they did not provoke the same outrage as killings perpetrated by Soviet forces in Tbilisi the previous year or in Vilnius a year later.

The Tbilisi tragedy

Gorbachev was increasingly blamed in post-Soviet Russia for using insufficient force rather than too much to hold the Soviet Union together, but the use of violence by Soviet troops in Tbilisi in April 1989 was a spectacular example of how counter-productive violent repression could be. Many young people were attracted in Georgia to a nationalist movement which, on the one hand, was determined to push for Georgian autonomy from the Soviet Union and, on the other, to deny to Abkhazia the independence from Georgia which the Abkhaz were asserting. Thousands participated in peaceful demonstrations over several days, but on the night of 8/9 April Soviet troops launched a brutal attack on the protesters. Nineteen of the demonstrators were killed and several hundred injured.[64] A majority of the dead were young women and the principal cause of death was asphyxiation through inhalation of chemicals fired from gas canisters.[65] While the local political and military authorities appear to have agreed that no guns would be used, the weapons employed—poison gas and sharpened spades[66]—were, if anything, even more vicious. The massacre of the young demonstrators outraged public opinion in Georgia and gave an enormous stimulus to the movement for complete independence from the Soviet Union, paving the way for the election of Zviad Gamsakhurdia, a former dissident and a fanatical nationalist, as head of an anti-Communist Georgian government from 1990 (and as President of Georgia from May 1991). Although democratically elected by an overwhelming majority, Gamsakhurdia quickly became a divisive ruler, demonstrating dictatorial tendencies as well as 'a sense of paranoia, a conspiratorial frame of mind, virulent anti-communism and a tendency to self-glorification'.[67] He was overthrown in 1992 and replaced by the former Soviet Foreign Minister and earlier First Secretary of the Georgian Communist Party, Eduard Shevardnadze.

The events in Tbilisi of April 1989 thus demonstrated that the harsh use of force could, in the new climate of raised expectations and aroused civic courage, produce the opposite effect from that intended by the Soviet authorities. They also were to become a prime example of misinformation, whether deliberate or through ignorance, on the part of Gorbachev's enemies at home and abroad who held him responsible for the massacre in the Georgian capital. In fact, Gorbachev had 'categorically stated that the situation in Tbilisi must be resolved by political means and through dialogue'.[68] That this was his position has long been plain and is now even clearer. Not only is there ample memoir and interview evidence—including the testimony of Shevardnadze and Sobchak[69]—but the report of the Commission set up by the Congress of People's Deputies of the USSR, under the chairmanship of Sobchak and the secretaryship of Stankevich (two members of the Inter-Regional Group of Deputies who were thereby politically closer to Yeltsin than to Gorbachev), lays no blame on Gorbachev.[70]

Gorbachev and Shevardnadze had flown into Moscow late on 7 April 1989, arriving shortly before midnight. The last lap of their trip was from London, but their visit to Britain had been immediately preceded by one to Cuba. They were met at the airport by a Politburo delegation which included Ligachev and Chebrikov. Although Ligachev had chaired an *ad hoc* meeting of selected members of the Politburo and of the Secretariat that day to consider the events in Georgia, it was Chebrikov who briefed the General Secretary and the Foreign Minister on the demonstrations and tensions which had developed in Tbilisi while they were abroad.[71] Gorbachev, as Shevardnadze records in his memoirs, declared: 'No matter what, the situation must be settled by political means.'[72] He immediately proposed that Shevardnadze and Razumovsky should fly to Tbilisi to make sure that this happened.[73] Although the local Communist Party leadership in Georgia was becoming increasingly unpopular, Shevardnadze still retained immense authority, for Georgians took pride in the role he was playing on the world stage. He was at that time the person best placed to resolve the impasse peacefully. Razumovsky was named not only because he was a Gorbachev ally, but because he had union-wide responsibility for party cadres within the Central Committee Secretariat and thus a superior authority to the Georgian party First Secretary, Dzhumber Patiashvili.

Unhappily, when Shevardnadze telephoned Patiashvili, he was told that everything was under control and that there was absolutely no need to hurry to Tbilisi. Since Shevardnadze had just returned from one long foreign trip and was due in Berlin on 10 April for a meeting with the Foreign Ministers of the Warsaw Pact countries, he doubtless received this news with some relief. In the event, he did not go to Berlin, for after the events in Tbilisi in the early hours of 9 April, he flew to Georgia after all, but in the aftermath of a tragedy he was too late to prevent. Anatoly Sobchak suggests that Shevardnadze was deeply shaken and upset by what had happened not only as a Georgian, but by what might have been. 'If', writes Sobchak, 'Shevardnadze had on 7 April been in Moscow and not in London and if at night on the 8th he had flown to Georgia, as Gorbachev suggested, the slaughter in front of the Government building evidently could have been avoided.'[74]

There is no doubt that if Shevardnadze had been in Moscow on 7 April Gorbachev would have involved him in the response which had to be made to a telegram from Patiashvili calling for extraordinary measures to be taken against extremist elements and declaring that events were getting out of control. The Georgian party First Secretary specifically asked for Ministry of Interior and regular army troops to be brought into Tbilisi and for a curfew to be imposed.[75] In the absence of Gorbachev and Shevardnadze, however, the meeting chaired by Ligachev responded favourably to Patiashvili's request. Ligachev went on holiday on 8 April, Gorbachev spent the day at his dacha, and it was Chebrikov who dealt with Patiashvili. Both Ligachev and Chebrikov bore some political responsibility for what followed, as did, to a still greater extent, the Minister of Defence, Yazov, who took the decision to put General Igor Rodionov, the particularly hardline commander of the Transcaucasion military district, in charge of the operation.[76]

The immediate culpability—or *'personal* responsibility', in the words of the Sobchak commission—for the brutal means employed to disperse the demonstration and for the deaths they brought about lay with Rodionov and with two other generals, K. A. Kochetov and Yu. T. Yefimov, who jointly controlled the troops on the spot.[77] The primary *political* responsibility, the commission decided, for 'the tragic consequences of the events of 9 April 1989 in Tbilisi is borne by the former secretaries of the Communist Party of Georgia, D. I. Patiashvili and B. V. Nikolsky'.[78] By the time the commission reported in late 1989, Patiashvili had been dismissed as First Secretary and Nikolsky as second secretary of the Georgian party, Chebrikov had been dropped from the Politburo and pensioned off, while General Rodionov was moved, but at the same time treated gently, by the Ministry of Defence. He lost his position in charge of the armed forces of the Transcaucasian district but was appointed head of the Military Academy of the General Staff of the Soviet Armed Forces.

Secession and the Constitution

In terms of demands for separate statehood, the most difficult challenge Gorbachev faced came from the Baltic republics. The Soviet Constitution, anomalously for a supposed federation (and totally misleadingly, given the reality of a highly centralized unitary state), granted on paper the right of secession to union republics. Any attempt to assert that right earlier than the second half of the 1980s would have been out of the question. There was no legal way in which secession could have been set in motion, and advocacy of it would have been branded as 'anti-Soviet propaganda'—itself a criminal offence prior to the Gorbachev era. If the right to secede were to become a serious one, there was a need for a law on secession specifying the steps which must be taken by a republican leadership wishing to pursue that goal.

One sign that the Communist Party leadership was beginning to treat the nationality question with the seriousness it deserved was the belated holding of a Central Committee plenum on the subject in September 1989, although Gorbachev's insistence then that Soviet citizens had 'not yet lived in a real federation' did not go far enough to satisfy the demands of the Balts in particular.[79] A more significant attempt to face up to growing demands for independence, particularly from the Baltic states, while simultaneously trying to slow down that process, was the eventual promulgation of a Law on Secession in April 1990. This fulfilled a promise Gorbachev had made on a three-day visit to Lithuania in January of that year which, however, achieved little in the way of mutual understanding.[80] The law's provisions included the need for two-thirds of the electorate of a republic to vote for secession in a referendum, a five-year transition period, and, finally, the endorsement of the Soviet legislature.[81] The fact that national sub-units (so-called autonomous republics or regions within the union republics), such as Abkhazia or Southern Ossetia in Georgia and Nagorno-Karabakh in Azerbaijan, were to be given the right to opt out of secession and remain in the USSR if they so voted, raised the possibility of secession leading to loss of territory by a republic seeking independent statehood, as did a provision in the law that 'the status of territories not belonging to [the republic] when it became part of the USSR' must be agreed between the parties. The Presidium of the Belorussian Supreme Soviet was quick to announce that it would demand the return of lands which had formerly been part of Belorussia should Lithuania leave the Soviet Union.[82] The following year republics, in fact, became independent following the enormous stimulus of the failed *putsch* and none of them did so with as much as a glance at the Law on Secession—nor, accordingly, with loss of territory. But for Gorbachev the Law on Secession had been, on the one hand, an effort to provide a legal mechanism for a paper right which had long existed in the Soviet Constitution and, on the other, a vain attempt to provide him with 'more time to create the kind of Soviet Union that no one would want to leave'.[83]

The last thing Gorbachev wanted was to lose any part of the Soviet Union following the loss—as his domestic enemies on 'the right' certainly saw it—of Eastern Europe. Gorbachev's refusal to use force to keep the Warsaw Pact countries under Soviet hegemony had produced one non-Communist regime after another in Eastern Europe, and the Soviet leader had survived in office, despite the increased ferocity of the attacks on him from sections of the military and other conservative forces. Yet he believed that if he were to stand idly by while parts of the Soviet Union dropped off, he would be forgiven neither by his contemporaries nor by future generations of Russians.[84] So far as the contemporaries were concerned, those fears were not misplaced. Within a very short time after the dissolution of the Soviet Union, it was for the disintegration of the Soviet state that Gorbachev was criticized most of all, and by no means fairly. As Alexander Yakovlev pointed out on the tenth anniversary of Gorbachev's coming to power (even though by that time Yakovlev's relations with Gorbachev had become strained): 'Now Mikhail Sergeevich [Gorbachev] is blamed for the breakup of the Union. This is unjust. He did everything possible to keep the country united, but renewed.'[85] Gorbachev had striven to maintain a union while trying to avoid the use of force (or to avoid escalating it on the rare occasions when troops were used). Since he was, however, attempting to keep the union intact while being unwilling to use the crude methods of repression employed in the past, his policy inevitably disappointed both those who claimed an absolute right to independent statehood and those who believed that any means were justified so long as they preserved the unity and integrity of the Soviet state. Although Gorbachev, even after he had lost office, continued to stress his genuine belief in the desirability of maintaining the union, he had also been well aware of the real danger of his being overthrown if he did not keep intact the state boundaries he inherited.

While both Gorbachev himself and his critics are agreed that he was too slow in attempting to deal with the nationality problem, the latter are divided between those who believe that he should have sought a new and voluntary union treaty at an earlier stage of his leadership and those who hold that the problem was that he did not crack down soon enough on manifestations of nationalism. In attempting to prevent secession, Gorbachev was reacting to events rather than anticipating them, but responding, nevertheless, within the terms of the Soviet Constitution—which, unlike his predecessors, he took seriously—and by political means rather than by violent repression. Thus, for example, the Politburo (including Gorbachev, Shevardnadze, and Yakovlev, but excluding Ligachev and Slyunkov, who were absent) voted for a series of measures designed to counteract the attempted secession of Lithuania from the union.[86] These included safeguards for the property of the USSR on the territory of Lithuania and proposals to use the mass media (a relapse into somewhat traditional Communist practice) to emphasize the 'economic and other negative consequences for the population of Lithuania' which would follow their exit from the Soviet Union.[87]

The retrospective blame placed on Gorbachev for failing to preserve the union increasingly rarely focused on the occasional resort to force by Soviet troops during his years in office—rather the reverse, his failure to use sufficient force to prevent secession. Thus, the journal of the Russian parliament—in a series of articles marking the ten years from the official launch of perestroika at the Central Committee plenum of April 1985—in the spring of 1995 gave most space to an article complaining that, faced by a declaration of sovereignty by Estonia in late 1988, Gorbachev merely stated that this was contrary to the Soviet Constitution and did not follow these words up with further censure or action.[88] Even authors who see themselves, and are generally seen, as belonging to the democratic camp in post-Soviet Russia increasingly blame Gorbachev for using insufficient coercion to hold the Soviet Union together. Thus, at a meeting at the Gorbachev Foundation to mark the tenth anniversary of the April 1985 plenum, the prominent political analyst Andranik Migranyan directly attacked Gorbachev along these lines, saying: 'Why did you not stop the disintegration? You were general secretary of the Soviet Communist Party—why did you not use force if you had to? Why did you not see it would come to this—wars every-where, refugees, people without a homeland. I, as an Armenian, know this very well.'[89] To this Gorbachev simply responded: 'Well, thank God Andranik Migranyan wasn't general secretary of the Soviet Communist Party.'[90]

Gorbachev's 'turn to the right'

What has become known as Gorbachev's 'turn to the right' refers to the period from October 1990 to March 1991, the winter during which he changed the balance of influence within his leadership team in a more conservative direc-tion both through personnel change and by becoming less accessible to those of his associates who had been the strongest advocates of political and economic transformation. Gorbachev's own account of this shift has varied somewhat, partly reflecting the political climate at the time of his pronouncements. Thus, in an interview in the autumn of 1991, after the August coup but while he was still in office as Soviet President, Gorbachev referred to the political events of the winter of 1990–1 and said that 'on both sides, the behaviour was certainly not impeccable, let me put it this way' and that 'democratic forces, those who really wanted change, sometimes regrettably found themselves on different sides of the barricades'.[91] He had been 'trying to steer a middle course', but had missed his chance when he should have come down firmly on one side. Contrasting this with the period from April 1991 onwards, he said: 'Of course later I did, but that's life. You can't edit it afterwards.'[92] Subsequently, while disclaiming responsibil-ity for the acts of violence of Soviet troops in Vilnius and Riga and accepting also that he had been mistaken in several of the appointments he had made, he defended, nevertheless, his emphasis on enforcing the law and his attempt to hold the Soviet Union together during that winter. By the time of the publica-tion of his memoirs in 1995 Gorbachev was responding, to some extent, to the mood of nostalgia within Russia both for the Soviet Union and for order, and was somewhat less critical of much of what he did during the winter months of 1990–1 than he had been in late 1991 in the very different political atmosphere following the failure of the hardline coup.[93]

For the outside observer, it seems fair to say that Gorbachev's 'turn to the right' was a tactical retreat, an understandable one, given the pressures he was under, but mistaken, since it left him with fewer political allies than he had before. The '500 Days Programme', discussed earlier, had been seen by its oppo-nents within the government, the army, the KGB, and the party apparatus—and ultimately by Gorbachev himself—as a threat to the continued existence of any kind of union, not least because it largely deprived the all-union authorities of their revenue-gathering powers. Since Gorbachev did not at that time see the 'left'—the radical democrats and the Baltic nationalists—as an immediate threat as great as that posed by the conservative and pro-union 'right', he felt the need to make concessions to the latter. These came the more naturally since he was a genuine believer in preserving the Soviet Union intact (including the Baltic states), although not at any price. It was his unwillingness to turn the clock back to maintaining the Soviet Union by use of the full apparatus of repression—which would simultaneously have destroyed both the democratization process and all the changes for the better in the international arena that he had played a decisive part in achieving—which distinguished Gorbachev from his pro-union allies of late 1990 and early 1991.

In moving closer to more conservative forces, Gorbachev was in danger, however, of becoming their prisoner, especially as this very shift led to a further deterioration in his relations with the democrats. He did not believe that there was a risk of him becoming a hostage to *any* group, and indeed his launching of the 'Novo-Ogarevo process' (discussed in the next section) in the spring of 1991 was an example of his remarkable ability to free himself from the constraints which a majority within the party-state high command endeavoured to place upon him. But, in the meantime, Gorbachev had paid a price in terms of loss of confidence in his leadership on the part of the democrats and, crucially, he had inadvertently ceded the position of Number One Democrat to his most dangerous rival, Boris Yeltsin.[94]

Of course, the intense pressures within an increasingly polarized society made all political choices difficult ones. Gorbachev was fiercely attacked at meetings he held with defence industry managers and army officers, whose demands were for a return to more traditional Soviet norms, not for more democracy. Moreover, by late 1990 the people as a whole were taking for granted the gains of the Gorbachev years—among them, freedom of speech, assembly, and publication, contested elections, and the end of the Cold War. They now had other concerns. During 1990 the nationalities issue had become more acute and economic problems had worsened as the instruments of the command economy were ceasing to function, while those of a market economy had scarcely begun to emerge.

The interconnectedness of the various aspects of the transition from the traditional Communist order was such that even democratization exacerbated the economic difficulties. Since regional officials had become more dependent on their local electorates than on the centre for their survival in office, they became increasingly unresponsive to the economic demands of the political authorities in Moscow, and would hoard goods locally rather than supply other areas, including the major cities. Whereas, under the command economy, Moscow had always been better served than the Russian provinces, by 1990–1 goods and foodstuffs were more readily available in some provincial towns than in the capital. During this time Gorbachev's popularity declined steeply. Although Gorbachev, while still in office (even six and a half years after coming to power), never reached as low a level of public support as that accorded Yeltsin in early

1995—some three and a half years after his election as President and a little over three years after the collapse of the Soviet Union—the period between May 1990 and December 1991 was one in which Yeltsin overtook Gorbachev in popularity and left him far behind. Whereas in December 1989 49 per cent of respondents in Russia (52 per cent in the Soviet Union) wholly approved of Gorbachev's activities and an additional 32 per cent (in both Russia and the USSR) partly approved, this support dropped sharply during the summer of 1990, and by December 1990 had gone down to 14 per cent of complete support in Russia (17 per cent in the union as a whole) and 38 per cent partial support in Russia (39 per cent in the USSR).[95] Following the failed coup, the leading public opinion polling institute in Russia surveyed opinion only in Russia, for the USSR was already well on the way to disintegration, and the September poll (their last while Gorbachev was still in office) indicated some recovery in Gorbachev's position, although his popularity then was much less than Yeltsin's. Following the failure of the August coup, the survey conducted in September 1991 showed 18 per cent wholly approving of Gorbachev's activity and 45 per cent partly approving.[96]

Those who thought of themselves as democrats and who, for the first four or five years of Gorbachev's years in power, had seen his leadership as the most important guarantee of movement in a democratic direction, increasingly deserted Gorbachev for Yeltsin. The latter's views were being influenced meanwhile by his new friends in the liberal and democratic wing of the intelligentsia, with whom he had little contact until he was elected to the Congress of People's Deputies in 1989. One reason, accordingly, for Gorbachev's 'turn to the right' was the feeling that he had been deserted by the 'left'. Of course, to the extent that he made concessions to more conservative forces, he exacerbated that problem by increasing the alienation of his former supporters. Thus, the tactical retreat during this winter of discontent turned out to be a strategic error. It satisfied neither one side nor the other. Gorbachev was never willing to be as ruthless and single-minded in pursuit of preservation of the union as a majority of the power-holders in Moscow wished. Many of them were disillusioned with Gorbachev even before he returned to the mainstream of reform in April 1991 and left his conservative colleagues still more in the cold than the radical reformists had been over the previous six months.

Tranquillizing or encouraging the hardliners?

These zig-zags may have been necessary up to a point, given the fundamental disagreements among power-holders and contenders for power both on the appropriate boundaries of the Soviet state and on what kind of political and economic system should emerge. There were grounds also for uncertainty as to whether the democrats were strong enough to prevail against the apparatus of Soviet power should it act increasingly independently of Gorbachev. By making such concessions as he deemed politically necessary at different times to powerful institutional interests, Gorbachev may have 'tranquillized the hardliners' long enough to render them almost impotent by the time they chose to strike. Thus, a case can be made even for Gorbachev's 'turn to the right'—in so far as it was both tactical and temporary—as being in the interests of a Soviet transition from Communism which proceeded without violent confrontation between the bastions of the old order and the forces of change within Russia itself. The personnel changes and policy compromises of the winter of 1990–1 also, however, offered some encouragement to the hardliners, who began to see for the first time significant concessions by Gorbachev in the face of their pressure. The tactical retreat, moreover, did not help Gorbachev personally, for his abandonment of the conservatives the moment winter turned to spring meant that they would never forgive him. Yet by that time only a minority of democrats retained the warm feelings and the gratitude towards Gorbachev which they had harboured during the greater part of his leadership.

Splitting the Communist Party at its Twenty-Eighth Congress in the summer of 1990 would have been a risky alternative but almost certainly a better one. Gorbachev, in fact, assumed that a split in the party would occur at the Twenty-Ninth Congress of the CPSU, which had been brought forward by several years and was due to be convened in November 1991.[97] As a result of the coup and the subsequent suspension of the Communist Party it was never held. Gorbachev argued that the essentially social democratic draft programme that had been prepared, with his full approval, by the summer of 1991 would have provoked a fundamental division. One group (numbering, he believed, several million members) would have been ready to support the programme, while another would have adopted a different programme, 'and then, naturally, they would be different parties'.[98] Since the Communist Party of the Soviet Union no longer existed by November 1991, it is evident enough in retrospect that Gorbachev had left it too late to force the membership of the party to choose quite clearly between a socialist party of a social democratic type and one which adhered to traditional Communist norms. But 1990 had been the time to force the issue. If from 1985 until 1989 Gorbachev was, on the whole, in the vanguard of political change—until 1988, in particular, its decisive initiator or facilitator—in 1990–1 he fell behind the pace of events. Postponing the party split—a division which would have been one of the more promising ways of introducing a competitive party system—until late 1991, and to what turned out to be a non-Congress, was one of several examples of excessive caution at this stage of his leadership when greater boldness was called for.

As well as the very real political pressures which would, however, have prevented *any* reformist leader from pursuing wholly consistent policies, there were personal attributes of Gorbachev which played their part in increasing his difficulties. Even if at times he was over-cautious, one of his characteristics was great self-confidence—his belief that he could both outmanœuvre all his opponents and win any argument. Shakhnazarov, a sympathetic, close collaborator, has alluded to Gorbachev firmly believing 'in his ability to convince anyone of anything'.[99] The fact that he had achieved so much—what was already taken for granted by democrats had, after all, seemed like utopian hopes for a distant future even to dissidents a mere five years earlier—made his over-confidence understandable, but optimism and self-belief were (and remain) important traits of Gorbachev's personality. Taking the years from 1985 to 1991 as a whole, this was for the good. A leader lacking in confidence or courage or one who leaned towards pessimism would never have embarked on the reform of the Soviet system or dared to move beyond that to undertake truly transformative change when he came up against the limits of the system.

Gorbachev believed also that people whom he had appointed would serve him loyally. Some did, but—as August 1991 demonstrated most dramatically—some did not. His appointments have already been discussed in Chapter 4, but with particular reference to his earlier years in office. It was then that such key reformers as Yakovlev, Shevardnadze, Chernyaev, and Shakhnazarov were elevated to positions which enabled them to exert great influence. Although others of a more conservative disposition were also promoted between 1985 and 1988, these were the years of Gorbachev's best appointments.[100] Some of his worst appointments were made in the winter of 1990–1. This half-year was perhaps the only period of Gorbachev's leadership when he was a centrist, in the sense of occupying a position roughly equidistant between that of the radical democrats and nationalists and that of the forces within the party-state machine which wanted to restore a more traditional order. He had previously not only been the main instigator of radical reform in the earliest years of his General Secretaryship and the person who took the decisive steps in 1988 to break with the traditional Communist order, but also 'left of centre' throughout 1989 and the greater part of 1990. His position in the political spectrum was that he remained more reformist than the party apparatus and government as a whole, even if less so than the new radicals who had gained a foothold in the system and a voice in Soviet politics as a result of the elections for the all-union and republican legislatures. While Gorbachev was often depicted as a centrist long before the autumn of 1990, that was a misperception of his position within the leadership, although he was happy to obfuscate the point, both because he genuinely tried to build a consensus, whether within the Politburo or the Presidential Council, and for tactical reasons, since it was to his advantage to appear even-handed and ready to listen to the views of both the liberal and the conservative wings of the leadership.

In the winter of 1990–1, however, Gorbachev did, indeed, occupy the centre ground. There were times when his position appeared to be on the 'centre-right', but this period of his leadership was marked by zig-zags, as he manœuvred between increasingly polarized political forces. With the exception of the months between the August coup and the collapse of the Soviet Union in December 1991, it was probably the most stressful and difficult phase of his tenure of the Kremlin. He was under intense pressure from both 'left' and 'right'—from, on the one hand, radical democrats and national separatists, and, on the other, from the government, the party apparatus, the army, the KGB, a conservative majority in the Supreme Soviet, and all those who felt that the pluralization of Soviet politics had gone too far and that the threat of disintegration of the union had got to be countered before it engulfed them all.

The relatively short-lived period of co-operation with Yeltsin, which began in August when Gorbachev supported the work of the Shatalin–Yavlinsky team on the '500 Days Programme' for rapid transition to a market economy, ended with Gorbachev's retreat from some of the starker implications of that strategy for radical change. Listening to the criticisms of the marketizing economists of the government programme of Ryzhkov and Abalkin and from the government side of the '500 Days' approach, Gorbachev shifted his position not only for reasons of political prudence—since the entire executive, including the Chairman of the Council of Ministers, the economic ministries, the army, the KGB, and most of the party apparatus were opposed to the fast-track 'Transition to the Market'—but also because he became genuinely convinced of weaknesses both in the government proposals and in those of the economic radicals. In retrospect, even a number of marketizing economists thought the '500 Days' programme unrealistic. Pavel Bunich, one such economist by no means well disposed towards Gorbachev, described it in 1995 as 'not a programme, but an introductory lecture', adding that, if it had been implemented, the results would 'probably have been worse than today'. It was, according to Bunich, a kind of marketeers' equivalent of the campaigns in Stalin's time to 'fulfil the 5-year plan in three years'.[101] Gorbachev undoubtedly vacillated both on the pros and cons of the programme and on the relative weight of the political forces gathered on each side. What may have been crucial is that the preponderance of power appeared to be on the side of the state authorities rather than the Shatalin–Yavlinsky team. Fierce opposition came not only from within the executive but also from the parliament, which was now a body to be reckoned with. Gorbachev believed that the '500 Days Programme' would not be accepted by the Supreme Soviet of the USSR.[102]

Institutional changes

The Communist Party apparatus had not, in the meantime, taken kindly to the formal removal of the party's leading role in March 1990. The composition of the Politburo had been changed radically at the Twenty-Eighth Party Congress in the summer of that year. It now contained the First Secretaries of all the union republican party organizations and the new Deputy General Secretary, Vladimir Ivashko, but not—as in the past—the Chairman of the Council of Ministers, the Minister of Foreign Affairs, the Minister of Defence, or the Chairman of the KGB. The absence of Ryzhkov, Shevardnadze, Yazov, and Kryuchkov, as well as of Alexander Yakovlev, all of whom were, however, members of the Presidential Council, led to the quite justified suspicion on the part of a Politburo which was increasingly rarely convened that they had been relegated, at best, to the position of a second eleven. They believed that Gorbachev was more interested in the views of the Presidential Council than of the Politburo, even if the former lacked the power and the means of implementing policy which the Politburo had until quite recently possessed. As nationalists and radical democrats became more assertive, and both party orthodoxy and party bureaucrats were increasingly held up to ridicule by a substantial section of the mass media, the backlash confronting Gorbachev became intense. From both the military and the new Politburo he was urged to institute a regime of centralized presidential rule, taking special powers which (their advocates realized) would alienate Gorbachev still further from his democratic allies. Alexander Yakovlev has recounted how a group of influential regional party secretaries, gathered in Moscow for the Twenty-Eighth Party Congress, had agreed that it was especially important to separate Gorbachev from Yakovlev and Shevardnadze.[103] While they did not succeed in doing so in the summer of 1990, that aim was partially achieved the following winter.

Having made a speech to the Supreme Soviet on 16 November 1990 which fell flat, Gorbachev the next day put forward a series of new proposals which were very well received. They included the abolition of the Presidential Council and granting instead real powers to the Federation Council, on which sat the heads of the union republics and which had been created earlier in 1990 at the same time as the Presidential Council. By explicitly according the Federation Council an enhanced role in policy formulation, Gorbachev was increasing the influence of a body whose membership was not determined by him. If the Politburo was an institution over whose composition he had considerable influence, but not absolute control, the Presidential Council had been appointed entirely at his discretion. Now, in contrast, he was to work with a collective body whose representatives were chosen in the republics, and in that sense his powers were significantly reduced. The attraction, though, of working through the Federation Council was that those who composed it had the power to implement policy within their respective republics and this looked like a viable way of holding the union together.

Other important changes were announced by Gorbachev at this time. They included the formation of a new government—a Cabinet of Ministers to take the place of the Council of Ministers; the creation of a Security Council on which most of the major political figures who had been members of the Presidential Council would sit (but no longer accompanied by free-ranging intellectuals);[104] and the introduction of a new post of Vice-President. Although the need to bring forward new proposals had been impressed on Gorbachev not only by the negative reception his speech of 16 November met in the Supreme Soviet but also by the fierce and open hostility he had encountered at a Politburo session the same day and at a meeting with representatives of the military on 13 November, Gorbachev has insisted that it was not Communist Party pressure which led to his change of tack.[105] The accumulation of criticism from a variety of quarters doubtless had its effect, but Gorbachev was particularly concerned to carry the Supreme Soviet with him, for he took constitutional provisions seriously, and the legislature was no longer an institution which could be bypassed in the way the party now could (however awkward that was while he remained its General Secretary).

Moreover, a number of Gorbachev's proposals for further institutional changes, including the possible abolition of the Presidential Council, had been discussed with certain of his aides and he had intended bringing them to the Congress of People's Deputies the following month.[106] Shakhnazarov had actually urged Gorbachev to include these proposals in his speech of 16 November, but 'others said there was no need to hurry'.[107] When Gorbachev 'felt that the reaction to his speech was negative', he decided to bring forward 'something we already knew'.[108] It was a last-minute decision in the sense that Gorbachev changed the timing of the announcements in response to what he judged to be the political mood, but the ideas themselves had not arisen so suddenly.[109] Shakhnazarov himself had been an advocate of the abolition of the Presidential Council because it was 'a hybrid' whose composition was 'quite eclectic' and which 'did not work from the very beginning'.[110]

Alexander Yakovlev, in contrast, was taken aback by the sudden abolition of the Council on which he sat and which left him with no official position other than the rather amorphous one of an adviser to the President (in which capacity, however, he retained his office in the Kremlin). Yakovlev said that he regarded the abolition of the Presidential Council as a mistake, for it 'had already started really working' and had taken the country close to the introduction of a market economy.[111] One reason, however, why the abolition of the Presidential Council took Yakovlev by surprise is that increasing disagreement on policy—most notably, on the '500 Days Programme', of which Yakovlev remained an enthusiastic supporter—meant that he was less frequently consulted by Gorbachev during the winter of 1990–1 than hitherto. As Gorbachev had retreated from the Shatalin–Yavlinsky proposals over the previous two months, he had begun also to distance himself somewhat from Yakovlev.[112] They were never again to enjoy as politically close a relationship as they had in the earliest years of Gorbachev's leadership, although Yakovlev was to regain some of his prominence after Gorbachev ended his unconvincing dalliance with the conservative forces at the end of that winter.

Personnel change

In the meantime, however, Gorbachev lost important allies and made some highly dubious new ones. He gave way to pressure for the removal of the liberal Minister of Interior, Vadim Bakatin, in spite of his admiration for him as a politician. His esteem for Bakatin was reflected in his appointment to membership of the newly formed Security Council even though he no longer had a ministerial portfolio. Bakatin's replacement was Boris Pugo, a relatively hardline Latvian who had been at various times head of the Latvian Komsomol, KGB, and Communist Party. The equally traditionalist former commander of Soviet forces in Afghanistan, General Boris Gromov (who, however, unlike Pugo had at least the good sense not to commit himself fully to the *putschists* in August 1991), became the First Deputy Minister of Interior. This was a response to widespread demands for a crack-down on crime and the imposition of order.

The new post of Vice-President went to Gennady Yanaev, whose background was in the Komsomol and the official Soviet trade union movement. Gorbachev did not know him well, but backed him partly on the grounds that he would be a reliable subordinate. He also believed that Yanaev, precisely because he lacked reformist credentials, would help to neutralize his 'right-wing' opponents. This was to turn out to be a serious misjudgement, as was the decision, announced on 3 January 1991, following a meeting of the Federation Council, to put Yanaev in charge of a group responsible for nominating members of the new Cabinet of Ministers.[113] Shortly thereafter Valentin Pavlov (who, as Minister of Finance, had done his best to sabotage the work of the Shatalin–Yavlinsky team by withholding essential information about government spending)[114] was appointed Prime Minister in succession to Nikolay Ryzhkov. Yanaev's views may have been among those Gorbachev listened to, but he consulted a great many people without necessarily accepting their advice. One whom Gorbachev went to see was Ryzhkov, still recovering both from his dismissal as head of the previous government and from a heart attack. Ryzhkov took the conventional view that Pavlov was a good financial specialist. However, while not as negative about him as he was about Oleg Baklanov, another possible candidate for the Prime Ministership whom Gorbachev mentioned (and a representative of the military-industrial complex who, like Pavlov, was to be a party to the August 1991 *putsch*), Ryzhkov was decidedly unenthusiastic, mentioning Pavlov's lack of knowledge of industry and also the fact that he was a heavy drinker.[115]

A politician whose voice may have counted for more, for his influence with Gorbachev reached its height during these winter months when the Soviet President's repositioning of himself in the centre of the Soviet political spectrum partially estranged him from his reformist team, was his former Moscow University Komsomol colleague Anatoly Lukyanov.[116] Lukyanov, as Chairman of the Supreme Soviet, now had a power base of his own, and he used that, together with the advantage of having known Gorbachev since their student years, to promote his views. These included a special determination to maintain the existing borders of the Soviet Union. Within the Supreme Soviet Lukyanov had shown great indulgence to the Soyuz (Union) group, the 600-strong faction which had been formed to defend, often in extremist language, the territorial integrity of the Soviet Union. In a small group discussion in November 1990, Gorbachev brushed aside implied criticism of Lukyanov by his aide Nikolay Petrakov, saying, 'I do not need aides who give me one-sided information', and added that Lukyanov 'always reports only the truth'.[117] (By the end of the year Petrakov had resigned of his own accord—Gorbachev, in fact, tried to persuade him to stay—although he returned to Gorbachev's team in an advisory capacity following the collapse of the August coup.)

Lukyanov's involvement is indicated by Gorbachev's statement that the issue of who should be Prime Minister 'was discussed for a long time in the Council of the Federation *and in the presidium of the USSR Supreme Soviet*' (emphasis added), following which it was decided that the candidacy of Pavlov should be presented to the Supreme Soviet as a whole.[118] Trying to carry as many of the republics with him as possible in the choice of Prime Minister, Gorbachev had consulted also the Federation Council about the main candidates; they included, Gorbachev informed the Supreme Soviet on 14 January (in addition to Pavlov and Baklanov), Yury Maslyukov, the Chairman of Gosplan, whose background, like Baklanov's, was in military industry.[119] Although the discussions in the Federation Council included 'critical evaluations', Pavlov was, nevertheless, their choice 'on the basis of a large degree of accord'.[120]

Shevardnadze's resignation

The promotions and demotions during the winter of 1990–1 undoubtedly reduced the weight of committed 'new thinkers' within Gorbachev's team. The most dramatic and public loss of a reformer was the resignation of Eduard Shevardnadze as Foreign Minister on 20 December 1990. Shevardnadze, as he makes clear in his memoirs, had enjoyed excellent relations with Gorbachev over many years and they spoke together—with unusual frankness for party officials before 1985—about many of the absurdities of Soviet life.[121] Shevardnadze had from 1985 onwards been a successful executant of what was essentially Gorbachev's foreign policy. The fact that he saw eye to eye with Gorbachev was of crucial importance, as was his ability to establish relations of trust with his Western counterparts. In the period just before his resignation, however, Shevardnadze (as was noted in Chapter 7) had been more whole-heartedly supportive than was Gorbachev of American willingness to use force against Iraq following the incursion of Iraqi forces into Kuwait. More generally, he felt that Gorbachev from the summer of 1990 had been too reluctant to come to his defence when he was under attack from hardliners within the Soviet Union (although by this time Gorbachev was himself attacked by name with increasing frequency). In his speech to the Fourth Congress of People's Deputies of the USSR in which he announced that he was giving up his post as Foreign Minister, Shevardnadze accused, without naming them, two deputies from the military (he had in mind Colonels Viktor Alksnis and Nikolay Petrushenko) of having boasted that the Minister of Interior (Bakatin) had been removed successfully 'and the time has come to settle accounts with the foreign minister'.[122] Shevardnadze's relations with the Soviet military were even worse than Gorbachev's and he was angered by the fact that the Ministry of Defence would act in ways which at times contradicted the spirit of agreements he had reached with his Western partners and, still more infuriating, he would learn of these actions for the first time from Western sources.[123]

Shevardnadze's speech was a protest aimed more generally at the growing strength of the conservative forces and their backlash against the foreign and domestic policy of Gorbachev. Shevardnadze referred not only to the severe criticism of him but also to the increasing attacks on 'the Gorbachev clique'. He blamed the democrats for having 'scattered', leaving the way open for a coming dictatorship. Saying that no one knew what form this dictatorship would take or who would be the dictator, Shevardnadze announced his resignation and added: 'let this be my contribution, if you like, my protest against the onset of dictatorship.'[124] The speech was a sensation both in the Soviet Union and abroad and raised consciousness world-wide of the possibility of a reversal of the profound changes which had occurred over the previous few years. For Gorbachev, Shevardnadze's resignation announcement was completely unexpected, and he was deeply pained that Shevardnadze had not discussed it with him in advance.[125] Although shaken by this sudden blow, he nevertheless took the earliest opportunity to speak with Shevardnadze and, indeed, persuaded him to carry on working in the capacity of Foreign Minister for another month until his successor—the career diplomat Bessmertnykh—had been appointed. When Gorbachev came to the Foreign Ministry on 26 January 1991 for the installation of the new Minister, he paid warm tribute to Shevardnadze, who was present. The sentence Shevardnadze valued most was: 'He was always by my side, my closest comrade in all the most difficult situations and, most important, in making the choice.'[126] *The choice* they had made of a new direction was for both of them the main thing, even at this time when Gorbachev was attempting (in an apt phrase of Yeltsin's) 'to reconcile the irreconcilable' and to manœuvre between polarized political forces.

In addition to the reasons for resigning which Shevardnadze offered, he may, nevertheless, have feared that Gorbachev—notwithstanding his high regard for him—might himself have taken the initiative in moving him from the Ministry of Foreign Affairs. Shevardnadze's name sometimes came up as a potential Prime Minister of the Soviet Union or Vice-President in conversations Gorbachev had in 1990. His diplomatic skills and Georgian nationality apparently offered the possibility of promoting the harmony between nations *within* the Soviet Union which he had successfully pursued further afield. By the winter of 1990–1 the offer of the prime ministership to Shevardnadze, as distinct from the vice-presidency—a less powerful post in day-to-day terms—had become unlikely. It would have met with fierce resistance from within the Soviet establishment. Removing him from the Foreign Ministry to a less crucially important post would, however, have had the superficial advantage of partially placating the Soviet conservatives. Shevardnadze may, accordingly, have been influenced, in addition to all the genuine reasons for resigning which he gave, by a desire to get his resignation in first. He was protesting not only against the growing strength and assertiveness of the hardliners but also, more implicitly, against Gorbachev's attempt to appease them, as exemplified by several personnel changes and, more generally, by his occupying a centrist position between them and the democrats.

Soon after he left office Shevardnadze was to compare the earlier Gorbachev with the Gorbachev of the winter of 1990–1. Expressing his understanding of why Gorbachev 'did not speak up' as before—'a politician has to size up the actual situation and the balance of forces'—Shevardnadze nevertheless observed that 'back in the early days of perestroika, while acknowledging the existence of an opposition, he wasn't afraid to go against the grain. He appealed to the people and won their support. All the more boldly, he hammered out the credo of the new thinking and put it into action.'[127] But now, said Shevardnadze, 'the seasoned debater who had persuaded the Party and the country that democracy and innovation were vitally needed, kept silent', although, he remarks elsewhere, 'not for an instant did I forget how complicated [Gorbachev's] position was, how contradictory and many-sided the pressure he was under'.[128]

Bloodshed in the Baltic states

The attempt of the conservative forces within the Soviet system to roll back the changes which had occurred since 1988 and to force Gorbachev into a general crack-down on all manifestations of nationalism took a more sinister turn in early 1991, lending greater plausibility to Shevardnadze's warnings of a coming dictatorship. On several occasions excessive force was used by local commanders with the backing of some of their superiors in Moscow precisely in order to sharpen the conflict, to discredit Gorbachev in the eyes of democrats and his supporters in the West, and to force him into bringing in direct presidential rule in the Baltic states. Direct rule was a course of action he had contemplated—and, in a speech of 10 January, had explicitly warned the Lithuanians might happen—but which he never in fact introduced. Boldin had done his best to bring it about, with his steady supply of one-sided and misleading information. He made sure that enormous piles of telegrams and letters from Russians living in Latvia, Lithuania, and Estonia (as well as from work collectives and organizations all over Russia), speaking of reprisals against Russians in the Baltic states and warning of the danger of civil war if order were not quickly restored, landed daily on Gorbachev's desk.[129] In a speech to the Supreme Soviet on 14 January, devoted entirely to Lithuania, and separate from the one in which he proposed Pavlov as Prime Minister, Gorbachev spoke of telegrams continuing to flow in, and 'in recent days' with the complaint that he had not instituted presidential rule.[130] (Lukyanov, who was chairing the session, interrupted to add that the Supreme Soviet had also received 'thousands of telegrams'.[131])

Of the several violent actions against the Balts, that on the night of 12/13 January 1991, in which fourteen people were killed and many more wounded when Soviet troops moved to take over the television station in Vilnius, provoked the greatest outcry. A significant part of the Soviet mass media criticized the actions from a liberal standpoint and on 20 January a massive demonstration in Moscow against repression in the Baltic republics drew an estimated 100,000 participants. Gorbachev had attempted through warnings and verbal intimidation to bring the Lithuanians and other Baltic nationalists into the legal process for secession which had been promulgated the previous year. Their reply was that, since they had been incorporated in the Soviet Union against their will, they had no need to seek permission to leave. The Lithuanians had, of course, obeyed Soviet laws for the greater part of five decades, until it seemed, several years into the Gorbachev era, that the sanctions against ignoring them would be far less severe than in the past.

Gorbachev's own rhetoric during this period was, however, often a throwback to earlier times. Thus on 10 January he spoke of an attempt at 'restoration of the bourgeois order' in Lithuania, a remark that made no sense in terms of the pluralization of politics over which he had himself presided,[132] and was a conscious tilt in the direction of the conservative forces he was trying to keep within an increasingly fragile and unmanageable coalition. All the big battalions (in the most literal sense) were pushing him in the direction of giving priority to preservation of the union—and this was an extremely high priority for him also, with the difference that he wished to achieve this *without* resort to violence and *with* respect for the law. Shakhnazarov has recounted a conversation with Gorbachev (on 5 October 1990) in which Gorbachev spoke of a recent meeting he had had with 'a leader of our *afgantsy*' (Soviet veterans of the Afghan war). That person had told him that he must use whatever means necessary to impose order and he could then count on the army to support him. Gorbachev responded: 'That is not my choice. We are following another path.'[133]

The killings in Vilnius—in which both General Valentin Varennikov, who was to be a leading figure in the attempted coup of August 1991, and General Viktor Achalov, later one of the most active *putschists* against Gorbachev and against Yeltsin in October 1993, appear to have played a significant part[134]— were not only against Gorbachev's will, but were intended (as was a later violent onslaught in Riga) to be but the start of a more general imposition of 'order' within the Soviet Union.[135] People who were prepared to remove Gorbachev from his presidential office unconstitutionally were more than capable of using unauthorized violence against nationalist separatists some months earlier. The unremitting struggle by conservative forces for Gorbachev's ear and the effort to isolate him from the liberal-minded members of his entourage continued. Not all of the attempts succeeded. Efforts were made to persuade him to remove his press spokesman, Vitaly Ignatenko—who later discovered that his telephone had been tapped throughout these months—but Gorbachev both defended and retained him.[136]

The day tensions reached their height in Vilnius (13 January) was a Sunday and when the Lithuanian President, Vytautas Landsbergis, tried to telephone Gorbachev to speak about the killings the previous night, not only was he not put through to Gorbachev's dacha, but Gorbachev was also not even informed that he had called.[137] The misleading information which, in fact, was given to Gorbachev that day was that there had been 'some outrages' in Vilnius which 'the nationalists had organized as a provocation'.[138] The Vilnius deaths did immediate damage to Gorbachev—as they were intended to[139]—among his remaining democratic supporters, and several of the liberals in his entourage, including Chernyaev and Ignatenko, contemplated resignation.[140]

Chernyaev, who had served Gorbachev well for the five years he had spent as his aide and foreign policy adviser, went so far as to write a letter to the Soviet President to denounce the latest turn of events and to resign his post. He concluded by saying that—in contrast with his service (in the International Department of the Central Committee) during the times of Brezhnev and Chernenko—he had never, since coming to work with Gorbachev, felt 'excruciating shame on account of the policy of the Soviet leadership'. He added: 'Alas! This has now happened.'[141] Although for Chernyaev it was hard to bring himself to make this break with Gorbachev, it seems it would have occurred but for the resistance of his secretary and assistant, Tamara Aleksandrova. She demanded to know what good Chernyaev thought would come from his departure, how he could contemplate leaving Gorbachev in the lurch and insulting him at a time like this, 'and so on in that spirit'.[142] She refused to type the lengthy letter Chernyaev was composing (and which occupies three and a half pages of small type in his memoirs).[143] When Chernyaev began to write the letter by hand, Tamara Aleksandrova apparently relented. She typed the letter, but then put it in her safe and locked it. She did not come in to work the following day and Chernyaev reconciled himself to waiting a little longer before delivering his protest and resignation to Gorbachev. But Tamara Aleksandrova did not return to work for a week and by then Chernyaev believed she had been right![144]

Gorbachev is open to criticism both for his tougher line and heightened rhetoric against the Lithuanians in the days preceding the attack and for his slowness in condemning the killings publicly once they had occurred, but there is some evidence that he was shocked and angered by what happened.[145] Yet his speech to the Supreme Soviet about the events in Vilnius avoided a direct condemnation of the violence on the part of the state authorities and came as a great disappointment to the liberals within his team as well as in the broader society. Alexander Yakovlev, who returned from holiday to his Kremlin office after the deaths in Vilnius, was one of those who argued that this was not the time to desert Gorbachev.[146] Yakovlev, Bakatin, Primakov, Chernyaev, Shakhnazarov, and Ignatenko had a series of meetings in which they decided that the optimal resolution of this political crisis would be for Gorbachev to fly to Lithuania, meet with Landsbergis, and explicitly disassociate himself from the violence.[147] They put their proposal directly to Gorbachev, who endorsed the idea and asked them to prepare the materials. Ignatenko and Yakovlev believed that he would be flying to Vilnius the next day.

This did not happen. Those who had sought a show-down with the Lithuanians had a firm ally and collaborator in Yury Plekhanov, the head of the Ninth Directorate of the KGB, which was responsible for the security of the Soviet leadership, as well as in Plekhanov's chief, Kryuchkov. On the day the most enlightened members of his entourage expected him to be flying to Vilnius, Gorbachev told Ignatenko that he would not now be making that journey, explaining: 'A number of comrades are against, because it is impossible to guarantee the safety of the President.'[148] Ignatenko believes that Gorbachev was obliged to take heed of the opinion of those charged with protecting his security, but this may not have been the only reason why Gorbachev wavered. To have gone to Vilnius at that moment would have been to take sides once again at a time when he was trying to steer a middle course. It would have amounted to a rejection of the viewpoint of the army, the KGB, the Ministry of Interior, and the government, as well, of course, as that of most of the leading figures in the CPSU. While deploring the loss of life, Gorbachev was reluctant to place *public* blame on the Soviet army or Ministry of Interior forces for fear of antagonizing further the very power structures he had been trying to mollify. Reflecting on this week in Soviet politics just over a year later, Ignatenko said that undoubtedly Gorbachev was not involved in the decision to use tanks and armed force in Vilnius, but that he failed to act sufficiently decisively in the aftermath of the killings and to dismiss those responsible.[149]

Those determined to push Gorbachev into the camp of violent suppressors of all manifestations of nationalism—or, better still, to discredit him and destabilize his presidency so that he would be forced to make way for those who would willingly do this—struck again on the night of 20/1 January, this time in Latvia, when OMON (special Ministry of Interior) troops killed four people in Riga.[150] In a news conference on 22 January Gorbachev said some of the things which would have been better said a week earlier, including an expression of condolence to the families affected by 'the tragic turn the confrontation in Lithuania and, in recent days, in Riga has taken'. He added: 'The developments in Vilnius and Riga are certainly not an expression of the line taken by the presidential power and nor was it created for this purpose. Therefore I resolutely reject all speculation and suspicion and slander on this score.'[151] At the same time Gorbachev confirmed 'the constitutional right of a republic to secede from the union', but added that 'we cannot permit either unruliness or arbitrariness in this matter, even on the part of elected bodies'. Secession could only take place in accordance with the Soviet Constitution and on the basis of a referendum and the process envisaged by Soviet law.[152]

The fact that each such tragedy was a one-day occurrence, with Gorbachev calling a halt to the violence as soon as he was made aware of it, distinguishes his behaviour sharply (as has already been mentioned in passing) from the direct culpability of Yeltsin in post-Soviet Russia, as he pursued a ruthless internal war against the Russian Federation's most assertively independent republic, Chechnya, month after month from the time it was launched in December 1994, leading to a death toll far in excess of the total number killed by the Soviet army and Ministry of Interior troops in all Soviet republics during the entire Gorbachev era.[153] Yet Gorbachev was in more imminent danger of being overthrown if he failed to prevent the unilateral secession of Soviet republics than was Yeltsin three to four years later. Although Gorbachev could not say so in public, his aide Shakhnazarov voiced what was also in the Soviet President's mind at the time when he said, in an interview published in Germany on 21 January 1991, that if 'this very man' who had pursued the two major objectives of democratization and integration in the international community 'were to tolerate the disintegration of the USSR', then 'Gorbachev would fall'.[154] Shakhnazarov believed that 'a brusque, uncontrolled disintegration of the USSR would be disastrous' and that it would lead to 'military dictatorship—without parliaments, without democratic guarantees, and without the right for the media to criticize the president'.[155] If the August coup of 1991 had succeeded, the logic of the *putschists'* actions would, indeed, have pushed them in that direction. Luckily, their incompetence meant that—in the short term, at least—Shakhnazarov's prognosis was excessively gloomy, albeit entirely plausible in the context of early 1991. By that January Shakhnazarov had, however, realized what Gorbachev was reluctant to admit even to himself and perhaps accepted only from the spring of 1991—that the Baltic states would part company with the Soviet Union sooner or later. Shakhnazarov stated: 'It is my firm conviction that the Baltic states will be permitted to leave the USSR on the basis of the Constitution without major problems.'[156] Gorbachev subsequently confirmed that position in essence, but with some difference of emphasis, saying that his aim was to try by all political means to prevent the secession of Lithuania from the union, but if that failed and the people there decided otherwise, then there needed to be a legal divorce following negotiations.[157]

The pressures increase

Feeling increasingly under siege in the winter of 1990–1, Gorbachev had appointed the malleable Leonid Kravchenko (so malleable that he later did the bidding also of those who temporarily deposed Gorbachev in August) as head of central Soviet television and radio in order to stem the tide of increasingly outspoken criticism of him and of the all-union authorities.[158] Kravchenko obliged by announcing that 'state television does not have the right to engage in criticism of the leadership of the country' and by taking off the air the most popular current affairs programme, *Vzglyad* (Viewpoint).[159] Gorbachev, in the heat of the moment in January 1991, when he was under fierce attack from some newspapers following the deaths in Vilnius, suggested that it might also be necessary to suspend the Press Law.[160] What is more important, however, is that not only did he not do so (withdrawing the proposal 'almost at once'[161]) but also that he had allowed this liberal law which ended censorship and institutionalized the freedom of the press to be enacted in the first place.

Indeed, it had been Gorbachev's decision to push through a Law on the Press (on which work began in 1989 with the legislation enacted in June 1990) that would defend freedom of publication while including also certain safeguards. The latter were essentially the constraints to be found also in the laws of a number of Western countries, such as prohibition on the advocacy of violent overthrow of the state and on propagandizing racial, national, or religious intolerance.[162] Although he was under fierce pressure from the Politburo not to give up the Communist Party's levers of control over the mass media, Gorbachev allowed his aide Shakhnazarov, in his capacity as chairman of a parliamentary subcommittee on constitutional legislation, to take overall responsibility for the drafting of what turned out to be a path-breaking law which 'effectively legitimized the expression of anti-communist opinions'[163] and 'in its effects on the print media . . . was one of the most effective pieces of legislation of the *perestroika* period'.[164]

Tension remained high in February and March 1991, but there was no repeat of the violence in the Baltic states of January. Even so, as a result of what had happened the previous month, a summit meeting which should have taken place between Gorbachev and George Bush in February was postponed. Pavlov made a fatuous speech in the same month in which he blamed Western financiers for trying to destabilize the Soviet economy, and Yeltsin took the opportunity of a live television interview on 19 February to call on Gorbachev to resign. Instead, Gorbachev pressed ahead with his plans for a referendum on support for a renewed Union, which was held on 17 March and, as noted earlier in this chapter, produced a favourable result from his point of view in the nine republics which agreed to conduct it. Several republics, however, added additional questions of their own, including a highly significant one in Russia. There the voters were asked whether they wanted direct elections for a Russian presidency to be held that June. Yeltsin had been Chairman of the Supreme Soviet of Russia since the previous summer, but he and his advisers were aware that his political position would be further strengthened if he could be elected by the whole people.[165] Of those who participated in the referendum, 70 per cent voted in favour of a popularly elected presidency.

As the economic position worsened, a new round of miners' strikes occurred, and, as distinct from the mainly economic concerns in 1989, demands now included calls for Gorbachev's resignation and for the removal of Communist Party organizations from the work-place.[166] In the face of such pressures, Gorbachev still appeared far too ready to believe information supplied to him by the likes of Kryuchkov, Pugo, and Boldin. When they told him that radicals were planning a march which would end with the storming of the Kremlin, he gave the story far more credence than it was worth, despite Alexander Yakovlev's attempts to disabuse him.[167] The Cabinet of Ministers, with Gorbachev's evident approval, called a ban on demonstrations in Moscow from 26 March to 15 April, and Yeltsin, in turn, called their bluff by announcing a demonstration for 28 March.[168] At least a quarter of a million people were estimated to have participated in that gathering, watched by some fifty thousand police and Ministry of Interior troops.[169] To the relief of Gorbachev and a broader Soviet public, the demonstration passed off peacefully. In the words of David Remnick, it had been 'blissfully boring' and 'a political draw'.[170]

Just as letters and telegrams sent to Gorbachev were filtered by Boldin's office, so were statistical information, excerpts from the press, and material 'from other sources' (including, evidently, intelligence sources).[171] It was as late as March 1991 that Chernyaev and the head of the presidential press service, Ignatenko, discovered that Boldin had created his own department of information in his secretariat which controlled this particular flow of papers and could thereby exercise a baneful influence on Gorbachev's perception of a number of issues.[172] Gorbachev's faith in Boldin, says Shakhnazarov, gave the chief of staff 'practically unlimited power, and he used it voluptuously'.[173] Undoubtedly, some of the worst decisions taken by Gorbachev owed much to his misplaced trust in people whom he should not have appointed to responsible posts in the first place, as well as to his insufficient attention to the machinery of government on which he depended.

Shakhnazarov, for all his esteem for Gorbachev, says that, as Soviet President, Gorbachev was 'an indifferent organizer'.[174] He had, of course, known how to work within the apparatus of the Communist Party, which, in comparison with most Soviet institutions, was relatively efficient in the processing of papers and the implementation of decisions. But, on becoming Soviet President, he had no experience or knowledge of how to secure the structural underpinnings which would endow that office with real executive power. It has to be added, however, that Gorbachev was carrying an almost superhuman work-load. When not conducting international diplomacy abroad, he was in his office from morning until at least ten o'clock in the evening, after which he sometimes worked until one or two in the morning at home on papers which assistants delivered to him there.[175] He badly needed, but lacked, a chief of staff who would combine organizational skills with genuine support for the kind of enlightened change which, tactical retreats and some strategic errors notwithstanding, was what gave purpose and profound significance to Gorbachev's leadership.

The Novo-Ogarevo process

The greatest machinery of government in the world would not, of course, have resolved the fundamental political conflicts within Soviet society. At some point the transformation of such a long-established Communist system into a non-Communist system (that this had in essence occurred is a point to which I return in the concluding chapter) and the threat of the breakup of the multi-national state, itself an unintended consequence of the democratization of a highly authoritarian regime, were bound to lead to a showdown. Whatever criticism can be levelled at Gorbachev concerning the most disappointing six months of his leadership—from October 1990 to March 1991—has to be tempered by amazement that he was able to carry with him for so long, and however reluctantly, the defenders of the old order. It is hardly surprising that matters came to a head when the very existence of Soviet statehood was at issue. By 1991 even the arguments over what kind of political or economic system was being created became subordinate to the question of what kind of union, if any, could be preserved.

While he was making concessions to conservative and hardline forces, Gorbachev was turning his mind to more constructive ways of dealing with this crisis. Already in the first months of 1991, when he was still listening to, and sometimes following, bad advice from the conservatives, Gorbachev understood that some of those putting pressure on him 'wished to drive me as President into a corner'.[176] Accordingly, from March he turned increasingly to people who constituted, on the whole, his best advisers and aides and who, once again, came to constitute an informal discussion group, in which all felt free to say exactly what they thought about the extraordinarily difficult situation they faced. The most regular members of this group were Alexander Yakovlev, Vadim Medvedev, Shakhnazarov, Chernyaev, Primakov, Ignatenko, and 'of course', Chernyaev remarks, 'Boldin' (the only one of that group to support the August coup).[177] The upshot was that Gorbachev decided to take the initiative once again and embark on what he called the 'Novo-Ogarevo process'.[178]

The name derived from the country house not far from Moscow, built in Khrushchev's time in the style of a nineteenth-century Russian landowner's home,[179] at which Gorbachev launched discussions and negotiations with the political heads of as many union republics and 'autonomous republics' of the USSR as were prepared to attend. Of the fifteen union republics, nine were represented, the absentees being the three Baltic states, Armenia, Georgia, and Moldova. The Novo-Ogarevo process got under way on 23 April with the first of these '9 + 1' meetings. Gorbachev was, of course, the 'one', although Lukyanov, as Chairman of the Supreme Soviet of the USSR, was also present at all the formal meetings. What was crucial was that Gorbachev had persuaded both Yeltsin and Kravchuk to take part, for, without the participation of Russia and Ukraine, nothing could have been achieved. The plan was to produce a new Union Treaty—a voluntary agreement on the respective powers and rights of the centre and the republics—within a very few months.

Gorbachev had launched the Novo-Ogarevo process on the eve of a plenary session of the Central Committee of the CPSU at which he came under severe attack from conservative forces. A majority of speakers at this plenum, held on 24–5 April 1991, were highly critical of his leadership of the Communist Party. The onslaught appeared to have been a preplanned and concerted effort to undermine him fatally. Gorbachev decided to force the issue of whether his authority as General Secretary could or could not be sustained. He threatened, in all seriousness, to resign, and although a majority of members of the Central Committee would almost certainly have preferred another General Secretary, they lacked the resolution to seize the opportunity offered to them. In frenzied behind-the-scenes activity more than seventy supporters of Gorbachev put their signatures to a document backing him. In the face of this pressure and the imminence of an overt split in the party leadership, the Politburo—meeting in emergency session during a recess—put to the plenum the proposal that, 'in the interests of the country, people and party', the issue of Gorbachev's leaving the post of General Secretary be removed from the agenda. To Gorbachev's short-term advantage and longer-term disadvantage, this motion was carried overwhelmingly.[180]

The vote meant, however, that Gorbachev could concentrate on the Novo-Ogarevo process. The background to these negotiations—designed to preserve some kind of union and a 'common economic space', from the latter of which the six non-participating republics were to be excluded unless they subsequently decided they wished to be part of the union—lay even more in the 'war of laws' between Russia and the USSR than in the conflict with the Baltic states. A huge impetus to the ultimate breakup of the Soviet Union had been given by the

Supreme Soviet of the Russian Federation in June 1990, some two weeks after Yeltsin became its chairman, when it declared political sovereignty and the supremacy of Russian law over union legislation. Over the next few months other republics followed the Russian example. Between June and October Uzbekistan, Moldova, Ukraine, Belorussia, Turkmenistan, Tajikistan, and Kazakhstan declared their sovereignty, while Armenia, which had already done so, took the further step of declaring its independence. In the case of the Central Asian republics there was no sign that they wished this to be a step towards full independence; rather, their leaders could hardly appear less interested in asserting sovereign rights against the union than Russia, given that the relationship between the Russian republic and the USSR had hitherto seemed to be a symbiotic one. But in the winter of 1990–1, when Yeltsin had shown political courage in defending the claims to independence of the Baltic states, relations between the Russian and all-union authorities had reached a new low, symbolized by Yeltsin's call for Gorbachev's resignation just two months before the Novo-Ogarevo process got under way.

Yeltsin's increasing rejection of the union had been based not only on the more radical policies which he was prepared to pursue but, still more, on the fact that the all-union authorities, and Gorbachev in particular, stood between him and full power and authority in Russia, including the symbolically important occupancy of the Kremlin. Yet a political alliance between Gorbachev and Yeltsin in 1990 or earlier—not merely the tentative and extremely short-lived one during the month of August when their nominees worked on the '500 Days Programme'—would have been, it seemed to a number of Gorbachev's most reformist allies, the best defence against the counter-attack of the conservatives. But, as already noted in Chapter 6, Gorbachev had ruled out as unrealistic Shakhnazarov's suggestion that he create the post of Vice-President of the USSR specially for Yeltsin.[181]

Yet, despite the mutual suspicion of Gorbachev and Yeltsin, Gorbachev was enough of a pragmatist to realize by the late winter of 1990–1 that there was no hope of achieving the 'renewed federation' for which a majority of Soviet citizens had voted in the 17 March referendum without the co-operation of Yeltsin. Moreover, when the massive demonstration of 28 March in Moscow had, in Gorbachev's view, brought the capital to the edge of the abyss of civil conflict, he drew the conclusion that a new political initiative was needed. For his part, Yeltsin did not wish to be blamed for the breakup of the union—indeed, although he had a much more *direct* hand than Gorbachev in bringing it about, he was to succeed in diverting much of the odium in the post-Soviet reaction against it on to Gorbachev—and so he accepted Gorbachev's invitation to take part in the Novo-Ogarevo process. This was not the first attempt to draw up a new Union Treaty. Four drafts were published—in November 1990 and in March, June, and August 1991—but only the last two were the result of negotiations in which the republics played a full part in deciding the content of the document through the Novo-Ogarevo process. Each version devolved more power to the republics than its predecessor, and it was the last version—published on 14 August—and the imminent signing of it on 20 August which determined the timing of the failed *putsch*.[182]

The detailed work on the documents and the preparatory work for the meetings were extremely demanding and were carried out by a surprisingly small group of people chosen by Gorbachev. The four leading figures were Shakhnazarov, who, as well as being a shrewd politician and political analyst, was also a lawyer by academic background; Grigory Revenko, a Ukrainian by nationality who had the more common background for a party official of an engineering education and who had risen through the Komsomol and party apparatus of Ukraine, and who was an efficient organizer on whom Gorbachev came increasingly to rely (he replaced Boldin as his presidential chief of staff in the wake of the coup, and accompanied the former Soviet President to the Gorbachev Foundation in 1992); Vladimir Kudryavtsev, a prominent academic lawyer who was Vice-President of the Academy of Sciences and a former Director of the Institute of State and Law in Moscow; and the current Director of the Institute of State and Law, Boris Topornin.[183]

One of the most significant aspects of this process is that it was set in motion by Gorbachev without consultation with the Communist Party. The actual negotiations bypassed not only the CPSU—and the Russian Communist Party headed by Ivan Polozkov—but even, to a large extent, the legislatures of the union republics.[184] It was the turn of the hardliners, especially within the all-union executive but also in the legislature, to feel left out in the cold. KGB Chairman Kryuchkov told Fedor Burlatsky (whom he had known since they both worked for Andropov in the Socialist Countries Department of the Central Committee) that he found it increasingly difficult to meet with Gorbachev and get across to him his view that the survival of the union was at risk.[185] One of the many charges to be laid against Gorbachev by conservative forces in the wake of the collapse of the Soviet Union was that he had embarked on the Novo-Ogarevo process, in which—while there were concessions by both sides in the course of negotiations—many of the former prerogatives of the all-union authorities were yielded by Gorbachev to the republics.

While there were grounds for concern on the part of those who wished to retain a unified state that the centre had become too dependent for revenue on the goodwill of the republics, which were granted ownership of the natural resources of their territories, including mineral deposits, this treaty was, nevertheless, the last realistic hope for a voluntary agreement which would bring together the majority of republics and peoples who inhabited the territory of the USSR. Those letters—which had since 1922 stood for the Union of Soviet Socialist Republics—became in the draft treaty the Union of Soviet *Sovereign* Republics.[186] Even if the post of President of the USSR had become something more like the presidency of the European Union than the executive presidency created for Gorbachev in March 1990, that would still have been a significant office and one which, as the example of the European Union illustrates, would have left its incumbent with an extremely important diplomatic and co-ordinating role to play. Moreover, the direct election of the Soviet President would have given that person a political advantage not possessed by the President of the European Union, whose member states resist such popular election precisely because of the still greater independent standing it would bestow upon the victor. The fact that the President of the USSR, according to the August 1991 draft of the Union Treaty, was to be elected by the people of the union as a whole would have given the holder of the office an authority throughout the entire union territory that it would have been difficult for any one republican president—even that of Russia—to equal outside the boundaries of his own republic.

In Novo-Ogarevo itself, a willingness to compromise for the sake of agreement on the preservation of some kind of union was an encouraging break with the confrontational politics of the previous winter, and the tone of exchanges between Gorbachev and Yeltsin acquired a new civility. Among the presidents participating in the talks, Nursultan Nazarbaev of Kazakhstan played a particularly constructive role. It was often, says Shakhnazarov, thanks to him that agreement on a particular matter was reached, for both Yeltsin and Kravchuk were prepared to pay heed to what he had to say.[187] In spite of their history of rivalry, it was easier for Gorbachev and Yeltsin to reach an accord during these summer months of 1991 than for many of the people who stood behind them.[188] Gorbachev and his entourage were being urged by the leading figures in the party-state machine who had been flexing their muscles a few months earlier to be more unyielding. 'What have you done, boys?', a member of the Politburo said to Shakhnazarov. 'You have thrown away power, and with it the Union.'[189] Yeltsin, meantime, was being advised by *his* extremists and by his most ambitious supporters to take an aggressive line and not to compromise.[190] This was a struggle for power and place not only between rival top leaders but between rival teams, Yeltsin's being composed both of those who had broken away from the all-union political élite and of those who had become politicized only during the perestroika years (although the latter were to be almost entirely ousted by the former within two years of Russia becoming the Soviet Union's continuer state). They were no less anxious to occupy the seats of those who exercised power and influence close to Gorbachev than was Yeltsin to supplant the Soviet President, and they saw it as being in their interests to make it unambiguously clear that Yeltsin had become the number one politician in Russia.

Away from the Novo-Ogarevo process, Yeltsin was able to take a giant step towards demonstrating just that. In the elections for the presidency of Russia—which had been authorized in the March 1991 referendum and which were held on 12 June—he overwhelmingly defeated his five rivals, thus becoming the first Russian leader in history to make popular election the basis of his legitimacy. In retrospect, it was all the clearer that Gorbachev, and many of his advisers, had erred in March 1990 in deciding that in the first instance the Soviet President would be chosen by the members of the Congress of People's Deputies of the USSR and only in the following election by the people as a whole. There was, as it turned out, to be no second chance.

Yeltsin secured a decisive advantage over Gorbachev with his direct election to the Russian presidency. With 74.66 per cent of the Russian electorate participating, he secured 57.30 per cent of the votes on the first ballot, thus avoiding the need for a second ballot. The runner-up to Yeltsin was the former Chairman of the Council of Ministers, Nikolay Ryzhkov, and third was the hyperbolic ultra-populist Vladimir Zhirinovsky, making his début on the stage of Russian politics. Of significance was the fact that the main representative in the election of the views of those who launched the August *putsch*, the extremely hardline General

Albert Makashov, attracted only 3.74 per cent of the votes, and also that the person who was almost certainly Gorbachev's favoured candidate (although the Soviet President did not reveal how he had voted), Vadim Bakatin, came bottom of the poll with 3.24 per cent.[191] The fact that Bakatin, although an engaging personality and a liberal reformer, remained within the Communist Party was by this time a serious disadvantage for anyone appealing to that part of the electorate which was rejecting the old order. Yeltsin, who was far better known and at the height of his popularity, had left the CPSU the previous year and secured most of the anti-establishment vote. That he had courageously condemned the acts of violence by Soviet troops in the Baltic states the previous winter had apparently done him no harm with Russian voters. He appealed, moreover, not only to a reformist constituency. His success owed something also to his fitting the image of a strong leader traditionally favoured by Russians and to his choice as vice-presidential running-mate of Colonel (later General) Alexander Rutskoy, an Afghan veteran who had formed the group 'Communists for Democracy' within the Russian legislature.[192] Rutskoy, in a sense, balanced the ticket, for although not then as overt a nationalist as he was later to reveal himself to be, he offered some reassurance to voters who might have been worried by Yeltsin's apparent radicalism.

Five days after the Russian presidential election a remarkable attempt to reduce Gorbachev's power came from a quite different political direction from Yeltsin's and—in a foretaste of what was to happen in August—from within Gorbachev's own administration. The Prime Minister, Valentin Pavlov, without consulting the Soviet President beforehand, persuaded the Supreme Soviet to increase the powers of the Cabinet of Ministers—in particular, granting him and his ministerial colleagues the right of legislative initiative.[193] Pavlov argued that the only way to deal with the deteriorating economic position was to increase the power of the government, as distinct from the President, since Gorbachev's working day was already fourteen hours long and there was a lot that he had simply no time to do. The argument was not intrinsically implausible, although there was little reason to suppose that increased powers for Pavlov, as distinct from a new government and different Prime Minister, would have done anything to reverse the deterioration of the Soviet economy. Not without reason, Pavlov's speech was interpreted abroad as 'an abortive constitutional *coup d'état*', for it was to be countermanded by Gorbachev five days later in a speech to the Supreme Soviet in which he succeeded without difficulty in persuading the deputies to hand back the powers they had so recently granted to Pavlov. He was exceedingly mild in his criticisms of Pavlov, saying that the Prime Minister had gone further than he should because he had not thought through what he was saying, and added that there was no crisis in their relations.[194] But the upshot was that Gorbachev's constitutional powers remained unimpaired and Pavlov's were not enhanced. Although Gorbachev had realized soon after the appointment of Pavlov that his tenure of the prime ministership would have to be a short-lived one,[195] he was not ready to propose a replacement until after the signing of the Union Treaty, when he wanted someone who would be able to consolidate the links between the union and the republics—preferably Nazarbaev.[196]

Political confrontation sharpened the following month partly because the Novo-Ogarevo negotiations moved closer to agreement and the conservative forces grew more desperate at the prospect of a further reduction in the powers of the all-union authorities. Yeltsin played his part in stoking up their discontent by issuing a decree on 20 July banning the organizational units of political parties in the work-place throughout Russia. This was aimed, of course, at the Communist Party, whose primary party organizations were based on the place of employment rather than residential area, and, as such, was a reasonable follow-up to the removal of the Communist Party's 'leading role' from the Soviet Constitution the previous year.[197] Alexander Yakovlev described Yeltsin's action as a 'normal approach', and Gorbachev—even though he was still, of course, General Secretary of the Communist Party—reacted calmly, saying that he would only overrule Yeltsin's action with a decree of his own if the Committee for the Supervision of the Constitution judged it to be illegal.[198] That Committee was still considering the matter when the coup occurred and its failure settled the issue.

Increasingly, those who were trying to resist the transformation of the system and, in particular, the loss of power to the republics emphasized the importance of statehood and patriotism rather than Marxism-Leninism. This was the main thrust of an open letter published in the conservative newspaper *Sovetskaya Rossiya* on 23 July. Called 'A Word to the People', and signed not only by Russian nationalist writers—among them Yury Bondarev, Alexander Prokhanov, and Valentin Rasputin (who had been a member the previous year of Gorbachev's Presidential Council)—but also by two members of the government, the First Deputy Minister of Interior, General Boris Gromov, and a Deputy Minister of Defence, General Valentin Varennikov, the letter came close to being a call to arms against those who were reducing the country to 'slavery and subordination'. It attacked unnamed leaders of the Communist Party who were destroying their own party and handing over power to 'frivolous and clumsy parliamentarians'. In an even more thinly veiled reference to Gorbachev, the authors of the letter asked how the country had allowed into power those 'who seek advice and blessings across the seas'. (This was published exactly a week after Gorbachev arrived in London for a meeting with the leaders of the G7 countries, during which they promised to assist the Soviet Union's integration into the world economy, but—to Gorbachev's disappointment—offered little immediate help in concrete terms.) Most ominously, the open letter expressed the conviction that the army would not allow the destruction of the fatherland but would 'act as a reliable guarantor of security and as the mainstay of all the healthy forces of society'.[199]

In the case of Gromov and Varennikov, as with that of Pavlov, Gorbachev may have been biding his time until after the signing of the Union Treaty before removing them from office, but their signatures to such a letter merited instant dismissal from the government and it looked like a sign of weakness when Gorbachev allowed them to remain. That the words of the Russian writers and their allies both inside and outside government had a strong echo in the highest echelons of the Communist Party was not surprising and became abundantly clear at the plenary session of the Central Committee held on 25–6 July. Two reformist members of the Central Committee, Andrey Grachev and Otto Latsis, who explicitly attacked 'A Word to the People' in their speeches at the plenum, were heckled and had difficulty in making themselves heard.[200] The participants were also incensed by Yeltsin's banning of Communist primary party organizations and their condemnation of it took precedence over attacks on the social democratic character of the draft Party Programme which Gorbachev presented to the plenum, although that, too, drew criticism.

Gorbachev got agreement for the holding of an extraordinary Party Congress in November or December to adopt a new programme, the Congress at which (as noted earlier) he had expected the party to split into those who could accept an essentially social democratic orientation and those who could not. One reason why the decision to hold an early Party Congress was endorsed was that many of the Central Committee members were looking forward to electing a new General Secretary then and to abandoning the draft programme under a new leadership.[201] In his speech to the Central Committee plenum Gorbachev made few concessions indeed to what was undoubtedly majority opinion within that body. He defended the Novo-Ogarevo process and, facing up to the past, stated that 'our party indisputably bears responsibility for the fact that it was not able to erect a barrier to despotism and allowed itself to be used as an instrument of totalitarianism'.[202] Gorbachev also accused those who expressed concern about the 'social democratization' of the party of 'communist fundamentalism'.[203] He pointed out that the old idea of the Communist Party as political vanguard had lost its meaning and that it was only by political persuasion that it could get its members elected to positions of authority. It was time, he said, to accept that the epoch when the masses had no other means of improving their lot than by storming the Bastille or the Winter Palace was long past.[204]

Boldly, he drew the Central Committee's attention to the fact that in the programme he was recommending to the party the goal of communism was, in effect, being abandoned as unrealistic. He argued that Marxism-Leninism, which had been turned into 'a collection of canonical texts', had to be supplemented by the riches of 'the world's socialist and democratic thought'. Realization of 'the socialist idea' had to be within the context of 'the common development of civilization'. The term 'communism', he admitted, was mentioned only in passing in the Draft Programme. That was because 'our experience, and not only ours, provides no grounds for thinking that this aim is realistically attainable in the foreseeable future'.[205] In order to provide a link between the founding fathers and his current thinking, Gorbachev drew upon a striking phrase from an unimpeachable source which he did not trouble to name (Marx and Engels, *The Communist Manifesto*) that in no way contradicted his emphasis on a socialism inseparable from liberty and democracy. What he chose to call 'the communist idea' was the maxim that 'the free development of each is the condition for the free development of all', and this, he said, remained an attractive aspiration for all mankind.[206] Not content with jettisoning the goal of communism, apart from the well-known words of Marx with which even the most libertarian of thinkers would be hard put to disagree, Gorbachev also dared to invite the Central Committee members to face up to the fact that the party could find itself out of power, observing that, where they failed to be elected, they must constitute 'a constructive opposition', supporting the decisions of the authorities when they were sensible and opposing them when this was necessary 'for the defence of the interests of working people'.[207] Many intellectuals in the Soviet Union had come to conclusions such as these by 1990 and 1991, but it was far less easy for the General Secretary of the Soviet Communist Party not only to do so but also to present them publicly to those whose claim to rule had rested on the belief that history was entirely on their side and that the victory of Communism was inevitable.

In a more down-to-earth preparation for the immediate future, Gorbachev held an important meeting at Novo-Ogarevo with Yeltsin and Nazarbaev at the end of July. They discussed changes in the government which should be made after the signing of the Union Treaty. Among those in leadership positions who were considered prime candidates for replacement were the Prime Minister, Pavlov, the Chairman of the KGB, Kryuchkov, and the Minister of Defence, Yazov. The idea of Nazarbaev taking the place of Pavlov was mooted by Yeltsin, and Gorbachev went along with it, although Nazarbaev himself reserved his position. It was agreed that further discussions on this and the composition of the union government as a whole would take place after the signing of the Union Treaty.[208] Yeltsin suspected, with good reason, that this conversation was being recorded by the KGB. Gorbachev and Nazarbaev scoffed at the idea at the time, but later accepted that Yeltsin had been right.[209] The tape of the conversation, along with many others, was found after the failed coup in one of Boldin's safes in the Kremlin.[210] The information the confidential meeting conveyed may well have been a stimulus to Kryuchkov, in particular, to take a leading role in organizing the plot.[211]

Gorbachev left for his holiday residence of Foros on the Crimean coast on 4 August,[212] planning to return to Moscow on 19 August for the Union Treaty signing ceremony the following day.[213] The mood among reformers was mixed. At a meeting of a recently formed pressure group, the Movement for Democratic Reforms, held on 17 August, Shevardnadze, Yakovlev, and others agreed that 'a right-wing coup was an imminent threat',[214] even though they had no concrete evidence of what was being prepared—other than, for example, the move of the Central Control Commission of the CPSU, which had just occurred, to expel Yakovlev from the Communist Party and such open challenges as that contained in 'A Word to the People'.[215] In contrast, Anatoly Sobchak—who had been democratically elected Mayor of Leningrad (soon to be St Petersburg again)—looked ahead with optimism when he spoke on 14 August about the forthcoming signing of the Union Treaty. Referring to this as a 'historic event', he said: 'I would like to see our treaty as long-lived as the American Declaration of Independence, and serve as the same reliable political and legal basis of the renovated Union.'[216] It was, however, to make sure that this 'historic event' became a non-event that the coup was launched.

From coup to collapse

This is not the place for a detailed history of the coup, on which there is already a voluminous literature, not all of which succeeds in distinguishing the wood from the trees.[217] Moreover, the focus here is on Gorbachev, although he was kept in isolation at his presidential holiday home on the Crimean coast. Unusually, therefore, during his time as Soviet leader, he was off-stage, while Yeltsin was at the centre of it, playing the leading role in the resistance to the *putschists* in Moscow. It is significant, nevertheless, that suborning or isolating Gorbachev was seen by the conspirators who moved against him as their first task (his enormous international reputation having been a major factor inhibiting them from more overtly overthrowing him). Thus, the coup began for Gorbachev and his family on 18 August and for Yeltsin and the rest of the country on 19 August. The plotters attempted to intimidate Gorbachev into declaring emergency rule and, having failed to do so, kept him in segregation and lied to the world that he was too ill to be able to continue to carry out his presidential duties.

The idea of emergency rule was not new. Gorbachev had earlier taken part in numerous discussions with the harder-line members of his administration in which they had urged upon him the declaration of 'presidential rule' or a state of emergency (each intended to imply resort to repressive measures to restore 'order'), but, to the dismay of Kryuchkov and the others, he had always refrained from doing so. In fact, while prepared to talk publicly about such a possibility in Lithuania as a way of attempting to slow down the movement towards complete independence of the Baltic states and of 'tranquillizing the hardliners', Gorbachev was opposed in principle to the implementation of emergency rule. Just a few days before the coup occurred, Gorbachev had, with the help of Chernyaev, who was with him in Foros, completed a long article he intended to publish shortly after the signing of the Union Treaty in which, *inter alia*, he observed: 'The introduction of a state of emergency, in which even some supporters of *perestroika*, not to mention those who preach the ideology of dictatorship, see a way out of the crisis, would be a fatal move and the way to civil war. Frankly speaking, behind the appeals for a state of emergency it is not difficult sometimes to detect a search for a return to the political system that existed in the pre-*perestroika* period.'[218]

Gorbachev's first intimation that something untoward was happening was when the head of his bodyguard, KGB General Vladimir Medvedev (who had not been part of the plot and was as surprised as Gorbachev by the arrival of uninvited guests) informed him at ten minutes to five on the afternoon of 18 August that a group of people had arrived at Foros demanding to see him.[219] When Gorbachev asked why he had let them inside the gates, he was told that Plekhanov (who, as noted earlier, headed the department of the KGB responsible for the personal security of the leadership) was with them.[220] Gorbachev was working in his office at Foros at the time. A little earlier he had telephoned Shakhnazarov, who was on holiday a few miles further down the coast, to discuss the speech he was preparing for the Union Treaty signing ceremony on 20 August and to ask him if he would join him on the plane to Moscow the next day.[221] Wishing to find out who had sent visitors he was not expecting, Gorbachev went to the array of telephones in his office, which included a special government line, a line for strategic and satellite communications, a normal line for outside calls, and the internal line for the Foros holiday complex. All were dead.[222]

Gorbachev told first his wife and then his daughter and son-in-law what the situation appeared to be and that it was clearly very serious. Although this event, when it happened, came out of the blue so far as Gorbachev was concerned, he had thought often about the fate of Khrushchev and had been well aware of the possibility (especially at an earlier stage of his leadership before a wider public had been politicized) of an attempt to overthrow him. He informed his family that he would 'not give in to any kind of blackmail, nor to any threats or pressure'.[223] The fact that, indeed, he did not, Chernyaev later remarked, meant that the coup failed on day one. The plotters were able to bring tanks on to the streets of Moscow, but did not know what to do next.[224] Their favoured scenario had been to intimidate Gorbachev into endorsing emergency rule, leaving them free to do the 'dirty work' for a time, after which (or so they told him) he could return to Moscow.[225]

The person who made that remark was Oleg Baklanov, Gorbachev's deputy head of the Security Council and the most important representative of the military-industrial complex in the leadership, who acted as if he were the senior member of the delegation.[226] The others in the group were Politburo member Oleg Shenin, Gorbachev's chief of staff, Valery Boldin, the Deputy Minister of Defence, Valentin Varennikov, and Plekhanov. Since Gorbachev had issued no instruction for the group to come up to see him, they spent some time waiting. Gorbachev used it, first, in the unavailing attempt to make telephone calls and then in speaking with his family. Eventually the group made their own way to his office and arrived at the door uninvited—'an unheard-of lack of respect', as Gorbachev later put it.[227]

Gorbachev began by ordering Plekhanov out, a command he obeyed, and asked the others who had sent them. He was told that they had come from the State Committee for the State of Emergency. Gorbachev pointed out that neither he nor the Supreme Soviet had set up such a committee, but in response was informed that he must either issue a decree establishing a state of emergency or hand over his powers to the Vice-President. Later in the conversation Varennikov demanded his resignation, to which Gorbachev responded: 'You'll get neither one thing nor the other out of me—tell that to the people who sent you here.' At the end of the conversation, Gorbachev recalled, 'using the strongest language that the Russians always use in such circumstances, I told them where to go. And that was the end of it.'[228] Varennikov actually saw fit to complain to the legal investigator of his case that Gorbachev had used 'unparliamentary expressions' in addressing him and the other members of the delegation.[229] Gorbachev's own account of his conduct during the meeting with Baklanov and the others was confirmed during the individual questioning of the coup participants by the Russian procuracy, even though later the conspirators' predictable—although absurd—defence tactic was to claim that Gorbachev was a willing participant in the coup against himself![230]

Both in the course of the investigation of the coup and, indeed, in the conversation the delegation which visited Foros had with Gorbachev, it was made abundantly clear that the timing of the unauthorized declaration of emergency rule was designed to prevent the Union Treaty from being signed on 20 August. A number of concrete steps, which would have included governmental changes, were due to follow rapidly. Gorbachev had already arranged a session of the Federation Council for the day after the Union Treaty ceremony. If the imminent signing of the Treaty, combined with the fact that Gorbachev was out of Moscow, determined the date of the coup, it was far from the only cause of the action. Each member of the State Committee for the State of Emergency had his own particular interest either in ending Gorbachev's presidency or in bringing him under the control of their self-empowered group (which, given their view that he had been destroying both the Soviet system and the Soviet state, would have been only a temporary and partial reprieve for Gorbachev on the way to total ousting and almost certain imprisonment or worse).[231]

Of the group which visited Gorbachev, only Baklanov was one of the eight members of the State Committee for the State of Emergency. The others on that temporarily ruling Committee were Kryuchkov, who had been the major initiator of the plot; the Minister of Defence, Yazov; the Prime Minister, Pavlov; the Minister of Interior, Pugo; the Vice-President, Yanaev; Vasily Starodubtsev, the head of the 'Peasants' Union', which in reality was a pressure group in defence of collective farms and opposed to private farming; and Alexander Tizyakov, a leading representative of state industry and the head of a group of defence-related plants. Both Starodubtsev and Tizyakov had been among the signatories of 'A Word to the People', as had one of the members of the delegation who visited Gorbachev, General Varennikov.

Gorbachev was especially shocked by the participation of Kryuchkov, Yazov, and, of course, Boldin, all of whom he had ill-advisedly trusted.[232] Gorbachev's guilt in relation to the coup consisted, indeed, of a number of bad appointments and misplaced trust. The choices of Pavlov, Pugo, and Yanaev were serious mistakes, although the earlier promotions of Yazov and Kryuchkov were more understandable. The error in the latter two cases was to *retain* faith in them—Kryuchkov, particularly—when it was clear to a number of serious reformers that they were hostile to the kind of transformative political change on which the Soviet Union had embarked from 1989. It is, however, likely that any plausible candidate for Minister of Defence in 1987 (when Yazov was appointed) or for Chairman of the KGB in 1988 (when Kryuchkov succeeded Chebrikov) would have come to the defence of their institutional interests. In some ways what is most remarkable is that Gorbachev kept their advocacy and protests largely within constitutional bounds for so long. The military-industrial complex was almost bound to view with alarm Gorbachev's efforts to cut it down to a more economical size, not to mention the withdrawal of Soviet troops from the whole of Eastern Europe, culminating in the unification of Germany within NATO. The KGB could not be other than concerned by the loss of their client organizations in Eastern Europe, by the process of democratization and pluralization in the Soviet Union which delegitimized most of their domestic political surveillance and controls, and by the loss of power of the centre (including, increasingly, the

KGB centre) to the Soviet republics, several of which threatened to become independent states.

If one of the first laws of bureaucratic politics is that 'where you stand depends upon where you sit',[233] it is reasonable to suggest that the participation of the heads of these two organizations had a structural rather than a purely personal or idiosyncratic basis. Gorbachev, moreover, had by no means a free hand when he appointed a Minister of Defence or KGB chief, especially when—as in these two cases—he was not yet Soviet President. When he was later elected to that office by the Congress of People's Deputies in March 1990, he acquired an authority independent of that granted him by the party Central Committee and Politburo, to whom he had in the 1980s been more fully accountable. The Soviet establishment were not ready for a civilian head of the army, and, although in the past KGB chairmen had more often than not been drawn from the party apparatus, they had rapidly 'gone native' and become spokesmen for KGB interests.

At the time of the appointment of Kryuchkov, this particular choice looked to Gorbachev like the best way of ensuring that the KGB stayed on his side. No one had ingratiated himself more with the General Secretary than Kryuchkov, who claimed that, in contrast with Chebrikov, *he* was a committed supporter of perestroika. Gorbachev had also regarded it then as an advantage that Kryuchkov was quite bright, that Andropov had thought highly of him, and that his background was in foreign intelligence rather than domestic repression. Yazov was distinctly less intelligent than Kryuchkov—'no Spinoza', as Yakovlev ironically put it[234]—but Gorbachev had believed him to be reliable and loyal. When Yazov was approached by Kryuchkov, however, he found himself torn between, on the one hand, loyalty to his basically conservative beliefs and the military institutional interest as he perceived it and, on the other, loyalty to Gorbachev and constitutional authority. The former set of loyalties won.

During the period in which Gorbachev was held in isolation his bodyguards 'found some old radio receivers in the service areas, fixed up aerials and started to pick up foreign broadcasts', while his son-in-law, Anatoly, 'managed to listen to a Western station on his pocket Sony'.[235] Thus, from the BBC and Radio Liberty in particular, as well as from Voice of America, Gorbachev was able to learn more of what was going on than he could from Soviet radio and television, which had been tightly censored from the morning of 19 August by Kravchenko on the instructions of 'the Committee'. Plekhanov had left his deputy, General Generalov, in charge of the fresh detachment of KGB officers at Foros, and, although Generalov was a long-standing acquaintance of Chernyaev, he made it plain to him that there would be no signing of the Union Treaty and that nobody would be allowed to leave Foros. Chernyaev argued that as a member of parliament—he was a deputy in the Congress of People's Deputies of the USSR as well as being Gorbachev's aide—he was especially entitled to leave the compound, but this did not cut any ice.[236] A demand by Gorbachev communicated to Generalov on 19 August that his telephones be immediately restored and that a plane be provided so that he could fly to Moscow received no reply.[237]

Gorbachev's presidential car, containing excellent telephone communications, remained in its garage with armed guards responsible to General

Generalov in front of it.[238] Not only Chernyaev, who had been staying in the same complex of residences as Shakhnazarov a few miles further along the coast but who happened to be at Foros when the coup began, but the entire domestic staff, who lived locally, were not allowed to leave the Foros compound for forty-eight hours.[239] Having heard the conspirators' claim that he was too ill to work and that, accordingly, Yanaev had assumed the duties of President, Gorbachev—with the help of his son-in-law, who had a video-camera—recorded a statement in which he denounced the misinformation about his health and said that what had occurred could not be described 'as anything but a *coup d'état'*. All subsequent acts were, accordingly, illegal, since neither the President nor the Congress of People's Deputies had given Yanaev the authority he claimed. Gorbachev called on Lukyanov to summon urgently the Supreme Soviet and Congress of People's Deputies of the USSR to consider the situation that had arisen, and, in the meantime, he demanded the immediate suspension of the activity of the State Committee for the State of Emergency.[240] He made four recordings of his message and the film was then cut into four parts, so that different people could try to get a copy out.[241] In fact, the film was seen by the outside world only after the conspirators had been arrested, so quickly did the coup collapse.

Later the members of the State Committee for the State of Emergency claimed that Gorbachev had in fact been free to leave Foros at any time and that his isolation was self-imposed. A number of radical democrats—anxious to speed up Gorbachev's replacement by, rather than co-operation with, Yeltsin—also took up this theme, which was inherently absurd, although some foreign observers were either gullible enough or sufficiently ill disposed towards Gorbachev to take it seriously. Not only is there abundant evidence that neither Gorbachev nor anyone loyal to him was free to leave the vicinity of Foros during the coup, but also the very idea that the self-proclaimed new leadership would have been quite content for Gorbachev to turn up in Moscow to announce that everything they had been telling the world—in particular, concerning Gorbachev's serious ill health—was a pack of lies is an insult to normal intelligence. Even Yeltsin, who missed few opportunities to embroider the truth in order to enhance his own standing and diminish Gorbachev's in his two volumes of memoirs,[242] fully accepts in the book written several years after the coup that Gorbachev was a victim of a plot against him (although guilty of making bad appointments and of earlier indecision).[243] That is in spite of the fact that Yeltsin made sure he had access to all relevant information. Gorbachev's presidential archive was taken over by him in December 1991, and already in August 1991, following the coup, one of the first archives to be seized was that of the Stavropol territorial party organization.[244]

In reality the coup came as a great shock to Gorbachev and his family. The trauma proved especially great for Raisa Maksimovna Gorbachev. Few people anywhere assumed on 19 August that the coup would be over in a few days, and it would have been rash for the Soviet President's family to have done so, although Gorbachev himself has always argued that he had been confident that the conspirators could not succeed. But desperate people might have resorted to desperate measures, and Gorbachev and his wife had every reason to believe that their long-term liberty and possibly their lives were in great danger. The strain reached its climax just as the coup was collapsing on 21 August. On that last day, when the tanks left the streets of Moscow and pressure was relaxed on the Russian White House where Yeltsin had become the symbol of resistance for Russia and the world, a delegation from the Russian parliament—headed by the Vice-President, Alexander Rutskoy, and including also two prominent Gorbachev allies, Vadim Bakatin and Yevgeny Primakov—and a group of the leading conspirators each took off for Foros, both sides hoping to reach Gorbachev before the other. Gorbachev wrote: 'At the moment when the BBC announced that a group of plotters were on their way apparently for the purpose of showing the Russian delegation and the Soviet people and the public at large the state Gorbachev was in we all took it to mean that some treachery had been thought up. It was at that moment that Raisa Maksimovna suffered a serious attack of pain from which she took some time to recover.'[245] Raisa Gorbachev suffered a nervous collapse and partial paralysis, believing that the fact that the conspirators were on their way to see them meant that they were going to reduce her husband's health to the state they had claimed it was in. (Until such practices were stopped during the Gorbachev era it was far from unusual for political prisoners to be held in mental asylums and to be given injections which reduced them for a time to a zombie-like condition and often permanently undermined their health.)[246]

Gorbachev, with his usual resilience, survived the ordeal of the coup psychologically and physically unscathed, but it took him some time to realize what a devastating blow it had dealt him politically. Yeltsin had not only been the person who was in contact with world leaders during Gorbachev's detention, but he had strengthened further his standing with the Russian people. Even deputies in the Russian parliament who were relatively hostile to him and who had voted against Yeltsin as Chairman of the Supreme Soviet in 1990 and were to be in open revolt against him in 1993 recognized him as a victor to whom they had better offer obeisance in the weeks after 21 August. Yeltsin and his closest supporters were ready, what is more, to press home the advantage this great political victory had given them. Even if Gorbachev had adapted himself to the changed atmosphere in Moscow more quickly than he did on his return from Foros, it is doubtful if a struggle for power—which, in the new circumstances, Yeltsin was likely to win—could have been avoided.

It was still the case in these last months of the Soviet Union's existence, as it had been earlier, that co-operation and a willingness to compromise between Gorbachev and Yeltsin, for the sake of preserving as much of an economic and political union as could be achieved voluntarily, would have been in the interests of a majority of Soviet citizens. Gorbachev was, indeed, more ready for such co-operation than was Yeltsin, who—following the defeat of the *putschists* and the political capital he was able to make out of the fact that these were people whom Gorbachev had appointed[247]—was increasingly unwilling to accord Gorbachev even a share of power, but the history of their relations was such that it was difficult for either person to put the past behind him. Moreover, as Shakhnazarov perceptively remarked, 'magnanimity is not in the character of Yeltsin and humility is not in the character of Gorbachev'.[248]

The coup itself had failed for a number of reasons. Among them undoubtedly were the fact that Yeltsin, with the legitimacy of recent popular election as Russian President behind him, provided a rallying-point for resistance to those ready to resort to repressive methods to restore the power which had been slipping fast from their grasp; the willingness of several hundred thousand people to take the risk of coming out on to the streets of Moscow and Leningrad in defiance of the orders of the State Committee for the State of Emergency and thus raise the political costs of military action; the lack of a plausible leader, still less a popular one, among the *putschists*, together with their indecisiveness (ironically enough, since that was one of their list of complaints about Gorbachev); the fact that jamming of foreign radio had been ended by Gorbachev and so objective information about the coup was readily available to the Soviet population; and the strong international support for Gorbachev and Yeltsin. The fruits of several years of liberty and democratization had also emboldened Russian journalists to produce underground newspapers and led a sufficient number of citizens not to accept that their political destinies could be decided once again by a small group of people 'up there'. But nothing was more important in bringing about the failure of the coup than Gorbachev's refusal to provide its leaders with any shred of legitimacy. This, in turn, meant that the army and the KGB were more divided than they otherwise would have been. Gorbachev's 'tragedy' lay, as Chernyaev observes, in the fact that on 18 August Gorbachev dealt 'in essence the decisive blow against the *putsch*' but having spurned 'the "services" of the traitors', he had by the evening of 21 August 'lost what was left of his own power'.[249]

Gorbachev made two political errors immediately upon his return to Moscow, although allowance has to be made for his isolation in Foros, since even foreign radio broadcasts were no substitute for direct experience of the changed mood in the capital. The first mistake was, after returning by plane to Moscow on the night of 21/2 August, not to go straight to the Russian White House. By the time he did go on 23 August he found Yeltsin determined to squeeze the maximum political advantage from the occasion and to evoke a response from the deputies in the Russian legislature which was part enthusiastic and part fawning. Gorbachev would almost certainly have received a more sympathetic reception if he had made the White House his first port of call after his flight landed in Moscow, since that building had been the physical and symbolic centre of resistance to the coup. It is noteworthy, however, that no one in the Russian delegation who took part in the relief of Foros—and with whom he returned in the plane in which they had flown to the Crimea, rather than in his own presidential aircraft, which had once again become available to him—suggested this or mentioned that he might be expected at the White House.[250] (The group of *putschists*, who had taken a plane of their own to the Crimea, did in fact reach Foros before the Russian delegation. By this time, however, they had lost the will for further desperate measures and it seems that they merely wished to get their excuses and explanations in first—before Gorbachev heard the views of those who had resisted their take-over. But Gorbachev refused to meet them and, apart from those who enjoyed parliamentary immunity—which was later legally rescinded—they returned to Moscow under arrest.)

Gorbachev's second, and more important, mistake was to revert to a familiar theme in his first press conference after returning to Moscow and speak about the need for 'renewal' of the Communist Party.[251] Gorbachev had not for some time believed that the Communist Party should be a ruling party in the old sense; indeed, he had increasingly bypassed it. He hoped instead to see a reformed, essentially social democratic party—several million strong—emerge out of the old CPSU. He was aware that he both lacked and needed a strong party as a political base and initially believed that, following the failed coup, it would be easier for him to win over the bulk of the party, since the hardliners had been so discredited.[252]

What Gorbachev failed to realize was that the Communist Party as such had, in the immediate aftermath of the coup, lost what had been left of its credibility. Almost all of the leading office-holders in the party had either supported the coup or had done nothing to resist it. The party was, accordingly, in the view of a majority both of the population and of political activists (including many, such as Alexander Yakovlev, who had themselves been senior party officials), beyond salvation. Gorbachev's remarks about the party were misinterpreted by some to mean that he was 'still a Communist at heart' when, in fact, he had done more than anyone to dismantle the distinctively Communist system. But to insist on reform of the party at a time when most people wished to see it simply swept aside undoubtedly did him further political damage. Yakovlev told Gorbachev in private that to talk of the 'renewal' of the party was 'like offering first aid to a corpse'.[253]

The remaining months of 1991 saw a further erosion both of Gorbachev's power and of what was left of the central authorities of the Soviet Union. At the meeting of the Russian parliament which Gorbachev addressed on 23 August, he insisted—as had, indeed, been true—that the Communist Party was not an undifferentiated body of people and that its members should not collectively be held responsible for the sins of its leadership (of which by this time he was better aware). Nevertheless, Yeltsin issued decrees there and then suspending the activity of the Russian Communist Party and seizing the assets of the CPSU. A day later Gorbachev, responding to the persuasion of colleagues such as Yakovlev as well as to the pressure from Yeltsin, resigned as General Secretary and called on the Central Committee of the CPSU to disband itself. At the meeting of the Russian legislature which Gorbachev addressed on 23 August Yeltsin also insisted that Gorbachev read the minutes of a meeting of the Council of Ministers, held on 19 August, from which it became very clear that almost every member—whether from conviction, cowardice, or, as a number would later claim, lack of information—had gone along with the coup. Yeltsin's insistence that these were Gorbachev's own appointees was not denied by the Soviet President, although it was true only in a formal sense. Most of the ministers (a majority of them responsible for different branches of the economy) had been chosen by Ryzhkov and had more recently been reappointed (along with some new members) by Gorbachev in association with the Federation Council, on which the heads of the union republics, including Yeltsin, sat.

There were several suicides by leading supporters of the coup, among them that of Pugo on 22 August and of Marshal Akhromeev, who on the same day wrote a dignified letter to Gorbachev explaining why he believed that everything to which he had devoted his life was being destroyed—he had been deeply concerned about the way things were going from 1990 and now all was lost; accordingly, he considered he had no honourable alternative to this last act he was about to perform.[254] Many more people simply lost office, and the *putschists* spent varying periods of time in prison, although all were eventually released without ever having been convicted by a court. Among those gaoled as an accomplice of the State Committee for the State of Emergency was Anatoly Lukyanov, who had indeed taken part in the discussions with Kryuchkov and others on the eve of the coup and who chose that time to attack the Union Treaty which should have been about to be signed and in the negotiation of which he had participated. (By the mid-1990s those who took part in the August 1991 conspiracy were being accorded heroes' receptions in conservative circles in post-Soviet Russia.)

There were also, however, welcome returns to high office of those who had been close to Gorbachev until the winter of 1990–1. Alexander Yakovlev rejoined Gorbachev at once as his principal adviser. Importantly, Vadim Bakatin, whose appointment to such an office would have been fiercely resisted before the coup, was made Chairman of the KGB in an effort to bring it under democratic political control, to remove the most active pro-*putschists*, and to divide its functions among several organizations in order to curb its power. Bakatin had no experience of the KGB and brought in as his adviser Oleg Kalugin, a KGB general who had thrown in his lot with the democrats at the end of the 1980s and had been removed from office and kept under surveillance subsequently. (He was one of those who joined the resistance at the Moscow White House on 19 August, and it was he who awakened Alexander Yakovlev at 6.20 that morning to tell him that a coup had taken place. Kalugin and Yakovlev had been in a group of Soviet exchange students at Columbia University, New York, in 1958–9, Yakovlev as a genuine, albeit already mature, student and Kalugin as a young KGB agent.[255]) Bessmertnykh was dismissed as Foreign Minister for having failed to condemn the coup and he was replaced, first, by Boris Pankin— who, as Ambassador in Prague, had been virtually alone among Soviet ambassadors in coming out against the *putschists*. A rather colourless figure, he was replaced in November by none other than Eduard Shevardnadze, returning to his old post of Soviet Foreign Minister, evidently not imagining that the state he was once again representing would cease to exist at the end of the following month.

Gorbachev was now no longer constrained by the hardliners in his choice of ministers and advisers. The irony was that he was able to assemble his strongest team (which included the former Prime Minister of Russia, Ivan Silaev, as the new Soviet Prime Minister) at a time when his power was but a shadow of what it had been even in the months preceding the coup, not to speak of a year or two earlier. The change in the balance of forces between the union and Russia, and between the Soviet and Russian presidents, was reflected in the fact that major appointments—such as that of KGB Chairman and Foreign Minister—required the approval of Yeltsin as well as of Gorbachev. Yeltsin could not actually object to Shevardnadze's return, given his record, but in fact there was concern within the Yeltsin team that Gorbachev might—against all the odds—be rebuilding the credibility of the union authorities.[256]

The desire of Yeltsin and of the Russian government to replace, rather than share power with, a Gorbachev administration was, however, reinforced by the accelerated trend towards independence of the other Soviet republics. The coup had in two crucial respects been a stimulus to the breakup of the Soviet Union. On the one hand, it had shown that there could yet be attempts to impose the old repressive rule from Moscow, so that the degree of *de facto* independence which most republics already enjoyed might once more be denied to them. Second, Yeltsin had taken a number of decisions of all-union significance in his capacity as Russian President and this, too, was worrying for republican leaderships sensitive about inroads on their sovereignty.

The independence of the Baltic states was the first to be officially recognized by the Soviet Union following the coup; this was done on 6 September. Four days later Armenia declared its independence. Moldova and Georgia already considered themselves to be independent. Gorbachev had actually succeeded in getting the Novo-Ogarevo process going again, although now the scales were tipped ever more heavily against him than before. The Central Asian republics and Kazakhstan were now the main advocates of preserving a union and, once again, Nazarbaev was a leading advocate of the desirability of this. Yeltsin, too, appeared to go along with the idea of a confederation and common market—a Union of Sovereign States rather than the Union of Soviet Sovereign Republics, as the draft Union Treaty which should have been signed on 20 August had it. In the months between the coup and the collapse of the union Gorbachev and Yeltsin actually shared the Kremlin, an arrangement which the latter clearly intended to be a temporary one. While Yeltsin went through the motions of participation in the Novo-Ogarevo process, behind the scenes he and his closest advisers were preparing to take full power in Russia rather than to share it with even much weakened union authorities.[257]

Although the chances of preserving a Soviet state had been greatly reduced by the activities of the *putschists*—in spite of the fact that to preserve such a state had been their chief aim—Gorbachev was prepared to accept as a fall-back a political entity akin to the European Union. Recent as well as past history told heavily against this, however. One of the decisive blows against preservation of a union was a referendum and presidential election in Ukraine on 1 December. Whereas a large majority of citizens of Ukraine who had participated in the March referendum had voted for a 'renewed union', approximately 90 per cent now opted for independence. There was still some doubt as to whether all those who voted in this way really wanted total separation from Russia and the union, but there is evidence that the Ukrainian leadership were encouraged by members of Yeltsin's team to state explicitly that this was exactly what it wished.[258] Indeed, there had been a vast shift of opinion in favour of independence as a result of the political events of recent months, especially those of August.

Gorbachev and Yeltsin had agreed that the union was unthinkable without Ukraine, but they had said this for different reasons. For Gorbachev it was because he not only wanted Ukraine in the union (and in a televised appeal to Ukrainians emphasized the Ukrainian blood in his own family[259]) but also because he could not bring himself to believe that Ukraine would, in the end, choose to sever its historic links with Russia. Even within his group of trusted associates he argued that Ukraine's borders were safe only within a union with Russia and with the force of his advocacy persuaded himself—as Andrey Grachev, now his presidential press spokesman in succession to Ignatenko, suggested happened not infrequently—if not all his interlocutors.[260] Yeltsin, more realistically, believed that Ukraine really would opt for independence. Agreement, therefore, that the union was unimaginable without Ukraine would make it possible to sweep away what was left of the union, including its President.

The final blow to the preservation of a union came when the presidents of Russia, Ukraine, and Belorussia—Yeltsin, Kravchuk, and Shushkevich—held a meeting near Brest in Belorussia (or Belarus, as it had become known) on 8 December and announced that the Soviet Union was ceasing to exist and that they were going to establish in its place a Commonwealth of Independent States. Gorbachev was outraged that such a decision should have been taken unconstitutionally as well as unilaterally—without consultation either with him or with the heads of the other republics still within the union. Nazarbaev was likewise offended that he had been excluded from the decision, although he was clearly going to remain President of Kazakhstan whatever happened, and it was now evident that there would soon be no state left for Gorbachev to head. In the remaining weeks of his leadership Gorbachev gradually reconciled himself to the fact that his presidency was coming to an end and argued for the creation of institutional structures in the new 'Commonwealth' which would give it some meaning. In fact, in the short term at least, these were to remain very weak.

Gorbachev announced on 18 December that he would resign as Soviet President as soon as the transition from union to Commonwealth had been completed. At a meeting in Alma-Ata on 21 December, to which Gorbachev was not invited, the number of states willing to join the Commonwealth—which had gradually been increasing—reached eleven, all the former Soviet republics except the three Baltic states and Georgia. Gorbachev's departure from office came on 25 December when he signed a decree divesting himself of his authority as President of the USSR and transferring his powers as Commander-in-Chief of the armed forces to Yeltsin, together with control of nuclear weapons (which passed to Russia as not only the largest successor state to the Soviet Union but in this respect, and in respect of its seat on the Security Council at the United Nations, the 'continuer state').

In a televised resignation speech on the evening of 25 December Gorbachev told his fellow citizens that he had tried to combine defending the independence of peoples and sovereignty of republics with preservation of the union and that he could not accept its dismemberment. He regretted the fact that the old system had crumbled before a new system could be made to work and deplored the August coup which had aggravated the existing crisis and, most perniciously, brought about 'the collapse of statehood'. Gorbachev acknowledged that mistakes had been made and that many things could have been done better, but he also listed the achievements of 'the transition period'. These included the ending of the Cold War, the liquidation of 'the totalitarian system', the breakthrough to democratic reforms, the recognition of the paramount importance of human rights, and movement towards a market economy.

The Soviet flag was lowered from the Kremlin that same day and replaced by the Russian tricolour. By 27 December, when Gorbachev returned to the Kremlin to clear his desk, he found his office already occupied by Boris Yeltsin. Gorbachev had believed that he had the use of it until 30 December. But these were the minutiae of a political rivalry which had been resolved in Yeltsin's favour. More momentous events had occurred. In less than seven years a vast country and much of the world had changed immeasurably. How much that was due to Gorbachev has been the major theme of his book. How his years in power should be evaluated is the subject of the next, and concluding, chapter.

Chapter 9

Conclusions

IT is quite common in Russia today, and even in some quarters in the West, to regard Gorbachev as a political failure.[1] Superficially, such a view seems entirely plausible. Nothing was further from Gorbachev's mind in 1985 than that the Soviet Union should cease to exist. On the contrary, he wanted it to enter the next millennium 'as a great and prosperous power'.[2] He wished to reform the Soviet system, not to destroy it, and he had a particular desire to achieve qualitative improvement in its economic performance. In these very important respects outcomes were far removed from Gorbachev's intentions.

Thus, the case for viewing Gorbachev as a failure rests, above all, on a comparison between his goals when he became General Secretary of the Soviet Communist Party and what actually happened during his years at the top of the Soviet political system. Even by these criteria, however, things are not so simple. As I have argued in earlier chapters, Gorbachev was a more serious reformer as early as 1984–5 than was generally appreciated at the time either in the Soviet Union or in the West, and he was interested not only in economic reform but also in glasnost (although, then, more as an instrument of reform than as a desirable end in itself), in a liberalization of the political system (for which he used the term 'democratization', although that became fully appropriate only from 1988), in replacing Soviet hegemony over other Communist parties and systems by co-operation, in reducing the size and political weight of the military-industrial complex, in bringing Soviet troops back from Afghanistan, and in ending the Cold War between East and West. Those goals were far from easy to attain, but Gorbachev realized them.[3]

More fundamentally, however, it may be asked why Gorbachev's success or failure should be judged by the limitations on his political horizons at a particular point in time, even the moment at which he became General Secretary. Why 1985 and not 1988? By the summer of 1988 Gorbachev had accepted the need for contested elections and had, as was shown in Chapters 4 and 6, laid the foundations for the development of political pluralism in the Soviet Union. He had discarded much of Marxist-Leninist ideology and was moving closer to a social democratic vision of socialism. He realized that eventually the Communist Party would have to compete with other political parties in Russia and he had come increasingly to admire what he saw of West European political and economic systems and became correspondingly more critical of the Soviet Communist heritage. He had comprehensively rethought the nature of the Soviet Union's relations with the outside world and had welcomed President Ronald Reagan to Moscow. Reagan had responded by saying that he no longer regarded the USSR as an 'evil empire' and by the end of 1988 the American Secretary of State, George Shultz, was convinced that the Cold War was over.[4] That this was, indeed, so had become still clearer by the end of the following year, by which time most of the countries of Eastern Europe had, one by one, rejected Communism and the Soviet connection and Gorbachev had preferred the disappearance of what had been 'the Soviet bloc' to a return to military intervention and the politics of repression. But already in 1988, in his speeches to the Nineteenth Party Conference and to the United Nations, Gorbachev had paved the way for the independence of the countries of Eastern Europe by recognizing sovereign states' 'freedom to choose' their political and economic system.

If we consider the four transformations—considered in Chapters 5, 6, 7, and 8—which were required if the Soviet Union was to make the transition from a highly repressive Communist system to some form of democracy and of a market economy, two of the four had by the end of the 1980s been successful beyond the dreams of Soviet dissidents or the most optimistic of Western observers at the time when Gorbachev came to power. That is to say, the political system had become substantially pluralist and partially democratized and international relations had been still more comprehensively transformed. In both cases, the initiative had come from Gorbachev, although Western leaders, on the whole, reacted sympathetically to the dramatic scale of the change in both Soviet domestic and foreign policy. If the attitudes of the second Reagan administration were significantly different from the first, this was in response to the fundamentally new challenge and opportunities presented by Moscow. The initial scepticism of the Bush administration also had before long to give way to recognition that Gorbachev had changed Soviet foreign policy fundamentally. It had long been taken for granted in Western capitals that, while amelioration of Communist regimes in Eastern Europe might be possible, the Soviet Union regarded the fruits of its victory in the Second World War in the shape of East European Communist regimes to a greater or lesser degree dependent on Moscow as non-negotiable. But this, too, had changed.

Economic reform and nationalities policy—along with some thoroughly bad appointments—were, in contrast, areas of relative failure for Gorbachev. Yet, even the economic system changed in several important respects (in ways noted in Chapter 5 and highlighted below) and Gorbachev had acquiesced in a substantial devolution of power from the all-union central authorities to the constituent republics of the Soviet Union before the process, from his point of view, got out of hand and resulted in the breakup of the USSR. As was argued in the previous chapter, however, it is possible that a smaller and different union might have been preserved but for the actions of Yeltsin and his supporters both before and after the August 1991 *putsch* and, still more, the self-defeating activity of Kryuchkov and his fellow plotters. While the liberalization and partial democratization of the Soviet Union made highly unlikely the preservation of a union covering the entire territory Gorbachev inherited from his predecessors, the total collapse of the union owed more to Yeltsin—and, of course, to the *putschists*—than to Gorbachev.[5]

Yeltsin had moved into political space created by Gorbachev and but for Gorbachev's reforms would have remained a little-known Communist Party official in the Urals. But he used his opportunities effectively, making at times a highly positive contribution to the peaceful transformation of the Soviet Union and of Russia more particularly. For Yeltsin, however, the pursuit of personal power took precedence over construction of a new federation or confederation. While a great many factors brought about the collapse of the statehood of the Soviet Union, it is appropriate to see Yeltsin, in Alexander Dallin's words, as 'the final catalyst of the collapse'.[6] More fundamentally, of course, the Soviet Union disintegrated because of the virtually insuperable difficulties imposed by attempting simultaneously a fourfold transformation of the system, although such were the interconnections between them that a staged sequencing of these transformations was not a realistic alternative.

Gorbachev's success or failure as a politician should, then, be judged not simply on the basis that, contrary to his wishes and notwithstanding his strenuous political efforts to avoid such an outcome, the Soviet Union gave way to fifteen independent successor states. Indeed, the fact that he refused to resort to the only means capable by 1990–1 of holding the entire USSR together—namely, widespread and sustained repression—is entirely to his credit. Even on the national question, moreover—as has been seen in the previous chapter—his views developed. It was, above all, because the Union Treaty Gorbachev negotiated, in the course of the Novo-Ogarevo process, gave very substantial powers to the republics that so many leading all-union officials rebelled against him in August 1991 and attempted to undo his conciliatory policy.

Defining Gorbachev's success or failure by reference to his thinking at a particular time is open also to the more basic objection that he was an evolutionary rather than revolutionary by conviction, someone who rejected utopian grand designs on principle, a pragmatist and not an ideologue, and a politician who combined the temperament of a reformer with an extraordinary capacity for learning and adjustment. He has been described by a Russian writer as 'a figure very rare in our history—a principled evolutionist'.[7] The same author underlines the point that 'Gorbachev was the main force, holding in check over a long period potential *putschists*'.[8] For almost the whole of his first five years as Soviet leader, Gorbachev was both in the vanguard of reform and the guarantor of its continuity. For much of 1990–1, in contrast, he was on the defensive as a polarization of politics which he had sought to avoid overtook him, but even then he did not resort to traditional Communist methods to reassert his control. The idea that Gorbachev might have become the dictator in the 'coming dictatorship' of which Shevardnadze warned in December 1990 was inherently absurd, for dictatorial methods were foreign both to his personality and to his intellectual conviction.[9]

Indeed, it was Gorbachev's awareness of the importance of means as well as of ends in politics which distinguished him from all of his Communist predecessors as well as from his *de facto* successor, Boris Yeltsin. Gorbachev's mind-set was far removed from the Bolshevik psychology of *kto kogo* (who will crush whom). He did not see politics as a zero-sum-game. Whether in foreign policy or domestic politics, he combined consensus-seeking with pushing forward increasingly fundamental change. As has been argued in earlier chapters, he moved from being a reformer of the Soviet system to a systemic transformer and, as I underline below, he went on—quite consciously during the second half of his General Secretaryship—to dismantle the pillars of Communism.

Gorbachev, as a relatively young General Secretary of the Communist Party in 1985, was better placed to take an overview of the profound problems confronting the Soviet system than other holders of institutional power. Lower-level party officials, economic ministries, the KGB, and the military-industrial complex all had their particular interests, whereas the party leader and *de facto* chief executive of the Soviet Union had a more general interest in the advancement (however defined) of the state in which he held the most powerful and responsible post. Khrushchev and Andropov had accepted such a general responsibility, although the changes they were prepared to contemplate were far less fundamental than those Gorbachev was willing to embrace. It was also, of course, possible to enjoy the perquisites of power and office (as Brezhnev did) while presiding over gradual internal decline. Yet it was slow decline, rather than terminal crisis, which confronted Gorbachev when he succeeded Chernenko as leader of the Soviet Communist Party, and there is absolutely no reason to suppose that any conceivable alternative to Gorbachev in the mid-1980s would have turned Marxism-Leninism on its head and fundamentally changed both his country and the international system in an attempt to reverse a decline which did not pose an immediate threat either to the system or to him. As Rajan Menon has remarked: 'Even a cursory scan of the world's political geography shows that all manner of oppressive, inefficient systems prove to have remarkable staying power and that decline is one thing, collapse quite another.'[10]

What could not be expected of any General Secretary of the Soviet Communist Party was that he would undertake reforms so far-reaching that they would turn the system into something different in kind. It is to Gorbachev's lasting credit that when he found that reform led to resistance from all the vested interests which it threatened, and he was, accordingly, faced with the choice of restoring the status quo ante or moving on to accept the risk of system-transformative change, it was the latter course he adopted. For the decision to move to contested elections and to create a legislature with real powers, taken by Gorbachev in 1988 (before there was any mass pressure for such a fundamental change, and at a time when Yeltsin was still sidelined in the State Construction Committee), was *the* crucial move towards making the Soviet system something different in essence from what it had been before.

The dismantling of Communism

Of the fact that the Soviet political system changed fundamentally under Gorbachev there is no doubt and, at least from the summer of 1988 onwards, there was a *conscious* aim on Gorbachev's part to *transform* it, even if he could not always move at his own preferred pace, which would sometimes have been faster than that forced on him and sometimes slower. Instead, he had, especially during his last two years in office, to respond to pressures and events beyond his control which were, nevertheless, in large part a result of the new freedoms he had opened up. There are two points in 1991, at one or other of which it is conventionally assumed that Communism in the Soviet Union ended. One is when Yeltsin suspended the activities of the Communist Party on Russian soil on 23 August 1991 following the failure of the attempted *putsch*. The other is when the Soviet flag was lowered from the Kremlin on 25 December of the same year and Gorbachev resigned and formally handed power over to Yeltsin—and to Russia as the major successor state to the Soviet Union (or 'continuer state', as Russian officials called it, thus setting it apart from the fourteen other successor states).

However, although there was a Communist Party of the Soviet Union until August 1991, and though its General Secretary was also President of the country, it had ceased to be a ruling party in anything like the sense it had been throughout Soviet history. That was clearly the case at the centre—and it was because the party had lost control over the General Secretary (and, with that, their decisive influence over the fate of the USSR) that some of its leading figures launched the *putsch*—although there were many rural areas, in particular, where the local party boss still held sway. Yet, from the spring of 1989 it is scarcely meaningful to describe the Soviet Union as a *Communist system*. It is not only that the greater part of Marxist-Leninist dogma had been abandoned by then—and by the party leader himself—but also that the most important defining characteristics of a Communist system, whether structural or ideological, had ceased to apply as a result of the policies introduced during the period of radical reform which got seriously under way in 1987 and became more fundamental in 1988.

This, of course, raises the question: what is, or was, a Communist system? There are, as I see it, five defining features which, taken together, made Communist systems a distinct subset among the world's political systems, differentiating them from other authoritarian or totalitarian systems and, still more fundamentally, from pluralist systems in which socialist parties of a social democratic type may at any given time have held office. These characteristics are: (1) the supreme authority and unchallengeable hegemony of the Communist Party (for which the official euphemism was 'the leading role of the party'); (2) a highly centralized, strictly disciplined party with very narrowly defined rights of intraparty debate (which was what 'democratic centralism' meant in practice); (3) state or, at any rate, non-private ownership of the means of production (with exceptions sometimes made for agricultural, but not for industrial, production); (4) the declared aim of building communism as the ultimate (legitimizing) goal; and (5) a sense of belonging to (or, in the Soviet case, leading) an international Communist movement.

By the time the First Congress of People's Deputies of the USSR had ended its first convocation in June 1989, little of this was left. The monopolistic or *leading role* of the party had been challenged by new movements such as the Popular Fronts in the Baltic states which, initially, were welcomed by Gorbachev as forces which would be in the vanguard of perestroika but which, occupying political space created by him, continued to operate even after they began to espouse separatist views much less acceptable to the General Secretary, not to speak of a majority of his Politburo colleagues. The 'leading role', or monopoly of power, of the party was also incompatible with the cultural freedom which had developed by 1989 and which included the publication of many mass-circulation articles and books which were profoundly anti-Communist, among them Orwell's *Animal Farm* and *Nineteen Eighty-Four*. Although the Communist Party remained far larger than all the new political parties put together, it was a historic breakthrough when other political parties were founded and enjoyed a legal existence after the 'leading role' of the CPSU was removed from Article 6 of the Soviet Constitution in March 1990. More important than the new parties as such was the broadly based movement called Democratic Russia, whose founding congress was held in October 1990 and which played an important part in the successful election campaign for the Russian Presidency of Boris Yeltsin in 1991. This body was, on the whole, critical of Gorbachev, but its very existence indicated that the constitutional amendment which deprived the Communist Party of its unique entitlement to power was matched by political change on the ground.

The second defining characteristic of a Communist system, *democratic centralism*, was, if anything, even more comprehensively undermined. Strict party discipline was, in effect, formally abandoned when Communist deputies were allowed to speak and vote according to their conscience in the new legislature elected in 1989. Centralization disappeared as republican party organizations increasingly set their own agendas from 1989, while the absence of open (as distinct from highly esoteric) political argument, which had been so characteristic of intra-party life, gave way to such a clash of opinion among members of the same party on issues of fundamental importance that conservative Communists frequently (and even Gorbachev on rare occasions) complained that the party had turned into a debating society.

Democratic centralism, as a concept, had been abandoned by the reformist wing of the Communist Party by the late 1980s: it had become a slogan mainly of those who wished to return to the pre-Gorbachev order. In practice, the notion of democratic centralism had provided a *carte blanche* for party officials to suppress disagreement and genuinely free discussion within the party. Such suppression effectively ended in 1988, by which time party members were expressing radically different views both in the mass media and in party forums—notably, at the Nineteenth Party Conference that summer. In the following year the reality that the Communist Party contained the complete spectrum of political opinion was manifest in the speeches delivered at the First Congress of People's Deputies and at subsequent sessions of the new Soviet legislature. Old traditions died hard, however, within the party apparatus, and it was not until 1990 that many party officials made direct attacks on Gorbachev and gave public voice to their extreme disquiet about the direction in which he was taking the party and country.[11]

Gorbachev had encouraged debate within both party and society, and the 'pluralism of opinion' he had first espoused in 1987 acquired a life of its own. The CPSU ceased to be a monolithic party (even in the eyes of non-party members) and shortly thereafter ceased to be a monopolistic party. In fact, precisely because it had enjoyed a monopoly of power within the society, it had contained a potentially explosive mixture of diverse political tendencies. These could only be controlled and the entire party kept together on the basis of Leninist discipline and an intransigent hostility towards factions and splits. Thus, the demise of democratic centralism had consequences not only for the Communist Party but for the political system and society as a whole. The emergence into the open of the party's real diversity had occurred by 1987 and was still more obvious from 1988, by which time rank-and-file party members, especially from the intelligentsia, were disagreeing in public on matters of cardinal importance. The introduction of contested elections in 1989 curtailed fundamentally the possibility of controlling party officials and activists through the power of patronage. A party secretary who had been rejected by his[12] local electorate immediately became an embarrassment who had to be removed; he was thus, in effect, replaced from his party post by the non-party majority in the electorate as a result of their rejecting him as a deputy, whether in elections for the national legislature or for a regional or city soviet.

Different Soviet newspapers and journals, almost all of them edited and staffed by party members, took radically divergent lines on the major issues of the day—from Russian nationalist to social democratic to neo-liberal. All this was a far cry from 'democratic centralism'. In the early years of perestroika some authors tried to redefine that concept in order to emphasize its democratic component, but its connotation in Communist political discourse was too well established for that to be more than a hurriedly passed milestone along the road of democratization.[13] Gorbachev himself dealt a death-blow to democratic centralism—and gave a great stimulus to freedom and democracy—when he told the vast majority of the deputies elected to the Congress of People's Deputies who were members of the Communist Party that they were free to speak and vote as they saw fit and did not have to operate as a party bloc. Given that most of these deputies had won their seats in competition with other Communist Party members, including those with radically different political outlooks, it is unlikely that a traditional insistence on party unity would have been universally obeyed, but for all except the boldest Gorbachev's statement was important. It indicated his willingness to make the new legislature more like a real parliament and quite different from the unreformed Supreme Soviet (which was little more than a decorative rubber stamp) and was a powerful encouragement to democratization as distinct from democratic centralism.

The third defining characteristic of a Communist system outlined above— *state ownership of the means of production*—was the one which had been least undermined by 1989 or even by the time the Soviet Union came to an end in 1991. Yet there had been a definite move in the direction of a mixed economy through the creation of co-operatives which in many cases were more like private businesses than genuine co-operatives. Whether the one or the other, they were not, in any case, state concerns. Most of them were in the service sphere— restaurants, shops, hairdressers, car-repair businesses—or in small-scale trading rather than in manufacturing industry, which remained overwhelmingly under state ownership. This was a backward area in the transition from Communism, but it is significant, none the less, that the monopoly control of the party-state over economic activity had been broken. It could be argued that even prior to Gorbachev's time the monopoly had been undermined as a result of the activities of the 'second economy' with its various black and grey markets. The difference by 1989 was that, as a result of the Law on Co-operatives and other legislation, non-state economic activity had now acquired a legal base. The principle of a mixed-ownership economy, including a private sector, had been accepted by 1990 and, to a modest extent, was being introduced in practice. Moreover, Gorbachev, far from reacting with horror and with appeals to traditional ideology, had initially accepted the '500 Days Programme' with its total rejection of the traditional Communist economic order, its avoidance even of a single mention of 'socialism', and its commitment to speedy marketization. While it is true that he later commissioned a compromise programme which postponed some of the toughest decisions called for by the Shatalin–Yavlinksy group, he did so (rightly or wrongly) more on pragmatic than ideological grounds.

The fourth defining characteristic of a Communist system—the *declared aim of building communism* in the sense of a self-governing communist society which would no longer have any use for state institutions—may have been already ritualistic for Communist leaders by the 1970s. (Khrushchev was perhaps the last true believer in the withering away of the state, although even he was too practical a person to swallow whole Marx's utopian vision of a society in which no professional government and officialdom would be needed. Khrushchev tried to hurry the process along by abolishing 'state' institutions and handing their functions over to 'party' bodies without fully realizing that the party institutions were, in a broader and more meaningful understanding of *the state*, themselves part of the state structure. Thus, there was an element of self-deception in Khrushchev's endeavours, since renaming the state as *party* and reallocating functions were not the same as the state's *withering away*.) Under Gorbachev, as has been noted already in Chapter 1, the character of Soviet discourse changed. Increasingly, influential reformers spoke of a better and different 'socialism' rather than of 'communism', and by 1990 many of them had abandoned socialism as well. Gorbachev, in the meantime, had so radically redefined it that it was something different in kind from the Soviet-style socialism he was expected to defend when his Politburo colleagues voted him into the General Secretaryship in March 1985.

The goal of building communism was not of remotely comparable importance in the everyday life of the Soviet Union to the three structural features of Communist systems I have already discussed. Yet it was an element in Marxism-Leninism which was accorded theoretical significance and which helped to distinguish Communist systems, not least the Soviet one, from societies in which governments had been formed by democratic socialist parties which aspired to introduce a form of socialism or, more commonly, nothing more (or less) than a fairer society with fewer extremes of inequality. The prospect of communism was also the ultimate legitimation of the 'leading role' of the Communist Party. If political activity is regarded (in the words of Michael Oakeshott) as an enterprise in which 'men sail a boundless and bottomless sea' in which 'there is neither harbour for shelter nor floor for anchorage, neither starting-place nor appointed destination',[14] a party could not claim a right to rule on the grounds that it had a compass, still less a route-map. It was, however, because Communist theoreticians maintained that there *was* an appointed destination—the destination of communism—that they could justify the permanent exercise of the 'leading role' of the Communist Party, since it was that party alone which possessed the knowledge and experience to guide less well-equipped citizens to this goal.

Gorbachev in his early years as Soviet leader made occasional reference to communism (in the sense of a society towards which everyone was supposedly working), even though he put it into a still remoter future than that envisaged by his predecessors. Khrushchev had argued that the Soviet Union had entered the period of 'full-scale construction of communism'. Brezhnev, more cautious, said they were in the stage of 'developed socialism'. Gorbachev, as noted in Chapter 4, made still more modest claims and spoke, especially in his earliest years as General Secretary, about the country being at the stage of 'developing socialism'. In 1985 Gorbachev would still sometimes refer to the notion of communism even when speaking within narrow party circles—as, for example, when he told the Politburo on 6 April 1985 that if they did not solve the major social problem of the day, alcoholism and drunkenness, they could forget about communism.[15] He used the concept less and less, however, and in public mainly as an oratorical device. The last occasion on which he employed the concept apparently at face value—for, as noted in the previous chapter, he used the word in a speech in July 1991, but in the context of explaining to the Central Committee that communism was *not* a realistic goal—was when rhetorically squaring the circle at the Nineteenth Party Conference on 28 June 1988. After discussing, in non-traditional terms, what he meant by socialism (although his understanding of the concept was not yet as social democratic as it had become by the time of the Twenty-Eighth Party Congress in the summer of 1990), Gorbachev said: 'Precisely such a democratic, humanistic type of socialism we have in view when we speak about the qualitatively new condition of our society as an important step in the advance to communism.'[16] This remark, in fact, made little sense other than in the context of reassuring conference delegates—many of whom were shaken by the radicalism of Gorbachev's reform proposals—that the old faith had not been totally abandoned.[17]

In reality 1988 was a turning-point for Gorbachev; he became increasingly attracted to the social democratic variant of socialism which was utterly at odds both with the norms of Communist political organization and the illusory goal of a communist society. By 1989–90 this change in Gorbachev's thinking had developed further. One of his favourite creative writers was Chingiz Aitmatov, who (as noted in Chapter 6) had distinguished himself at the First Congress of People's Deputies in 1989 by singling out a number of Western countries as far superior examples of socialism in practice than the Soviet Union. Aitmatov suggested that the great service which the Soviet Union had performed for the rest of the world was to demonstrate how *not* to go about constructing socialism.[18] Such a speech in the past would have been deemed worthy of at least ten years in a labour camp. Aitmatov's reward was different. When Gorbachev became President of the USSR nine months later, he named Aitmatov as one of the small group of members of his Presidential Council.

If the fifth defining characteristic of a Communist system was a sense of *belonging to an international movement* and, in the Soviet case, of *leading* such a movement, that aspect of Communism collapsed with the 'velvet revolutions' which saw the speedy transition from Communist to overtly non-Communist regimes in Eastern Europe in 1989–90. This was a direct result of change in Soviet foreign policy whereby, first, the leaderships of the East European countries and, then, the populations realized that the Soviet Union would no longer intervene militarily to prop up unpopular regimes. Most of those Communist systems would have disappeared much earlier had it not been for the entirely realistic perception of the people of Eastern Europe (prior to the Gorbachev era) that the Soviet Union was fully prepared to use force of arms to defend 'the gains of the Great Patriotic War'.

Gorbachev, by the end of 1988, had already openly moved away from the 'two camps' approach to international relations. The important speech he made to the United Nations in December of that year has been referred to more than once. In that address, which had special significance for the countries of Eastern Europe, he not only emphasized each country's right to choose its own political system but ruled out the use of force as an instrument of foreign policy. Gorbachev added that the Soviet Union did not (meaning *no longer*) pretend to possess the 'indisputable truth', but wished rather—along with other countries— to seek jointly to affirm ideas common to all humankind and to preserve the viability of civilization on a universal basis.[19] The notion of one civilization, of which the Soviet Union should be a part, and of one international economic system, which they wished to join, figured prominently in Gorbachev's thought and speeches during the second half of his General Secretaryship. These ideas preceded the collapse of communism in Eastern Europe and, indeed, played their part in precipitating it. The actual events in what had been 'the Soviet bloc' merely confirmed that there was no longer an international Communist movement worthy of the name in which the Soviet Union could participate, still less dominate, since of the Communist countries which were left, the most important, China, viewed developments in the Soviet Union under Gorbachev with alarm and distaste.

The dramatic changes which Gorbachev introduced, and which had, of course, unintended as well as intended consequences, had made the Soviet political system even by the spring of 1989—and, still more clearly, a year later—different in kind from the polity Gorbachev inherited in 1985. Although far from fully democratic, it had become *pluralist* as a result of the introduction of contested elections and the existence of relatively autonomous political organizations whose activities could not be prevented even by the state authorities except at a cost higher than they, under Gorbachev's leadership, were prepared to pay.[20] It had attained a level of political freedom, together with political (and religious) tolerance, unheard of throughout the earlier Soviet period. In effect, well before Yeltsin took over Gorbachev's offices in the Kremlin and the old Central Committee building, the system had ceased to be Communist.

Gorbachev's place in history

What applies to the system is still more true of Gorbachev himself. Nothing could be further removed from an understanding of Gorbachev than the description offered of him at the beginning of 1995 by Richard Pipes as 'a typical product of the Soviet nomenklatura, a man who to this day affirms his faith in the ideals of communism'.[21] The former Chairman of the Soviet Council of Ministers, Nikolay Ryzhkov—who criticized Gorbachev for his unwillingness to use to the full the power he possessed and for his excessive liking for listening to a great many opinions and arguments before making up his mind[22]—perceptively remarks: 'Gorbachev—long before all our native parliamentary games began—was a leader of a parliamentary type. How this formation took place in a party-bureaucratic system, God alone knows. But so he was formed, although from his post-student youth he had risen up the traditional career ladder of Komsomol and party.'[23] Contrary to the view of Pipes, Gorbachev was a highly untypical product of the Soviet *nomenklatura* and the only leader of the Soviet Communist Party to come to reject, while he still held the office of General Secretary, the most distinctive features of Communism. Gorbachev has appositely described himself as 'a product of that very *nomenklatura* and at the same time its antiproduct—its "grave digger", so to speak'.[24]

Gorbachev could, of course, have achieved nothing if there had not been within the Soviet system people who were deeply dissatisfied with it, whether specialists within the research institutes or a minority of senior officials (among the latter, such important political actors of the Gorbachev era as Yakovlev, Shevardnadze, Chernyaev, and Shakhnazarov) who had occupied high positions within the party apparatus.[25] There had also been crucial changes in Soviet society which, as noted in Chapter 1, made the Soviet Union when Gorbachev came to power a very different place from what it had been immediately after the death of Stalin, although in 1985 it remained far removed from being a civil society. If political change in Poland was, in large measure, a result of the struggle of autonomous forces within the society against the power of the party-state, this was not how change was initiated in the Soviet Union.[26]

Social changes and the availability of enlightened (as well as a more numerous category of unenlightened) party officials notwithstanding, individuals desperate for radical reform remained highly dependent on change at the top of the party hierarchy. Political power was concentrated to a remarkable degree in the Central Committee building and the tone of political life set to a surprising extent by the party General Secretary. This meant that would-be reformers, especially over the period of approximately twenty years between the fall of Khrushchev and the death of Chernenko, had found themselves frustrated by the strict limits of Soviet official political discourse and the narrow bounds of all sanctioned political activity. They needed a Gorbachev even more than he needed them. Thus, Alexander Yakovlev, who is today rightly regarded as an important reformer, would have made little mark on Russian history had Gorbachev not brought him into the inner circle of power and given him great opportunities to exercise influence over policy. Yakovlev himself, speaking in March 1995—by which time, partly as a result of their very different assessments of a number of actions of Yeltsin, he had become estranged from Gorbachev— said: 'I consider Gorbachev to be the greatest reformer of the century, the more so because he tried to do this in Russia where from time immemorial the fate of reformers has been unenviable.'[27]

In a political system which concentrates great power in the hands of the political leader, the character, intelligence, courage, and relative open-mindedness of the person at the apex of that system becomes crucially important. Yet, as has been emphasized throughout this volume, a Soviet leader was accorded great power provided he did not engage in actions which posed a threat to the system. Since Gorbachev did present such a threat, he was always in danger of being removed and the fact that he survived for almost seven years while transforming the system is a tribute to his exceptional political finesse. Almost three decades ago Samuel Huntington wrote:

> The revolutionary must be able to dichotomize social forces, the reformer to manipulate them. The reformer, consequently, requires a much higher order of *political skill* than does the revolutionary. Reform is rare if only because the political talents necessary to make it a reality are rare. A successful revolutionary need not be a master politician; a successful reformer always is.[28]

These words apply especially forcefully in the Soviet and Russian context. Social scientists may resist an emphasis on the element of contingency and particularity in the coming to power of a reformer in 1985. It is tempting to see Gorbachev as the handmaiden of history or the embodiment of social forces which, if Gorbachev rather than Dmitry Ustinov had died in December 1984, would have brought forth an alternative leader in the mid-1980s whose policies would have been broadly the same as Gorbachev's, producing similar results. This, however, is a temptation which should be resisted, for it has got little but a 'restrospective determinism' to commend it.[29]

No scholar predicted in 1985 the actual sequence of events whereby the Soviet system was reformed, then transformed, whereupon the Soviet state itself collapsed. Certainly this provided further evidence to support the view that *reform communism was an unstable and temporary expedient*, although that is not at all the same thing as saying that it was pointless to embark on radical reform in the Soviet Union (however unlikely even such an attempt appeared to most observers before Gorbachev undertook it). On the contrary, a process of ever more radical reform was the *only* way in which the Communist system could have been peacefully transformed in a country where—in sharp contrast with East-Central Europe—Communist institutions and norms were deeply entrenched. Reform of the Soviet system could, however, have been either a stage on the path to more thoroughgoing change (not necessarily to democracy, possibly to a non-Communist authoritarian regime) or a transient liberalization before more orthodox Communist norms were restored. There was nothing inevitable either about the timing of the end of the Soviet state or about the way in which, under Gorbachev's leadership, the system was transformed.

Taking all his mistakes and some undoubted failures into account—along, however, with the almost insuperable obstacles he had to overcome—Gorbachev has strong claims to be regarded as one of the greatest reformers in Russian history and as the individual who made the most profound impact on world history in the second half of the twentieth century. He played the decisive part in allowing the countries of Eastern Europe to become free and independent. He did more than anyone else to end the Cold War between East and West. He went along with, encouraged, and (in important respects) initiated fundamental rethinking about politics—radically new thinking in the Soviet context about the political and economic system he inherited and about better alternatives. He presided over, and facilitated, the introduction of freedom of speech, freedom of the press, freedom of association, religious freedom, and freedom of movement, and left Russia a *freer country* than it had been in its long history.

For Olga Chaykovskaya, Gorbachev is 'the one great Russian reformer'. Focusing precisely on his contribution to Russian freedom, she compares him favourably in this respect with Peter the Great, Catherine the Great, and even Alexander II (although the last-named 'made a huge step forward on the path to freedom'). But Gorbachev, she says, *succeeded*: he inherited 'a moribund, slavish country and made it alive and free'.[30] Similarly, Alexander Tsipko has emphasized as perhaps the greatest of Gorbachev's achievements that he 'delivered us from fear—from fear of thought and speech' and gave people the possibility for the first time in seventy years to state their convictions out loud.[31]

There are other Russian intellectuals who cannot forgive Gorbachev for the fact that he gave them freedom when their self-esteem suggests they should have won it for themselves. Similarly, for a General Secretary of the Soviet Communist Party to have played the most decisive part in dismantling the Communist system was not a script much to the liking of a number of Western observers and they have done their best to rewrite it. Yet the Gorbachev factor *was* the most crucial of all. Gorbachev must be judged in his political context—not by the purely intellectual criteria of total consistency of word and thought, but as the inheritor of the most powerful post in a highly repressive regime who abandoned both the means and the ends of Communism. In his own words he was 'a man who led a colossal military force, a deadly police and surveillance apparatus, and a state that was the sole great master of all'. But 'I started to dismantle all that, to rid myself of that power, and now Russia is a different country'[32]—although one which has gone through great turmoil and in which it will remain for future generations to appreciate fully Gorbachev's historic role.

Notes

Preface

1 Oleg Gordievsky, *Next Stop Execution* (Macmillan, London, 1995), 312.

Chapter 1   Introduction

1 In many respects the best account of these developments is still Leonard Schapiro, *The Communist Party of the Soviet Union*, 2nd edn. (Eyre & Spottiswoode, London, 1970).

2 For well-informed discussion of the overthrow of Khrushchev, drawing upon the fresh materials (including memoirs) which became available in the Soviet Union and Russia from the late 1980s, see William J. Tompson, 'The Fall of Nikita Khrushchev', *Soviet Studies*, 43/6 (1991), 1101–21; and Tompson, *Khrushchev: A Political Life* (Macmillan, London, 1995).

3 While the relative stability and predictability of the Brezhnev years has become quite attractive to many citizens of post-Soviet Russia, there is no need for foreign observers to share this limited vision. A number of Russian memoirists, including Brezhnev's doctor, Yevgeny Chazov, and the Director of the Institute of the United States and Canada, Georgy Arbatov, distinguish between the early, more vigorous Brezhnev and the later, enfeebled leader and hold the former in reasonably high esteem. But neither the early nor the late Brezhnev tackled the fundamental problems of the Soviet economy or dared to attempt to liberalize, pluralize, or democratize the Soviet political system. While the Soviet Union increased its military might, it continued to use its superior strength to oppress its neighbours. The 'early' Brezhnev invaded Czechoslovakia and the 'late' Brezhnev invaded Afghanistan. Cf. Yevgeny Chazov, *Zdorov'e i vlast'* (Novosti, Moscow, 1992); and G. A. Arbatov, *Zatyanuvsheesya vyzdorovlenie (1953–1985 gg.): svidetel'stvo sovremennika* (Mezhdunarodnye otnosheniya, Moscow, 1991).

4 The inadequacies of that literature are noted by Ronald Amann in his article, 'Soviet Politics in the Gorbachev Era: The End of Hesitant Modernization', *British Journal of Political Science*, 20/3 (July 1990), 289–310, esp. 291–3. Even as sophisticated an observer as Seweryn Bialer, in a book containing many insights, *The Soviet Paradox: External Expansion, Internal Decline* (Taurus, London, 1986), suggested that there 'is almost no expectation that the tensions in Soviet–American relations will subside in the foreseeable future' (p. 343). On the issue of economic reform, he wrote: 'It is conceivable that the new leadership will initiate an economic reform leading toward market socialism, like the Hungarian New Economic Mechanism. But this is extremely unlikely' (p. 128).

5 Some of the responses to my review article, 'Change and Challenge' (*Times Literary Supplement*, 27 Mar. 1987, pp. 313–14), fall into this category. See the series of letters published in the columns of the *TLS* between 15 May and 24 July 1987.

6 Seweryn Bialer's view was again representative. He believed that by the autumn of 1987 the Soviet Union had become 'the most interesting country in the world' and argued that 'Gorbachev's personal importance to the cycle of reforms cannot be over-emphasized'. See Seweryn Bialer and Michael Mandelbaum (eds.), *Gorbachev's Russia and American Foreign Policy* (Westview Press, Boulder, Colo., 1988), 231, 269. Not all commentators could bring themselves to acknowledge that a Soviet leader might actually be serious about reforming the system. A symposium published in *The National Interest* in the summer of 1987 embraced a variety of viewpoints, including an extreme example, in the joint contribution by Alain Besançon and Françoise Thom (pp. 27–30), of a priori rejection of any evidence of change in the Soviet system.

7 The *émigré* Russian sociologist, Vladimir Shlapentokh, is among those who see the First Congress as a turning-point in Gorbachev's relations with the intelligentsia and, in particular, the liberals among them. See Shlapentokh, *Soviet Intellectuals and Political Power: The Post-Stalin Era* (Princeton University Press, Princeton, 1990), 268.

8 The point was made explicitly by Bialer when he wrote in October 1990 that increasingly 'Gorbachev is a problem rather than a solution'. See Seweryn Bialer, 'The Last Soviet Communist', *U.S. News and World Report*, 8 Oct. 1990, pp. 53–4. See also Robert G. Kaiser, *Why Gorbachev Happened: His Triumphs and his Failures* (Simon & Schuster, New York, 1991), 414.

9 *Reytingi Borisa Yel'tsina i Mikhaila Gorbacheva po 10-bal'noy shkale* (All-Russian Centre for the Study of Public Opinion, Moscow, 1993).

10 For the details, see Ch. 8.

11 The All-Union Centre for the Study of Public Opinion, headed (from its foundation in 1988) by Academician Tatyana Zaslavskaya and (from 1992) by Professor Yury Levada; after the dissolution of the union, it became the All-Russian Centre for the Study of Public Opinion (VTsIOM).

12 Yury Levada, 'Chto zhe dal'she? Razmyshleniya o politicheskoy situatsii v strane', *Izvestiya*, 10 Apr. 1990, p. 3.

13 *Reytingi Borisa Yel'tsina.*

14 Margaret Thatcher's early recognition that Gorbachev was a different kind of Soviet leader from his predecessors has been well documented. For one of her own earliest accounts of it, see the interview given to her daughter, Carol Thatcher, 'Thatcher on Gorbachev', in *Life* (Oct. 1987), 32–4. See also Margaret Thatcher, *The Downing Street Years* (HarperCollins, London, 1993), esp. 450–3. For Denis Healey's early impressions of Gorbachev, based on their meeting during Gorbachev's visit to London of Dec. 1984, see Healey, 'Gorbachev Face to Face', *Newsweek*, 25 Mar. 1985, p. 15. In what a German author describes as 'a rash interview', Helmut Kohl in the autumn of 1986 described Gorbachev as 'a propagandist of the Goebbels type' (Gerd Ruge, *Gorbachev: A Biography* (Chatto & Windus, London, 1991)), but Kohl later established a relationship with Gorbachev characterized by warmth and trust. For discussion both of the Goebbels episode and of the subsequent rapport between Gorbachev and Kohl, see the important book by Timothy Garton Ash, *In Europe's Name: Germany and the Divided Continent* (Jonathan Cape, London, 1993), esp. 107, 118.

15 *Izvestiya TsK KPSS*, 11 (1990), 150–9.

16 Ibid. 155.

17 Ibid. 156.

18 See Alexander Shtromas, *Political Change and Social Development: The Case of the Soviet Union* (Peter Lang, Frankfurt am Main, 1981), esp. 67–82.

19 See Peter Reddaway, 'Dissent in the Soviet Union', *Problems of Communism*, 32/6 (Nov.–Dec. 1983), 1–15.

20 Ibid. 14.

21 Ibid.

22 Amalrik (1938–80) was a Soviet dissident who died in exile in a car accident in Spain. Zinoviev (b. 1922) is a Russian dissident philosopher and satirical novelist who has lived in Germany since 1977.

23 Reddaway, 'Dissent in the Soviet Union'.

24 See Alexander Solzhenitsyn, 'Kak nam obustroit' Rossiyu?' in *Literaturnaya gazeta*, 18 Sept. 1990, pp. 3–6; and *Komsomol'skaya pravda*, 18 Sept. 1990, pp. 3–6. This work by Solzhenitsyn was subsequently translated into English and published as *Rebuilding Russia: Reflections and Tentative Proposals* (Harvill, London, 1991). Editors of Russian literary journals vied with one another to publish Solzhenitsyn's earlier works. *The Gulag Archipelago* appeared in *Novy mir* in 1989 in No. 8, pp. 7–94; No. 9, pp. 68–165; No. 10, pp. 25–149; and No. 11, pp. 63–175.

25 Asked in an investigation of 1991 conducted by the All-Union Centre for the Study of Public Opinion if they had heard anything about the human rights movement in the Soviet Union, only 21 per cent of respondents gave a positive answer. See Levada, *Chelovek i legenda: obraz A. D. Sakharova v obshchestvennom mnenii* (Data, Moscow, 1991), 13–14. Widespread popular support for the former dissidents and even for Andrey Sakharov is, as this study confirmed, a relatively recent phenomenon.

26 See ibid.; and Sakharov, *Moscow and Beyond 1986 to 1989* (Knopf, New York, 1991).

27 Shlapentokh, *Soviet Intellectuals and Political Power*, 81. See also for a general account of the newspaper survey *Literaturnaya gazeta*, 29 Mar. 1989, p. 12. The polls were conducted under the leadership of two of the Soviet Union's most respected sociologists. The team which carried out the *Literaturnaya gazeta* survey was headed by Yury Levada. It had the disadvantage that the sample was self-selected, inasmuch as the newspaper published the sociologists' questionnaire and invited

readers to complete it. No fewer than 200,000 did so! The random sample poll of the population at large was conducted by Boris Grushin. At that time Levada and Grushin—both of whom did pioneering sociological research in the 1960s—worked in Zaslavskaya's All-Union Centre for the Study of Public Opinion. Levada, as noted above, is now Director of the (All-Russian) Centre, whereas Grushin moved to found his own separate research centre, Vox Populi.

28 The Mayor of St Petersburg, Anatoly Sobchak, who was one of Sakharov's political allies in the Congress of People's Deputies of the USSR, has also observed that it was only from the time of his death that Sakharov had a large following. See Sobchak, *Khozhdenie vo vlast'* (Novosti, Moscow, 1991), 258. That the following was growing throughout 1989 was, however, suggested by the result of a survey based on letters to a weekly newspaper of the popularity of members of the Congress of People's Deputies of the USSR (though the result was at odds with the more modest levels of support for Sakharov found in the studies of the All-Union Centre for the Study of Public Opinion which employed less amateurish sampling methods). Sakharov occupied top place in the popularity league table based on readers' letters to the weekly *Argumenty i fakty* (No. 40) in Oct. 1989. The manner in which the survey was conducted and its publication became a source of friction between Gorbachev and the paper's editor, Vladislav Starkov.

29 *Obshchestvennoe mnenie v tsifrakh*, 6/13 (Feb. 1990) (All-Union Centre for the Study of Public Opinion, Moscow, 1990), 14.

30 Margaret Thatcher, mentioned by 16.8 per cent of respondents, received exactly four times as much support as her closest challenger, the Estonian politician Marju Lauristin.

31 Levada *et al.*, *Chelovek i legenda*, 13–14.

32 Ibid. 24.

33 V. V. Dubin *et al.*, *Obshchestvennoe mnenie v tsifrakh*, 2/9 (Jan. 1990) (All-Union Centre for the Study of Public Opinion, Moscow), 6. Over 500 names were mentioned by the 2,696 respondents drawn from every Soviet republic. Only the first 29 names are published in the booklet giving the findings (cited above). That list includes all those who were mentioned by more than 3.5 per cent of respondents. The one other Soviet politician apart from Lenin and Gorbachev to be placed on such a pantheon at that time was Stalin (11.9 per cent).

34 There is some evidence of this, although the survey is not directly comparable with the one cited in the text which sampled opinion in (what were at that time) all fifteen Soviet republics. However, a similar question was posed to citizens of Moscow, Leningrad (which officially regained its old name of St Petersburg on 1 Oct. 1991) and Kiev on 2 Sept. 1991. Respondents were asked to 'name the three, in your view, most outstanding people of all times and peoples'. In first place came Peter the Great (named by 13 per cent), followed by Jesus Christ (11 per cent). Lenin shared third place with Einstein, each being named by 8 per cent of the sample. They were followed by Andrey Sakharov (6 per cent), and three historical figures on 5 per cent: Alexander Nevsky, Petr Stolypin, and Napoleon Bonaparte. See *Argumenty i fakty*, 39 (Oct. 1991), 1. A different survey, conducted by Boris Grushin's Vox Populi opinion research institute in June and July 1992, asked respondents throughout the Russian federation to name Russia's greatest politician (of all time). Peter the Great was by far the most popular choice, being mentioned by 44 per cent of respondents. Lenin, however, came second (a long way behind with 15 per cent) and Stalin (6 per cent) came third. See Mark Rhodes, 'Russians Say Peter was Greater than Lenin', *RFE/RL Research Report*, 2/7 (12 Feb. 1993), 54–5.

35 Brown, 'Political Developments', in Archie Brown and Michael Kaser (eds.), *The Soviet Union since the Fall of Khrushchev* (Macmillan, London, 1975), 218–75, esp. 255–62.

36 Some notable contributions have already been made to that literature. See, for instance, Timothy J. Colton, *The Dilemma of Reform in the Soviet Union*, rev. and expanded edn. (Council on Foreign Relations, New York, 1986); Moshe Lewin, *The Gorbachev Phenomenon: A Historical Interpretation* (Hutchinson, London, 1988); Geoffrey Hosking, *The Awakening of the Soviet Union* (Heinemann, London, 1990); Vladimir Shlapentokh, *Public and Private Life of the Soviet People: Changing Values in Post-Stalin Russia* (Oxford University Press, New York, 1989); Mary Buckley, *Redefining Russian Society and Polity* (Westview, Boulder, Colo., 1993); Leslie Holmes, *The End of Communist Power: Anti-Corruption Campaigns and Legitimation Crisis* (Polity Press, Oxford, 1993); and Philip G. Roeder, *Red Sunset: The Failure of Soviet Politics* (Princeton University Press, Princeton, 1993). See also Shlapentokh, *Soviet Intellectuals and Political Power*.

37 For stimulating accounts of the national question in the USSR, see Alexander J. Motyl, *Sovietology, Rationality, Nationality: Coming to Grips with Nationalism in the USSR* (Columbia University Press, New York, 1990); Motyl (ed.), *Thinking Theoretically about Soviet Nationalities* (Columbia University Press, New York, 1992); Bohdan Nahaylo and Victor Swoboda, *Soviet Disunion: A History of the Nationalities Problem in the USSR* (Hamish Hamilton, London, 1990); Graham Smith (ed.), *The Nationalities Question in the Soviet Union* (Longman, London, 1990); Michael Mandelbaum (ed.), *The*

Rise of Nations in the Soviet Union: American Foreign Policy and the Disintegration of the USSR (Council on Foreign Relations, New York, 1991); Gail W. Lapidus and Victor Zaslavsky (eds.), *From Union to Commonwealth: Nationalism and Separatism in the Soviet Republics* (Cambridge University Press, Cambridge, 1992); Ronald Grigor Suny, *The Revenge of the Past: Nationalism, Revolution and the Collapse of the Soviet Union* (Stanford University Press, Stanford, Calif., 1993); and Ian Bremner and Ray Taras (eds.), *Nations and Politics in the Soviet Successor States* (Cambridge University Press, Cambridge, 1993).

38 Until recently very little justice had been done to the Yeltsin factor (or Yeltsin *phenomenon*, although there are at least three books entitled *The Gorbachev Phenomenon*), but for two early accounts of Yeltsin's break with the Communist Party establishment in 1987, see Timothy J. Colton, 'Moscow Politics and the El'tsin Affair', *The Harriman Institute Forum*, 1/6 (June 1988), 1–8; and Seweryn Bialer, 'The Yeltsin Affair: The Dilemma of the Left in Gorbachev's Revolution', in Bialer (ed.), *Politics, Society and Nationality Inside Gorbachev's Russia* (Westview, Boulder, Colo., 1989), 91–119. The best biography of Yeltsin so far is John Morrison, *Boris Yeltsin* (Penguin, London, 1991). For two journalistic accounts, the former uncritically pro-Yeltsin, the latter more sceptical, see Vladimir Solovyov and Elena Klepikova, *Boris Yeltsin: A Political Biography* (Weidenfeld & Nicolson, London, 1992); and Jonathan Steele, *Eternal Russia: Yeltsin, Gorbachev and the Mirage of Democracy* (Faber & Faber, London, 1994).

39 Particularly valuable for the interview material they contain are Angus Roxburgh, *The Second Russian Revolution* (BBC Books, London, 1991); Hedrick Smith, *The New Russians* (Random House, New York, 1990); Robert G. Kaiser, *Why Gorbachev Happened: His Triumphs and his Failures* (Simon & Schuster, New York, 1991); and David Remnick, *Lenin's Tomb: The Last Days of the Soviet Empire* (Viking, London, 1993).

40 See, most notably, Stephen White, *Gorbachev and After*, 3rd edn. (Cambridge University Press, Cambridge, 1992); Richard Sakwa, *Gorbachev and his Reforms 1985–1990* (Philip Allan, London, 1990); and Harley D. Balzer (ed.), *Five Years that Shook the World: Gorbachev's Unfinished Revolution* (Westview, Boulder, Colo., 1991). The first such book to be completed after Gorbachev had ceased to be Soviet leader (which also contains some interesting interpretations) is John Miller, *Mikhail Gorbachev and the End of Soviet Power* (Macmillan, London, 1993).

41 An exception to that generalization is Dusko Doder and Louise Branson, *Gorbachev: Heretic in the Kremlin* (Viking, New York, 1990). Gerd Ruge's *Gorbachev* (Chatto & Windus, London, 1991) is useful also, especially for the interviews conducted by the author. Ruge had good access to Gorbachev's friends and acquaintances in both Moscow and Stavropol. Unfortunately, the book contains a number of factual errors in addition to material of value. The first point applies, *a fortiori*, to Gail Sheehy's *The Man Who Changed the World: The Lives of Mikhail S. Gorbachev* (HarperCollins, New York, 1990).

42 This is a trap into which even one of the best recent books on Gorbachev—Miller, *Gorbachev and the End of Soviet Power*—sometimes falls.

43 That latter view is eloquently represented by Françoise Thom in her book *The Gorbachev Phenomenon: A History of Perestroika* (Pinter, London, 1989), and by Brian Crozier in *The Gorbachev Phenomenon: 'Peace' and the Secret War* (Claridge Press, London, 1990).

44 See Archie Brown, 'Gorbachev: New Man in the Kremlin', *Problems of Communism*, 34/3 (May–June 1985), 1–23; and Archie Brown, 'Can Gorbachev Make a Difference?', *Detente*, 3 (May 1985), 4–7.

45 My 1980 Stimson Lecture reference to Gorbachev is cited in the Preface. The first published references I made to Gorbachev as a future General Secretary of reformist disposition are to be found in Archie Brown and Michael Kaser (eds.), *Soviet Policy for the 1980s* (Macmillan, London, 1982), 240–2, 244–5, 269–70.

46 In 1982 Jerry F. Hough was another who argued that 'Gorbachev would almost surely be a reform leader'. See Hough, 'Changes in Soviet Elite Composition', in Seweryn Bialer and Thane Gustafson (eds.), *Russia at the Crossroads: The 26th Congress of the CPSU* (Allen & Unwin, London, 1982), esp. 43–4. In many other areas our views diverged. Hough subsequently wrote very extensively on Gorbachev, emphasizing his commitment to economic reform. In my view, however, he seriously underestimated Gorbachev's interest in political democratization—at times portraying him as a dictator—and by 1990 he was still more mistakenly playing down the threats to Gorbachev's power from both 'right' and 'left'—not least, from nationalist drives for independence. Among Hough's highly controversial contributions to the Gorbachev debate are his book, *Russia and the West: Gorbachev and the Politics of Reform*, 2nd (Touchstone) edn. (Simon & Schuster, New York, 1990); 'Gorbachev's Strategy', *Foreign Affairs*, 64/1 (1985), 33–55; 'The Politics of Successful Economic Reform', *Soviet Economy*, 5/1 (Jan.–Mar. 1989), 3–46; 'Gorbachev's Endgame', *World Policy Journal*, 7/4 (Fall 1990), 639–72; and 'Understanding Gorbachev', *Soviet Economy*, 7/2 (Apr.–June 1991), 89–109.

47 On Gorbachev's learning in office, see George Breslauer, 'Soviet Economic Reforms Since Stalin: Ideology, Politics and Learning', *Soviet Economy*, 6/3 (July–Sept. 1990), 252–80; and George

Breslauer and Philip E. Tetlock (eds.), *Learning in U.S. and Soviet Foreign Policy* (Westview, Boulder, Colo., 1991).

48 The most detailed academic account of the 1989 elections (a 384-page book) was produced by Russian scholars. In the world of political studies the book was as refreshing a break with the Soviet past as the actual 1989 elections were with the previous 'real world' of Soviet politics. See V. A. Kolosov, N. V. Petrov, and L. V. Smirnyagin (eds.), *Vesna 89: Geografiya i anatomiya parlamentskikh vyborov* (Progress, Moscow, 1990).

49 See the successive draft party programmes which Gorbachev persuaded a reluctant Central Committee to adopt, published in *Pravda*, 26 July 1991, pp. 1–2, and *Pravda*, 8 Aug. 1991, pp. 3–4.

50 The term 'totalitarian' is now used freely and indiscriminately in Russia to describe the Soviet system at any stage of its history. Stalin's Soviet Union was surely close enough to ideal-typical totalitarianism (in the Weberian sense of 'ideal type') to be called totalitarian. The 'late Communism' or 'really existing socialism' of the Brezhnev years is a less clear-cut case. On the whole, it seems to me that the differences between the years of 'high Stalinism' (from the early 1930s until Stalin's death in 1953), on the one hand, and the post-Stalin years from Khrushchev to Chernenko, on the other, are sufficiently great as to merit a conceptual distinction between them. As I understand the terms 'totalitarianism' and 'authoritarianism' (though, of course, they can be defined in different ways to produce different classifications), the Soviet system post-Stalin and pre-Gorbachev was highly authoritarian—a special category of post-totalitarian authoritarianism—rather than totalitarian. For elaboration of some of these points, see my book, *Soviet Politics and Political Science* (Macmillan, London, 1974), 30–41; and my chapter, 'Political Power and the Soviet State: Western and Soviet Perspectives', in Neil Harding (ed.), *The State in Socialist Society* (Macmillan, London, 1984), 51–103, esp. 55–7. The application by liberal Soviet writers and politicians of the term 'totalitarian' to the Soviet system as it operated even during the Gorbachev era stretched its meaning too far. Yet, the use of such rhetoric in the mass media could only be welcomed, for it served as evidence that the system had, in fact, become far from totalitarian. In a wry comment on many of his fellow countrymen, the head of the Centre for Political Research at the Institute of State and Law in Moscow, William Smirnov, remarked to me late in the Gorbachev era: 'When there was real totalitarianism, we pretended it was a democracy. Once it became pluralist, everyone shouted that it was totalitarian.' For a discussion of totalitarian and authoritarian regimes which also views post-Stalin Russia as 'post-totalitarian', see Ralf Dahrendorf, *The Modern Social Conflict: An Essay on the Politics of Liberty* (Weidenfeld & Nicolson, London, 1988), 72–92, esp. 85, 91.

51 I have stated the argument against regarding the pre-Gorbachev Soviet Union as pluralist in any [illegible] at [illegible] length in my chapter, 'Political Power and the Soviet State: Western and Soviet Perspectives', in Harding (ed.), *The State in Socialist Society*, 51–103, esp. 57–66.

52 For a perceptive recent article on the theme, see Michael Ignatieff, 'On Civil Society: Why Eastern Europe's Revolutions Could Succeed', *Foreign Affairs*, 74/2 (Mar.–Apr. 1995), 128–36.

53 See Michael Bourdeaux, *Gorbachev, Glasnost and the Gospel* (Hodder & Stoughton, London, 1990), esp. 1–21; and Michael Bourdeaux, chapter on religion in Archie Brown and Michael Kaser (eds.), *The Soviet Union since the Fall of Khrushchev*, 2nd edn. (Macmillan, London, 1978), 157–80.

54 See e.g. Hugh Seton-Watson, *The Decline of Imperial Russia* (Methuen, London, 1952); Jacob Walkin, *The Rise of Democracy in Pre-Revolutionary Russia: Political and Social Institutions under the Last Three Czars* (Thames & Hudson, London, 1963); and Geoffrey Hosking, *The Russian Constitutional Experiment: Government and Duma 1907–1914* (Cambridge University Press, Cambridge, 1973).

55 Tibor Szamuely, *The Russian Tradition*, ed. with an introduction by Robert Conquest (Secker & Warburg, London, 1974).

56 Ibid., p. ix.

57 There is a substantial amount of evidence showing that Soviet citizens took a stronger interest in newspaper and magazine articles on foreign countries than in those on their own country. For a good summary of the relevant survey data, see Shlapentokh, *Public and Private Life*, esp. 139–52.

58 For fuller discussions of some of the social pre-conditions for perestroika, see David Lane, *Soviet Society under Perestroika* (Unwin Hyman, London, 1990), esp. ch. 5, 'The Changing Social Structure', 123–60; Gail W. Lapidus, 'State and Society: Toward the Emergence of Civil Society in the Soviet Union', in Bialer (ed.), *Politics, Society and Nationality*, 121–47; Tatyana Zaslavskaya, *The Second Socialist Revolution: An Alternative Strategy* (Tauris, London, 1990), esp. ch. 1, pp. 1–20; and Zaslavskaya, 'Perestroyka i sotsializm', in F. M. Borodkin, L. Ya. Kosals, and R. V. Ryvkina (eds.), *Postizhenie* (Progress, Moscow, 1989), 217–40, esp. 224–6.

59 Ellen Mickiewicz, *Split Signals: Television and Politics in the Soviet Union* (Oxford University Press, New York, 1988), 3, 17.

60 Archie Brown, John Fennell, Michael Kaser, and H. T. Willetts (eds.), *The Cambridge Encyclopedia of Russia and the Soviet Union* (Cambridge University Press, Cambridge, 1982), 407.

61 For the fullest account of the ecological disaster area which the Soviet Union became, see Murray Feschbach and Alfred Friendly, Jr., *Ecocide in the USSR* (Basic Books, New York, 1992).

62 The gulf between private and public discourse was the phenomenon which surprised me most when I made my first study visit to Moscow in the mid-1960s. It did not fit with the totalitarian image of the Soviet Union I had carried with me and which probably owed more to Orwell's *Nineteen Eighty-Four* than to the social realities of post-Stalin Russia. For a brief but accurate description of the gap between private and public domains pre-perestroika, see Hosking, *The Awakening of the Soviet Union*, esp. 12–13.

63 T. H. Rigby, *The Changing Soviet System: Mono-Organisational Socialism from its Origins to Gorbachev's Restructuring* (Edward Elgar, Aldershot, 1990), 215.

64 For important discussions of this, see T. H. Rigby and Bohdan Harasymiw (eds.), *Leadership Selection and Patron-Client Relations in the USSR and Yugoslavia* (Allen & Unwin, London, 1983); John H. Miller, 'Putting Clients in Place: The Role of Patronage in Cooption into the Soviet Leadership', in Archie Brown (ed.), *Political Leadership in the Soviet Union* (Macmillan, London, 1989), 54–95; and T. H. Rigby, *Political Elites in the USSR: Central Leaders and Local Cadres from Lenin to Gorbachev* (Edward Elgar, Aldershot, 1990).

65 The reminiscences of two of the prominent former assistants of Andropov and Kuusiinen, Fedor Burlatsky and Georgy Arbatov (with the latter's curriculum vitae including Prague as well), throw interesting light on these networks. See Arbatov, *Zatyanuvsheesya vyzdorovlenie*; and Fedor Burlatsky, *Vozhdi i sovetniki: o Khrushcheve, Andropove i ne tol' ko o nikh* (Politizdat, Moscow, 1990). See also Stephen F. Cohen and Katrina vanden Heuvel, *Voices of Glasnost: Interview with Gorbachev's Reformers* (Norton, New York, 1989); and Archie Brown, 'Andropov: Discipline *and* Reform?', *Problems of Communism*, 32/1 (Jan.–Feb. 1983), 18–31.

66 From my conversations with party officials who came out strongly on the reformist side during the Gorbachev era, I am aware that the extent to which they read the work of dissidents varied. Some read parts of the dissident literature and others did not do so at all. Andrey Grachev has said that during the Brezhnev years he took the opportunity to read the major works of Soviet dissidents when he was abroad (interview with Grachev, Oxford, 16 Jan. 1993).

67 See Geoffrey Hosking, *Beyond Socialist Realism: Soviet Fiction since Ivan Denisovich* (Granada, London, 1980), esp. 50–83.

68 For two well-informed accounts of this from different perspectives, see Alexander Yanov, *The Russian New Right: Right-Wing Ideologies in the Contemporary USSR* (Institute of International Studies, University of California, Berkeley, 1978); and John B. Dunlop, *The Faces of Contemporary Russian Nationalism* (Princeton University Press, Princeton, 1983).

69 See, for instance, Crozier's *The Gorbachev Phenomenon*, and the same author's more recent book, *Free Agent: The Unseen War 1941–1991* (HarperCollins, London, 1993).

70 The exceptions in Eastern Europe were Albania and Yugoslavia, with Czechoslovakia a somewhat marginal case. See Joseph Rothschild, *Return to Diversity: A Political History of East Central Europe since World War II* (Oxford University Press, New York, 1989); and Archie Brown and Jack Gray (eds.), *Political Culture and Political Change in Communist States* (Macmillan, London, 1977), esp. Introduction, pp. 15–16.

71 Anatoly Sobchak, *Khozhdenie vo vlast'. Rasskaz o rozhdenii parlamenta* (Novosti, Moscow, 1991), 9.

72 There are a number of accounts of the radical divergences of view contained within the Soviet Communist Party in the years before these differences became overt and a matter for public debate. See, for instance, Stephen Cohen, 'The Friends and Foes of Change', in Stephen F. Cohen, Alexander Rabinowitch, and Robert Sharlet (eds.), *The Soviet Union since Stalin* (Indiana University Press, Bloomington, Ind., 1980), 11–31; Cohen and vanden Heuvel, *Voices of Glasnost*; and Jerry F. Hough, *The Struggle for the Third World: Soviet Debates and American Options* (Brookings, Washington, 1986). See also Archie Brown (ed.), *New Thinking in Soviet Politics* (Macmillan, London, 1992); and Brown, 'Political Science in the USSR', *International Political Science Review*, 7/4, 1986, 443–81.

73 See Sobchak, *Khozhdenie vo vlast'*, 9.

Chapter 2   The Making of a Reformist General Secretary

1 T. H. Rigby, 'Concluding Observations', in T. H. Rigby, Archie Brown, and Peter Reddaway (eds.), *Authority, Power and Policy in the USSR: Essays Dedicated to Leonard Schapiro* (Macmillan, London, 1980), 197.

2 The house in Privolnoe in which Gorbachev's mother lived for some thirty years until she was persuaded (without Gorbachev's knowledge) to sell it in 1993 was one in which her elder son had been only a visitor. Although there was some talk of turning the house in which he was born into a museum in honour of the first and last Soviet President, it was, noted the journalist Irina Mastykina, already too late for that; his actual birthplace had been knocked down years earlier. See *Komsomol'skaya pravda*, 11 Aug. 1993, p. 3.

3 *Izvestiya*, 1 Dec. 1990, pp. 1–4, at p. 4; and also Gorbachev's interview with Yury Shchekochikhin in *Literaturnaya gazeta*, 4 Dec. 1991, p. 4.

4 Ibid. (both *Izvestiya* and *Literaturnaya gazeta*).

5 Interview with Gorbachev, *Komsomol'skaya pravda*, 7 Nov. 1992, p. 1.

6 *Izvestiya TsK KPSS*, 5 (May 1989), 58.

7 *Izvestiya*, 1 Dec. 1990, pp. 1–4, at p. 4.

8 Ibid.

9 Mikhail Gorbachev, 'The Legacy of a Monster that Refuses to Die', *Guardian*, 27 Feb. 1993, p. 21 (article reprinted from *La Stampa*).

10 *Bol'shaya Sovetskaya Entsiklopediya*, 3rd edn., vol. xxiv (Sovetskaya Entsiklopediya, Moscow, 1976).

11 Hedrick Smith, *The New Russians* (Random House, New York, 1990), 35.

12 *Izvestiya TsK KPSS*, 5 (May 1989), 58.

13 *Stavropol'skaya pravda*, 24 Feb. 1976, p. 3.

14 Boris Kuchmaev, *Kommunist s bozh'ey otmetinoy: dokumental'no-publitsisticheskiy ocherk* (Yuzhno-Russkoe kommerchesko-izdatelskoe tovarishchestvo, Stavropol, 1992), 16.

15 Gorbachev's interview for Ukrainian television in which he mentioned both his wife's and his own Ukrainian ethnic links was reported in *The Times*, 9 Dec. 1991, p. 10. On Gorbachev's Ukrainian blood, see also his interview in *Moskovskiy komsomolets*, 28 June 1995, p. 2.

16 My source for that statement is Yelena Korenevskaya, who had met Maria Panteleevna.

17 Zdeněk Mlynář, 'Il mio compagno di studi Mikhail Gorbaciov', *L'Unità* (Rome), 9 Apr. 1985, p.9.

18 The desirability within the Soviet Communist Party of having some background as a worker was such that Gorbachev's official biographies up to and beyond the time when he became General Secretary did not reveal that his schooling continued in the second half of the 1940s. While the brief newspaper and encyclopaedia yearbook biographies noted his years at Moscow University in the first half of the 1950s, the years 1946–50 are covered solely by the description 'assistant to a combine-harvester operator'. See e.g. *Yezhegodnik Bol'shoy Sovetskoy Entsiklopedii 1981* (Sovetskaya Entsiklopediya, Moscow, 1981), 573; and *Pravda*, 12 Mar. 1985, p.1.

19 Gerd Ruge, *Gorbachev* (Chatto & Windus, 1991), 31.

20 *Izvestiya TsK KPSS*, 5 (May 1989), 58; and Kuchmaev, *Kommunist s bozh'ey otmetinoy*, 28. Sergey Gorbachev was 36 by the time he was admitted to the Communist Party during the Second World War.

21 See Sheila Fitzpatrick, *Education and Social Mobility in the Soviet Union 1921–1934* (Cambridge University Press, Cambridge, 1979).

22 Vera S. Dunham, *In Stalin's Time: Middleclass Values in Soviet Fiction* (Cambridge University Press, Cambridge, 1976), 13.

23 Gorbachev has always taken a greater pride in his wife's scholastic achievements than in his own. On his first visit to Britain in 1984, when he was not yet General Secretary of the Soviet Communist Party, one of the things he told his British hosts—as I learned shortly afterwards from one of the British ministers present—was that, whereas he had got a silver medal at school, his wife had received a gold one.

24 Mlynář suggests that this work led to Gorbachev being recommended to Moscow University by the authorities in his own area (Mlynář, *L'Unità*, 9 Apr. 1985, p. 9).

25 Kuchmaev, *Kommunist bozh'ey otmetinoy*, 30–1.

26 Smith, *The New Russians*, 39. See also Ruge, *Gorbachev*, 26–7.

27 Michail Gorbatschow (Mikhail Gorbachev), *Erinnerungen* (Seidler Verlag, Berlin, 1995), 64. Gorbachev's memoirs have appeared in German before being published in other languages, including Russian and English (the Bertelsmann publishing combine has world rights). The German edition became available just before this book went to press and I have been able to make limited use of it.

28 Ruge, *Gorbachev*, 37.

29 Ibid. 26.

30 Dusko Doder and Louise Branson, *Gorbachev: Heretic in the Kremlin* (Viking, New York, 1990), 13–16; Ruge, *Gorbachev*, 40.

31 For some reason both Hedrick Smith (*The New Russians*, 47) and Robert Kaiser (*Why Gorbachev Happened*, 31) give the year of the Gorbachevs' marriage, incorrectly, as 1954. But Gorbachev himself supplied the information that he first met his wife in 1951 and that they married in 1953. See *Izvestiya TsK KPSS*, 5 (May 1989), 58.

32 Gorbachev, 'The Legacy of a Monster that Refuses to Die', *Guardian*, 27 Feb. 1993.

33 Ibid.

34 Doder and Branson, *Gorbachev: Heretic in the Kremlin*, 11. In another interview, Yakovlev said: 'In general, we young fellows went off to war with an absolute, one hundred percent faith in Stalin. . . . there was real popular enthusiasm during the Stalin years. The Soviet people put out an enormous effort. Yes, all sorts of terrible things happened. Yes, the humane aims of socialism were not realized. But we sincerely believed in it all' (Stephen F. Cohen and Katrina vanden Heuvel (eds.), *Voices of Glasnost: Interviews with Gorbachev's Reformers* (Norton, New York, 1989), 36–7).

35 Eduard Shevardnadze, *The Future Belongs to Freedom* (Sinclair-Stevenson, London, 1991), 19.

36 Ibid. 17–19; Yegor Ligachev, *Inside Gorbachev's Kremlin* (Pantheon, New York, 1993), 256–8.

37 Interview with Gorbachev, *Komsomol'skaya pravda*, 7 Nov. 1992, p. 1.

38 Ibid.; and Gorbatschow, *Erinnerungen*, 81.

39 Ruge's book, *Gorbachev*, gives a good summary of the evidence on this point (pp. 41–3). Other authors have wrongly described as a 'classmate' of Gorbachev one of his *émigré* critics, Lev Yudovich, whose claims to know about Gorbachev's student career have led to his being much cited. But, according to *Soviet Analyst*, which published Yudovich's negative portrait of Gorbachev the student on 19 Dec. 1984, Yudovich graduated from the Moscow University Law Faculty in 1950—i.e. before Gorbachev arrived there—and his tenuous claim to knowledge of Gorbachev is based on nothing more than the assertion that he 'fairly frequently' visited it thereafter.

40 Raisa Gorbachev refers to the friendship with Mlynář in her volume of reminiscences, *I Hope* (HarperCollins, London, 1991), 49–50, as does Gorbatschow, *Erinnerungen*, 75.

41 See Adam Ulam, *Stalin: The Man and his Era* (Allen Lane, London, 1974), 736–7.

42 Smith, *The New Russians*, 49; Ruge, *Gorbachev*, 41.

43 Mlynář, *L'Unità*, 9 Apr. 1985, p. 9.

44 Gorbatschow, *Erinnerungen*, 70–1.

45 This information comes from one of my own conversations with Zdeněk Mlynář. Gorbachev had a particular interest in political history and the history of law.

46 When I made my first study visit to Moscow from January to April 1966, I was assigned as my academic adviser none other than Professor S. F. Kechekyan. I was doing research at that time on eighteenth-century Russian political and social thought. I looked forward to working with him again when I returned to Moscow in September 1967, but by then he had died.

47 Mlynář, *L'Unità*, 9 Apr. 1985, p. 9.

48 Ibid.

49 Ibid.

50 Ibid.

51 Kuchmaev, *Kommunist s bozh'ey otmetinoy*, 61.

52 M. S. Gorbachev, *Zhivoe tvorchestvo naroda* (Politizdat, Moscow, 1984), 11.

53 Ibid. 41.

54 Mlynář, *L'Unità*, 9 Apr. 1985, p. 9.

55 Yelena Lukyanova, 'On ne narushal zakon', *Literaturnaya gazeta*, 11 Oct. 1991, p. 2.

56 Raisa Gorbachev, *I Hope*, 61–2; and Gorbatschow, *Erinnerungen*, 75.

57 *Izvestiya TsK KPSS*, 5 (May 1989), 58; Raisa Gorbachev, *I Hope*, 14.

58 Ibid. 16–17.

59 Gorbachev, 'Legacy of a Monster', *Guardian*, 27 Feb. 1993. Gorbachev, in his article written shortly before the fortieth anniversary of Stalin's death, prefaced his remark quoted in the text of this chapter by observing that 'the horror continually re-surfaces' and that it was only 'a few days ago we learned of the fate of Raisa Maximovna's grandfather'.

60 Raisa Gorbachev, *I Hope*, 19, 22.

61 My source is one of her British hosts on that occasion.

62 Valery Boldin, *Ten Years that Shook the World: The Gorbachev Era as Witnessed by his Chief of Staff* (Basic Books, New York, 1994), 132. Boldin adds: 'The merits of her approach are open to debate, though it is certainly better than finding oneself staring for the first time at some cultural site one has never even heard of.'

63 Raisa Gorbachev, *I Hope*, 78–80.

64 My source is Andrey Grachev (interview in Oxford, 13 Jan. 1993), citing one of his own conversations with Raisa Gorbachev.

65 Raisa Gorbachev, *I Hope*, 96.

66 Mlynář accords her some of the credit for the innovatory agricultural policy (within the relatively narrow limits for manœuvre in Brezhnev's time) which Gorbachev pursued in the Stavropol area in the 1970s.

67 Raisa Maksimovna Gorbacheva, *Byt kolkhoznogo krest'yanstva: sotsiologicheskiy ocherk* (Knizhnoe izdatelstvo, Stavropol, 1969).

68 Ibid. 136.

69 Ibid. 50.

70 See e.g. ibid. 33–45.

71 Ibid. 71–2, 131–2, 134.

72 Ibid. 95–107.

73 Ibid. 88.

74 Raisa Gorbachev, *I Hope*, 7; and Gorbachev interview, *Moskovskiy komsomolets*, 28 June 1995, p. 2.

75 *Izvestiya*, 20 Sept. 1991, p. 3.

76 *Pravda*, 2 Dec. 1987, pp. 1–2, at p. 2. For the text as carried by Soviet television and domestic radio, see BBC Summary of World Broadcasts, SU/0016 C/6, 3 Dec. 1987. The *Pravda* text is also republished in M. S. Gorbachev, *Izbrannye rechi i stat'i* (Politizdat, Moscow, 1988), v. 486.

77 BBC SWB, SU/0016 C/6, 3 Dec. 1987.

78 Mlynář was conscious of the fact that to draw attention to his friendship with Gorbachev was potentially harmful to the latter, in view of Mlynář's background as a prominent participant in the Prague Spring, dissident in Husák's Czechoslovakia, and political *émigré*. His decision to write nothing about him until (and if) he became General Secretary was, therefore, a deliberate one. Gorbachev, in 1985, was prepared to acknowledge the potential danger openly. When the Italian Prime Minister at that time, Bettino Craxi, told him that he had been reading a very interesting article about him by his old friend Mlynář (referring to Mlynář's 9 April *L'Unità* contribution), Gorbachev responded, 'Oh, Zdenek? And did he deal kindly with me?' When Craxi replied 'Very much so', Gorbachev observed that 'a Prague Spring intellectual issuing a very positive verdict on me could cause some tongues to wag'. For this exchange, see Foreign Broadcast Information Service (Washington, DC—hereafter FBIS), *Daily Report Soviet Union*, 2 July 1985, p. 87.

79 Zdeněk Mlynář, *Night Frost in Prague: The End of Humane Socialism* (Hurst, London, 1980), 17.

80 Ibid. 28.

81 Raisa Gorbachev, *I Hope*, 66.

82 Interview with Gorbachev, *Komsomol'skaya pravda*, 7 Nov. 1992, p. 1.

83 Raisa Gorbachev, *I Hope*, 81.

84 Ibid. 81–2.

85 B. N. Petukhov, who, Raisa Gorbachev records, presented inscribed copies of two of his books, published in 1970 and 1981, to Gorbachev (ibid. 82).

86 Ibid.

87 Andrei Sakharov, *Moscow and Beyond: 1986 to 1989* (Knopf, New York, 1991), 10. (Where a Russian name, as author of a work in English, has been transliterated differently from the scheme I am using, I have followed that bibliographical convention—thus, in this and other instances, 'Andrei', not 'Andrey'.)

88 Ibid. 45.

89 Arbatov in Cohen and vanden Heuvel (eds.), *Voices of Glasnost*, 307–27, at p. 312.

90 Arkady Shevchenko, *Breaking with Moscow* (Knopf, New York, 1985), 184–5.

91 The quotation is from a normally perceptive Western scholar—indeed, from an article which contains much good sense as well as the occasional piece of nonsense such as that quoted above. See Peter Rutland, 'Sovietology: Notes for a Post-Mortem', *The National Interest*, 31 (Spring 1993), 109–22, at p. 109.

92 *Yezhegodnik Bol'shoy Sovetskoy Entsiklopedii 1981* (Sovetskaya Entsiklopediya, Moscow, 1981), 573.

93 Kuchmaev, *Kommunist s bozh'ey otmetinoy*, 63–4.

94 According to the Stavropol journalist Kuchmaev, the elevation of Gorbachev to the highest post in the Stavropol territory came as a surprise to the inhabitants, an indication, perhaps, that they took less interest in the mechanics of the system than outside observers. But, as Kuchmaev notes, the decision was taken in the Central Committee building where Gorbachev had the support of

Kulakov, while Yefremov was also extremely well disposed towards Gorbachev. See Kuchmaev, *Kommunist s bozh'ey otmetinoy*, 87–8.

95 Gorbachev, 'Legacy of a Monster', in *Guardian*, 27 Feb. 1993.

96 The term was first used as a collective noun for the group of Russian critical thinkers on social issues who gained prominence in the *1860s* before being applied a century later to the critics and would-be reformers of the *1960s*.

97 My source for this statement is Georgy Shakhnazarov, Gorbachev's aide and close colleague, whom I interviewed in the Kremlin on 16 Dec. 1991. See also Ruge, *Gorbachev*, 60–1.

98 *Literaturnaya gazeta*, 4 Dec. 1991, p. 3.

99 Vadim Pechenev, *Gorbachev: K vershinam vlasti* (Gospodin Narod, Moscow, 1991), 24.

100 Raisa Gorbachev, *I Hope*, 107.

101 Ruge, *Gorbachev*, 55.

102 Mlynář, *L'Unità*, 9 Apr. 1985, p. 9.

103 Gorbachev, interviewed by Jonathan Steele, *Guardian*, 24 Dec. 1992, p. 19.

104 Gorbatschow, *Erinnerungen*, 159.

105 *The Second Russian Revolution* transcripts: interview with Vladimir Dolgikh (deposited in the Special Collections of the LSE Library). That Gorbachev and Ligachev first met on the delegation to Czechoslovakia is confirmed by Ligachev in his memoirs, although in the text of that book (Yegor Ligachev, *Inside Gorbachev's Kremlin* (Pantheon, New York, 1993), 7) he erroneously refers to this journey having taken place 'in the early 1970s'. However, the caption to a picture in the same book of Gorbachev and Ligachev together in Prague correctly identifies the date as November 1969.

106 Ibid.

107 Ruge, *Gorbachev*, 74.

108 Ligachev, *Inside Gorbachev's Kremlin*, 7.

109 Anatoly Chernyaev, interview with the author in the Gorbachev Foundation, Moscow, 30 Mar. 1992. More recently Chernyaev has published memoirs in which he refers to his first meeting with Gorbachev. See A. S. Chernyaev, *Shest' let s Gorbachevym: po dnevnikovym zapisyam* (Kultura, Moscow, 1993), 8.

110 Author's interview with Chernyaev, 30 Mar. 1992.

111 Chernyaev, *Shest' let s Gorbachevym*, 8.

112 Shakhnazarov, interview by the author, 16 Dec. 1991.

113 Raisa Gorbachev, *I Hope*, 116.

114 *Paris Match*, 19 Mar. 1992, pp. 48–53, at p. 52. Michel Tatu has suggested that Gorbachev travelled to France in 1966, 1975, and 1976 and says that Gorbachev confirmed the 1966 trip in an interview with him in 1987, implying that was when Gorbachev 'drove for 5,500 kms through France in a Renault' (Michel Tatu, *Mikhail Gorbachev: The origins of Perestroika*, East European Monographs (Boulder, Colo., 1991), 42). Gorbachev, in the *Paris Match* interview which he gave jointly with his wife, speaks of 'three couples in three Renaults' driving around France in the year which his wife identified as 1978. It is more plausible that, as an established regional party secretary who enjoyed the confidence of Andropov, Gorbachev would be able to do this in the second half of the 1970s than in 1966. Chernyaev (*Shest' let s Gorbachevym*, 8) suggests that Gorbachev's inclusion in a delegation to Belgium in 1972 was his first time in the West.

115 The interview was given to *L'Unità* on 18 May 1987. It is published in M. S. Gorbachev, *Izbrannye rechi i stat'i*, v (1988), 53–82.

116 Ibid. 53.

117 This was mentioned by both Chernyaev and Shakhnazarov in my interviews with them (already cited) and confirmed also by Vadim Medvedev in my interview with him in the Gorbachev Foundation on 22 Mar. 1993.

118 Ruge, *Gorbachev*, 204. Ruge is, however, incorrect in describing Gorbachev's 1975 stay in Stuttgart as 'his first visit to the West'. Gorbachev had, as already noted, been to Belgium in 1972.

119 Kuchmaev, *Kommunist s bozh'ey otmetinoy*, 59.

120 Ibid.

121 Alexander Nikonov, in an interview with the present author, Moscow, 20 Apr. 1994.

122 Ibid.

123 Ibid.

124 Ruge, *Gorbachev*, 126–8. At a conference (which I attended) devoted to an evaluation of Nikita Khrushchev in the year of the centenary of his birth, held in the Gorbachev Foundation on 18 Apr. 1994, and chaired by Mikhail Gorbachev, Gorbachev displayed a very respectful attitude to the

75-year-old Nikonov, who was one of the conference speakers (on Khrushchev's agricultural policies).

125 Ruge, *Gorbachev*, 127.

126 The above account is based both upon my interview with Nikonov on 20 Apr. 1994 and on Nikonov's introduction to the collected works of Chayanov published in 1993. In the latter, more formal account, Nikonov does not mention the role of Gorbachev. See A. V. Chayanov, *Izbrannye trudy* (Kolos, Moscow, 1993), and, in particular, the introduction, 'Nasledie A. V. Chayanova' by A. A. Nikonov, pp. 6–17, esp. 13–15.

127 Mlynář, *L'Unità*, 9 Apr. 1985, p. 9.

128 Ibid.

129 Gorbachev interview with Anna Pugach, *Komsomol'skaya pravda*, 19 Aug. 1993, pp. 1–2, at p. 2.

130 These quotations are from my own notes of Gorbachev's opening speech at the 18 Apr. 1994 conference on Khrushchev.

131 Two articles by Gorbachev while he was still the Stavropol regional party secretary voice his support for this approach which he also adopted in practice. See M. S. Gorbachev, 'Sel'skiy trudovoy kollektiv: puti sotsial'nogo razvitiya', *Kommunist*, 2 (1976), and 'Peredovoy opyt—vazhnyy rezerv', *Kommunist*, 14 (1978). Both articles are reprinted in M. S. Gorbachev, *Izbrannye rechi i stat'i*, i (Politizdat, Moscow, 1987), 123–33, 201–12.

132 On this see V. P. Gagnon, Jr., 'Gorbachev and the Collective Contract Brigade', *Soviet Studies*, 39/1 (Jan. 1987), 1–23.

133 Ruge, *Gorbachev*, 78–9.

134 Smith, *The New Russians*, 63–4.

135 Zhores Medvedev, *Gorbachev* (Blackwell, Oxford, 1986), 81–7. See also Kuchmaev, *Kommunist s bozh'ey otmetinoy*, 139–42.

136 Medvedev, *Gorbachev*, 84–6.

137 Ibid. 85–6.

138 'O nekotorykh merakh posledovatel'nogo osushchestvleniya agrarnoy politiki KPSS na sovremennom etape', from the transactions of the Central Committee of the CPSU, May 1978, in Gorbachev, *Izbrannye rechi i stat'i*, i. 180–200.

139 Ibid. 101.

140 Ibid. 199.

141 Ibid. 200. Cf. Andropov's speech to the Central Committee of the Soviet Communist Party on 22 Nov. 1982, cited in Archie Brown, 'Andropov: Discipline *and* Reform?', *Problems of Communism*, 32/1 (Jan.–Feb. 1983), 18–31, at p. 30.

142 Gorbachev, *Izbrannye rechi i stat'i*, i. 200.

143 Cohen and vanden Heuvel (eds.), *Voices of Glasnost*, 118–19.

144 Donald Morrison (ed.), *Mikhail S. Gorbachev: An Intimate Biography* (Time Books, New York, 1988), 103.

145 See *Bol'shaya Sovetskaya Entsiklopediya*, xiii (Sovetskaya Entsiklopediya, Moscow, 1973), 581; and *Bol'shaya Sovetskaya Entsiklopediya*, xxix (Sovetskaya Entsiklopediya, Moscow, 1978), 84.

146 G. A. Arbatov, *Zatyanuvsheesya vyzdorovlenie (1953–1985 gg.): Svidetel'stvo sovremennika* (Mezhdunarodnye otnosheniya, Moscow, 1991), 80.

147 Initially it was called simply the Institute of the USA (of the Academy of Sciences of the USSR). From 1975 it became the Institute of the USA and Canada. See ibid. 381.

148 Ibid. 297–333. See also Roy Medvedev, *Gensek s Lubyanki: Yu. V. Andropov. Politicheskiy portret* (Leta, Nizhny Novgorod, 1993), 157–8.

149 They are discussed further in Ch. 4.

150 Burlatsky has written extensively about Andropov's team of consultants and of his (not always easy) relations with other members of that group in his volume of reminiscences, *Vozhdi i sovetniki* (Politizdat, Moscow, 1990). This book subsequently appeared in an English translation by Daphne Skillen under a different title. See Fedor Burlatsky, *Khrushchev and the First Russian Spring* (Weidenfeld & Nicolson, London, 1991).

151 On the team of consultants, see Burlatsky, *Vozhdi i sovetniki*, 249–58; and Arbatov, *Zatyanuvsheesya vyzdorovlenie (1953–1985)*, 81.

152 A. D. Sakharov, 'Neizbezhnost' perestroyki', in Yury Afanasev (ed.), *Inogo ne dano* (Progress, Moscow, 1988), 122–34, at p. 125.

153 *Literaturnaya gazeta*, 4 Dec. 1991, p. 3.

154 Arkady Vaksberg, *The Soviet Mafia* (Weidenfeld & Nicolson, London, 1991).

155 Gorbatschow, *Erinnerungen*, 150.

156 Arbatov, *Zatyanuvsheesya vyzdorovlenie (1953–1985)*, 303.

157 Interview with Arbatov in Cohen and vanden Heuvel (eds.), *Voices of Glasnost*, 307–27, at p. 312.

158 *Literaturnaya gazeta*, 4 Dec. 1991, p. 3. Both Raisa Gorbachev in her memoirs (*I Hope*) and Mikhail Gorbachev in the German edition of his memoirs (*Erinnerungen*) include photographs of themselves along with Andropov in the Stavropol countryside.

159 Chernyaev, *Shest' let s Gorbachevym*, 28.

160 In an interview with S. P. K. Gupta, the Press Trust of India correspondent in Moscow, on 17 May 1985 (cited by Dev Murarka, *Gorbachev: The Limits of Power* (Hutchinson, London, 1988), 76).

161 Gorbatschow, *Erinnerungen*, 127.

162 It was at Suslov's behest that Andropov was moved out of the Secretariat of the Central Committee in 1967 when he became Chairman of the KGB. In my article 'Andropov: Discipline *and* Reform?' (*Problems of Communism*, Jan.–Feb. 1983), I observed that 'Andropov's removal from the Secretariat in 1967 was not unwelcome to Suslov' and that it was not accidental that Andropov's return to the Secretariat, after fifteen years as KGB Chairman, 'took place at the first plenary session of the Central Committee held after Suslov's death in 1982—and not before' (p. 24). For confirmation of that point from people who were close to Andropov at the time, see Ch. 3, n. 6.

163 Gorbatschow, *Erinnerungen*, 186.

164 On this see Jerry F. Hough, 'Soviet Succession: Issues and Personalities', *Problems of Communism*, 31/5 (Sept.–Oct. 1982), 20–40, at p. 37; and Marc D. Zlotnik, 'Chernenko Succeeds', *Problems of Communism*, 33/2 (Mar.–Apr. 1982), 17–31, at p. 20.

165 Gorbatschow, *Erinnerungen*, 155. The somewhat tautological account of Kulakov's death provided by *Pravda* had given rise to the speculation among Muscovites that his death was by suicide. After noting that Kulakov had died suddenly, aged 60, and mentioning some previous ill health, the report continued: 'The immediate cause of death was acute cardiac insufficiency and sudden cardiac arrest' (*Pravda*, 18 July 1978). It was also considered odd that Kulakov's Red Square funeral was not attended by Brezhnev, Kosygin, or Suslov, although many other leading party figures were there, including Kirilenko, Andropov, Gromyko, Ustinov, Romanov, and Mazurov. According to Andrey Grachev, it was believed in Central Committee circles that Kulakov was suffering from cancer (interview with the author, 16 Jan. 1993). The gloss which Valery Boldin puts on this is to say that Kulakov 'died from an overdose of alcohol while recovering from stomach surgery' (Boldin, *Ten Years that Shook the World*, 175). Gorbachev does not directly confirm this, but tactfully hints that Kulakov's life-style contributed to his failure to recover from the illness, which may *not* have been cancer (*Erinnerungen*, 155). Gorbachev regarded it as reprehensible that Brezhnev did not interrupt his holiday in order to attend the funeral (ibid.).

166 *Pravda*, 20 July 1978, 1–2.

167 See on this Medvedev, *Gorbachev*, 92–3.

168 Ibid. 90.

169 See ibid. 91–2; Doder and Branson, *Gorbachev: Heretic in the Kremlin*, 39–40; and Arbatov, *Zatyanuvsheesya vyzdorovlenie (1953–1985)*, 303.

Chapter 3   In the Portals of Power

1 Gorbachev interview with Jonathan Steele, *Guardian*, 24 Dec. 1992, p. 19.

2 Ibid.

3 Yevgeny Chazov, *Zdorov'e i vlast': Vospominaniya 'Kremlevskogo vracha'* (Novosti, Moscow, 1992), 86–7.

4 Ibid. 86.

5 See Nikolay Ryzhkov, *Perestroyka: Istoriya predatel'stv* (Novosti, Moscow, 1992), 36.

6 Georgy Arbatov and Fedor Burlatsky, both former heads of Andropov's group of consultants within the Central Committee apparatus in the 1960s, are among those who have noted Suslov's wariness of Andropov and his desire to keep him out of the Central Committee Secretariat. See e.g. Arbatov, *Zatyanuvsheesya vyzdorovlenie (1953–1985 gg.): Svidetel'stvo sovremennika* (Mezhdunarodnye otnosheniya, Moscow, 1991), 307; and Burlatsky in Stephen F. Cohen and Katrina vanden Heuvel, *Voices of Glasnost: Interviews with Gorbachev's Reformers* (Norton, New York, 1989), 183. Discussing Suslov's relations with Andropov in the 1960s in a more recent book of his own, Burlatsky observed: 'Suslov did not like Andropov and was afraid of him, suspecting that he was angling for

his post in the Politburo' (Burlatsky, *Khrushchev and the First Russian Spring* (Weidenfeld & Nicolson, London, 1991), 136; see also p. 215). Chazov, a well-placed insider, observes that Andropov and Suslov were people of opposed views and that it would have been very difficult for Andropov to become party leader if Suslov had still been alive (Chazov, *Zdorov'e i vlast'*, 146, 176).

7 Ibid. 119–22.

8 Ibid. 132–3.

9 *The Second Russian Revolution* transcripts: interview with Gorbachev.

10 See Arbatov, *Zatyanuvsheesya vyzdorovlenie (1953–1985)*, 229; Eduard Shevardnadze, *The Future Belongs to Freedom* (Sinclair-Stevenson, London, 1991), 26; A. S. Chernyaev, *Shest' let s Gorbachevym: po dnevnikovym zapisyam* (Kultura, Moscow, 1993); and interview with former KGB General Oleg Kalugin, *Moscow News*, 25 (1990), 13.

11 Chernyaev, *Shest' let s Gorbachevym*, 38.

12 Shevardnadze, *The Future Belongs to Freedom*, 26.

13 Sergey Parkhomenko, 'Afganskiy sled', *Nezavisimaya gazeta*, 10 Oct. 1992, p. 2. See also David Remnick, *Lenin's Tomb: The Last Days of the Soviet Empire* (Random House, New York, 1993), 510.

14 Vadim Pechenev, *Gorbachev: k vershinam vlasti* (Gospodin Narod, Moscow, 1991).

15 Valery Legostaev, 'Demokrat s radikal'nymi vzglyadami', *Den'*, 14 (July 1991), 4.

16 This pattern of decision-making was confirmed by Andrey Grachev, at that time a senior official in the International Department of the Central Committee, in an interview with the author on 16 Jan. 1993.

17 For an early complaint that the foundations of the Soviet system were being undermined by Mikhail Gorbachev's reforms, see Vyacheslav Gorbachev, 'Perestroyka i podstroyka', *Molodaya gvardiya*, 7 (1987), 220–47. The Russian nationalist newspaper *Den'*—which made common cause with Gorbachev's unreconstructed Communist opponents—published a series of accusatory articles under the title 'The Case of Gorbachev', from no. 8 (23–9 Feb. 1992) to no. 23 (7–13 June 1992). That last issue called for the Procurator-General of Russia, Valentin Stepankov, to begin criminal proceedings against Gorbachev, taking account of his 'anti-people, anti-state activities' delineated in detail by the contributors to *Den'*. The essence of their case was that Gorbachev had destroyed the Soviet system and the Soviet Union.

18 Shakhnazarov referred to this in my interview with him in the Kremlin, 16 Dec. 1991.

19 Arkady Vaksberg *The Soviet Mafia* (Weidenfeld & Nicolson, London, 1991), 210–11.

20 See Alec Nove's chapter on 'Agriculture' in Archie Brown and Michael Kaser (eds.), *Soviet Policy for the 1980s* (Macmillan, London, 1982), 170–85, esp. 173–5; and V. P. Gagnon, jr., 'Gorbachev and the Collective Contract Brigade', *Soviet Studies*, 39/1 (Jan. 1987), 1–23, at p. 2.

21 Speech in Belgorod on 18 Mar. 1983, published in *Pravda*, 20 Mar. 1983, p. 2, and in M. S. Gorbachev, *Izbrannye rechi i stat'i*, i (Politizdat, Moscow, 1987), 352–64, esp. 356–7.

22 See Nove, 'Agriculture', in Brown and Kaser (eds.), *Soviet Policy for the 1980s*, esp. 173–7; and Gagnon, 'Gorbachev and the Collective Contract Brigade', esp. 3–5.

23 Tikhonov interview, *The Second Russian Revolution* transcripts.

24 Ibid.

25 Academician Boris Topornin, in a conversation with the author.

26 Anatoly Sobchak, *Khozhdenie vo vlast': Rasskaz o rozhdenii parlamenta* (Novosti, Moscow, 1991), 198.

27 Among those who, like Topornin and Sobchak, have emphasized Gorbachev's ability as a listener (in interviews or conversations with me) are Anatoly Chernyaev, Georgy Shakhnazarov, Nikolay Petrakov, Andrey Grachev, Mikhail Piskotin, the late Vladimir Tikhonov, and Tatyana Zaslavskaya. On Gorbachev as a good listener and easy interlocutor, see also the interviews with Stanislav Shatalin, Anatoly Sobchak, Vladimir Tikhonov, and Tatyana Zaslavskaya in *The Second Russian Revolution* transcripts. To set against that, Roald Sagdeev told me (in March 1992) that he did not regard Gorbachev as a good listener. The assessment is subjective in the sense that something depends on the extent to which at any given time Gorbachev accepted his interlocutor's ideas and proposals. Thus, in one of a number of interviews he gave in 1995 concerning Gorbachev and perestroika, Alexander Nikolaevich Yakovlev was very enthusiastic about Gorbachev as a listener during his first two years as General Secretary, but this he attributes to Gorbachev then still feeling himself to be a provincial and having, on that account, 'an inferiority complex' (*Argumenty i fakty*, 11 (Mar. 1995), 3). Yakovlev said he had very much welcomed Gorbachev's style of work in the early days, but later everything changed. The reference to 'provincialism' (a little surprising coming from Yakovlev who was also a Muscovite only by adoption and, like Gorbachev, was born into a peasant family) was not uncommon among Muscovite intellectuals. After they turned against

Gorbachev politically, many of them gave vent to a metropolitan snobbery and scoffed at Gorbachev's provincial origins and his southern Russian accent. Yakovlev, however, is unusual in attributing feelings of inferiority to Gorbachev. People who worked with him at least as closely as did Yakovlev took a different view, believing him to be genuinely self-confident. Moreover, although a number of those whom I have interviewed agree that Gorbachev talked more and listened less as time went on—and, to that extent, are in agreement with Yakovlev—many of the statements about his exceptional listening ability (including Sobchak's, both in his book cited above and in his interview, *The Second Russian Revolution* transcripts) date from 1990. Thus, Yakovlev's remark would appear to be a considerable exaggeration and reflects the fact that his political and personal relations with Gorbachev had evolved in the course of a decade from warm to distinctly cool. Interestingly, the pattern which a number of those who worked with Gorbachev attributed to his years as General Secretary is discerned by an observer of his activities as First Secretary of the Stavropol territory from 1970 to 1978. Boris Kuchmaev says that at first Gorbachev travelled widely around the Stavropol countryside, spoke with the peasants, listened a lot, and spoke little. Later he 'spoke more and listened less' (Kuchmaev, *Kommunist s bozh'ey otmetinoy: dokumental'no-publitsisticheskiy ocherk* (Yuzhno-Russkoe kommerchesko-izdatelskoe tovarishchestvo, Stavropol, 1992) 96). Since this change in Gorbachev's style the longer he held a particular office occurred in 'the provinces' as well as in Moscow, it perhaps calls further into question Yakovlev's specific psychological explanation of the behaviour pattern.

28 Interview with Zaslavskaya in Stephen F. Cohen and Katrina vanden Heuvel (eds.), *Voices of Glasnost* (Norton, New York, 1989), esp. 117–18. See also Zaslavskaya interview in *The Second Russian Revolution* transcripts.

29 See Tatyana Zaslavskaya, *The Second Socialist Revolution: An Alternative Soviet Strategy* (Tauris, London, 1990), 2–3; and Cohen and vanden Heuvel, *Voices of Glasnost*, 118, where Zaslavskaya speaks of having met Gorbachev 'no more than seven or eight times'. She referred to 'seven or eight' meetings with Gorbachev in a conversation I had with her in November 1988.

30 That it was Zaslavskaya who first connected him to Gorbachev was mentioned by Aganbegyan in a meeting I had with him in November 1987.

31 Zaslavskaya interview in Cohen and vanden Heuvel, *Voices of Glasnost*, 118.

32 Zaslavskaya interview in *The Second Russian Revolution* transcripts.

33 Ibid. Alexander Nikonov has also confirmed to me (interview, Moscow, 20 Apr. 1994) that the more radical points that he and his academic colleagues had tried to insert in the Food Programme were eliminated from the final version, notwithstanding the fact that Gorbachev was entirely sympathetic to them.

34 *The Second Russian Revolution* transcripts. Gorbachev's rhetorical question is cited also by Angus Roxburgh, *The Second Russian Revolution* (BBC Books, London, 1991), 11.

35 Vadim Medvedev, *V komande Gorbacheva* ('Bylina', Moscow, 1994), 24. The special irony of this, as Medvedev observes, is that it was Kirilenko who, in a speech on Brezhnev's seventieth birthday, suggested that in the Soviet Union that was really the prime of life. Like Brezhnev, Kirilenko was born in 1906, and he went into even faster mental decline than the General Secretary after passing the age of 70.

36 There were recent examples for Gorbachev to contemplate. In 1977 Konstantin Katushev (born 1927) was replaced as a Secretary of the Central Committee and head of the Central Committee's Socialist Countries Department by Konstantin Rusakov (born 1909). The following year Kirill Mazurov (born 1914) was dropped from the Politburo and replaced by Nikolay Tikhonov (born 1905), who became, first, a candidate member and in 1979 a full member of the Politburo.

37 Chernyaev, *Shest' let s Gorbachevym*, 9.

38 Ibid. 10.

39 John Chrystal also compared Gorbachev favourably with all the other senior figures in Soviet politics whom he had met over a period of many years—ever since, through his uncle, Roswell Garst, he first became acquainted with Khrushchev—in a conversation I had with him when he and I were both speakers at a conference on Gorbachev's reforms held in Minneapolis on 24 Feb. 1988.

40 Chazov, *Zdorov'e i vlast'*, 159 (see also p. 164).

41 Yegor Ligachev, *Inside Gorbachev's Kremlin* (Pantheon, New York, 1993), 35.

42 Chazov, *Zdorov'e i vlast'*, 166–9. On Chebrikov, Fedorchuk, and Shchelokov, see Archie Brown (ed.), *The Soviet Union: A Biographical Dictionary* (Weidenfeld & Nicolson, London, 1990; and Macmillan, New York, 1991), 66, 92, 335–6.

43 Yu. V. Andropov, *Izbrannye rechi i stat'i*, 2nd edn. (Politizdat, Moscow, 1983), 194.

44 Ibid.

45 Ibid. 195.

46 Nikolay Ryzhkov, *Perestroyka: istoriya predatel'stv* (Novosti, Moscow, 1992), 41.

47 Ibid.

48 Ibid. 42.

49 Ryzhkov interview, *The Second Russian Revolution* transcripts.

50 Ibid.

51 These are among the names mentioned by Ryzhkov in his memoirs, *Perestroyka: Istoriya predatel'stv*, 46, and (more sparingly) in *The Second Russian Revolution* transcripts.

52 Ed A. Hewett, *Reforming the Soviet Economy: Equality versus Efficiency* (Brookings Institution, Washington, 1988), 266.

53 Ryzhkov, *Perestroyka: istoriya predatel'stv*, 47.

54 Ibid.

55 Ligachev, *Inside Gorbachev's Kremlin*, 17.

56 Ibid. 20.

57 Ibid. 26.

58 Ibid. 28–9.

59 On this see e.g. Ryzhkov, *Perestroyka: istoriya predatel'stv*, 42; Chazov, *Zdorov'e i vlast'*, 180; and Arbatov, *Zatyanuvsheesya vyzdorovlenie (1953–1985)*, 334.

60 Chazov, *Zdorov'e i vlast'*, 184; Volsky interview in *The Second Russian Revolution* transcripts; and Kira Vladena's interview with Volsky in *Nezavisimaya gazeta*, 18 June 1993, p. 5.

61 This was noted in the medical bulletin published after Andropov's death. See *Pravda*, 11 Feb. 1984, p. 1.

62 Ryzhkov, *Perestroyka: istoriya predatel'stv*, 51.

63 Besides the election of Ligachev as a Secretary of the Central Committee, Vitaly Vorotnikov and Mikhail Solomentsev were promoted from candidate to full membership of the Politburo and the KGB Chairman, Viktor Chebrikov, became a candidate member.

64 Roxburgh, *The Second Russian Revolution*, 17.

65 Ibid.

66 On Bogolyubov, see Ligachev, *Inside Gorbachev's Kremlin*, 39–43. He was removed from the Central Committee apparatus in dishonour and expelled from the Communist Party in the Gorbachev era.

67 This account is based both on Roxburgh, *The Second Russian Revolution*, and on the full text of the interview with Volsky in *The Second Russian Revolution* transcripts.

68 David Remnick, *Lenin's Tomb: The Last Days of the Soviet Empire* (Random House, New York, 1993), 192.

69 Volsky interview, *The Second Russian Revolution* transcripts.

70 Gorbachev interview, autumn 1991, *The Second Russian Revolution* transcripts.

71 Ibid.

72 My source is Vadim Medvedev himself (interview in the Gorbachev Foundation, 22 Mar. 1993).

73 Roxburgh, *The Second Russian Revolution*, 17.

74 This point, based on conversation with Gorbachev, was also made by Vadim Medvedev in my interview with him of 22 Mar. 1993.

75 Ibid.

76 Chazov, *Zdorov'e i vlast'*, 185; see also p. 123.

77 Ligachev, *Inside Gorbachev's Kremlin*, 30.

78 Roxburgh, *The Second Russian Revolution*, 18. Volsky has also given a slightly different version of what he overheard, one in which Ustinov seems still less well disposed towards Gorbachev. In an interview to *Literaturnaya gazeta* on 4 July 1990, cited by Georgy Arbatov in his memoirs, Volsky quotes Ustinov as saying 'Kostya will be more amenable than that . . .'. As Arbatov observes, Kostya is Chernenko and 'that . . .' refers to Gorbachev (Arbatov, *Zatyanuvsheesya vyzdorovlenie (1953–1985)*, 334).

79 Dolgikh was a Secretary of the Central Committee from 1972 until his forced retirement in 1988 and a candidate member of the Politburo from May 1982 until 1988. He thus received both of his major promotions in Brezhnev's time; his career advanced no further under Gorbachev.

80 Interview with Dolgikh, *The Second Russian Revolution* transcripts.

81 For a variety of accounts of this meeting, see the interviews with Aliev, Ligachev, Pechenev, Ryzhkov, and Vorotnikov in *The Second Russian Revolution* transcripts; in addition: Ligachev, *Inside Gorbachev's Kremlin*, 30–1; and Ryzhkov, *Perestroyka: istoriya predatel'stv*, 57–60. I was also given an account of it by Vadim Medvedev (interview, 22 Mar. 1993), who attended the meeting. Legostaev,

an assistant at that time to Ligachev, states firmly that three members of the Politburo—Grishin, Romanov, and Tikhonov—actually spoke against Gorbachev's elevation to the second place in the party and that two more, the First Secretary of the Ukrainian party organization, Shcherbitsky, and the Kazakhstan First Secretary, Kunaev, were not on Gorbachev's side (*Den'*, 14 (July 1991), 4). Chernenko's aide, Pechenev, who was at the meeting, also states that Tikhonov, Grishin, and Romanov expressed their opposition to Gorbachev chairing the Secretariat. He adds that Ustinov supported Chernenko's suggestion, 'even though I knew he was never a particular fan of Gorbachev's' (Pechenev, *The Second Russian Revolution* transcripts).

82 Ryzhkov, *Perestroyka: istoriya predatel'stv*, 60.

83 The point that in this respect Ustinov's death strengthened Romanov has been made by Ligachev's former aide, Legostaev, but, noting that it weakened the group of older members of the Politburo, he suggests that it also 'opened up before Gorbachev expanded opportunities' (*Den'*, 14 (July 1991), 4). Ligachev himself (*Inside Gorbachev's Kremlin*, 77) is virtually alone among those from the Kremlin's corridors of power who have offered an opinion on the matter to express confidence that Ustinov, if he had still been alive in March 1985, would have supported Gorbachev for the leadership.

84 See *Deputaty Verkhovnogo Soveta SSSR: Desyatyy sozyv*, 379.

85 Ryzhkov, *Perestroyka: istoriya predatel'stv*, 60–1.

86 Ibid. 60–3.

87 See e.g. Mikhail Shatrov, 'Neobratimost' peremen', *Ogonek*, 4 (1987), 4–5, at p. 5; and Shatrov, *Suomen Kuvalehti* (Finland), 11 (13 Mar. 1987), 2–7, at p. 2; and also the hints dropped by Yegor Ligachev in his speech to the Nineteenth Party Conference in 1988 (*Pravda*, 2 July 1988, p. 11).

88 *Kommunist*, 3 (Feb. 1984), 14; and *Partiynaya zhizn'*, 5 (Mar. 1984), 12.

89 Ryzhkov, *Perestroyka: istoriya predatel'stv*, 73.

90 Ibid.

91 Ligachev, *Inside Gorbachev's Kremlin*, 47.

92 Aganbegyan interview, *The Second Russian Revolution* transcripts.

93 Arbatov, *Zatyanuvsheesya vyzdorovlenie (1953–1985)*, 336–7.

94 Aganbegyan and Arbatov interviews, *The Second Russian Revolution* transcripts; and Arbatov, *Zatyanuvsheesya vyzdorovlenie (1953–1985)*, 336–7.

95 Ibid.

96 Ibid.

97 Ligachev, *Inside Gorbachev's Kremlin*, 53.

98 Ibid. 53–4.

99 *Materialy vneocherednogo plenuma tsentral'nogo komiteta KPSS 11 Marta 1985 goda* (Politizdat, Moscow, 1985), 6.

100 Ligachev, *Inside Gorbachev's Kremlin*, 54.

101 Ibid. 54–5.

102 Ibid. 56–7, 61–2; and Ryzhkov, *Perestroyka: istoriya predatel'stv*, 77.

103 Ibid.

104 Ligachev, *Inside Gorbachev's Kremlin*, 56–7.

105 Gorbachev interview, *Moskovskiy komsomolets*, 28 June 1995, p. 2; and Raisa Gorbachev, *I Hope*, 4–5.

106 This brief account draws largely on my own interviews and conversations, including that with Alexander Nikolaevich Yakovlev himself. See also Smith, *The New Russians*, 73–4.

107 Yakovlev interview, *The Second Russian Revolution* transcripts.

108 Joseph LaPalombara, *Democracy, Italian Style* (Yale University Press, New Haven, 1987), 237–8.

109 Chernyaev, *Shest' let s Gorbachevym*, 15–16.

110 Ibid. 33.

111 Ibid.

112 For two of the more interesting examples, see the assessments by Laurence Marks in *Observer*, 23 Dec. 1984, p. 4; and David Buchan in *Financial Times*, 22 Dec. 1984, p. 26.

113 Raisa Gorbachev, *I Hope*, 125. On the same page she mentions that she accompanied her husband 'with Konstantin Chernenko's permission' and that the 'delegation's trip turned out to be extremely interesting, substantive and productive of good results'.

114 Raisa Gorbachev herself noted: 'It was reported in our press but more fully in British and American publications' (ibid.).

115 Both Anatoly Chernyaev and Andrey Grachev, in conversations I have had with them, have expressed the conviction that, even at his advanced age, Gromyko was still thinking primarily in

terms of his own career when a few months later he backed Gorbachev strongly for the General Secretaryship following Chernenko's death.

116 *Materialy vneocherednogo plenuma tsentral'nogo komiteta KPSS 11 marta 1985 goda*, 7.

117 Ibid. 8.

118 Gromyko wrote quite interestingly and positively about Gorbachev in his memoirs, even though the latter repeat some straight lies about Soviet foreign policy which the glasnost of the Gorbachev era was already exposing as such. By the time of his death in July 1989, Gromyko—who had been removed from the Central Committee in April of that year—may have had second thoughts about his 1985 encomium. For the memoir observations of Gromyko—who describes himself 'as a communist to the marrow of my bones'—on Gorbachev, see Andrei Gromyko, *Memories* (Hutchinson, London, 1989), 340–4.

119 Gorbachev's aides, Anatoly Chernyaev and Georgy Shakhnazarov, and former Politburo member Vadim Medvedev are among those who have made that point to me.

120 Gorbatschow, *Erinnerungen*, 249, 639, 641.

121 Immediately after Mrs Thatcher's forced resignation from office in late 1990, Reagan recalled: 'She told me that Gorbachev was different from any of the other Kremlin leaders. She believed that there was a chance for a great opening. Of course, she was proven exactly right' (*Newsweek*, 3 Dec. 1990, p. 37).

122 Ronald Reagan, *An American Life* (Simon & Schuster, New York, 1990), 609; and George P. Shultz, *Turmoil and Triumph: My Years as Secretary of State* (Charles Scribner, New York, 1993), 508–9.

123 Ibid. 509.

124 *Financial Times*, 22 Dec. 1984, p. 26.

125 At lunch at Chequers, following another seminar there on the Soviet Union in which I participated, on 27 Feb. 1987, the Prime Minister described Gorbachev as the only Soviet politician she had met with whom she could have a good argument. The memoirs of Reagan and Shultz, cited above, n. 122, are just two of many sources documenting Thatcher's favourable comment on Gorbachev even when she was far out of earshot of the mass media.

126 I am quoting from a conversation I had with Malcolm Rifkind (then Minister of State at the Foreign Office) in February 1985, just two months after Gorbachev's visit to Britain, about Gorbachev. Rifkind commented also on the fact that Gorbachev had not been ideological, had not stuck to a script, and had been ready to respond to any points made to him. When the subject of religion came up, Gorbachev mentioned that he had, as a child, been christened. Among the English books he had read, it transpired, were *Parkinson's Law* and C. P. Snow's *Corridors of Power* (both of which were translated into Russian during the Brezhnev era).

127 Medvedev, *V komande Gorbacheva*, 22.

128 Both Yakovlev and Medvedev have personally confirmed to me their participation. For the involvement of Bikkenen, see Vadim Pechenev, *Gorbachev: k vershinam vlasti*, 92. In general, one of the more useful aspects of the memoirs of the former Chernenko aide Pechenev is the information conveyed concerning who worked on which documents. His account of the content of the December 1984 speech itself is, however, superficial and misleading. The economist Stepan Sitaryan and Georgy Smirnov of the Department of Propaganda of the Central Committee also took part in the preparation of the speech, according to Valery Boldin. (See Valery Boldin, *Ten Years that Shook the World: The Gorbachev Era as Witnessed by his Chief of Staff* (Basic Books, New York, 1994), 49.)

129 According to the party reformer Otto Latsis, people close to Chernenko tried to play down the significance of the speech and *Pravda* made cuts without asking Gorbachev's permission (Latsis interview, *The Second Russian Revolution* transcripts).

130 M. S. Gorbachev, *Zhivoe tvorchestvo naroda* (Politizdat, Moscow, 1984). In an article published soon after Gorbachev's accession to the Soviet leadership, I quoted extensively and exclusively from those parts of the speech which *Pravda* had failed to print. See Archie Brown, 'Gorbachev: New Man in the Kremlin', *Problems of Communism*, 34/3 (May–June 1985), esp. 18–21. A useful account of the speech is given by Robert Kaiser in *Why Gorbachev Happened: His Triumphs and his Failures* (Simon & Schuster, New York, 1991), 75–80, although it is surprising to read that Kaiser's research assistant's 'greatest triumph was finding the full text of Gorbachev's December 1984 speech in the bowels of the Library of Congress after the ordinary search process had ended in failure' (ibid. 458). A work published in 100,000 copies was not such an extreme bibliographical rarity, and the speech was republished with only the most insignificant excisions in Gorbachev's collected speeches and writings. See M. S. Gorbachev, *Izbrannye rechi i stat'i*, ii (Politizdat, Moscow, 1987), 75–108.

131 Gorbachev, *Zhivoe tvorchestvo naroda*, 11.

132 Ibid. 8.

133 Pechenev, *Gorbachev: k vershinam vlasti*, 93.

134 Gorbachev, *Zhivoe tvorchestvo naroda*, 15, 16, 17, 27, 30.

135 Ibid. 8, 10, 26.

136 Ibid. 12–13.

137 See especially Tatyana Zaslavskaya, 'The Novosibirsk Report', *Survey*, 28/1 (Spring 1984), 88–108; this is the translated text of a paper she delivered at a closed seminar in Novosibirsk in 1983 and whose leakage to the West (although not by Zaslavskaya) earned both her and the Director of her Institute, Abel Aganbegyan, a party reprimand. Among other innovative writing by Soviet scholars in the first half of the 1980s, traces of whose work appear in Gorbachev's speech of December 1984, that of Aganbegyan, Mikhail Piskotin, and Boris Kurashvili is worth noting.

138 Gorbachev, *Zhivoe tvorchestvo naroda*, 14.

139 Author's interview with Vadim Medvedev, 22 Mar. 1993. The same point was made to me by, among others, Gorbachev's former economic aides Nikolay Petrakov and Oleg Ozherelev.

140 Pechenev interview, *The Second Russian Revolution* transcripts.

141 Nenashev interview, *The Second Russian Revolution* transcripts.

142 Author's interview with Vadim Medvedev, 22 Mar. 1993.

143 Ibid.

144 Boris Yeltsin, *Against the Grain: An Autobiography* (Jonathan Cape, London, 1990), 112.

145 Arbatov interview, *The Second Russian Revolution* transcripts.

146 Ibid.

147 That is not to deny that political reform was a higher priority for Gorbachev from January 1987 onwards than at the outset of his General Secretaryship—when the composition of the Politburo was such that it would have been impossible to launch such reform—or to suggest that his ideas for change were as fundamental in 1985 as they became in 1988. But as Gorbachev's views had developed—in the course of visits abroad and of conversations with advisers and colleagues—over the several years immediately preceding his elevation to the top post, it was not only the economic condition of the Soviet Union with which he had become increasingly discontented. Anatoly Lukyanov, interviewed by *Pravda* in 1995, was asked whether Gorbachev already had in 1985 a prepared programme 'for the demolition of the socialist system'. Lukyanov replied that, so far as Gorbachev's words were concerned, Gorbachev's three objectives when he came to power were acceleration of the development of socialism, the strengthening of scientific-technological progress, and the deepening of democracy. What is more, the Politburo would not have allowed him 'to derail socialism'. For that, he had to change the composition of the Politburo, and before long he started to do so, bringing in Yakovlev, Shevardnadze, Vadim Medvedev, Primakov, and others. See *Pravda*, 20 Mar. 1995, p. 4. Much, of course, hangs on the different meanings Gorbachev and Lukyanov attached to 'socialism' and 'democracy'.

148 Alexander Yakovlev, *Muki prochteniya bytiya. Perestroyka: nadezhdy i real'nosti* (Novosti, Moscow, 1991), 32.

149 Ibid.

150 Gorbachev speech to cultural workers on 28 Nov. 1990, published in *Izvestiya*, 1 Dec. 1990, pp. 1, 2, 4 (at p. 4).

151 Shevardnadze, *The Future Belongs to Freedom*, 37.

152 The words used, according to Raisa Gorbachev, were: 'tak dal'she zhit' nel'zya' (*Ya Nadeyus'*, (Kniga, Moscow, 1991), 13). David Floyd, in the translation of those memoirs (Raisa Gorbachev, *I Hope*, 5), renders Gorbachev's remark as 'We just can't go on like this'. Angus Roxburgh, quoting directly from an impromptu speech made to a reunion of his Moscow University Law Class, held on 16 June 1990 (which Roxburgh attended), cites Gorbachev's recollection of saying the night before he became General Secretary: 'We cannot go on living like this, we must change' (*The Second Russian Revolution*, 9).

153 Shevardnadze, *The Future Belongs to Freedom*, 23–6, esp. 26. Lukyanov, speaking in 1995, referred to the Pitsunda conversation between Gorbachev and Shevardnadze as possible evidence that Gorbachev did have a hidden agenda (*Pravda*, 22 Mar. 1995, p. 4).

154 Vladimir Dolgikh, who, at the time of Gorbachev's accession to power, was a Secretary of the Central Committee and a candidate member of the Politburo, later admitted that he did not then 'have a clue' that Gorbachev would introduce sweeping reform of the Soviet system. See Roxburgh, *The Second Russian Revolution*, 9.

155 For Shchelokov's statement about Gorbachev, see Gorbachev interview, *Moskovskiy komsomolets*, 28 June 1995, p. 2. For the announcement on the removal of Shchelokov's military rank, see *Vedomosti verkhovnogo soveta SSSR* (Moscow), 46 (14 Nov. 1984), 860.

156 Chazov, *Zdorov'e i vlast'*, 206–7.

157 Ibid. 207.

158 Ligachev, *Inside Gorbachev's Kremlin*, 62. Cf. ibid. 32–4, 80; and Yeltsin, *Against the Grain*, 112.

159 This point is made by Ligachev's former aide Legostaev, who observes that, notwithstanding Grishin's disclaimers that he aspired to the top post, it is possible that there were members of the Politburo who saw him as a 'transitional figure from Chernenko to Romanov' (*Den'*, 14 (July 1991), 4).

160 Chazov, *Zdorov'e i vlast'*, 210.

161 Arbatov interview, *The Second Russian Revolution* transcripts.

162 On Grishin's activity at this time, see also Ryzhkov, *Perestroyka: istoriya predatel'stv*, 74; and Ligachev, *Inside Gorbachev's Kremlin*, 57, 62.

163 *Pravda*, 4 Jan. 1985, pp. 1–2.

164 *Pravda*, 21 Feb. 1985, p. 2; *Pravda*, 22 Feb. 1985, p. 2; and *Pravda*, 23 Feb. 1985, pp. 1–2.

165 *Pravda*, 1 Mar. 1984, p. 2; *Pravda*, 2 Mar. 1984, p. 2; and *Pravda*, 3 Mar. 1984, pp. 1–2.

166 Dolgikh interview, *The Second Russian Revolution* transcripts.

167 Chazov, *Zdorov'e i vlast'*, 210.

168 Ibid.

169 Ibid. 211.

170 In addition to the discussion earlier in this chapter concerning the suppression of Andropov's recommendation that Gorbachev should take his place as acting head of the Politburo, see also Ligachev, *Inside Gorbachev's Kremlin*, 39–41, 67–8.

171 Gorbachev's former aide Boldin is quite wrong in asserting that Shcherbitsky 'had *chosen not to fly back* from the United States for Chernenko's funeral, thus arguably helping Gorbachev's cause' (emphasis added) (Boldin, *Ten Years that Shook the World*, 60).

172 Vorotnikov interview, *The Second Russian Revolution* transcripts.

173 Grishin, quoted by Legostaev, *Den'*, 14 (July 1991), 4.

174 Ibid.

175 Quoted by Chernyaev, *Shest' let s Gorbachevym*, 29. Chernyaev is also dismissive of the idea of Grishin as a candidate for the General Secretaryship.

176 See Yeltsin, *Against the Grain*, 89, 112, 121.

177 Ligachev, *Inside Gorbachev's Kremlin*, 67.

178 Ibid. 34. 'Of course,' Ligachev adds with heavy irony, 'it's possible that in Sverdlovsk, where Boris Yeltsin was working at the time, they knew more than we did about what was happening in the Kremlin.'

179 Chernyaev, *Shest' let s Gorbachevym*, 31.

180 Pechenev interview, *The Second Russian Revolution* transcripts.

181 The full transcript of the Politburo meeting of 11 March which chose Gorbachev for the General Secretaryship is published in *Istochnik*, 0/1 (1993), 68–75.

182 Cf. Ligachev, *Inside Gorbachev's Kremlin*, 66 82; and Ryzhkov, *Perestroyka: istoriya predatel'stv*, 78–82, esp. 79. See also the interviews with Dolgikh and Vorotnikov, *The Second Russian Revolution* transcripts.

183 Dolgikh interview, *The Second Russian Revolution* transcripts.

184 Chernyaev, *Shest' let s Gorbachevym*, 29. The same four names are given by Pechenev (interview, *The Second Russian Revolution* transcripts).

185 Gorbachev, *Izbrannye rechi i stat'i*, ii 129–33, esp. 130–1.

186 See Ligachev, *Inside Gorbachev's Kremlin*, 72–9; and Chernyaev, *Shest' let s Gorbachevym*, 30–1.

187 Speech of A. A. Gromyko, *Materialy vneocherednogo plenuma tsentral'nogo komiteta KPSS 11 Marta 1985 goda*, 6–8.

188 See *Istochnik*, 0/1 (1993), 68–75; and *Kommunist*, 5 (Mar. 1985), 3–11.

189 Ryzhkov, *Perestroyka: istoriya predatel'stv*, 79.

190 Ibid. 50.

191 Ibid. 361.

192 Andrey Grachev so described Gorbachev in conversation with me in Oxford, 16 Jan. 1993.

Chapter 4   The Power of Ideas and the Power of Appointment

1 In addition to the data cited in Ch. 1 showing that Lenin was still in 1989 (by which time people had no inhibitions about responding honestly to survey research) regarded by Russians as the greatest person who ever lived, as late as December 1989 a remarkable 72 per cent of Soviet citizens named Lenin as the most outstanding scholar/scientist of all. The list of eighteen names included those of Darwin, Newton, Einstein, Marx, and Mendeleev. Respondents could name more than one such person, but Lenin easily topped the poll. His nearest rivals were Mendeleev (named by 53.5 per cent) and Marx (51.4 per cent). See *Obshchestvennoe mnenie v tsifrakh* (All-Union Centre for the Study of Public Opinion), 3/10 (Jan. 1990), 7.

2 Alexander Yakovlev, *Predislovie, Obval, Posleslovie* (Novosti, Moscow, 1992), 125.

3 Seweryn Bialer, *The Soviet Paradox: External Expansion, Internal Decline* (Tauris, London, 1986), 169–70.

4 Georgy Shakhnazarov, *Tsena svobody* (Rossika Zevs, Moscow, 1993), 579.

5 Ibid.

6 Bialer, *The Soviet Paradox*, 16. Bialer continued: 'Perhaps such forces exist but are dormant and no outside observer is capable of penetrating the system deeply enough to establish their existence and evaluate their scope. But this is not likely.'

7 Stephen F. Cohen, *Rethinking the Soviet Experience: Politics and History since 1917* (Oxford University Press, New York, 1985), 129.

8 The emergence of the Stalin issue into public political discourse between 1985 and 1988 is usefully traced by R. W. Davies in his book *Soviet History in the Gorbachev Revolution* (Macmillan, London, 1989).

9 That Gorbachev was an 'anti-Stalinist' was one of the points on which Zdeněk Mlynář laid stress in the first conversation I had with him about Gorbachev in June 1979, a time when the terms 'Stalinism' and 'anti-Stalinism' had been banished from political discourse in the Soviet Union (as well, of course, as in Mlynář's native Czechoslovakia). Gorbachev's anti-Stalinism was likewise quite evident to Alexander Nikonov during the Brezhnev years when he was closely acquainted with Gorbachev in Stavropol (interview, 20 Apr. 1994).

10 See M. S. Gorbachev, *Izbrannye rechi i stat'i*, iii (Moscow, 1987), 154–70, at p. 162.

11 Ibid.

12 M. S. Gorbachev, *Gody trudnykh resheniy* (Alfa-Print, Moscow, 1993), 24.

13 Loone, reviewing Raymond Taras (ed.), *The Road to Disillusion: From Critical Marxism to Postcommunism in Eastern Europe*, in *Soviet Studies*, 45/4 (1993), 741–2, at p. 742.

14 To give but one example, a political tract co-authored by a French Sovietologist and a British political scientist (published in the very year when Gorbachev took decisive steps to undermine Leninist political organization) includes the statement: 'As good Marxist-Leninists, Soviet leaders must practise as well as preach Lenin's doctrine. To understand Lenin is therefore to understand Soviet leaders today, not least Mikhail Gorbachev and his policies.' See Françoise Thom and David Regan, *Glasnost, Gorbachev and Lenin: Behind the New Thinking* (Policy Research Publications, London, 1988), 41.

15 Yakovlev, *Predislovie, Obval, Posleslovie*, 267.

16 Ibid.

17 Boris Yeltsin, *Against the Grain: An Autobiography* (Jonathan Cape, London, 1990), 113–14.

18 For an elaboration of the latter term, and of his reasons for preferring it to 'revolution from above', see John Gooding, 'Perestroika as Revolution from Within: An Interpretation', *Russian Review*, 51/1 (Jan. 1992), 36–57.

19 Gorbachev, in an interview with Jonathan Steele, *Guardian*, 24 Dec. 1992, p. 19.

20 A. S. Chernyaev, *Shest' let s Gorbachevym: po dnevnikovym zapisyam* (Kultura, Moscow, 1993), 89.

21 Yakovlev, *Predislovie Obval Posleslovie*, 267–8.

22 Referring to the April plenum of 1985, Yeltsin wrote in the earlier of his two volumes of memoirs: 'A big step had been taken in the right direction, although, of course, it was a revolution from above' (Yeltsin, *Against the Grain*, 114).

23 Yakovlev, *Predislovie, Obval, Posleslovie*, 268.

24 Ibid. 268–9.

25 Gooding, 'Perestroika as Revolution from Within', 56.

26 Ibid. 36–7.

27 Gorbachev's self-description in *Gody trudnykh resheniy*, 25.

28 Chernyaev, *Shest' let s Gorbachevym*, 89.

29 Yakovlev, *Predislovie, Obval, Posleslovie*, 266.

30 Interview with Mikhail Gorbachev by Colin Greer, *Austin-American Statesman (Parade Magazine)*, 23 Jan. 1994, pp. 4–6, at p. 4. Gorbachev continued: 'So the development of the ideas on which I based my leadership was not an easy process. It didn't happen overnight.'

31 Gooding, 'Perestroika as Revolution from Within', 38.

32 In a talk at St Antony's College, Oxford, on 19 Nov. 1993, Bridget Kendall—the BBC radio correspondent in Moscow from 1989 to 1993—noted that as late as July 1989, when she took up her post, she was replacing a colleague who had been expelled from the Soviet Union accused of spying and that 'unofficial' Russian friends were still being stopped from entering the foreigners' compound in which she lived. For academic specialists visiting the Soviet Union, it should be added, the ease of contact with Soviet citizens was by that time very great; even earlier, they had a less difficult time than the journalists, although their telephones, too, were tapped as a matter of course.

33 On this, see also Alexander Rahr, 'Gorbachev's Personal Staff', Radio Liberty Research (RL 216/88), 30 May 1988.

34 Interview with Alexandrov-Agentov, *Argumenty i fakty*, 20 (May 1993), 6.

35 Andrei S. Gratchev (Grachev), *L'Histoire vraie de la fin de L'URSS: Le Naufrage de Gorbatchev* (Editions du Rocher, Paris, 1992), 292.

36 Ibid.

37 Interview with Andrey Grachev, 14 Jan. 1993.

38 Interview with Anatoly Chernyaev, 30 Mar. 1992.

39 Chernyaev, *Shest' let s Gorbachevym*, 63.

40 Interview with Smirnov in Stephen F. Cohen and Katrina vanden Heuvel, *Voices of Glasnost: Interviews with Gorbachev's Reformers* (Norton, New York, 1989), 76–96, at p. 77.

41 Ibid. 76.

42 Interview with Ivan Frolov, *Zhurnalist*, 5 (May 1994), 43–7, at p. 44.

43 Ibid. 45.

44 Ibid.

45 As early as November 1987 Chernyaev wrote a memorandum to Gorbachev in which he said, *inter alia*, that in period of revolutionary changes it was disgraceful that *Pravda* should be the most conservative of all Soviet newspapers. He linked this remark with criticism of Ligachev, indicating that Viktor Afanasev, as editor-in-chief, was able to continue dragging his feet because of support from within the Politburo (meaning, above all, from Ligachev). See Chernyaev, *Shest' let s Gorbachevym*, 201–2. See also the memoirs of Viktor Afanasev, *Chetvertaya vlast' i chetyre genseka* (Kedr, Moscow, 1994), in which he responds by criticizing Gorbachev for his cadres policy and foreign policy as well as for his 'indecisiveness' (p. 100) but, nevertheless, describes him as 'lively, energetic, erudite' and with the ability 'to enter vividly into conversation with any interlocutor, whether worker or academician, rank-and-file soldier or marshal, ordinary clerk or president of a foreign state' (ibid.).

46 Frolov, *Zhurnalist*, 5 (May 1994), 43–4.

47 Rakhmanin's influence within the Soviet leadership did not long survive Gorbachev's coming to power. When he published an article in *Pravda* on 21 July 1985 under his usual pseudonym of 'Vladimirov', in which he criticized both Hungarian and East German reforms, Gorbachev angrily attacked the article at the next meeting of the Politburo and criticized not only Rakhmanin but three of those present: Konstantin Rusakov, a Secretary of the Central Committee and head of the Socialist Countries Department; Mikhail Zimyanin, the Secretary responsible for Propaganda; and Viktor Afanasev, the editor of *Pravda*, who in that capacity had the right to attend Politburo meetings (see Chernyaev, *Shest' let s Gorbachevym*, 49–51).

48 For more on this, see Archie Brown, 'Political Science in the Soviet Union', *International Political Science Review*, 7/4 (1986), 443–81.

49 G. Kh. Shakhnazarov, *Sotsialisticheskaya demokratiya: nekotorye voprosy teorii* (Politizdat, Moscow, 1972).

50 G. Kh. Shakhnazarov, 'Logika politicheskogo myshleniya v yadernuyu eru', *Voprosy filosofii*, 5 (1984), 62–74, esp. 72–3.

51 In a conversation I had with Shakhnazarov in the Institute of State and Law in Moscow early in the perestroika period, he accepted that the Soviet intervention in Czechoslovakia in 1968 was wrong. When I interviewed him in the Kremlin on 16 Dec. 1991 he went so far as to say that his point of view had been that of a social democrat since the early 1960s. It has to be said that this viewpoint was often very well disguised; equally, it *had* to be unless Shakhnazarov had been prepared to

exchange work in the Central Committee apparatus for persecution as a dissident. Just as Gorbachev's views were to change partly as a result of the impact of his trips abroad, so Shakhnazarov said that *his* earlier foreign travels had influenced his outlook.

52 This was mentioned to me by Shakhnazarov in my interview with him of 16 Dec. 1991, but a month earlier Shakhnazarov had already elaborated on the point in print. See *Izvestiya*, 18 Nov. 1991, p. 4.

53 M. S. Gorbachev, 'Sotsialisticheskaya ideya i revolyutsionnaya perestroyka', *Pravda*, 26 Nov. 1989, pp. 1–3.

54 On this see Archie Brown and George Schöpflin, 'The Challenge to Soviet Leadership: Effects in Eastern Europe', in Paulo Filo della Torre, Edward Mortimer, and Jonathan Story (eds.), *Eurocommunism: Myth or Reality?* (Penguin, Harmondsworth, 1979), 249–76.

55 *Izvestiya*, 18 Nov. 1991, p. 4.

56 Worth citing because it is so typical of writing which carries over-simplification to the point of distortion was the description of Gorbachev in *The Economist* ('Gorbachev or Yeltsin? The Lords of Misrule', 6–12 Apr. 1991, p. 17): 'Above all he is still, unlike Mr Yeltsin, a faithful Communist, in a country that has largely turned its back on that religion.' And in the same article: 'For all that he has done, the Soviet Union is in worse shape in 1991 than it was in 1985.' So much for freedom of speech and of assembly, contested elections, an end to persecution of dissidents, the possibility to travel abroad (or to emigrate), the beginnings of a rule of law, and much else!

57 *Izvestiya*, 18 Nov. 1991, p. 4.

58 Ligachev made this remark on the television programme *600 Seconds*, on the St Petersburg channel, which I happened to see in Moscow on 31 Mar. 1992. I return to the issue of Gorbachev and social democracy later in this chapter in the context of considering the intellectual influence on him of his discussions with Western politicians.

59 Frolov interview, *Zhurnalist*, 5 (May 1994), 46.

60 Ibid.

61 See the published draft in *Nezavisimaya gazeta*, 23 July 1991, p. 2. The First Secretary of the Leningrad regional party organization, Boris Gidaspov, complained on Moscow Television on 25 July that 'it has turned not just into a social democratic, but into a real liberal program' (FBIS-SOV-91-144, 26 July 1991).

62 Conversation with Alexander Chubaryan at St Antony's College, Oxford, 16 May 1994.

63 Interview with Alexander Nikonov, 20 Apr. 1994.

64 Valery Boldin, *Ten Years that Shook the World* (Basic Books, New York, 1994). My review of it, 'The Traitor's Tale', appeared in the *Times Literary Supplement*, 20 May 1994, p. 6.

65 See Chernyaev, *Shest' let s Gorbachevym*, 201–2.

66 For an excellent, and highly sympathetic, portrait of Yakovlev, see David Remnick, *Lenin's Tomb: The Last Days of the Soviet Empire* (Random House, New York, 1993), 290–305. For a rather less sympathetic view from a well-informed colleague who belonged to the same political tendency within the Communist Party, see Chernyaev, *Shest' let s Gorbachevym*.

67 Only as the Soviet system came to an end did Yakovlev make the existence of this 1985 memorandum public. See e.g. Yakovlev, *Predislovie, Obval, Posleslovie*, 127–8. Yakovlev goes on to say in this book (published in 1992) that when he put forward the proposal in 1985 he saw it as entirely compatible with 'perfecting socialism' and viewed it as an important step towards the 'democratic transformation' of Soviet socialism. Subsequently he quoted extensively from the actual document in a newspaper article based on another book and (still more fully) in that new volume of memoirs. See *Obshchaya gazeta*, 28 Jan.–3 Feb. 1994, p. 9; and Yakovlev, *Gor'kaya chasha: Bolshevizm i Reformatsiya Rossii* (Verkhne-Volzhskoe knizhnoe izdatelstvo, Yaroslavl, 1994), 205–13.

68 Up to that point Yakovlev's heterodox views had been reserved for private conversation with Gorbachev or confined to confidential memoranda. They were scarcely at all to be found in his published works. Once he had become a Secretary of the Central Committee (in 1986) Yakovlev more and more openly voiced in public his increasingly radical critique of the Soviet system.

69 If a two-party system and contested elections were the most dramatically new element in Yakovlev's memorandum, they were only part of a range of proposals for political reform. See *Obshchaya gazeta*, 28 Jan.–3 Feb. 1994, p. 9.

70 Yakovlev had been much more supportive, to put it mildly, of the Yeltsin administration than had Gorbachev. In particular, he had endorsed Yeltsin's dissolution of the Supreme Soviet and Congress of People's Deputies of the Russian Federation in September 1993, whereas Gorbachev had criticized both the Russian President and the leadership of the legislature for the political ineptitude which had led to the impasse. At the end of 1993 Yakovlev accepted an invitation from Yeltsin to

become Director of Ostankino television and left the Gorbachev Foundation, where, since the collapse of the Soviet Union, he had held the post of Vice-President.

71 *Obshchaya gazeta*, 28 Jan.–3 Feb. 1994, p. 9.

72 This conversation, in which I participated, took place at a lunch for Yakovlev in St Antony's College (following his lecture at the college which constitutes the last chapter of *Predislovie, Obval, Posleslovie*) on 29 Jan. 1992.

73 *Yezhegodnik Bol'shoy Sovetskoy Entsiklopedii 1981* (Sovetskaya Entsiklopediya, Moscow, 1981), 9–10.

74 Yegor Ligachev, *Inside Gorbachev's Kremlin* (Pantheon, New York, 1993), 95–7. Yakovlev, for his part, complained about Ligachev's excessive influence, including his influence over party appointments.

75 Chernyaev, *Shest' let s Gorbachevym*, 49.

76 Eduard Shevardnadze, *The Future Belongs to Freedom* (Sinclair-Stevenson, London, 1991), 38.

77 Ibid. 39.

78 Ibid.

79 The personnel change in Gorbachev's first three years as General Secretary is discussed in greater detail in my two concluding chapters of Archie Brown (ed.), *Political Leadership in the Soviet Union* (Macmillan, London, 1989), 162–231. In the same book, T. H. Rigby (ch. 2, p. 48) makes the point that *within his first year* Gorbachev had attained a position 'in which there were no carry-overs from his predecessor's regime who could conceivably challenge his primacy'. Rigby goes on to observe: 'It took Stalin six years after the death of Lenin to achieve such a position, Khrushchev four years after the death of Stalin, and Brezhnev ten or twelve years after the replacement of Khrushchev.'

80 Apart from Romanov, these Secretaries were the technocratic Vladimir Dolgikh; the exceptionally aged (even by Soviet standards) foreign policy specialist Vasily Kuznetsov; the veteran ideologist, ousted early on in the Gorbachev era from the headship of the International Department of the Central Committee, Boris Ponomarev; the reactionary former editor of *Pravda* and propaganda secretary Mikhail Zimyanin; and the conservative head of the Socialist Countries Department of the Central Committee (already in failing health by the time of his removal in early 1986), Konstantin Rusakov. For the dates of these personnel changes, see the successive editions of the *Yezhegodnik Bol'shoy Sovetskoy Entsiklopedii* (Sovetskaya Entsiklopediya, Moscow, 1984–90); and for biographies of the politicians involved Archie Brown (ed.), *The Soviet Union: A Biographical Dictionary* (Weidenfeld & Nicolson, London, 1990; and Macmillan, New York, 1991).

81 Vadim Medvedev became a Secretary of the Central Committee immediately after the Twenty-Seventh Party Congress in 1986 and was responsible until 1988 for overseeing the department of the Central Committee which kept an eye on other Communist countries. Following the Nineteenth Party Conference in 1988, Medvedev became a full member of the Politburo while retaining his Secretaryship.

82 Yeltsin, *Against the Grain*, 72.

83 Ibid. 76.

84 Ibid.

85 Gorbachev interview, *Moskovskiy komsomolets*, 28 June 1995, p. 2; see also *Pravda*, 2 July 1988, p. 11; and Vadim Medvedev, *V komande Gorbacheva* ('Bylina', Moscow, 1994), 66.

86 Chernyaev, *Shest' let s Gorbachevym*, 202.

87 Yeltsin, *Against the Grain*, 90.

88 Cf. ibid. 88–90; and Medvedev, *V komande Gorbacheva*, 66.

89 For the full text of Yeltsin's speech, see *Izvestiya TsK KPSS*, 2 (1989), 239–41, 279–81.

90 See e.g. Robert Legvold, 'Soviet Learning in the 1980s', in George W. Breslauer and Philip E. Tetlock (eds.), *Learning in U.S. and Soviet Foreign Policy* (Westview, Boulder, Colo., 1991), 684–732, esp. 694–7, 704–7.

91 Bogomolov's institute sent a memorandum to 'the appropriate authorities' on 20 Jan. 1980 in which they spoke of the 'hopelessness and harmfulness' of the Soviet military intervention in Afghanistan. Bogomolov first drew public attention to the memorandum in *Literaturnaya gazeta*, 16 Mar. 1988, in an article cited by Andrei Melville and Gail W. Lapidus, *The Glasnost Papers: Voices on Reform from Moscow* (Westview Press, Boulder, Colo., 1990), 295–6.

92 O. Bogomolov, 'Ne mogu snyat' s sebya vinu', *Ogonek*, 35 (1990), 2–3.

93 Among those from the Bogomolov institute who made important contributions to the pool of ideas and analyses after 1985 were the foreign policy specialist (later Chairman of the Foreign Affairs Committee of the Russian Supreme Soviet and now Russian Ambassador to Mexico) Yevgeny Ambartsumov; the political scientists Igor Klyamkin, Andranik Migranyan, Lilia Shevtsova, and Alexander Tsipko; the young constitutional theorist and founder of the Social Democratic Party

Oleg Rumyantsev; and the economists Otto Latsis, Gennady Lisichkin, and Ruben Yevstigneev. Several of the most prominent reformers from Bogomolov's institute belonged to the network of scholar-politicians who had spent several years in Prague (on *World Marxist Review*), among them Ambartsumov and Latsis. A radical economic reformer, whose exceptionally well-written essays helped to set the political agenda from 1987, Nikolay Shmelev, also spent the greater part of his career in Bogomolov's institute, although he moved to Arbatov's in 1982.

94 Even a fairly critical observer of Gorbachev, Viktor Afanasev, a scholar-journalist of conservative Communist disposition and editor-in-chief of *Pravda* from 1976 until 1989, notes that Gorbachev held 'in great esteem scholars, writers and journalists' (Afanasev, *Chetvertaya vlast' i chetyre genseka*, 100).

95 Besides the influential political analyst Fedor Burlatsky, there were several others at the Institute of Social Sciences whose ideas had an impact on official policy, among them Alexander Galkin and the Institute's Director, Yury Krasin.

96 Its leading figure, Sergey Alekseev, was to become increasingly influential in the perestroika era.

97 Jeff Checkel, 'Ideas, Institutions, and the Gorbachev Foreign Policy Revolution', *World Politics*, 45/1 (Jan. 1993), 271–300. On the more general problem with this type of analysis, see Legvold, 'Soviet Learning in the 1980s', especially the section 'The Perils of Parsimony', 720–6.

98 Checkel, 'Ideas, Institutions, and the Gorbachev Foreign Policy Revolution', 294.

99 In his diary account of the Central Committee plenum of 1 July 1985 at which Gorbachev announced that Gromyko would be moving from the Ministry of Foreign Affairs to become the Chairman of the Presidium of the Supreme Soviet (a dramatic end to Gromyko's twenty-eight years in charge of that ministry, which was made known to the outside world only on 2 July at a session of the Supreme Soviet), Chernyaev noted: 'And not a word about the "services" of Gromyko in foreign policy. Everyone drew attention to that, whispering to one another' (*Shest' let s Gorbachevym*, 48–9).

100 Ponomarev's precise response was: 'What "new thinking"? We have correct thinking! Let the Americans change their thinking' (quoted in Chernyaev, *Shest' let s Gorbachevym*, 61).

101 These attributes were referred to by many of those who had worked with Gorbachev in my interviews with them (as well as in a number of the interviews to be found in *The Second Russian Revolution* transcripts). More than one of Gorbachev's associates referred to him as a 'workaholic'.

102 On Gorbachev's respect for scholarly specialists in Stavropol, see Boris Kuchmaev, *Kommunist s bozh'ey otmetinoy* (Yuzhno-Russkoe kommerchesko-izdatelskoe tovarishchestvo, Stavropol, 1992), 68.

103 Ibid. 88.

104 Gorbachev interview with Jonathan Steele, *Guardian*, 24 Dec. 1992. 'It was', said Gorbachev, 'like being in the front line of a war. I lived through several lives, and I don't know how I survived.'

105 Interview with Yakovlev, *Literaturnaya gazeta*, 25 Dec. 1991, p. 3.

106 Even for long-standing reformers, the change in 1990–1 could be dramatic. Thus, in a conversation I had in the Bogomolov institute in June 1991, Ruben Yevstigneev said that, looking at what he had written a year ago, he could hardly believe how much his views had changed in the meantime.

107 Author's interview with Shakhnazarov, 16 Dec. 1991.

108 When he voted for Khrushchev's wildly over-optimistic and somewhat utopian Party Programme at the Twenty-Second Party Congress in 1961, he had (he said years later) sincerely believed in it. See Vadim Pechenev, *Gorbachev: k vershinam vlasti* (Gospodin Narod, Moscow, 1991), 24.

109 Andrey Grachev, *Kremlevskaya khronika* ('EKSMO', Moscow, 1994), 247.

110 Mikhail Gorbachev, 'Delaet li chelovek politiku? Delaet li chelovek istoriyu? Razmyshleniya o nasledii Villi Brandta', *Svobodnaya mysl'*, 17 (1992), 17–21, at p. 21.

111 Ibid. and 'M. S. Gorbachev–V. Brandt: Iz arkhiva Gorbacheva', *Svobodnaya mysl'*, 17 (1992), 22–9.

112 Gorbachev, 'Delaet li chelovek politiku? Delaet li chelovek istoriyu?', 17. The link between affect and persuasion has been extensively explored in the literature of social psychology. See e.g. R. P. Abelson, D. R. Kinder, M. D. Peters, and S. T. Fiske, 'Affective and Semantic Components in Political Person Perception', *Journal of Personality and Social Psychology*, 42/4 (1982), 619–30, esp. 619, 624.

113 Grachev, *Kremlevskaya khronika*, 247.

114 Ibid. Grachev adds that Gorbachev 'did not just appreciate "Felipe", he loved him'.

115 Ibid.

116 Substantial excerpts from one of those conversations (in Madrid on 26 Oct. 1990) were published two years after Gorbachev's fall from power. See Gorbachev, *Gody trudnykh resheniy*, 234–53.

117 Ibid. 239.

118 Ibid. 246–7; and Michail Gorbatschow, *Erinnerungen* (Seidler Verlag, Berlin, 1995), 761.

119 Interview with Andrey Grachev, 11 Mar. 1992.

120 Gorbatschow, *Erinnerungen*, 760.

121 Ibid. 639.

122 See Chernyaev, *Shest' let s Gorbachevym*, 134–41; and Margaret Thatcher, *The Downing Street Years* (HarperCollins, London, 1993), 478–85, esp. 481–3.

123 Chernyaev, *Shest' let s Gorbachevym*, 138, 140–1.

124 Ibid. 141.

125 Gorbachev, *Gody trudnykh resheniy*, 24.

126 Chernyaev, *Shest' let s Gorbachevym*, 75–6.

127 Cf. Stephen F. Cohen, introduction to Ligachev, *Inside Gorbachev's Kremlin*, pp. vii–xxxix, at pp. xxix–xxx.

128 In a book which, along the way, contains many sensible observations, Martin Malia begins by recognizing that 'socialism' means different things to different people and then proceeds, somewhat obsessively, to obscure that central point. See Malia, *The Soviet Tragedy: A History of Socialism in Russia, 1917–1991* (The Free Press, New York, 1994).

129 Alec Nove, 'New Thinking on the Soviet Economy', in Archie Brown (ed.), *New Thinking in Soviet Politics* (Macmillan, London, 1992), 29–38, at 35–6.

130 Interview with Gorbachev, *Kuranty*, 13 Oct. 1992, pp. 4–5. It is interesting to compare this with the view of the former Warden of Wadham College, Oxford, Sir Stuart Hampshire—a philosopher and democratic socialist in the British tradition—writing in a book which he co-edited with Leszek Kolakowski *called* 'The Socialist Idea': 'For me socialism is not so much a theory as a set of moral injunctions, which seem to me clearly right and rationally justifiable: first, that the elimination of poverty ought to be the first priority of government after defence; secondly, that as great inequalities in wealth between different social groups lead to inequalities in power and in freedom of action, they are generally unjust and need to be redressed by governmental action; thirdly, that democratically elected governments ought to ensure that primary and basic human needs are given priority within the economic system, even if this involves some loss in the aggregate of goods and services which would otherwise be available . . . At present socialism needs a variety of evidence, open minds with moral conviction, and distrust of all unitary theories.' See Hampshire's 'Epilogue' to Kolakowski and Hampshire (eds.), *The Socialist Idea: A Reappraisal* (Weidenfeld & Nicolson, London, 1974), 249.

131 Transcript of the broadcast of Gorbachev's speech published in FBIS-SOV-90-231, 30 Nov. 1990, 43–8, at p. 44.

132 Ibid.

133 'Sotsialisticheskaya ideya i revolyutsionnaya perestroyka', *Pravda*, 26 Nov. 1989, pp. 1–3.

134 After linking the birth of 'the socialist idea' with 'the human dream of freedom, justice, peace and democracy, that is, a truly human society', Gorbachev added: 'On the other hand, the liberal current of thought and practice has also given humankind a great deal', partly because it borrowed ideas from the socialists and used them at times 'better than did the socialists themselves' (*Svobodnaya mysl'*, 17 (1992), 21).

135 Kuchmaev, *Kommunist s bozh'ey otmetinoy*, 61.

136 Gorbachev interview with Jonathan Steele, *Guardian*, 24 Dec. 1992, p. 19.

137 Ibid.

138 Smirnov interview in Cohen and vanden Heuvel (eds.), *Voices of Glasnost*.

139 One of the questions in the interview referred in the past tense to the elections for the Congress of People's Deputies of the USSR which had been held in the spring of 1989.

140 Yakovlev interview in Cohen and vanden Heuvel, *Voices of Glasnost*, 39–40.

141 For an excellent account of the fundamentally undemocratic character of Lenin's thought, see A. J. Polan, *Lenin and the End of Politics* (Methuen, London, 1984).

142 See e.g. Archie Brown, 'Political Power and the Soviet State', in Neil Harding (ed.), *The State in Socialist Society* (Macmillan, London, 1984), 51–103; and Jerry F. Hough, *The Struggle for the Third World: Soviet Debates and American Options* (The Brookings Institution, Washington, 1986).

143 Stephen Padgett and William E. Paterson, *A History of Social Democracy in Postwar Europe* (Longman, London, 1991), 263. Gorbachev would appear to have noted the degree of convergence that had taken place between social democracy and liberalism when he writes, approvingly, that Willy Brandt succeeded in uniting 'loyalty to the ideas of social justice, democracy and freedom with respect for the potentialities of liberalism' (*Svobodnaya mysl'*, 17 (1992), 21).

144 Cf. Gorbatschow, *Erinnerungen*, 391–2, 401–3, 412, 419, 423.

145 His regard for Lenin certainly did not mean (*pace* Martin Malia) that Gorbachev had a 'thoroughly Communist concept of his role as leader'. See Malia, *The Soviet Tragedy*, 431.

146 Gorbachev interview with Jonathan Steele, *Guardian*, 24 Dec. 1992, p. 19.

147 Ibid.

148 Gorbachev, *Zhivoe tvorchestvo naroda* (Politizdat, Moscow, 1984), esp. 6, 10, 11, 12, 14, 18, 20, 30, 40, 41–2.

149 That the speech did cause a stir—and that it aroused criticism in conservative circles—has already been noted in Ch. 3.

150 Nikolay Ryzhkov, *Perestroyka: istoriya predatel'stv* (Novosti, Moscow, 1992), 70–1.

151 Ibid. 72.

152 Gorbachev, *Izbrannye rechi i stat'i*, ii (1987), 251.

153 In the seven volumes of Gorbachev's speeches and writings, dating from his Stavropol days until June 1989, which were published in Moscow between 1987 and 1990, only vol. i and vol. vii do not contain any references to *uskorenie* in the index. The index to vol. vi suggests that the last time Gorbachev used the term in a speech was in June 1988 at the Nineteenth Party Conference, but, in fact, the word does not appear on any of the three pages (395–7) indicated. In reality, it would appear, his last use of 'acceleration' was on 13 Apr. 1988. See Gorbachev, *Izbrannye rechi i stat'i*, vi (1989), 195. The index to vol. ii is also in error in suggesting that the first time Gorbachev employed the notion of acceleration was in the speech he made after being elected General Secretary at the Central Committee plenum of 11 Mar. 1985. In fact, in his speech of December 1984 to the ideology conference Gorbachev spoke of the 'enormous possibilities for the acceleration [*uskorenie*] of socio-economic development' which depended upon 'uniting the initiative and self-generated activity of the masses with a scientific base and a creative approach to the resolution of urgent problems'. See Gorbachev, *Zhivoe tvorchestvo naroda*, 10.

154 See e.g. his article 'Novomu metody—shirokuyu dorogu', *Ekonomicheskaya gazeta*, 9 (1978), repr. in Gorbachev, *Izbrannye rechi i stat'i*, i. 154–9, in the course of which the need for 'psychological perestroika' is stressed twice; and his article, 'Prodovol'stvennaya programma i zadachi ee realizatsii', *Kommunist*, 10 (1982), repr. in *Izbrannye rechi i stat'i*, i. 302–20 (at p. 315).

155 Gorbachev, *Zhivoe tvorchestvo naroda*, 26.

156 Gorbachev, *Izbrannye rechi i stat'i*, ii. 269.

157 Ibid. iii. 326–58, esp. 330–1.

158 Medvedev, *V komande Gorbacheva*, 35–6.

159 Gorbachev, *Izbrannye rechi i stat'i*, iii. 330.

160 Gorbachev's speech to the January 1987 plenum of the Central Committee (ibid. iv. 299–354).

161 Gorbachev's speech to the Eighteenth Conference of Trade Unions, 25 Feb. 1987 (ibid. 424–43, at p. 428).

162 It also became in the later part of Gorbachev's years in power and especially after the collapse of the Soviet Union an unpopular term with the Russian people as a whole. A survey conducted by VTsIOM in November 1994 found more than twice as many respondents taking a positive view of Gorbachev's role in history as evaluated positively perestroika as a period of history. The apparent contradiction would seem to arise from the fact that, in the evaluation of Gorbachev, a larger number of people recalled that he had introduced glasnost, political freedom, and contested elections, whereas perestroika meant a failed restructuring of the economy as well as an upheaval which included the unpopular breakup of the Soviet state. The most popular period of Soviet history, according to this VTsIOM survey of the Russian Federation, was the Brezhnev era, positively evaluated by 36 per cent of respondents (perhaps, not least, for its stability and predictability), whereas perestroika was seen as more positive than negative by only 16 per cent. Even the Stalin era attracted more support (18 per cent) than perestroika, although the Stalin years also had higher negative evaluations (57 per cent thought them more bad than good as compared with 47 per cent taking the same view of perestroika); fewer people were fence-sitters regarding the Stalin era than on perestroika. However, in the same November 1994 survey 33 per cent evaluated Gorbachev's role in history positively (the comparable figure for other twentieth-century Russian leaders being: Nicholas II 36 per cent; Lenin 44 per cent; Stalin 25 per cent; Khrushchev 39 per cent; Brezhnev 29 per cent; and Yeltsin 30 per cent). See Yu. A. Levada, ' "Chelovek sovetskiy" pyat' let spustya: 1989–1994 (predvaritel'nye itogi sravnitel'nogo issledovaniya)', *Ekonomicheskie i sotsial'nye peremeny: monitoring obshchestvennogo mneniya*, VTsIOM, 1 (Jan.–Feb. 1995), 9–14, at p. 10.

163 *Pravda*, 26 Feb. 1986, p. 5.

164 Mikhail Gorbachev, *Perestroika: New Thinking for Our Country and the World* (Collins, London, 1987), 49–50.

165 Yakovlev interview with Kira Vladina, *Nezavisimaya gazeta*, 10 Aug. 1994, p. 5.

166 Nove, in his contribution to the symposium 'What's Happening in Moscow?', *The National Interest*, 8 (Summer 1987), 15.

167 Quoted by Nove, ibid.

168 Brezhnev speech of 14 June 1974, republished in L. I. Brezhnev, *Voprosy razvitiya politicheskoy sistemy sovetskogo obshchestva* (Politizdat, Moscow, 1977), 315. I recall being told by Fedor Burlatsky in the early 1980s that the speech-writer responsible for putting those words into Brezhnev's mouth was Alexander Bovin, at that time political correspondent of *Izvestiya*, today the Russian ambassador to Israel. Alexander Yakovlev, in contrast (speaking informally in Oxford in January 1992), confessed to having tried and failed—in the years before 1973 when he was acting head of the Propaganda Department of the Central Committee—to write 'glasnost' into one of Brezhnev's speeches. According to their political disposition, party insiders played the game of trying to make their leader's speeches more enlightened or more orthodox. But in the Brezhnev—as distinct from the Gorbachev—era it made remarkably little difference to the way the political system worked in practice.

169 Gorbachev, *Izbrannye rechi i stat'i*, i. 88.

170 As noted by David Wedgwood Benn, *From Glasnost to Freedom of Speech: Russian Openness and International Relations* (Pinter, in association with the Royal Institute of International Affairs, London, 1992), 12.

171 Gorbachev, *Zhivoe tvorchestvo naroda*, 30.

172 Wedgwood Benn, *From Glasnost to Freedom of Speech*, 12–13. See also Vladimir Lakshin, 'From Glasnost to Freedom of Speech', *Moscow News*, 15 (1989), 4.

173 Gorbachev, *Zhivoe tvorchestvo naroda*, 30.

174 Ibid. 30. Emphasis on 'self-management' and more democracy at the work-place was also well to the fore in the earliest years of Gorbachev's General Secretaryship, but was later subordinated both to a radical reform of political institutions and to the demands of marketizing economic reformers. On 'the false promise of enterprise democratization', see Donald Filtzer, *Soviet Workers and the Collapse of Perestroika: The Soviet Labour Process and Gorbachev's Reforms, 1985–1991* (Cambridge University Press, Cambridge, 1994), 82–8.

175 Gorbachev, *Zhivoe tvorchestvo naroda*, 16.

176 I have discussed that particular aspect of Gorbachev's speech of December 1984 with, among others, Vadim Medvedev, who took part in the writing of it.

177 See Terence Ball, James Farr, and Russell L. Hanson (eds.), *Political Innovation and Conceptual Change* (Cambridge University Press, Cambridge, 1989), esp. 2, 30.

178 *Pravda*, 15 July 1987, pp. 1–2, at p. 2.

179 For other early uses of the term by Gorbachev see e.g. *Pravda*, 30 Sept. 1987, p. 1; and Gorbachev, *Perestroika*, 77.

180 *Pravda*, 6 Feb. 1990, pp. 1–2, at p. 1.

181 Some of this is common ground with the view of Joseph Schull, 'The Self-Destruction of Soviet Ideology', in Susan Gross Solomon (ed.), *Beyond Sovietology: Essays in Politics and History* (M. E. Sharpe, New York, 1993), 8–22. Where I part company from Schull is in his apparent belief that the lack of consistency of Gorbachev's public utterances in some way invalidates his decisive role as an instigator of change. If Gorbachev had, for the sake of argument, publicly embraced the principle of political pluralism in 1985 or 1986, he would not have had the opportunity to show how consistently he could adhere to it, for he would have been removed from office within twenty-four hours. Since there was no mass movement from below to change the system until Gorbachev created the conditions of freedom in which it could emerge, there would in all probability be a Soviet system in place to this day. Only dissidents (whose movement had been fairly comprehensively crushed before Gorbachev came to power) or the totally apolitical could be wholly consistent under Soviet conditions. To search for consistency or coherence in the language of a politician leading a movement away from an extreme and highly ideological authoritarianism when timing was everything and one step too far at the wrong moment could lead to a return to the status quo ante is a somewhat sterile exercise.

182 See e.g. *Pravda*, 6 Feb. 1990, p. 1.

183 Citing one or two such instances in his memoirs, Yegor Ligachev blames 'the tantalizing all-permissiveness of the radical press', which was 'presented as the highest manifestation of democracy'. See Ligachev, *Inside Gorbachev's Kremlin*, 125.

184 Keith Michael Baker, *Inventing the French Revolution* (Cambridge University Press, Cambridge, 1990), 7.

185 Ibid. 6.

186 Gorbatschow, *Erinnerungen*, 391–2, 402–3, 412, 419, 423, 437–9, 445.

Chapter 5   Gorbachev and Economic Reform

1 Andrey Grachev, *Dal'she bez menya... Ukhod Prezidenta* (Kul'tura, Moscow, 1994), 136.

2 Ibid.

3 Although output fell still more precipitously after the complete breakup of the Soviet Union, already in Gorbachev's last year in office it was falling dramatically, with barter 'becoming increasingly the norm in economic transactions in 1991 as political barriers to trade rose between union republics, regions, and even cities' (Richard E. Ericson, 'The Russian Economy Since Independence', in Gail W. Lapidus (ed.), *The New Russia: Troubled Transformation* (Westview Press, Boulder, Colo., 1995), 37–77, at p. 37). Ericson notes that 'in 1991 oil output decreased by 11%, that of chemical goods by 10–15%, coal by 11%, and light industry and food industry by 11–12%. State purchases of meat fell by 18%, of milk by 14%, and the grain harvest fell by 24%' (ibid.).

4 That is not to overlook the International Department of the Central Committee—which is discussed in both Chs. 4 and 7—but that department was not charged with the execution of Soviet foreign policy, especially where state-to-state relations were concerned. In some respects, the department of the Central Committee responsible for liaison with ruling Communist Parties (popularly known as the 'Socialist Countries Department') was more concerned with policy implementation than the International Department, in so far as it related to Eastern Europe, in particular. The Ministry of Defence and the KGB also exerted (or attempted to exert) influence over foreign policy, but their part in the implementation process in the Gorbachev era was a minor one as compared with the Ministry of Foreign Affairs.

5 This is a central theme of Stephen Whitefield's *Industrial Power and the Soviet State* (Clarendon Press, Oxford, 1993). On the industrial ministries, see also Julian Cooper, *The Soviet Defence Industry: Conversion and Reform* (Pinter, for the Royal Institute of International Affairs, London, 1991), esp. 6–11.

6 Alexander Yakovlev, *Predislovie, obval, posleslovie* (Novosti, Moscow, 1992), 138.

7 Whitefield, *Industrial Power and the Soviet State*, 180.

8 Ibid.

9 Ibid.

10 Cf. Jerry F. Hough, *The Soviet Prefects: The Local Party Organs in Industrial Decision-Making* (Harvard University Press, Cambridge, Mass., 1969); and Peter Rutland, *The Politics of Economic Stagnation in the Soviet Union: The Role of Local Party Organs in Economic Management* (Cambridge University Press, Cambridge, 1993).

11 Boris Yeltsin, *Against the Grain: An Autobiography* (Jonathan Cape, London, 1990), 58.

12 Rutland, *The Politics of Economic Stagnation in the Soviet Union*, 212.

13 On this point, see Ed A. Hewett, *Reforming the Soviet Economy: Equality versus Efficiency* (Brookings Institution, Washington, 1988), 20; and Gorbachev, 'O zadachakh partii po korennoy perestroyke upravleniya ekonomikoy', *Izbrannye rechi i stat'i* (Politizdat, Moscow, 1988), v 129–85, at p. 182.

14 See George W. Breslauer, 'Soviet Economic Reforms Since Stalin: Ideology, Politics, and Learning', *Soviet Economy*, 6/3 (1990), 252–80. Another article which looks at learning in the context of economic reform (James Clay Moltz, 'Divergent Learning and the Failed Politics of Soviet Economic Reform', *World Politics*, 45/1 (Jan. 1993), 301–25) is less persuasive, partly because it does not explore the evidence for Gorbachev's interest in marketizing reform and partly because it fails to identify any types or stages of economic reform between an *uskorenie* (acceleration) of the old economic system, on the one hand, and acceptance of one or other variant of 'foreign capitalism', on the other.

15 For a fascinating case-study of the emergence of the late-Soviet and post-Soviet banking system, see Joel S. Hellman, 'Bureaucrats vs. Markets? Rethinking the Bureaucratic Response to Market Reform in Centrally Planned Economies', in Susan Gross Solomon (ed.), *Beyond Sovietology: Essays in Politics and History* (M. E. Sharpe, Armonk, NY, 1993), 53–93.

16 See e.g. Seweryn Bialer and Joan Afferica, 'The Genesis of Gorbachev's World', *Foreign Affairs*, 64/3 (1986), 605–44, esp. 608–13; Marshall Goldman (who not unrealistically suggested in 1985 that 'Gorbachev will probably continue to hold out the vision of fundamental economic reform, but the likelihood is that he will have to settle for considerably less', although Gorbachev's economic policy by 1990 was radicalized beyond Goldman's expectations), 'Gorbachev and Economic Reform', *Foreign Affairs*, 64/1 (Fall 1985), 56–73, esp. 72; and Philip Hanson (who expressed scepticism that Gorbachev would move 'even by stealth' in the direction of the kind of economic reform undertaken in Kádár's Hungary), 'The Economy', in Martin McCauley (ed.), *The Soviet Union under Gorbachev* (Macmillan, London, 1987), 97–117, esp. 115.

17 Mikhail Gorbachev, *Perestroika: New Thinking for our Country and the World* (Collins, London, 1987), 19. By February 1988 Gorbachev was painting a still gloomier picture of the early 1980s, saying that the beginning of the decade had seen an actual decrease of national income in absolute terms (Gorbachev, *Izbrannye rechi i stat'i*, vi (1989), 77).

18 Tables of the slow-down in Soviet economic growth, in terms both of official Soviet statistics and CIA estimates, are conveniently available in David Dyker, *Restructuring the Soviet Economy* (Routledge, London, 1992), 42.

19 Abel Aganbegyan, *The Challenge of Perestroika* (Hutchinson, London, 1988), 2–3.

20 The point is made in a careful study of Khanin's work (including his book *Dinamika ekonomicheskogo razvitiya SSSR*, published in Novosibirsk in 1991) by Mark Harrison, 'Soviet Economic Growth since 1928: The Alternative Statistics of G.I. Khanin', *Europe-Asia Studies*, 45/1 (1993), 141–67.

21 Vasily Selyunin and Grigory [a Russification of Khanin's given name] Khanin, 'Lukavaya tsifra', *Novy mir*, 2 (Feb. 1987), 181–201; and Alec Nove, *Glasnost' in Action: Cultural Renaissance in Russia* (Unwin Hyman, London, 1989), 214.

22 Harrison e.g. observes: 'In the past it was possible for antagonists to dismiss Khanin's work, and for more sympathetic sceptics to maintain reservations, on the grounds that his sources and methods were not fully available. Publication of *Dinamika* in 1991 has removed most (but not all) of the grounds for such reservations. From what is now available it is clear that Khanin's estimates are honest and, for the most part, consistent and well founded' ('Khanin's Economic Growth Statistics', 159).

23 For a useful comparison of the Soviet and Chinese reforms, see Włodzimierz Brus, 'Marketisation and Democratisation: The Sino-Soviet Divergence', *Cambridge Journal of Economics*, 17/4 (Dec. 1993), 423–40.

24 For a valuable account of the Hungarian reform between 1968 and 1988—with a strong emphasis on its flaws—see Włodzimierz Brus and Kazimierz Laski, *From Marx to the Market: Socialism in Search of an Economic System* (Clarendon Press, Oxford, 1989), 61–86. See also János Kornai, *The Road to a Free Economy. Shifting from a Socialist System: The Example of Hungary* (Norton, New York, 1990).

25 The alarm extended to senior officials within the Central Committee apparatus, as Andrey Grachev, himself a full-time consultant within the International Department of the Central Committee in the first half of the 1980s, has confirmed in conversation.

26 I have used the term 'General Secretary' to embrace Brezhnev's tenure of office as party leader from 1964 until 1982, but for the first eighteen months he was, strictly speaking, *First* Secretary of the Central Committee. That term had been introduced under Khrushchev and in fit may from 1953 until the Twenty-Third Party Congress in early 1966, when the Communist Party reverted to the nomenclature of Stalin's time, *General* Secretary.

27 For some interesting observations on the political outlooks of Brezhnev and Kosygin and on their relationship, see Georgy Arbatov, *Zatyanuvsheesya vyzdorovlenie (1953–1985 gg.): Svidetel' stvo sovremennika* (Mezhdunarodnye otnosheniya, Moscow, 1991), 102–48, esp. 119–20.

28 I first noted this distinction and the other differences between the political context of the Kosygin and Gorbachev reforms in an article, 'Soviet Political Developments and Prospects', *World Policy Journal*, 4/1 (Winter 1986/7).

29 According to Nikolay Petrakov, Gorbachev's economic aide during 1990 and an informal adviser before then (interview with the author, 18 June 1991), Gorbachev had confidence in Ryzhkov for the first several years of his leadership. But by late 1989 Gorbachev realized that more drastic action was needed and that Ryzhkov would be against such radical reform.

30 On the party apparatus and economic reform, see Rutland, *The Politics of Economic Stagnation in the Soviet Union*, esp. 207, 223. On military industry, see Julian Cooper, *The Soviet Defence Industry: Conversion and Reform* (Pinter, in association with the Royal Institute of International Affairs, London, 1991), chapter on 'The Defence Industry as a Political Force', 70–88, esp. 77–8.

31 Ibid.

32 The writings of these authors were especially important partly because they were powerfully written (particularly Shmelev's articles) and appeared in journals widely read by the intelligentsia. They helped to mould opinion in favour of a more comprehensive rejection of the existing Soviet economic system than had prevailed hitherto. Among the most interesting of these articles are: Shmelev, 'Avansy i dolgi', *Novy mir*, 6 (June 1987), 142–58; Shmelev, 'Novye trevogi', *Novy mir*, 4 (Apr. 1988), 160–75; Popov and Shmelev, 'Anatomiya defitsita', *Znamya*, 5 (May 1988), 158–83; Popov, 'S tochki zreniya ekonomista: o romane Aleksandra Beka "Novoe naznachenie" ', *Nauka i zhizn'*, 4 (1987); Selyunin, 'Eksperiment', *Novy mir*, 8 (Aug. 1985), 173–94; Selyunin and Khanin, 'Lukavaya tsifra', *Novy mir*, 2 (Feb. 1987), 181–201; and Selyunin, 'Rynok: khimera i real'nost'', *Znamya*, 6 (June 1990), 193–205. Apart from the more specialist journals, important contributions

to radicalizing economic thought were made by Otto Latsis in his articles in the party journal, *Kommunist*.

33 Both before and during the perestroika period, some of the boldest breaks with past thinking on economic reform were made at the Institute of State and Law in Moscow by academic lawyers and political scientists. The works of three of these scholars, Piskotin, Kurashvili, and Obolonsky, are noted in Archie Brown, 'Political Science in the USSR', *International Political Science Review*, 7/4 (1986), 443–81. Special attention is paid to Kurashvili's publications by Ronald Amann, 'Towards a New Economic Order: The Writings of B. P. Kurashvili', *Detente*, 8 (Winter 1987); and by Anders Åslund, *Gorbachev's Struggle for Economic Reform: The Soviet Reform Process, 1985–88* (Pinter, London, 1989), esp. 112–14. Kurashvili is an interesting and unusual case inasmuch as his views have remained virtually unchanged since the beginning of the 1980s. The opinions which made him an exceptionally bold reformer then place him in opposition to Soviet and Russian economic developments since 1990 from a 'conservative' position. A former colonel in the KGB—he taught at the KGB High School until he was asked to leave because of his unacceptably reformist views—he came to the Institute of State and Law in the early 1970s. He was described to me in the early 1980s by one of his colleagues there as 'the bravest man in the institute'. He genuinely believed in, and argued for, a 'socialist market economy', but he was as much in favour of the 'socialist' component (with the emphasis strongly on a variety of forms of *public*, not private, ownership—'destatization without privatization' was how he put it in a *Pravda* article in 1990) as of the move to the market. By 1993 he found himself in the curious position of defending the Communist Party of the Soviet Union when a civil court action against it was taken by the Yeltsin administration, and, accordingly, in the company of die-hard conservative Communists (even though Kurashvili had also been one of the first people in the Soviet Union to argue publicly for a multi-party political system) rather than that of the radicals who were his allies five years earlier (or, in the case of the bolder among them, ten years earlier). While there are Communist or nationalist reactionaries whose views may not have changed much over the past decade, it is highly unusual to find a genuine reformer whose viewpoint has remained almost the same in public and private over that turbulent period. Among the more significant contributions to the economic reform debate to come out of the Institute of State and Law are: B. P. Kurashvili, 'Gosudarstvennoe upravlenie narodnym khozyaystvom: perspektivy razvitiya', *Sovetskoe gosudarstvo i pravo*, 6 (1982), 38–48; Kurashvili, 'Ob"ektivnye zakony gosudarstvennogo upravleniya', *Sovetskoe gosudarstvo i pravo*, 10 (1983), 36–44; Kurashvili, 'Kontury vozmozhnoy perestroyki', *EKO* (June 1985), 59–79; Kurashvili, 'Osnovnoe zveno khozyaystvennoy sistemy', *Sovetskoe gosudarstvo i pravo*, 10 (1986), 12–21; Kurashvili, *Ocherk teorii gosudarstvennogo upravleniya* (Nauka, Moscow, 1987); Kurashvili, 'Pravye i levye, ili gde iskat' optimal'nuyu put' v ekonomike?', *Pravda*, 4 Oct. 1990, pp. 3–4; and Kurashvili, *Strana na rasput'e . . . (Poteri i perspektivy perestroyki)* (Yuridicheskaya literatura, Moscow, 1990); M. I. Piskotin, *Sotsializm i gosudarstvennoe upravlenie* (Nauka, Moscow, 1984; rev. and expanded edn., 1988); A. V. Obolonsky, 'Mekhanizm regulirovaniya sluzhebnykh mezhlichnostnykh otnosheniy v gosudarstvennom apparate', *Sovetskoe gosudarstvo i pravo*, 9 (1985), 58–66; Obolonsky, 'Byurokraticheskaya deformatsiya soznaniya i bor'ba s byurokratizmom', *Sovetskoe gosudarstvo i pravo*, 1 (1987), 52–61; Obolonsky, *Chelovek i gosudarstvennoe upravlenie* (Nauka, Moscow, 1987); Obolonsky, 'Mekhanizm tormozheniya: chelovecehskoe izmerenie', *Sovetskoe gosudarstvo i pravo*, 1 (1990), 80–7; V. P. Rassokhin, *Mekhanizm vnedreniya dostizheniy nauki: politika, upravlenie, pravo* (Nauka, Moscow, 1985); and Rassokhin, 'Vedomstvennost' kak istoricheskiy fenomen sovetskoy ekonomiki', in F. M. Borodkin, L. Ya. Kosals, and R. V. Ryvkina (eds.), *Postizhenie* (Progress, Moscow, 1989).

34 How compatible this was with radical economic reform is, however, questionable. Many marketizing economists disagreed with the election of managers by the work-force even as a stage in the transformation of Communist economic systems. See e.g. Kornai, *The Road to a Free Economy*, 99–100. Donald Filtzer notes that a significant minority—some 20 per cent—of factory managers had been elected by late 1988, together with between 5 and 8 per cent of shop superintendents and foremen. But 'in late 1989, as perestroika entered its more "radical", pro-market phase, the Soviet government did away with these elections altogether . . .' (Filtzer, *Soviet Workers and the Collapse of Perestroika: The Soviet Labour Process and Gorbachev's Reforms, 1985–1991* (Cambridge University Press, Cambridge, 1994), 83).

35 Dyker, *Restructuring the Soviet Economy*, 185.

36 As noted in Ch. 3, this term was used by Gorbachev in his speech of December 1984 and his economic advisers with whom I spoke were in no doubt that by it Gorbachev meant 'market'. Even the use of 'commodity-money relations' was a relatively bold step forward for a Politburo member at that time. Alexander Yakovlev, then still Director of IMEMO, tried in 1984 to get two social scientists to write an article on the role of 'commodity-money relations'. But he was not successful: 'Both of them were members of the Academy of Sciences, very progressive people, but they never wrote

that article. They were afraid, and efforts had to be made to get public opinion used to the idea, step by step, article by article, speech after speech'—even to the use of the term 'commodity-money relations' (A. N. Yakovlev interview, in *The Second Russian Revolution* transcripts).

37 Interesting extracts from Politburo transcripts of 1987 gave an indication of Gorbachev's economic thinking at that time. See Gorbachev, *Gody trudnykh resheniy* (Alfa-Print, Moscow, 1993), 67–86.

38 Gorbachev, *Izbrannye rechi i stat'i*, v (1988), 163. Moreover, at the Twenty-Seventh Party Congress in early 1986 the one speaker to use the term 'socialist market' was Gorbachev's client and old Stavropol colleague Vsevolod Murakhovsky (see *Pravda*, 3 Mar. 1986, p. 3). It can be taken for granted that in so doing he was acting with Gorbachev's full knowledge and as a stalking-horse for him. Gorbachev could not yet employ a term still unacceptable to the Politburo as a whole when his use of it would imply an official commitment by the Soviet leadership to marketization.

39 Gorbachev, *Izbrannye rechi i stat'i*, vii. 113.

40 Ibid. 573.

41 Ibid. 594.

42 Gorbachev interview, *Der Spiegel*, No. 3, 18 Jan. 1993, p. 127. Gorbachev went on (pp. 127–8): 'I don't want to idealize your country but I am in favour of the kind of state that provides social security, a state based on the rule of law with a functioning parliamentarism, which represents a federation of largely independent federal *Länder* with a strong centre. I myself witnessed in Bonn and Munich how you balance your interests.'

43 See e.g. Gorbachev, *Izbrannye rechi i stat'i*, vi. 54, 344, 395.

44 Gaydar's speech to the Russian Congress of People's Deputies, 3 Dec. 1992, reported from Russian radio in BBC Summary of World Broadcasts, Part 1, Former USSR, 5 Dec. 1992, pp. C1/3–C1/4, at p. C1/4.

45 It is in this sense that it is used by John R. Freeman in his book *Democracy and Markets: The Politics of Mixed Economies* (Cornell University Press, Ithaca, NY, 1989).

46 Robert A. Dahl, 'Why All Democratic Countries Have Mixed Economies', in John W. Chapman and Ian Shapiro (eds.), *Democratic Community* (New York University Press, New York, 1993), 259–82, esp. 259, 280.

47 Dahl notes: 'Although it is true that a market economy exists in all democratic countries, it is also true that what exists in every democratic country is a market economy modified by government intervention. These mixed economies take many different forms, from the corporatist systems of the Scandinavian countries, Germany, Austria, and the Netherlands to the more fragmented systems of Britain and the United States. Moreover, the extent and forms of intervention vary not only from country to country but also over time' (ibid. 278).

48 Ibid.

49 Gorbachev, 'K global'nomu gumanizmu', in *Gody trudnykh resheniy*, 330–3, at p. 333. Cf. Dahl, who, after noting that the collapse of Communism and of socialist command economies had greatly enhanced the appeal both of democracy and the market, goes on: 'Indeed, it seems often to be assumed that democracy and free markets mutually reinforce one another. My aim here is to show that both historical experience and theoretical considerations contradict this assumption' ('Why All Democratic Countries Have Mixed Economies', 259–60). For a more comprehensive corrective to the view that the unfettered market is the optimal agent of human development, see the important inter-disciplinary study of Robert E. Lane, *The Market Experience* (Cambridge University Press, Cambridge, 1991).

50 E. K. Ligachev, 'Nam nuzhna polnaya pravda', *Teatr*, 8 (Aug. 1986), 2–7, at p. 3.

51 Åslund, *Gorbachev's Struggle for Economic Reform: The Soviet Reform Process, 1985–88*. In a second edition published (without the subtitle) in 1991, the same author reacts stridently to Gorbachev's backtracking on support for the controversial '500 Days Programme' (discussed later in this chapter and in Ch. 8) in the autumn of 1990. Although Gorbachev found it difficult to make up his mind on the pros and cons of the 500 Days Programme and was under enormous pressure to withdraw his earlier approval of this document, he was *probably* politically as well as economically mistaken to backtrack on it. That, however, scarcely merits Åslund's sweeping judgement: 'After such a spectacular failure even to try to salvage his own people, Gorbachev can expect little mercy in his own country *or in history*' (emphasis added: 2nd edn. (1991), 221). The second edition of this work is a curate's egg. The first seven chapters, which incorporate the material of the earlier edition completed in October 1988 with only minor updating, are a careful and valuable study of the reform debates and of Gorbachev's part in them, in which the author takes pragmatic account of the realities of Soviet politics. In the final two chapters added to the second edition and completed in January 1991, ideological commitment gets in the way of understanding Gorbachev's dilemmas. Thus, the author insists (p. 230) that nothing short of a proclamation of the victory of capitalism

could pave the way for systemic change. Since a number of Russian intellectuals had already given voice to such thoughts, presumably it was the General Secretary of the Soviet Communist Party who was remiss in failing to do so. Even in January 1991, however, such a proclamation by Gorbachev would have been one of the surer ways of putting an end (for some years at least) to a transition to democracy and a predominantly market economy. With Yeltsin not yet elected President of Russia and the forces opposed to change looking for an excuse to return to the old order, nothing would have suited them better than such overt apostasy on the part of the leader they bitterly distrusted.

52 Gorbachev interview, *Der Spiegel*, No. 3, 18 Jan. 1993, p. 127.

53 Hewett, *Reforming the Soviet Economy*, 349.

54 Ibid. 350–3.

55 Ibid. 352.

56 Michail Gorbatschow, *Erinnerungen* (Seidler Verlag, Berlin, 1995), 330.

57 See e.g. the Ryzhkov, Shevardnadze, and Shakhnazarov interviews, *The Second Russian Revolution* transcripts; and Nikolay Ryzhkov, *Perestroyka: Istoriya predatel'stv* (Novosti, Moscow, 1992), 93–5. See also Eduard Shevardnadze, *The Future Belongs to Freedom* (Sinclair-Stevenson, London, 1991), 3–4.

58 Ryzhkov, *Perestroyka: Istoriya predatel'stv*, 95.

59 See Daniel Tarschys, 'The Success of a Failure: Gorbachev's Alcohol Policy, 1985–88', *Europe-Asia Studies*, 45/1 (1993), 7–25. Tarschys, a prominent Swedish specialist on Russian and comparative social policy, notes (p. 10): 'In 1979 23 billion rubles were paid in income tax and some 65 billion rubles in turnover taxes on consumer goods. Of the latter, alcoholic beverages accounted for 25.4 billion rubles. Indirect taxes on alcohol thus yielded more than all income taxes.'

60 Raisa Gorbachev spoke about her brother in her volume of tape-recorded reminiscences, saying: 'He is a gifted and talented person. But his potentialities were not fated to be realized. His talents turned out to be unwanted and were ruined. My brother drinks and spends many months in hospital. His fate is a tragedy for Mother and Father. For me it is a constant source of pain which I have carried in my heart for more than thirty years now. His tragedy brought me a lot of sorrow, all the more so since we were very close in our childhood . . .' (*I Hope* (HarperCollins, London, 1991), 26).

61 Shevardnadze, *The Future Belongs to Freedom*, 3–4.

62 Tarschys, 'The Success of a Failure', 22–3.

63 Ibid. 23.

64 Ibid.

65 I first heard Shmelev make these points when we were both guest speakers at a conference on 'Political reform in the Soviet Union' at El Colegio de Mexico, Mexico City, in December 1987. Shmelev elaborated and expanded them to include, *inter alia*, the contribution the alcohol curbs would make to fuelling inflation in an important article the following year. See Shmelev, 'Novye trevogi', *Novy mir*, 4 (1988), 160–75.

66 Shmelev, 'Novye trevogi', 162 (cited by Tarschys, 'The Success of a Failure', 21).

67 Tarschys makes this point when he suggests that 'with the whole fabric of Soviet society loosening up . . . mobilizing the old command system against such a deeply rooted habit as a taste for vodka stood little chance of succeeding' ('The Success of a Failure', 23). There would appear to have been substantial republican variations even earlier than 1988. When I was in Georgia and Armenia in 1987, wine was freely available in shops in Tbilisi (without any of the queuing which was required in Moscow with its reduced retail outlets and opening hours) and available in every rural as well as Tbilisi restaurant. In Armenia alcohol was much less accessible in the normal way, but seemed to be under every hotel counter. In mine it could be served if you did not require a receipt for your meal.

68 I am indebted to Professor Charles Gati, who told me this story when we were colleagues at Columbia University in 1985. He got it directly from the Hungarian Central Committee Secretary for agriculture, who put the question to Gorbachev. Gorbachev's admiration for the Hungarian agricultural reform and the fact that he would have liked to pursue something similar in the Soviet Union is confirmed by Alexander Nikonov (my interview with him of 20 Apr. 1994).

69 Zaslavskaya interview, *The Second Russian Revolution* transcripts.

70 This is noted by Anders Åslund, *Gorbachev's Struggle for Economic Reform*, 31–2, 60–1.

71 The Secretaryship of the Central Committee with responsibility for agriculture fell vacant immediately Gorbachev became General Secretary in March 1985. A Party Congress was not due until early 1986 and it was only at Congresses that new members could be elected to the Central Committee and could then be added to the pool of contenders for a secretaryship of that body. There is not the slightest reason to suppose that Alexander Nikonov aspired to a post other than

his academic one, which carried with it the possibility of advising Gorbachev. However, he characterized Viktor Nikonov as 'a technocrat and not a serious reformer' (my interview with A. A. Nikonov, 20 Apr. 1994).

72 Gorbachev, *Izbrannye rechi i stat'i*, iii (1987), 211.

73 Interview with A. A. Nikonov, 24 Apr. 1994.

74 Nikonov added that Ryzhkov frequently spoke against his views in the Politburo, although Gorbachev accepted them both then and earlier.

75 Ibid.

76 In a survey conducted in January 1990 (and published in summary form the following month) the All-Union Centre for the Study of Public Opinion posed the question: 'Which form of transfer of land to citizens for their individual use seems to you the most correct at the present time?' 25.1 per cent opted for long-term leasing from the state, 32.6 per cent for lifetime possession with the right of inheritance but without the right to sell the land, and only 21.1 per cent favoured 'private property with the right of inheritance and the right to sell'. (10 per cent were completely against transferring land for individual use and 14.6 per cent found the question too difficult to answer.) See *Obshchestvennoe mnenie v tsifrakh*, 4 (11) (Feb. 1990) (VTsIOM, Moscow).

77 See e.g. Gorbachev speeches of 17 Sept. and 28 Nov. 1990, reported in *Pravda*, 18 Sept. 1990, 1 Dec. 1990, and 18 Dec. 1990.

78 *Informatsionnyy byulleten' monitoringa: Ekonomicheskie i sotsial'nye peremeny* (VTsIOM, Moscow), 3 (May–June 1994), 14.

79 Åslund, *Gorbachev's Struggle for Economic Reform*, 163–7.

80 *Zakon Soyuza Sovetskikh Sostsialisticheskikh Respublik o kooperatsii v SSSR* (Izvestiya sovetov narodnykh deputatov SSSR, Moscow, 1988). For a good account of the law and the debate surrounding it, see Åslund, *Gorbachev's Struggle for Economic Reform*, 167–80.

81 Ibid. 169–70.

82 V. Kudryavtsev, 'Pravovaya sistema: puti perestroyki', *Pravda*, 5 Dec. 1986, p. 3.

83 Gorbachev, *Izbrannye rechi i stat'i*, v. 183.

84 See A. Yu. Kabalkin, 'Zakon ob individual'noy trudovoy deyatel'nosti—vazhnyy rychag osushchestvleniya sotsial'no-ekonomicheskoy politiki', *Sovetskoe gosudarstvo i pravo*, 3 (1987), 12–21, at p. 17; V. V. Laptev, 'Zakon o predpriyatii i kodifikatsiya khozyaystvennogo zakonodatel'stva', *Sovetskoe gosudarstvo i pravo*, 12 (1987), 67–75, at p. 69; and Åslund, *Gorbachev's Struggle for Economic Reform*, 170.

85 Ryzhkov interview, *The Second Russian Revolution* transcripts.

86 Gorbachev, *Izbrannye rechi i stat'i*, ii (1987), 269.

87 Ibid. 272.

88 Aganbegyan interview, *The Second Russian Revolution* transcripts.

89 Bogomolov interview, *The Second Russian Revolution* transcripts.

90 *Pravda*, 1 July 1987, pp. 1–4.

91 Aganbegyan interview, *The Second Russian Revolution* transcripts. The danger of assuming that all economic policy outcomes were willed by Gorbachev is illustrated by Vladimir Kontorovich, who, in an article which also contains much good sense, sets off on a wrong track by assuming that the Five-Year Plan which Gorbachev in fact failed to shape significantly 'reflected his true objectives' and that 'the rest was just talk'. See Kontorovich, 'The Economic Fallacy', *The National Interest*, 31 (Spring 1993), 35–45, at p. 43.

92 Nikolay Petrakov has said (*The Second Russian Revolution* transcripts) that in the middle of 1989 Gorbachev began again to work intensively on economic issues. He called economists in to see him and attended meetings at which economists, including Petrakov, spoke.

93 Aganbegyan interview, *The Second Russian Revolution* transcripts.

94 *Izvestiya TsK KPSS*, 1/1 (Jan. 1989), 81–6.

95 *Pravda*, 30 June 1988, pp. 3–4, at p. 3; and Leonid Abalkin, *Neispol'zovannyy shans: poltora goda v pravitel'stve* (Politizdat, Moscow, 1991), 8–10.

96 Abalkin, *Neispol'zovannyy shans*, 10 and 19.

97 Ibid. 19–20.

98 Author's interview (as already noted) with Nikolay Petrakov, 18 June 1991.

99 Interview with Nikolay Petrakov, *Stolitsa*, 18 (24) (1991), 1–5, at pp. 1–2.

100 Ibid. 5. Petrakov added: 'now it is even funny to recall that such a word as "self-financing" was considered bourgeois'. It was, said Petrakov, thanks to Academician Nikolay Fedorenko, the Director of TsEMI, who defended him, that he was able to retain his position in the institute.

101 Author's interview with Petrakov, 18 June 1991.

102 Ibid.; and Petrakov interview (autumn 1990), *The Second Russian Revolution* transcripts.

103 Petrakov interview, *The Second Russian Revolution* transcripts.

104 Author's interview with Petrakov, 18 June 1991.

105 Petrakov interview, *The Second Russian Revolution* transcripts.

106 Petrakov and Shatalin are among those who place great emphasis on Gorbachev's ability to absorb economic ideas and analyses. Petrakov made the point strongly to me in June 1991, even though he had left Gorbachev's team at the end of 1990 because of Gorbachev's 'turn to the right' in the winter of 1990–1; he remained in no doubt about Gorbachev's intellectual commitment to speedy marketization. See also Petrakov and Shatalin interviews, *The Second Russian Revolution* transcripts.

107 As Stanislav Shatalin put it at the very time when Gorbachev was trying to find a compromise between his '500 Days Programme' and the programme of Ryzhkov's government: 'I think he understands everything. He simply does not have the right to say everything that I have the right to say. However, his views are very far from dogmatic. He doesn't like fixed or *a priori* schemes, and he's open to all sorts of ideas, as long as these are well substantiated—as long as you've got proof' (Shatalin interview, *The Second Russian Revolution* transcripts).

108 Bakatin interview, *The Second Russian Revolution* transcripts. Bakatin went on to make clear that he had in mind the Communist Party *apparat*, the army, and the military-industrial complex.

109 Author's interview with Petrakov, 18 June 1991.

110 Petrakov interview, *The Second Russian Revolution* transcripts.

111 Ibid.

112 *Reytingi Borisa Yel'tsina i Mikhaila Gorbacheva po 10-bal'noy shkale* (VTsIOM, Moscow, 1993).

113 Petrakov interview, *The Second Russian Revolution* transcripts.

114 Ryzhkov, *Perestroyka: Istoriya predatel'stv*, 324–5; and Ryzhkov interview, *The Second Russian Revolution* transcripts.

115 Petrakov and Shatalin interviews, *The Second Russian Revolution* transcripts.

116 *Perekhod k rynku: Chast' 1. Kontseptsiya i Programma* (Arkhangelskoe, Moscow, 1990).

117 Petrakov interview, *The Second Russian Revolution* transcripts.

118 See e.g. Abalkin, *Neispol'zovannyy shans*, 206–7, and Ryzhkov, *Perestroyka: Istoriya predatel'stv*, 328–31 and 339; and Ryzhkov interview, *The Second Russian Revolution* transcripts.

119 That was, for example, the view of Alexander Yakovlev (Yakovlev interview, *The Second Russian Revolution* transcripts). Other members of Gorbachev's team were more sceptical. Pavel Palazhchenko, Gorbachev's English-language interpreter, for one was convinced that Yeltsin would have found a way of breaking with Gorbachev once the new policies had begun to bite and would have placed the blame on Gorbachev for the hardship which was bound to be one result of such a fast marketization (author's interview).

120 Abalkin interview, *The Second Russian Revolution* transcripts.

121 Gorbatschow, *Erinnerungen*, 553–4.

122 See e.g. Stanislav Shatalin, ' "500 dney" i drugie dni moey zhizni', *Nezavisimaya gazeta*, 2 Apr. 1992, pp. 5 and 8. While very critical of Gorbachev's retreat from the '500 Days Programme', Shatalin in the same article not only describes Gorbachev as 'intelligent' but also (and already from a post-Soviet perspective) as 'one of the greatest politicians in Russian history' (p. 8).

123 Gorbachev's appointment of Pavlov is discussed further in Ch. 8.

124 Gorbatschow, *Erinnerungen*, 565–6.

125 Cf. interviews with Gorbachev and Yavlinsky, *Russia & CIS Today: TV & Radio Monitoring* (RFE/RL Research Institute), 22 Aug. 1994, No. 0592, pp. 4–15.

126 These developments are discussed further in Ch. 8.

Chapter 6   Gorbachev and Political Transformation

1 Some of the evidence has already been presented, notably in the discussion of Gorbachev's speech to the Moscow conference on ideology held on 10 Dec. 1984, three months before he succeeded Chernenko as Soviet leader. See Gorbachev, *Zhivoe tvorchestvo naroda* (Politizdat, Moscow, 1984).

2 In the context of discussion of transitions from authoritarianism to democracy, Adam Przeworski argues that 'liberalization is inherently unstable'; it stimulates more radical demands from below and the formation of autonomous organizations within the society. See Przeworski, *Democracy and the Market: Political and Economic Reforms in Eastern Europe and Latin America* (Cambridge University Press, Cambridge, 1991), 58–9.

3 Gorbatschow, *Erinnerungen* (Seidler Verlag, Berlin, 1995), 438–9.

4 Since a critical attitude to the Prague Spring had been made a loyalty test for party members from the time of the Soviet intervention in 1968, it was not so much, therefore, that Gorbachev had the Czech example in mind as that, driven by what he saw as the need for change in the Soviet Union, he found himself traversing the same reformist path. His recognition that the Czech Communist reformers, including his old Moscow University friend Zdeněk Mlynář, had been pursuing policies similar to his own (during the first three years of his General Secretaryship) came later. According to Vadim Medvedev (interview with the present author, 22 Mar. 1993) there were *no* foreign models in the minds of Gorbachev and his allies when they embarked on perestroika in 1985. From 1988 that changed significantly; both the reformist wing of the leadership and, still more, radically reformist intellectuals, offering advice from outside the party-state machine, cast a wide net in looking for relevant foreign experience which could be drawn upon in the transformation of the Soviet political and economic system.

5 Taking a static view of *demokratizatsiya* and suggesting that for Gorbachev it had nothing in common with *democratization*, Brendan Kiernan holds that '*Demokratizatsiya* is subject to mutually exclusive interpretations: "Gorbachev the revitaliser" and "Gorbachev the democratiser". Both, of course, imply radical change, but in different directions' (Kiernan, *The End of Soviet Politics: Elections, Legislatures, and the Demise of the Communist Party* (Westview, Boulder, Colo., 1993), 212). In the first two years of Gorbachev's leadership, it is not out of place to talk about 'revitalization', although *liberalization* is more appropriate, since some of the institutions Gorbachev was trying to 'revitalize', such as the soviets, had never had much vitality. But by 1988–9 a democratization process was under way and by that time *demokratizatsiya* for Gorbachev meant something which is entirely correctly translated into English as 'democratization', bearing in mind that *democratization* is a process and is not identical with fully-fledged democracy in so far as any actually existing democracy is fully-fledged.

6 For distinctions between liberalization and democratization in the transition process, see Guillermo O'Donnell and Philippe C. Schmitter, *Transitions from Authoritarian Rule: Tentative Conclusions about Uncertain Democracies* (Johns Hopkins University Press, Baltimore, 1986), 7–11. See also Giuseppe di Palma, *To Craft Democracies: An Essay on Democratic Transitions* (University of California Press, Berkeley, 1990), esp. 80–3.

7 For the texts of what did exist on paper in the form of Constitution and Party Rules, and commentaries on them, see Robert Sharlet, *The New Soviet Constitution of 1977: Analysis and Text* (King's Court Communications, Brunswick, Oh., 1978); Aryeh L. Unger, *Constitutional Development in the USSR: A Guide to the Soviet Constitutions* (Methuen, London, 1981); and Graeme Gill, *The Rules of the Communist Party of the Soviet Union* (Macmillan, London, 1988).

8 Yegor Ligachev, *Inside Gorbachev's Kremlin* (Pantheon, New York, 1993), 296.

9 The distinction between post-totalitarian and authoritarian regimes which had never been totalitarian is made by Juan J. Linz and Alfred Stepan. See their article, 'Political Identities and Electoral Sequences', *Daedalus*, 121/2 (Spring 1992), 123–39, esp. 132. See also Juan Linz, 'Transitions to Democracy', *Washington Quarterly* (Summer 1990), 143–64, esp. 144–5.

10 In an article entitled 'No Role Models for Soviet Transition', *Los Angeles Times*, 2 Apr. 1991, p. B7, I wrote about the first three necessary elements in a Soviet transition from Communism discussed above in terms of the Soviet need for a *triple transformation*. Daniel Yergin and Thane Gustafson (*Russia 2010 and What it Means for the World* (Nicholas Brealey Publishing, London, 1994), 4–6) make a similar point when they talk about Russia's agenda involving a *triple transition*. They obscure the last point, however, when they speak in terms of transition from 'a four-century old empire to a nation-state'. Whereas non-Russians constituted just under 50 per cent of the *Soviet* population, they make up only 20 per cent of the population of Russia. Even so, Russia remains sufficiently multi-ethnic with many nations living in their historic homelands for the idea of a 'nation-state' to be inapplicable. The only way Russia could be governed democratically is through recognition that it is a *multinational state* with institutions designed to accommodate that political and social reality. In any event, as I suggest in the text, the Soviet Union (and, to a lesser extent, post-Soviet Russia) required an inter-linked *fourfold* transformation. The loss of the alliteration of my earlier formulation must be borne in the interests of better understanding.

11 Paul Kennedy, *The Rise and Fall of the Great Powers: Economic Change and Military Conflict from 1500 to 2000* (Unwin Hyman, London, 1988), 513–14.

12 Ibid. 513. Kennedy continues: 'the prospects of an escape from the contradictions which the USSR faces are not good.' In that, of course, he was on firm ground, for even though Gorbachev exceeded most people's (including Kennedy's) expectations, the military and the enormous defence industry lobby fought a rearguard action against the changes Gorbachev—and his foreign policy allies Shevardnadze and Yakovlev—wished to impose on them and played their part in eventually bringing Gorbachev down (along, ironically, with the Soviet Union, which had been the last thing they had intended).

13 Anatoly Chernyaev, seminar talk on 'Soviet Foreign Policy-Making under Gorbachev', St Antony's College Oxford, 17 Oct. 1994.

14 Georgy Shakhnazarov, *Tsena svobody: Reformatsiya Gorbacheva glazami ego pomoshchnika* (Rossika Zevs, Moscow, 1993), 42.

15 Three of the best and most scholarly accounts of political reform in the Gorbachev era (each with different strengths) are John Miller, *Mikhail Gorbachev and the End of Soviet Power* (Macmillan, London, 1993); Richard Sakwa, *Gorbachev and his Reforms 1985–1990* (Philip Allan, London, 1990); and Stephen White, *After Gorbachev*, 3rd edn. (Cambridge University Press, Cambridge, 1993).

16 As the author of a useful study of the development of an independent political society in the former Soviet Union, Steven Fish, observes: 'In a number of respects 1989 stands out as the crucial takeoff phase for autonomous political activity in Russia' (Fish, *Democracy from Scratch: Opposition and Regime in the New Russian Revolution* (Princeton University Press, Princeton, 1995)). The author is much less well informed—indeed, highly misleading—on Gorbachev.

17 In its domestic aspect, attention is paid to this conceptual innovation in Ch. 4 and, in its international dimension, in Ch. 7.

18 The last woman in the party leadership had been in Khrushchev's time. Yekaterina Furtseva was a full member of the Politburo (at that time called Presidium of the Central Committee) from 1957 until 1961.

19 The difference is still more striking if one excludes those promoted from candidate membership or from the Central Auditing Commission to full membership of the Central Committee. There were 41 such complete newcomers out of 319 in 1981 and 95 out of 307 in 1986.

20 As touched upon earlier, Ligachev—who was supervising the party organization within the Central Committee Secretariat—had a large say in preparing the list of names to be presented to the Party Congress for election to the new Central Committee.

21 Many of the people I have interviewed who attended Politburo meetings, whether as participants or as observers, have commented on this. Anatoly Chernyaev mentions Gorbachev remarking with puzzlement, following Yeltsin's clash with the leadership in late 1987 which led to his removal from his leadership posts (apart from membership of the Central Committee, which he retained), upon the fact that no one had less to say in the Politburo than Yeltsin. The same point was made forcefully by Ryzhkov, Ligachev, and Vorotnikov in their speeches to the October plenum of 1987 following Yeltsin's unscheduled speech. See *Izvestiya TsK KPSS*, 2 (1989), for the stenographic report of the plenum proceedings, especially pp. 242, 257, 259.

22 For as long as he remained a party official, Yeltsin was very sensitive about his place in the hierarchy, as he reveals in his first volume of memoirs. See Boris Yeltsin, *Against the Grain: An Autobiography* (Jonathan Cape, London, 1990), 72, 76, 82.

23 *Izvestiya TsK KPSS*, 2 (1989), 242, 257, 259, 274, 286. See also A. N. Yakovlev, *Gor'kaya chasha: Bolshevizm i Reformatsiya Rossii* (Verkhne-Volzhskoe knizhnoe izdatelstvo, Yaroslavl, 1994); and Shakhnazarov, *Tsena svobody*.

24 See e.g. Shakhnazarov, *Tsena svobody*, 53.

25 Gorbatschow, *Erinnerungen*, 291.

26 A. N. Yakovlev interview, *The Second Russian Revolution* transcripts.

27 An early example of government cover-up of a nuclear accident, aided by the fact that the mass media and public opinion were then much less attuned to the dangers of radioactive contamination, occurred in Britain in the 1950s. The occasion was a major fire affecting the nuclear reactor at Windscale, Cumbria, on 10 Oct. 1957. Harold Macmillan, Prime Minister at the time, went to great lengths to ensure that the detailed report by Sir William Penney on the causes and consequences of the accident would be known only to a small group within government: 'In fact, Macmillan had instructed the Atomic Energy Authority not to permit any leakage of the Penney report, to the extent that all prints of it obtained from the Stationery Office were to be destroyed; so even was the type used by the printers' (Alistair Horne, *Macmillan 1957–1986*, vol. ii of the Official Biography (Macmillan, London, 1989), 54). Although a less major disaster than the Chernobyl explosion, the Windscale accident was, as Horne observes, 'much more menacing to life than the fall-out caused by the melt-down at Three Mile Island in the United States which so shook world opinion in 1979'

(ibid. 53–4). Macmillan's main reason for suppressing information about the grave lapse of safety standards at Windscale was that he feared this would 'endanger moves in America to share her nuclear secrets with Britain' (ibid.). See also Tony Hall, *Nuclear Politics: The History of Nuclear Power in Britain* (Penguin, Harmondsworth, 1986); and (for an example of greater American openness) Peggy M. Hassler, *Three Mile Island: A Reader's Guide to Selected Government Publications and Government-Sponsored Research* (The Scarecrow Press, Metuchen, NJ, 1988); and William Sweet, *The Nuclear Age: Atomic Energy, Proliferation, and the Arms Race*, 2nd edn. (Congressional Quarterly Inc., Washington, 1988).

28 David R. Marples, *The Social Impact of the Chernobyl Disaster* (Macmillan, London, 1988), 114. See also Grigori Medvedev, *The Truth about Chernobyl* (Basic Books, New York, 1991).

29 For one graphic account, see Grigori Medvedev, *No Breathing Room: The Aftermath of Chernobyl* (Basic Books, New York, 1993).

30 Gorbachev interview, *The Second Russian Revolution* transcripts. The point is expressed more strongly by Shakhnazarov, who argues that Chernobyl 'inflicted a decisive blow against the mania for secrecy, inducing the country to open itself up to the world' (*Tsena svobody*, 53).

31 See *Kommunist*, 12 (Aug. 1986), 3–10; and 13 (Sept. 1986), O. Latsis, 'Po novomu vzglyanut'', 32–41; and T. Zaslavskaya, 'Chelovecheskiy faktor razvitiya ekonomiki i sotsial'naya spravedlivost'', 61–73.

32 For elaboration on these changes, see Riitta H. Pittman, '*Perestroika* and Soviet Cultural Politics: The Case of the Major Literary Journals', *Soviet Studies*, 42/1 (Jan. 1990), 111–32.

33 Voronov at an earlier stage of his career had fallen foul of the party authorities, but immediately before he became head of the Central Committee Cultural Department in the summer of 1986 he was chief editor of *Znamya*. He moved from the Central Committee apparatus to become editor of the Writers' Union weekly newspaper, *Literaturnaya gazeta*, in December 1988, in which post he was succeeded in March 1990 by Fedor Burlatsky, a liberal-leaning political scientist whose career as editor-in-chief ended at the time of the August 1991 coup when he found himself the victim of a 'mini-*putsch*' by his enemies on the newspaper. On Voronov, see the book by his deputy (who later became an aide to Gorbachev), Vladimir K. Yegorov, *Out of a Dead End into the Unknown: Notes on Gorbachev's Perestroika* (edition q, Chicago, 1993), esp. 15.

34 Klimov interview, *The Second Russian Revolution* transcripts.

35 For more on the 'cultural renaissance', see Alec Nove, *Glasnost' in Action: Cultural Renaissance in Russia* (Unwin Hyman, London, 1989); and Julian Graffy and Geoffrey Hosking (eds.), *Culture and the Media in the USSR Today* (Macmillan, London, 1989).

36 A. S. Chernyaev, *Shest' let s Gorbachevym: po dnevnikovym zapisyam* (Kultura, Moscow, 1993), 125–6.

37 Andrey Grachev gives an interesting account of the process in a section of his memoirs entitled 'Dances with Wolves'. See Grachev, *Kremlevskaya khronika* ('EKSMO', Moscow, 1994), 94–104, esp. 95–7.

38 Ibid. 96–7.

39 Ibid. 96.

40 Ibid. 97.

41 Ibid.

42 Ibid. 97–8.

43 Chernyaev, *Shest' let s Gorbachevym*, 125.

44 Andrei Sakharov, *Memoirs* (Knopf, New York, 1990), 615.

45 Ibid. 612, 615–16.

46 In his memoirs, Sakharov writes: 'I said, "Thank you again. Goodbye". (Contrary to the demands of protocol, I brought the conversation to a close, not Gorbachev. I must have felt under stress and perhaps subconsciously feared that I might say too much.) Gorbachev had little choice, so he said "Goodbye" ' (ibid. 616).

47 Chernyaev, *Shest' let s Gorbachevym*, 126.

48 Information on these earlier postponements was first given by Gorbachev in his speech to the Eighteenth Congress of Soviet Trade Unions the following month. See *Pravda*, 26 Feb. 1987, p. 1.

49 M. S. Gorbachev, 'O perestroyke i kadrovoy politike partii', in Gorbachev, *Izbrannye rechi i stat'i*, iv. 299–354, at p. 302.

50 Ibid. 317.

51 Ibid. 323.

52 Ibid. 354.

53 Dolgikh interview, *The Second Russian Revolution* transcripts.

54 Chernyaev, *Shest' let s Gorbachevym*, 163–6.

55 See e.g. E. K. Ligachev, 'Nam nuzhna polnaya pravda', *Teatr*, 8 (Aug. 1986), 2–7.

56 'Oktyabr'' i perestroyka: revolyutsiya prodolzhaetsya', in Gorbachev, *Izbrannye rechi i stat'i* (Politizdat, Moscow, 1987–90), v (1988), 386–436.

57 Ibid. 436.

58 The term 'old Bolshevik' embraces those who were party members before the 1917 revolution, having joined Lenin's Bolshevik branch of the revolutionary movement when it was still in opposition to, and subject to persecution by, the tsarist state. It was sometimes misleadingly stretched by Western writers to include aged party bureaucrats—for no better reason, apparently, than that they were fairly old and Communists—including (absurdly) Konstantin Chernenko, who was born in 1911.

59 See Stephen F. Cohen, *Bukharin and the Bolshevik Revolution: A Political Biography 1888–1938* (Wildwood House, London, 1974). A Russian translation of this book was sent to Gorbachev as holiday reading by his aide Ivan Frolov during the summer of 1987. Gorbachev not only read it, but was also impressed and influenced by it (see Angus Roxburgh, *The Second Russian Revolution* (BBC Books, London, 1991), 68). While Gorbachev, in his anniversary speech of November 1987, was still sufficiently constrained by more conservative colleagues to be able to do no more than open the door to Bukharin's rehabilitation—mentioning him in a more positive than negative light—he soon brought that process to completion. Bukharin was fully rehabilitated in February 1988, the centenary of his birth and fiftieth anniversary of his execution, thus bringing to a belated conclusion a long campaign waged by Bukharin's widow, Anna Larina (who was still alive and thus able to see her efforts finally rewarded), for her husband's posthumous rehabilitation, together with acknowledgement that the charges brought against him by Stalin's henchmen were a pack of lies.

60 Gorbachev, *Izbrannye rechi i stat'i*, v. 402.

61 Ibid.

62 The full stenographic report of this Central Committee session was published almost eighteen months after the event. Yeltsin, among others, has attested to its accuracy. It appeared in *Izvestiya TsK KPSS*, 2 (Feb. 1989), 209–87.

63 Andrey Grachev, conversation with the author, 29 Mar. 1995.

64 *Izvestiya TsK KPSS*, 1 (1989), 239–41.

65 Ibid. 242.

66 Ibid. 249.

67 A. N. Yakovlev interview, *The Second Russian Revolution* transcripts.

68 *Izvestiya TsK KPSS*, 1 (1989), 254–7. Ryzhkov had reinforced Gorbachev's doubts about the desirability of bringing Yeltsin from Sverdlovsk to Moscow, but the strong advocacy of Ligachev had carried the day. See *Moskovskiy komsomolets*, 28 June 1995, p. 2.

69 *Izvestiya TsK KPSS*, 1 (1989), esp. 256–7.

70 Boris Yeltsin, *The View from the Kremlin* (HarperCollins, London, 1994), 179.

71 *XIX Vsesoyuznaya konferentsiya Kommunisticheskoy Partii Sovetskogo Soyuza, 28 Iyunya–1 Iyulya 1988 goda: Stenograficheskiy otchet* (Politzdat, Moscow, 1988), ii. 61–2.

72 Ibid.

73 *Izvestiya TsK KPSS*, 2 (1989), 280.

74 Ibid. 282.

75 Chernyaev, *Shest' let s Gorbachevym*, 174–5.

76 A. N. Yakovlev, *Gor'kaya chasha: Bol'shevizm i Reformatsiya Rossii* (Verkhne-Volzhskoe knizhnoe izdatelstvo, Yaroslavl, 1994), 216. In an interview three years earlier Yakovlev said that it had been Yeltsin's violation of his agreement with Gorbachev which prompted him to make his speech critical of Yeltsin at the October 1987 plenum, adding: 'When I told him [Yeltsin] about this he told me that there was never any agreement on this. Well, I cannot verify this, nor do I intend to' (Yakovlev interview, *The Second Russian Revolution* transcripts).

77 Vadim Medvedev, *V komande Gorbacheva* ('Bylina', Moscow, 1994), 64.

78 Yakovlev, *Gor'kaya chasha*, 216; and Yakovlev interview, *The Second Russian Revolution* transcripts.

79 Medvedev, *V komande Gorbacheva*, 66–7.

80 Ibid. 66. The temperamental similarity of Ligachev and Yeltsin was noted by a number of people I interviewed who knew them both.

81 Ibid.

82 *Izvestiya TsK KPSS*, 2 (1989), 283.

83 Gorbachev acknowledged, in his closing speech to the Nineteenth Party Conference on 1 July 1988, that it had been a mistake not to provide information at the time about the content of Yeltsin's speech at the October 1987 plenum, suggesting that, had they done so then, 'the process would not have developed in the way it had'. See *XIX Vsesoyuznaya konferentsiya Kommunisticheskoy Partii Sovetskogo Soyza, 28 Iyunya–1 Iyulya 1988 goda: Stenograficheskiy otchet* (Politizdat, Moscow, 1988), ii. 184.

84 Roxburgh, *The Second Russian Revolution*, 73–4.

85 Ibid. 75–6. Roxburgh adds (p. 76): 'That the conservatives had scored a major victory and cornered the radicals became clear on 3 November, when Yakovlev gave a news conference to explain the importance of Gorbachev's jubilee speech the previous day. Asked about the Yeltsin affair, he clammed up and even lied . . . Western reporters were horrified. Many left the hall shaking their heads: "If this is 'Mr Glasnost', God help them".' Looking back on the October 1987 plenum from the perspective of 1994, by which time he was head of Ostankino television in Moscow (a position to which he had been appointed by Yeltsin in late 1993 and from which he resigned in March 1995), Yakovlev, in his latest volume of memoirs and reflections, argues that in essence Yeltsin had been correct seven years earlier, but he had been wrong from a tactical point of view. Before making a speech of such a character, he should have prepared the ground more carefully. See Yakovlev, *Gor'kaya chasha*, 217.

86 See *Pravda*, 14 Nov. 1987, pp. 1–3; Yeltsin, *Against the Grain*, 153–5; Roxburgh, *The Second Russian Revolution*, 76–8; and John Morrison, *Boris Yeltsin* (Penguin Books, London, 1991), 70–3.

87 Morrison, *Boris Yeltsin*, 71–2; and Roxburgh, *The Second Russian Revolution*, 77–8.

88 The radically reformist economist Nikolay Shmelev was among those who drew attention to the conservative fightback at the beginning of 1988. He warned that 'we are witnessing a stepping-up of resistance by conservative forces' and expressed concern that 'the strength of that resistance . . . is now underestimated' (*Moscow News*, 1 (3 Jan. 1988), 3).

89 Linking references to Jews (starting with Stalin's pejorative use of 'cosmopolitanism') with attacks on political liberalism, Andreeva also wrote: 'Militant cosmopolitanism is now linked with the practice of "refusenikism"—of "refusing" socialism' (*Sovetskaya Rossiya*, 13 Mar. 1988, p. 3).

90 Vorotnikov interview, *The Second Russian Revolution* transcripts.

91 Vitaly Ignatenko interview, *The Second Russian Revolution* transcripts.

92 Andrey Grachev, *Kremlevskaya khronika*, 122–9; Vitaly Ignatenko, Ivan Laptev, Alexander Yakovlev, and Yegor Yakovlev interviews, *The Second Russian Revolution* transcripts.

93 On the Ligachev role in this, see Grachev, *Kremlevskaya khronika*; David Remnick, *Lenin's Tomb: The Last Days of the Soviet Empire* (Random House, New York, 1993), 70–86; Roxburgh, *The Second Russian Revolution*, 83–7; and William and Jane Taubman, *Moscow Spring* (Summit Books, New York, 1989), 146–60.

94 Andrey Grachev tried to persuade Ivan Laptev, who already enjoyed a relatively liberal reputation as editor of *Izvestiya*, to publish a reply to the Andreeva letter, arguing that, since *Izvestiya* was not specifically a Communist Party newspaper, there was no reason to hold back. Laptev, however, replied: 'No, we are powerless against Ligachev' (Grachev, *Kremlevskaya khronika*, 126).

95 Remnick, *Lenin's Tomb*, 76–7; Roxburgh, *The Second Russian Revolution*, 85–6; and Andrei Melville and Gail W. Lapidus (eds.), *The Glasnost Papers: Voices of Reform from Moscow* (Westview Press, Boulder, Colo., 1990) where Andrei Melville—at that time a department head in Arbatov's Institute of the USA and Canada—writes (p. 14): 'For three full weeks there were very few indeed who dared openly challenge this conservative manifesto . . .'.

96 Remnick, *Lenin's Tomb*, 76–7.

97 Chernyaev, *Shest' let s Gorbachevym*, 203–4.

98 Gorbachev, 'Potentsial kooperatsii—delu perestroyki', in *Izbrannye rechi i stat'i*, vi (1989), 141–73.

99 Gorbachev, in conversation with Chernyaev, mentioned Vorotnikov as the first to praise the article, followed by Ligachev, Gromyko, and Solomentsev. Vadim Medvedev adds the name of another Politburo member, Nikonov, as well as that of the future *putschist* Baklanov. See Chernyaev, *Shest' let s Gorbachevym*, 203–4; and Medvedev, *V komande Gorbacheva*, 68.

100 Substantial extracts from the transcript of the second day's discussion at that Politburo meeting were published for the first time in M. S. Gorbachev, *Gody trudnykh resheniy* (Alfa-Print, Moscow, 1993), 98–110 ('O stat'e N. Andreevoy i ne tol'ko o ney').

101 Medvedev, *V komande Gorbacheva*, 69.

102 Chernyaev, *Shest' let s Gorbachevym*, 206.

103 Medvedev, *V komande Gorbacheva*, 71.

104 Ibid. 68–71; and Roxburgh, *The Second Russian Revolution*, 86.

105 The Andreeva episode, as Vadim Medvedev notes, was just the 'tip of the iceberg' of the growing conservative opposition. Gorbachev, he observes, 'true to himself', did not make the Andreeva discussion in the Politburo a matter of personalities and Ligachev was not singled out for blame (Medvedev, *V komande Gorbacheva*, 71).

106 Even Yakovlev on his own could not initiate a political response to the Andreeva article, knowing—as he did—that it had been published with the blessing of Ligachev. Asked why it was some time after his return from Mongolia that the Politburo first discussed the article, Yakovlev replied: 'First, Mikhail Sergeevich [Gorbachev] had to come back, that was the first and most important thing.' Yakovlev also confirmed that the eventual Politburo discussion, in which a variety of viewpoints and nuances were expressed, 'lasted two days' (Yakovlev interview, *The Second Russian Revolution* transcripts).

107 Gorbachev, *Gody trudnykh resheniy*, 106.

108 Ibid. 106–7.

109 Chernyaev, *Shest' let s Gorbachevym*, 208.

110 Although Gorbachev himself chaired the next meeting of the Secretariat of the Central Committee following the Andreeva discussion in the Politburo, thereafter Ligachev resumed his place at the head of the Secretariat (which was responsible for the day-to-day execution of Politburo decisions) until the Secretariat was itself downgraded as an institution following the Nineteenth Party Conference. See Chernyaev, *Shest' let s Gorbachevym*, 208.

111 See Gorbachev, 'Revolyutsionnoy perestroyke—ideologiyu obnovleniya', speech to the Central Committee plenum, 18 Feb. 1988, in *Izbrannye rechi i stat'i*, vi. 58–92; and Shaknazarov, *Tsena svobody*, 45.

112 Gorbachev, quoted by Shakhnazarov, ibid.

113 Medvedev, *V komande Gorbacheva*, 72. Medvedev mentions the names also of Boldin, Sitaryan, and Mozhin.

114 Chernyaev, *Shest' let s Gorbachevym*, 209.

115 Ibid.

116 Ibid. 210.

117 Ibid.

118 They had been approved by a plenary session of the Central Committee on 23 May. See *Pravda*, 27 May 1988, p. 1.

119 Shakhnazarov, *Tsena svobody*, 48.

120 Ibid.

121 *Pravda*, 27 May 1988, pp. 1–3, at p. 3.

122 Shakhnazarov, *Tsena svobody*, 48.

123 Ibid.

124 Cf. Stephen White, 'Communists and their Party in the Late Soviet Period', *Slavonic and East European Review*, 72/4 (Oct. 1994), 644–63.

125 Shakhnazarov, *Tsena svobody*, 46.

126 *XIX Vsesoyuznaya konferentisya Kommunisticheskoy Partii Sovetskogo Soyuza, 28 Iyunya–1 Iyulya 1988 goda: Stenograficheskiy otchet* (Politizdat, Moscow, 1988), i. 269–70; and ii. 56.

127 See e.g. *XIX Vsesoyuznaya konferentsiya Kommunisticheskoy Partii Sovetskogo Soyuza*, ii. 121–35.

128 The generalization applies to Stalin, Khrushchev, Brezhnev, and Gorbachev (up to the qualitative change in the Soviet system in the spring of 1989 marked by contested elections to the new legislature). The General Secretaryships of Andropov and Chernenko were too short, and too dominated by the ill health of the incumbents, for them to be meaningfully counted. For discussion of this generalization (including some directly contrary views) which I first advanced in 1980 see e.g. Archie Brown, 'The Power of the General Secretary of the CPSU', in T. H. Rigby, Archie Brown, and Peter Reddaway (eds.), *Authority, Power and Policy in the USSR: Essays Dedicated to Leonard Schapiro* (Macmillan, London, 1980), 135–57, esp. 136; Valerie Bunce, *Do New Leaders Make a Difference? Executive Succession and Public Policy under Capitalism and Socialism* (Princeton University Press, Princeton, 1981); Philip G. Roeder, 'Do New Soviet Leaders Really Make a Difference? Rethinking the Succession Connection', *American Political Science Review*, 79/4 (Dec. 1985), 958–76; Valerie Bunce and Philip G. Roeder, 'The Effects of Leadership Succession in the Soviet Union', *American Political Science Review*, 80/1 (Mar. 1986), 215–24; and Thane Gustafson and Dawn Mann, 'Gorbachev's First Year', *Problems of Communism*, 35/3 (May–June 1986), 1–19, esp. 1–2. Of my generalization of 1980 that 'each General Secretary has wielded less individual power over policy than his predecessor, but *within* his period of office his power *vis-à-vis* his colleagues has grown', the *first* part cannot be extended beyond Brezhnev's incumbency, for Gorbachev wielded *more* power (in

the sense of getting decisions adopted that were against the preferences of senior colleagues and the interests of major institutions) than any of his predecessors after Khrushchev.

129 One of Yeltsin's innovative and constructive suggestions in his speech to the Nineteenth Party Conference was that the composition of the Politburo should be renewed at the same time as a new General Secretary was elected, so that the latter would not be forced to work with the political legatees of his predecessors. See *XIX Vsesoyuznaya konferentsiya Kommunisticheskoy Partii Sovetskogo Soyuza*, ii. 58.

130 For the text of these resolutions and the speeches of the chairmen of the commissions which prepared each of them, see *XIX Vsesoyuznaya konferentsiya Kommunisticheskoy Partii Sovetskogo Soyuza*, ii. 105–75.

131 I prefer the term 'policy networks' in the Soviet context to 'policy communities' or 'issue networks'. It would be a slight exaggeration to see specialists in Moscow and Novosibirsk as belonging to the same *community*, less so to see them as being (in specific cases) part of the same *network*. Equally, what kept these networks going was not so much occupation with single issues as with broad areas of policy, concerning which there was both formal and informal interaction among like-minded people. This took the form of communication through journal and newspaper articles as well as through conferences, seminars, and, in some cases, relations of friendship. The notion of 'policy networks', however, draws on the work both of John W. Kingdon on policy communities and of Hugh Heclo on issue networks. Kingdon (*Agendas, Alternatives and Public Policies*, HarperCollins, New York, 1984) is writing in the context of American politics, but within his framework of analysis there are points of relevance to policy innovation in the Soviet Union under Gorbachev (as well, of course, as some major differences). On issue networks—a concept which, terminology aside, has much in common with the notion of policy communities, and which was also developed within the study of American politics—see Hugh Heclo, 'Issue Networks and the Executive Establishment', in Anthony King (ed.), *The New American Political System* (American Enterprise Institute, Washington, 1978), 87–124, esp. 102–4. 'More than mere technical experts,' Heclo writes (p. 103), 'network people are policy activists who know each other through the issues.' Such networks existed in the Soviet Union and were increasingly important in the Gorbachev years, although—until 1988 at least—they remained very dependent on the top party leadership, and Gorbachev, in particular, if they were to be able to have a significant influence on actual policy.

132 See Gorbachev, *Gody trudnykh resheniy*, 98–110.

133 *XIX Vsesoyuznaya konferentsiya Kommunisticheskoy Partii Sovetskogo Soyuza*, ii. 138.

134 Ibid. 139–40.

135 Издательство, ЦК, КПСС, ПД. I. ?.

136 On this, see also Shakhnazarov, *Tsena svobody*, 72.

137 These changes were to have been incorporated in a new Soviet constitution, on which work had begun but was never completed. The abolition of the Congress of People's Deputies and the replacement of the Soviet of Nationalities of the Supreme Soviet by a Soviet of Republics was by 1991 already incorporated in the draft Union Treaty. That document had for Gorbachev become a higher priority than the new constitution; it was the centre-piece of his struggle to maintain some kind of union covering all or most of the territory of the USSR.

138 Even such perceptive comparativists as Juan Linz and Alfred Stepan seem somewhat disapproving of the fact that, while 'the first elections were indeed all-union', they had, nevertheless, 'many limitations' which they proceed to enumerate. It is significant, however, that when Gorbachev took the major step in 1988 of announcing and instituting contested elections, he was still ahead of both public and élite opinion. There had been no serious demand for such elections from the society prior to Gorbachev's pushing this decision through the Nineteenth Party Conference. See Juan J. Linz and Alfred Stepan, 'Political Identities and Electoral Sequences: Spain, the Soviet Union and Yugoslavia', *Daedalus*, 121/2 (Spring 1992), 123–39, esp. 131.

139 The article by Nina Andreeva published on 13 Mar. 1988 in *Sovetskaya Rossiya* (discussed earlier in this chapter).

140 Even before the Nineteenth Party Conference, differences of view could be read between the lines of the speeches of leading Soviet politicians and in the press. But from the spring and summer of 1988 onwards the divisions within the Soviet élite became increasingly clear and unconcealed, and open to inspection in the pages of mass-circulation newspapers as well as in the specialist journals. It is, indeed, unimaginable that the Soviet élite could have been anything other than divided over reforms which were turning the system into something different in kind from what it had been over seven decades, one in which there were going to be new losers as well as new winners. More significantly, in *post*-Soviet Russia the élite *remained* divided on what should constitute rules of the democratic game and this did not augur well for the consolidation of the democratic elements within what had become a disorganized system of mixed government. The low priority given to

consensus-seeking, democratic institution-building, and respect for the rule of law by the post-Soviet leadership meant that Russia failed to build during the first few post-Communist years on foundations for the possible consolidation of democracy which had been established by 1991. The failure was that, in the first instance, of the Russian President, Boris Yeltsin, although the Chairman of the Supreme Soviet (until that body was disbanded by Yeltsin in the autumn of 1993), Ruslan Khasbulatov, also bears responsibility for his part in rejecting the kind of negotiated compromises essential to democratic consolidation. On this general issue, see John Higley and Richard Gunther (eds.), *Elites and Democratic Consolidation in Latin America and Southern Europe* (Cambridge University Press, Cambridge, 1992). On the early post-Soviet stage of the Russian transition, see Archie Brown, 'Political Leadership in Post-Communist Russia', in Amin Saikal and William Maley (eds.), *Russia in Search of its Future* (Cambridge University Press, 1995), 28–47.

141 Guillermo O'Donnell and Philippe C. Schmitter, *Transitions from Authoritarian Rule: Tentative Conclusions about Uncertain Democracies* (Johns Hopkins Press, Baltimore, 1986), 23.

142 On Gorbachev and the Khrushchev parallel, see Ligachev, *Inside Gorbachev's Kremlin*, 123–4, 127–8.

143 Some of the underpinnings of democracy in Britain, including the rule of law and the rights of parliament *vis-à-vis* the monarch (as distinct from parliamentary *democracy*), developed, of course, over a far longer period.

144 O'Donnell and Schmitter, *Transitions from Authoritarian Rule*, 44. The phrase 'on the installment plan' comes from Dunkwart A. Rustow, who, in an important article, 'Transitions to Democracy: Toward a Dynamic Model' (*Comparative Politics*, 2/3 (Apr. 1970), 337–63), wrote (p. 356): 'Whether democracy is purchased wholesale as in Sweden in 1907 or on the installment plan as in Britain, it is acquired by a process of conscious decision at least on the part of the top political leadership.' This generalization could, however, be applied to the Soviet Union only if the phrase 'at least on the part of' were replaced by 'at least *by* a part of'.

145 Giuseppe di Palma, *To Craft Democracies*, 82.

146 Ibid.

147 Shakhnazarov interview, *The Second Russian Revolution* transcripts.

148 Ibid. See also Medvedev, *V komande Gorbacheva*, 74.

149 Cf. Shakhnazarov, *Tsena svobody*, 74. If Ligachev and Yakovlev had failed to be elected on the party list, each of them (especially Yakovlev) could almost certainly have been returned from a territorial constituency—a more conservative rural one in Ligachev's case and a more reform-oriented city constituency in Yakovlev's.

150 How large a first step towards political democratization, as distinct from mere liberalization, this was can be seen more clearly when it is compared with the substantial measures of liberalization under Gorbachev which preceded it. These changes included the advent of glasnost, a growing religious tolerance, and the development of some civic participation and formation of small independent associations and groups from 1986–7, but what they did not include was an opportunity for either the electorate or a representative assembly to call the executive to account. On the fruits of the liberalization in the early years of the Gorbachev era, see Geoffrey Hosking, Jonathan Aves, and Peter J. S. Duncan, *The Road to Post-Communism: Independent Political Movements in the Soviet Union 1985–1991* (Pinter, London, 1992), esp. ch. 1 by Hosking, 'The Beginnings of Independent Political Activity', pp. 1–28. How great an advance were the 1988 reforms over what had gone before is further highlighted by a look back at the first phase of relaxation in the post-Stalin era. As Robert Dahl puts it, discussing post-totalitarian authoritarian regimes (which he calls 'fully hegemonic regimes'): 'In a full hegemony the first step may be nothing more or less than some kind of understanding that in conflicts within the ruling groups, the losers will not be punished by death or imprisonment, exile, or total destitution. In this respect the change in the USSR from Stalin's hegemony to the post-Stalinist system was a profound step toward liberalization.' See Robert A. Dahl, *Polyarchy: Participation and Opposition* (Yale University Press, New Haven, 1971), 218.

151 Ivan Laptev interview, *The Second Russian Revolution* transcripts.

152 Ibid.

153 See Roxburgh, *The Second Russian Revolution*, 101–2. Roxburgh points out that the official transcript of the conference does not capture the sleight of hand which Gorbachev employed and is incorrect in stating that Ligachev, in the chair at the final session, put the resolution to a vote. In fact, says Roxburgh: 'Gorbachev concluded, "That's what I've said . . . [confirming that *he* wrote the text] Are there any objections? Allow me to put it to the vote"' (ibid. 102).

154 A more precise transcript than the official Soviet one at this point (see previous note) is provided by the BBC monitoring of Gorbachev's speech, taken from Soviet television. See BBC SWB SU/0194 C/44, 4 July 1988.

155 Ibid.

156 According to Laptev, Gorbachev looked nervous as he read from his slip of paper: 'You could see that he felt some doubts whether he could pull it off' (cited by Roxburgh, *The Second Russian Revolution*, 101). On the speed with which Gorbachev moved, see also Medvedev, *V komande Gorbacheva*, 78.

157 See Laptev, *The Second Russian Revolution* transcripts.

158 Ibid.

159 The memorandum was published in the very first issue of a new party journal launched at the beginning of 1989 which was to be a useful source of archival material, both from the recent and more distant Soviet past. See *Izvestiya TsK KPSS*, 1/1 (Jan. 1989), 81–6.

160 Ibid. 86.

161 See Whitefield, *Industrial Power and the Soviet State*, 127–9, 211–13.

162 Ibid. 224.

163 As Whitefield notes (p. 226): 'Ministries . . . sought to exploit the possibilities open to them to become concerns, corporations, associations, supporters of co-operatives, joint-stock companies, and privatized. They did so, none the less, with one eye on preserving any advantages of the old order, and to surviving if the old order was restored.'

164 *Izvestiya TsK KPSS*, 1/1 (1989), 86. The other eight departments (with the name of the department heads in brackets) following the October 1988 reorganization of the Central Committee apparatus were: the Department for Party Construction and Cadre Work (G. P. Razumovsky); the Ideological Department (A. S. Kapto); the Socio-Economic Department (V. I. Shimko); the Agricultural Department (I. I. Skiba); the Defence Department (O. S. Belyakov); the State-Legal Department (A. S. Pavlov); the General Department (V. I. Boldin); and the Department of Affairs (meaning mainly financial affairs, N. E. Kruchina).

165 Ligachev, *Inside Gorbachev's Kremlin*, 109–10.

166 Medvedev, *V komande Gorbacheva*, 80.

167 Yakovlev interview, *The Second Russian Revolution* transcripts.

168 Gorbachev may, however, have been excessively cautious in removing Chebrikov in two stages. The latter, according to Vadim Medvedev, was 'in a good mood' about his shift from the chairmanship of the KGB to a secretaryship of the Central Committee, for he had expected 'something worse'. See Medvedev, *V komande Gorbacheva*, 80.

169 *Izvestiya TsK KPSS*, 5 (1989), 45–6.

170 In his farewell speech at the plenum, Fedoseev damned the notion of socialist pluralism with faint praise and called for the ideological unity of the party. See *Pravda*, 27 Apr. 1989, p. 4.

171 V. A. Kolosov, N. V. Petrov, and L. V. Smirnyagin (eds.), *Vesna 89: geografiya i anatomiya parlamentskikh vyborov* (Progress, Moscow, 1990), 109.

172 See e.g. O'Donnell and Schmitter, *Transitions from Authoritarian Rule: Tentative Conclusions about Uncertain Democracies*, 61–4; and Juan J. Linz and Alfred Stepan, 'Political Identities and Electoral Sequences: Spain, the Soviet Union, and Yugoslavia', *Daedalus*, 121/2 (Spring 1992), 123–39.

173 Obolonsky, 'Russian Politics in the Time of Troubles', in Saikal and Maley (eds.), *Russia in Search of its Future*, 25. Obolonsky writes: 'Despite the impressive number of parties and blocs which took part in the 1993 election campaign, at the moment we hardly have more than a quasi-multi-party system. Most of our parties are ad hoc groups which have been organised to support more or less popular leaders.'

174 The official figure for the turn-out was 54 per cent, which was extremely low given that the electorate were also participating in a plebiscite on a new Constitution. Yet that statistic probably exaggerates the participation rate. Even a number of successful candidates were later to complain that official voting turn-out figures (with over 50 per cent being required to validate acceptance of the Constitution) bore little relationship to the reality they observed. The Helsinki Commission, nevertheless, accepted the official results, while expressing at various points in their report a certain disappointment with the outcome. In their words: 'On December 12, 1993, Russia's voters went to the polls in a parliamentary election and constitutional referendum amid widely reported apathy and cynicism. The Central Election Commission later reported that voter turnout was only 54 per cent, thereby passing the 50 per cent minimum for the referendum to be valid' (Commission on Security and Cooperation in Europe, *Russia's Parliamentary Election and Constitutional Referendum, December 12, 1993* (Washington, 1994), 1). While this represented a substantial drop in participation as compared with the 1989, 1990, and 1991 contested elections in the last years of the Soviet Union (and in particular, *vis-à-vis* 1989), there was one important element of continuity. In both cases the rules governing the elections had been established by those in positions of political power rather than by agreement between government and opposition—not that there *was*

significant political opposition in 1988 when the decision to move to contested national elections was taken. But just as the rules governing the election of 1989 had been determined by Gorbachev and his supporters, so those of 1993 had been decided by Yeltsin and those close to him. They were not the result of a pact or understanding among all the major political players. On this, see Michael Urban, 'December 1993 as a Replication of Late-Soviet Electoral Practices', *Post-Soviet Affairs*, 10/2 (Apr.–June 1994), 127–58.

175 While not meeting all the criteria of a 'founding election', it did meet some of them in a way in which no subsequent Russian election did. Thus, for example, as O'Donnell and Schmitter put it: 'Founding elections are … moments of great drama. Turnout is very high' (*Transitions from Authoritarian Rule: Tentative Conclusions about Uncertain Democracies*, 62).

176 On this, see Medvedev, *V komande Gorbacheva*, 75–6; and Shakhnazarov, *Tsena svobody*, 72.

177 Cf. ibid. 76.

178 See Kolosov, Petrov, and Smirnyagin, *Vesna 89*, 107; and Stephen White, *After Gorbachev*, 3rd edn. (Cambridge University Press, Cambridge, 1993), 50–64.

179 White, *After Gorbachev*, 50–1.

180 *Izvestiya*, 21 Apr. 1989, p. 3.

181 *Pravda*, 27 Apr. 1989, p. 6.

182 Ibid. 4.

183 Ibid.

184 *Pravda*, 10 June 1989, p. 14.

185 Shakhnazarov interview, *The Second Russian Revolution* transcripts. See also Shakhnazarov, *Tsena svobody*, 74–80.

186 For the results of survey research on the extent to which the Congress was viewed and heard, together with the reaction of the respondents, see *Izvestiya*, 31 May 1989, p. 7; and *Izvestiya*, 4 June 1989, p. 1.

187 *Izvestiya*, 26 May 1989, p. 4.

188 I have drawn here and in several other paragraphs in this section upon my article 'Political Change in the Soviet Union', *World Policy Journal*, 6/3 (Summer 1989), 469–501.

189 *Izvestiya*, 27 May 1989, p. 4.

190 Soviet television, 29 May 1989, as reported in BBC Summary of World Broadcasts, SU/0475 C/3–C/6, 6 June 1989.

191 Shakhnazarov interview, *The Second Russian Revolution* transcripts.

192 Ibid.

193 Ibid.

194 Ibid.

195 Shakhnazarov for one believes that the aura of authority attached to a Russian head of state was damaged by the sight of unknown young deputies arguing with, and occasionally even haranguing, Gorbachev, who calmly accepted this and patiently explained the situation as he saw it. See Shakhnazarov, *Tsena svobody*, 77–8.

196 Gorbatschow, *Erinnerungen*, 463–5.

197 Ibid. 466–7.

198 Ibid. 464–5.

199 Author's interview with Chernyaev, 30 Mar. 1992.

200 Laptev interview, *The Second Russian Revolution* transcripts.

201 On this, see e.g. Shakhnazarov, *Tsena svobody*, 139.

202 Ryzhkov, *Perestroyka: Istoriya predatel'stv*, 291.

203 Ibid.

204 Ibid. 292. These remarks of Ryzhkov are to be found in a chapter which he entitles 'All Power to the Soviets!', recalling Lenin's slogan of 1917. The turning-point in the power of the soviets did, indeed, come as late as 1989. In contrast with by far the greater part of the Soviet period, it was only during the last three years of the USSR and the first two years of post-Soviet Russia that the soviets exercised substantial power.

205 Among them were Anatoly Chernyaev, Georgy Shakhnazarov, Nikolay Petrakov, Nikolay Shmelev, and Georgy Arbatov. See Chernyaev, *Shest' let s Gorbachevym*, 352, 356.

206 Shakhnazarov, *Tsena svobody*, 118.

207 Chernyaev, *Shest' let s Gorbachevym*, 345, 356.

208 Asked by Anastázie Kudrnová if he thought it was practicable to continue to hold both the presidency and the leadership of the CPSU, Gorbachev's reply was: 'In principle we must aim to

separate party and state posts. But at the moment, in a period of transition, when the soviets are not strong, when authority and the party are undergoing changes, it would mean engaging in an unnecessary struggle, which would play into the hands of those who want to liquidate perestroika' (*Lidové noviny*, 5 July 1990). I am grateful to Gordon Wightman for supplying me with this reference.

209 Gorbachev, 'Ya ne znayu schastlivykh reformatorov . . .', introductory chapter to *Gody trudnykh resheniy*, 12.

210 Anatoly Sobchak, *Khozhdenie vo vlast': Rasskaz o rozhdenii parlamenta* (Novosti, Moscow, 1991), 175.

211 Cf. Christopher Young, 'The Strategy of Political Liberalization: A Comparative View of Gorbachev's Reforms', *World Politics*, 45/1 (Oct. 1992), 47–65. Young's argument that Gorbachev's far-reaching reforms were 'very deliberately constructed to undermine the organizational basis of his opponents' power while safeguarding the interests of his own faction' is unconvincing. The idea that Gorbachev 'proposed to eliminate the CPSU as a source of political and administrative power' because 'Ligachev and his followers were concentrated in the party apparatus' and had to be kept away from the task of implementing economic reform misses the points (*a*) that it was only Gorbachev's policy of economic and political liberalization that from 1989 prevented him from enjoying the unchallengeable authority which normally accrued to the General Secretary; and (*b*) that, if he had abided by the traditional rules of the game, he would not have had great difficulty in removing Ligachev from the Politburo and, indeed, from political life in a pre-pluralist Soviet system. Ligachev was no Suslov (who had been in the Politburo before Brezhnev entered it and had many tentacles in the Central Committee Secretariat and apparatus) but someone whom Gorbachev had himself brought into the Politburo and whose continued presence there depended on the General Secretary's goodwill.

212 A good brief account of the miners' strikes is to be found in Roxburgh, *The Second Russian Revolution*, 147–8. For a fuller discussion, see Donald Filtzer, *Soviet Workers and the Collapse of Perestroika: The Soviet Labour Process and Gorbachev's Reforms, 1985–1991* (Cambridge University Press, Cambridge, 1994), esp. 94–122.

213 Filtzer, *Soviet Workers and the Collapse of Perestroika*, 100–1.

214 Shakhnazarov interview, *The Second Russian Revolution* transcripts.

215 Shakhnazarov, *Tsena svobody*, 137–8.

216 From the beginning of 1991 the Chairman of the Council of Ministers was formally renamed Prime Minister and the Council became the Cabinet of Ministers. This coincided with the replacement of Nikolay Ryzhkov by Valentin Pavlov as head of that Soviet government.

217 Shakhnazarov, *Tsena svobody*, 73.

218 Shakhnazarov interview, *The Second Russian Revolution* transcripts.

219 Medvedev, *V komande Gorbacheva*, 74.

220 Shakhnazarov, *Tsena svobody*, 137–8.

221 It was not, of course, his only formal function. In 1988 he had become Chairman of the Presidium of the (unreformed) Supreme Soviet, which was not at that time an independent power base.

222 Ligachev, *Inside Gorbachev's Kremlin*, 110.

223 Ibid. 111.

224 See *Yezhegodnik Bol'shoy Sovetskoy Entsiklopedii 1986* (Sovetskaya Entsiklopediya, Moscow, 1986), 15–16; and *Izvestiya TsK KPSS*, 9 (1990), 17.

225 Ibid.; *Izvestiya TsK KPSS*, 11 (1990), 9; and *Izvestiya TsK KPSS*, 1 (1991), 9.

226 *Izvestiya TsK KPSS*, 2 (1991), 10–11; *Izvestiya TsK KPSS*, 6 (1991), 11; and *Pravda*, 27 July 1991, p. 1.

227 Yakovlev, *Gor'kaya chasha*, 417.

228 *Izvestiya TsK KPSS*, 9 (1990), 19, 21.

229 Ibid. 19.

230 On Gorbachev's 'narrow' circle or group of close advisers and associates, see Chernyaev, *Shest' let s Gorbachevym*, 66 and 432–3; and Shakhnazarov, *Tsena svobody*, 144.

231 *Reytingi Borisa El'tsina i Mikhaila Gorbacheva po 10-bal'noy shkale* (VTsIOM, Moscow, 1993).

232 Among those in the Gorbachev team who urged the desirability of the creation of the presidency and election to it in 1990 by popular vote was Andrey Grachev. In a memorandum submitted to the Politburo in January 1990 (for a copy of which I am grateful to Dr Grachev), Grachev notes the need for consolidating executive power and Gorbachev's authority (for he was in no doubt that Gorbachev would win such an election) on the basis of popular mandate in a union-wide election. Two other interesting documents from the hand of Grachev—a memorandum to Alexander Yakovlev, dated 10 Jan. 1990, in which Grachev stresses the need to turn the Communist Party into a different kind of party, and a draft programme for Gorbachev's first months as President (written in March)—are published as annexes to the French (but not the Russian) edition of the second

of Grachev's two books of political reminiscences and reflections. See Andrei Gratchev, *La Chute du Kremlin: L'Empire du non-sens* (Hachette, Paris, 1994), 225–43.

233 Medvedev, *V komande Gorbacheva*, 111.

234 See Gale Stokes, *The Walls Came Tumbling Down: The Collapse of Communism in Eastern Europe* (Oxford University Press, Oxford, 1993), 132–6. The more radical parties in the democratic opposition to the Communists in Hungary opposed the direct election of the President and favoured a renewed parliament making the choice. Their reasoning was not only principled, the argument that a directly elected President would be likely to be stronger than was healthy for a new democracy, but also tactical inasmuch as in 1989—the year of democratic breakthrough in Hungary—the most popular politician by far, and the person most likely to win such an election, was the radical reformer within the Communist leadership, Imre Pozsgay. The Free Democrats and Young Democrats in Hungary succeeded in forcing a referendum on the issue, in which by an extremely narrow majority it was decided that, following elections to the National Assembly, parliament—rather than the people as a whole—would elect the President. As the former Communists—who had changed their name from Hungarian Socialist Workers' Party to Hungarian Socialist Party—did badly in that election, that put paid to Pozsgay's hopes of the presidency.

235 Sobchak, *Khozhdenie vo vlast'*, 182.

236 For the full transcript of this Third Congress of People's Deputies, see *Vneocherednoy tretiy s"ezd narodnykh deputatov SSSR, 12–15 marta 1990 g.: Stenograficheskiy otchet* (Izdanie Verkhovnogo Soveta SSSR, Moscow, 1990), 3 vols. See also Sobchak, *Khozhdenie vo vlast'*, 159–206; and Roxburgh, *The Second Russian Revolution*, 171–5.

237 Sobchak, *Khozhdenie vo vlast'*, 189. Shakhnazarov (interview, *The Second Russian Revolution* transcripts) says that, as a deputy himself, he tried of his own accord to convince his neighbours that they should vote for Gorbachev, but that—in sharp contrast with Brezhnev, with whom before every Central Committee plenum everything was calculated in advance in fine detail—Gorbachev had not put in place any behind-the-scenes activity: 'There was no organised effort to support him.'

238 Sobchak, *Khozhdenie vo vlast'*, 189.

239 Roxburgh, *The Second Russian Revolution*, 175.

240 Sobchak, *Khozhdenie vo vlast'*, 199–200.

241 Interview with A. N. Yakovlev on Russian television, 24 Aug. 1991, reported in full in FBIS-SOV-91-166, 27 Aug. 1991, pp. 40–9 (quotation from p. 49).

242 Roxburgh, *The Second Russian Revolution*, 187. Roxburgh (pp. 186–92) provides one of the most vivid and perceptive accounts of the Twenty-Eighth Party Congress.

243 Ibid. 189.

244 Shakhnazarov, *Tsena svobody*, 253–4. See also Roxburgh, *The Second Russian Revolution*, 193.

245 See *Izvestiya TsK KPSS*, 1 (1990), 9.

246 See *Izvestiya TsK KPSS*, 7 (1990), 7–9; and Roxburgh, *The Second Russian Revolution*, 182–3.

247 See *Izvestiya TsK KPSS*, 8 (1990), 129–32.

248 *Izvestiya*, 4 June 1989, p. 2.

249 Ibid.

250 The initial enthusiasm of e.g. Shatalin for membership of the Presidential Council was based on what turned out to be a misunderstanding that he would thereby exercise some real power. See the interview with him in *Moscow News*, No. 14, 8 Apr. 1990, p. 6.

251 When a majority of members of the Presidential Council were questioned in August 1990 (by which time the total membership—in addition to Gorbachev—was seventeen), it became clear that they had different ideas about the nature of the institution—even on the question as to whether it was purely a consultative body or had some executive power. See *Moskovskie novosti*, 33 (1990), 8–9.

252 That is not to say that their power within the society was as great as it once was. The growth of spontaneous economic activity, whether under the guise of co-operatives or overtly private, undermined the old system of administrative allocation of resources.

253 Shakhnazarov, *Tsena svobody*, 164.

254 Ibid. 142. Shakhnazarov says that it was he who suggested the name 'Presidential Council' to Gorbachev.

255 Boldin is described by Shakhnazarov as the 'unprepossessing . . . ultimate bureaucrat' and as someone who reminded him of Konstantin Chernenko (*Tsena svobody*, 140–1).

256 Chernyaev, *Shest' let s Gorbachevym*, 334.

257 Shaken by the 25 February demonstration, Gorbachev, according to Chernyaev, spoke more like a party boss than a new thinker at the Politburo meeting held on 2 Mar. 1990. See Chernyaev, *Shest' let s Gorbachevym*, 335–6. Cf. Shakhnazarov, *Tsena svobody*, 13.

258 For a perceptive account of Gorbachev as a transformational leader, see George W. Breslauer, 'Evaluating Gorbachev as Leader', *Soviet Economy*, 5/4 (Oct.–Dec. 1989), 299–340.

Chapter 7   Gorbachev and Foreign Policy

1 That is not for a moment to suggest that Gorbachev wished to abandon the Soviet Union's position as one of the two great military powers, along with the United States. Although there was, in all probability, an element of lip-service in the reference to the military, Gorbachev—in his closing remarks to the Politburo which had just chosen him as General Secretary—spoke of the need for new decisions which would raise the economic and military might of the Soviet Union and improve the life of the people. (For the stenographic report of this Politburo meeting, see *Istochnik*, 0/1993, 66–75.) However interested Gorbachev may or may not have been in enhancing the Soviet Union's military might, he was, though, *more* concerned to reduce international sources of tension and the military budget. According to Anatoly Chernyaev (speaking at a specialist seminar on the Gorbachev era at St Antony's College, Oxford, on 15 Oct. 1994), by the time Gorbachev visited Britain in December 1984 for his first meeting with Margaret Thatcher, he had already come to the view that the Soviet Union could not continue with such a large military-industrial complex. Roald Sagdeev, the former Director of the Soviet Space Research Institute, who was brought into the circle of Gorbachev's advisers on scientific issues early in the perestroika period, rightly observes: 'Soon Gorbachev's interests moved in the direction of international security and military buildup, trying to break the deadlock with medium-range nuclear missiles in the European theater. I believe that outside the understandable general strategic considerations, Gorbachev wanted the chance to reduce the future military budget as a part of his program for the economic revival of the country.' See Roald Z. Sagdeev, *The Making of a Soviet Scientist: My Adventures in Nuclear Fusion and Space from Stalin to Star Wars* (John Wiley, New York, 1994), 267.

2 For an interesting insider's account of the workings of the Soviet military-industrial complex, see the memoirs of Sagdeev, *The Making of a Soviet Scientist*, esp. 45, 164–6, 185–200, 240–3, 325–7.

3 As Chernyaev observed (St Antony's seminar of 15 Oct. 1994), every member of the Central Committee voted without question for Shevardnadze when Gorbachev proposed him, although they were taken completely by surprise. Neither in the West nor even in well-informed circles in the Soviet Union had speculation about Gromyko's successor included the name of Shevardnadze.

4 It is helpful that all six of these people have written memoirs. Yakovlev has published three volumes of reminiscences and reflections: *Muki prochteniya bytiya. Perestroika: Nadezhdy i real'nosti* (Novosti, Moscow, 1991); *Predislovie, Obval, Posleslovie* (Novosti, Moscow, 1992); and *Gor'kaya chasha: Bol'shevizm i Reformatsiya Rossii* (Verkhne-Volzhskoe knizhnoe izdatelstvo, Yaroslavl, 1994). Vadim Medvedev has published two useful memoirs: *V komande Gorbacheva. Vzglyad iznutri* ('Bylina', Moscow, 1994); and *Raspad: Kak on nazreval v 'mirovoy sisteme sotsializma'* (Mezhdunarodnye otnosheniya, Moscow, 1994). Chernyaev has published his rich and detailed *Shest' let s Gorbachevym* (Kultura, Moscow, 1993); and Shakhnazarov a thoughtful and detailed memoir of comparable importance, *Tsena svobody* (Rossika Zevs, Moscow, 1993). The memoirs of Shevardnadze, published as *The Future Belongs to Freedom* (Sinclair-Stevenson, London, 1991), show, in contrast, the signs of the haste in which they were written, although they, too, are certainly not without value. Dobrynin has also written memoirs which, however, as this book goes to press, are not yet available.

5 Interview with Anatoly Chernyaev, 30 Mar. 1992. Shakhnazarov has pointed out that this information came not only to the International Department but also to the Socialist Countries Department of the Central Committee, and that it included diplomatic telegrams as well as KGB and military intelligence reports. He adds, however, that its distribution was restricted *within* the departments. The head and deputy heads of the department saw it and they could show what seemed to be relevant to sector heads within the department. See Shakhnazarov, *Tsena svobody*, 52.

6 Interview with Chernyaev, 30 Mar. 1992.

7 Medvedev, *Raspad*, 26.

8 Ibid.

9 Here I would disagree with Amin Saikal and William Maley in their otherwise valuable contribution, 'From Soviet to Russian Foreign Policy', in Saikal and Maley (eds.), *Russia in Search of its Future* (Cambridge University Press, Cambridge, 1995), 102–22, at p. 119, where they write: 'The International Department was almost certainly the single most important bureaucratic agency involved in foreign policy formulation in the USSR.' This generalization appears to include the

Gorbachev era when, given Gorbachev's closeness to Shevardnadze, it was especially difficult for the International Department to overshadow the Ministry of Foreign Affairs. It is a generalization which draws upon an article by Leonard Schapiro, 'The International Department of the CPSU: Key to Soviet Policy', *International Journal*, 32/1 (Winter 1976/7), 41–55, in which, however, Schapiro (p. 44) did not recognize the increase in political weight which Gromyko's promotion to full Politburo membership in 1973 brought both the minister and his ministry. In rightly emphasizing that the International Department was concerned with the West as well as the Third World, Schapiro, nevertheless, draws his examples mainly from the Department's relations with the major Communist Parties of Western Europe which were, indeed, its direct responsibility rather than the more important state-to-state relations with Western governments which were not. On this, see Medvedev, *Raspad*, 26. Writing in Brezhnev's time, Franklyn Griffiths revealed that whereas a major role in the formulation of the international section of the General Secretary's report to the Twenty-Fourth Party Congress in 1971 was played by IMEMO (which, as well as being an institute of the Academy of Sciences, came under the supervision of the International Department), a greater part in the drafting of the corresponding section of the report to the Twenty-Fifth Congress of 1976 was played by the Department of General International Relations of the Ministry of Foreign Affairs. Griffiths adds: 'Such a change in participation would be quite in line with the growth of the Foreign Ministry's authority following the elevation of A. A. Gromyko to the Politburo in 1973 and with the failure of the director of the Institute of the World Economy [i.e. IMEMO] to advance from candidate membership in the Central Committee at the Twenty-Fifth Congress.' See Griffiths, 'Ideological Development and Foreign Policy', in Seweryn Bialer (ed.), *The Domestic Context of Soviet Foreign Policy* (Westview, Boulder, Colo., 1981), 19–48, at p. 20. For further discussion of the role of the Minister and Ministry of Foreign Affairs pre-Gorbachev, see Archie Brown, 'The Foreign Policy-Making Process', in Curtis Keeble (ed.), *The Soviet State: The Domestic Roots of Soviet Foreign Policy* (Gower, Aldershot, for the Royal Institute of International Affairs, 1985), 191–216, esp. 206–9, 216.

10 See e.g. Yu. V. Aksyutin (ed.), *Nikita Sergeevich Khrushchev: Materialy k biografii* (Politizdat, Moscow, 1989); Fedor Burlatsky, *Vozhdi i Sovetniki: O Khrushcheve, Andropove i ne tol'ko o nikh* (Politizdat, Moscow, 1990); Roy A. Medvedev, *Khrushchev* (Blackwell, Oxford, 1982); William J. Tompson, 'The Fall of Nikita Khrushchev', *Soviet Studies*, 43/6 (1991), 1101–21; and Tompson, *Khrushchev: A Political Life* (Macmillan, London, 1995).

11 Gromyko was recruited into the Soviet diplomatic service in 1939 shortly after it had been purged by Stalin. According to Chernyaev (St Antony's seminar, 15 Oct. 1994)—and it is a view which is borne out in Gromyko's memoirs—Gromyko always took the view that everything that had been done in foreign policy while he was Foreign Minister was correct. Accordingly, so long as he remained there, Gorbachev would have found it exceedingly difficult to introduce a fresh approach.

12 Interview with Anatoly Chernyaev, 30 Mar. 1992.

13 Bessmertnykh, as Vadim Bakatin records in his memoirs, refused to put his name to a letter condemning the August 1991 *putsch* at a time when Gorbachev was still under house arrest in the Crimea. The letter was signed by Bakatin, Yevgeny Primakov, and Arkady Volsky. See Bakatin, *Izbavlenie ot KGB* (Novosti, Moscow, 1992), 14–15.

14 This was a spontaneous remark by Sir Geoffrey Howe (as he then was) in a dinner-table conversation I had with him on 27 Oct. 1988, after he had delivered the annual Cyril Foster lecture at Oxford University. See also Geoffrey Howe, *Conflict of Loyalty* (Macmillan, London, 1994), esp. 437–42, 563.

15 Interview with Chernyaev, 30 Mar. 1992.

16 Ibid.

17 The five Gorbachev–Reagan summits were in Geneva (19–21 Nov. 1985), Reykjavik (11–12 Oct. 1986), Washington (8–11 Dec. 1987), Moscow (30 May–2 June 1988), and New York (7 Dec. 1988). The four Gorbachev–Bush summits were held off the coast of Malta (2–3 Dec. 1989), in Washington (31 May–3 June 1990), in Helsinki (9 Sept. 1990), and in Moscow (29 July–1 Aug. 1991). For a valuable discussion of all these summit meetings, see Raymond L. Garthoff, *The Great Transition: American–Soviet Relations and the End of the Cold War* (Brookings Institution, Washington, 1994).

18 It is also questionable whether the high-profile campaign of the Japanese authorities was the wisest diplomatic course. Gorbachev, in meetings with Japanese leaders, suggested that they consider, with a view to emulating, the example of Germany. (My source is Andrey Grachev, interview in Moscow, 18 Sept. 1992.) For the first quarter of a century after the Second World War, no country was more feared and distrusted in the Soviet Union than Germany. But beginning with the Chancellorship of Willy Brandt, the Germans gradually established good relations with the Soviet leadership and acquired a vastly improved image with the Soviet public. Eventually, Gorbachev is said to have reminded his Japanese hosts, that led to the reunification of Germany, something scarcely imaginable a few years earlier. The implication for the Kuriles was clear.

19 For a useful brief account of Soviet policy in Asia in the later Gorbachev years, see Coit D. Blacker, *Hostage to Revolution: Gorbachev and Soviet Security Policy, 1985–1991* (Council on Foreign Relations, New York, 1993), 135–9.

20 See e.g. George P. Shultz, *Turmoil and Triumph: My Years as Secretary of State* (Macmillan, New York, 1993), 702, where Shultz describes the contrast between Shevardnadze and Gromyko as 'breathtaking' and adds: 'He could smile, engage, converse. He had an ability to persuade and to be persuaded.' See also Howe, *Conflict of Loyalty*, 438–9, 548; and Don Oberdorfer, *The Turn. How the Cold War Came to an End: The United States and the Soviet Union, 1983–1990* (Jonathan Cape, London, 1992), 123, for the comments on Shevardnadze of French Foreign Minister Roland Dumas as well as those of Shultz and Howe. Shultz's successor as American Secretary of State, James Baker, formed an equally warm relationship with Shevardnadze. Following the latter's resignation as Soviet Foreign Minister in December 1990, Baker said: 'I never found anything he ever told me to be untrue' (Michael R. Beschloss and Strobe Talbott, *At the Highest Levels: The Inside Story of the End of the Cold War* (Little, Brown, London, 1993), 296).

21 Andrei Gratchev (Grachev), *La Chute du Kremlin: L'Empire du non-sens* (Hachette, Paris, 1994), 78.

22 Oberdorfer, *The Turn*, 123.

23 Shultz, *Turmoil and Triumph*, 702–4. Shultz also told his State Department team in January 1986: 'We are now facing a bold and agile Soviet leader who is even tougher and more of a challenge to us than his predecessors' (ibid. 704). The phrase 'the Soviets', when applied to people rather than the institutions of local government—as in 'the Soviets had an inferiority complex'—usually obscures more than it reveals. It is necessary to know whether a generalization about 'the Soviets' extends to all Soviet nationalities or only to Russians or, more specifically, to Soviet officials or a still narrower ruling group. Many officials did indeed have an inferiority complex, so the 'Soviet experts in the U.S. government' cited by Shultz were not entirely wrong, even if Gorbachev was, as Shultz insisted, among the more spectacular exceptions to that rule.

24 On one of my visits to the United States around the time Shultz was making the remarks just quoted, I listened to a former US Ambassador to Moscow argue on television that Gorbachev was much more dangerous than any of his predecessors because he was 'smart', possessed 'charm', and was 'flexible'. He was thus an especially alarming person to let loose on the Europeans, in particular, who were notoriously easy to seduce. But the events of the next few years did nothing to bolster the implicit argument that the Europeans or, for that matter, the Americans would have benefited from having a Soviet leader who was stupid, boorish, and inflexible.

25 A similar point is made by Jonathan Haslam, 'Soviet Policy Toward Western Europe', in George W. Breslauer and Philip E. Tetlock (eds.), *Learning in U.S. and Soviet Foreign Policy* (Westview, Boulder, Colo., 1991), 169–603, esp. 197 ff.

26 Adamishin held that rank until 1990 when he became Soviet Ambassador to Italy. In post-Soviet Russia he was promoted to First Deputy Foreign Minister, from which post he moved to London as Russian Ambassador in 1994. Petrovsky remained a deputy foreign minister until August 1991 when he became Soviet First Deputy Foreign Minister. In 1992 he became Deputy General Secretary of the United Nations.

27 Arkady Shevchenko, the high-ranking Soviet diplomat who defected to the United States in 1978, contrasted the ideological preoccupations of the pre-Gorbachev International Department with the more pragmatic concerns of the Foreign Ministry. Yet he also notes that Ponomarev was 'keenly aware of the value of expertise' and that he had been 'energetic in recruiting able associates' in the International Department. See Shevchenko, *Breaking with Moscow* (Knopf, New York, 1985), 188–91, esp. 189.

28 The source for this statement is Andrey Grachev (deputy head of the International Department, 1989–91), speaking at a seminar at St Antony's College, Oxford, on 10 Oct. 1994.

29 Shevchenko, writing on the eve of Gorbachev's coming to power, observes that he first 'met Zagladin during our days at MGIMO'. Subsequently, he says, he 'watched his rise with a mixture of admiration and distaste'. Shevchenko is one of those who notes that Zagladin, following the Twentieth Party Congress in 1956, was 'genuinely enthusiastic about possibilities for changing what was obsolete in Soviet life and government' and that a 'surge of idealism' in the early post-Stalin years 'carried Zagladin and others into Party work'. But, he adds, what 'began as something of a crusade . . . turned into a career' (Shevchenko, *Breaking with Moscow*, 190).

30 Petrakov's successor, Oleg Ozherelev, had at one time been Dean of the Economics Faculty of Leningrad University, but—unlike Petrakov—he had subsequently served (under Vadim Medvedev, whose protégé he was) in the Central Committee apparatus. Valery Boldin come to Gorbachev from *Pravda* (whose party status at that time made it virtually an adjunct of the Central Committee), but he had earlier served in the Central Committee apparatus under the reactionary head of the Propaganda Department of the Central Committee in Khrushchev's time, Leonid

Ilichev. In those years Boldin had been a colleague also of Alexander Nikolaevich Yakovlev, with whom he was on familiar (second-person singular) terms.

31 Personal information from a scholar who took part in the meeting and who urged total support for a military response to the Iraqi incursion if Saddam Hussein did not obey an imposed deadline for withdrawal.

32 Andrey Grachev (personal communication of 6 Jan. 1995) has confirmed that Gorbachev's and Shevardnadze's positions were not identical. Shevardnadze was more closely tied to the American position and more ready for a military showdown than Gorbachev, who hoped to avoid an all-out attack on the Soviet Union's former Arab ally, while at the same time emphasizing the autonomy of Soviet foreign policy. For a detailed account of decision-making on the Gulf crisis of 1990–1, based on interviews with participants both in Washington (especially) and Moscow, see Beschloss and Talbott, *At the Highest Levels*, 244–344. See also Garthoff, *The Great Transition*, 435.

33 Beschloss and Talbott, *At the Highest Levels*, 270–80.

34 Among those who later engaged in public criticism of Gorbachev and (still more) Shevardnadze on the issue of military action against Iraq was Georgy Kornienko, who—until he was pensioned off by Gorbachev in November 1988—was First Deputy Head of the International Department of the Central Committee. This was another instance in which that department was sidelined by Gorbachev. See Kornienko's comprehensive attack on Gorbachev's foreign policy, 'Zakonchilas' li "kholodnaya voyna"?: Razmyshleniya ee uchastnika', *Nezavisimaya gazeta*, 16 Aug. 1994, p. 5; and the reply of Anatoly Chernyaev, 'Dlya nego kholodnaya voyna deystvitel'no ne zakonchilas'', *Nezavisimaya gazeta*, 3 Sept. 1994, p. 4.

35 Interview with Andrey Grachev, 14 Jan. 1993. See also Medvedev, *Raspad*, 26.

36 See *Nezavisimaya gazeta*, 16 Aug. 1994, p. 5; and also Kornienko's memoirs, *Kholodnaya voyna: svide-tel'stvo ee uchastnika* (Mezhdunarodnye otnosheniya, Moscow, 1994), where he argues (pp. 260–1) that the 'new thinking' in practice became a 'betrayal of the state interests of the Soviet Union'.

37 Interview with Anatoly Chernyaev, 30 Mar. 1992.

38 Interview with Andrey Grachev, 14 Jan. 1993.

39 Ibid.

40 This would appear to date from the beginning of the 1970s and Willy Brandt's Ostpolitik. Prior to the improved relations with the Soviet Union established by the West German Social Democrats, Soviet leaders (following the example of both Lenin and Stalin) had tended to regard social democrats as far more dangerous adversaries than conservatives, seeing the former as rivals, and in free elections almost invariably more successful rivals, for working-class support. Equally, from the mainstream of social democratic parties, there was generally suspicion of and antipathy towards the Communists, not only on account of Soviet policy in post-war Eastern Europe but because of the first-hand experience of struggle between social democratic and labour parties, on the one hand, and Communists and Trotskyists, on the other, in the West European trade union movements. For a well-documented argument which suggests that—partly as a reaction against this earlier anti-Communism—the West German Social Democrats, in their desire to provide the Soviet Union with reassurance on its security, became excessively tolerant of Soviet domination of Eastern Europe, see Timothy Garton Ash, *In Europe's Name: Germany and the Divided Continent* (Jonathan Cape, London, 1993), esp. Ch. 6.

41 This point is also made by Andrey Grachev (interview with author, 13 Jan. 1993), who observed that Dobrynin did not find it interesting to deal with the main subjects of the International Department's activity and that he was not regarded as a strong political figure within the Central Committee apparatus. Vadim Medvedev also indicates that having to deal with a multitude of tiny parties did not suit Dobrynin and observes that 'the new International Department did not find itself' (*Raspad*, 26).

42 Interview with Chernyaev, 30 Mar. 1992.

43 Ibid.

44 Ibid.

45 For Falin's views (among others), see Hannes Adomeit, 'Gorbachev, German Unification and the Collapse of Empire', *Post-Soviet Affairs*, 10/3 (1994), 197–230; and for Kornienko's critique, see *Nezavisimaya gazeta*, 16 Aug. 1994, p. 5; and Kornienko, *Kholodnaya voyna*, 234–57.

46 See Gorbachev, *Izbrannye rechi i stat'i*, iii (1987), 180–280, esp. 243–58.

47 General Albert Makashov, 'Doktrina predatel'stva', *Den'*, 7–13 June 1992, p. 2.

48 Gorbachev was careful, however, immediately to add: 'But, of course, we attach great importance to the state and nature of relations with the United States.'

49 Gorbachev, *Izbrannye rechi i stat'i*, iii. 247.

50 Mikhail Gorbachev, 'Za bez"yadernyy mir, za gumanizm mezhdunarodnykh otnosheniy', in Gorbachev, *Izbrannye rechi i stat'i*, iv (1987), 376–92.

51 See *XIX Vsesoyuznaya konferentsiya Kommunisticheskoy Partii Sovetskogo Soyuza, 28 Iyunya–1 Iyulya 1988 g.: Stenograficheskiy otchet*, 2 vols. (Politizdat, Moscow, 1988), especially Gorbachev's report to the conference, i. 19–92, at pp. 40–5.

52 The UN speech is published in Gorbachev, *Izbrannye rechi i stat'i*, vii (1990), 184–202.

53 It was revealing of the Soviet leadership's concern about the emergence of a spontaneous working-class movement in a 'fraternal socialist state' that it was in August 1980 that they resumed the jamming of foreign radio (which they had ceased to do—with the exception of Radio Liberty and Radio Free Europe—in the period preceding the Helsinki Agreement of 1975) to ensure that as little independent information as possible about the activities of Polish workers would reach their Soviet counterparts.

54 See Alexander Dallin, 'New Thinking in Soviet Foreign Policy', in Archie Brown (ed.), *New Thinking in Soviet Politics* (Macmillan, London, 1992), 71–85, esp. 72.

55 Legvold, 'Soviet Learning in the 1980s', in Breslauer and Tetlock (eds.), *Learning in U.S. and Soviet Foreign Policy*, 684–732, at 710.

56 Gorbachev, *Perestroika: New Thinking for our Country and the World* (Collins, London, 1987), 147.

57 Previous Soviet leaders from time to time accepted that there were global problems, but attempted to place them within the traditional 'class' framework. Thus, Chernenko in 1984 said: 'The problems of war and peace, like all the global problems, do not exist by themselves. They are inseparable from the world's social contradictions and from the development of the class struggle' (quoted in *Textual Analysis of General Secretary Mikhail Gorbachev's Speech to the Forum 'For a Nuclear-Free World, for the Survival of Mankind', Moscow, February 16, 1987* prepared by the staff of the American Committee on US Soviet Relations (the main author being Joel Hellman), Washington, 1987).

58 *Literaturnaya gazeta*, 5 Nov. 1986, p. 2.

59 Stephen Shenfield, *The Nuclear Dilemma: Explorations in Soviet Ideology* (Routledge, for the Royal Institute of International Affairs, London, 1987), 45–6.

60 Ibid. 47.

61 Gorbachev, *Perestroika*, 145.

62 See Sakharov, *Progress, Coexistence and Intellectual Freedom* (Deutsch, London, 1968); Burlatsky, 'Filosofiya mira', *Voprosy filosofii*, 12 (1982), 57–66; and Shakhnazarov, 'Logika politicheskogo myshleniya v yadernuyu eru', *Voprosy filosofii*, 5 (1984), 62–74. See also for commentary on the intellectual origins of the new thinking in foreign policy: *Textual Analysis of General Secretary Mikhail Gorbachev's Speech to the Forum 'For a Nuclear-Free World, for the Survival of Mankind', Moscow, February 16, 1987*; Stephen Shenfield, *The Nuclear Dilemma*; Neil Malcolm, *Soviet Policy Perspectives on Western Europe* (Routledge, for the Royal Institute of International Affairs, London, 1989); Dallin, 'New Thinking in Soviet Foreign Policy', in Brown (ed.), *New Thinking in Soviet Politics*, and Breslauer and Tetlock (eds.), *Learning in U.S. and Soviet Foreign Policy*, chs. 17 and 18 (by Franklyn Griffiths and Robert Legvold).

63 Shevardnadze, too, was in 1988 sensitive to the potential charge, which soon gathered overt force within conservative Communist circles, that playing down the class approach was a deviation from Lenin's teaching. Thus, in a major speech at the Soviet Ministry of Foreign Affairs (primarily aimed at a domestic audience of ministry officials and *mezhdunarodniki*) he got in first by characterizing the idea that 'peaceful coexistence' was a 'specific form of class struggle' as not only 'erroneous' but also 'anti-Leninist', although the last point was omitted from the printed text—an abridged version of the speech itself (Shevardnadze, speech of 25 July 1988, 'XIX vsesoyuznaya konferentsiya KPSS: vneshnyaya politika i diplomatiya', *Vestnik Ministerstva Inostrannykh Del*, 15 (15 Aug. 1988), 27–46, esp. 34).

64 Chernyaev, *Shest' let s Gorbachevym*, 152–3.

65 See Dmitry Volkogonov, *Lenin: Politicheskiy portret*, 2 vols. (Novosti, Moscow, 1994), esp. ii. 124, 166. The views which Gorbachev judged it prudent to express were, of course, subject both to tactical considerations and to evolutionary development during his time in office. Thus, Volkogonov is able to quote him as supporting in the Politburo in 1987 the principle of 'the liquidation of the kulaks as a class' (ibid.), even though Gorbachev deplored the methods by which this was done by Stalin and though two years later he unambiguously rejected the principle as well. Volkogonov's large book on Lenin (which contains numerous digressions) is available in an abbreviated English-language edition, well translated and edited by Harold Shukman (Volkogonov, *Lenin: A New Biography*, The Free Press, New York, 1994).

66 Rigby, 'Some Concluding Observations', in Brown (ed.), *New Thinking in Soviet Politics*, 102–10, at p. 109.

67 M. Gorbachev, 'Sotsializm i perestroyka', *Pravda*, 26 Nov. 1989, pp. 1–3.

68 Ibid. 2.

69 Ibid. 1.

70 Ibid. 2.

71 Ibid.

72 Gorbachev, report of the Central Committee to the Nineteenth Party Conference (28 June 1988) in *XIX Vsesoyuznaya konferentsiya Kommunisticheskoy Partii Sovetskogo Soyuza*, i. 18–92, at p. 43.

73 Gorbachev, 'Vystuplenie v Organizatsii Ob"edinennykh Natsiy', *Izbrannye rechi i stat'i*, vii (1990), 184–202, at p. 188.

74 On that point I would disagree with Hannes Adomeit, who, in the course of a generally illuminating and well-researched article, suggests that 'by 1988' Gorbachev was reacting to events over which he had 'lost control'. During 1989 that, indeed, became the case so far as East-Central Europe was concerned (although even then Gorbachev had choices and the fact that he, rather than, say, Ligachev, was General Secretary made an enormous difference), but in 1988 he was still, to a large extent, setting the political agenda both domestically and in the international arena. It is another matter that the major changes he inaugurated in that year—above all, at the Nineteenth Party Conference in June but also in his UN speech in December—unleashed forces which were within the next two to three years to go far further than he envisaged and in directions which, in a number of cases, were by no means those he had intended. See Hannes Adomeit, 'Gorbachev, German Unification and the Collapse of Empire', *Post-Soviet Affairs*, 10/3 (July–Sept. 1994), 197–233, at pp. 225–6. Michael R. Beschloss and Strobe Talbott are precise and to the point when they write: 'During his first four years in power, Gorbachev was an event-making leader. He came to office in 1985 determined to substitute "real politics" for terror as the organizing principle of Soviet life. Until the end of 1988, he retained a degree of control over the forces of change he had so boldly set in motion' (Beschloss and Talbott, *At the Highest Levels*, 467).

75 Sagdeev, *The Making of a Soviet Scientist*, 273.

76 It was occasionally suggested in the West and more often in the Soviet Union that the expression 'military-industrial complex' is inappropriate in the Soviet context because the military and military industry were two separate entities, but when I questioned Sagdeev about this in March 1992 he stressed that from personal experience he was only too well aware of the close interaction between the military, on the one hand, and military-related industry and science, on the other, and, accordingly, the complete aptness of the concept to Soviet conditions. In his memoirs, *The Making of a Soviet Scientist*, Sagdeev devotes an entire chapter to the military-industrial complex and, noting the existence (pp. 186–7) of the Commission on Military-Industrial Issues of the Council of Ministers, the creation of Dmitry Ustinov, he comments: 'With a name like that, I was never able to understand how our propagandists could ever have denied the existence of our own military-industrial complex.'

77 Strobe Talbott, *Deadly Gambits* (Picador, London, 1985), 317–21.

78 Oberdorfer, *The Turn*, 55. See also Alexander Dallin, *Black Box: KAL 007 and the Superpowers* (University of California Press, Berkeley, 1985).

79 Howe, *Conflict of Loyalty*, 350. See also Oleg Gordievsky, *Next Stop Execution* (Macmillan, London, 1995), 271–3.

80 Dallin, *Black Box*, 104–5.

81 Howe, *Conflict of Loyalty*, 350.

82 Ibid.

83 Gordievsky, *Next Stop Execution*, 272–3.

84 As Howe puts it: 'Both Margaret and I had been impressed' [by Gordievsky's alarming reports]. 'We each found opportunities to warn allies and friends of the genuineness of Soviet fears' (Howe, *Conflict of Loyalty*), 350.

85 Christopher Andrew and Oleg Gordievsky, *KGB: The Inside Story of its Foreign Operations from Lenin to Gorbachev* (Hodder & Stoughton, London, 1990), 504.

86 Michael MccGwire, *Perestroika and Soviet National Security* (Brookings Institution, Washington, 1991), 392.

87 MccGwire (ibid.) observes: 'It has been said that the danger of war in U.S. policy lies in the conduct of policy as if there was no danger of war, and this was never more true than during the first Reagan administration.'

88 Interview with Andrey Grachev, 14 Jan. 1993.

89 He had, however, as noted in an earlier chapter, shared with his friend Shevardnadze (who in March 1985 was still a candidate, or non-voting, member of the Politburo) his disapproval of the Soviet military intervention in Afghanistan soon after that decision was taken.

90 Volkogonov, *Lenin: Politicheskiy portret*, ii. 123. Volkogonov is quoting from the Politburo minutes, to which he had access.

91 *Istochnik*, 0/1993, p. 74.

92 Ibid.

93 Moreover, he had impressed British public opinion and the Prime Minister by his personality, intelligence, and style rather than by any deviation from official Soviet policy. As the Prime Minister wrote in her memoirs: 'If at this stage I had paid attention only to the content of Mr Gorbachev's remarks . . . I would have had to conclude that he was cast in the usual communist mould. But his personality could not have been more different from the wooden ventriloquism of the average Soviet *apparatchik*. He smiled, laughed . . . followed an argument through and was a sharp debater. . . . His line was no different from what I would have expected. His style was. . . . I found myself liking him' (Thatcher, *The Downing Street Years* (HarperCollins, London, 1993), 461).

94 According to Nancy Reagan, commenting on the 1988 Moscow summit between her husband and Mikhail Gorbachev, 'After four meetings [Reagan and Gorbachev] had developed a mutual respect and affection. . . . I also believe that each is profoundly grateful that the other was in power during those years, and they were able to work together to reduce the threat of nuclear war' (*My Turn: The Memoirs of Nancy Reagan* (Dell, New York, 1989), 370–1).

95 Thus, when Richard Pipes asks 'why the Politburo chose, in response to Reagan's anticommunism, a man committed to perestroika and disarmament', his question is based on a false premiss. The Politburo members, as I have argued in this chapter and in Chapter 3, were blissfully unaware that they were electing a radical reformer and disarmer. See the review essay by Pipes, 'Misinterpreting the Cold War: The Hard-liners Had It Right', *Foreign Affairs*, 74/1 (Jan.–Feb. 1995), 154–60, at p. 158. Where Reagan did make a distinctive contribution was in the way he combined an anti-Communism in principle with a relatively sympathetic and pragmatic approach in practice to Gorbachev's changes in foreign and domestic policy during his last three years in the White House. His response was, indeed, more pragmatic than some of his opponents expected and a number of his supporters wished, and it played its important part in the improved climate of international relations. In this Reagan was well served by his Secretary of State, George Shultz, and less well served by his Secretary for Defense, Caspar Weinberger, whose resignation in November 1987 removed the senior member of the administration slowest to recognize the extent of the difference Gorbachev was making to Soviet policy at home and abroad.

96 Among those who have got the significance of SDI for the change in the Soviet Union out of proportion is Margaret Thatcher, notably in the following passage from her memoirs: 'President Reagan's Strategic Defence Initiative, about which the Soviets and Mr Gorbachev were already so alarmed, was to prove central to the West's victory in the Cold War. . . . Looking back, it is now clear to me that Ronald Reagan's original decision on SDI was the single most important of his presidency' (*The Downing Street Years*, 463). This was not Margaret Thatcher's view at the time. She was relatively guarded in her public comments, but highly suspicious of SDI in private, as I recall clearly from the meeting in 10 Downing Street (on the eve of Gorbachev's arrival in Britain) in which I participated on 14 Dec. 1984. Immediately after her meeting with Gorbachev Mrs Thatcher flew to the United States to see President Reagan and, in particular, to convey her impressions of the man who might well be the next Soviet leader. Commenting on this visit in his memoirs, Reagan notes not only Margaret Thatcher reporting Gorbachev's expression of 'strong Soviet reservations over the SDI' but also that the British Prime Minister 'seemed to share some of his misgivings'. See Ronald Reagan, *An American Life: The Autobiography* (Simon & Schuster, New York, 1990), 609.

97 The most detailed and thorough account of the changing Soviet–US relationship is Raymond Garthoff, *The Great Transition: American–Soviet Relations and the End of the Cold War* (Brookings Institution, Washington, 1994).

98 Interview with Chernyaev, 30 Mar. 1992.

99 Chernyaev, *Shest' let s Gorbachevym*, 214.

100 See e.g. Thatcher, *The Downing Street Years*, 462–3, 465–6, 470–2, 482–3.

101 The quotations are from a memorandum George Shultz sent to President Reagan summarizing his thoughts on an informal evening the Reagans and Shultzes had just spent with the Gorbachevs and Shevardnadzes at a dacha near Moscow in the summer of 1988. For Shultz's full text, see Reagan, *An American Life*, 710–11.

102 M. S. Gorbachev, 'U perelomnoy cherty', in Gorbachev, *Gody trudnykh resheniy*, 46–55, at p. 54. The speech was delivered on 23 May 1986. The passage quoted from Gorbachev's above-mentioned book of 1993 did not appear in the summary of the speech which was published in *Vestnik MID*, 5 Aug. 1987, pp. 4–6.

103 Chernyaev, *Shest' let s Gorbachevym*, 105.

104 Ibid. 105–6.

105 Referring to the Reykjavik conference, the Secretary of State, George Shultz, wrote that the American expert advisers on the Soviet Union thought that even though Akhromeev had been brought to Iceland, he would not be in the working group which thrashed out the issues between the Gorbachev–Reagan sessions. In fact: 'He wound up as its chairman and did practically all the talking' (Shultz, *Turmoil and Triumph*, 763).

106 Chernyaev, *Shest' let s Gorbachevym*, 110.

107 Oberdorfer, *The Turn*, 194.

108 Beschloss and Talbott, *At the Highest Levels*, 438.

109 Sagdeev, *The Making of a Soviet Scientist*, 273.

110 Shultz, *Turmoil and Triumph*, 772. Shultz notes: 'I was criticized in the aftermath of Reykjavik for not "stopping" Ronald Reagan from offering to eliminate nuclear weapons. I responded that President Reagan had taken that position publicly and privately many times: before and after national elections. I knew that no one could stop him from taking this position in which he believed deeply and on which he had campaigned.'

111 Garthoff, *The Great Transition* (p. 289) has an interesting discussion of the extent to which Gorbachev was constrained by Politburo guide-lines to go no further than he did. There is disagreement even among those involved in the decision-making process on whether Gorbachev had any more leeway in negotiations. His interpreter, Pavel Palazhchenko, believes that he did not, observing that he was 'General Secretary, and not Emperor'.

112 Oberdorfer's *The Turn* (esp. 189–205) provides an excellent account of the Reykjavik summit, based mainly on high-level American sources but also on interviews with some Soviet participants (including Shevardnadze). Since that book was published more information on the initiation and preparation of the project from the Soviet side has become available—in particular, in the memoirs of Gorbachev's foreign policy aide, Chernyaev, who was a member of the official Soviet delegation at Reykjavik. See *Shest' let s Gorbachevym*, 105–20.

113 Oberdorfer, *The Turn*, 206.

114 Ibid.

115 Chernyaev, *Shest' let s Gorbachevym*, 114–15.

116 Ibid. 115.

117 Ibid.

118 Reagan, *An American Life*, 707. Among other positive observations on Gorbachev, Reagan notes: 'Whatever his reasons, Gorbachev had the intelligence to admit Communism was not working, the courage to battle for change, and, ultimately, the wisdom to introduce the beginnings of democracy, individual freedom, and free enterprise' (ibid. 508).

119 Reagan, *An American Life*, 707.

120 The Soviet military intervention to put an end to the Czech reforms, in contrast, made a greater impact in Western Europe than the Soviet venture into Afghanistan, partly because it took place in the heart of Europe and partly because for some months before the Soviet tanks moved into Prague in August 1968 the West European mass media had taken a close interest in developments in Czechoslovakia. For the United States the reverse was the case. The incursion into Afghanistan in 1979 produced a sharper reaction than the invasion of Czechoslovakia eleven years earlier. In 1968 the Vietnam War was still by far the most salient foreign policy issue for the United States, in addition to which the fact that the Czech reforms had been launched by the leadership of the Communist Party (strictly speaking, only a section of it) seemed to reduce American interest. In some respects the 'Prague Spring' was a forerunner on a smaller scale of the extension of civil and political liberties which was to occur during the earlier part of the perestroika period. Between January and August 1968 the Czech reformers, facing less formidable domestic obstacles than their Soviet counterparts, were able to cover roughly the same ground as that traversed by Gorbachev and his reformist allies between 1986 and early 1988.

121 Chernyaev, *Shest' let s Gorbachevym*, 41.

122 Ibid. 57–8.

123 Shultz, *Turmoil and Triumph*, 895.

124 Ibid. 910.

125 'Discussion of Struggles within the Politburo on Withdrawal from Afghanistan', Central Television interview with A. N. Yakovlev of 27 Dec. 1991, in BBC SWB, SU/1266, 31 Dec. 1991, p. A3/3. Politburo commissions included non-members as well as members of the Politburo. The commission on Afghanistan is discussed also by Georgy Kornienko, who, in his memoirs, offers a different account of the line-up on speedy withdrawal from Afghanistan from Yakovlev. See Kornienko, *Kholodnaya voyna*, 200–8.

126 Yakovlev, BBC SWB, SU/1266, 31 Dec. 1991, p. A3/3.

127 Kornienko, *Kholodnaya voyna*, 200–7; and Chernyaev, *Shest' let s Gorbachevym*, 271–2.

128 Yakovlev, BBC SWB, SU/1266, 31 Dec. 1991, p. A3/3.

129 Shultz, *Turmoil and Triumph*, 987.

130 Ibid.

131 See e.g. ibid. 751–80, esp. 774–6.

132 Ibid. 776.

133 Shevardnadze, *The Future Belongs to Freedom*, 89.

134 Shultz, *Turmoil and Triumph*, 1006.

135 Ibid. 1007–8.

136 Ibid. 1015.

137 Shultz, *Turmoil and Triumph*, 1005. The extent to which President Reagan's schedule was determined by Mrs Reagan's San Francisco astrologer, with whom she was in frequent telephone contact, was revealed by Reagan's White House Chief of Staff in his memoirs. See Donald T. Regan, *For the Record: From Wall Street to Washington* (Hutchinson, London, 1988), esp. 73–4, 367–8.

138 Fred Halliday, *The Making of the Second Cold War*, 2nd edn. (Verso, London, 1986).

139 I am grateful to Professor Yury Levada, the Centre Director, for supplying me in 1993 with these and other data from the records of the All-Russian Centre for the Study of Public Opinion on levels of support for Gorbachev over time.

140 *Obshchestvennoe mnenie v tsifrakh* (All-Union Centre for the Study of Public Opinion), 6 (13) (Feb. 1990), 14.

141 Oberdorfer, *The Turn*, 294.

142 Ibid.

143 Beschloss and Talbott, *At the Highest Levels*, 9.

144 Shultz, *Turmoil and Triumph*, 1103–4.

145 Cf. Beschloss and Talbott, *At the Highest Levels*, 9.

146 Shultz, *Turmoil and Triumph*, 1138. Shultz also noted. 'Brent Scowcroft had been named early on as NSC adviser, and I knew he would be influential. He had opposed the INF Treaty, had raised severe doubts about the prospective START Treaty, and was highly skeptical about the reality of change in the Soviet Union and Eastern Europe. . . . President Reagan and I were handing over real momentum. I hoped it would not be squandered.'

147 On this, see Chernyaev, *Shest' let s Gorbachevym*, 288, 290–1.

148 Beschloss and Talbott, *At the Highest Levels*, 469.

149 Barbara Bush, in her memoirs, describes Gorbachev as 'a strong, very able person and also quite charming' and continues: 'United Nations Secretary General Perez de Cuellar had said once: "He is either the world's greatest actor or is sincere". George and I agreed that he was sincere. He was smart, fast, and had a great sense of humour.' See *Barbara Bush: A Memoir* (Charles Scribner's Sons, New York, 1994), 344.

150 Beschloss and Talbott, *At the Highest Levels*, 121.

151 Ibid. 135.

152 When I quoted this immediately before a British television discussion programme in early 1990 in which Andrey Grachev—at that time a deputy head of the International Department of the Central Committee—and I were participants, Grachev asked, reasonably enough, what the 'Sinatra doctrine' meant. Agreeing with the substance of this 'new concept' when it was explained, he added: 'Gerasimov knows American culture so well he sometimes mystifies *us*.'

153 Beschloss and Talbott, *At the Highest Levels*, 165.

154 Chernyaev, *Shest' let s Gorbachevym*, 302–3.

155 Ibid. 302.

156 Beschloss and Talbott, *At the Highest Levels*, 166.

157 Ibid. 223–4.

158 Ibid. 222–3. Beschloss and Talbott (pp. 215–28) provide a very useful account of the summit as a whole.

159 Beschloss and Talbott, *At the Highest Levels*, 412–13. See also Barbara Bush, *Barbara Bush: A Memoir*, 427–8.

160 See L. A. Sedov, 'Peremeny v strane i v otnoshenii k peremenam', *Ekonomicheskie i sotsial'nye peremeny: monitoring obshchestvennogo mneniya*, 1 (Jan.–Feb. 1995) (VTsIOM, Moscow), 23–6.

161 Beschloss and Talbott, *At the Highest Levels*, 448–9. Gorbachev saw this statement as an attempt to

'stimulate separatism in Ukraine', and James Baker conceded in private that Gorbachev's complaint had some merit and that it had been a mistake for the United States to 'jump the gun' (ibid. 449).

162 Quoted by Beschloss and Talbott, ibid. 418, who add that Bush had Zviad Gamsakhurdia, the intolerant nationalist who had recently been elected president of Georgia, particularly in mind when he made these remarks, which were, however, also intended as a warning to Ukrainians not to get carried away by nationalist excess.

163 This speech is not included in Gorbachev's collected writings and speeches, even though the relevant volume (iii) was published only in 1987. As noted above, a summary of it was, however, published (well over a year after it was delivered) in the journal of the Ministry of Foreign Affairs. See *Vestnik MID*, 5 Aug. 1987, pp. 4–6. The speech itself—even then, with excisions—was first published in Gorbachev, *Gody trudnykh resheniy*, 46–55.

164 *Vestnik MID*, No. 1, 5 Aug. 1987, p. 6; *Gody trudnykh resheniy*, 48.

165 *Vestnik MID*, No. 1, 5 Aug. 1987, p. 6; *Gody trudnykh resheniy*, 54.

166 *Vestnik MID*, No. 1, 5 Aug. 1987, p. 5. The passages of Gorbachev's speech on Eastern Europe are among those most radically pruned from the text of this speech published in the collection of his speeches and transcripts of his meetings with foreign leaders, *Gody trudnykh resheniy*, compiled by Alexander Galkin and Anatoly Chernyaev.

167 Macmillan had excellent relations with both Eisenhower and Kennedy and by no means bad relations with the volatile Khrushchev, but the opportunities for influencing Soviet policy at that time were much more limited. Where Macmillan was of most consequence in East–West relations was as a source of sound advice to Kennedy at the time of the Cuban Missile Crisis in 1962 and as a vigorous advocate of the Nuclear Test Ban Treaty of 1963. On these processes, see Alistair Horne, *Macmillan, 1957–1986*, vol. ii of the Official Biography (Macmillan, London, 1989), 362–85, 503–12, 518–26.

168 Harold Wilson's official biographer, Philip Ziegler, observes that Wilson in 1975 'still saw himself as the only man who could communicate on equal terms and to equally good effect with Russia and the United States' (Philip Ziegler, *Wilson: The Authorised Life of Lord Wilson of Rievaulx* (Weidenfeld & Nicolson, London, 1993), 461). Prior to Gorbachev's coming to power it was, however, almost impossible for any Western leader to acquire the trust of a Soviet General Secretary (Wilson's meetings were, in any event, usually with Kosygin rather than with the more powerful Brezhnev) and Wilson, unlike Thatcher, had the disadvantage that he was not wholly trusted in Washington. For Wilson's unsuccessful attempt to mediate between Washington and Moscow on the Vietnam War, see Ben Pimlott, *Harold Wilson* (HarperCollins, London, 1992), 382–94.

169 While the more ideological conservatism of Margaret Thatcher and Ronald Reagan as compared with their successors, George Bush and John Major, has often been commented on—and is reasonable enough as a generalization—relations with the Soviet Union under Gorbachev became one area where both Thatcher and Reagan displayed an increasing pragmatism. In Margaret Thatcher's case, close attention to changing Russian realities made her much more supportive of Gorbachev than the unreconstructed cold warriors among her supporters in Britain and the United States could easily accept. The same is broadly true of Reagan—if allowance is made for his hazier and more impressionistic knowledge of change in the Soviet Union—and of the reaction of some of his camp-followers. Nevertheless, criticism on the far right was somewhat muted since even the more paranoiac members of that fraternity found it difficult to accuse Thatcher and Reagan of being 'soft on Communism'.

170 Some of the evidence for the first part of this statement is to be found in Chernyaev's account (verbatim at times) of the Gorbachev–Thatcher 1987 Moscow meetings in *Shest' let s Gorbachevym*, 131–40. For Reagan on Thatcher, see Reagan, *An American Life*, esp. 204, 350–2, 609, 635.

171 Gorbatschow, *Erinnerungen*, 748.

172 Chernyaev, *Shest' let s Gorbachevym*, 140.

173 Ibid.

174 Ibid. 140–1.

175 Ibid. 140.

176 Ibid. 141.

177 Garton Ash, *In Europe's Name*, 108. Garton Ash continues: 'Weizsacker recalls at this point interjecting "or perhaps fifty?", and receiving an indication of assent from Gorbachev, thus, as Weizsacker wryly observes, negotiating a fifty per cent cut. But the significant point is that Gorbachev did not say "never".'

178 Gorbachev, *Perestroika*, 200.

179 Chernyaev, *Shest' let s Gorbachevym*, 154.

180 On this, see also Garton Ash, *In Europe's Name*, 109, 494. Garton Ash is citing Yakovlev's response to a question at a lunch at St Antony's College on 29 Jan. 1992, at which I was also present and a witness to Yakovlev's surprising statement.

181 Andrey Grachev (conversation with the author) is among those who hold that Gorbachev envisaged future events unfolding in that way.

182 Vyacheslav Dashichev, 'On the Road to German Reunification: The View from Moscow', in Gabriel Gorodetsky (ed.), *Soviet Foreign Policy, 1917–1991: A Retrospective* (Cass, London, 1994), 170–9, at p. 172.

183 It is extremely doubtful whether Falin and Ligachev should be placed in the same category. Falin objected to the speed, method, and price of reunification of Germany, Ligachev to the very idea.

184 Ibid. 173, 174.

185 Chernyaev, 'Gorbachev and the Reunification of Germany: Personal Recollections', in Gorodetsky (ed.), *Soviet Foreign Policy, 1917–1991*, 158–69, at p. 161.

186 Ibid. 162. See also Chernyaev, *Shest' let s Gorbachevym*, 261–2.

187 Dashichev, 'On the Road to German Reunification', 176.

188 On this see Kornienko, *Nezavisimaya gazeta*, 16 Aug. 1994, p. 5; and Adomeit, 'Gorbachev, German Unification and the Collapse of Empire', *Post-Soviet Affairs*, 10/3 (July–Sept. 1994). Andrey Grachev, in my interview with him of 14 Jan. 1993, drew attention to the view of the leadership of the International Department (and Falin, most notably) that Gorbachev and Shevardnadze, in their desire for breakthroughs, would seek 'accord at any price', whether in the German reunification negotiations or in the disarmament process.

189 Yugoslavia, of course, had long been outside the Soviet bloc and Romania under Nicolae Ceauşescu was a maverick member of it, at one and the same time more oppressive than the others and less open to influence from Moscow.

190 A detailed analysis of the process of German reunification, or even of Gorbachev's role in it, cannot, of course, be provided in what is only a part of a single chapter. Although new material (including some used in this chapter) has become available since they wrote, fuller accounts are to be found in Adomeit, 'Gorbachev, German Unification and the Collapse of Empire'; and in Garton Ash, *In Europe's Name*. For the American role in the diplomacy of German reunification (important, although not as important as the direct Gorbachev–Kohl discussions), see Beschloss and Talbott, *At the Highest Level*.

191 See Adomeit, 'Gorbachev, German Unification and the Collapse of Empire', and Garton Ash, *In Europe's Name*.

192 Beschloss and Talbott, *At the Highest Level*, 230.

193 Ibid. 231.

194 Adomeit, 'Gorbachev, German Unification and the Collapse of Empire', 220.

195 *Materialy plenuma Tsentral'nogo Komiteta KPSS 11, 14, 16 Marta 1990 g.*, pp. 91–2.

196 Adomeit, 'Gorbachev, German Unification and the Collapse of Empire', 220. Earlier Shevardnadze had told American Secretary of State Baker at a meeting in Copenhagen on 5 June 1990 that the Soviet Union could agree to German unification (within NATO if the Germans so chose) taking place by the end of that year. See Beschloss and Talbott, *At the Highest Levels*, 230.

197 Garton Ash, *In Europe's Name*, 354–5.

198 Adomeit, 'Gorbachev, German Unification and the Collapse of Empire', 224–5.

199 Ibid. 224.

200 For vivid accounts of how the changes looked at the time from Eastern and East-Central Europe, see especially Timothy Garton Ash, *The Magic Lantern: The Revolution of '89 Witnessed in Warsaw, Budapest, Berlin and Prague* (Random House, New York, 1990), and Mark Frankland, *The Patriots' Revolution: How East Europe won its freedom* (Sinclair-Stevenson, London, 1990). For fuller accounts of the changing Soviet relationship with Eastern Europe under Gorbachev, see Alex Pravda (ed.), *The End of the Outer Empire: Soviet–East European Relations in Transition, 1985–90* (Sage, London, 1992), especially Pravda's perceptive chapter, 'Soviet Policy towards Eastern Europe in Transition: The Means Justify the Ends', 1–34; and Neil Malcolm (ed.), *Russia and Europe: An End to Confrontation* (Pinter, for the Royal Institute of International Relations, London, 1994), esp. chs. 1, 6, and 7. See also Ralf Dahrendorf, *Reflections on the Revolution in Europe* (Chatto & Windus, London, 1990).

201 See Zbigniew Brzezinski, *The Grand Failure: The Birth and Death of Communism in the Twentieth Century* (Collier Books, New York, 1990).

202 Some of those who were most involved in the numerically not very large Czech opposition movement were the first to recognize that Gorbachev and the changes in the Soviet Union had been

crucial—a necessary and almost sufficient condition for the ending of the Communist regime in Czechoslovakia. Among those who (in conversation with the present author) had no illusions about the relative weight of indigenous 'revolution', on the one hand, and the Gorbachev factor, on the other, were the late Rita Klímová, the first post-Communist Czechoslovak Ambassador to the United States, and Petr Pithart, the first post-Communist Prime Minister of the Czech Republic, both of whom had been active in the Charter 77 movement and in the 'velvet revolution' (Václav Havel's phrase which entered the English language through Klímová, who was interpreting for him during the days when Communism fell in Czechoslovakia).

203 Brzezinski, *The Grand Failure*, 42. Brzezinski is generally perceptive about Gorbachev and recognizes his 'progressive conversion to revisionism' by 1988 on 'issues fundamental to the established Soviet doctrine' (p. 63). He rightly notes also the changes which had taken place within the Soviet élite and Soviet society by the time Gorbachev came to power. He does not, however, examine the actual composition of the Soviet Politburo at the time Gorbachev became General Secretary and thus glides over the inconvenient fact that it did not contain even one other reformer, still less an alternative, seriously reformist candidate for the General Secretaryship. The behaviour of these colleagues (whom Gorbachev replaced as quickly as political prudence allowed) *after* March 1985, as well as before, suggests that if Gorbachev's elevation was not quite a 'freak event' (as Brzezinski insists it was not), radical reform—in the absence of Gorbachev—might well have been postponed for another decade or longer.

204 Chernyaev, *Shest' let s Gorbachevym*, 49–51.

205 Alex Pravda, 'Soviet Policy towards Eastern Europe in Transition: The Means Justify the Ends', 21.

206 The transcript of the meeting between Gorbachev and Zhivkov is published verbatim in *Sovershenno Sekretno*, 4 (1992), 19.

207 Ibid.

208 See e.g. articles by General Albert Makashov, 'Doktrina predatel'stva', Colonel Viktor Alksnis, 'Udary v spinu armii', and General Mikhail Titov, 'Ostalis' bez oruzhiya', in *Den'*, 7–13 June 1992, p. 2. Titov particularly berates Gorbachev for his one-sided concessions on disarmament and concludes that 'for such criminal acts' he must 'answer before the people'.

209 Zdeněk Mlynář, *Night Frost in Prague: The End of Humane Socialism* (Hurst, London, 1980), 163; and G. A. Arbatov, *Zatyanuvsheesya vyzdorovlenie (1953–1985 gg.): Svidetel'stvo sovremennika* (Mezhdunarodnye otnosheniya, Moscow, 1991), 147.

210 See Gorbatschow, *Erinnerungen*, 863–78; Shakhnazarov, *Tsena svobody*, 101; and Medvedev, *Raspad*, 89.

211 See Pravda, 'Soviet Policy towards Eastern Europe in Transition: the Means Justify the Ends', 19. Pravda notes that the change was engineered within the Hungarian party itself but had the approval of Moscow. He adds: 'From Gorbachev's standpoint Grósz seemed to have the potential to continue reform and, more important, the power base to do so in a controlled fashion.'

212 This point is made by Pravda, ibid.

213 Cited by Hannes Adomeit, drawing upon the East German party archives, in Adomeit, 'Gorbachev, German Unification and the Collapse of Empire', 210.

214 Adomeit (ibid. 212–13) suggests that this was *not* an attempt by Gorbachev to influence the SED leadership, citing German archival material in which Gorbachev said later that he had really been talking about himself when he made that remark. While Gorbachev may, indeed, have been engaging in somewhat surreptitious self-criticism, he was a shrewd enough politician to know how his remark would be interpreted and there is no reason to doubt that it was a tactful criticism of Honecker.

215 Robert Legvold, 'Observations on International Order: A Comment on MacFarlane and Adomeit', *Post-Soviet Affairs*, 10/3 (1994), 270–6, at p. 274.

216 Chernyaev, speaking at the seminar on foreign policy-making under Gorbachev at St Antony's College, 15 Oct. 1994. See also Gorbatschow, *Erinnerungen*, 842–3; and Vadim Medvedev, *Raspad*, 15–16.

217 Pravda, 'Soviet Policy towards Eastern Europe in Transition: The Means Justify the Ends', 17–18. See also Alex Pravda, 'Relations with Central and South-Eastern Europe', in Malcolm (ed.), *Russia and Europe*, 123–50, at p. 134.

218 As the title of the first of Alex Pravda's two chapters quoted above, 'Soviet Policy towards Eastern Europe in Transition: The Means Justify the Ends', has it.

219 Ibid. 31.

220 Medvedev, *Raspad*, 393–4.

221 Ibid. 395.

Chapter 8   The National Question, the Coup, and
             the Collapse of the Soviet Union

1 Robert Conquest, Foreword to Ian Bremner and Ray Taras (eds.), *Nations and Politics in the Soviet Successor States* (Cambridge University Press, Cambridge, 1993), p. xvii. Cf. Georgy Shakhnazarov, *Tsena svobody: Reformatsiya Gorbacheva glazami ego pomoshchnika* (Rossika Zevs, Moscow, 1993), 348.

2 Mark Galeotti, *The Age of Anxiety: Security and Politics in Soviet and Post-Soviet Russia* (Longman, London, 1995), 192–3.

3 This was the implicit position of many Western commentators on the Soviet scene and close to the viewpoint also of some of the boldest of radical libertarians in Russia during the last years of the Soviet Union, among them Yelena Bonner, Gavriil Popov, and Galina Staravoytova. (Cf. Shakhnazarov, *Tsena svobody*, 193.)

4 As the authors of an article in *Moscow News* (one of them, Illarionov, a former economic adviser to the Russian Prime Minister, Viktor Chernomyrdin, and current Director of the Institute of Economic Analysis in Moscow) observed with reference to one republic, Chechnya: 'Formally "pacified" Chechnya remained within Russia for 132 years, exactly as long as Poland, which also refused to tolerate the loss of independence. This is much shorter than the amount of time that many other states on the territory of the former USSR spent in the Russian embrace. Their independence has already been internationally recognized' (Andrei Illarionov and Boris Lvin, 'Should Russia Recognize Chechnya's Independence?', *Moscow News*, 8 (24 Feb.–2 Mar. 1995), 4).

5 Even Robert Conquest, who in several important books has dealt with the plight of some of the smaller nationalities during the Soviet period, appears surprisingly to overlook this point when he writes that 'the breakup of the USSR (and Yugoslavia) would add no more than a score or so to the present large roster of independent states' (Preface to Bremner and Taras, *Nations and Politics in the Soviet Successor States*, p. xvii).

6 Accordingly, the Central Asian republics remained pro-union in the late Soviet period at a time when, one by one, the other republics began to embrace the cause of independence. In that respect, at least, the well-known book by Hélène Carrère d'Encausse, *L'Empire éclaté: La Révolte des nations en U.R.S.S.* (Flammarion, Paris, 1978), was less percipient than its title, for the central thesis was that the faster growth of population of Soviet Central Asia, as compared with European Russia, together with the rise of Islam, represented the major threat to the survival of the Soviet state.

7 Illarionov and Lvin compared 'the present "winter war" [. . that launched by the Soviet Union in December 1939 against Finland, and the bombing of residential areas of Helsinki with the similar attacks on residential quarters of Grozny. They went on: 'The extermination of thousands of utterly innocent citizens on the territory of Chechnya is unambiguously characterized as genocide by international and national law' ('Should Russia Recognize Chechnya's Independence?', 4). Among the many to condemn the war on Chechnya in the pages of the Russian press was Mikhail Gorbachev, who asked: 'What kind of terrorists are they, who must be fought using all arms of the service, including tanks, the air force, artillery and, what is more, on the territory of a peaceful city?' He went on to argue that 'the tragic consequences of this bloody venture' would include 'the loss of Russia's prestige as a state' and that part of the problem was the Russian constitution adopted in December 1993 which left 'the president and the government out of control', possessing such power that they felt no need to concern themselves with public opinion. See Mikhail Gorbachev, 'Crisis Exposes Social Ills', *Moscow News*, 1 (6–12 Jan. 1995), 3.

8 Dunkwart A. Rustow, 'Transitions to Democracy: Toward a Dynamic Model', *Comparative Politics*, 2/3 (Apr. 1970), 337–63, at pp. 350–1.

9 Rustow (ibid. 351) argues that 'the background condition' of national unity is best fulfilled when 'accepted unthinkingly' or silently taken for granted, and adds that 'most of the rhetoric of nationalism has poured from the lips of people who felt least secure in their sense of national identity'— Germans and Italians in the nineteenth century 'and Arabs and Africans in the present, never Englishmen, Swedes, or Japanese'. The use of 'Englishmen' is, of course, question-begging, for the boundaries of the *British* polity have not been undisputed, especially (it is fair to add) in the twenty-five years since Rustow wrote. In addition to the divisions over Northern Ireland, accompanied by terrorism for the greater part of the past quarter-century, there has been a peaceful nationalist movement in Scotland, with a significant minority of Scots rejecting British statehood and favouring complete independence.

10 As Juan Linz and Alfred Stepan note: 'not one army officer was killed during the Basque insurgency in the 1968–75 Franco period, or in the 1975–77 transition period. But in the postelectoral period of democratic rule between 1978 and 1983, thirty-seven army officers died.' See Linz and Stepan,

'Political Crafting of Democratic Consolidation or Destruction: European and South American Comparisons', in Robert A. Pastor (ed.), *Democracy in the Americas* (Holmes & Meier, New York, 1989), 41–61, at p. 49.

11 Ibid.

12 Robert A. Dahl and Edward R. Tufte, *Size and Democracy* (Stanford University Press, Stanford, Calif., 1973), 138. What is more: 'No single type or size of unit is optimal for achieving the twin goals of citizen effectiveness and system capacity.'

13 Robert A. Dahl, *Democracy and its Critics* (Yale University Press, New Haven, 1989), 209. Thus, 'despite the perfectionism of democratic ideas, the best attainable unit will be for some citizens the second best'.

14 See J. Roland Pennock and John W. Chapman (eds.), *Liberal Democracy* (New York University Press, New York, 1983), esp. Frederick G. Whelan, 'Prologue: Democratic Theory and the Boundary Problem', 13–47; Robert A. Dahl, 'Federalism and the Democratic Process', 95–108; and David Braybrooke, 'Can Democracy be Combined with Federalism or with Liberalism?', 109–18.

15 Dahl, *Democracy and its Critics*, 209.

16 Whelan, 'Democratic Theory and the Boundary Problem', 41.

17 W. Ivor Jennings, *The Approach to Self-Government* (Cambridge University Press, Cambridge, 1956), 56 (cited by Rustow, 'Transitions to Democracy', 351).

18 Whelan, 'Democratic Theory and the Boundary Problem', 40.

19 Zbigniew Brzezinski, *The Grand Failure: The Birth and Death of Communism in the Twentieth Century* (Collier Books paperback edn., New York, 1990), Epilogue, p. 278.

20 Ibid. 274.

21 Within, that is to say, the USSR as a whole; they constituted actual majorities in certain republics.

22 'Every specific, concrete and feasible alternative solution to the problem of the best unit will, almost certainly, on balance benefit the interests of some citizens more than others' (Dahl, *Democracy and its Critics*, 209).

23 See *Pravda*, 27 Mar. 1991, pp. 1–2. In the Soviet Central Asian states the proportion supporting a 'renewed federation' was in every case more than 90 per cent. In Kazakhstan, however, the question was altered by the republic's Supreme Soviet in a way which could have influenced the outcome. There the wording was: 'Do you believe it essential to preserve the USSR as a Union of equal sovereign states?' The Kazakh authorities, nevertheless, requested that the answers to *their* question be included in the overall figures of the USSR referendum, and the President of Kazakhstan, Nursultan Nazarbaev, was, in fact, one of the most eloquent opponents of the complete breakup of the Soviet Union.

24 *Pravda*, 27 Mar. 1991, pp. 1–2.

25 Ian Bremner and Ray Taras note that, whereas in his earliest years in power Gorbachev spoke of the relations between nationalities as if it were a unified issue, 'by 1991, Gorbachev's statements consistently highlighted the differences among the Soviet nationalities, with particular emphasis placed upon the uniqueness of the Baltic situation' (Preface to *Nations and Politics in the Soviet Successor States*, p. xxi).

26 Shevardnadze interview (17 Sept. 1991), *The Second Russian Revolution* transcripts.

27 See A. V. Veber, V. T. Loginov, G. S. Ostroumov, and A. S. Chernyaev (eds.), *Soyuz mozhno bylo sokhranit': belaya kniga doumenty i fakty o politike M. S. Gorbacheva po reformirovaniyu i sokhraneniyu mnogonatsional'nogo gosudarstva* (Gorbachev Foundation, Moscow, 1995).

28 Ronald Grigor Suny, *The Revenge of the Past: Nationalism, Revolution and the Collapse of the Soviet Union* (Stanford University Press, Stanford, Calif., 1993), 130.

29 Questions could scarcely be asked earlier than 1988 on such sensitive political issues and, even had they been, the results of such survey research would have been of little value. Prior to the Gorbachev era respondents would have had little incentive to answer frankly unless their views happened to coincide with what the party-state authorities wanted to hear.

30 While one of the many strands in Russian nationalism was an anti-Soviet one, and while Yeltsin in 1990–1 was able to win support for the idea that Russia was being exploited by the 'centre', this was not a widespread view during the greater part of the Soviet period or, indeed, in the years since the collapse of the USSR. By September 1994 70 per cent of the population of Russia, according to a survey of the All-Russian Centre for the Study of Public Opinion, regretted the breakup of the Soviet Union (although only a minority thought it could be reconstructed). According to the principal researcher, L. A. Sedov, it is the massively negative attitude to the demise of the Soviet Union which is the most important single factor in explaining the growth of disenchantment with the other changes of the past ten years. By September 1994 the percentage of the population which

preferred the time before 1985 to the present had risen to the highest level (58 per cent) since the Centre began (in 1991) asking the question. See L. A. Sedov, 'Peremeny v strane i v otnoshenii k peremenam', *Ekonomischeskie i sotsial'nye peremeny: monitoring obshchestvennogo mneniya* (VTsIOM, Moscow), 1 (Jan.–Feb. 1995), 23–6, esp. 23.

31 Shakhnazarov, *Tsena svobody*, 208.

32 In a by-election for the Russian State Duma, held in Kolomna in the Moscow region in May 1995, the convincing victor was the second man in space, former Soviet cosmonaut German Titov. Standing as the candidate of the Communist Party of the Russian Federation, he easily defeated his seven opponents. Titov, who twice received the Order of Lenin and was a Hero of the Soviet Union, joined the CPSU in 1961 and never surrendered his party card. See *Moscow News*, 19 (19–25 May 1995), 1, 3.

33 It is worth noting also that the blood shed in almost seven years under Gorbachev was far less than that shed on the territory of the former Soviet Union in the period just half that long which has elapsed since the USSR ceased to exist.

34 Vorotnikov interview, *The Second Russian Revolution* transcripts.

35 Kolbin interview, *The Second Russian Revolution* transcripts.

36 Angus Roxburgh, *The Second Russian Revolution* (BBC Books, London, 1991), 54, 208.

37 Kolbin interview, *The Second Russian Revolution* transcripts.

38 Ibid.; and Gorbachev interview, *Moskovskiy komsomolets*, 28 June 1995, p. 2. Kolbin gives a slightly contradictory account of the water-cannon in his interview. After referring to Gorbachev's criticism of him for the use even of this level of force, he said: 'But in fact there was no water in them. They did not—they couldn't work. But he said I shouldn't have done it.' A little later he maintained: 'No force was used. With the exception of the water-cannons, and I was heavily reprimanded for that.'

39 Gorbatschow, *Erinnerungen* (Siedler Verlag, Berlin, 1995), 480.

40 This has been overlooked by the great majority of those who have written about the episode. An exception is Roxburgh, *The Second Russian Revolution*, 54. See also the interviews with Kolbin, Razumovsky, and Vorotnikov in *The Second Russian Revolution* transcripts. Kunaev refused Kolbin's request that he go out to attempt to calm the crowd of demonstrators, who went on to burn cars and damage buildings. During the disturbances it became clear that Kunaev's relations with some of his former colleagues were tense. Kolbin observes: 'Probably that was precisely why he had asked for a Russian to be nominated. For somebody coming from outside Kazakhstan. He did not want people with whom he had been in conflict—in a political conflict.' Vorotnikov, as a Politburo member, recalls Kunaev's view that nobody in Kazakhstan could fill his position: 'He even said that in that situation a good Russian person should be sent to Kazakhstan, rather than a Kazakh.'

41 Gorbatschow, *Erinnerungen*, 480.

42 See Roxburgh, *The Second Russian Revolution*, 54. Kunaev, having refused to try to calm the demonstrators, told Nazarbaev: 'This is your doing—you solve it.' And to Razumovsky, the Secretary of the Central Committee responsible for party cadres who had come from Moscow to supervise the election of Kolbin, he said: 'You've just fired me. I have no more responsibilities.'

43 Gorbatschow, *Erinnerungen*, 481.

44 Mary Dejevsky, 'Glasnost and the Tatars', *The Times*, 27 July 1987, p. 10. A month later, following demonstrations in Baltic cities as well, Dejevsky wrote: 'It is not just the authorities which have to educate themselves as to the need to tolerate other opinions and listen to argument if Soviet society is to become more democratic, it is the Russian public as well . . . During the Tatar protests, the police had to ensure not only that they kept the demonstration under control but that they restrained the crowd of onlookers as well' (Mary Dejevsky, 'When Dogma Comes Up Against Demo', *The Times*, 25 Aug. 1987, p. 8).

45 Edward J. Lazzerini, 'Crimean Tatars', in Graham Smith (ed.), *The Nationalities Question in the Soviet Union* (Longman, London, 1990), 322–38.

46 Ibid. 335–6.

47 Volsky interview, *The Second Russian Revolution* transcripts.

48 Ibid.

49 In the post-Soviet era, by which time forces from nearby Armenia had brought Nagorno-Karabakh under Armenian control, the unenviable task of resolving the dispute was passed to the Organization for Security and Cooperation in Europe (OSCE). When a delegation from OSCE visited Baku on 27 April 1995, they were berated by the President of Azerbaijan, Heydar Aliev, who accused them of failing to condemn Armenia and said that the organization had achieved nothing to prevent 'aggression and losses' since it began its attempts to settle the Karabakh conflict in 1992. See 'Armenian-Azerbaijani Conflict', BBC SWB, 29 Apr. 1995, SU/2290 F/1.

50 Nora Dudwick, 'Armenia: The Nation Awakes', in Bremner and Taras (eds.), *Nations and Politics in the Soviet Successor States*, 261–87, esp. 277. See also Suny, *The Revenge of the Past*, 132–8; and Roxburgh, *The Second Russian Revolution*, 81–3.

51 Shireen T. Hunter, 'Azerbaijan: Search for Industry and New Partners', in Bremner and Taras (eds.), *Nations and Politics in the Soviet Successor States*, 225–60, at p. 248.

52 That law, while instituting a mechanism for secession from the union, was even more concerned with slowing the process down and discouraging republics from opting for secession. Thus, one of its provisions was that autonomous republics or regions within republics (such as e.g. Nagorno-Karabakh within Azerbaijan and Abkhazia in Georgia) would have the right to choose to remain in the USSR even if the rest of the republic opted for separate statehood. See Ann Sheehy, 'Supreme Soviet Adopts Law on Mechanics of Secession', *Radio Liberty Report on the USSR*, 2/17 (27 Apr. 1990), 2–5.

53 Yegor Ligachev, *Inside Gorbachev's Kremlin* (Pantheon, New York, 1993), 172.

54 Gorbatschow, *Erinnerungen*, 484; Ligachev, *Inside Gorbachev's Kremlin*, 172.

55 Ibid. 173.

56 Volsky interview, *The Second Russian Revolution* transcripts.

57 Tamara Dragadze, 'Azerbaijanis', in Smith (ed.), *The Nationalities Question in the Soviet Union*, 163–79, at p. 177.

58 Volsky interview, *The Second Russian Revolution* transcripts.

59 Ibid.

60 Roxburgh, *The Second Russian Revolution*, 167. See also Suny, *The Revenge of the Past*, 137.

61 Roxburgh, *The Second Russian Revolution*, 167–8. Cf. A. S. Chernyaev, *Shest' let s Gorbachevym: po dnevnikovym zapisyam* (Kultura, Moscow, 1993), 326.

62 Gorbatschow, *Erinnerungen*, 500–1.

63 Gorbachev said this in reply to one of the questions put to him at a meeting held by the club of Moscow intellectuals 'Free Word' ('Svobodnoe slovo') on 20 Jan. 1995. See *Perestroyka—desyat' let spustya: vstrecha s M. S. Gorbachevym* (Stenographic Report, Svobodnoe slovo, Moscow, 1995), 62.

64 The number of deaths is that given by the Sobchak commission of investigation. See *Istoricheskiy arkhiv*, 3 (1993), 115.

65 Ibid. 116.

66 See Roxburgh, *The Second Russian Revolution*, 132.

67 See Stephen Jones, 'Georgia: A Failed Democratic Transition', in Bremner and Taras (eds.), *Nations and Politics in the Soviet Successor States*, 288–310, esp. 305.

68 Roxburgh, *The Second Russian Revolution*, 132.

69 See Sobchak interview, *The Second Russian Revolution* transcripts; Eduard Shevardnadze, *The Future Belongs to Freedom* (Sinclair-Stevenson, London, 1991), 192–7; and Anatoly Sobchak, *Khozhdenie vo vlast': Rasskaz o rozhdenii parlamenta* (Novosti, Moscow, 1991), 79–104.

70 See *Istoricheskiy arkhiv*, 3 (1993), 102–22. The same issue of this journal publishes telegrams from the Georgian Communist Party First Secretary at the time, D. I. Patiashvili, to the Secretariat of the Central Committee of the CPSU (pp. 95–102).

71 Ligachev was conscious of the fact that his wings had been clipped and that, with difficulty, he had to try to prevent the appearance that he was still involving himself in every area of policy. As he puts it: 'after the spring of 1989 I tried not to stick my nose into matters that did not concern agriculture unless I really had to, although that wasn't always possible . . . But I think it's clear why Chebrikov and I had agreed that he should present the information at the airport' (Ligachev, *Inside Gorbachev's Kremlin*, 161–2).

72 Shevardnadze, *The Future Belongs to Freedom*, 193.

73 Attestation of Gorbachev's insistence that Shevardnadze and Razumovsky should go to Tbilisi has been provided by a number of the participants in the airport discussion late at night on 7 April. See Nikolay Ryzhkov, *Perestroyka: Istoriya predatel'stv* (Novosti, Moscow, 1992) 215; Ligachev, *Inside Gorbachev's Kremlin*, 162, 191–5; and Shevardnadze, *The Future Belongs to Freedom*, 193 (although Shevardnadze obscures the fact that Gorbachev had asked him to fly to Tbilisi on 8 April—the very next day). The Minister of Defence, Dmitry Yazov, speaking about the meeting at Moscow airport in his evidence to the Sobchak commission, said: 'A decision was taken to send Comrades Razumovsky and Shevardnadze there [Tbilisi] in order to resolve all problems on the spot' (Sobchak, *Khozhdenie vo vlast'*, 98).

74 Ibid. 97.

75 *Istoricheskiy arkhiv*, 3 (1993), 95–6.

76 Roxburgh, *The Second Russian Revolution*, 132.

77 Ibid. 117.

78 Ibid. 116.

79 See John Miller, *Mikhail Gorbachev and the End of Soviet Power* (Macmillan, London, 1993), 156–7; and Richard Sakwa, *Gorbachev and his Reforms, 1985–1990* (Philip Allan, London, 1990), 262–3.

80 Ann Sheehy, 'Supreme Soviet Adopts Law on Mechanics of Secession', 2–5, at p. 3. See also Jonathan Steele, *Eternal Russia: Yeltsin, Gorbachev and the Mirage of Democracy* (Faber & Faber, London, 1994), 206–9.

81 Sheehy, 'Supreme Soviet Adopts Law on Mechanics of Secession', 3–4.

82 Ibid., at pp. 4–5.

83 Ibid. 5.

84 Chernyaev, *Shest' let s Gorbachevym*, 410. See also Shakhnazarov, *Tsena svobody*, 196, 348.

85 Interview with Alexander Nikolaevich Yakovlev in *Argumenty i fakty*, 11 Mar. 1995, p. 3.

86 The series of proposals designed to discourage or slow down the Lithuanian drive for independence was drawn up by Andrey Girenko (a Secretary of the Central Committee since September 1989 and a Ukrainian by nationality), Yury Maslyukov (the Chairman of Gosplan and a Politburo member), Vadim Medvedev (the Politburo member and Secretary of the Central Committee who was at that time overseeing ideology), and Georgy Razumovsky (the Central Committee Secretary, and candidate member of the Politburo, in charge of party cadres). See *Istoricheskiy arkhiv*, 1 (1992), 3–5.

87 Ibid.

88 Alexander Utkin, 'Pyat' rokovykh shagov Gorbacheva', *Rossiyskaya federatsiya*, 7 (1995), 4–8, at p. 8. Utkin states that the Estonian declaration of sovereignty was in October 1988; in fact, it came in November of that year.

89 Reported by John Lloyd in an article entitled 'Gorbachev Shivers in his Own Shadow', *Financial Times*, 24 Apr. 1995, p. 17.

90 Ibid.

91 Gorbachev interview, *The Second Russian Revolution* transcripts.

92 Ibid.

93 Cf. Gorbachev interview, *The Second Russian Revolution* transcripts; and Gorbatschow, *Erinnerungen*, 561–70.

94 For two useful collections of documents, one of which is devoted entirely to the Gorbachev–Yeltsin relationship and the other of which devotes substantial space to it, see M. K. Gorshkov, V. V. Zhuravlev, and L. N. Dobrokhotov (eds.), *Gorbachev–Yel'tsin: 1500 dney politicheskogo protivostoyaniya* (Terra, Moscow, 1992); and B. I. Koval (ed.), *Rossiya segodnya: politicheskiy portret v dokumentakh, 1985–1991* (Mezhdunarodnye otnosheniya, Moscow, 1991), 393–511 (for the period Dec. 1990–Apr. 1991, pp. 487–509).

95 I am grateful to Professor Yury Levada, Director of VTsIOM, for supplying me with the results of twelve opinion polls conducted by his institute (between December 1989 and January 1992) on the extent to which people approved of the activity of Gorbachev. For a Gorbachev–Yeltsin comparison, see also *Reytingi Borisa Yel'tsina i Mikhaila Gorbacheva po 10-bal'noy shkale* (VTsIOM, Moscow, 1993).

96 *V kakoy mere vy odobryaete deyatel'nost' M. S. Gorbacheva* (VTsIOM survey), courtesy of Professor Levada.

97 Gorbatschow, *Erinnerungen*, 1089.

98 M. Gorbachev, 'Novaya politika v novoy Rossii', *Svobodnaya mysl'*, 13 (1992), 3–19, at p. 14. See also Gorbatschow, *Erinnerungen*, 1089. In an interview with Angus Roxburgh for the BBC *Newsnight* programme on 6 Aug. 1992, Gorbachev made essentially the same point. I am grateful to the BBC for supplying me with the full video-recording of that interview.

99 Shakhnazarov, *Tsena svobody*, 147. Andrey Grachev has written that during his years in power Gorbachev had been so successful in convincing the entire world of 'his ability to perform political miracles that perhaps he ended up believing it himself' (Grachev, *Dal'she bez menya . . . Ukhod Prezidenta* (Kultura, Moscow, 1994), 3). The economist Pavel Bunich has made the point about Gorbachev's self-confidence in altogether more hostile terms, describing him as 'secretive and self-satisfied' (*Argumenty i fakty*, 12 (Mar. 1995), 3).

100 The only exception to that generalization is the period of several months after the August 1991 coup, when Gorbachev was able to bring back into his inner circle proponents of far-reaching change, while being freed for the first time from the pressures of more conservative forces within the party apparatus, the military, KGB, and the ministerial apparatus. The party machine had ceased to exist, new leaderships existed in all of the other organizations, and the political climate

was one in which defenders of the status quo ante had been seriously weakened and the only (but decisively important) threat to Gorbachev came from Yeltsin's team and from the separatist tendencies in all of the European republics within the Soviet Union.

101 Bunich, *Argumenty i fakty*, 12 (Mar. 1995), 3.

102 Chernyaev, *Shest' let s Gorbachevym*, 376.

103 Alexander Yakovlev, *Muki, prochteniya, bytiya. Perestroyka: nadezhdy i real'nosti* (Novosti, Moscow, 1991), 348.

104 As Boldin correctly notes in his tendentious and generally unreliable memoirs, the Security Council consisted of Bakatin, Bessmertnykh, Kryuchkov, Pavlov, Pugo, Primakov, Yazov, and Yanaev. He does not, however, mention that Gorbachev also proposed one other person to be a member of the Council—none other than Valery Boldin, but the Supreme Soviet of the USSR threw his name out. See Boldin, *Ten Years that Shook the World: The Gorbachev Era as Witnessed by his Chief of Staff* (Basic Books, New York, 1994), 263.

105 Gorbatschow, *Erinnerungen*, 562.

106 Shakhnazarov interview, *The Second Russian Revolution* transcripts.

107 Ibid.

108 Ibid.

109 Ibid.

110 Ibid.

111 A. N. Yakovlev interview, *The Second Russian Revolution* transcripts.

112 On the growing disagreements between Gorbachev and Yakovlev and on the attempts to exacerbate them by Gorbachev's enemies both among the conservative forces and among the radical democrats, see Vadim Medvedev, *V komande Gorbacheva. Vzglyad iznutri* ('Bylina', Moscow, 1994), 173–4.

113 *RFE/RL Report on the USSR*, 3/2 (11 Jan. 1991), 31.

114 Roxburgh, *The Second Russian Revolution*, 198.

115 Ryzhkov, *Perestroyka: Istoriya predatel'stv*, 14–17, esp. 16. Gorbachev, in the course of canvassing the opinion of his aides, Chernyaev and Shakhnazarov, on who should be Prime Minister, remarked that 'many' people had proposed Pavlov. Among the names suggested by Chernyaev and Shakhnazarov were Leonid Abalkin, Anatoly Sobchak (who, Chernyaev pointed out, would give the new government the advantage of becoming a bridge-building coalition), and Arkady Volsky (whom Gorbachev was quicker to reject, saying 'I know more about him than you do'). See Chernyaev, *Shest' let s Gorbachevym*, 404–5.

116 When I was in Moscow in January 1991 a number of politicians and specialists with links to Gorbachev's inner circle, with whom I spoke, mentioned the growing influence (a negative and conservative influence in the view of one of them, Fedor Burlatsky) of Lukyanov on the Soviet leader.

117 Chernyaev, *Shest' let s Gorbachevym*, 396.

118 Gorbachev's speech of 14 Jan. 1991 to the Supreme Soviet of the USSR on the formation of a new cabinet is reported verbatim (recorded from Moscow Central Television) in FBIS-SOV-91-010, 15 Jan. 1991, pp. 16–19. For the references to consultations with the Presidium of the Supreme Soviet and the Federation Council, see p. 17.

119 Ibid. 18.

120 Ibid. 17.

121 Shevardnadze, *The Future Belongs to Freedom*, esp. 23–6, 37–40.

122 Shevardnadze's 'Resignation Speech to Congress', FBIS-SOV-90-245, 20 Dec. 1990, pp. 11–12, at p. 11. The speech appears also verbatim as an appendix to Shevardnadze's memoirs, *The Future Belongs to Freedom*, 201–4. Colonel Petrushenko, in his immediate reaction to Shevardnadze's speech, did not take the resignation threat seriously, calling it 'political gamesmanship' and saying: 'I am sure Shevardnadze was following orders from Gorbachev' (FBIS-SOV-90-245, 20 Dec. 1990, p. 14).

123 Shevardnadze, *The Future Belongs to Freedom*, p. xvi.

124 FBIS-SOV-90-245, 20 Dec. 1990, p. 12.

125 Shevardnadze, *The Future Belongs to Freedom*, 199; and Vitaly Ignatenko, 'Ot Vil'nyusa do Forosa. Samye trudnye dni Gorbacheva', *Novoe vremya*, 12 (Mar. 1992), 22–6, at p. 23.

126 Shevardnadze, *The Future Belongs to Freedom*, 198.

127 Ibid., p. xviii.

128 Ibid., pp. xviii, 192.

129 Ignatenko, 'Ot Vil'nyusa do Forosa'; and author's interviews with Andrey Grachev. Shakhnazarov (interview, *The Second Russian Revolution* transcripts) also refers to Gorbachev having been 'buried in an avalanche of letters, telegrams and other requests calling for Presidential rule in the Baltics'. On Boldin's general attitude to the radical reformers within Gorbachev's entourage see Chernyaev, *Shest' let s Gorbachevym*, 402–3.

130 FBIS-SOV-91-010, 15 Jan. 1991, pp. 19–23, at p. 20. Talking to journalists during a break in the proceedings of the Supreme Soviet on 14 Jan., Gorbachev said that he 'would not like to introduce presidential rule with all its attributes' in Lithuania, and he had decided to limit himself a few days earlier 'to nothing more than a warning to the Lithuanian Supreme Soviet, even if strongly-worded' (FBIS-SOV-91-010, 15 Jan. 1991, p. 23).

131 Ibid.

132 Cf. Miller, *Mikhail Gorbachev and the End of Soviet Power*, 172–3.

133 Shakhnazarov, *Tsena svobody*, 17–18.

134 See Stephen Foye, 'Russia's Fragmented Army Drawn into the Political Fray', *RFE/RL Research Report*, 2/15 (9 Apr. 1993), 1–7, at p. 5; David Remnick, *Lenin's Tomb: The Last Days of the Soviet Empire* (Random House, New York, 1993), 307; and FBIS-SOV-91-010, 15 Jan. 1991, p. 21. Also directly responsible was Major General Uskhopchik, the commander of the Vilnius garrison (Miller, *Gorbachev and the End of Soviet Power*, 173).

135 On the criticism of Gorbachev from completely opposed positions, see Medvedev, *V komande Gorbacheva*, 176–7.

136 Ignatenko, 'Ot Vil'nyusa do Forosa', 25.

137 Ibid. 25–6. Cf. Chernyaev, *Shest' let s Gorbachevym*, 407. The first account Gorbachev heard of the events in Lithuania came from sources strongly defensive of the action of the Soviet troops and which greatly underestimated the number of Lithuanian casualties. Since, however, Gorbachev's relations with Landsbergis were significantly worse than his relations with the former First Secretary of the Lithuanian Communist Party, Algirdas-Mikolas Brazauskas (notwithstanding the latter's prominent part in the drive for Lithuanian independence), it is not certain what difference, if any, the call from Landsbergis on the Sunday would have made. Gorbachev did have a telephone conversation with him the following day—early on the morning of 14 Jan.—and described it as 'very unproductive' (FBIS-SOV-91-010, 15 Jan. 1991, p. 21). Landsbergis was one of the most difficult interlocutors Gorbachev encountered in any of the Soviet republics seeking secession. Landsbergis's ambition—according to an astute observer of Baltic politics, Anatol Lieven—to become 'Father of the Nation' had been fed both by his 'complete self-identification with Lithuanian culture and by his own personal vanity'. Lieven also observes: 'There were beautiful sides to Landsbergis' nationalism, but others which were profoundly ugly.' See Lieven, *The Baltic Revolution: Estonia, Latvia and Lithuania and the Path to Independence*, 2nd edn. (Yale University Press, New Haven, 1994), 259, 274.

138 Ignatenko, 'Ot Vil'nyusa do Forosa', 26. For two useful accounts of the violence in Vilnius in January 1991 and of several other repressive acts leading to loss of life in the Baltic states during the same year, see Lieven, *The Baltic Revolution*, 244–55; and Steele, *Eternal Russia*, 189–202.

139 See Grachev, *Dal'she bez menya*, 261–2.

140 See Chernyaev, *Shest' let s Gorbachevym*, 405–15; and Ignatenko, 'Ot Vil'nyusa do Forosa', 26. Both Chernyaev and Ignatenko note also that Andrey Grachev, who had been invited to leave his post as deputy head of the International Department and join Gorbachev's staff to strengthen the presidential apparatus, telephoned to say that he would not now be coming, adding: '1968 and 1979 were enough for me' (Chernyaev, *Shest' let s Gorbachevym*, 407–8; Ignatenko, 'Ot Vil'nyusa do Forosa', 26). Grachev was, of course, referring to the Soviet invasions of Czechoslovakia and of Afghanistan.

141 Chernyaev, *Shest' let s Gorbachevym*, 408–11, esp. 411.

142 Ibid. 412.

143 Ibid. 408–11.

144 Ibid. 408–12. On this episode, see also Ignatenko, 'Ot Vil'nyusa do Forosa', 26. Tamara Alexandrova had worked closely with Chernyaev for many years.

145 When Ignatenko and others gave Gorbachev on 14 Jan. an account of what had actually happened in Vilnius at the weekend (the details they had learned from the former Minister of Interior, Bakatin), 'Gorbachev was shocked', in the words of Ignatenko ('Ot Vil'nyusa do Forosa', 26). See also the interview, conducted early in 1991, with Alexander Yakovlev (*The Second Russian Revolution* transcripts). Yakovlev says that he was on vacation at the time of the 'tragic events in Vilnius this January', but Gorbachev called him the very next day and 'he took it very close to heart'. At another point in the same interview Yakovlev noted that the avoidance of bloodshed was a

constant concern of Gorbachev. Andrey Grachev (interview with the author, 14 Jan. 1993) observed that for Gorbachev an unwillingness to shed blood was not only a criterion but the condition of his involvement in politics. Gorbachev, in his memoirs, says that he was angered by what happened in Vilnius on the night of 12/13 January and that he demanded explanations, in turn, from Kryuchkov, Pugo, and Yazov, all of whom denied having given the orders. He adds that 'back then I trusted Yazov' (Gorbatschow, *Erinnerungen*, 1021). See also Gorbachev interview, *Moskovskiy komsomolets*, 28 June 1995, p. 2.

146 Ignatenko, 'Ot Vil'nyusa do Forosa', 26.

147 Ibid.; Chernyaev, *Shest' let s Gorbachevym*, 414–15; Shakhnazarov interview, *The Second Russian Revolution* transcripts; and author's interview with Andrey Grachev, 14 Jan. 1993.

148 Ignatenko, 'Ot Vil'nyusa do Forosa', 26.

149 Ibid.

150 Even in retrospect Gorbachev blamed 'radical separatists' for provoking the attack, which, however, he deplored. He had specifically prohibited the use of troops, and the action appeared to have been determined on the spot. See Gorbatschow, *Erinnerungen*, 1023–5.

151 Gorbachev news conference of 22 Jan., FBIS-SOV-91-015, 23 Jan. 1991, pp. 3–4, at p. 3. In a newspaper interview published on 16 Jan., Vadim Bakatin said that he had spoken with Gorbachev both on the Sunday evening and the Monday (13 and 14 Jan.) and that 'everything that happened in Vilnius came as a complete surprise to him'. He added that in the two years he had worked quite closely with Gorbachev in the law-enforcement sphere Gorbachev had always, even in the most complex cases, tried 'to avoid unnecessary violence with no basis in law'. Bakatin, therefore, reacted with both surprise and disapproval to the fact that Gorbachev had not clearly disassociated himself from the repressive actions in Vilnius in his first pronouncement after they had occurred to the USSR Supreme Soviet (*Komsomol'skaya pravda*, 16 Jan. 1991, p. 1). In a subsequent interview (*The Second Russian Revolution* transcripts) Bakatin said that from his first telephone conversation with Gorbachev on Sunday 13 Jan. he discovered that Gorbachev knew nothing about the fact that tanks had been used in the assault. There were other serious deficiencies in the information Gorbachev had been given: 'He believed that the first to attack were the separatists and the extremists, and then certain measures had to be taken in response. His number of victims was smaller: he believed that only two people had died. My information was 12' (ibid.).

152 FBIS-SOV-91-015, 23 Jan. 1991, p. 3.

153 This is notwithstanding the fact that Yeltsin, in an earlier incarnation (in August 1990), had told the Tatars to take all the power they could cope with for their 'autonomous republic' (*Pravda*, 9 Aug. 1990, p. 2).

154 Shakhnazarov interview in *Der Spiegel*, 21 Jan. 1991, pp. 131–4; published in English in FBIS-SOV-91-015, 23 Jan. 1991, pp. 30–3 (p. 31).

155 Ibid.

156 Ibid. Shakhnazarov added: 'The Caucasian republics, just like the Asian ones, will probably prefer to stay in a closer relationship with Russia. If we manage to give everybody a feeling of freedom and if, at the same time, we manage to improve our economic situation, then Russia's attraction as a powerful, promising region will become so strong that the others will move closer again and not widen their distance.' Writing about Gorbachev's reactions to the efforts of the Baltic states already in 1990 to regain their independence, Chernyaev observes that Gorbachev found it difficult to adjust himself psychologically to the exit from the Soviet Union of the Baltic states. He sincerely believed that if this were to happen it would be to 'the great detriment above all of the peoples of those republics' (*Shest' let s Gorbachevym*, 339).

157 Gorbatschow, *Erinnerungen*, 1019. The Lithuanian leadership rejected the language of divorce on the grounds that they had been *forced* into their relationship with Russia and into being part of the Soviet Union. Shakhnazarov's response to this in his *Der Spiegel* interview in mid-Jan. 1991 was to say: 'Let us assume the Lithuanians are right. In this case, please let me give you the following example: A man forces a woman to live with him. After half a century they have a home, children, common relatives, and contacts with their neighbors... This entails certain obligations that can be solved only on a legal basis' (FBIS-SOV-91-015, 21 Jan. 1991, p. 30).

158 Kravchenko was dismissed following his co-operation with the leaders of the August coup and replaced as head of state television and radio (Gostelradio) by Yegor Yakovlev, the independent-minded editor of *Moscow News*.

159 Remnick, *Lenin's Tomb*, 392. Kravchenko later claimed that 'the dissatisfaction of Gorbachev' with *Vzglyad* played a role in the closure of the programme. Gorbachev, he argued, could not directly demand that the programme be closed down, but 'from people whose duties were a little lower' he got a quite clear instruction to this effect. Given the very different personalities and outlooks of

people working for Gorbachev, that leaves unsettled the issue of whether it was Gorbachev's wish to take that particular programme off the air. See interview with Kravchenko in *Novyy vzglyad*, 16 (1992), 1.

160 David Wedgwood Benn, *From Glasnost to Freedom of Speech: Russian Openness and International Relations* (Pinter, London, for the Royal Institute of International Affairs, 1992), 23; and Stephen White, *After Gorbachev* (Cambridge University Press, Cambridge, 1993), 131.

161 Wedgwood Benn, *From Glasnost to Freedom of Speech*, 23.

162 Shakhnazarov, *Tsena svobody*, 55.

163 Wedgwood Benn, *From Glasnost to Freedom of Speech*, 18–21, at p. 18.

164 Miller, *Gorbachev and the End of Soviet Power*, 98–100, at p. 100. Shakhnazarov describes the sometimes stormy passage of the law, and his discussions concerning it with Gorbachev, in his memoirs. See *Tsena svobody*, 54–60. For some years before he became an aide to Gorbachev, Shakhnazarov had—in addition to working in the Central Committee apparatus—headed a sector on the Theory of Political Systems at the Institute of State and Law. Two of the three able younger scholars who drafted the variant of the Press Law—which, in spite of amendments and objections, became the basis of the new legislation—he drew from that sector. They were Yury Baturin (who later became an aide to Shakhnazarov in the Kremlin and, later still, in post-Soviet Russia a presidential aide to Boris Yeltsin) and Vladimir Entin. The third member of the group was Mikhail Fedotov, who was later to become Minister for the Press in the Russian government in 1993. The same three specialists were the authors of the draft of the Law on Glasnost the previous year.

165 See Remnick, *Lenin's Tomb*, 420.

166 Stephen Fish, *Democracy from Scratch: Opposition and Regime in the New Russian Revolution* (Princeton University Press, Princeton, 1995), 48.

167 Indeed, even after he had left office, Gorbachev continued to believe that the dangers of demonstrations getting out of hand had been quite real. See the full page interview with Gorbachev in *Literaturnaya gazeta*, 8 July 1992, p. 11.

168 Remnick, *Lenin's Tomb*, 420–2.

169 Ibid.; and Richard Sakwa, *Russian Politics and Society* (Routledge, London, 1993), 9.

170 Remnick, *Lenin's Tomb*, 422.

171 Chernyaev, *Shest' let s Gorbachevym*, 434.

172 Ibid.

173 Shakhnazarov, *Tsena svobody*, 144.

174 Ibid. 145.

175 See e.g. ibid. 54 and 290. Shakhnazarov writes (p. 290) that Gorbachev 'as always worked from 10 o'clock in the morning until 10 or 11 in the evening'.

176 Interview with Gorbachev, *Literaturnaya gazeta*, 8 July 1992, p. 11.

177 Chernyaev, *Shest' let s Gorbachevym*, 432–3.

178 *Literaturnaya gazeta*, 8 July 1992, p. 11; and Shakhnazarov, *Tsena svobody*, 221–39.

179 Ibid. 225.

180 On the April plenum of the Central Committee, see *Izvestiya TsK KPSS*, 6 (1991), 10–11, Medvedev, *V komande Gorbacheva*, 184–6; and FBIS-SOV-91-082-S, Daily Report Supplement, 'Soviet Union: CPSU Plenum', 29 Apr. 1991.

181 Shakhnazarov, *Tsena svobody*, 164. See also pp. 155–6.

182 The draft Union Treaty due to be signed on 20 Aug. was published in *Moskovskie novosti* on 14 Aug. and in *Sovetskaya Rossiya* on 15 Aug. 1991. For a fuller discussion of the changing content of the Union Treaty, see Miller, *Gorbachev and the End of Soviet Power*, 183–200, esp. 184, 192–7.

183 Shakhnazarov, *Tsena svobody*, 225. This team of four also had several younger consultants assisting them, among whom Yury Baturin played a particularly active role.

184 Ibid. 237.

185 Author's interview of 14 May 1992, with Fedor Burlatsky.

186 *Sovetskaya Rossiya*, 15 Aug. 1991, p. 3.

187 Shakhnazarov, *Tsena svobody*, 233.

188 Ibid. 224–5.

189 Ibid. 225.

190 Ibid.

191 For the voting figures and percentage support of all six candidates, see FBIS-SOV-91-119, 20 June 1991, pp. 56–7. The candidate not mentioned in the text was Aman-Geldy Tuleev, who came fourth with 6.81 per cent of the votes.

192 In post-Soviet Russia tensions very quickly arose between Yeltsin and Rutskoy and culminated in the showdown in 1993 at the Moscow White House between executive and legislature, during which Rutskoy threw in his lot completely with the Russian Supreme Soviet and was arrested when the White House came under fire from troops loyal to Yeltsin on 4 October. He was released from prison in February 1994 (at the behest of the State Duma which had been elected in December 1993) and almost immediately launched himself into political campaigning—with an eye on the next Russian presidential elections—on a pro-nationalist platform.

193 For a useful account of the episode, see Dawn Mann, 'An Abortive Constitutional Coup d'Etat?', *RFE/RL Report on the USSR*, 3/27 (5 July 1991), 1–6.

194 The text of Gorbachev's speech to the Supreme Soviet on 21 June 1991 is published in full in FBIS-SOV-91-121, 24 June 1991, pp. 36–7.

195 Gorbatschow, *Erinnerungen*, 565–6.

196 Valentin Pavlov, *Avgust iznutri. Gorbachevputch* (Delovoy mir, Moscow, 1993), 95; and Shakhnazarov, *Tsena svobody*, 233. Shakhnazarov adds that Gorbachev should have moved sooner to give a key post at the all-union level to Nazarbaev.

197 For a good account of the political context, see Elizabeth Teague and Julia Wishnevsky, 'El'tsin Bans Organized Political Activity in State Sector', *RFE/RL Report on the USSR*, 3/33 (16 Aug. 1991), 21–5.

198 Ibid. 23, 25.

199 *Sovetskaya Rossiya*, 23 July 1991, p. 1.

200 Interview with Andrey Grachev, 25 Jan. 1992. See also *Pravda*, 29 July 1991, p. 1.

201 Andrey Grachev (interview of 25 Jan. 1992) said that Lukyanov was so warmly received at the July 1991 Central Committee plenum that it was evident that he was being seen as a future leader and likely General Secretary. The only reason in Grachev's view why the Central Committee gave their provisional endorsement to the draft Party Programme was that they had no intention of implementing it. The mood of the meeting was indicated by the fact that he and Latsis were the *only* two Central Committee members to attack the inflammatory 'Word to the People' open letter as well as by the rough reception this earned them.

202 *Pravda*, 26 July 1991, pp. 1–2, at p. 2.

203 Ibid.

204 Ibid.

205 Ibid.

206 Ibid. See also Karl Marx, *Communist Manifesto* (centenary edition with an introduction by Harold J. Laski, Allen & Unwin, London, 1948), 146.

207 *Pravda*, 26 July 1991, p. 2.

208 Interview with Nursultan Nazarbaev by Kira Vladena, *Nezavisimaya gazeta*, 28 July 1993, p. 5.

209 Ibid.

210 On this conversation, see Boris Yeltsin, *The View from the Kremlin* (HarperCollins, London, 1994), 38–9; Pavlov, *Avgust iznutri*, 95; Nazarbaev interview, *Nezavisimaya gazeta*, 28 July 1993, p. 5; and Gorbachev interview, *The Second Russian Revolution* transcripts.

211 Yeltsin himself goes so far as to say that perhaps this meeting 'is what triggered the August 1991 coup' (*The View from the Kremlin*, 39).

212 *Komsomol'skaya pravda*, 6 Aug. 1991, p. 1.

213 See e.g. Shakhnazarov, *Tsena svobody*, 262–3; and Mikhail Gorbachev, *The August Coup* (HarperCollins, London, 1991), 17.

214 Remnick, *Lenin's Tomb*, 449.

215 When Yakovlev was asked in an interview conducted on 16 August but which was published only after the coup was over whether 'A Word to the People' contained, in essence, 'an appeal to overthrow Gorbachev', he replied: 'Yes, of course.' See *Literaturnaya gazeta*, 34, 28 August 1991, p. 2.

216 FBIS-SOV-91-158, 15 Aug. 1991, p. 27.

217 The most richly documented book on the coup was published in Moscow in 1992. Extensive verbatim extracts from the interviews of the legal investigators with all concerned in the coup, whether as victims or conspirators, are published there by the Russian Procurator-General at that time, Valentin Stepankov, and deputy Procurator-General, Yevgeny Lisov. While it is, to say the least, surprising that the chief law officers should have produced a popular book on the subject of their investigation before the case had been heard in court, it contains much interesting

information. See Stepankov and Lisov, *Kremlevskiy zagovor* (Ogonek, Moscow, 1992). The best account of the coup in English is to be found in Remnick, *Lenin's Tomb*, 439–90.

218 Gorbachev, *The August Coup*, 111. The article which Gorbachev and Chernyaev completed a few days before the coup is published as Appendix C to Gorbachev's short book on the coup, pp. 97–127.

219 For Vladimir Medvedev's account of the episode, see his volume of memoirs, *Chelovek za spinoy* (Russlit, Moscow, 1994), esp. 274–87.

220 Gorbachev, *The August Coup*, 18; cf. Stepankov and Lisov, *Kremlevskiy zagovor*, 9; and Medvedev, *Chelovek za spinoy*, 276–7. Plekhanov, as head of the KGB Ninth Department, was Medvedev's chief. Before leaving Foros himself, he ordered Medvedev to leave and the latter obeyed. Neither at the time nor later did Gorbachev hold this against his former principal bodyguard (whose face was well known to the outside world, although his name was not, for he was to be seen lurking behind Gorbachev in thousands of photographs, especially those taken abroad), since it was virtually impossible for him to disobey an order from his commanding officer. Following the coup, however, Gorbachev created a cadre of presidential bodyguards answerable ultimately to him—as did Yeltsin with the Russian presidency—who were no longer part of the KGB. Medvedev apart, Gorbachev's bodyguards remained with him, loyal to him—and armed—throughout his period of isolation at Foros, but they were under the surveillance of an 'outer layer' of fresh KGB detachments who had been brought in by Plekhanov.

221 Gorbachev, *The August Coup*, 17–18; and Shakhnazarov, *Tsena svobody*, 262. Gorbachev and Shakhnazarov are thirty to forty minutes apart in their estimate of when their telephone conversation took place, Gorbachev saying that it was 'at 4.30 p.m.' (*The August Coup*, 17) and Shakhnazarov stating that it was 'at 15.50', but a few pages further on, quoting from the speech he made to the Russian Supreme Soviet on 21 August, he gives the time of his conversation with Gorbachev as 16.00 hours (*Tsena svobody*, 262, 266).

222 A telephone operator at Foros later recounted how a KGB officer appeared behind her just as she was connecting Gorbachev with Shakhnazarov. Immediately that conversation was completed the Chairman of the Belorussian Supreme Soviet, Dementey, telephoned, returning a call from Gorbachev. The officer told him to put down the telephone and not to trouble the President with any more phone calls. The lines were then disconnected. See Shakhnazarov, *Tsena svobody*, 270–1 and Gorbachev, *The August Coup*, 18.

223 Ibid. 18–19.

224 Author's interview with Chernyaev, 30 Mar. 1992.

225 Gorbachev, *The August Coup*, 18.

226 Stepankov and Lisov, *Kremlevskiy zagovor*, 13.

227 Gorbachev, *The August Coup*, 19.

228 Ibid. 20–3.

229 Stepankov and Lisov, *Kremlevskiy zagovor*, 14. Even Boldin confirms that Gorbachev ordered Plekhanov out and went on the offensive against Baklanov and, still more, against Varennikov. See Boldin, *Ten Years that Shook the World*, 26–7.

230 On that, see Stepankov and Lisov, *Kremlevskiy zagovor*; Shakhnazarov, *Tsena svobody*, 270–6; and Chernyaev, *Shest' let s Gorbachevym*, 177–88.

231 Numerous articles have appeared in the hardline conservative press of post-Soviet Russia, especially *Den'* and its successor, *Zavtra*, both edited by Alexander Prokhanov—one of the main authors of 'A Word to the People'—calling for Gorbachev to be brought to trial for treason.

232 Stepankov and Lisov, *Kremlevskiy zagovor*, 12; and Chernyaev, *Shest' let s Gorbachevym*, 484–5. The appointment of Vice-President Yanaev, although he was not particularly close to the Soviet President, had been another of Gorbachev's bad mistakes. At a press conference on 22 August, the day after his return to Moscow, Gorbachev said: 'In particular, I can see that the Congress of People's Deputies of the USSR was right when it initially refused to elect the vice-president, but I insisted on it. That was my mistake, and not my only mistake. I can see that now. I would also say quite frankly that I particularly trusted Yazov and Kryuchkov' (*Pravda*, 23 Aug. 1991, p. 2).

233 Harold Seidman introduced 'Miles's law' into the literature of political analysis in his *Politics, Position and Power: The Dynamics of Federal Organization*, first published in 1970. He attributed the remark to Rufus Miles, a former Assistant Secretary for Administration in the United States Department of Health, Education and Welfare. The actual wording Seidman uses is 'Where one stands depends on where one sits' (*Politics, Position and Power*, 3rd edn. (Oxford University Press, New York, 1980), 21).

234 Quoted in Remnick, *Lenin's Tomb*, 455.

235 Gorbachev, *The August Coup*, 27.

236 Chernyaev, *Shest' let s Gorbachevym*, 483.

237 Ibid.

238 Ibid.

239 Ibid.

240 Gorbachev, *The August Coup*, 25.

241 Ibid. 24.

242 Boris Yeltsin, *Against the Grain: An Autobiography* (Jonathan Cape, London, 1990); and Yeltsin, *The View from the Kremlin*. For example, in *Against the Grain* Yeltsin expresses his surprise and disapproval that when he was brought to Moscow in 1985 to head the department of the Central Committee which dealt with the construction industry, Gorbachev made no move to meet him (p. 76). But Vladimir Dolgikh, Yeltsin's immediate superior as a Secretary of the Central Committee— 'one of the most professional and efficient secretaries of the central committee', according to Yeltsin (p. 121)—has explicitly stated that what Yeltsin said in his book was 'not true'. He personally introduced Yeltsin to Gorbachev with whom they had a talk when Yeltsin first came to Moscow (Dolgikh interview, *The Second Russian Revolution* transcripts). In *The View from the Kremlin* Yeltsin states (pp. 75–6) that the uncertainty of Gorbachev's fate during the August 1991 coup 'managed to raise his ratings more in one hour than all his years of reform'. Gorbachev's popularity did receive a minor boost following the coup, but Yeltsin's implication here and elsewhere that this was the high point of Gorbachev's popularity and that Gorbachev had never earlier been popular is extraordinarily wide of the mark. As both anecdotal evidence for the early period and the survey data of VTsIOM indicate, Gorbachev was highly popular for the greater part of his leadership. When, as already noted, his ratings did fall, they never during any point of his years in office reached the depths which Yeltsin's had plumbed by early 1995. One other example of Yeltsin's carelessness with the facts when they concern Gorbachev may suffice. He writes (*The View from the Kremlin*, 114–15) about the killings in Tbilisi, Baku, Vilnius, and Riga discussed earlier in this chapter and states: 'I am certain that Gorbachev could not have helped knowing about *all* these actions' (emphasis added). In the light of the Sobchak report, and the public evidence of Shevardnadze and others, Yeltsin should certainly have been aware that this had been demonstrated to be the opposite of the truth so far as the Tbilisi deaths (nineteen, rather than nine, as Yeltsin states, p. 114) are concerned. Shevardnadze—as already noted—had been specifically instructed by Gorbachev to fly to Tbilisi to settle the dispute peacefully. For the crack-down in Baku, although not for the indiscriminate firing, Gorbachev bears—and has not denied—responsibility. The killings in the Baltic states were in a different category. Rather than being acts of state violence instigated or approved by Gorbachev, they were designed partly to compromise him and to embroil him in a general crackdown on those republics.

243 For Yeltsin's account of the coup, including Gorbachev's isolation, see *The View from the Kremlin*, 50–103.

244 On the seizure of the Stavropol party archive, see FBIS-SOV-91-167, 28 Aug. 1991, p. 81.

245 Gorbachev, *The August Coup*, 29.

246 Those who made the ludicrous suggestion that Gorbachev could have been involved in a dangerous game of collusion with Kryuchkov, Baklanov, and company might have given a moment's thought to Gorbachev's utter devotion to his wife and to the fact that, as he acknowledged in a televised interview (referred to in an earlier chapter), he discussed *everything* with her. In addition to the most fundamental fact that the *putschists* were threatening his historic achievements and were hoping to reverse virtually all of the policies he had pursued since 1988—including, not least, the Union Treaty which had been his main preoccupation, almost obsession, over the preceding months—it is unthinkable that for the sake of some illusory political gain Gorbachev would have subjected his wife to the uncertainty, stress, and suffering which she endured between 18 and 21 August 1991, after which her health was never to be as strong again as it had been before that experience.

247 Ironically, Yeltsin in Sept.–Oct. 1993 faced a revolt by people whom *he* had appointed or promoted, including his Vice-President, the Chairman of the Russian Supreme Soviet, and the head of the Russian security service (the post-Soviet equivalent of the KGB). It ended with the storming of the Russian White House, of which Yeltsin had been a defender two years earlier, and with a substantially higher death-toll (mainly on the side of Yeltsin's opponents) than in August 1991 when three people were killed in Moscow.

248 Shakhnazarov, *Tsena svobody*, 176.

249 Chernyaev, *Shest' let s Gorbachevym*, 487.

250 Ibid. 489.

251 *Pravda*, 23 Aug. 1991, p. 2.

252 Cf. Gorbachev, *The August Coup*, 46–7; and Grachev, *Dal'she bez menya*, 8–9.

253 Remnick, *Lenin's Tomb*, 495.

254 The full text of Akhromeev's letter to Gorbachev, setting out the reasons for his suicide, is published in Stepankov and Lisov, *Kremlevskiy zagovor*, 240–2.

255 See Oleg Kalugin, *Spymaster* (Smith Gryphon, London, 1994).

256 The fullest account of the high (and low) politics of the last months of the Soviet Union is to be found in Grachev, *Dal'she bez menya*. See also Mikhail Gorbachev, *Dekabr'-91: Moya pozitsiya* (Novosti, Moscow, 1992).

257 Grachev, *Dal'she bez menya*, 184.

258 Ibid. 180.

259 *The Times*, 9 Dec. 1991, p. 10.

260 Grachev, *Dal'she bez menya*, 13.

Chapter 9   Conclusions

1 The Russian examples are too numerous to mention, but they range from radical proponents of the free market to Russian nationalists and unreconstructed Communists. The latter two groupings are united by their belief that nothing was more important than the preservation of Soviet statehood and that all other values, including those pertaining to democracy and human rights, should have been subordinated to that goal. Thus e.g. Colonel Viktor Alksnis, one of Gorbachev's fiercest critics who was a leading member of the Soyuz group in the Supreme Soviet, scoffs at Gorbachev's hatred of using violence, saying that this was all very well if you wanted to be a follower of Tolstoy but no good for a politician (cited in Mark Galeotti, *The Age of Anxiety: Security and Politics in Soviet and Post-Soviet Russia* (Longman, London, 1995), 192). Galeotti adds: 'Past Russian and Soviet leaders have rarely shied away from the use of violence. It may have made Gorbachev a better human being, but it also made him a failure as a politician' (ibid.). More sweepingly, an American specialist on Soviet society, John Bushnell, has written: 'Few national leaders have failed so spectacularly as Mikhail Gorbachev: in 1985 he set out to reanimate Soviet society and economy, by the end of 1991 he had managed without benefit of war to destroy the Soviet state and lose for Russia the territorial gains of more than three centuries'. See Bushnell, 'Making History out of Current Events: The Gorbachev Era', (*Slavic Review*, 51/3 (Fall 1992), 557–63, at p. 557).

2 Gorbachev used this phrase in his speech to the conference on ideology in Moscow in Dec. 1984. See M. S. Gorbachev, *Izbrannye rechi i stat'i* (Politizdat, Moscow, 1987), ii. 75–108, at p. 86.

3 They embraced, and even exceeded, the hopes of liberal Russian intellectuals. Thus, the writer Olga Chaykovskaya has written about her thoughts when Gorbachev became Soviet leader, saying that what she 'needed from this person was that he would set free Sakharov and end the war in Afghanistan, nothing more' ('Dostoinstvo vyshe politiki', *Literaturnaya gazeta*, 21 Nov. 1992, p. 11).

4 These responses of Reagan and Shultz have been cited and discussed in Ch. 7.

5 Alexander Dallin, 'Causes of the Collapse of the USSR', *Post-Soviet Affairs*, 8/4 (1992), 279–302, esp. 299.

6 Ibid.

7 Valery Surikov, 'Soyuz, Gorbachev, Rossiya', *Nezavisimaya gazeta*, 17 Oct. 1991, p. 5.

8 Ibid.

9 Shakhnazarov, a close and perceptive observer, is among those who have remarked that 'harsh and dictatorial methods are not in the character of Gorbachev' (*Tsena svobody: Reformatsiya Gorbacheva glazami ego pomoshchnika* (Rossika Zevs, Moscow, 1993), 147). Vladimir Yegorov—also a Gorbachev aide, although a less prominent one—has written of his chief: 'By character he was a man incapable not only of using dictatorial measures, but even of resorting to hard-line administrative means' (Vladimir K. Yegorov, *Out of a Dead End into the Unknown: Notes on Gorbachev's Perestroika* (edition q, Chicago, 1993), 125). See also Nikolay Ryzhkov, *Perestroyka: Istoriya predatel'stv* (Novosti, Moscow, 1992), 364.

10 Rajan Menon, 'Post-Mortem: The Causes and Consequences of the Soviet Collapse', *Harriman Review*, 7/10–12 (Nov. 1994), 1–10, at p. 8.

11 On this, see e.g. Shakhnazarov, *Tsena svobody*, 347.

12 I use 'his' advisedly, since virtually all party secretaries were men.

13 Such articles were to be found especially in the journal *Sovetskoe gosudarstvo i pravo*, whose chief editor at that time, Mikhail Piskotin, had himself earlier attempted to place no less weight on the democratic than the centralistic component of 'democratic centralism' in his book *Sotsializm i gosudarstvennoe upravlenie* (Nauka, Moscow, 1984), published the year before Gorbachev came to power. See especially pp. 209–32. See also D. D. Tsabriya, 'Demokraticheskiy tsentralizm: Nekotorye voprosy teorii i praktiki', *Sovetskoe gosudarstvo i pravo*, 1 (1986), 30–7; D. A. Kerimov and N. G. Kobers, 'XXVII s'ezd KPSS i razvitie sotsialisticheskoy demokratii', *Sovetskoe gosudarstvo i pravo*, 4 (1986), 3–10; and M. P. Lebedev, 'Nekotorye tendentsii i perspektivy razvitya politicheskoy sistemy sotsializma', ibid. 14–21 (esp. 15).

14 Michael Oakeshott, *Political Education: An Inaugural Lecture delivered at the London School of Economics and Political Science on March 6, 1951* (Bowes & Bowes, Cambridge, 1951), 22.

15 A. S. Chernyaev, *Shest' let s Gorbachevym: po dnevnikovym zapisyam* (Kultura, Moscow, 1993), 39.

16 Gorbachev, *Izbrannye rechi i stat'i*, vi. 397.

17 The extent of the shift in doctrine is, however, reflected in the fact that of the seven volumes of Gorbachev's speeches and writings which were published in the Soviet Union, vol. vii alone—which covers the period from 1 Oct. 1988 to 9 June 1989—does not have the word 'communism' in the index.

18 *Izvestiya*, 4 June 1989, p. 2.

19 M. S. Gorbachev, 'Vystuplenie v organizatsii ob"edinennykh natsiy', 7 Dec. 1988, in Gorbachev, *Izbrannye rechi i stat'i*, vii. 185–202, esp. 187–9.

20 I follow Robert Dahl in his understanding of political pluralism as systems in which there are relatively autonomous political organizations. Dahl goes on to define *relative autonomy* thus: 'An organization is relatively autonomous if it undertakes actions that (a) are considered harmful by another organization and that (b) no other organization, including the government of the state, can prevent, or could prevent except by incurring costs so high as to exceed the gains to the actor from doing so.' See Dahl, *Dilemmas of Pluralist Democracy. Autonomy vs. Control* (Yale University Press, New Haven, 1982), 26.

21 Richard Pipes, 'Misinterpreting the Cold War: The Hard-Liners Had it Right', *Foreign Affairs*, 74/1 (Jan.–Feb. 1995), 154–60, at p. 158.

22 Ryzhkov, *Perestroyka: Istoriya predatel'stv*, 364–5.

23 Ibid. 365.

24 Meeting with M. S. Gorbachev, 'Perestroyka—desyat' let spustya' (stenographic report of meeting at the discussion club 'Svobodnoe Slovo', Moscow, 20 Jan. 1995), 80.

25 The point is clearly recognized by Gorbachev (ibid.).

26 X. L. Ding has suggested that 'the dichotomous conceptualization of civil society versus the state' is a hindrance to understanding of the process of political change in a number of Communist countries (his own principal focus being on China). He offers instead the notion of 'institutional amphibiousness' to convey the 'mutual infiltration' of party-state, on the one hand, and society on the other. Arguing that 'state-society relations are highly interpenetrated and interwoven' in late Communism, Ding holds that an appreciation of this institutional amphibiousness is an important aid to interpreting the dynamics of the transition processes. See Ding, 'Institutional Amphibiousness and the Transition from Communism: The Case of China', *British Journal of Political Science*, 24/3 (July 1994), 293–318, esp. 315, 317–18.

27 Alexander Yakovlev, 'Eto krupneyshiy reformator', *Ogonek*, 11 (Mar. 1995), 45.

28 Samuel P. Huntington, *Political Order in Changing Societies* (Yale University Press, New Haven, 1968), 345.

29 The phrase 'the fallacy of retrospective determinism' is that of Reinhard Bendix (*Nation-Building and Citizenship* (John Wiley, New York, 1964), 13), cited by Dallin, 'Causes of the Collapse of the USSR', 297.

30 Olga Chaykovskaya, 'Dostoinstvo vyshe politiki', 11.

31 *Nezavisimaya gazeta*, 6 Apr. 1995, p. 3. For a more detailed historical comparison, see W. E. Mosse, *Alexander II and the Modernization of Russia* (updated edn., I. B. Tauris, London, 1992); W. E. Mosse, *Perestroika under the Tsars* (I. B. Tauris, London, 1992); and W. Bruce Lincoln, *The Great Reforms: Autocracy, Bureaucracy and the Politics of Change in Imperial Russia* (Northern Illinois University Press, De Kalb, Ill., 1990).

32 Gorbachev interview, *La Repubblica* (Rome), 14 Oct. 1992, pp. 1–3; translated and republished in FBIS-SOV-92-204, 21 Oct. 1992, pp. 18–20 (at p. 18).

Glossary

apparat	apparat (apparatus), bureaucracy
apparatchik	full-time official (especially of Communist Party, but also of Soviet governmental institutions)
glasnost'	glasnost, openness, transparency
institutchiki	scholars who worked in policy-oriented research institutes
kolkhoz	kolkhoz, collective farm
nomenklatura	nomenklatura, list of appointments which required the approval of a party committee or higher state body; also used to refer to the people on such approved lists as an especially privileged social stratum
perestroyka	perestroika, reconstruction (or restructuring)
samizdat	self-publishing (generally typescripts of works which could not be published officially in the Soviet Union and which circulated clandestinely)
Secretariat	unless otherwise stated refers to the Secretaries (the most senior officials) of the Central Committee of the CPSU who until 1988 met as a group in most weeks
shestidesyatniki	people of the sixties
Smersh	[*Smert' shpionam!*] Death to the spies! (Soviet wartime counter-intelligence)
sovkhoz	sovkhoz, state farm
tamizdat	works published 'over there', i.e. works written by Soviet citizens or exiled Russians which could not be published in the USSR but which were published abroad in Russian and found their way (although not in large numbers) into the Soviet Union
uskorenie	acceleration

Index

Abalkin, Leonid 64, 148, 149, 151, 152, 273,
    382 n. 115
Abkhazia 265, 267, 380 n. 52
Academy of Sciences of Russia 103
Academy of Sciences of the USSR 20, 60, 98,
    112, 180, 187, 257
Academy of Social Sciences 69
acceleration (*uskorenie*) 80, 122, 123, 128,
    344 n. 153
accountability 20, 24, 90, 195, 200
Achalov, General Viktor 280
Adamishin, Anatoly 217, 367 n. 26
Adomeit, Hannes 217, 370 n. 74, 376 n. 214
Afanasev, Viktor 100, 124, 339 n. 45, 342 n. 94
Afanasev, Yury 188, 191, 192
Afgantsy 280
Afghanistan 55, 56, 112, 221, 233, 259, 276,
    306, 372 nn. 120 & 125
    Soviet withdrawal from 175, 221, 233, 235
Aganbegyan, Abel 60, 64, 72, 73, 98, 112, 113,
    114, 146, 147, 148, 154
agenda-setting 4, 13, 46, 92–3
agriculture 46, 51, 58, 59, 60, 64, 142
    agricultural reform 142–5; collective contract
    144; link system 45, 46, 58
Aitmatov, Chingiz 209, 314
Akhmadulina, Bella 35–6
Akhromeev, Marshal Sergey 231, 232, 234, 301,
    372 n. 105, 389 n. 254
alcoholism 4, 10, 142, 314
Aleksandrova, Tamara 281
Aleksandrov-Agentov, Andrey 86, 98, 114
Alekseev, Sergey 199, 342 n. 96
Alexander II 125, 318
Aliev, Heydar 47, 65, 379 n. 49
Alksnis, Colonel Viktor 278, 389 n. 1
All-Russian Society for the Preservation of
    Historical and Cultural Monuments 21
All-Russian Theatre Society 164
All-Union Centre for the Study of Public
    Opinion; *now* All-Russian Centre for the
    Study of Public Opinion x–xi, 11, 238
Alma-Ata; *now* Almaty 260, 261, 304
Amalrik, Andrey 9, 320 n. 22
Andreeva, Nina 172, 173, 357 n. 89
    see also Nina Andreeva affair

Andropov, Yury 3, 4, 8, 19, 25, 46, 50, 51, 52,
    54, 55, 56, 57, 62, 64, 66, 67, 69, 70, 71,
    74, 98, 113, 214, 227, 230, 263, 297, 309,
    330 n. 162
    anti-corruption campaign 4, 49, 63
    as Chairman of KGB 4, 47, 49, 51, 54, 62, 65,
    101
    death of 51, 65, 69, 71, 83, 228
    declining health of 64, 66, 67, 216
    as General Secretary 4, 49, 55, 58, 62, 63, 64,
    67, 82, 85, 86, 100, 200
    Lenin anniversary speech 63
    and need for reform 38, 46, 47, 64, 134, 144
    and Socialist Countries Department 19, 48,
    109, 288
    and support for Gorbachev 45, 47, 50, 51, 64,
    67, 73
anti-alcohol campaign 4, 141–2
Anti-Ballistic Missile Treaty (1972) 233
'anti-cosmopolitan campaign' *see* Stalin, J. V.
anti-semitism 30
anti-Stalinism 40, 45, 91, 92, 99
Arbatov, Georgy 20, 37, 48, 50, 64, 81, 82, 112,
    234, 243, 319 n. 3, 330 n. 6
Armenia 192, 256, 262, 263, 264, 286, 287,
    303
    see also Nagorno-Karabakh dispute
army 124, 181, 212, 269, 273, 274, 282, 300
Åslund, Anders 139, 349 n. 51
August coup, *see* coup (August 1991)
authoritarianism 16, 17, 91, 95, 116, 131, 158,
    181, 196, 323 n. 50
Azerbaijan 47, 65, 262, 263, 264, 267, 380 n. 52
    Communist Party of 263
    Popular Front of 264

Bakatin, Vadim 150, 208, 276, 278, 281, 290,
    299, 302, 366 n. 13, 384 n. 151
Baker, James, Secretary of State 237, 239, 240,
    241, 367 n. 20, 374 n. 161
Baker, Keith Michael 128
Baklanov, Georgy 164, 387 n. 229, 388 n. 246
Baklanov, Oleg 277, 295, 296, 357 n. 99
Baku, killings in 260, 262, 264, 388 n. 242
balance of influence 97–103
balance of power 97, 104–11

Baltic states 267, 279, 280, 283, 284, 286, 287, 294, 303, 304
    nationalists in 270
    Popular Fronts in 310
banks, banking 133
Basic Positions (*Osnovye polozheniya*) 140, 141
Baturin, Yury 385 nn. 164 & 183
Baybakov, Nikolay 147
BBC radio 297, 299
Belarus, *see* Belorussia
Belgium 42, 43, 254
Belgorod 58
Belorussia 256, 259, 267, 287, 304
Bendix, Reinhard 390 n. 29
Berlin Wall, opening of 239, 240, 245
Berlinguer, Enrico 75
Beschloss, Michael 239, 370 n. 74
Bessmertnykh, Alexander 215, 278, 302, 366 n. 13
Bialer, Seweryn 90, 91, 319 n. 4, 338 n. 6
Bikkenin, Nail 79, 176
Biryukova, Aleksandra 161
Bogolyubov, Klavdy 68, 84, 86
Bogomolov, Oleg 20, 21, 48, 64, 112, 147
    see also Institute of Economics of the World Socialist System
Bogomolov's Institute, *see* Institute of Economics of the World Socialist System
Boldin, Valery 33, 103, 105, 199, 202, 208, 210, 279, 284, 285, 286, 288, 293, 295, 296, 364 n. 255, 367 n. 30, 382 n. 104, 387 n. 229
    as gatekeeper 103, 211, 383 n. 129
Bolshevik Revolution (1917) 21, 90, 121, 196, 257
    Seventieth anniversary of 167, 168, 170, 171
Bolshevism 118, 121
Bondarev, Yury 177, 291
Bonner, Yelena 165
Bovin, Alexander 49, 345 n. 168
Brakov, Yevgeny 188
Brandt, Willy 37, 116, 120, 343 n. 143, 368 n. 40
Brazauskas, Algirdas-Mikolas 383 n. 137
Bremner, Ian 378 n. 25
Breslauer, George 322 n. 47, 365 n. 258
Brest (8 December 1991) 304
Brezhnev, Leonid Ilich 3, 7, 25, 29, 37, 38, 42, 45, 46, 47, 50, 52, 53, 54, 55, 56, 61, 63, 69, 72, 85, 98, 112, 113, 125, 136, 141, 146, 182, 198, 214, 216, 218, 248, 309, 314
    adulation of 53, 54, 55
    death of 62, 63, 67, 71
    declining health of 51, 53, 54, 216
    General Secretaryship of 39, 41, 49, 57, 61, 86, 97, 112, 136, 174
    succession to 54, 62
Brezhnev era 8, 19, 20, 21, 24, 38, 47, 48, 49, 57, 61, 67, 79, 87, 92, 93, 101, 122, 132, 134, 191, 200, 214, 224, 233, 281
'Brezhnev doctrine' 240, 250
British-Soviet relations 77

Brokaw, Tom 35
Brzezinski, Zbigniew 255, 376 n. 203
Bukharin, Nikolay 168, 356 n. 59
Bulgarian Communist Party 248
Bunich, Pavel 274, 381 n. 99
Burlatsky, Fedor 20, 48, 101, 192, 223, 288, 329 n. 150, 330 n. 6, 342 n. 95, 355 n. 33, 382 n. 116
Bush, Barbara 373 n. 149
Bush, President George 7, 37, 116, 140, 216, 230, 237, 239, 284, 307, 374 n. 169
    negotiations with 240–2
Bushnell, John 389 n. 1

Cabinet of Ministers 199, 275, 276, 284, 290
    see also Council of Ministers
'cadres policy' 108, 177
Canada 74, 75, 81, 105, 115, 219, 240, 254
capitalism 63, 133, 222, 223
Carrère d'Encausse, Hélène 377 n. 6
Carter, President Jimmy 216
Catherine II, the Great 318
Catholic Church (in Poland) 56
Ceauşescu, Nicolae 249
censorship 96, 283
Central Asia 253, 257, 259, 262, 287, 303
Central Committee of the CPSU 4, 5, 16, 61, 66, 69, 70, 80, 81, 83, 84, 96, 104, 106, 107, 115, 131, 161, 168, 181, 187, 189, 195, 196, 200, 204, 301
    apparatus of 92, 101, 111, 184, 185, 201, 226
    changing composition of 73, 109, 177, 187
    departments of: Administrative Organs 7; Agriculture 38, 51, 53, 59, 61, 103, 109, 184; Construction 110; Culture 164; General 68, 84, 86, 103, 121, 199; Heavy Industry and Energy 184; Ideology 80, 109, 213; International 19, 20, 42, 55, 62, 75, 86, 99, 108, 111, 112, 185, 213, 214, 217, 218, 219, 220, 228, 232, 245, 281, 346 n. 4, 365 n. 9, 368 n. 34; International Information 165; Machine Building and Industry 263; Party Organizational Work 66, 74, 132; Propaganda 74, 99, 115, 163, 367 n. 30; Science and Education 69, 86; Socialist Countries 19, 42, 48, 49, 100, 101, 185, 213, 214, 248, 288, 346 n. 4; Socio-Economic 184
    General Secretaryship of 52, 54, 76, 104, 107, 108, 115, 121, 128, 136, 139, 142, 143, 152, 155, 168, 174, 178, 182, 191, 195, 196, 197, 198, 199, 205, 216, 227, 229, 248–9, 286, 301, 310, 318
    Plenary Sessions of 62, 67, 72, 73, 86, 87, 97, 123, 126, 138, 165, 166, 167, 171, 200, 267, 292; April 1985 Plenum 147, 268; January 1987 Plenum 166, 167; June 1987 Plenum 146, 147, 148, 167; October 1987 Plenum 169–72, 357 n. 83; March 1990 Plenum 246; April 1991 Plenum 286; July 1991 Plenum 291, 292, 386 n. 201

reorganization of 184–6
Secretariat of 57, 62, 65, 68, 70, 71, 83, 85, 86, 97, 100, 104, 108, 109, 174, 183, 185, 186, 200, 266
see also Politburo
Central Control Commission of the CPSU 293
Central Economic–Mathematical Institute 112, 149
Central Europe 245, 247
'centre-left coalition' 207
Chakovsky, Alexander 58
Chayanov, Alexander 44
Chaykovskaya, Olga 318, 389 n. 3
Chazov, Yevgeny 53, 54, 62, 63, 67, 69, 82, 83, 84, 319 n. 3
Chebrikov, Viktor 62, 107, 165, 173, 186, 234, 265, 266, 296, 297, 361 n. 168
Chechnya 254, 282, 377 nn. 4 & 7
checks and balances 128, 199
Cheka 43
see also KGB
Chequers 77, 335 n. 125
Chernenko, Konstantin 1, 25, 37, 47, 51, 56, 61, 62, 63, 64, 66, 67, 68, 73, 74, 76, 78, 80, 86, 93, 98, 113, 114, 214, 230, 263, 281, 337 n. 158, 369 n. 57
as General Secretary 4, 8, 16, 34, 65, 69, 70, 71, 72, 73, 74, 77, 79, 82, 122, 147, 200, 228
closeness to Brezhnev 51, 52, 54, 63
death of 71, 72, 75, 83, 85, 86, 105, 228, 316
illness of 72, 73, 74, 82, 83, 84, 121, 125, 216, 228
succession to 70, 71, 82, 83, 91, 122, 139, 229, 309
Chernobyl nuclear accident 163, 231, 366 n. 30
Chernyaev, Anatoly 50, 62, 98, 99, 100, 101, 105, 110, 114, 166, 219, 245, 284, 295, 298, 339 n. 45, 365 n. 1
as aide and ally of Gorbachev xii, 42, 86, 94, 98, 168, 177, 196, 202, 205, 210, 213, 215, 218, 281, 273, 294, 316, 382 n. 115
and International Department 20, 55, 108, 111
and 'kitchen cabinet' 202, 286
memoirs 117, 159, 164, 170, 219, 233, 234, 235, 243, 244, 248, 297, 300
and national question 384 n. 156
and new ideas 99, 100, 115, 231, 273
and Nineteenth Party Conference 176, 194
Chernyshevsky, Nikolay 125
Chikin, Valentin 34, 124, 173
'children of the Twentieth Congress' 39, 99
China 135, 144, 216, 259, 315
'Chinese variant' (of economic reform) 90
Chrystal, John 62, 332 n. 39
Chubaryan, Alexander 103
church, persecution of 17
Churchill, Winston 243
CIA (Central Intelligence Agency) 227
Cinema Workers' Union Congress 164
civil society 16, 17, 316, 323 n. 52

coal-miners, strikes of 197, 198, 239, 284
coalition-building 121, 206, 207–10
cognitive dissonance 115
Cohen, Stephen F. 91, 356 n. 59
Cold War, ending of 230, 237, 239, 240, 270, 304, 306, 307, 317
'collective contract', *see* agriculture, agricultural reform
collective farms 144
collectivization of agriculture 26
Columbia University 74, 302
Comecon 242
Comintern 75
command economy 131, 133, 138, 139, 158
commissions, on agriculture 186
on ideology 185
on international affairs 186
on legal affairs 186
on military-industrial issues 370 n. 76
on party construction and cadres policy 186
on social and economic policy 186
Committee of Special Administration 263
Committee for Supervision of the USSR Constitution 199, 291
commodity-money relations 80, 137, 349 n. 38
commodity production 224
Commonwealth of Independent States (CIS) 304
communism 138, 292, 313, 314
Communist system 15, 16, 115, 119, 121, 161, 242, 293, 316
collapse of 12, 186, 247
dismantling of 309–15
Communist Party of the Soviet Union (CPSU) 21, 22, 38, 74, 86, 90, 91, 93, 94, 96, 101, 111, 117, 126, 131, 148, 156, 161, 169, 170, 179, 180, 188, 193, 196, 203, 206, 207, 221, 225, 269, 273, 282, 285, 286, 288, 290, 291, 293, 301, 306, 310, 311, 316
bureaucracy 14, 19, 94, 132, 133, 240, 246, 270, 273, 274, 285
see also Central Committee, Party Conference, Party Congresses, Party Programme, Politburo
'Communists for Democracy' 290
conceptual innovation 15
see also new thinking
conceptual revolution 121–9
confederation 255, 256
Congress of Collective Farm Workers 173
Congress of People's Deputies of Russia 188–93
Congress of People's Deputies of the USSR 103, 179, 180, 182, 183, 187, 189, 192, 193, 194, 195, 265, 275, 297, 298
abolition of 359 n. 137
election of first President of USSR 203–6, 289, 297
First Congress 5, 125, 138, 177, 187–93, 197, 209, 271, 310, 311, 314
Third Congress 196, 206
Fourth Congress 278

Conquest, Robert 17, 252
Conservative Caucus (USA) 236
Constitution (1977) 125, 155, 194, 267, 268,
    269, 282, 283
  amendments to 184, 193, 194, 196
  Article 6 193, 194, 196, 200, 311
  Day of (1936) Constitution 170
Constitutional Commission 205
co-operatives, legalization of 197, 312
corruption 4, 63, 67, 82
Council of Ministers of the RSFSR 85, 151
Council of Ministers of the USSR (formerly
    Council of People's Commissars) 2, 3, 64,
    65, 69, 83, 107, 136, 149, 151, 169, 194, 195,
    199, 208, 209, 213, 274, 275, 301
  see also Cabinet of Ministers
countervailing powers 14
coup, August 1991 15, 68, 100, 103, 174, 182,
    215, 232, 253, 254, 269, 271, 272, 273, 277,
    283, 288, 289, 294–300, 302, 304, 386 n. 217,
    387 nn. 220–2 & 229
courts 71
Crimean Tatars 261, 262
Cuba 265
Cuban missile crisis 111
Cultural Foundation 204
cultural life 35, 94, 107, 162
cultural policy 104
Czechoslovak Communist Party 44
Czechoslovakia 11, 34, 40, 41, 124, 160, 249
  Soviet military intervention in 40, 75,
    372 n. 120
  1960s reforms in 75, 124, 135, 247–8
  see also 'Prague Spring'

Dahl, Robert A. 138, 139, 255, 256, 349 n. 47,
    360 n. 150, 378 nn. 12, 13 & 22, 390 n. 20
Dahrendorf, Ralf (Lord) xiv, 323 n. 50
Dallin, Alexander xiv, 227
Daniel, Yuly 92
Dashichev, Vyacheslav 245
defence industry 63, 71, 159
  see also military–industrial complex
Dejevsky, Mary 379 n. 44
Delyusin, Lev 49
Dementey, Nikolay 387 n. 222
democracy 17, 90, 95, 116, 138, 158, 307,
    336 n. 147
democratic centralism 156, 181, 311, 312
'Democratic Platform in the CPSU' 208
'Democratic Russia' 188, 311
democratization 17, 123, 126, 128, 136, 137,
    155, 156, 159, 160, 166, 167, 178, 182,
    196–7, 203, 216, 252, 255, 258, 270, 283,
    306, 307, 322 n. 46, 353 nn. 5 & 6,
    360 n. 150
demographic change 12
derevenshchiki 21
'developed socialism' 79, 314
'developed socialist society' 79

'developing socialism' 79, 314
Ding, X. L. 390 n. 26
dissidents; dissent 7, 8, 9, 10, 11, 24, 47, 49, 56,
    57, 63, 157, 165, 186, 212, 307
Dobrynin, Anatoly 109, 111, 114, 185, 213, 214,
    219, 220, 232, 368 n. 41
Dole, Senator Robert 236
Dolgikh, Vladimir 69, 83, 86, 187, 263, 333 n.
    79, 336 n. 154, 341 n. 80, 388 n. 242
draft programme of the CPSU (1991) 16, 292
drunkenness 18, 141, 314
Dubček, Alexander 30
Duma 90
Dumbarton Oaks conference (1944) 76
Dunham, Vera 27
Dyker, David 137

East–West relations 77, 214, 219, 222, 230–47
Eastern Europe 17, 21, 42, 106, 213, 225, 236,
    242, 244, 247–51, 255, 296, 315
  Communist parties of 194, 196
  fall of communism in i, 5, 160, 182, 186, 194,
    237, 240, 244, 268, 307, 315
  political reform/development in 112, 160,
    249
  Soviet relaxation of control over 224, 230,
    239–40, 242, 247–8, 258, 267, 268, 296,
    307
economic growth 95
  declining rate of 12, 18, 63, 134, 135
economic legislation 145–7
economic policy-making 140–7
economic reform 4, 95, 133, 322 n. 46,
    346 n. 14
  failure of 130, 307
  Kosygin reform (1965) 49, 50, 123–4, 134,
    135, 136
economy 64, 65, 130–54, 346–52
  market 80, 128, 137
  mixed 137, 138
  socialist market economy 155
Ehrenburg, Ilya 35
Eisenhower, President Dwight D. 216, 374 n. 167
Eisenhower, Susan 226
elections:
  campaign 197
  contested 14, 93, 96, 106, 124, 132, 155, 156,
    159, 166, 169, 179–84, 186, 201, 306, 309,
    312
  'founding election' 188, 362 n. 175
  of president 202–7
  shop floor 137
Engels, Friedrich 292
enterprise autonomy 65
Entin, Vladimir 385 n. 164
environmental pollution 18
Estonia 17, 160, 191, 194, 241, 256, 269, 279
Eurocommunism 75
European Union 288, 289, 303
executive, federal 14

Falin, Valentin 185, 187, 214, 220, 245, 246, 247, 375 n. 188
famine 26
federalism/pseudo-federalism 198, 256, 257, 267
Federation Council 201, 209, 275, 276, 277, 296, 301
Federenko, Nikolay 351 n. 100
Fedorchuk, Vitaly 62
Fedorov, Boris 151
Fedoseev, Petr 187
Film-makers' Union 173, 180
First Congress of the Russian Communist Party 208
Fitzwater, Marlin 240
'500 Days Programme' 150–4, 207, 269, 273, 274, 276, 287, 313, 352 n. 107
Food Programme 60, 143, 332 n. 33
Foreign and Commonwealth Office (British) 77
Foreign Intelligence Service (Russian) 112, 219
foreign policy 212–51, 365–76
   change in 160
   Gorbachev's 98, 99, 101, 113, 212–51
   Soviet 95, 113, 114, 117, 131, 159
foreign radio 96
   see also BBC
Foros 293, 294, 295, 296, 297, 298, 299, 300
France 12, 43, 231
   Fifth French Republic 198, 209
freedom 7, 119, 158, 259, 283, 292, 315
   Gorbachev's support for 115, 118, 119, 175, 249, 307, 312, 317–18
   lack of 90
   religious freedom 237, 318
   of speech 125, 126, 132, 318
   of travel 242, 318
Friedman, Milton 139
Frolov, Ivan 99, 100, 101, 102, 163, 176, 202, 205, 356 n. 59
funeral commission 84, 85, 86
Furtseva, Yekaterina 354 n. 18

G7 summit (June 1991) 153
Galeotti, Mark 389 n. 1
Galkin, Alexander 20, 342 n. 95
Gamsakhurdia, Zviad 265, 374 n. 162
Garton Ash, Timothy 244, 246, 374 n. 177, 375 n. 180
Gaydar, Yegor 99, 138, 151, 197
Gelman, Alexander 173
Generalov, Vyacheslav, KGB General 297, 298
General Secretaryship
   see Central Committee of the CPSU, General Secretaryship of
Geneva accords 175
Georgia 2, 47, 141, 192, 215, 257, 260, 265, 266, 267, 286, 303, 304, 380 n. 52
Georgian Party organization 108, 257, 260, 266
Gerasimov, Gennady 49, 240, 373 n. 152
Germany 116, 117, 118, 138, 366 n. 18
   FRG 43, 214

GDR 249, 250
   reunification of 220, 230, 240, 243, 244–7, 296, 375 nn. 188 & 190
Gidaspov, Boris 340 n. 61
Girenko, Andrey 381 n. 86
glasnost 18, 87, 122, 125, 127, 128, 132, 136, 137, 162, 163, 175,179, 258, 306
Goldansky, Academician Vitaly 204
González, Felipe 37, 98, 116, 119, 120, 242–3
Gooding, John 94, 95
Gopalko, Panteli 25, 26
Gorbachev, Andrey 25
Gorbachev, Maria Panteleevna 27
Gorbachev, Mikhail Sergeevich 7, 8, 25, 29, 40, 49, 50, 111, 122,
   appointments 97, 103, 104–11, 381 n. 100, 387 n. 232
   and coup 14, 294–303, 387 nn. 220, 221, 229, 388 n n. 242, 243 & 246
   December 1984 speech 60, 78–80, 81, 87, 109, 121, 122, 123, 125, 126, 229
   distaste for use of force 268, 383 n. 145, 388 n. 242, 389 nn. 1 & 9
   early life: family background 25, 33, 40, 325 nn. 15 & 18, 326 n. 31, 388 n. 246; education 27, 28, 29–31, 43; labour awards 27, 28, 46
   and economic reform 130–54, 269–70, 306, 307, 312–13
   foreign policy 212–51, 277, 366 n. 17
   historic role 315–18, 344 n. 162
   mistakes 130, 203–11, 268, 269, 272, 276–7, 281, 300–1, 387 n. 232
   and national question 262, 263, 277, 279, 280, 294, 303–4, 384 n. 156
   and Novo-Ogarevo process 285–93
   political reform 3, 4, 102, 132, 155–211
   popularity xi, 1, 5, 6, 10, 270, 271, 321 n. 33, 344 n. 162, 388 n. 242
   relationship with Andropov 4, 50, 51, 62–9
   relationship with Yeltsin 12, 110–11, 169–72, 192, 245, 287, 381 n. 94
   on social democracy 102, 116 17, 121, 138, 206
   'turn to the right' 260, 269–72
   'zig-zags' 127, 156, 271, 273
Gorbachev, Raisa Maksimovna (née Titorenko) 36, 40, 41, 51, 60, 205, 327 n. 64
   and the coup 298, 299, 388 n. 246
   family background 32, 33, 34, 141, 350 n. 60
   foreign travel 33, 34, 42, 76
   relationship with Gorbachev 29, 34, 35, 325 n. 23, 326 n. 31
   and sociological research 33, 34, 60
Gorbachev, Sergey Andreevich 26, 27, 28, 325 n. 20
Gorbachev Foundation 45, 109, 269, 287
Gordievsky, Oleg xi, 227, 370 n. 84
Gorky (Nizhny Novgorod) 9, 37, 56, 157

Gosagroprom, *see* State Committee for the Agro-Industrial Complex
Gosplan (State Planning Committe) 60, 64, 146, 147, 208, 277
Grachev, Andrey xii, 20, 88, 98, 112, 116, 130, 165, 218, 292, 304, 324 n. 66, 347 n. 25, 357 n. 94, 363 n. 232, 375 n. 188, 381 n. 99
 events in Vilnius 383 n. 140, 384 n. 145
 Party Programme 386 n. 201
Gratsiansky, Pavel 28
Great Britain 33, 75, 76, 77, 78, 115, 117, 118, 231, 254
'Great Patriotic War' 315
 see also the Second World War
Griffiths, Franklyn 366 n. 9
Grishin, Viktor 69, 70, 81, 82, 85, 86, 90, 109, 110, 113, 162, 337 n. 159
Gromov, General Boris 276, 291
Gromyko, Andrey 50, 54, 55, 56, 66, 73, 113, 168, 179, 187, 217, 219, 228, 261, 262
 as Foreign Minister 50, 66, 114, 213, 214, 215, 218, 220, 221, 342 n. 99, 366 n. 11
 Nina Andreeva affair 173, 357 n. 99
 Politburo member 54, 177, 366 n. 9
 support for Gorbachev 73, 76, 77, 86, 87
Grósz, Károly 249
Grushin, Boris x, 34, 321 n. 27

Hampshire, Sir Stuart 343 n. 130
Havel, President Václav 376 n. 202
Hayek, Friedrich von 139
Healey, Denis 7, 320 n. 14
Heclo, Hugh 359 n. 131
Hegel, Georg Wilhelm Friedrich 31
Helms, Senator Jesse 236
Heseltine, Michael 77
Hewett, Ed 140
Hobbes, Thomas 33
Holland 42, 43
Honecker, Erich 249, 376 n. 214
Hough, Jerry F. 322 n. 46
Howe, Sir Geoffrey (*now* Lord) 77, 215, 227
'the human factor' 80
L'Humanité 92
Hungary 11, 100, 135, 143, 160, 204, 245, 247
 agricultural reform in 142, 144
 1956 revolution 225
Huntington, Samuel 317
Husák, Gustáv 30
Hussein, Saddam 218, 219

Ignatenko, Vitaly 280–1, 282, 284, 286, 304, 383 n. 145
Illarionov, Andrei 377 n. 4
illicit distilling 142
INF, *see* Intermediate-Range Nuclear Forces Treaty
infant mortality 18
inflation 140
Inozemtsev, Nikolay 20

institutchiki 112, 113, 114
Institute of Economics and Organization of Industrial Production, Novosibirsk 73, 113
Institute of Economics of the Academy of Sciences 64, 148
Institute of Economics of the World Socialist System, *now* Institute of International Economic and Political Studies 20, 21, 48, 112, 245, 341 nn. 91 & 93
Institute of Europe 243
Institute of Marxism-Leninism 99, 120
Institute of Oriental Studies of the Soviet Academy of Sciences 49, 219
Institute of Social Sciences 20, 112, 342 n. 95
Institute of State and Law 20, 59, 112, 145, 199, 288
Institute of the International Workers' Movement 112
Institute of the United States and Canada 20, 21, 37, 48, 112, 234, 243
Institute of World Economy and International Relations (IMEMO) 20, 21, 75, 76, 105, 112, 113, 202, 219
'institutional amphibiousness' 390 n. 26
intelligentsia 9, 12, 21, 92, 115, 118, 164, 202, 203, 209, 257, 258, 312
Inter-Regional Group of Deputies 204
Intermediate-Range Nuclear Forces (INF Treaty) 236, 237
Ipatovsky method 46
Iraq 218, 278
Israel 49
Italian Communist Party (PCI) 43, 75
Italy 42, 43, 75
Ivashko, Vladimir 200, 274
Izvestiya 35, 49, 183

Japan 216, 366 n. 18
Jaruzelski, General Wojciech 249
Jennings, Sir Ivor 255

Kádár, János 100, 249
Kaganovich, Lazar 3
KAL 007, flight, 227, 229
Kalugin, Oleg, KGB General 302
Karpov, Vladimir 164
Kazakhstan 69, 84, 260, 287, 289, 303, 304, 378 n. 23
 party leadership in 261
Kazannik, Aleksey 192
Kechekyan, Stepan Fedorovich 31
Kendall, Bridget 339 n. 32
Kennedy, President John F. 374 n. 167
Kennedy, Paul 159, 354 n. 12
KGB 3, 22, 25, 36, 41, 62, 71, 103, 133, 186, 190, 208, 227, 240, 274, 293, 297, 300, 302, 304, 309
 and Andropov 4, 47, 49, 54, 65, 66, 100, 101
 and foreign intelligence 228, 248
 and foreign policy 214, 217, 237, 346 n. 4

and killings in Vilnius 282
and opposition to change 124, 152, 181, 234, 235, 269, 273, 274, 296
and suppression of dissent 9, 10, 30, 96, 165, 257
Khanin, Girsh 134, 135, 347 n. 22
Khasbulatov, Ruslan 360 n. 140
Khrushchev, Nikita Sergeevich 3, 17, 25, 38, 45, 63, 207, 286, 295
and agricultural policy 39, 43, 44, 53
criticism of Stalin 25, 39, 40, 41, 91
fall of 15, 44, 91, 92, 182, 316
and foreign policy 114, 215, 216, 374 n. 167
and goal of communism 313, 314
rehabilitation of 168, 328 n. 124
'secret speech' 25, 39, 91, 99, 166
style of leadership 3, 40, 187, 198, 215
years as First Secretary 3, 18, 19, 37, 218, 222
Kiev 156, 242
Kingdon, John W. 359 n. 131
Kirilenko, Andrey 51, 61, 110
Klaus, Václav 248
Klimov, Elem 164
Klímová, Rita 376 n. 202
Kochetov, K. A. 266
Kohl, Helmut 7, 37, 116, 239, 243, 245, 246, 247, 250, 320 n. 14
Kolbin, Gennady 260, 261, 379 nn. 38 & 40
Koldunov, General Alexander 78
Kommunist 72, 73, 79, 99, 100, 163, 176
Komsomol (Young Communist League) 27, 28, 30, 32, 36, 37, 38, 39, 126, 180, 316
Thirteenth Congress (1958 of) 40
Kondratev (*also known as* Kondratieff), Nikolay 44
Korea, South 216
Kornai, János 147
Kornienko, Georgy 55, 219, 220, 232, 234, 235, 368 n. 34
Korotich, Vitaly 163
Kosolapov, Richard 73, 163
Kosygin, Aleksey 7, 49, 52, 69, 123–4, 134, 135, 136
Kovalev, Anatoly 231, 232
Krasin, Yury 342 n. 95
Krasnodar 109
Krasnogvardeysk 28, 36
Kravchenko, Leonid 283, 297, 384 nn. 158 & 159
Kravchuk, Leonid 256, 259, 286, 289, 304
Kryuchkov, Vladimir 208, 228, 234, 235, 274, 284, 288, 293, 294, 387 n. 232
and August coup 49, 103, 296, 297, 302, 307, 388 n. 246
and killings in Vilnius 282, 384 n. 145
Kuchmaev, Boris 114, 119, 327 n. 94, 332 n. 27, 343 n. 135
Kudryavtsev, Vladimir 145, 146, 288
Kulakov, Fedor 38, 39, 45, 46, 47, 50, 51, 57, 330 n. 165

kulaks 32
Kunaev, Dinmukhamed 69, 84, 85, 260, 379 nn. 40 & 42
Kurashvili, Boris 348 n. 33
Kurile Islands 216, 366 n. 18
Kuusiinen, Otto 19
Kuwait, invasion of 218, 219, 278
Kuznetsov, Vasily 341 n. 80

Lakshin, Vladimir 164
Landsbergis, Vytautas 281, 383 n. 137
Lane, Robert E. 349 n. 49
language of politics 127–9
LaPalombara, Joseph 75
Laptev, Ivan 183, 184, 194, 357 n. 94
Larina, Anna 356 n. 59
Latsis, Otto 99, 164, 292, 348 n. 32, 386 n. 201
Latvia 17, 43, 160, 192, 194, 241, 256, 279, 282
Lauristin, Marju 321 n. 30
Law on Co-operatives (1988) 145, 146, 312
Law on Individual Labour Activity 145, 146
Law on Land 145
Law on Leaseholds 145
Law on the Press 283
Law on Secession 263, 267
Law on the State Enterprise 65, 146, 147
law-governed state 185, 186
learning, *see* political learning
legal reform 179
Legostaev, Valery 56, 333 n. 81, 337 n. 159
Legvold, Robert 222
Lenin, Vladimir Ilich 2, 16, 29, 94, 102, 120, 168, 238
idealization of 14, 40, 90, 119, 120, 121, 223, 321 nn. 33 & 34, 338 n. 1
and NEP 17, 119, 134
thought of 32, 80, 96, 119, 120, 139, 222
Lenin All-Union Academy of Agricultural Sciences 44, 60
Lenin Anniversary Speech (April 1982) 63
Leningrad, siege of 232
see also St Petersburg
Leningrad Military District 78
Leningrad Regional Party organization 172, 208
Leninism 75, 89, 91, 92, 93, 99, 117, 120, 121, 126, 159, 223, 250
see also Marxism–Leninism
Levada, Yury x, 6, 10, 320 n. 27, 381 n. 95
liberalism 343 n. 143
liberalization 155, 157, 182, 196–7, 216, 258, 306, 307, 353 n. 6, 360 n. 150
Liberman, Vladimir 30, 31, 32
Lieven, Anatol 383 n. 137
life expectancy 18
Ligachev, Yegor 30, 41, 56, 63, 67, 82, 94, 97, 102, 104, 106, 109, 179, 183, 187, 200, 201, 246, 263, 265, 266, 268, 360 n. 149, 380 n. 71
anti-alcohol measures 141

Ligachev, Yegor (*cont.*):
  conflict with Yeltsin 110, 111, 167, 169–72,
    177, 189, 356 n. 80
  and Nina Andreeva affair 173, 174, 175,
    357 n. 99
  relationship with Andropov 66, 67, 73
  relationship with Gorbachev 42, 66, 70, 73,
    83, 105, 156, 328 n. 105
  reluctant reformer 66, 105, 118, 132, 139,
    145, 149, 168, 176, 185, 186, 245
  and Secretariat of Central Committee 174,
    175, 358 n. 110
  and succession to Chernenko 84, 85, 86,
    334 n. 83
Likhachev, Dmitry, Academician 204, 205
Linz, Juan 353 n. 9, 359 n. 138, 377 n. 10
Lisov, Yevgeny 386 n. 217
Literaturnaya gazeta 10, 48, 57, 58
Lithuania 2, 17, 160, 192, 194, 240–1, 259, 267,
    268, 279, 280, 283, 294
  killings in 280, 282, 383 n. 137
Locke, John 33
Loone, Eero 93
Lukyanov, Anatoly 86, 176, 192, 199, 208, 277,
    280, 286, 336 n. 147, 382 n. 116, 386 n. 201
  and coup 174, 298, 302,
  and Nina Andreeva letter 173, 174
  relationship with Gorbachev 32, 173, 192,
    277
Luther, Martin 93, 127
Lvin, Boris 377 n. 4
Lyubimov, Yury 57

MccGwire, Michael 370 n. 87
Macmillan, Harold 243, 374 n. 167
Major, John 374 n. 169
Makashov, General Albert 221, 290
Malenkov, Georgy 3
Maley, William 365 n. 9
Malia, Martin 343 n. 128
Marchenko, Anatoly 165
market 80, 128, 149
market economy 99, 128, 130, 131, 138, 150,
    276, 305, 307
market socialism 139
marketization 158, 255, 313
Markov, Georgy 164
Martynov, Vladen 20
Marx, Karl 11, 32, 75, 96, 119, 139, 172, 292,
    313
Marxist theory 31, 63, 80
Marxism-Leninism 13, 21, 32, 74, 79, 93, 96,
    101, 102, 110, 120, 126, 128, 161, 175, 206,
    221, 222, 223, 245, 249, 253, 259, 291, 292,
    306, 309, 310, 313
Maslyukov, Yury 208, 277, 381 n. 86
mass media 18, 35, 96, 104, 107, 127, 162, 163,
    258, 284, 384 n. 159
  see also television
Medvedev, Roy 7, 8, 9, 192

Medvedev, Vadim 69, 78, 80, 86, 109, 110, 123,
    176, 204, 214, 250, 336 n. 147, 353 n. 4,
    361 n. 168, 367 n. 30
  and Gorbachev xii, 176, 286
  and ideology 104, 109, 185, 200
  on Ligachev–Yeltsin dispute 170, 171
  and Politburo 202, 341 n. 81
  Nina Andreeva affair 172, 174, 357 n. 99,
    358 n. 105
Medvedev, Vladimir, KGB General, 294,
    387 n. 220
Medvedev, Zhores 45, 52
Melnikov, Alexander 190
Menon, Rajan 309
Mensheviks 121
MGIMO 217
Migranyan, Andranik 269
Miles, Rufus 387 n. 233
military 3, 5, 22, 25, 70, 71, 76, 78, 133, 152,
    190, 240, 245, 278, 365 n. 1
military-industrial complex 159, 212, 226, 232,
    295, 296, 309
miners *see* coal miners
Minister of Agriculture of RSFSR 109
Minister, Ministry of Foreign Affairs of Russia 218
Minister, Ministries, Soviet, 131
  of Agriculture 45
  of Defence 68, 78, 208, 214, 266, 267, 274,
    278, 293, 296, 297, 346 n. 4
  economic 274, 309
  of Finance 142, 146, 153, 276
  of Foreign Affairs 49, 76, 108, 111, 114, 131,
    208, 213, 214, 215, 217, 218, 219, 220, 231,
    242, 274, 277, 278, 302
  of Heavy and Transport Machine-Building 64
  industrial 132, 133
  of Interior (MVD) 22, 63, 71, 208, 276, 278,
    282, 296; troops of, *see* OMON
  ministerial network 25, 132, 136
Mitterrand, François 7, 37, 116, 231, 243, 245
Mlynář, Zdeněk x, xii, 30, 31, 32, 35, 41, 44,
    119, 327 n. 78, 338 n. 9, 353 n. 4
Moldova 256, 286, 287, 303
Molodaya gvardiya 21
Molotov, Vyacheslav 3, 217
Mongolia 173
Morgun, Fedor 169
Moscow News 163
Moscow Party organization 110, 111, 170
  First Secretary of 171, 172
Moscow University 2, 27, 28, 29, 30, 31, 33, 35,
    98, 238
  Law Faculty of 2, 28, 29, 41, 192
Most Favoured Nation Status (MFN) 240, 241
Movement for Democratic Reforms 293
Murakhovsky, Vsevelod 44, 143

Nagorno-Karabakh dispute 262–4, 267, 379 n. 49,
    380 n. 52
Najibullah, Mohammad 234, 235

Nash sovremennik 21
national conflicts 260–7
national question 12, 130, 158, 160, 179, 203, 252–69, 308
nationalism 255–60, 261
  in Baltic states 12, 258, 267, 270, 279
  in Georgia 12, 258
  in Russia 12, 57, 74, 259, 378 n. 30
  in Ukraine 12, 258
nationalities policy 190, 307
NATO 222, 227, 239, 240, 246, 296
Natta, Alessandro 75
Nazarbaev, Nursultan 153, 261, 289, 290, 293, 303, 304, 378 n. 23, 379 n. 42
Nenashev, Mikhail 80
neo-Bolshevism 121
NEP (New Economic Policy) 17, 119, 134, 223
networks, political 19, 42
networks, policy 179, 359 n. 131
New Political Thinking (*Novoe politicheskoe myshlenie*) *or* New Thinking 5, 96, 99, 101, 117, 122, 162, 165, 220–5, 244, 246
New York Times 236
Nikolsky, B. V. 266
Nikonov, Alexander 43, 44, 60, 103, 143, 144, 328 n. 124, 332 n. 33, 338 n. 9, 350 n. 71
Nikonov, Viktor 143, 173, 357 n. 99
Nina Andreeva affair 168, 172–4, 179, 201
Nixon, President Richard M. 216
Nizhny Novgorod, *see* Gorky
NKVD, *see* KGB
Nobel Peace Prize (1990) 238
nomenklatura 37, 181, 191, 206, 245, 259, 315, 316
Nove, Alec 118, 125, 135
Novo-Ogarevo process 161, 270, 285–93, 303, 308
Novy mir 19, 40, 92, 134, 164
nuclear war, risk of 91
nuclear accident 354 n. 27
  see also Chernobyl nuclear accident

Oakeshott, Michael 313
Obolonsky, Alexander 191, 361 n. 173
O'Donnell, Guillermo 181, 182, 362 n. 175
Ogonek 163
Oktyabr' 19
OMON (Ministry of Interior troops) 282, 284
Orwell, George 96, 164, 311
Ossetia, Southern 267
Ozherelev, Oleg xii, 153, 367 n. 30

Pakistan 235
Palazhchenko, Pavel 352 n. 119, 372 n. 111
Pankin, Boris 302
Partiynaya zhizn' 72
Party Conference, Nineteenth 22, 102, 110, 122, 123, 148, 166, 169, 175–9, 181, 183, 184, 187, 194, 199, 200, 201, 213, 221, 225, 248, 307, 311, 314
Party Congresses 72, 73, 97, 179, 272

Twentieth (1956) 25, 39, 40, 41, 45, 92, 166
Twenty-second (1961) 40, 102, 166
Twenty-fourth (1971) 39
Twenty-sixth (1981) 106, 162, 201
Twenty-seventh (1986) 79, 93, 97, 102, 124, 144, 161, 166, 167, 177, 201, 221, 222
Twenty-eighth (1990) 102, 156, 200, 201, 206, 207, 272, 274, 314
Party Programme 40, 102, 222
Patiashvili, Dzhumber 266
Pavlov, Valentin 153, 154, 276, 277, 280, 293, 363 n. 216, 382 n. 115
  anti-West speech 284
  attempt to increase powers 290
  and coup 277, 296
PCI, *see* Italian Communist Party
peasants; peasantry 27, 33
Peasants' Union 296
Pechenev, Vadim 40, 56, 73, 79, 80, 334 n. 81, 335 n. 128
Pelshe, Arvid 43
perestroika 80, 81, 89, 94, 117, 122, 123, 124, 128, 166, 196, 199, 222, 234, 240, 243, 261, 262, 263, 294, 297, 344 n. 162
  economic aspect of 46, 65, 123, 178
  initiators of 94, 105, 181
  political aspect of 120, 123, 178, 252
perestroika era xi, 3, 11, 29, 57, 90, 93, 142, 200, 218, 279, 289, 312
Peter I, the Great 11, 94, 318, 321 n. 34
Petrakov, Nikolay xii, 64, 139, 146, 149, 150, 151, 152, 153, 202, 210, 218, 277, 347 n. 29, 351 n. 100, 352 n. 106
Petrov, Yury Vladimir AIT
Petrushenko, Colonel Nikolay 278, 382 n. 122
Pinsky, Leonid 18
Pipes, Richard 315, 316, 371 n. 95
Piskotin, Mikhail 390 n. 13
Pithart, Petr 376 n. 202
Pitsunda 81, 336 n. 153
Plekhanov, Yury 282, 294, 295, 297, 387 nn. 220 & 229
pluralism, political 14, 16, 17, 63, 90, 95, 96, 106, 127, 128, 156, 160, 186, 194, 204, 211, 306, 307, 323 n. 51, 390 n. 20
  of opinion 128, 311
Podgorny, Nikolay 7
Poland 11, 56, 135, 136, 160, 222, 245, 247, 316
Politburo of the CPSU 25, 38, 39, 42, 55, 61, 62, 64, 65, 68, 69, 70, 71, 72, 73, 77, 80, 81, 83, 84, 85, 86, 87, 90, 93, 96, 100, 108, 131, 148, 162, 174, 176, 177, 179, 199, 200, 201, 202, 209, 229, 260, 265, 274, 354 n. 21, 372 n. 111, 376 n. 203
political culture 11, 117, 125
political learning 12, 13, 60, 111–17, 133, 220–3
political reform 95, 100, 123, 132, 137, 159, 165, 166–72, 179, 185–7, 258, 317, 336 n. 147
political stability 94

political transformation 90, 95, 158, 160–211, 307–18
Polozkov, Ivan 208, 288
Ponomarev, Boris 19, 20, 55, 62, 75, 99, 111, 113, 114, 187, 213, 214, 219, 341 n. 80
Pope, the 93, 127
Popov, Gavriil 22, 137, 192
Postnikov, Viktor 45
power of appointment 89, 97–111, 114, 162, 178, 212–15
power of ideas 89–97, 101–2, 105–6, 113–15, 117–29, 212, 220–5
Pozsgay, Imre 364 n. 234
Prague 41, 42, 98, 101
'Prague Spring' 30, 34, 40, 41, 50, 75, 101, 135, 149, 155, 225, 234, 240, 249, 254, 353 n. 4
Pravda 35, 48, 58, 72, 79, 83, 100, 101, 103, 119, 124, 163, 174, 224
Pravda, Alex 376 n. 211
presidency 14, 199, 210
   executive presidency, creation of 198, 205, 208
   President of Russia 111, 118, 188, 284, 303, 311
   President of USSR 68, 103, 178, 182, 195, 200, 201, 202, 205, 218, 283, 285, 288, 289, 297, 301, 304, 314, 362 n. 208
Presidential Council 201, 208, 209, 210, 219, 273, 274, 291, 314, 364 n. 250
   abolition of 275, 276
   see also Federation Council
Primakov, Yevgeny 20, 112, 202, 208, 219, 264, 281, 286, 299, 336 n. 147
privacy, growth of 18
private land ownership:
   Gorbachev's attitude to 145
   public attitude to 145, 351 n. 76
Privolnoe 25, 26, 28, 45
Procuracy of USSR 36, 71
Prokhanov, Alexander 291, 387 n. 231
Przeworski, Adam 353 n. 2
psychology, of Bolshevism 121, 308
public opinion 11, 37, 136, 137
Pugo, Boris 276, 284, 296, 301, 384 n. 145
purges 30–1, 39–40, 91
putsch 100, 160, 203, 206, 267, 277, 290, 307, 310
   see also coup (August 1990)
putschists 103, 202, 215, 256, 276, 283, 294, 299, 300, 302, 303, 307, 308

Quayle, Senator Dan 236

Radio Liberty 297
Rakhmanin, Oleg 100, 339 n. 47
Rasputin, Valentin 209, 291
Razgon, Lev xi
Razumovsky, Georgy 109, 186, 263, 265, 379 n. 42, 380 n. 73, 381 n. 86
Reagan, Nancy 237, 371 n. 94, 373 n. 137

Reagan, President Ronald 7, 51, 83, 217, 237, 239, 371 n. 95
   administration of 226, 228, 230
   foreign and defence policy 229, 230
   relationship with Gorbachev 37, 77, 231, 239, 243, 374 n. 169
   Reykjavik summit 231–3, 372 n. 110
   SDI 226, 232, 233, 371 n. 96
   summits 216, 231, 235, 236
   visit to Moscow 175, 238, 307
Reddaway, Peter 8, 9
referendum, March 1991 256, 284, 287, 289
reform, *see* economic reform, political reform
'reform communism' 15, 63, 317
Remnick, David 68, 284, 387 n. 217
Revenko, Grigory 288
'revolution from above' 94, 338 nn. 18 & 22
'revolution from within' 94
Rifkind, Malcolm 77, 335 n. 126
Riga, killings in 260, 269, 280, 282, 388 n. 242
Rigby, T. H. 19, 24, 224
right to strike, introduction of 198
Rodionov, General Igor 266
Romania 194, 246, 375 n. 189
Romanov, Grigory 65, 70, 71, 78, 82, 90, 109, 113, 162, 337 n. 159, 341 n. 80
Roosevelt, President Franklin D. 76
Roxburgh, Angus 67, 171, 360 n. 153
RSFSR 208
rule-of-law state 128, 224
Rusakov, Konstantin 213, 339 n. 47, 341 n. 80
Russia 286, 287, 304
   flight from the land 144
   Russian Bureau of the Central Committee of the CPSU 208
   Russian Communist Party 208
   Russian Theatre Workers' Union 164
   see also nationalism, Russian; President of
Russophiles 21
Rust, Matthias 78
Rustow, Dunkwart 254, 256, 377 n. 9
Rutland, Peter 327 n. 91
Rutskoy, Alexander (Colonel, later General) 290, 299
   conflict with Yeltsin 386 n. 192
Ryabov, Yakov 110
Ryzhkov, Nikolay 66, 68, 74, 174, 179, 197, 289, 362 n. 204
   appointment to the Secretariat 63, 65, 70, 83
   as Chairman of the Council of Ministers 107, 136, 169, 195, 208, 316
   and economic reform 65, 122, 136, 140, 141, 144, 146, 148–9, 153, 273, 347 n. 29
   view of Gorbachev's role 67, 71, 87, 88
   work with Gorbachev 64, 65, 72, 139, 146, 147, 148, 152, 153, 201, 277, 301

Sagdeev, Roald 189, 226, 232, 235, 365 n. 1, 370 n. 76
Saikal, Amin 365 n. 9

St Petersburg 22, 59
see also Leningrad
Sakharov, Andrey 124, 165, 223, 238, 328 n. 34,
    355 n. 46
    death of 10, 321 n. 28
    as dissident 7, 8, 37, 49, 120, 125
    in exile 9, 37, 56, 157, 164, 165, 166, 212
    as radical deputy in legislature 5, 188, 189,
        191, 193
samizdat 157
Scandinavia 118
Schapiro, Leonard 24, 319 n. 1, 366 n. 9
Schmitter, Philippe C. 181, 182, 362 n. 175
Schull, Joseph 345 n. 181
science and technology 123, 146
scientific and technological revolution 72
Scowcroft, Brent 373 n. 146
SDI, *see* Strategic Defence Initiative
Second World War 17, 25, 27, 69, 74, 98, 101,
    121, 232, 234, 237, 242, 254, 259, 261, 307
Security Council of USSR 275, 276, 295
Sedov, L.A. 378 n. 30
Seidman, Harold 387 n. 233
self-government/ self-management (*samoupravle-*
    nie) 79, 345 n. 174
Selyunin, Vasily 135, 137
Seventieth Anniversary of the Bolshevik
    Revolution 111
Shakh, Georgy, *pseud.* of Georgy Shakhnazarov
    101
Shakhnazarov, Georgy 90, 91, 101, 103, 115,
    175, 195, 198, 202, 205, 206, 210, 223, 259,
    275, 285, 316, 339 n. 51, 362 n. 195, 364 n.
    237, 384 nn. 166 & 167, 398 n. 161
    and killings in Vilnius 281
    and Nineteenth Party Conference 102, 176,
        177, 183
    and Novo-Ogarevo process 287, 288, 289
    and political reform 91, 100, 102, 159, 176,
        177, 179, 183, 192, 199, 273, 275, 284
    and Socialist Countries Department 48, 100,
        213, 365 n. 5
    as presidential aide xii, 42, 100, 105, 192, 205,
        210, 283, 284, 286, 382 n. 115
    perception of Gorbachev 57, 102, 272, 280,
        285, 299, 389 n. 9
Sharapov, Viktor 100
Shatalin, Stanislav Sergeevich 64, 98, 152, 153,
    202, 209, 210, 352 n. 107, 364 n. 250
Shatalin-Yavlinsky group, *also known as* Shatalin
    group 151, 152, 207, 273, 274, 276, 313
Shatrov, Mikhail 164
Shchelokov, Nikolay 62, 63, 82, 336 n. 155
Shcherbitsky, Vladimir 84, 85, 200
Shenfield, Stephen 222
Shenin, Oleg 295
shestidesyatniki 40, 164
Shevardnadze, Eduard 30, 38, 55, 103, 109, 125,
    141, 169, 174, 201, 208, 218, 226, 227, 231,
    233, 234, 245, 256, 257, 268, 273, 274, 279,

293, 316, 336 nn. 147, 152, 369 n. 63
    and Afghanistan 234, 235
    and Gulf War 218, 219, 368 n. 32
    as Foreign Minister of USSR 108, 114, 131,
        139, 162, 213, 214–16, 220, 231, 232, 245,
        274, 365 n. 3
    killings in Tbilisi 265–7, 380 n. 73
    and post-Soviet Georgia 265
    and reunification of Germany 245, 375 nn.
        188 & 196
    reinstatement as Foreign Minister 302
    relations with foreign counterparts 215, 235,
        236, 239, 240
    relations with Gorbachev 47, 56, 81, 105, 108,
        215, 220, 260, 277, 278
    resignation of 277–9, 308, 382 n. 122
Shevchenko, Arkady 37, 367 nn. 27 & 29
Shishlin, Nikolay 49, 165
Shlapentokh, Vladimir 320 n. 7
Shmelev, Nikolay 137, 142, 189, 204, 347 n. 32,
    350 n. 65, 357 n. 88
'shock therapy' 137
Shtromas, Alexander 8
Shultz, George, Secretary of State 77, 232, 237,
    307, 371 n. 95
    and Gorbachev 217, 231, 239, 367 n. 23
    and Reykjavik summit 236, 372 nn. 105 &
        110
    and Shevardnadze 235, 239, 367 n. 20
    and withdrawal from Afghanistan 234, 235
Shushkevich, Stanislav 256, 304
Šik, Ota 50, 149
Silaev, Ivan 151, 302
Simonov, Konstantin 340, 373 n. 131
Sinyavsky, Andrey 92
Slyunkov, Nikolay 186, 268
Smersh 62
Smirnov, Georgy Lukich 99, 120
Smirnov, William 323 n. 50
Sobchak, Anatoly 22, 59, 204, 205, 210, 264,
    266, 293, 321 n. 28, 382 n. 115
social democracy 101, 102, 103, 117, 120, 121,
    126, 161, 272, 343 n. 143, 368 n. 40
social deterioration 18
socialism 15, 16, 75, 101, 116, 118, 119, 121,
    166, 206, 209, 222, 240, 272, 306, 313, 314,
    336 n. 147, 343 n. 130
    Andropov on 63
'socialist idea' 118, 129, 343 n. 134
socialist pluralism 96, 127, 128, 361 n. 170
socialist system 118, 129, 223
socialist state based upon the rule of law
    (*sotsialistichskoe pravovoe gosudarstvo*) 180
Sokolov, Marshal Sergey 78, 228
Solidarity 56, 221
Solomentsev, Mikhail 141, 168, 173, 177,
    357 n. 99
Solovev, Yury 190
Solzhenitsyn, Alexander 1, 9, 10, 40, 96, 120,
    125, 157, 164, 320 n. 24

Sovetskaya Rossiya 34, 80, 124, 172, 173, 174, 181, 291
Soviet–American relations 230–42
Soviet–East European relations 242, 247–51, 307, 314–15, 317
Soviet–German relations 245, 366 n. 18, 374 n. 177, 375 nn. 183 & 188, 190, and 196
Soviet President, *see* presidency
Soviet Union, *see* USSR
Soviet–West European relations 243–7
Soviet of Nationalities 191, 192
Soviet of the Union 191, 192, 202
Soyuz (Union) group in Supreme Soviet 277, 389 n. 1
space programme 63
Spain 116, 254
'stability of cadres' 38
stagnation (*zastoy*) 8, 55, 93, 122, 171
Stalin era 27, 245
Stalin, Joseph Vissarionovich 2, 19, 26, 27, 29, 30, 39, 41, 51, 72, 91, 93, 95, 102, 119, 120, 158, 168, 178, 191, 217, 234, 274, 321 n. 33, 326 n. 34
   'anti-cosmopolitan' campaign 30
   crimes of 17, 25, 41, 91, 92, 187
   death of 2, 3, 18, 29, 30, 35, 84, 98, 257, 316, end of NEP 17
   Khrushchev's criticisms of 39, 40, 91, 92, 166
   personality cult of 47, 92
   purges and use of terror 2, 26, 28, 38, 119
Stalinism 91, 92, 93, 168
Stankevich, Sergey 192, 265
'Star Wars', *see* Strategic Defence Initiative
Starodubtsev, Vasily 296
START Treaty; *see* Strategic Arms Reduction Treaty
State Commission on Economic Reform (July 1989) 148
State Committee for the Agro-Industrial Complex (Gosagroprom) 44, 60, 143
State Committee for the State of Emergency 295, 296, 298, 300, 302
State Committee on Prices 140, 149
state farms 144
State Planning Committee, *see* Gosplan
statistics, Soviet 134, 135, 142
Stavropol 2, 25, 28, 31, 32, 33, 34, 35, 38, 39
Stavropol Agricultural Institute 33, 41, 43, 60,
Stavropol region 35, 38, 44, 45, 50, 119, 132, 246, 256,
Stavropol Party organization 110, 298
Stepan, Alfred 353 n. 9, 359 n. 138, 377 n. 10
Stepankov, Valentin 386 n. 217
Strategic Arms Reduction Treaty (START) 241
Strategic Defence Initiative (SDI) 226, 227, 231, 232, 233, 235, 371 n. 96
succession (to General Secretaryship) 82–88
Sumgait 262
summit talks 216, 231
   with Bush: (1989, Malta) 239, 240; (1990,

Washington) 240, 246; (1991, Moscow) 241
   with Reagan: (1986, Reykjavik) 231, 232, 233, 236, 372 n. 112; (1987, Washington) 235, 237; (1988, Moscow) 235
Suny, Ronald 257
Supreme Soviet of Russian Republic 150, 186, 188, 191, 192, 193, 197, 198, 199, 240, 287
Supreme Soviet of the USSR 22, 48, 83, 153, 166, 174, 179, 183, 184, 192, 208, 246, 257, 274, 275, 277, 280, 286, 290, 295, 298, 312
   Presidium of 261, 277
Suslov, Mikhail 38, 50, 51, 52, 54, 55, 56, 57, 61, 62, 67, 70, 71, 174, 330 n. 162
Sverdlovsk 2, 64, 110, 132, 151, 169, 171
Sverdlovsk Juridical Institute 113, 199
systemic transformation 15, 157–60, 309–18
Szamuely, Tibor 17

Taganka Theatre 57
Tajikistan 287
Talbott, Strobe 239, 370 n. 74
tamizdat 157
Taras, Ray 378 n. 25
Tarschys, Daniel 350 n. 59
Tbilisi, killings in 260, 264–6, 380 n. 73, 388 n. 242
television 18, 190–1
   see also mass media
Terekhov, Vladislav, Ambassador 247
Thatcher, Margaret 73, 83, 231, 245, 371 n. 96
   popularity in USSR 10, 186
   relationship with Gorbachev 7, 37, 51, 76, 77–8, 116, 117, 239, 243, 320 n. 14, 321 n. 30, 335 nn. 121 & 125, 365 n. 1, 371 n. 93, 374 n. 169
   visit to Moscow 117
Theatre Workers' Union 180
Third World 214, 219
Tikhonov, Nikolay 51, 59, 68, 69, 70, 72, 83, 107, 109, 122, 136, 147, 162, 187
Tikhonov, Vladimir 64
The Times 261
Titorenko, Raisa Maksimovna, *see* Gorbachev, Raisa Maksimovna
Titov, German 379 n. 32
Tizyakov, Alexander 296
Togliatti 123
Tompson, William J. 319 n. 2
Topilin, Yury 32
Topornin, Boris 288
totalitarianism 16, 95, 116, 131, 292, 304, 323 n. 50
trade unions 126, 180
   see also Film-makers' Union; Theatre Workers' Union; Writers' Union
transformation 16, 157, 194, 198, 248, 252
   centre-periphery 158, 252–69
   economic 158, 247, 252
   foreign policy 159, 230–51, 252
   at home and abroad 186–211

political system 95, 158, 196, 198–207, 211, 247, 252
transition, from authoritarian rule 16, 157, 181
'transition to the market' 274
Travkin, Nikolay 204
Trotsky, Leon (Lev Davidovich) 96
Tsipko, Alexander 318
Tufte, Edward R. 255
Turchin, Valentin 7, 8
Turkmenistan 287
Tvardovsky, Alexander 19, 40, 92, 164

Ukraine 197, 241, 242, 256, 259, 286, 287, 303, 304
Ukrainian Communist Party 84
Ulyanov, Mikhail 164
'Union of Sovereign States' 303
'Union of Soviet Sovereign Republics' 288, 303
Union Treaty 161, 287, 289, 291, 293, 294, 296, 297, 302, 303, 359 n. 137
United Nations, Gorbachev's speech to 221, 225, 232, 250, 307, 315
Security Council 304
United States of America 215, 216, 219, 220, 227, 229, 240, 246
presidential system of 198
relations with USSR 153, 217, 218, 221, 230–42
Uralmash 64
uskorenie, see acceleration
USSR 15, 86, 91, 92, 101, 118, 153, 158, 182, 203, 224, 234, 236, 238, 247, 258, 259, 267, 307, 308, 309
collapse of 161, 223, 232, 241, 252, 258, 283, 301, 303, 307, 308, 317
superpower status 159, 259
Ustinov, Dmitry 54, 55, 56, 68, 69, 70, 71, 78, 82, 113, 228, 229, 317, 370 n. 76
Uzbekistan 287

Vaksberg, Arkady 49, 57, 58
Varennikov, General Valentin 234, 280, 291, 295, 387 n. 229
Velikhov, Yevgeny 76, 187
Vietnam War 372 n. 120
Vilnius, killings in 260, 264, 269, 280, 281, 282, 283, 383 n. 145, 388 n. 242
Voice of America 297
Volkogonov, General Dmitry 223, 369 n. 65
Volsky, Arkady 67, 68, 262, 263, 264, 333 n. 78, 382 n. 115
Voronov, Yury 164, 355 n. 33
Vorontsov, Yuly 232
Vorotnikov, Vitaly 85, 168, 173, 357 n. 99
Vzglyad (Viewpoint) 283

'war of laws' 286
Warsaw Pact 194, 224, 240, 243, 246, 249, 250, 266, 267

Weinberger, Caspar 371 n. 95
Weizsacker, President Richard von 244, 374 n. 177
welfare state (West European) 119
West Germany 43
Western Europe 115, 117, 226, 230, 236, 242, 243, 244, 247
Westernizers 21
Whitefield, Stephen 132, 361 n. 163
Wilson, Harold 243, 374 n. 168
'within-system reformers' 57, 63
workers/work collectives 12, 126
World Marxist Review 19, 98, 99, 101, 112
Writers' Union of the Russian Republic 21
Writers' Union of the USSR 164, 180

Yakovenko, Alexander 28
Yakovenko, Yakov 28
Yakovlev, Alexander Nikolaevich 20, 29, 38, 90, 94, 95, 98, 106, 109, 110, 115, 124, 125, 132, 162, 163, 165, 168, 169, 170, 179, 183, 186, 189, 199, 201, 213, 218, 226, 235, 244, 274, 281, 282, 284, 286, 291, 293, 301, 316, 326 n. 34, 345 n. 168, 352 n. 119
as Ambassador to Canada 74, 75, 81, 105
and Central Committee Secretariat xii, 107, 108, 164, 175, 208, 234
and coup 206, 302, 386 n. 215
and ideology 79, 115, 120, 175, 185
and IMEMO 75, 76, 106, 348 n. 36
and Nina Andreeva letter 172, 173, 174, 358 n. 106
1985 memorandum 105, 106, 194, 340 n. 67
and Nineteenth Party Conference 176, 177
and Politburo 106, 107, 108, 201, 234, 263, 336 n. 147
promotion of 106, 107, 114, 213, 273
and Presidential Council 274, 275, 276
relationship with Gorbachev 74, 93, 100, 104, 105, 106, 108, 123, 202, 268, 276, 302, 316, 331 n. 27, 382 n. 112
and Yeltsin 340 n. 70, 357 n. 85
Yakovlev, Yegor 163, 384 n. 158
Yanaev, Gennady 276, 296, 298, 387 n. 232
Yarin, Veniamin 209
Yavlinsky, Grigory 151, 152, 153
Yazov, Marshal Dmitry Timofeevich 208, 235, 266, 274, 293, 297, 380 n. 73
and coup 296, 297, 387 n. 232
killings in Vilnius 383 n. 145
Yefimov, Yu.T. 266
Yefremov, Leonid 39, 50
Yefremov, Oleg 57, 164
Yegorov, Vladimir 389 n. 9
Yeltsin, Boris Nikolaevich 9, 48, 93, 99, 109, 111, 115, 118, 153, 181, 187, 192, 202, 203, 207, 219, 280, 291, 293, 302, 305, 307, 308, 309, 310, 354 n. 22, 378 n. 30, 384 n. 153
banning of CPSU primary organizations 291, 292, 301, 310

Yeltsin, Boris Nikolaevich (*cont.*):
  as Chair of Supreme Soviet of Russia 150, 240,
    284, 287, 299
  and Congress of People's Deputies 187, 188
  and coup 294, 298, 299
  end of Communist Party career 110, 111,
    357 n. 85
  and Gorbachev's succession 80, 85
  as Moscow First Secretary 110, 162, 167
  and Novo-Ogarevo process 286–93, 303
  popularity of 6, 10, 151, 203, 270, 271, 289,
    290, 388 n. 242
  as President of Russia 22, 118, 188, 241, 289,
    300, 303, 304, 311, 360 n. 140
  relationship with Gorbachev 105, 110, 132,
    151, 153, 167, 169–74, 192, 210, 284, 289,
    299, 301, 303, 352 n. 119, 388 n. 242
  relationship with Ligachev 110, 111, 167,
    177, 356 n. 80

  response to crises 254, 282–3, 386 n. 192,
    388 n. 24
Yerevan 263
Yevtushenko, Yevgeny 35
Young, Christopher 363 n. 211
Yugoslavia 85, 96, 173, 253, 375 n. 189
Yuzhkov, Serafim Vladimirovich 31

Zagladin, Vadim 86, 112, 218, 367 n. 29
Zalygin, Sergey 164
Zaslavskaya, Tatyana, Academician x, 46, 60, 64,
  80, 98, 113, 143, 164, 192
Zaykov, Lev 109, 172
Zhirinovsky, Vladimir 289
Zhivkov, Todor 248
Zhurkin, Vitaly 243
Zimyanin, Mikhail 58, 339 n. 47
Zinoviev, Alexander 1, 9
Znamya 164